ECCLESIASTICAL LAW HANDBOOK

AUSTRALIA
LBC Information Services
Sydney

CANADA and USA
Carswell
Toronto • Ontario

NEW ZEALAND
Brooker's
Auckland

SINGAPORE and MALAYSIA
Thomson Information (S.E. Asia)
Singapore

ECCLESIASTICAL LAW HANDBOOK

by

Lynne Leeder, M.A. (Cantab.)

of Lincoln's Inn, Barrister

London
Sweet & Maxwell
1997

Published in 1997 by
Sweet & Maxwell Limited of
100 Avenue Road, Swiss Cottage, London NW3 3PF
Typeset by LBJ Enterprises Ltd of Aldermaston and Chilcompton.
Printed and bound by Butler and Tanner Ltd, Frome and London.

No natural forests were destroyed to make this product;
only farmed timber was used and replanted

British Library Cataloguing in Publication Data

A CIP catalogue record
for this book is
available from the
British Library

ISBN 0 421 57720 7

The index was prepared by Elisabeth Ingham.

To B. and P.

Foreword

Ecclesiastical law has not always enjoyed a good reputation in the Church. The contrast between law and gospel in the New Testament, has often led to a suspicion of law and ecclesiastical lawyers as binding the gospel, rather than expressing it. Yet God has so created human communities, the church included, that they need to have an order and structure for their life to be enabled and invigorated. It was the late Chancellor Garth Moore, a notable ecclesiastical lawyer, who reminded me on more than one occasion when I was a young student of theology, that it was naive to think of the Church existing outside a legal structure, and that disestablishment, were it to happen, would not put the Church of England outside the law, but would rather define it more closely within the law. He would have rejoiced that there is more interest today in ecclesiastical law than there has been for several decades. This book is clear evidence of this renewed interest.

Those who in any way have a responsibility for pastoral care, order and government in the Church of England will be grateful for this careful, detailed and thorough setting out of the laws by which the life of the Church is currently ordered. Bishops entering on episcopal office for the first time will find here a clear reference book to guide them in the exercise of their ministry. It will be no less valuable to parish priests, churchwardens, and members of parochial church councils, who need information on the law as it governs the life and organisation of the parish. Whether what is required is knowledge of the provisions of the Pastoral Measure, or questions relating to ecclesiastical discipline, or to the law governing worship or churchyards, Miss Leeder's book will be a primary source of reference. It is written in a way which guides the non-lawyer through the complexities of the various acts and measures, and with an appropriate sense of the theological grounding and historical shaping of the way the Church is organised. Every effort has been made to bring it up to date by including, for instance, the legislation consequent upon the decision of the General Synod to permit the ordination of women to the priesthood, and, in another area of the Church's life, the ecumenical canons. Miss Leeder is to be congratulated on her achievement.

I am happy to commend this wide-ranging and judicious description of the law governing the Church of England, and believe it has the potential to become the standard work of reference to all concerned with the organisation and life of the Church.

† *Geoffrey Basingstoke*

Preface

When I first discussed the possibility of writing a book with my editors at Sweet & Maxwell it was clear to all of us how many changes ecclesiastical law had undergone in the last few years. Following on from the success of the *Faculty Jurisdiction of the Church of England* by the late Chancellor George H. Newsom (now in its second edition), it was decided that what was required was a comprehensive and accessible work, detailing the ecclesiastical law of England as the twentieth century draws to a close.

A mere ten years ago the reader searching for twentieth century works upon ecclesiastical law could only turn to the Reverend Dr E. Garth Moore's *Introduction to English Canon Law* and to the relevant volume of *Halsbury's Laws of England*. Since then, in addition to Chancellor Newsom's book, Mr Mark Hill has produced his *Ecclesiastical Law*, a sourcebook of Measures, Canons and case law, whilst last year saw the publication of Dr Norman Doe's *The Legal Framework of the Church of England*, a comparative study of the laws of the Church of England and the Roman Catholic Church, and the Reverend Dr Rupert D. H. Bursell's *Liturgy, Order and the Law*. It would seem therefore that ecclesiastical law is enjoying something of a revival. Much of the interest in the subject has no doubt been generated by the Ecclesiastical Law Society through its journal and conferences, and by the postgraduate course in canon law at Cardiff Law School.

Unlike Mr Hill's work, this book does not reproduce the original material, nor does it seek to emulate the academic treatment which Dr Doe and Chancellor Bursell have applied to their chosen subjects. Rather this is a work which seeks to take the reader step by step through the complex maze of ecclesiastical law. It is above all a handbook, and is intended for use by lawyers, clergy and laity alike, to provide a practical account of the law.

The law does not stand still. This book endeavours to set out the law as it stood at March 1, 1997. However, such is the fast moving nature of the subject that I have also taken the somewhat unusual step of discussing a number of changes which are likely to occur over the next few years.

At the risk of incurring the wrath of strict grammarians I have used the third person plural throughout when referring to actions which may be carried out by a person of either sex, reserving the use of the singular *he* or *she* for those occasions when I am referring only to a person of that sex. I hope I will be forgiven this solecism, committed in the interests of clarity.

I cannot conclude this preface without expressing my gratitude to various people,

My thanks must first of all go to the late Reverend Dr E. Garth Moore who introduced me to canon law and encouraged me to study the subject alongside theology, and to Father Robert Ombres O.P. who has been a stalwart supporter for many years.

To Dr Paul Irving of Winckworth and Pemberton, the Reverend James Neal and Miss Kimberley McManus I owe an enormous debt. Without their painstaking reading of the manuscript and many helpful comments and suggestions this book could not have been completed. My thanks also go to all those others, too numerous to mention, who have offered advice and assistance on various points. Any errors and omissions which remain are of course my own.

I am most grateful to the eminent church historian, the Right Reverend Dr Geoffrey Rowell for agreeing to write the Foreword.

The excellent index has been compiled by Elisabeth Ingham, whose energy and enthusiasm appear to know no bounds.

Lynne Leeder
London.

Contents

Chapter One: The Origins and Sources of Ecclesiastical Law

Chapter Two: The Constitution of the Church of England

Chapter Three: The Diocese

Chapter Four: The Parish

Chapter Five: The Benefice

Chapter Six: Non-Parochial Units

Chapter Seven: Ecclesiastical Persons

Chapter Eight: Property and Finance of the Church of England

Chapter Nine: Doctrine and Worship

Chapter Ten: Sacraments and Offices

Chapter Eleven: Ecclesiastical Jurisdiction

Chapter Twelve: The Anglican Communion and Ecumenical Relations

Abbreviations

Thirty-nine Articles of Religion	Articles agreed upon by the Archbishops and Bishops of both Provinces and the whole Clergy in the Convocation holden at London in the year 1562 for the avoiding of diversities of opinions and for establishing of consent touching true religion; which is generally bound up with a printed copy of the Book of Common Prayer
ASB 1980	Alternative Service Book 1980
Canon	One of the Canon's Ecclesiastical promulged by the Convocations of Canterbury and York in 1964 and 1969 and by the General Synod of the Church of England from 1970. A Canon is denoted by its letter and number and the composite paragraphs appear by their number in brackets
CCEJM	Care of Churches and Ecclesiastical Jurisdiction Measure 1991
CRR	Church Representation Rules (Schedule 3 to the Synodical Government Measure) 1969
DAC	Diocesan Advisory Committee
DBF	Diocesan Board of Finance
EJM	Ecclesiastical Jurisdiction Measure 1963
FJM	Faculty Jurisdiction Measure 1964
FJR	Faculty Jurisdiction Rules 1992
Legal Opinions	Legal Opinions Concerning the Church of England (7th ed. 1994)
Newsom	G. H. Newsom and G. L. Newsom *Faculty Jurisdiction of the Church of England* (Second Edition 1993)
Ordinal	The Form and Manner of Making, Ordering and Consecrating of Bishops, Priests and Deacons, referred to in the Act of Uniformity 1662 (repealed); which is generally bound up with a printed copy of the Book of Common Prayer
PCC	Parochial Church Council
PCCPM	Parochial Church Councils (Powers) Measure 1956
SGM	Synodical Government Measure 1969

Table of Cases

Table of Statutes

Table of Statutory Instruments

Table of Canons

Table of Measures

Table of Church Regulation Rules

Chapter One:
The Origins and Sources of Ecclesiastical Law

"The ecclesiastical law and the temporal law have several proceedings and to several ends; the one being temporal to inflict punishment upon the body, lands, or goods; the other being spiritual, *pro salute animae*, the one to punish the outward man, the other to reform the inward . . . Then both these distinct and several jurisdictions consist and stand well together, and do join in this: to have the whole man inwardly and outwardly reformed."[1]   **1.1**

This quotation encapsulates the divergent motives underlying temporal and ecclesiastical law and the purposes behind the differing sanctions which the temporal and spiritual courts may seek to impose.[2] However, despite its clarity it may also be misleading, since it would tend to suggest that a ready distinction may be drawn between the subject matter within the two spheres of jurisdiction. In practice the position is somewhat more complex.

Despite its unitary nature, there exists within English law a distinction between one branch, with its own administration, which is known as ecclesiastical law and the remainder which may conveniently be termed general law, and is the province of the temporal or secular courts.[3] The first branch is ecclesiastical law used in its technical sense.[4] However, ecclesiastical law may also be used in a general sense[5] to refer to the law relating to all matters concerning the Church of England regardless of whether they fall within the jurisdiction of ecclesiastical or secular courts. This book is primarily concerned with ecclesiastical law used in its technical sense, but it also includes some areas of law which fall within the more general definition. The history of the division of jurisdiction between the temporal and spiritual courts and the present scope of the ecclesiastical courts are both considered more fully in Chapter 11.

In this chapter we consider the origins of the ecclesiastical law of England and its sources from the inception of Christianity to the modern era. It must be remembered that whilst a distinct and practical area of law, ecclesiastical

---

[1] *Caudrey's Case* (1591) 5 Co. Rep. 1a at 6b.
[2] For a discussion of the purpose of ecclesiastical law see Doe, *The Legal Framework of the Church of England* (1996), Chap. 2.
[3] *Att.-Gen. v. Dean and Chapter of Ripon Cathedral* [1945] 1 Ch. 239 at 245.
[4] Denning "The Meaning of Ecclesiastical Law". (1944) 60 L.Q.R. 235; Doe, *The Legal Framework of the Church of England* (1996), pp. 12–16.
[5] See n. 4.

jurisprudence has its roots in theology and in a belief in divine law. Understanding these basic principles is essential to its proper interpretation.

The origins of ecclesiastical law

1.2 The right of the Church to make rules and regulations for its own members, known as the *jus statuendi*, rests upon Christ's direction to the Apostles to "bind" and to "loose",[6] or to declare what was and was not allowed. That duty and right was first undertaken by the Apostles and the elders of the early Church, as is evident, for example, in the rules relating to the conduct of divine worship set out by St Paul in his first letter to the Corinthians.[7]

Legislative language runs throughout the Old Testament,[8] and Christ's commission to the Apostles to regulate the affairs of the Church is a continuation of that legislative authority. Thus, this right is delegated to what might today be called a subordinate legislature; subordinate since it is not an unlimited power, but is set within the framework of the divine and natural laws. Divine law is that law which is revealed or made explicit in the Scriptures, whilst the term natural law, as utilised by theologians, refers to that law which is unrevealed but is implicit in the natural order; both these laws being ascertained by theological inquiry. The Church is therefore constrained from making laws which contain orders, prohibitions or permissions contrary to either divine or natural law.

The history of the ecclesiastical law of England may be divided into three phases.[9] The first two, known as the *jus antiquum* and the *jus novum*, are common to the whole of the Western Catholic Church. The third phase, known as the period of mixed sources, runs from the Reformation, when the Church of England became a national Church independent of Rome, and contains what is today called the ecclesiastical law of England.

1.3 The early Church had no universal law other than that which derived directly from the Bible. Rather, until the time of Constantine the Great, matters were regulated by local custom and by rules made by each bishop. By the fourth century, having weathered periods of persecution the Church sought a greater uniformity, not least in order to deal with the problem of apostates who wished to return to the faith. Four regional councils were therefore formed, followed by the first General Council of the whole Church at Nicaea in A.D. 325. The decisions of these councils were set out in written laws to which the term "canons" was applied. Canon means a straight rod or line by which to measure something, in other words a standard or criterion by which to judge things; described by St Paul as a standard of Christian living.[10] The body of canons of these and subsequent general and local councils came to be referred to as canon law to distinguish them from Roman civil law.

[6] Matt. 18:18, 16:19, 19:28. Luke 22:28–30, 10:16.
[7] 1 Co. 11: 2–34. See also the proceedings of the Apostolic Council at Jerusalem: Acts 15.
[8] *Moore's Introduction to English Canon Law*, Briden & Hanson (3rd ed., 1992) Mowbray, pp. 1–2.
[9] A detailed history of the canon law of the Church of England is contained in *The Canon Law of the Church of England*, being the report of the Archbishops' Commission on Canon Law (See also Kemp, "The Spirit of the Canon Law and Its Application in England", (1987–88) 1 Ecc. L.J. 5, 1947).
[10] Gal. 6:16.

In addition to canon law the Church has a further source of law, known as "decretals". These decretals were the answers given by the papacy in response to questions put to them for decision, and were similar to modern case law. Both canons and decretals were intended to address specific situations. This, together with the fact that each province of the Church appears to have recognised only those canons of general or local councils on which it was represented and to have heeded only those decretals which were addressed to it, meant that the legislation in the early Church existed on an ad hoc basis. Attempts were made by various authors to rationalise the system by collecting together these canons and decretals and forming them into a more cohesive body. The most important of these collections, known as the *Dionysiana*, was undertaken in Rome at the beginning of the sixth century, by a monk called Dionysius Exiguus.

In the Anglo-Saxon Church the law also comprised several different compo- **1.4** nents. In addition to decretals on matters which had been referred to Rome by English bishops such as Gregory the Great's letter to St Augustine of 601, there were also canons which had been enacted or adopted by local councils of bishops. Examples of these councils include those of Hatfield and Cloveshoo presided over by the Archbishop of Canterbury, and the two legatine synods held in 786 presided over by papal legates. A further source were the dooms enacted by the Sovereign, bishops and nobility in the witenagemot. These tended to be concerned with the protection of the clergy and of Church property, as well as with secular enforcement of the Christian moral code. To this list may be added the penitentials, thought to have originated in Ireland, which set out lists of the penances to be imposed for particular sins. These lists, which differed from each other as well as from the canons and decretals, were the cause of much confusion before they finally fell into disrepute.

Following the Norman conquest, Archbishop Lanfranc attempted to revise Anglo-Saxon ecclesiastical laws as part of his general reform of the Church. Lanfranc introduced into England laws based upon a collection which has since come to be known as the "Forged Decretals". This collection had at its core an earlier body of laws known as the *Hispania* to which further decretals were appended in order to bring the law up to date. Viewed in context such forgeries are less shocking than they might appear to the modern mind. The Forged Decretals focused attention on the legislative power of the papacy and were the chief collection of law used in England until the end of the eleventh century, when they were displaced by the *Panormia*, a collection produced by Bishop Ivo of Chartres. This itself was based upon various sources, including the other great collection of that period, the *Decretum* of Burchard of Worms.

These collections were in turn displaced by the *Concordia Discorantium* **1.5** *Canonum*, or *Concordance of Discordant Canons* (produced in circa 1140 by Gratian, a monk in Bologna), which became known generally as the *Decretum*. This was the most comprehensive work then produced, drawing as it did from all recognised sources: decretals, canons, dicta of the Church Fathers, Frankish capitularies and Roman Civil Law. From these often contradictory sources Gratian produced a coherent and reasoned system of law. He made practical use of principles which had been under discussion amongst canonists for almost a century, in order to develop a system of ecclesiastical jurisprudence or science of law which assisted in bringing about logical cohesion. Laws were categorised into two types; immutable laws laid down by God in the Bible or in natural law, which, because they contain things essential to salvation or forbid things which are evil cannot be changed, and mutable laws, made in the course of history, which may be adapted to conditions of time and place by dispensation, for the good of the Church or an individual. In the *Decretum* the papacy stands out as the supreme legislative authority of the Church, a role which Medieval Popes were not slow to exploit. Gratian's work, although that of a private individual which never received official sanction, formed the basis of the *jus novum* of the later medieval centuries.

The *Decretum* formed the first and the largest part of the *Corpus Juris Canonici*. Although this latter term was sometimes used to describe any collection of laws, its technical use dates from the beginning of the sixteenth century, and refers to the collection published in Paris by Chappuis.[11] This contained the *Decretum* of Gratian, the *Decretals* of Gregory IX, the *Sext* of Boniface VIII, the *Clementines* of Clement V, the *Extravagantes* of John XXII and the *Extravagantes Communes*.[12] The *Corpus*, consisting of three official and three private codes, set out the law of the Church from the fourth century to the end of the Middle Ages. While much of the *Decretum* itself was rendered obsolete by subsequent papal legislation as set out in the rest of the *Corpus*, it nonetheless remained the classical exposition of the principles of canonical jurisprudence, and as such is still studied today.

1.6   Throughout this period the English Church recognised the same law as the rest of the Western Catholic Church. Only in very limited respects, for example in connection with the payment of tithes, did its application differ in England. One of the jurisprudential principles of the Church was that positive statute law could be abrogated by a contrary custom which was rational, had been in existence for a number of years and amounted to more than non-usage of that statute law.[13] However, notwithstanding the operation of this custom, the law of the Church as it has been received in England, was not substantially altered.

A further principle of the Church's common law was that each local church was to follow the metropolitan church of its province in liturgical matters. It is interesting to note that in the province of Canterbury however, the local custom was to follow the practices of Sarum, the Bishop of Salisbury being the provincial precentor.

The terminology used in respect of the law of the Church may be confusing and needs to be understood. The law of England is divided into two types; written or statute law, and the unwritten or common law.[14] Ecclesiastical law, which is part of the law of England, falls into these same two divisions. The common law of England is simply the common custom of the Realm.[15] It is

---

[11] The modern standard edition of this work is the *Corpus Juris Canonici* (ed. by Aemil Friedberg), 2 Vols (Leipzig 1879–81).

[12] *The Canon Law of the Church of England*, being the report of the Archbishop's Commission on Canon Law (1947), Chap. II, sets out the history and details of the *Corpus Juris Canonici*.

[13] *ibid*. This was a rule of pre-Reformation canon law; there appears to be no reported post-Reformation case recognising a custom *contra legem*. See Bursell, "What is the Place of Custom in English Canon Law?" (1989) 4 Ecc. L.J. 12.

[14] *Blackstone's Commentaries On the Laws of England* (14th ed.), 1803 Vol. I, p. 63.

[15] The potential for confusion is increased by the fact that in England there existed a system of common law courts in which the common lawyers from the Inns of Court practised. Older cases refer to the respective spheres of jurisdiction of the common law

important to note that it is not the same as the common law (or *jus commune*) of the Church of Rome, which means the law common to the Church of Rome.[16]

In England the ecclesiastical courts tended to modify the way in which the common law of the Church was applied. As in the rest of Western Europe there was debate as to the jurisdiction of the secular and ecclesiastical courts. In England matters such as ecclesiastical patronage came to be dealt with by the temporal courts under the rules of English common law, whilst the ecclesiastical courts exercised jurisdiction over wills disposing of personal property to an extent not contemplated by the *Corpus*, or seen in the rest of Europe. It is suggested that this development was a *quid pro quo* for the loss of their jurisdiction over advowsons.[17]

In the twelfth and thirteenth centuries the Church's common law was **1.7** interpreted and supplemented by the legislation of national and legatine synods. Provincial synods were also held once a year (in obedience to a canon of the Fourth Lateran Council inserted in the *Decretals* of Gregory IX) to consider decrees of General Councils and to enact constitutions. These constitutions were essentially ad hoc measures to remedy abuses, rather than a national system of Church law. They only created new laws when the matter was not already covered.

Our chief source of knowledge regarding the way in which the Church's common law was applied in the Middle Ages is the *Provinciale* by William Lynwood: a collection of the provincial constitutions of the province of Canterbury promulgated from 1222 to 1416, together with a gloss and commentary.[18] Lynwood did not regard the law of the Church in England to be independent of the *Corpus*, rather he considered the papal codes to be the highest legislative authority, in the light of which all local constitutions and customs must be interpreted.

The Reformation brought about the termination of papal authority in the Realm, and the recognition of the Sovereign as the Supreme Governor of the Church of England. With this shift in focus came moves to adapt canon law to meet the needs of the reformed Church. In 1534 the Act for the Submission of the Clergy and the Restraint of Appeals[19] provided for the appointment of a commission of 32 persons to be given power, subject to Royal Assent, to appraise the canon law contained in the *Corpus* together with provincial and synodical constitutions, and to abolish that of which they disapproved. This Act also made provision for those canons, constitutions and ordinances which had been made and which were neither contrary nor repugnant to the laws of the Realm, to continue in force until the work of the Commission was complete. A further Act

---

and the ecclesiastical courts, but today the distinction to be drawn is between the secular courts enforcing general law and the ecclesiastical courts enforcing ecclesiastical law; common law meaning no more than the unwritten customary law applicable to either general or ecclesiastical law.

[16] *Rennell v. Bishop of Lincoln* (1825) 3 Bing. 233 at 271; *Evers and Owen's Case*, Godb. 431.

[17] Pollock and Maitland *History of English Law*, Vol. II, p. 333.

[18] An English translation of the Canons collected by Lynwood of 1534 but without his commentary was reprinted in 1929: Bullard & Bell, *Lynwood's Provinciale*.

[19] 25 Hen. VIII, c. 19.

of 1543[20] conferring a new power to appoint a commission, which this time would have the additional right to make new canons, contained a similar provision, but with the additional reference to the ecclesiastical laws, or jurisdictions spiritual as accustomed and used in the Church of England.

1.8   This additional reference is of some importance, for it dervies from the theory that the Realm of England has always been free from subjection to laws other than those devised, made or ordained within it, and that the laws of any foreign prince or prelate only become laws of the Realm through the consent of the people, who have bound themselves to observe them by custom and long usage. In other words the application of such laws depends upon its reception into English law.[21] Thus the canon law of papal Rome as a body of laws never formed part of the law of England.[22] Those parts of the *jus commune* which were neither contrary nor repugnant to the laws of England, nor harmful to the royal perogative were given statutory recognition.[23] However, their authority depends not upon this statutory recognition, but upon incorporation into the law of the Realm as customary rather than written law. It is for this reason that any directive, rule or usage of pre-Reformation canon law must, in order to be binding, be pleaded and proved to have been recognised, continued and acted upon in England since the Reformation.[24]

Since no new code of post-Reformation canon law received the authority of either Parliament or the Convocations, Roman canon law continued to remain in force as part of the law of the Realm subject to the limitations imposed by the Act for the Submission of the Clergy. Thus much of the common law of the Church was accepted as part of the law of England,[25] being incorporated into either the statute or common law.

Thus it was that even into the nineteenth century much of the *Corpus Juris Canonici* (which was known as papal canon law) continued in force, as part of the customary law of England, in so far as it has not been abrogated or modified by statute or by the courts in the intervening period. So also did the legatine and provincial constitutions (known as domestic canon law) continue on the same basis with the additional proviso that those chapters of the papal law to which they related themselves continued in force.

1.9   Papal and domestic law was not the only law applied in the ecclesiastical courts following the Reformation, for the Canons of 1603 were also of great import-ance. Passed by the Convocation of Canterbury in 1604 and confirmed by Letters Patent under the Great Seal by James I, they were finally passed by the Convocation of York in 1606. Consisting of 141 canons in all, 97 of which were

---

[20] 35 Hen. VIII, c. 16 (Canon Law) (repealed).

[21] *Le Case de Commendam* (1612) Davies 696.

[22] This was the unanimous opinion of the judges advising the House of Lords in *R. v. Millis* (1844) 10 Cl. & Fin. 534 at 680 where that House was equally divided. It was also adopted by Blackburn J. in his advice to the House of Lords in *Bishop of Exeter v. Marshall* (1868) L.R. 3 H.L. 17 at 35 and was expressly approved by Lord Chelmsford L.C. at 46.

[23] See n. 20 *ante*.

[24] *Re St Mary's Westwell* [1968] 1 W.L.R. 513 at 516; *Bishop of Exeter v. Marshall* (*ante*) at 53, see also Bursell, "What is the Place of Custom in English Canon Law?" (1989) 14 Ecc. L. J. 12.

[25] *Caudrey's Case* (1591) 5 Co. Rep. 1a; *Att.-Gen. v. Dean and Chapter of Ripon Cathedral* [1945] 1 Ch. 239.

adapted from previous canons, orders and injunctions, whilst the remainder were mainly concerned with the regulation and reform of the procedure in the ecclesiastical courts. Although much of the material was of sixteenth century origin, the law contained within it, was generally a re-enactment or adaption of provincial constitutions of the Middle Ages. The Canons of 1603, to which various amendments were made over the centuries, were not intended to be, nor were they, comprehensive.[26]

In addition to the papal and domestic law and the Canons of 1603 there was also what has been termed ecclesiastical common law,[27] meaning a law older than the papal and domestic codes. However, whilst accurate this term may be confusing since all three sources form part of the common law of England. Further, much of the law in testamentary, and to a lesser extent matrimonial causes, over which the ecclesiastical courts exercised jurisdiction, was derived from the *Corpus Juris Civilis*, in other words it had its source in Roman civil law.

Some matters relating to the Church had fallen within the jurisdiction of the temporal courts and were dealt with under both common and statute law administered by them. One effect of the Reformation was that statute law also came to be part of the law administered by the ecclesiastical courts, and the ecclesiastical judges had to consider its impact upon the ecclesiastical law, and in particular whether it abrogated or modified any element of that law. Although initially there were few such statutes, by the eighteenth and more particularly the nineteenth century their numbers had significantly increased. One result of this increase was that much ecclesiastical law that had been uncertain and which had relied upon custom, was to be given statutory effect.

Precisely which part of the common law of the Church was abrogated by **1.10** statute, or was contrary or repugnant to the laws or customs of the Realm, or never binding since it had not been observed in England, was never officially delineated. After the Reformation the first attempt to set out fully the ecclesiastical law was made by John Godolphin in his *Repertorium Canonicum*,[28] a work which is modelled on the abridgments produced by the common lawyers. Other works of great authority were the *Parergon Juris Canonici Anglicani*[29] by John Ayliffe, and the *Codex Juris Ecclesiastici Anglicani*[30] by Edmund Gibson, Bishop of Lincoln and subsequently of London. However, the most successful of such publications was *Ecclesiastical Law*, the first edition of which was published in 1763[31] by Richard Burn a clergyman and Chancellor of the Diocese of Carlisle.

At the beginning of the nineteenth century full reports began to be produced of cases before the ecclesiastical courts and these judgments assist in defining the content and origin of English ecclesiastical law. A comprehensive account of the general principles was given, for example, by Sir John Nicholl at the beginning of the nineteenth century.

---

[26] *The Canon Law of the Church of England*, being the report of the Archbishops' Commission on Canon Law (1947), Chap. V.

[27] *Evers and Owen's Case*, Godb. 431 at 432.

[28] Godolphin, *Repertorium Canonicum: or an Abridgment of the Ecclesiastical Laws of this Realm* (London, 1678).

[29] Ayliffe, *Parergon Juris Canonici Anglicani: or A Commentary by Way of Supplement to the Canons and Constitutions of the Church of England* (London, 1726).

[30] Gibson, *Codex Juris Ecclesiastici Anglicani*, 2 Vols (Oxford, 1713).

[31] Burn *Ecclesiastical Law* (London, 1763). Sir Robert Phillimore *The Ecclesiastical Law of the Church of England* incorporates much of Burn's work.

"The law of the Church of England, and its history, are to be deduced from the ancient general Canon Law—from the particular constitution made in this country to regulate the English Church—from our own Canons—from the Rubric [*in the Book of Common Prayer*], and from any Acts of Parliament that may have been passed upon the subject; and this whole may be illustrated, also, by the writings of eminent person."[32]

1.11   At the beginning of the nineteenth century the ecclesiastical law of England was extremely flexible. As we shall see in Chapter 11 the doctrine of the binding force of precedent was then unknown to the ecclesiastical courts, which enabled its judges to adapt the law in each case as they saw fit within the principles of canonical jurisprudence. The general canon law or common law of the Church still applicable in England was sufficiently antiquated to require much judicial elucidation. The practice of deriving the law from the *Corpus* in respect of matters to which it still applied and explaining it by reference to the writings of eminent persons created judge-made law, the basis of which was far from certain. Only when the binding force of precedent was introduced into the ecclesiastical courts by Lord Stowell did ecclesiastical law develop into a system which fitted the main traditions of English legal practice.

When a question arises before the courts as to what is the ecclesiastical law of England it is ascertained by taking judicial note of what the law is, that is by hearing argument founded on legal principles and authorities.[33] In particular it is not ascertained by calling witnesses to prove it, which is how foreign law is determined.[34]

Sources of contemporary ecclesiastical law

1.12   Our consideration of the origins of ecclesiastical law has at least indicated its main sources.[35] First amongst these are the legislative or written sources. The Church of England is the Established Church of the State and accordingly the State (through Acts of Parliament) legislates on matters concerning the Church of England. Therefore much ecclesiastical law is to be found in general public Acts of Parliament and some in private Acts of Parliament.[36] Since the "Enabling Act" in 1919 a further legislative source is the Measures of the Church Assembly or the General Synod. The Church's powers to legislate by Measure and also by Canon, which is yet another source of ecclesiastical law, and the status of such legislation are matters considered in Chapter 2.

In addition another important source is the secondary or subordinate legislation of persons or bodies acting under a delegated legal authority. Examples are Statutory Instruments consisting of rules or orders, Orders in Council of the Sovereign and byelaws of local or other public authorities.

[32] *Kemp v. Wickes* (1809) 3 Phil, Ecc. R. 264 at 276.
[33] See *Mackonochie v. Lord Penzance* (1881) 6 App. Cas. 424 at 466, H.L.
[34] *ibid*.
[35] For a summary and discussion of the sources of Ecclesiastical Law see Denning "The Meaning of Ecclesiastical Law", (1944) 60 L.Q.R. 235; Doe, *The Legal Framework of the Church of England* (1996), Chap. 3.
[36] An example is the City of London (Guild Churches) Act 1952.

Acts of Synod, which are also discussed in Chapter 2, do not, despite their title, have statutory force. Rather they, together with all resolutions of Convocations whether or not formally dignified with the title of an Act of Convocation, have a great moral force. The same is true of statements by the House of Bishops of the General Synod. Other guidance material issued by the Church such as Codes of Practice may give rise to legitimate expectations that they will be applied fairly, as we shall also see in Chapter 12.

All pre-Reformation canon law so far as this is neither repugnant, nor contrary to the laws of England, forms part of the ecclesiastical law of England. As we have seen, some of this law is unwritten, but much of both papal and domestic law may be found in written sources. In either case such pre-Reformation law as survived the Reformation is now incorporated in statute, or forms part of the common or unwritten law of England.

The common law is an important source not just of surviving pre-Reformation **1.13** canon law, but of much ecclesiastical law. As we have seen, the reports of decided cases provide the greatest source for defining the content of English ecclesiastical law and it is from these that much of the common law may be deduced. However, common law means no more than customary law and if a custom can be proved it forms part of the ecclesiastical law of England.

All these sources must be added the works of eminent authors. Finally one must add the caveat that in order to have a proper understanding of ecclesiastical law it must be set in its proper framework, that is in its theological context.[37]

---

[37] Doe, "Towards a Critique of the Role of Theology in English Ecclesiastical and Canon Law", (1992) 2 Ecc. L.J. 328.

Chapter Two: The Constitution of the Church of England

The Church of England, established according to the laws of the Realm, claims **2.1** to belong to the true and apostolic Church of Christ.[1] From this flows the legal doctrine that the Church of England is a continuous body from its foundation in Saxon times to the present day.[2] England did not experience a Reformation in the same sense as Protestant Europe. Statutes passed during the reign of Henry VIII[3] excluded England from papal jurisdiction, which was regarded as a usurpation of the Sovereign's power, and recognised the Church as a separate national Church. Consequently the Church in England became the Church of England, but there was no intention to decline or vary from Christ's Church or the articles of the Catholic faith.[4] Thus the two provinces of the Church of England remain, as they were in origin, provinces of the Western Catholic Church. However, the religion of the Church of England did undergo a process of reform departing in its Articles of Religion from certain elements of the teaching of the Church of Rome. Accordingly the Church of England is both catholic and reformed, and in some sense therefore a Protestant Church.

In this chapter we consider the meaning of establishment and the relationship between Church and State. We also look at the Church's constitution, the process of Synodical Government, the General Synod and the legislative powers and processes of the Church together with proposals for a new Archbishops' Council and the consequent centralisation of many of the Church's functions. Finally we examine the Church's provincial organisation, convocations and the role of the archbishops.

The relationship between Church and State[5]

Establishment

The term establishment when used in relation to a church is capable of several **2.2** interpretations. In one sense any church which is recognised by the law and

---

[1] Canon A1.

[2] *Marshall v. Graham* [1907] 2 K.B. 112 at 126, D.C. *Halsbury's Laws of England* (4th ed.), Vol. 14, para. 345.

[3] Ecclesiastical Appeals Act 1532 (repealed); Submission of the Clergy Act 1533 (part repealed); Appointment of Bishops Act 1533 (part repealed); Ecclesiastical Licences Act 1533 (part repealed); Supremacy of the Crown Act 1534 (repealed).

[4] Ecclesiastical Licences Act 1533, s.13.

[5] See also Hastings, *Church and State: The English Experience* (1991); *Church and State*, Reports of the Archbishops' Commissions (1916, 1970); *Church and State* the report of a

whose rights are protected can be said to be established. However, what is called the establishment principle, when applied to a church, means the duty upon the State to support and assist that church,[6] and a church is established in the fullest sense when all the provisions constituting its organisation receive the sanction of law and establish that system throughout the state to the exclusion of all others[7] (although this does not mean that the established Church thereby becomes a department of State).[8] The Church of England has been treated judicially as a denomination[9] but it is accepted that the Church of England is established by law,[10] and it is treated as the public or State-recognised form of religion.[11]

Accordingly the constitution of the Church of England, as established by law, consists of those ordinances, authorities and provisions by which it operates and which are judicially recognised by the courts.[12] By contrast an unestablished church or religious association is free from State control as regards doctrine, government and discipline, and it is this freedom which differentiates it from the established Church.[13]

Supremacy of the Sovereign

2.3   Prior to the Reformation the relationship in England between Church and State was akin to a marriage; each party remaining separate but regarded as being one for certain purposes, and with some marital tensions evident.[14] Following the Reformation, papal authority in the Realm was terminated and the Sovereign recognised as Supreme Governor of the Church of England,[15] bringing about a far closer identification of Church and State. That identification was fundamental to the concept of establishment.

As Supreme Governor and acting according to the laws of the Realm, the Sovereign is the highest power under God in the Realm, having supreme authority in all causes ecclesiastical and temporal. The Sovereign is thus the ultimate court of appeal in all ecclesiastical suits[16] but exercises this function, as

commission appointed by the Church Assembly in 1947 (1952). Doe, *The Legal Framework of the Church of England* (1996), pp. 7–10. Pearce, "The Church of England and the European Union; Establishment and Ecclesiology", (1994) 3 Ecc. L.J. 337.

[6] *Marshall v. Graham* (*ante*); *Halsbury's Laws of England* (4th ed.), Vol. 14, para. 345.

[7] *General Assembley of the Free Church of Scotland v. Overtoun* [1904] A.C. 515, H.L.

[8] See n. 6, above.

[9] *R. v. Registrar General, ex p. Segerdal* [1970] 3 All E.R. 886 at 887; *Re Perry Almshouses* [1898] 1 Ch. 391 at 400; *Re Perry Almshouses, Re Ross' Charity* [1899] 1 Ch. 21, C.A.

[10] See, *e.g. Re Barnes, Simpson v. Barnes* [1930] 2 Ch. 80 at 81.

[11] *Halsbury's Laws of England* (4th ed.), Vol. 14, para. 334.

[12] *Mackonochie v. Lord Penzance* (1881) 6 App. Case. 424, H.L.

[13] *General Assembly of the Free Church of Scotland v. Overtoun ante* at 684; *R. v. Dibdin* [1910] P. 57, C.A.; affd *sub nom. Thompson v. Dibdin* [1912] A.C. 533, H.L. The powers of such unestablished churches lie within their constitutions.

[14] Briden and Hanson, *Moore's Introduction to English Canon Law* (3rd ed., 1992), Chap. 2.

[15] Supremacy of the Crown Act 1534 (repealed); Act of Supremacy 1558, s.8 (part repealed), s.9 (repealed); Canon A7; 39 Articles of Religion, Preface, Article xxxvii; Makower, *Constitutional History of the Church of England* (English translation 1895) p. 251 *et seq.*

[16] *Blackstone's Commentaries on the Laws of England* (14th ed. 1803) Vol. 3, pp. 66–67.

in temporal matters, through her judges. However, although supreme government of the Church of England is attributed to the Sovereign, and the Sovereign is regarded as *persona sacra*, the monarch does not have the status of an ordained minister.[17]

The Sovereign must be in communion with the Church of England: in order to ensure that the Sovereign is not a Roman Catholic, a doctrinal declaration is made on accession to the effect that the Sovereign is a faithful Protestant and will, according to the true intent of the enactments which secure the Protestant succession to the throne, uphold and maintain those enactments to the best of their powers according to the law.[18]

The Sovereign is Supreme Ordinary[19] and visitor, and as such visits the archbishops[20] and receives their resignations. The Sovereign also visits all those places which are exempt from episcopal visitations (known as royal peculiars). The Sovereign is patron paramount of all the archbishoprics, bishoprics and benefices in England and has extensive powers of patronage in addition to numerous executive functions, often exerciseable by Orders in Council. Various powers formerly vested in the Pope are generally exercisable by the Sovereign, who also has control over the granting of certain licences and dispensations under the Ecclesiastical Licences Act 1533. However, the Sovereign does not have a general power to dispense from the laws ecclesiastical,[21] which remain binding unless altered by the Sovereign in Parliament.

Following the Glorious Revolution of 1689 and the introduction of a constitutional monarchy, Royal supremacy in effect gave way to Parliamentary supremacy. Thus the Sovereign, Lords and Commons together form the Sovereign power, and may legislate for the Church as they see fit, all other persons and bodies being in law subordinate to the supremacy of the Sovereign in Parliament.

The Church has a significant presence in Parliament. The two archbishops and 24 bishops have seats in the House of Lords, whilst the Second Church Estates Commissioner is by convention a member of the House of Commons and steers legislation through that House on behalf of the General Synod. Although clergy are precluded from sitting in the House of Commons they are entitled to vote for members of Parliament.

Territorial limits of the Church of England

The Church of England must not be confused with the wider Anglican **2.4** Communion of which it forms a part, nor with the other national Churches of the United Kingdom.[22] The Union with Scotland Act 1706 secured both the established Church of England and the government of the Presbyterian Church of Scotland, as fundamental and essential conditions of that union. Thus Scotland

---

[17] Articles of Religion, 37.
[18] Bill of Rights 1688, s.1; Act of Settlement 1700, ss.2, 3; Accession Declaration Act 1910, s.1. See also the Coronation Oath Act 1688, s.3.
[19] See Chap. 3.
[20] *Blackstone's Commentaries on the Laws of England* (14th ed. 1803), Vol. 1, p. 382.
[21] Bill of Rights 1688, s.1.
[22] See Chap. 12.

has its own established Kirk. Although the Churches of England and Ireland were united from 1800 until 1871, when the Church of Ireland was disestablished, the constitution of the Church of England was unaffected by this temporary union.[23] For the purposes of defining the territorial limits of the Church of England, "England" includes the town of Berwick-upon-Tweed, but not any part of England or Wales to which the Welsh Church Act 1914 applies,[24] the Church in Wales having been disestablished in 1920.

The Channel Islands[25] form part of the diocese of Winchester in the province of Canterbury,[26] whilst the diocese of the Isle of Man forms part of the province of York,[27] the Bishop of Sodor and Man having a seat in the Upper House of the Convocation of York. He is also a member of the Legislative Council which forms part of the parliament of Tynwald and for this reason is excluded from the ranks of the bishops who may be summoned to a seat in the House of Lords at Westminster. The diocese of Europe is a diocese in the province of Canterbury.[28]

It is outside the scope of this work to consider the application of English statute laws and in particular the application of Acts and Measures relating to the Church of England, to the Isle of Man and the Channel Islands. However, it should be noted that the provisions of the Synodical Government Measure 1969 (SGM) relating to the establishment, constitution and functions of the General Synod extend to the Isle of Man[29] and the remainder of its provisions were extended to it, with modifications, by an Act of Tynwald.[30] The SGM was also applied, with modifications, to the Channel Islands by a scheme approved by General Synod and confirmed by Order in Council.[31]

Membership of the Church of England

2.5   The Church of England is not a corporation, but must be considered as an aggregate of all its members, both lay and clerical.[32] Membership is generally taken to include all baptised persons who offer general allegiance to the ordinances and liturgy of the Church of England,[33] which may be demonstrated

---

[23] Irish Church Act 1869, s.69, contains a saving clause that in all enactments and other documents provisions relating to the United Church of England and Ireland shall be read distributively in respect of the Church of England and the Church of Ireland.

[24] Interpretation Measure 1925, s.2.

[25] "The Islands" or Channel Islands meaning the Island of Jersey, and the Island and Bailiwick of Guernsey and its dependencies, Alderney and Sark: Channel Islands (Church Legislation) Measure 1931, s.1.

[26] *ibid.*, preamble.

[27] *Coke on Littleton* (14th ed. 1639) Vol. 1, p. 94a; Godolphin, *Repertorium Canonicum* (3rd ed. 1687), p. 14.

[28] Diocese in Europe Measure 1980.

[29] SGM, s.9(3), (4).

[30] Church (Synodical Government Measure) Act 1971 (c. 10). See generally, Gumbley, "Church Legislation in the Isle of Man", (1994) 3 Ecc. L.J. 240.

[31] SGM, s.9(3), (5); Synodical Government (Channel Islands) Order, S.I. 1970 No. 1117.

[32] *R. v. Dibdin* [1910] p. 57 at 136, C.A.

[33] *Re Perry Almshouses* [1898] 1 Ch. 391 at 400; *Re Perry Almshouses, Re Ross' Charity* [1899] 1 Ch. 21, C.A.; *MacLaughlin v. Campbell Re Barnes, Simpson v. Barnes* [1930] 2 Ch. 80 [1906] 1 I.R. 588.

by certain formal acts and conduct such as baptism, confirmation, and attendance at church services.[34] However, membership may have different meanings in different contexts. In some respects non-conforming Christians are, and used to describe themselves as, members of the Church of England who do not conform, although they are now generally referred to in England as members of the Free Churches. Much will depend upon the subject matter in question,[35] and in one sense all those who do not actively exclude themselves from membership may be taken as being members of the Church of England as the national church.[36]

In order to have their name placed upon the church electoral roll a person must declare themselves to be a member of the Church of England or a church in communion with it.[37] "Member" is not defined for this purpose. Thus anyone resident within the parish prepared to declare themselves as such is a member. Attendance at public worship is only required for enrolment of those not resident in the parish. To be elected as a parochial representative of the laity to the Parochial Church Council (PCC) or the deanery synod, or to be elected to the diocesan synod or House of Laity of the General Synod there is a requirement that the person whose name is on the church electoral roll is "an actual communicant". This refers to a person who has received Communion according to the use of the Church of England or of a Church in communion with it, at least three times during the 12 months preceding their election or appointment and whose name is on the electoral roll of a parish. Such a person must also be either confirmed, or ready and desirous of being confirmed, or be entitled to and actually receiving Holy Communion.[38] For ecclesiastical judicial office a lay person is required to be a "communicant", by which is meant a person who has received communion according to the use of the Church of England or a church in communion with it at least once within the 12 months preceding the date on which they either make a declaration that they fulfil that requirement, are offered the appointment, or are requested to act.[39]

Synodical government

The Enabling Act 1919

As we saw in Chapter 1 all changes in ecclesiastical law after the Reformation were effected by Act of Parliament. Although the Church did retain a subordinate legislature in the form of the Convocations of the two provinces of Canterbury and York their power was limited to making canons which were and still are binding only upon ecclesiastical persons.   **2.6**

---

[34] *Re Selby's Will Trusts, Donn v. Selby* [1966] 1 W.L R. 43.
[35] *Re Allen, Faith v. Allen* [1953] Ch. 116.
[36] See further Warren (ed.), *A Church for the Nation* (1992).
[37] CRR, r. 1. This now includes a member of a church which subscribes to the doctrine of the Holy Trinity who is also prepared to declare themselves to be a member of the Church of England having habitually attended such parish worship. For those churches in communion with the Church of England see Chap. 12.
[38] CRR, r. 54.
[39] EJM, s.66(1). As to which see Chap. 11.

With the general increase in the legislative programme throughout the nineteenth and into the early twentieth century, Parliament no longer had the time to devote to matters relating to the Church, nor were its members any longer uniformly Anglican. In 1916 therefore the Archbishops' Commission on Church and State produced a report which later went on to form the basis of addresses presented by the two Convocations to the King in 1919, the result of which was the passing of the Church of England Assembly (Powers) Act 1919, commonly known as the Enabling Act. The Act accorded statutory recognition to the National Assembly of the Church of England, and gave it the right to pass Measures which, subject to Parliamentary scrutiny and approval, would have the force and effect of Acts of Parliament. Thus a new ecclesiastical legislature was created, placing primary responsibility for matters concerning the Church in the hands of its members, both clergy and laity, who were each represented in the Church Assembly. Parliament however remains supreme both in the control it exercises over such Measures and in its unfettered right to legislate directly upon Church matters, without recourse to the Church Assembly, if it so wishes.

Transfer of powers to the General Synod

2.7   In addition to its powers in respect of Measures the Church Assembly had concurrent powers with the Convocations with regard to the making of canons. To bring about an end to this dual exercise of functions, and to ensure that the authority to legislate by canon would be exercisable by the Church of England as a whole rather than provincially, the Convocations of Canterbury and York vested their functions, authority, rights and privileges in the Church Assembly. From the date of that transfer[40] the Church Assembly was, pursuant to the SGM, reconstituted and renamed the General Synod of the Church of England, and thus synodical government was born.[41]

With the creation of the Church Assembly governance of the Church of England was opened up in part at least to its practising members. The SGM made provision for the reconstitution of that Assembly, established new rules for representation of the laity and created diocesan and deanery synods to replace the former diocesan and rurideaconal conferences. Thus a structure was set in place which complemented the administrative structure of the Church.

As regards the administrative structure of the Church of England, under the Sovereign are the two archbishops who oversee the dioceses of their respective provinces. Beneath them the bishops of the dioceses, each diocese being divided into archdeaconries with an archdeacon, and further subdivided into rural deaneries into which the parishes are grouped.

It is often said the Church is episcopally led but synodically governed. Synodical government, with the General Synod at its head, affords both clergy

---

[40] Transitional provisions provided that any existing canons, Acts of Convocation or regulations made by Convocations in exercise of their functions and any orders, regulations or rules of the Church Assembly were to continue in force as if made by the General Synod: SGM, Sched. 4, para. 1.

[41] Synodical Government is currently the subject of a review by a committee under the chairmanship of Lord Bridge of Harwich. See also McHenry, "The Future of Synodical Government in the Church of England", (1993) 3 Ecc. L.J. 86.

and laity the opportunity for representation at national, diocesan and deanery level, and in the PCCs, at parish level. In this chapter we consider the constitution and role of the General Synod and although some of the matters covered are of relevance to the system of synodical government as a whole, diocesan and deanery synods are discussed in Chapter 3 and PCCs in Chapter 4.

Proposals to centralise the Church's administration

The Archbishops' Commission on the Organisation of the Church of England, **2.8** under the chairmanship of the Bishop of Durham, the Right Reverend Michael Turnbull, has produced a report[42] which makes recommendations to restructure the central administration of the Church in order to meet the challenges of the new millenium. The Commission felt that to encapsulate the Church as episcopally led and synodically governed tended to obscure the role of the bishops in synodical government itself. Although the Commission stated that it would wish to resist the members of the General Synod becoming a distinct legislative caste, and emphasised their important deliberative role, its report concluded that the Synod cannot take on the role of an executive body.

The Commission's report emphasises the importance of the episcopacy and in particular the significance of the House of Bishops in its role as a chief college of pastors. In addition to its primary role in relation to worship and doctrine the House of Bishops would continue to issue papers on matters of importance to the Church. Episcopal responsibilities of oversight mean that the bishops have the most general knowledge of their dioceses and hence collegially of the Church as a whole. Flowing from this concept of the primary importance of the episcopate the recommendations of the Turnbull Commission are based upon the model of the bishop in synod.

The Commission proposes an Archbishops' Council in order to produce an overall policy for the Church and to provide cohesion to the current "cat's cradle" of autonomous or semi-autonomous central bodies with their overlapping functions. The aim of the new council would be to enhance the operation of episcopal leadership and synodical government, the Council reporting to, but not being subordinate, to the General Synod. However, although not subordinate the Council would be accountable to the General Synod which would retain the power to reject policy proposals and legislation introduced to the Synod by the Council, to reject the national budget prepared by the Council, and have the right to receive regular reports on the work of the Council and to question the Council on any matter for which it had responsibility.

The Archbishops of Canterbury and York would be joint Presidents of the **2.9** Archbishops' Council. The Archbishops would be immediately supported by four chairmen responsible for the main areas of the Council's activity; these being: ministry, mission, heritage, and legal and finance. The four chairmen would be appointed by the Archbishops after consultation through (at least in the first instance) a Nominations Committee, with their appointments approved by the General Synod.

---

[42] *Working as One Body*, The Report of the Archbishops' Commission on the Organisation of the Church of England (1995) and see *Working as One Body: A Framework for Legislation* (1996) (G.S. 1188).

The Prolocutors of the Convocations of Canterbury and York (who lead the House of Clergy of the General Synod) and the Chairman and Vice-Chairman of the House of Laity would be members of the Council, together with two members of the House of Bishops elected by and from its members and one member from each of the Houses of Clergy and Laity elected by and from the members of those Houses. In addition there would be a chairman of the proposed new Business Committee of the General Synod. It is currently envisaged that the First Church Estates Commissioner would be a member of the Council, whilst a Secretary General would be the Council's chief executive and head of staff, having a right to attend its meetings and to speak, but not actually being a member of the Council. The Archbishops would also have the power to co-opt up to three further members.

The Council would thus consist of a maximum of 19 members, nine directly elected by the General Synod. Such members of the Council who were not also members of Synod would be made *ex officio* members so that they could present the Council's business to the Synod. The intention would be to have a slimmer organisation involving fewer committees. The new Council which would meet about six times a year, and the House of Bishops would both be served by a central secretariat.

The Council would assume the main functions of the General Synod's Standing and Policy Committees, the Central Board of Finance and the Advisory Board of Ministry, all of which would cease to exist. The preparation of the business of General Synod itself would be placed in the hands of a new Business Committee whilst the current appointments sub-committee would remain as a fully fledged Appointments Committee. The work of the other Boards and Councils of the General Synod would also come under the authority of the Council. Various executive bodies would continue to serve the Church at national level, but again they would interrelate through the Council. The Council would in addition take over responsibility for oversight of the Church's resources, a matter considered in more detail in Chapter 8.

2.10   The main function of the Council would be to help develop a clearer sense of direction drawing on the guidance of the House of Bishops. Specifically it would be responsible for the assessment of the overall financial and human resource needs of the Church, and would seek to ensure that policies and strategies were developed to meet those needs and priorities. In addition to overseeing the direction of staff and other resources at national level the Council would support the dioceses and co-ordinate their work. The Council would also have a legislative role and would normally introduce legislation to the General Synod although Synod would nonetheless retain its powers of legislative initiative.

If adopted the proposals of the Commission and in particular the creation of an Archbishops' Council will have a profound effect upon the current organisation of the Church. Having received the broad consensus of the General Synod the proposals are now the subject of a steering group which will seek to proceed to draft legislation and to further consultation and consideration. Although the main thrust of the Commission's report is not likely to be implemented before 1998, the proposals of the Turnbull Commission may be regarded as representing, in draft form at least, the new structure of the Church as it moves into the twenty-first century.

The General Synod

The General Synod's constitution is set out in Schedule 2 to the SGM, and **2.11** consists of the Convocations of Canterbury and York joined together in a House of Bishops and a House of Clergy, together with a House of Laity. It should be noted that the emphasis is upon the two Convocations, rather than the individuals who are for the time being members of them, the intention being to make clear that General Synod possesses the full spiritual authority as well as the functions of the Convocations. However, in practical terms, the membership of the Houses of Bishops and Clergy is identical to that of the Upper and Lower Houses respectively of the two Convocations combined, and accordingly we consider the qualifications for membership of these bodies together. By contrast the members of the House of Laity are elected in accordance with the Church Representation Rules (CRR).

The close connection between General Synod and the Convocations is emphasised by the fact that the calling together of the Convocations has the effect of bringing into being General Synod, and likewise the Convocations' dissolution also dissolves General Synod.[43] However, the link between the lives of the Convocations and Parliament has now been broken. Convocation still meets in response to a Royal writ, but this is no longer issued to the archbishops when Parliament is summoned. The Convocations may be summoned together and dissolved by the Sovereign without regard to the time at which Parliament is summoned or dissolved, and in contrast to Parliament are not dissolved automatically on the death of the Sovereign.[44] Unless dissolved earlier by Royal writ, Convocations have a life of five years from the date they were called together and new Convocations are called together as soon as convenient following such dissolution.[45]

House of Bishops and the Upper Houses of the Convocations

The Upper House of the Convocation of each province consists of the arch- **2.12** bishop and all the diocesan bishops,[46] together with elected members. These members, six in Canterbury and three in York, are elected by and from all the suffragan bishops of that province and any other persons in episcopal orders working in a diocese who are members of the House of Bishops of that diocese.[47] Membership of the Upper and Lower Houses is strictly segregated. Consequently all those in episcopal orders are disqualified from being elected, chosen or co-opted to be members of the Lower Houses, and all those who are members of the House of Bishops of a diocesan synod are excluded from electing or choosing any member of the Lower Houses.[48] When any member of one of the Upper

---

[43] SGM, s.1(4), Sched. 2, art. 3(2).
[44] Church of England Convocations Act 1966, s.1.
[45] *ibid*.
[46] The diocese in Europe is deemed for the purposes of representation in both Convocation and the General Synod to be within the province of Canterbury: Diocese in Europe Measure 1980, ss.1, 2; Canons H2, H3.
[47] Canon H3.
[48] Canon H2 (1A).

Houses ceases to be eligible for membership he is deemed to have vacated his seat, and in the case of suffragans, provision is made for elections to casual vacancies.[49]

House of Clergy and Lower Houses of the Convocations

2.13   Canon H2[50] provides for the representation of the clergy, known as proctors, in the Lower Houses of the Convocations. Membership consists of directly and specially selected proctors, who must not exceed in total 170 for Canterbury and 80 for York, together with *ex officio* and co-opted proctors.

The largest group in both Houses are the directly elected proctors, that is elected representatives, of the clergy. Each diocese forms an electoral area, the number of persons to be elected from it being determined by the General Synod in proportion to the number of electors within it. Each diocese must have three elected proctors, save for Sodor and Man and Europe which have one and two respectively. The archbishop has the power to divide a diocese up into separate electoral areas, provided the assignment leaves each area with no fewer than three proctors.

All clergy admitted to deacon's or priest's orders who are entitled to vote in that electoral area are eligible as proctors, together with archdeacons who hold office in the area and who are not otherwise appointed. Clergy beneficed or licensed to a parish, or to serve as team vicar in a diocean electoral area and who are only precluded from voting in that area because they are entitled to vote in a university area, may elect whether to stand as a proctor in the university or diocesan area. However, all deacons and priests are excluded if they hold any paid office, employment or appointment which is or may be made or confirmed by certain bodies of the Church.[51] All those eligible may only offer themselves for election in one electoral area at a time.

Electors are all the clergy in the electoral area who are exercising the office of assistant bishop, or are beneficed in the area, or licensed under seal by the diocesan bishop and resident in the area, or holding office in a cathedral church (or in Canterbury, certain collegiate churches) in the area. However, any member of the House of Bishops of a diocesan synod, deans, provosts, archdeacons, members of religious communities and those clergy who are entitled to vote in a university electoral area but who elect not to do so, are not permitted to be electors. Neither are in the case of Canterbury, chaplains who are *ex officio* members of that House. All those eligible as electors are restricted to voting in one electoral area.

In the province of Canterbury the universities of Oxford, Cambridge and London and the other universities in the province taken together, consist of four

---

[49] Canon H3.

[50] The Canon (as published by Church House Publishing) is a conflated text of the two parallel canons promulged by the Convocations of Canterbury and York. The canon provides for rules to be made by the General Synod governing appointments and elections to the Lower House.

[51] Namely the General Synod, Convocations, the Central Board of Finance, the Church Commissioners, the Church of England Pensions Board or the Corporation of Church House, although the disqualification does not apply to a Church Commissioner in receipt of a salary or other emoluments.

electoral areas, and in York the universities of Durham and Newcastle taken together comprise one electoral area and all the other universities in the province taken together comprise a second. From these six areas proctors are specially elected by and from the clergy qualified to vote by reason of positions which they hold within these universities.

In addition, the Lower House of Canterbury consists of 10 specially elected **2.14** proctors, and the Lower House of York five, elected by and from the deans and provosts of all the cathedral churches in the province, together with, in the case of Canterbury, the Deans of the collegiate churches of St Peter's Westminster, St George, Windsor and the cathedral church of Holy Trinity in Gibralter. Further special proctors are appointed. One archdeacon is appointed (by all the archdeacons if they agree, otherwise by the bishop) for each diocese (other than in the diocese of Sodor and Man where the Archdeacon of Man is appointed and the diocese in Europe where none is appointed) and one person is chosen by and from the clerical members of religious communities in each province. In addition, in Canterbury, the Deans of Jersey and Guernsey alternate as special proctors.

If a member of the clergy the Vicar-General of each province sits as an *ex officio* proctor. So too, in the case of Canterbury, does the Dean of the Arches and Auditor, the Third Church Estates Commissioner and the Chairman of the Church of England Pensions Board if they are clergy: otherwise all these persons are *ex officio* members of the House of Laity. In Canterbury the Chaplain of the Fleet, the Chaplain-General of the Forces the Chaplain in Chief, Royal Air Force, and the Chaplain General of Prisons, or if they are not clergy such chaplain is of the relevant service as, nominated by the Archbishop also sit.

In addition each Convocation has the power to co-opt clergy (three for Canterbury and two for York) admitted to priests orders as members of the Lower House. Where this power is exercised the Houses may fix a period of membership which is shorter than the lifetime of the Convocations.

As a general rule any member of the Lower Houses who ceases to be eligible for their seat, or whose election or choice is deemed void, is deemed to have vacated it. The exceptions are proctors elected by the clergy (other than those who are disqualified by reason of a specified office or employment), whom the Bishop's Council and Standing Committee of the relevant diocese determine in advance of the vacancy arising should remain a member. Provision is also made for election to casual vacancies unless the vacancy arises less than 12 months before an ordinary election is to be held.

Church Representation Rules—rules of general application

Before turning to consider the membership of the House of Laity it is helpful to **2.15** consider some general points regarding the CRR[52] which make provision for membership of that House, the constitution and proceedings of diocesan and deanery synods and PCCs, the election or appointment of persons to these bodies, and the establishment of a church electoral roll. We have already considered the requirement in the CRR that for election to any of these bodies a person must be an "actual communicant".

[52] SGM, Sched. 3. The CRR have been subject to considerable amendment and renumbering. Church House Publishing produces updated versions at regular intervals.

The strict application of certain rules is expressly modified. Thus it is stated that no proceedings of any body constituted under the CRR are invalidated by a vacancy in membership, nor by any defect in the qualification, election or appointment of any members.[53] Furthermore, although the CRR prescribe necessary forms no proceedings are in fact invalidated by the use of a different form which is substantially similar in effect to that prescribed, this being a matter to be determined by the bishop.[54] In addition the diocesan bishop is given powers to provide for matters not dealt with by the CRR, first in order to give effect to the intention of the rules and secondly to alter or extend the time for certain meetings or elections as well as to make certain other modifications of procedure. He also has power to appoint any person to do any act in respect of which there has been neglect or default on the part of the person or body charged with the duty under the rules, and to give directions for the purpose of removing any difficulties.[55] However, these powers do not enable a bishop to validate anything which was invalid at the time it was done, or to give any direction which is contrary to a resolution of the General Synod.

A person is not to be disqualified for being elected or chosen as a member of any body under the CRR because they are an *ex officio* member of it. Nor is an elected or chosen member deemed to have vacated their seat because they subsequently become an *ex officio* member of it.[56] Where the rules refer to a casual vacancy this also includes the situation where insufficient candidates have been nominated to fill the places available.[57]

It should also be noted that anyone who holds office under the CRR or is a member of a body consituted under it may resign by sending notice in writing, signed by them, to the secretary of the relevant body. The resignation takes effect either on the date specified in the notice, or if no date is specified, on the receipt of the notice by the secretary.[58]

The House of Laity of the General Synod

2.16 The House of Laity is constituted and its members elected and selected in accordance with Part V of the CRR.[59] Its membership is mainly composed of persons directly elected by diocesan electors, but also includes three members (two from Canterbury and one from York) chosen by the lay members of religious communities from among their number, *ex officio* members who, as we saw above, could not take seats in the House of Clergy because they were not ordained, and co-opted members. The House of Laity may co-opt up to five members at any one time, provided that at least two-thirds of the members of the standing committee of that House consent. Co-opted members must be actual lay communicants aged at least 18 years of age. The House of Laity elects from amongst its members a chairman and vice-chairman who also discharge the

---

[53] CRR, r. 53.
[54] *ibid*.
[55] *ibid*.
[56] CRR, r. 47.
[57] *ibid*., r. 49.
[58] *ibid*., r. 48(11).
[59] *ibid*., r. 35–42.

functions assigned to the Prolocutor (speaker) and Pro-Prolocutor of the House.[60]

Each diocese is an electoral area for such elections, a diocesan synod having the power to divide a diocese into two or more areas and apportion the number of members to be elected for such areas, provided that no less than three members will be elected in each area. The diocesan electors of all the dioceses except Europe,[61] are the members of the Houses of Laity of the deanery synods in the diocese, excluding co-opted members and lay members of religious communities who have elected representatives.

Register of lay electors

All electors must be entered in the register of lay electors maintained by the **2.17** diocesan electoral registration officer.[62] The qualifying date for all electors is 6.00 a.m. on the date of the dissolution of the General Synod, save in cases of a casual vacancy where the qualifying date is 6.00 a.m. on the date when the nomination papers are issued.

Provision is made for the inspection and correction of the register of these electors, except during the period between close of nominations and declaration of the result of an election. An appeal procedure exists in respect of either the removal or the refusal to remove a name from the register.[63] The appeal may be made by anyone who is refused enrolment or whose name is removed, or by a person whose name is on the register who objects to the enrolment or removal from it of anyone else. Notice must be given within 14 days of the act complained of,[64] to the chairman of the House of Laity of the diocesan synod. The matter is then referred to the bishop's council, which appoints three or more (so long as there is an odd number) of its lay members to consider and decide the appeal, the procedure being the same as that described below in regard to election appeals.

Elections

The total number of persons to be elected, including those specially elected as **2.18** the representatives of the Channel Islands and of the lay members of religious communities, must not exceed 170 for the province of Canterbury and 80 for York. No dioceses, other than Sodor and Man and Europe which elect one and two members respectively, have fewer than three directly elected members. The total number of persons to be elected by diocesan electors is fixed by resolution of the General Synod which must apportion the numbers between the two

---

[60] SGM, Sched. 2, art. 9(2).
[61] In the diocese of Europe the electors are those persons elected by the annual meetings of the chaplaincies, those eligible for election being actual lay communicants, aged at least 18, whose names are entered on the electoral roll of such a chaplaincy.
[62] CRR, r. 29. The co-opted members being listed separately.
[63] *ibid.*, r. 43.
[64] Or within 14 days of the publication of a revised or new register if this is the cause of the complaint: *ibid.*

provinces in a proportion of 68 to 32 or as close as possible to that proportion. The number to be elected for each province is further divided between the dioceses so that the number of members to be elected by each diocese is as near as possible in proportion to the total number of names certified as names on the electoral rolls of parishes in that diocese.

A lay person is qualified for election for a diocese if they are an actual communicant and were at least 18 years of age on the date of the dissolution of the General Synod. In addition their name must, at 6.00 a.m. on that date, have been entered on the electoral roll of any parish in the diocese, or they are declared (at any time within the period of two months beginning one month immediately before the date of dissolution), by the dean of any cathedral church to be an habitual worshipper there. As with persons otherwise eligible to be elected as proctors of the clergy, a lay person is disqualified from election to the House of Laity if they hold any of the same paid offices, employments or appointments.

Since recent failures to comply with election procedures have caused concern the rules are set out here in some detail. Subject to any directions by the General Synod or its presidents, elections to the House of Laity are carried out during the three months immediately following the dissolution of Synod, during the period within the three months fixed by the archbishops. The presiding officer sends out nomination papers. Each candidate for election must be nominated and seconded by diocesan electors qualified to vote in the area for which the candidate is standing. All nominations must be in writing and include the year of the candidate's birth. These are sent, together with evidence of the candidate's willingness to serve, to the presiding officer, within a period of not less than 28 days ending on a date specified by that officer. Nominations are scrutinised by the officer as soon as they are lodged. If the officer rules a nomination to be invalid a candidate is not disqualified from the election if a new valid nomination is not received within the permitted time; thus it is advisable to lodge a nomination as soon as possible in case it is invalid and submission of a new nomination is necessary.

2.19   Upon making a written request a candidate is entitled to a copy of the names and addresses of all qualified electors. A candidate may also request the presiding officer to despatch an election address from them to every elector. The officer must comply with this request, provided sufficient copies of the address in the correct form (which must not comprise more than one sheet of A4 paper) are delivered to them at the candidate's own expense, within such time as the officer determines (but not less than seven days after the close of nominations).

Duties are imposed upon the presiding officer to ensure that no material, save candidates' addresses, which is likely to prejudice the conduct of the elections, is circulated by him or by or under authority of a diocesan or deanery synod or at a synod meeting, from the time when nominations are invited to the last day for return of voting papers. Similiar obligations are now imposed upon the rural dean and lay chairman and the secretary of the deanery synod.

Contested elections are conducted using voting papers by the method of the single transferable vote under rules made as provided by the Standing Orders of the General Synod. Each paper, which must include the year of birth of the candidate, must be marked and signed on the reverse by the elector and returned within such period as the presiding officer specifies, this being not less than 21 days after issue. A candidate has the right to be present when the votes are counted. Provisions exist for a recount to be ordered by either the presiding officer, or scrutineer appointed by the Standing Committee of General Synod. Valid voting papers themselves must be preserved for two years. In cases where there has been no valid election the general powers of the diocesan bishop which were considered earlier, would enable him to give directions for a fresh election. Results must be displayed publically in the diocesan office and at the General Synod office until the end of the first group of sessions of the new Synod.

Appeals

Provision is made for appeals by an elector or candidate[65] in an election to the House of Laity.[66] The appeal may be against the allowance or disallowance of a vote given or tendered in such election, or the result of any election, or choice of members of the House of Laity arising out of an election or selection of members of the House of Laity. However, an error in the register of electors or electoral roll is expressly excluded as a ground of appeal unless it has been determined that there is an error or that question is awaiting determination, and the error would or might have been material to the election. Notice of appeal must be in writing and given to the chairman of the House of Laity of the diocesan synod within 14 days after the allowance or disallowance of the vote or announcement of the result appealed against.

Unless the appellant withdraws the appeal in writing the appeal must be referred to the Standing Committee of the General Synod within 14 days. The committee must appoint three or more (being an odd number) of members from an appeal panel consisting of the lay members of the committee (other than the chairman or vice-chairman of the House of Laity where they are the appellant or any member of the committee who comes from the diocese to which the appeal relates), and such of the Dean of the Arches and Auditor and the Vicar-Generals of Canterbury and York as are not clerks in holy orders, to decide the appeal.

2.20

Procedure on appeals

The procedure for all appeals pursuant to the CRR is set out in rule 45. In the case of election appeals the panel must determine three matters. First, whether the persons whose election was complained of were duly elected. Secondly, whether the facts complained of amounted to a minor infringement of the rules which did not affect the outcome of the election, with the consequence that the appeal should be dismissed. Thirdly, whether the election was void. In all cases where the election was invalid the panel must direct a new election to be held, with such directions on its conduct as it sees fit.

In all appeals the panel must consider all relevant circumstances and it is entitled to inspect all documents and papers relating to the subject matter of the

2.21

---

[65] The chairman or vice-chairman of that House also has a right of appeal under slightly different conditions.

[66] CRR, r. 44. These rules also apply to appeals by electors or candidates in elections to diocesan and deanery synods (the chairmen of the Houses of Clergy and Laity of the diocesan synod having rights of appeal under slightly different conditions) and to the election of churchwardens.

appeal, and to be furnished with all information relating to the subject matter as they shall require. The parties to the appeal must be given an opportunity to appear before the panel either in person or through a legal or other representative. The panel has the power at any time to extend the time within which notice of appeal is given and it may consent to the withdrawal of the appeal at any time, subject to a determination in respect of costs. In all cases the determination by the panel is final as to the matters at issue.

So far as costs are concerned the panel has the power to direct that any party to an appeal shall be entitled to payment of costs by any other party or by the Diocesan Board of Finance (DBF). It may also direct that any party be responsible for the expenses of the appeal panel, which are otherwise paid by the DBF.

Term of office and casual vacancies

2.22   Elected members of the House of Laity generally serve for the lifetime of the General Synod for which they are elected. The seat of any member who ceases to have their name on the roll of a parish or who is no longer declared an habitual worshipper in the diocese where they were elected is normally vacated; however, it is not vacated if the lay members of the bishop's council and the standing committee have determined before the vacancy occurs that the person is able and willing to continue to discharge those duties to the lay members satisfaction. A seat is also deemed vacated if the person takes an office or employment which would have disqualified them from standing for election, or if their election is declared void.[67]

Elections to fill casual vacancies amongst the elected members of the House of Laity should be held as soon as practicable and not less than six months after the vacancy arises.[68] However, no election is required where the vacancy arises within 12 months of the commencement of the period for holding a general election to the House of Laity (unless the lay members of the bishop's council and standing committee acting in accordance with any directions of the diocesan synod direct otherwise). Such elections as do take place must be conducted in the same manner as ordinary elections, except that if the vacancy occurs within two years beginning with 1 August of the year in which the last general election was held, or beginning with the declaration of the result of an election for a casual vacancy conducted in the same manner as a general election, the election is to be conducted with those papers.[69]

Although they will generally be members until the next dissolution of General Synod the House may fix a shorter period of membership for co-opted members. Save for the method of their appointment *ex officio* and co-opted members have the same rights and are subject to the same rules and regulations as elected members of the House.

---

[67] CRR, r. 46.
[68] *ibid.*, r. 48.
[69] *ibid.* In other words the person with the next highest number of votes will fill the vacancy if still eligible.

Functions of the General Synod

The General Synod is a legislative and deliberative body rather than one in which **2.23**
all the functions of church government are concentrated. Its primary function is
to consider, and make provision in respect of, matters concerning the Church of
England. Such provision may either be by Measure or canon, or by an order,
regulation of other subordinate instrument authorised by Measure or canon.
Alternatively, where provision by or under a Measure or canon is not required,
provisions may be made by an Act of Synod, or by regulation or other
instrument, or by such proceedings as may be appropriate.[70] It is also the function
of the General Synod to consider and express its opinion on any other matter of
religious or public interest.[71] No executive functions are exercised by General
Synod. In particular the bishops, the ecclesiastical courts and the Church
Commissioners exercise their power and authority independently of it.[72] Nor does
General Synod have a judicial function.

Proceedings of the General Synod

The Archbishops of Canterbury and York are joint presidents of the General **2.24**
Synod.[73] Any question concerning the interpretation of its constitution must be
referred to and determined by them, unless the legislation expressly provides
otherwise.[74] Any function exercisable by the two Archbishops may, during the
absence abroad or incapacity through illness of one of them, or during a vacancy
in one of the sees, be exercised by the other alone.[75]

The General Synod must meet in session at least twice a year at such times and
places as it may provide or as its Joint Presidents may direct.[76] In 1992 General
Synod resolved to reduce the number of times it sat each year from three to two.
Thus, it now sits in July at the University of York and in November at Church
House in London, a "reserve day" being retained in February to transact urgent
business.

It is for the archbishops to determine on which occasions it is desirable that
one of them should be chairman, and to arrange which of them will take the
chair.[77] However, one of the archbishops must take the chair on the formal
promulgation or final approval of a canon or Act of Synod and when a motion is
taken for final approval of a provision touching doctrinal formulae or the services
of the Church or the administration of the sacraments or sacred rites.[78] When the

---

[70] SGM, Sched. 2, art. 6.

[71] *ibid.*

[72] para. 15 of the Appendix to the Church of England Assembly (Powers) Act 1919
expressly debarred the Church Assembly from exercising any of the functions dis-
tinctively belonging to the bishops in right of their episcopal office, and by implication
the same principle applies to the General Synod.

[73] SGM, Sched. 2, art. 4(1); Canon C17 (4).

[74] *ibid.*, art. 12(2).

[75] *ibid.*, art. 13.

[76] *ibid.*, art. 3(1).

[77] *ibid.*, arts 4(1), 7(1), 12(1).

[78] *ibid.*, art. 4 (2).

chair is not taken by one of the archbishops it is taken by one of a panel of between three and eight chairmen, appointed from among the members of any House of Synod by the archbishops in consultation with the Standing Committee.[79] Such chairmen act in accordance with arrangements approved by and subject to any special directions of the archbishops.[80] The business and procedure of meetings of the General Synod or any House or Houses of the Synod is regulated by the chairman, subject to the constitution of the Synod and to any Standing Orders.[81]

Standing Orders of General Synod may provide for separate sittings of any of the three Houses or joint sittings of any two Houses, and may direct who is to take the chair and thus regulate proceedings at any separate or joint sitting.[82] General Synod may make, amend and revoke Standing Orders providing for any matters for which such provision is required or authorised by its constitution, and for the Synod's meetings, business and procedure or suspend them on the vote of a majority of its members.[83] Each House may also make, amend and revoke standing orders which are consistent with the constitution and with any Standing Orders of the General Synod for the separate sittings, business and procedure of that House.[84]

2.25 Standing Orders are kept under review by a Committee, and provide for an agenda, notice of business, debates, motions and amendments, addresses and voting.[85] The Standing Committee of Synod determines the agenda to which the Joint Presidents may make additions, and notice must be given of new business. Every member of the Synod has a right to speak, subject to certain limitations. A quorum is formed by one-fifth of the members of each house.

Usually motions of the General Synod are determined by a majority of the members of Synod present and voting, either by a show of hands or a division. On a motion, other than one relating solely to the course of business or procedure, any 25 members present may demand a division by Houses, in which case the motion is not carried unless it receives the assent of a majority of the members of each House present and voting.[86]

A motion for the final approval of any Measure or canon must receive the assent of a majority of the members of each House present and voting in order to be carried, although this requirement can be dispensed by permission of the chairman with the leave of the General Synod in accordance with Standing Orders.[87] In certain cases special majorities of the Synod or each of its Houses are required under the provisions of the constitution or of a Measure. A special majority of two thirds in each House is required to amend the CRR; special categories of legislation considered below also require special majorities, as may the suspension of certain Standing Orders.[88]

A general saving rule provides that no proceedings of the General Synod, or any of its Houses, boards, commissions, committees or other bodies are

---

[79] *ibid.*, art. 4(2).
[80] *ibid.*, art. 4(2).
[81] *ibid.*, art. 11(3).
[82] *ibid.*, art. 9(1).
[83] *ibid.*, art. 11.
[84] *ibid.*, art. 11.
[85] Standing Orders (1995 ed.), (G.S. 1180, 1180A), S.O., 4–37.
[86] SGM, Sched. 2, art. 5.
[87] *ibid.*
[88] *ibid.*

invalidated by a vacancy in membership or by any defect in the qualification, election or appointment of its members.[89]

During a period when the General Synod is dissolved the archbishops and any officers or bodies of Synod may do all things necessary or expedient for conducting Synod's affairs and for making arrangements for the resumption of business by the new Synod. Pending business does not abate, but is resumed by the new Synod at the stage reached before dissolution. Boards, commissions, committees and other bodies of Synod, so far as appropriate and subject to any standing orders or directions of the archbishops also continue their proceedings during a period of dissolution.[90] Members of the dissolved General Synod may continue to act as members of all such bodies.[91]

Committees and other bodies of the General Synod

The General Synod appoints a Standing Committee,[92] which consists of the **2.26** archbishops, the chairman of the Central Board of Finance and some 22 further members elected by the Houses of Synod by and from their memberships. The chairmen of the major Synod boards generally attend its meeting but do not have the right to vote. In addition to its Standing Committee, the General Synod must appoint certain committees and may in addition appoint such other committees, commissions and bodies,[93] with such officers, as it sees fit: these committees may include persons who are not members of the Synod.[94] Each House may also appoint such committees of its members as it thinks fit.[95]

Under its Standing Orders, the General Synod determines the constitution and terms of reference of its subordinate bodies, which it may make, revoke or amend at any time. Although the constitution and membership of these bodies varies, the chairmen of all of them are appointed by the presidents of the Synod acting in consultation with the Standing Committee. Normally a member holds office for five years and is prohibited from serving for more than two successive terms. Each body regulates its own procedure subject to the Standing Orders or any directions of Synod and generally appoints its committees in consultation with the Standing Committee.

A Legislative Committee must be appointed by the General Synod from members of all three of its Houses, and all Measures passed by Synod to which it is desired to give the force of an Act of Parliament must be referred to it.[96] The Standing Committee of the General Synod is also required to appoint a Legal Aid Commission to administer the legal aid fund.[97]

---

[89] SGM, Sched. 2, art. 12(3).

[90] *ibid.*, art. 3(3).

[91] *ibid.*, art. 3(4). Provided that, in the case of elected proctors of the clergy and members of the House of Laity who do not stand for re-election, they cease to act when the election of their successor is announced by the presiding officer.

[92] *ibid.*, art. 10(2).

[93] A review has just been completed of these by the Standing Committee, *General Synod: Board and Council Constitutions: Quinquennial Review* (1996) (G.S. 1136).

[94] See n. 92, above,

[95] SGM, Sched. 2, art. 10(3).

[96] *ibid.*, art. 10(1). For further details and a list of members of the committee see *The Church of England Yearbook* published annually by Church House Publishing.

[97] Church of England Legal Aid Measure 1994, s.1(2). As to legal aid see Chap. 11.

2.27   The General Synod has a number of advisory bodies. Amongst the current bodies are the Advisory Board of Ministry, the Board of Education, the Board of Mission, the Board for Social Responsibility, the Council for the Care of Churches, the Council for Christian Unity, the Crown Appointments Commission, the Doctrine Commission, the Hospital Chaplaincies Council and the Liturgical Commission.[98] As we have seen under the proposals of the Turnbull Commission these bodies would be reformed into four departments of the new archbishops' Council dealing with resources for ministry, mission resources, heritage and legal matters, and finance. These non-statutory bodies are in addition to the various statutory bodies including the Church Commissioners, the Pensions Board and the Cathedrals Fabric Commission.

   Although there is no statutory authority for its existence the Legal Advisory Board, previously known as the Legal Board of the Church Assembly, has been constituted since 1923. It comprises a body of persons learned in both ecclesiastical law and the general law of England whose function is to advise on legal questions referred to it by the General Synod and its bodies, the Church Commissioners, diocesan authorities and others. It is the policy of the Board not to advise in contentious matters unless the facts are agreed by and referred to it by both parties.[99] In addition to an annual report submitted to the General Synod which sets out matters of current importance the Board produces volumes of selected opinions.[1]

Legislation

2.28   As we saw earlier Parliament, through the Enabling Act, gave the Church primary responsibility for legislation which affected it. The extent to which Parliament intended to permit the General Synod to legislate by Measure was examined by the Court of Appeal, it being held that the phrase "legislation touching matters concerning the Church of England" meant precisely that rejecting the contention that this was not intended to include fundamental changes to the constitution, doctrine, conventions, customs or practices of the Church.[2]

   A Measure may extend to the amendment or repeal, in whole or in part, of any Act of Parliament, including the Enabling Act of 1919. However, it may not make any alteration to the composition or powers or duties of the Ecclesiastical Committee of Parliament or the procedure laid down in the 1919 Act for the consideration by Parliament of Measures.[3]

---

[98] This is not an exhaustive list. For an updated list of all advisory committees, permanent commissions, boards and councils and their composition and membership see *The Church of England Yearbook*.

[99] *Report on the Church's Legal Officers* (1973) (GS 149).

[1] The latest being the seventh edition, *Legal Opinions Concerning the Church of England* (1994).

[2] *R. v. The Ecclesiastical Committee of the Houses of Parliament, ex p. the Church Society, The Times*, November 4, 1993. Whether the power to repeal or amend Acts of Parliament is restricted to such matters is not clear a strict reading of the legislation would suggest not; and this appears to have been the view of Tuckey J. in this case.

[3] Church of England (Assembly) Powers Act 1919, s.3(6).

Within the General Church the Synod is the supreme legislature but strictly speaking it must be regarded as a subordinate legislature since it derives its authority from an Act of Parliament. Parliament did not transfer its powers, but retained its own legislative competence over ecclesiastical matters and further reserved to itself the scrutiny of all Measures. In this sense Measures themselves may also be regarded as secondary legislation.

However, once enacted a Measure has the force and effect of an Act of Parliament,[4] and in this sense may be seen as primary legislation. Secondary legislation is open to challenge in the secular courts by means of judicial review in cases where the body to which legislative power was delegated has exceeded its powers, in other words in cases where the legislation is *ultra vires*, but the courts cannot challenge the validity of a statute on the grounds of its substance and neither will they go behind the statute to question any defects in the legislative process.[5] The consequence of this in regard to Measures would appear to be that a challenge may be made to the *vires* of a draft Measure,[6] but not to the *vires* of a Measure which has received Royal Assent.[7] Whether the courts have the power to inquire into procedural irregularities in the procedures for enactment of a Measure is a matter of some doubt.[8] The answer may well depend upon whether the Measure is still in draft or has received Royal Assent, a Measure not being open to challenge once it has been accorded the force and effect of an Act of Parliament.[9]

Canons

The power to legislate by Canon now vests in the General Synod and is exercisable, in accordance with Synod's constitution, for the Church of England as a whole, but without prejudice to the making of different provision, where appropriate, for the two provinces.[10] As well as a general power to make Canons the General Synod is specifically authorised to do so pursuant to certain Measures, and as a matter of convention Canons are usually made pursuant to such Measures rather than under its general powers.[11] Like Measures, Canons are required to touch matters concerning the Church of England[12] and require the assent and licence of the Sovereign to their making, promulgation and execution. The transfer to the General Synod of the power to make Canons did not alter the limited legal effect of Canons,[13] and thus they remain binding only upon ecclesiastical persons.

2.29

[4] *ibid.*, s.4.
[5] *Cheney v. Conn* [1968] 1 W.L.R. 242 at 247. There is of course an exception to this general principle in the case of statutes which infringe European Union law.
[6] *R. v. the Ecclesiastical Committee of the Houses of Parliament, ex p. the Church Society (ante).*
[7] *R. v. Church Assembly Legislative Committee, ex p. Haynes* [1928] 1 K.B. 411, D.C. 80. *R. v. Archbishops of Canterbury and York, ex p. Williamson, The Times,* March 9, 1994, C.A. See further Doe, *The Legal Framework of the Church of England* (1996), pp. 57–62.
[8] Doe, *The Legal Framework of the Church of England* (1996), pp. 66–70.
[9] *Brown v. Runcie, The Times,* February 20, 1991; *R. v. Archbishops of Canterbury and York, ex p. Williamson (ante).*
[10] SGM, s.1(1), (2).
[11] *Brown v. Runcie, (supra).*
[12] SGM, Sched. 2, art. 6(a)(ii).
[13] *ibid.*

A Canon may not be made or put into execution by the General Synod which is contrary to the general law of England.[14] However, Canons made pursuant to the Church of England (Worship and Doctrine) Measure 1974 may be contrary to any rule of ecclesiastical law relating to any matter for which provision may be made under that Measure,[15] as may Canons dispensing with or modifying any formal procedure or document required on ordination or admission to any office in the Church of England.[16] The ability of the courts to inquire into the *vires* of such Canons and into the procedures of Synod regarding their enactment is again a matter of some difficulty. The courts have entertained a challenge to a draft Canon,[17] and it would appear that they would be prepared to inquire into Synod's compliance with procedures for its enactment, but whether such a challenge could be made once the Canon had received Royal Assent is a matter of doubt.[18]

Requirement of special majorities

2.30   Before they may be approved by the General Synod certain categories of legislation must be subjected to special procedures and special majorities. Any provision[19] touching doctrinal formulae, or the services or ceremonies of the Church of England, or the administration of the sacraments or sacred rites, must be referred to the House of Bishops and must be submitted for final approval in terms proposed by that House and not otherwise.[20]

If either or both of the Convocations of Canterbury and York, or the House of Laity so require, a provision which touches on any of these matters must be referred, in the terms approved by the House of Bishops for final approval, to the two Convocations sitting separately and to the House of Laity.[21] Each House of Convocation and the House of Laity must approve the provision before it may be submitted for final approval by the General Synod.[22] Any provision which fails to get the approval of Convocation and the House of Laity must not be proposed again in the same or similar form until a new General Synod is brought into being, save that if only one House of one Convocation fails to approve the provision the House of Clergy and Bishops of General Synod may approve the provision by a two-thirds majority in lieu of such House's approval.[23]

Any Canon which makes provision with respect to worship or doctrine[24] cannot be submitted for the Sovereign's Licence and Assent until it has been finally approved by a majority in each House of the General Synod of not less than two-thirds of those present and voting.[25] Nor can any regulation under any Canon

---

[14] Submission of the Clergy Act 1533, ss.1, 3; SGM, s.1(3).
[15] Church of England (Worship and Doctrine) Measure 1974, s.6(1).
[16] Church of England (Miscellaneous Provisions) Measure 1976, s.1(3).
[17] *Brown v. Runcie (ante)*.
[18] See further Doe, *The Legal Framework of the Church of England* (1996), pp. 72–76.
[19] A term intended to apply to Canons and Acts of Synod as well as Measures: SGM, Sched. 2, art. 12(1).
[20] *ibid*., art. 7(1).
[21] *ibid*., art. 7(2).
[22] *ibid*., art. 7(2).
[23] *ibid*., art. 7(5).
[24] *i.e.* under the Church of England (Worship and Doctrine) Measure 1974, ss.1(1), 2(1).
[25] *ibid*., s.3.

with respect to worship, nor any approval, amendment, continuance or discontinuance of a form of service by the Synod under any such Canon have effect, unless finally approved by each House of Synod with the same majority.[26]

A Measure or Canon which provides for permanent changes in the Ordinal or the services for baptism or Holy Communion must not be finally approved by the General Synod unless, at a stage determined by the archbishops, it has been approved by a majority of the dioceses at their diocesan synods.[27] The same requirement applies to a scheme for constitutional union or a permanent and substantial change of relationship between the Church of England and another Christian body, a substantial number of whose members reside in Great Britain.[28] The archbishops may also direct that a scheme which affects the Church of England and another Christian body but which would not otherwise be subject to this requirement is so subjected.[29]

A motion for final approval by the General Synod of a change in the Ordinal or the services for baptism or Holy Communion requires a majority in each House of the General Synod of not less than two-thirds of those present and voting.[30] In the case of a scheme dealing with inter-church relations the General Synod may resolve that final approval will require the assent of special majorities of the members present and voting, such resolution specifying the majorities required of each House or of the whole Synod or both.[31]

Any question as to whether any of the requirements apply to any Measure or Canon or scheme and whether they have been complied with is to be determined conclusively by the Archbishops, the Prolocutors of the Lower Houses of Convocation and the Prolocutor and Pro-Prolocutor of the House of Laity of the General Synod.[32]

Procedure in regard to Measures and Canons before Synod

The Standing Orders of the General Synod set out many of the procedures regarding the creation and passage of draft Measures.[33] Any member of Synod may introduce a motion to instruct the Synod's Standing Committee to introduce a Measure in accordance with the proposals specified within the motion. The Standing Committee will appoint members of the Synod to a steering committee which is put in charge of the Measure. A Measure which deals with any matter other than doctrine and liturgy is considered at five separate stages; general approval, revision committee (which makes a report including amendments), revision (where the Measure is considered clause by clause), final drafting and final approval. **2.31**

Essentially the same procedures apply to Canons,[34] although if before promulgation Standing Committee decides that the matter should be reconsidered

[26] *ibid.*, s.3,
[27] SGM, Sched. 2, art. 8(1).
[28] *ibid.*
[29] *ibid.*, art. 8(1A).
[30] *ibid.*, art. 8(1C).
[31] *ibid.*, art. 8(1B).
[32] *ibid.*, art. 8(2) (as amended).
[33] Standing Orders (1955 ed.) (G.S. 1180, 1180A) S.O. 45–63.
[34] *ibid.*, S.O. 65–67.

then a motion to this effect together with a motion for amendment or withdrawal of any paragraph of the Canon is put forward. Before final approval a petition for the Sovereign's Assent and Licence must also be prepared.

Submission of Measure to Parliament

2.32   The General Synod must refer any Measure intended to have the effect of an Act of Parliament to its Legislative Committee.[35] From this point the procedure for the submission of Measures to Parliament is set out in the Enabling Act of 1919.[36] The Legislative Committee must submit a Measure referred to it to the Ecclesiastical Committee of Parliament together with such comments and explanations as the Legislative Committee deem it expedient, or is directed by the General Synod, to add.

The Ecclesiastical Committee is a committee of both Houses of Parliament, comprising 15 members of the House of Lords nominated by the Lord Chancellor and 15 members of the House of Commons nominated by the Speaker. The Committee is appointed at the commencement of each Parliament and serves for its duration, casual vacancies being filled on the nomination of the Lord Chancellor or Speaker as the case may be. The Committee may, subject to the provisions of the Enabling Act, regulate its own procedure, and its powers and duties may be exercised and discharged by any 12 members. It may sit and transact business whether or not Parliament is sitting and notwithstanding any vacancy in its membership.

The Ecclesiastical Committee must consider any Measure submitted to it and may, at any time, either on its own motion or at the request of the Legislative Committee, invite that committee to a conference to discuss the provisions of the Measure, whereupon a conference of the two committees must be held. In fact such conferences are rare and generally occur when the Ecclesiastical Committee is considering reporting that a Measure is not expedient. Consideration usually involves a more informal process by which the Ecclesiastical Committee invites representatives of the General Synod to a meeting to amplify the written comments and explanations and to answer questions.

The Legislative Committee may, on its own motion or at the direction of the General Synod, withdraw a Measure from the consideration of Ecclesiastical Committee, at any time before the report of the Ecclesiastical Committee is presented to Parliament. However, it cannot vary a Measure, either before or after conference with the Ecclesiastical Committee.

After considering the Measure the Ecclesiastical Committee must draft a report (which generally sets out any dissenting view) to Parliament stating the nature and legal effect of the Measure and the Committee's views as to its expediency, especially with relation to the rights of all the Sovereign's subjects. The report is communicated in draft to the Legislative Committee and is not presented to Parliament until that Committee signifies that it wishes it to be presented.

The text of the Measure together with the report of the Ecclesiastical Committee are then laid before both Houses of Parliament. A Measure must be

---

[35] SGM, Sched. 2, art. 10(1).
[36] Church of England (Assembly Powers) Act 1919 ss.2, 3, 4.

either accepted or rejected, Parliament having no power to amend Measures laid before it. A recent example of rejection was the Appointment of Bishops Measure 1984, notwithstanding the report of the Ecclesiastical Committee that the Measure was expedient. The inability of Parliament to amend Measures led the Church Assembly to make amendments to the text of a Measure designed to meet objections raised in the House of Commons, following the rejection of the Prayer Book Measure 1927. This was then resubmitted to Parliament as the Prayer Book Measure 1928, but was also rejected.

If both Houses pass a resolution (which is generally moved in the Commons by the Member who is second Church Estates Commissioner and in the Lords by a bishop) directing that a Measure shall be presented to the Sovereign and the Measure thereupon receives Royal Assent and has the force and effect of an Act of Parliament.

Synodical instruments

In addition to its powers to legislate by Measure or Canon, the General Synod has the power to make provision by such order, regulation or other subordinate instrument (which means any rule, scheme or other instrument) as may be authorised by Measure or Canon.[37] Although there is no general requirement for Royal Assent, Synod's Standing Orders provide that where the legal rights of an individual are affected the parent Measure must provide for the laying of the subordinate instrument before Parliament for its approval or annulment on a resolution of either House, unless it is a scheme to be approved by Order in Council.[38] **2.33**

Synod also has the power to create an Act of Synod, or a regulation or other subordinate instrument or proceeding as may be appropriate in cases where provision under Measure or Canon is not required.[39] Synod's Standing Orders provide that if such an instrument is to be published as "the embodiment of the will or opinion of the Church of England", it is to be affirmed and proclaimed as an Act of Synod.[40] Such Acts of Synod do not have statutory force.[41] Rather they have great moral force to which the Courts may attach considerable weight, as they have been prepared to do recently with statements of the House of Bishops.

Quasi-legislation

Increasingly the Church of England is supplementing the law with a plethora of codes of practice, guidelines and other material. The extent to which these give rise to enforceable rights, and to what extent the courts would review the validity of what may be termed "quasi" or "tertiary" legislation is far from clear, although the trend in recent years has been towards increased judicial intervention.[42] Codes of Practice, guidelines and other material may also give rise to a **2.34**

[37] SGM, Sched. 2, art. 6(a)(iii).
[38] Standing Orders (1995 ed.) (G.S. 1180, 1180A) S.O. 46.
[39] SGM, Sched. 2, art. 6(a)(iv).
[40] Standing Orders (1995 ed.) (G.S. 1180, 1180A) S.O. 40.
[41] *Bland v. Archdeacon of Cheltenham* [1972] Fam. 157 at 166.
[42] See further Doe, *The Legal Framework of the Church of England* (1996), pp. 19–22.

"legitimate expectation" that they will be applied properly and fairly,[43] enforceable in the secular courts by means of judicial review.

The ecclesiastical courts have been prepared to attach considerable weight to guidelines and in particular to Statements of the House of Bishops in recent years. Most notably, in *Re St James, Shirley*[44] the consistory court gave effect to such a statement[45] notwithstanding that it was inconsistent with the terms of a Canon. Once such a statement or code is incorporated within the *ratio decidendi* of the decision it acquires the force of law.[46]

The province

2.35   A province is the circuit of an archbishop's jurisdiction, England being divided into the two provinces of Canterbury and York. Prior to the Reformation, in the Western Catholic Church the emphasis had been placed upon the Pope with the archbishops acting as his deputies. However, since the Reformation the grouping together of dioceses into a province is merely a matter of administrative convenience, since theologically, if not jurisprudentially, the emphasis is upon the diocese as the basic unit of the church in accordance with the structure of the early church.

Archbishops

2.36   The procedure for the election of an archbishop is governed by the same procedure as that for bishops described in Chapter 3, save that in the case of the archbishopric of Canterbury the Crown Appointments Committee meets under the chairmanship of a lay communicant Anglican appointed by the Prime Minister. The Sovereign then sends a *conge d'elire* to the dean and chapter of the metropolitan cathedral church, accompanied by the name of the person to be elected.

As with the requirements for a bishop, a man must be 30 years of age before he can become an archbishop[47] and cannot be appointed if aged 70 years or over[48] but there appears to be no other restriction upon the Sovereign's powers of appointment, since all archbishoprics and bishoprics were founded by the Sovereign and are royal donatives,[49] and the Royal supremacy is recognised by law.

---

[43] For an example of the application of this principle see *R. v. Criminal Injuries Compensation Board, ex p. Lain* [1967] 2 Q.B. 864.

[44] [1994] Fam. 134.

[45] *Response by the House of Bishops to Questions raised by Diocesan Chancellors* dated June 1992, which concerned the positioning of fonts.

[46] However, such guidelines need,to be distinguished from the guidelines laid down by the ecclesiastical courts in certain matters which the courts have emphasised are not rules of law: see, *e.g. Re All Saints, Melbourn* [1990] 1 W.L.R. 833 at 843.

[47] Preface to the *Ordinal*.

[48] Ecclesiastical Offices (Age Limit) Measure 1975, s.1, Sched.

[49] *Coke on Littleton, Institutes*, (4th ed. 1639) Vol. 1, pp. 94a, 97; *Blackstone's Commentaries on the Laws of England*, (14th ed. 1803), Vol. 1, p. 379, n. 7,

Since an archbishop is usually translated from another see there is no consecration. For the purposes of confirmation the Sovereign must notify the other archbishop and two other bishops or alternatively four bishops within the Realm or any of the dominions which the Sovereign may assign.[50] Strictly speaking an archbishop is enthroned rather than installed as other bishops.[51] The provisions governing this, and of the restitution of all spiritual and temporal possession and profits from the Sovereign and the doing of homage, are essentially the same, those applicable upon the installation of bishops discussed in Chapter 3.

Each archbishop is also styled Metropolitan, it being said that the title archbishop relates to his being chief of other bishops and that of metropolitan relates to the cities or cathedral, where the bishoprics are.[52] Both archbishops are subject to the Sovereign who is their immediate superior, and although in many respects the two archbishops are of equal and independent position and authority, the see of Canterbury does have certain privileges over that of York.[53].

The Archbishop of Canterbury is also styled "Primate of All England", [54] and as such has the privilege of crowning the Sovereign of England.[55] He has the right to grant all those licences dispensations and faculties, in both provinces, which were formerly within the jurisdiction of the Pope, and which are commonly known as legatine powers because they were delegated by the papal legate.[56] By virtue of this right he grants special marriage licences[57] and confers degrees "in prejudice" of the universities.[58] Known as "Lambeth degrees", these degrees confer no right to membership of any university but entitle the recipient to wear the academic robes of the university of which the archbishop is himself a member.[59] The Archbishop of Canterbury is a Lord of Parliament with a seat in the House of Lords,[60] and takes precedence after the Royal Family and before the Lord Chancellor.[61]

The Archbishop of York, who is styled "Primate of England",[62] is also a Lord **2.37** of Parliament and by statute has his allotted seat in the House of Lords next after the Archbishop of Canterbury.[63] He is placed immediately after the Lord

---

[50] Appointment of Bishops Act 1533, s.4.
[51] Godolphin *Repertorium Canonicum*, (3rd ed. 1687) p. 21. An archbishop has the title and style of grace "Most Reverend Father in God by divine providence" whereas a bishop is styled "Lord" and "Right Reverend Father in God by divine permission: *Blackstone's Commentaries on the Laws of England* (14th ed. 1803), Vol. 1, p. 382.
[52] *ibid*., p. 15.
[53] For a history of the struggle for precedence between the two provinces see *Constitutional History of the Church of England* Makower (English translation 1895), pp. 281 *et seq*.
[54] Canon C17(1).
[55] Ayliffe, *Parergon Juris Canonici Anglicani* (2nd ed., 1734), pp. 94, 95.
[56] Ecclesiastical Licences Act 1533, ss.3, 4; Canon C17(7). These licences and dispensations are confirmed by the Sovereign's authority and have force throughout England: Canon C17(7). See Chap. 11 as to the Court of Faculties which grants these.
[57] As to which see Chap. 10.
[58] *Blackstone's Commentaries on the Laws of England* (14th ed. 1803), Vol. 1, p. 381.
[59] For a discussion by Archbishop Lang of these rights see *Official Report*, 5 H.L., Vol. 87, col. 838.
[60] *Coke on Littleton, Institutes*, (4th ed. 1639) Vol. 1., p. 97a.
[61] *Debretti and Barontage* (1990 ed.) *Peerage*, Table of Precedents see p. 56.
[62] Godolphin *Repertorium Canonicum*, p, 14; Canon C17(1).
[63] House of Lords Precedence Act 1539, ss.2, 3.

Chancellor and has precedence over all dukes not being of the royal blood.[64] He may claim the special privilege of crowning a Queen Consort and of being her chaplain, although it appears he is not entitled to these privileges as of right.[65] Both archbishops are Privy Councillors.[66-67].

The archbishops, in common with all bishops, are by ancient fiction wedded to their see. Thus by custom he impales the arms of his see, with his own arms taking the place which would ordinarily be occupied by his wife's.[68] He also drops his own surname and signs his Christian name and that of his see using the latin abbreviation; "Cantuar" for Canterbury and "Ebor" for York. The archbishops are corporations sole with perpetual succession[69] and a seal,[70] and are sued by their christian name together with their name of office. The archbishop has his own diocese, and references to "bishop" in relation to the diocese of an archbishop in Measures passed after 1925 means to an archbishop.[71]

Each archbishop has, as superintendent of all ecclesiastical matters throughout the province, metropolitan jurisdiction to correct and supply the defects of other bishops.[72] He also has the right to hold metropolitan visitations, during which he has jurisdiction as "Ordinary" except in places and over persons who are exempt by law or custom,[73] and is entitled to inspect the bishops and inferior clergy of his diocese. Such archepiscopal visitations have become rare in modern times and by agreement the Archbishop of Canterbury does not visit the diocese of London.[74] The Archbishop's jurisdiction is exercised either in person, or by a vicar-general, official or other commissary to whom authority in that behalf has been committed by the archbishop.[75] Any proceedings for offences against the laws ecclesiastical must take the due legal form directed by ecclesiastical law, rather than being dealt with summarily by the archbishop or his commissary.[76]

2.38   Within his province an archbishop is the principal minister. He has the right of confirming the election of every person to a bishopric and to be the chief consecrator at the consecration of every bishop and is entitled to the oath of obedience from every bishop in his diocese. He may also consecrate persons to the office of bishop for the purpose of exercising episcopal functions elsewhere than in England.[77] Where a bishopric is vacant the archbishop may, by prescription or composition, be entitled to act as guardian of the spiritualities, that is to

---

[64] *Debretti and Barontage* (1990) ed.) *Peerage*, Table of Precedents and see p. 56.

[65] Ayliffe, *Parergon Juris Canonici Aglicani* (2nd ed. 1734), p. 95.

[66] The archbishops are also both dignitaries: *Broughton v. Grousley* (1599) Cro. Eliz. 663.

[67] *Gibson's Codex Juris Ecclesiastici Anglicani*, p. 118.

[68] See *Burke's Peerage*.

[69] Rolle's *Abridgment of the Common Law*, Vol. 1, p. 1512.

[70] Godolphin *Repertorium Canonicum*, (3rd ed. 1687) p. 27. Although the seals of all ecclesiastical Ordinaries ought to have the Sovereign's arms engraved on them since the ecclesiastical courts are the Sovereign's courts the Archbishop of Canterbury may use his own seal; *ibid.*, p. 28.

[71] Interpretation Measure 1925, s.3.

[72] Canon C17(2). As to visitations generally see Chap. 3.

[73] *ibid*.

[74] *Gobbet's Case* (1634) Cro. Car 339; *Halsbury's Laws of England* (4th ed.) Vol. 14, para. 431.

[75] Canon C17(3).

[76] See, *e.g. R. v. Dean of York* (1841) 2 Q.B. 1.

[77] Bishops in Foreign Countries Act 1841, ss.1, 3. In such cases the archbishop may dispense with the oath of obedience to himself: Colonial Clergy Act 1874, s.12.

provide for the ecclesiastical administration of the diocese during the vacancy, by and through such persons as he may nominate.[78] The archbishop may also make appointments to perform various functions in a diocese during a vacancy in the see, or during the illness or incapacity of the diocesan bishop. The archbishops have certain functions regarding the exercise of patronage and the filling of benefices. It is also for the archbishop to give permission to officiate within his province to any minister ordained priest or deacon by an overseas bishop, or a bishop not in communion with the Church of England whose orders are recognised or accepted by the Church of England.

The archbishop presides in the Convocation of the province and the two archbishops are Joint Presidents of the General Synod, whilst various functions are assigned to the archbishops under the constitution of the General Synod and the CRR. The Archbishops are also both *ex officio* Church Commissioners, the Archbishop of Canterbury acting as chairman.

In each province there is a court of the Archbishop, known in Canterbury as the "Court of the Arches" and in York as the "Court of Chancery". These courts, considered in Chapter 11, exercise appellate jurisdiction, although the Archbishop does not sit as a judge. In a few limited cases, however, the archbishop does exercise personal powers of adjudication, which have arisen by specific enactment.[79]

An archbishop must retire at 70 years of age unless the Sovereign authorises his continuance in office for a period not exceeding a year,[80] and must tender his resignation not less than six months before the date he is required to retire.[81] An archbishop may resign earlier by tendering his resignation to the Sovereign in the prescribed form.[82] Special provision is made for resignation on the grounds of incapacity, on the request of the two senior bishops of the province and the concurrence of the other archbishop.[83] In all cases of resignation, unless the Sovereign makes a declaration to the contrary the archbishop must vacate any other preferment held at that date.[84]

In addition to a vacancy occasioned by retirement and resignation, an archbishopric may become vacant by translation, death or deprivation. On a vacancy arising the dean and chapter of the metropolitan church are the guardians of the spiritualities.[85] Until the new archbishop is elected and confirmed[86] or appointed by letters patent, they exercise the spiritual jurisdiction of the province and diocese and have the power of receiving presentations to, or admitting and instituting to benefices, but not of consecrating or ordaining nor presenting to vacant benefices or confirming leases.[87] During a vacancy in the see of Canterbury, the powers of the dean and chapter extend to the grant of such licences and dispensations throughout both provinces as the Archbishop is

---

[78] Canon C19(2).
[79] *e.g.* appeals against the summary revocation of the licence of unbeneficed clergy and certain lay ministers by a diocesan bishop.
[80] Ecclesiastical Offices (Age Limit) Measure 1975, ss.1, 2, Sched.
[81] Bishops (Retirement) Measure 1986, s.5.
[82] *ibid.*, s.4.
[83] *ibid.*, s.6.
[84] *ibid.*, s.8(1).
[85] Canon C19(1).
[86] Gibson *Codex Juris Ecclesiastici Anglicani*, (2nd ed. 1761) p. 114.
[87] Canon C19(3); Godolphin *Repertorium Canonicum*, (3rd ed. 1687) pp. 21, 40.

entitled to grant.[88] The position in regard to the guardianship of the temporalities of the province is the same as that in respect of bishoprics which is discussed in Chapter 3.

Convocations

2.39   The Convocations or ancient parliaments of the two provinces have their origins in the provincial synods of the medieval church and are therefore older than the secular Parliament. Originally Convocation was a gathering of prelates, but in the thirteenth century in England it became, as it is now, a gathering of both bishops and inferior clergy. Unlike the provincial synods of medieval times, which were summoned by the Pope for purely ecclesiastical business, convocations, which were peculiar to England, were of direct interest to the Sovereign, at least so far as the taxation of the clergy was concerned. It was in convocation that the clergy's contribution to the royal exchequer was voted, and despite attempts by Edward I to transfer this function to Parliament, the clergy continued to tax themselves in convocation until 1664.

The power and the legislative functions of convocation were curtailed by the Sovereign and subject to Royal Supremacy following the Reformation, and their importance was diminished still further by the transfer of their power of making Canons to The General Synod. Although there was a period of suspension of activity from the early eighteenth to mid-nineteenth centuries, these ancient bodies still continue to meet and transact business.[89]

Given that the Upper and Lower Houses of the Convocations form the Houses of Bishops and Clergy in the General Synod, the question is raised from time to time as to the necessity of their continued separate existence. The virtues of a forum in which clerics alone may exchange views, or fears that the larger province of Canterbury might swamp the smaller northern province of York are frequently cited, but underlying this is perhaps a general reluctance to abolish an institution of such ancient lineage.[89a]

2.40   The constitution of the Upper and Lower Houses of Convocation has already been considered. A convocation may also make provision for the joining of a House of Laity, comprised of the members of the House of Laity of the General Synod who represent that province, to its two Houses for the purposes of such functions as it may determine.[90]

Convocation may only be summoned with the Sovereign's assent.[91] Convocations may meet separately within their province, or elsewhere, at such places and times as they may determine.[92] They may meet for the purpose of considering any matter concerning the Church of England, and making provision by appropriate instrument, (which may not be by Canon) for such matters in relation to their province, and may refer such matters to the General Synod.

---

[88] *ibid.*
[89] For a detailed historical analysis of the Convocations see Joyce, *England's Sacred Symbols: A Constitutional History of the Convocations of the Clergy* (1855).
[89a] Briden and Hanson, *Moore's Introduction to English Canon Law* (3rd ed. 1992), p. 24.
[90] Canon H1(3).
[91] Submission of the Clergy Act 1533, s.1.
[92] Canon H1(2).

They must meet for the purposes of discharging certain functions exercisable by them pursuant to the Ecclesiastical Jurisdiction Measure 1963.[93] As we have seen the General Synod may refer provisions concerning worship and doctrine to the Convocations,[94] which must meet to consider these and any other matter referred to them by the General Synod.[95]

If the Crown desires the advice of Convocation on matters ecclesiastical Letters of Business may be issued, stating the matter to be considered and authorising Convocation to debate, consider, consult and agree upon it, and after a mature debate, to present a report in writing to the Crown. Such Letters were issued in 1904 for consideration of the Prayer Book which ultimately led to the abortive Prayer Book Measures of 1927 and 1928, but it seems unlikely that they would be used today.

Unless the Sovereign appoints a vice-regent, which has not occurred since Henry VIII appointed Thomas Cromwell, the Archbishop has the right to preside at Convocation either in person or by a deputy appointed by him.[96] In the province of Canterbury the Bishop of London, or in his absence the Bishop of Winchester have the right to be appointed deputy.[97] The President of each House is called a prolocutor (speaker). The Prolocutor of the Lower House is chosen by that House and is then presented to the Upper House.[98] The prolocutor of the Lower House fulfils a similar role to the Speaker of the House of Commons by acting as an intermediary between the two Houses.

Convocation has felt able to discuss and pass resolutions on a wide variety of topics. An Act of Convocation is a resolution passed by both Houses and ratified and promulged by the president in full synod.[99] By ancient custom no act is held to be an Act of Convocation unless it receives the assent of the Archbishop.[1] As with Acts of Synod these Acts have moral but no legal force. Resolutions of Convocation, especially those dignified as an Act, are however of considerable weight in matters of theological importance and ecclesiastical polity. They are of evidential value in the courts, as indicating the mind of the church and thereby throwing light on points of doctrine.[2] **2.41**

[93] *ibid.* SGM, s.3(6). As to which see Chap. 11.
[94] Canon H1(2); SGM, Sched. 2, art. 7.
[95] Canon H1(2).
[96] Canon C17(4).
[97] *ibid.*
[98] *Coke's Institutes*, (1680), Vol. 4, p. 323.
[99] See *Acts of the Convocations of Canterbury and York* (Smethurst, Wilson, Riley eds) (revised ed. 1961), Editor's Note.
[1] Canon C17(5).
[2] *Bland v. Archdeacon of Cheltenham* [1972] Fam. 157 at 166.

Chapter Three: The Diocese

Whilst today many people have come to see the parish as the fundamental **3.1** building block from which the structure of the Church of England is constructed, originally this was not so. Prior to the parish attaining its current status it was the diocese, called the *parochia*, which was the smallest unit, and the bishop—the sole parson of his diocese—who had exclusive cure of all souls within it. As the Church developed and the number of people under the bishop's care grew, the diocese was divided into smaller ecclesiastical districts. To these districts ministers, ordained by the bishop, were sent to serve the cure and preach. Initially these ministers resided with the bishop in the place where his church or cathedral was. However, as more churches were founded and endowed districts annexed to them, some of the bishop's ministers were sent to officiate in these churches and reside in these districts. In this way parishes were formed.

The bishop still retained a certain number of ministers in his cathedral, now called the dean and prebenderies or canons, to assist him, and the cathedral continued to be the parish church of the whole diocese. The bishop remained chief minister and universal incumbent of the diocese, and as such has the right to institute or collate priests to the parishes who received the cure of souls from him. With some minor alterations this is still the case today and accordingly it is the diocese, rather than the parish, which remains the basic unit of the Church.

In this chapter we will consider the role and status of the diocese and its bishop. We will also examine the role of suffragan bishops and all those episcopally consecrated, together with the arrangements for extended episcopal care. Diocesan and deanery synods, which form the intermediate and lower tiers of synodical government are discussed, as are the various diocesan boards and committees. The roles of the archdeacon and rural dean and the division of the diocese into deaneries are also considered.

The diocese

A diocese is a legal division of a province, and the circuit of a bishop's **3.2** jurisdiction. Certain parts of a diocese, known as peculiars, are generally exempt from the bishop's jurisdiction, and certain other parts may be extra-diocesan.[1] Over the centuries new bishoprics have been created and others dissolved, and the boundaries of the dioceses of both provinces have undergone considerable alteration.

---

[1] See Chap. 6.

The Dioceses Commission

3.3   The Dioceses Commission which is appointed by the General Synod advises it upon the diocesan structure of the two provinces and upon action which might be taken to improve the episcopal care or administration of the affairs of any diocese.[2] The Commission is available to be consulted by either the bishop or the diocesan synod. As part of its functions it prepares and makes reorganisation schemes for dioceses, including the foundation of new bishoprics, the transfer of areas between dioceses, and the creation of suffragan sees.[3] Such schemes may, after preliminary consultation with the diocesan synod and with the consent of the Standing Committee of the General Synod, be submitted by the diocesan bishop to the Commission.[4]

Before making any scheme the Commission consults interested parties within the relevant dioceses, including diocesan and suffragan bishops, archdeacons and diocesan synods, together with the incumbent (or priest-in-charge), PCC and deanery synod of any parish or deanery which would be particularly affected. In addition it consults the provincial archbishop, the Church Commissioners and the Charity Commissioners. Finally consultation may extend to any person of whom the Commissioners see fit to inquire.[5] Although representations made to the Commissioners by these persons or bodies must be considered, and the draft scheme may be amended as a consequence, if the Commission decides to proceed the draft only requires the approval of the diocesan synod of each diocese concerned.[6] Even then the consent of a diocesan synod whose interest in the scheme as a whole is small may be dispensed with, and the scheme presented to the General Synod for its approval notwithstanding.[7] If the General Synod gives its approval the scheme is then submitted for confirmation by an Order in Council of the Sovereign.[8]

Paradoxically certain diocesan reorganisations and the alteration of diocesan boundaries are matters which fall under the remit of the Church Commissioners, pursuant to the Pastoral Measure 1983.[9] The lack of functional clarity was one of the matters criticised by the recent Turnbull report. Its committee members under the chairmanship of the Bishop of Durham, expressed the view that having two bodies, operating under differing procedures, capable of undertaking certain forms of reorganisation, but unable to initiate proposals, had been the cause of a lack of strategic initiative at national level.[10]

The dioceses

3.4   The province of Canterbury comprises 30 dioceses. Fourteen of these, namely, Canterbury, London, Winchester, Bath and Wells, Chichester, Ely, Exeter, Hereford, Lichfield, Lincoln, Norwich, Rochester, Salisbury and Worcester, were

[2] Dioceses Measure 1978, ss.1, 2.
[3] *ibid.*, s.3. The last occasion on which a new diocese in England was created was in 1927.
[4] *ibid.*, s.4.
[5] *ibid.*, s.5.
[6] *ibid.*, s.6.
[7] Dioceses Measure 1978, s.6.
[8] *ibid.*, s.7.
[9] See Chap. 5.
[10] *Working as One Body*, The report of the Archbishops' Commission on the Reorganisation of the Church of England (1995), at para. 3.9.

founded before the reign of Henry VIII. Four, Gloucester, Bristol, Peterborough and Oxford, were founded during his reign. Eleven, St Albans, Truro, Southwark, Birmingham, Chelmsford, St Edmundsbury and Ipswich, Coventry, Derby, Guildford, Portsmouth and Leicester, were founded from the first quarter of the nineteenth century onwards by Orders in Council made under authority of Act of Parliament or Measure. The diocese in Europe, comprising the former diocese of Gibraltar and the areas of Northern and Central Europe, formerly under the jurisdiction of the Bishop of London, which was founded in 1980, is the final diocese in the province.

The province of York is comprised of 14 dioceses. Four, York, Durham, Carlisle and Sodor and Man, were founded before the reign of Henry VIII and one, Chester, during it. The remaining nine, namely Bradford, Blackburn, Liverpool, Manchester, Newcastle, Ripon, Sheffield, Southwell and Wakefield, were founded from the beginning of the nineteenth century onwards.

Bishops[11]

As a matter of law the Church of England recognises two types of bishop, **3.5** diocesan and suffragan, although as we shall see, in practice other bishops do work within a diocese.

A man must be 30 of years of age before he can become a bishop,[12] and cannot be appointed if he is over 70 years of age.[13] At the present time women cannot be appointed to the office of bishop.[14] If he is not already ordained a man must be ordained as well as consecrated, and would thus be subject to the requirements of an ordinand. In modern times all those appointed bishop have already been ordained priests.

The appointed bishop must be a godly and well-learned man, and has to be vouched for as such by two bishops who present him for consecration.[15] He must declare that he is persuaded that he is truly called to this ministration according to the will of our Lord Jesus Christ and the order of this Realm, and must declare, in response to a series of questions from the archbishop, that he will carry out the duties and exercise the powers required of a bishop.[16]

Appointment of diocesan bishops

All diocesan bishops in England are appointed by the Crown, since all bishoprics **3.6** were founded by the Sovereign.[17] Today the Sovereign makes the appointment acting on the advice of the Prime Minister, who is in turn advised by a standing

---

[11] *Episcopal Ministry*, the report of the Archbishops' Commission on the Episcopate (1990) (GS 944) examines the nature of the episcopate, the role of the suffragan and the theological issues underlying the ordination of women as bishops and the desirability of creating new dioceses.

[12] Preface to the *Ordinal*; Canon C2(3).

[13] Ecclesiastical Offices (Age Limit) Measure 1970, s.1, Sched.

[14] Priests (Ordination of Women) Measure 1993, s.1(2); Canon C2(5).

[15] *Ordinal*, Form of Ordaining or Consecrating of an Archbishop or Bishop.

[16] *ibid.*

[17] *Coke on Littleton, Institutes*, Vol. 1, (4th ed. 1639) p. 94a.

committee of the General Synod known as the Crown Appointments Commission.[18] No legislation was required to institute this procedure which was adopted in 1976 since it does not curtail the Crown's powers of appointment.

In each diocese a vacancy in see committee has been established.[19] This consists of the diocesan or suffragan bishop as *ex officio* members, together with two clerics beneficed or licenced within the diocese who are elected by the house of clergy, and at least two actual communicant lay persons whose names are on an electoral roll of a parish in the diocese and who have been elected by the house of laity of the diocesan synod to serve on the committee.[20] Provision must also be made by the diocesan synod for adequate representation of each archdeaconry, which in practice means that in many dioceses the archdeacons themselves are also members of the Committee.

It is the function of this Committee to prepare a statement of the needs of the diocese for the information of the Crown Appointments Commission. It also elects four of its members to be members of the Appointments Commission in connection with that body's functions in regard to the vacancy of the particular diocesan bishopric.

In addition to these four elected members the Commission comprises both archbishops together with three clergy and three laity elected by and from the Houses of Clergy and Laity of the General Synod. The relevant vacancy in see committee may suggest names of suitable candidates to the Commission, which provides a shortlist of two names to the Prime Minister. The Prime Minister then has the right to recommend either name to the Sovereign or to ask the Commission for a further name or names.

Upon the avoidance of the bishopric, and the certification of the vacancy to the Crown (a practice sometimes now omitted), the Crown grants a licence under the Great Seal (called a *congé d'élire*), to the dean and chapter or cathedral chapter[21] of the void see, to elect a bishop.[22] The licence is accompanied by a letter missive containing the name of the person to be elected.[23] That person must be elected[24] within 12 days of delivery of the licence and letter missive, and after certification by the dean and chapter or cathedral chapter under their or its common seal is reputed and taken to be lord elect of the bishopric.[25]

Previously if the dean and chapter or cathedral chapter refused to elect the Crown's nominee they were exposed to the penalties of *praemunire*, which meant that they were placed outside the Sovereign's protection and could be subject to various penalties including imprisonment. The Crown may still, if election is

---

[18] See further, *Senior Church Appointments*, the report of a General Synod working party (1992) (GS 1019). The report criticised the procedure for the appointment and election of bishops and recommended the creation of a new advisory committee and electoral board. The consequent Appointment of Bishops Measure of 1984 was rejected by the House of Commons.

[19] Vacancy in See Committee Regulations 1993, proclaimed as an Act of Synod.

[20] See n. 18 *ante*.

[21] In the diocese of Sodor or Man the normal procedure is to appoint by letters patent.

[22] Appointment of Bishops Act 1533, s.3.

[23] *ibid*.

[24] As to the procedure to be followed see *Halsbury's Laws of England* (4th ed.) Vol. 14, para. 461, n. 4.

[25] Appointment of Bishops Act 1533, ss.3, 4. The right to confirm the election belongs to the archbishop: Canon C17(4).

deferred, nominate and present by letters patent its choice to the archbishop of the relevant province.[26] In such a case confirmation is not required and the person may be invested and consecrated forthwith.[27] In all other cases, after the election is certified, the Crown must signify the election of the bishop to the archbishop of the relevant province by letters patent, and require and command him to confirm the election and to invest and consecrate the person elected.[28]

The archbishop then commissions his Vicar-General to perform all acts necessary to perfect the confirmation.[29] Unless such a power is to be found in the word "confirm", the Appointment of Bishops Act 1533 does not appear to contemplate the possibility of the archbishop questioning the fitness of the Crown's choice in any way: rather he appears to be a ministerial agent.[30] Before confirmation the bishop takes the oaths of allegiance[31] and of obedience to the archbishop[32] and makes the declaration of assent.[33]

Guardianship of the spiritualities and temporalities

During a vacancy in the see the spiritualities, or spiritual jurisdiction, belong **3.7** either to the archbishop (in most cases), or to the dean and chapter of the cathedral church.[34] The See of Durham is an interesting case, for whilst the dean and chapter claim, and do in fact exercise, guardianship, their right to do so is formally denied by the Archbishop of York. The guardian exercises spiritual jurisdiction during the vacancy, which includes instituting to benefices, granting licences for the solemnisation of matrimony without the publication of banns and issuing commissions for ordination.[35] However, their powers do not extend to matters excluded from their jurisdiction by the laws of the Realm. It should be noted that the functions of a diocesan bishop, including his functions as president of the diocesan synod, under the CRR, are exercisable during a vacancy by such person in episcopal orders as the archbishop of the province may appoint.[36]

Following election and confirmation the new bishop becomes entitled to exercise all spiritual jurisdiction and the powers of the guardian accordingly cease.[37] However, until he is consecrated, his authority is limited and he is not

[26] Appointment of Bishops Act 1533, s.3.
[27] Appointment of Bishops Act 1533, ss.3, 4.
[28] ibid.
[29] Godolphin *Repertorium Canonicum*, (3rd ed. 1687) p. 25. As to the procedure carried the archbishop's power to correct defects, see *Halsbury's Laws of England* (4th ed.), Vol. 14, paras 464, 466.
[30] *R. v. Archbishop of Canterbury* (1848) 11 Q.B. 483; *R. v. Archbishop of Canterbury* [1902] 2 K.B. 503.
[31] As to which see Chap. 7.
[32] Canon C14(1).
[33] As to which see Chap. 7.
[34] Canon C19(2). The archbishop acting through such person or persons as he may nominate according to the prescription or composition by which he acquired the right: *ibid.*
[35] Canon C19(3). Such commissions are issued *sede vacante*.
[36] CRR, r. 53(7).
[37] Gibson *Codex Juris Ecclesiastici Anglicani*, (2nd ed. 1761) p. 114.

entitled to full exercise of episcopal functions,[38] and he cannot for example ordain priests or deacons.

The temporalities of the diocese are all those things which the bishop has by livery from the Sovereign, such as manors, parsonages and other certainties. In practical terms these are now all, with the exception of rights of patronage, vested in the Church Commissioners. The Sovereign is guardian and custodian of the temporalities during a vacancy in the see,[39] and these remain in the Sovereign's hands until the new bishop sues for them. The bishop pays homage to the Sovereign for his temporalities, taking a solemn oath in her prescence to be faithful to Her Majesty and acknowledging that he holds his temporalities from her.[40] Upon restitution (now always entire and untouched) the bishop has a fee simple, or freehold, in his bishopric.

Consecration and installation

3.8   An elected bishop may already be in episcopal orders, either because he is the diocesan bishop of another see and is therefore to be translated, or because he was a suffragan bishop in the same or in another diocese. However, if he is not in such orders he is consecrated by the archbishop (who may appoint another bishop to act on his behalf) with the assistance of at least two other bishops, although in practice more usually assist.[41] Consecration must occur on a Sunday or Holy Day unless the archbishop, for some weighty or urgent cause appoints another day.[42]

Following confirmation (or presentation) and consecration where this is required, and having sued for his temporalities, the bishop is then installed in the bishopric.[43] The ceremony of installation is sometimes referred to as an enthronement, but strictly speaking only archbishops are enthroned.[44] Special forms of service for installation and enthronement have been drawn up, but the essentials are as follows. Pursant to the archbishop's mandate the bishop is introduced into the cathedral church in the presence of a public notary and is placed in the episcopal seat with the customary formula. After divine service the bishop is conducted to the chapter house where he receives the customary acknowledgments of canonical obedience, the public notary recording the whole matter in a written instrument which is retained as authority to posterity.[45] On installation the bishop must be obeyed in all things, and may do and execute all things touching his office as are customary and not contrary to the Crown's prerogative or to the laws and customs of the Realm.[46]

---

[38] Ayliffe *Parergon Juris Canonici Anglicani* (2nd ed. 1734), pp. 120, 121.
[39] *Blackstone's Commentaries, on the Laws of England*, Vol. 1, (14th ed. 1803), Vol. 1 p. 380.
[40] Godolphin *Repertorium Canonicum* (3rd ed. 1687) p. 26.
[41] Canon C2(1).
[42] Canon C2(2).
[43] Appointment of Bishops Act 1533, s.5.
[44] Godolphin *Repertorium Canonicum*, p. 21, *ante*.
[45] *ibid*., pp. 26, 27.
[46] Appointment of Bishops Act 1533, s.5.

Powers, duties and privileges of diocesan bishops

The term episcopate derives from the latin *episcope* meaning oversight, and it is **3.9** the diocesan bishop in whom the authority to exercise the episcopal ministry in his diocese resides. Although the bishop has his throne or *cathedra* in his cathedral church he has considerably less authority over the cathedral, which is governed by the deans or provost and the chapter, than he does over the parishes in his diocese. The diocesan bishop is, subject to royal supremacy and the supervision of the archbishop, "chief in superintendency" in matters ecclesiastical within the diocese,[47] although he may delegate certain matters to a suffragan. Canon 18 sets out his powers, duties and privileges.

In some enactments the bishop is referred to as the "Ordinary", since he has ordinary jurisdiction in ecclesiastical causes in his diocese after the Sovereign.[48] The bishop's jurisdiction is exercised throughout the diocese—except in places and over persons exempt by law or custom—either by the bishop himself, or by a Vicar-General, official or other commissary.[49] Although the bishop is enjoined to correct and punish all such as be unquiet, disobedient or crimonious within his diocese, according to such authority as he has by God's word and which is committed to him by the laws and ordinances of the Realm, as we shall see below such power is now much restricted.

The bishop is the chief pastor to all in his diocese, clergy and laity, and is their father in God. He has the general supervision of the clergy in his diocese, and no-one can perform clerical functions within the diocese without his permission.[50] It is his duty to teach and to uphold sound and wholesome doctrine and to banish and drive away all erroneous and strange opinions. He is also required to be an example of righteous and godly living, and to set forward and maintain quietness, love and peace among all men. The bishop must reside within his diocese, but by ancient right residence in any house in London, during his attendance on Parliament or the Court, or for the purpose of performing any other duties of his office, is to be taken as residence within the diocese.

Within his diocese the bishop is also the principal minister. He has the right, save in places and over persons who are exempt by law or custom, to celebrate the rites of ordination and confirmation, and indeed only a bishop can ordain and confirm. He is required to be faithful in admitting persons into holy orders, and in celebrating the rite of confirmation as often and in as many places as shall be convenient. He has the right of conducting, ordering, controlling and authorising all services in churches, chapels, churchyards and consecrated burial grounds within the diocese. However, in so doing he must act in conformity with the law relating to public worship. He is also required to provide, so far as lies in his power, that in every place within his diocese there are sufficient priests to minister to the people.

The bishop has the right to consecrate new churches, churchyards and burial **3.10** grounds, to institute to all vacant benefices, and to admit persons by licence to all other vacant ecclesiastical offices. Generally he has the patronage of large

---

[47] *ibid*.
[48] Godolphin *Repertorium Canonicum*, pp. 23, 32 *ante*.
[49] As to the exercise of this jurisdiction see Chap. 11.
[50] *Smith v. Lovegrove* (1755) 2 Lee 162.

numbers of benefices, and is chairman of the diocesan board of patronage. He also makes appointments to chancellorships, archdeaconries, deaneries, and most canonries and honorary canonries. He has the right to grant faculties or licences, this power being exercised through the faculty jurisdiction of the consistory court.[51]

The bishop is president of the diocesan synod, and must, as we shall see, consult it on matters of general importance and concern to the diocese. He is also required not to withhold his consent to its resolutions lightly nor without grave cause. In recent times the doctrine of the bishop-in-synod has developed, a term which describes the means by which the diocesan bishop plans and implements effective strategies for the administration of his diocese and the mission of the Church within it.[52] As we have already seen in Chapter 2, it is this model upon which the current proposals for reform at national level are based.

All diocesan bishops of the provinces of Canterbury and York are Church Commissioners, and all diocesan bishops hold seats in the Upper House of Convocation and the House of Bishops in the General Synod. In addition the Bishops of London, Durham and Winchester have seats in the House of Lords, together with 21 other bishops summoned in order of seniority.[53]

Suffragan bishops

3.11   Strictly speaking all bishops of a province are suffragans[54] of the archbishop, but the term is now only applied to bishops who assist the diocesan bishop. In most dioceses the diocesan bishop has the assistance of one or more suffragan bishops.

The power of a bishop to commission a suffragan has now been abolished, and he may now only petition the Sovereign for the creation of a suffragan see, or for appointment to a see in his diocese which has been vacant for at least the preceding five years, with the approval of the diocesan synod and the General Synod acting on a report by the Dioceses Commission.[55] However, generally suffragan's are appointed to existing titular sees.

The diocesan bishop has the right to nominate two candidates to the Sovereign, who then (acting on the advice of the Prime Minister) appoints one of the candidates to the office.[56] There is no obligation on the part of the diocesan bishop to consult, but generally the bishop's council, the diocesan synod and the archbishop are consulted.[57]

Where a person is either to be consecrated or translated to a suffragan bishopric he must take and swear the oath of allegiance,[58] and take the oath of

---

[51] See Chap. 11.
[52] See *Episcopal Ministry*, the report of the Archbishops' Commission on the Episcopate (1990), (GS 944), para. 825.
[53] *Halsbury's Laws of England* (4th ed.), Vol. 14, paras 351, 479.
[54] The term originally referred to bishops with a "suffrage", that is a vote in the House of Lords.
[55] Diocese Measure 1978, ss.15, 18.
[56] Suffragan Bishops Act 1534, s.1.
[57] The process by which suffragan and area bishops are appointed is set out *Senior Church Appointments*, the Report of the Working Party established by the Standing Committee of the General Synod of the Church of England (1992) (G.S. 1019) together with proposals for reform.
[58] Canon C13(1).

obedience to the archbishop.[59] On his consecration (if this is required) and investment by the archbishop the suffragan must make the declaration of assent.[60] He is given a titular see on appointment, which invariably is named after a place within the diocese, and he is styled "bishop suffragan" of that see.[61]

The jurisdiction or episcopal power or authority of a suffragan bishop extends only to that licensed or limited to him by the diocesan bishop.[62] Although he takes no oath of obedience to the diocesan bishop he is the suffragan under a duty to endeavour to execute faithfully those things which the diocesan commissions him to undertake.[63] Unless he has a licence from the diocesan bishop to reside elsewhere, he must reside within the diocese.[64] A suffragan bishop may be elected to the Upper House of Convocation and thus have a seat in the House of Bishops of the General Synod. He has a seat in the house of bishops of the diocesan synod, and is an *ex officio* member of the diocesan pastoral committee.

A suffragan is appointed for the diocese as a whole, not to a particular area. **3.12** However, a diocesan reorganisation scheme may provide for the division of the diocese into episcopal areas, with episcopal oversight either undertaken by a suffragan alone, or by the diocesan and suffragan together.[65] In such a case the suffragan is known as an area bishop. The scheme, which binds the diocesan's successors, does not divest the diocesan bishop of his functions, which continue to be exercisable by him either at his discretion, or because they cannot be divested. To date the Diocese of London has been divided into five episcopal areas in accordance with such a scheme, but no scheme has been made for any other diocese.

A diocesan bishop may also temporarily delegate to a suffragan specified functions, the discharge of which may be subject to conditions.[66] The suffragan may be authorised to exercise these functions in a particular area (and is then generally known as an area bishop) or throughout the diocese, either alone or jointly with the diocesan bishop, although no delegation divests the discesan bishop of any of his functions, which he may continue to exercise if he so wishes.

Notwithstanding this power the diocesan bishop cannot delegate functions in respect of his duty regarding the application to the archbishop to grant a faculty for admitting into Holy Orders a person who could not otherwise be admitted because of certain remarriages, nor in regard to the making of declarations pursuant to the Priests (Ordination of Women) Measure 1993.[67] Neither can these functions be delegated pursuant to a diocesan reorganisation scheme.[68]

Unless the only functions specified in the instrument are the administration of the rite of confirmation and the holding of ordinations, the bishop must not temporarily delegate any functions without the consent of the diocesan synod.[69] Any delegation will cease to have effect at the end of the period specified, or

---

[59] Canon C14(1).
[60] Canon C15(1), (3).
[61] Suffragan Bishops Act 1534, s.1.
[62] Canon C20(1).
[63] Suffragan Bishops Act 1534, s.4; Canon C20(2).
[64] Suffragan Bishops Act 1534, s.6; Canon C20(3).
[65] Diocese Measure 1978, s.11.
[66] *ibid.*, s.10.
[67] Diocese Measure 1978, s.10.
[68] Diocese Measure 1978, s.11.
[69] *ibid.*, s.10.

when either the diocesan or the suffragan bishop cease to hold office, whichever occurs first, and the diocesan has the power to revoke or vary the licence, seemingly at any time without giving notice.[70]

Delegation or authorisation to others in episcopal orders

3.13   In cases where the diocesan bishop has executed an irreversible instrument of resignation, or he considers that he will be unable to discharge any or all of his functions due to illness or absence from the diocese and there is no other person in the diocese in episcopal orders authorised to discharge the bishop's functions, he may delegate these to a person or persons in episcopal orders who is a member of the Church of England.[71]

Before doing so he must consult the bishop's council and standing committee, unless he is unable to because of illness, but he need not consult the diocesan synod. He must specify which functions are delegated, but the same prohibitions regarding the delegation of certain functions discussed above in relation to suffragans still apply.[72]

The bishop may not delegate his functions for a period of more than six months. However, this period may be extended by the archbishop, who himself has the power to delegate the diocesan bishop's functions without consultation where the see is vacant or the bishop is unable or does not otherwise delegate.[73]

Other bishops working in the diocese

3.14   Although the law only recognises suffragan bishops as assistants to the diocesan other bishops can and do act within the diocese. Bishops other than suffragans who are resident in the diocese and assist the diocesan bishop are given a variety of designations; assistant, honorary assistant or auxiliary bishops. Often these bishops are formally retired, but in other cases they may be full-time stipendiary assistant bishops. In all cases they act only with the permission of the diocesan, and in some dioceses can only act in an episcopal capacity with the prior consent of the diocesan.

On the request and by the commission in writing (which requires the consent of the archbishop) of a diocesan bishop, an overseas bishop, or a bishop consecrated in a church not in communion with the Church of England whose orders are recognised and accepted by the Church of England, may ordain persons and perform other episcopal functions in the diocese.[74]

Extended episcopal care

3.15   Whilst the ordination of women to the priesthood is considered in Chapter 7, it is perhaps more convenient to examine one consequence of such ordination as part of our exploration of the episcopacy in general. A parish opposed to the ministry

---

[70] *ibid.*, s.10.
[71] Church of England (Miscellaneous Provisions) Measure 1983, s.8.
[72] *ibid.*
[73] *ibid.*
[74] Overseas and other Clergy (Ministry and Ordination) Measure 1967, s.4(1). The commission may not extend to women bishops of the Anglican Communion, as to which see Chap. 12.

of women priests, which has passed either or both of the relevant resolutions, may petition the diocesan bishop concerned to the effect that appropriate episcopal duties in the parish should be carried out in accordance with the Episcopal Ministry Act of Synod 1993. This rearrangement of duties is sometimes referred to as "alternative episcopal oversight".

This Act, which needs to be read in conjunction with Code of Practice issued by the House of Bishops, dated January 12, 1994, prescribes three types of arrangements, diocesan, regional and provincial, which may be made to provide an appropriate ministry for those opposed to the ordination of women priests.[75] Diocesan arrangements are those which may be made, so far as is possible, by the diocesan bishop within his own diocese for appropriate care and oversight of the clergy and parishes in the diocese. Regional arrangements (a region comprising two or more dioceses in a province which are designated an area by the archbishop for the purposes of the Act of Synod[76]) are those under which the diocesan bishops of each region, acting together, may from time to time nominate one or more bishops from within their region who are opposed to the ordination of women, to carry out for any parish in the region such episcopal duties as the diocesan bishop concerned may request.

Provincial arrangements are those by which the Archbishops of Canterbury and York appoint additional suffragan bishops for their dioceses to act as "provincial episcopal visitors" to carry out or cause to be carried out for any parish in the province, such episcopal duties as the diocesan bishop concerned may request. In the province of Canterbury there are two appointments, to the sees of Ebbsfleet and Richborough, and in York one, to the see of Beverley. These episcopal visitors, who have acquired the appellation "flying bishops", work with the diocesan bishop concerned to enable pastoral care and sacramental ministry to be provided, and act as a spokesmen and advisor for those opposed to the ordination of women, assisting the archbishops in the monitoring of the operation of the Act of Synod. When a vacancy occurs in the office of such an episcopal visitor the archbishop is required to consult the other episcopal visitor or visitors and all other bishops who are directly concerned before filling the office.[77] Whilst the Act does not appear to be clear it would seem that these would be all those in the province not opposed to the ordination of women, in whose diocese there are parishes receiving or expected to request alternative oversight.

No special majority is specified in respect of the PCC resolution to petition the bishop or to withdraw such petition. Accordingly, the normal rules as to a quorum of one-third of the members and a simple majority of those present and voting will suffice.[78] However, unless the bishop is satisfied that at least four weeks' notice of the time and place of the meeting was given,[79] that the meeting was attended by at least half the council and at least two-thirds of the members present and voting were in favour of the resolution and that the minister, whether or not they were present or voted, is in favour, he is not obliged to make any arrangements or to cancel any existing arrangements.[80]

3.16

---

[75] Episcopal Ministry Act of Synod 1993, ss. 2, 3, 4, 5.
[76] *ibid.*, s.12.
[77] *ibid.*, s.6.
[78] CRR, r. 15. App. II.
[79] Save in cases where a notice of vacancy was sent to the secretary of the council pursuant to s.7(4) of the Patronage (Benefices) Measure 1986.
[80] Episcopal Ministry Act of Synod 1993, s.10.

Subject to these provisions, on receipt of a petition for appropriate episcopal duties to be carried out in accordance with the Act of Synod the bishop is obliged to consult, personally or through a representative, with the minister and the PCC, before making appropriate arrangements.[81] It would appear that the effect of the Act of Synod is that the PCC has no choice as to which of these arrangements it will accept.

A petition may be withdrawn at any time, and subject to the bishop being satisfied as to the conditions under which such a resolution was passed, he must ensure any arrangements are cancelled.[82] The Act also provides that where a PCC has presented a petition it must review the working of the subsequent arrangements every five years.[83] However, the Act is silent as to what action the PCC should take as a consequence, the implication being that the PCC it should consider whether or not to withdraw its petition.

In practice whether a parish petitions or withdraws a petition will depend upon the declarations, if any, which its own diocesan bishop may have made, or whether that bishop is opposed to the ordination of women and consequently will not himself ordain women priests.[84]

The arrangements for extended episcopal care being contained in an Act of Synod supplemented by a Code of Practice, have no legislative force. Despite the willingness of the courts to attach great weight to such statements, the arrangements are strictly voluntary and depend for their effectiveness upon the goodwill of all concerned.[85] All clergy who are ordained, instituted or licensed in the diocese take an oath of allegiance to their diocesan bishop. Some clergy and parishioners may as the result of the position adopted by their diocesan bishop with regard to the ordination of women, consider themselves to be in "impaired communion" with him, yet this impairment notwithstanding he remains legally and administratively the chief pastor and incumbent paramount of the diocese.

3.17   No bishop can exercise his ministry in another bishop's diocese without that diocesan's consent. Thus the scheme for extended care, must as the legislation stands derive its authority from the diocesan bishop. When the bishops of the provinces of Canterbury and York met in Manchester in 1993 to draw up the scheme they envisaged precisely this state of affairs. The diocesan bishop was to accept full responsibility for the episcopal and pastoral care of all in his charge. The bishops spoke of extended rather than alternative episcopal care and this is in essence what the scheme provides for. The diocesan bishop authorises a suffragan bishop to minister on his behalf to certain members of his diocese: he does not relinquish either authority over, or responsibility for such persons.[86]

---

[81] *ibid.*, s.8.
[82] *ibid.*, s.9(1).
[83] *ibid.*, s.9(2).
[84] See Chap. 7.
[85] See however Chap. 2.
[86] See further statements issued by the House of Bishops in January and June 1993 (the latter under the title *Bonds of Peace*) and the associated theological paper *Being in Communion* (G.S. Misc. 418). Rees, "Alternative Episcopal Oversight, in *Through a Glass Darkly: A Crisis Considered* (M. Watts ed., 1993), p. 131; Turner, "Bonds of Discord: Alternative Episcopal Oversight Examined in the Light of the Nonjuring Consecrations", 13 (1955) E.L.J. 398.

Episcopal visitation

The term visitation refers to the bishop or other Ordinary undertaking a circuit **3.18**
throughout his diocese or district with full power to inquire into all matters
relating to the government and discipline of the Church. The bishop has the
right, but no duty, to visit at times and places limited by law or custom.[87]
Although most peculiars have now been abolished by statute, royal residences
and certain other places, for example Westminster Abbey, retain their status as
peculiars and are exempt from visitation by the customary Ordinary.[88] In the case
of royal peculiars these are visitable only by the Crown.

The purpose of the bishop's, archbishop's or archdeacon's visit, is to gain
knowledge of the state, sufficiency and ability of the clergy and other persons in
the locality.[89] During the time of the visitation the jurisdiction of all inferior
Ordinaries is suspended, and the visitor has the right to perform all such acts as
by law and custom are assigned to their charge in that behalf, including the
supply of such things which are lacking and the correction of such things as are
amiss.[90]

Every spiritual person is visitable by the Ordinary, but laymen, except arguably
churchwardens and sidesmen, are not.[91] Provision is made in the constitution and
statutes of every cathedral in regard to the bishop's functions as visitor,[92-93] and in
earlier times it was customary for the bishop to visit his cathedral first, although
this practice is no longer generally observed.

Contemporary visitations do not have about them the characteristics of court
proceedings, as once was the case with episcopal visitations. The bishop today is
regarded as primarily a pastoral figure rather than a judicial one, and it is
doubtful if reported cases upon the subject are of relevance today. The modern
practice is for the bishop to select certain centres to which he summons clergy,
churchwardens and other persons, although in fact visitatorial powers beyond
those of the archdeacon (considered below) are rarely used.[94]

When the bishop summons his visitation he must deliver to the minister and
churchwardens of every parish, such articles of inquiry as he would require them
to use as the basis for their presentments, together with the form of declaration
which must be made immediately prior to any such presentment.[95] Previously
presentments were associated with an inquisitorial procedure in respect of
offences committed by clergy and laity, but today presentments in their original
sense are uncommon if not entirely obsolete. A modern presentment is likely to

---

[87] Canons G5(1); C18(4). These provisions supercede the former requirement in Canon 60
of the Canons Ecclesiastical 1603 (repealed) that an episcopal visitation should normally
be held every three years.
[88] Ecclesiastical Licences Act 1533, ss.14, 17.
[89] Canon C18(1).
[90] Canon G5.
[91] *Anon* (1608) No. 123.
[92-93] As to which see Chap. 6.
[94] Smith, "Points of Law and Practice Concerning Ecclesiastical Visitation" (1990–92)
2 E.L.J. 189. It should be noted that in some dioceses no episcopal visitations have
taken place in recent years.
[95] Canon G6. Presentments should be made by the outgoing not the new churchwardens,
since these are akin to the rendering of a spiritual as opposed to a financial account.

be confined to such matters as complaints by churchwardens against their incumbent. It should also be noted that whilst the Ordinary previously had the power of summary correction over the clergy of his diocese, such power can now only be exercised by proceedings in the ecclesiastical courts.[96] However, should he consider such punishment to be sufficient it is still possible for the bishop to deal with a matter through private admonition.

Retirements and other vacancies arising in a see

3.19   A vacancy in a diocesan or suffragan bishopric may be occasioned by translation, resignation, death, deprivation or retirement (a bishop must retire at 70 years of age).[97] With regard to retirement where the archbishop, in the case of a diocesan, or the diocesan in the case of a suffragan, considers it desirable he may authorise their continuance in office for a period not exceeding a year.[98] At a date not less than six months prior to the date on which a diocesan or suffragan bishop is required to vacate his office, the archbishop must declare the bishopric vacant, or if the bishop is authorised to continue for a period the date so authorised.[99] Should he wish to do so a bishop may seek to resign earlier than is required by law. In order to effect such a resignation however, he must consult with the archbishop who will decide whether to accept such a resignation, and should the archbishop be so minded he must then tender his resignation to the archbishop in the prescribed form.[1] In all cases of resignation, unless the archbishop makes a declaration to the contrary, the bishop must vacate any other preferment held at that date.[2]

Special provision is made for resignation on the grounds of incapacity. Where the archbishop of the province is of the opinion that a diocesan or suffragan bishop is incapacitated from performing his episcopal duties by reason of physical or mental infirmity he may, with the concurrence of two senior diocesan bishops of the province request that bishop to resign, and the bishop must comply.[3] Before making such a request the archbishop must send the bishop notice of his intention to do so.[4] If within 15 days the bishop demands a medical examination the archbishop must not demand his resignation until that report has been considered by the archbishop and the two senior bishops.[5]

Archdeacons and archdeaconries

3.20   For administrative purposes dioceses are legally divided, usually into between two to four archdeaconries, although an archdeaconry may comprise the whole diocese or any part of one. It is upon the archdeacons that the day to day supervision of parishes falls.

[96] See *Re Dean of York* (1841) 2 Q.B. 1.
[97] Ecclesiastical Offices (Age Limit) Measure 1975, s.1, Sched. This does not apply to a bishop who was already holding office on January 1, 1976: *ibid.*, s.1(4).
[98] *ibid.*, s.3(1).
[99] Bishops (Retirement) Measure 1986, s.2(1).
[1] *ibid.*, s.1.
[2] *ibid.*, s.8(1).
[3] *ibid.*, s.3(1). The bishop is treated for the purposes of Church of England pensions provisions as having retired on the grounds of infirmity: *ibid.*, s.7.
[4] *ibid.*, s.3(2).
[5] *ibid.*, s.3(2).

It is the usual practice for an archdeacon to be appointed by the diocesan bishop, who prefers them by collation. However, some archdeaconries are still in the gift of lay persons and the patron in such cases presents their candidate to the bishop who institutes in the same manner as to any other benefice. The dean and chapter of the cathedral church to which the archdeacon belongs induct the archdeacon by placing them in a stall of the cathedral church.[6] In general, before appointing an archdeacon the diocesan bishop undertakes a thorough consultation under procedures which vary from one diocese to another. The consultation process usually includes reference to representatives of deaneries within the archdeaconry and the bishop's council, as well as to the archbishop's secretary for appointments and the Prime Minister's secretary for appointments, both of whom maintain lists of persons deemed suitable for preferment.[7]

As the term archdeacon or chief deacon implies the office was originally exclusively held by deacons. Now an archdeacon must have been in holy orders (including the diaconate) for six complete years, and must be in priest's orders at the time of the appointment.[8] There would not appear to be any legal objection to a woman priest becoming an archdeacon.[9] The maximum age for appointment is now 69 years of age,[10] and the archdeacon is required to retire at 70, although their terms of office may be extended for up to one year where the diocesan bishop considers that there are special circumstances which make this desirable.[11]

Before collation the archdeacon must make and subscribe the declaration of assent and take the oath of allegiance and the oath of obedience to the bishop. The archdeacon is a corporation sole, and the office is one of freehold tenure[12] so that the archdeacon cannot simply be removed at the bishops pleasure.[13] Customarily an archdeacon is styled "the Venerable". **3.21**

An archdeacon is said to be next after the bishop in all matters ecclesiastical in respect of their archdeaconry, having statutory authority under the Crown.[14] However, an archdeacon is inferior to the chancellor of the diocese since the chancellor represents the bishop himself and has the greater jurisdiction.[15] The archdeacon's jurisdiction is described as an Ordinary jurisdiction[16] and may be

[6] *Sale v. Bishop of Coventry and Lichfield* (1590) 1 And. 241, *sub nom. Smallwood v. Bishop of Coventry and Lichfield and Marsh* (1590) 1 Leon. 205. Such archdeacons are said to have *locum in choro*.

[7] The current procedures are set out in the Report of the Working Party established by the Standing Committee of the General Synod of the Church of England, *Senior Church Appointments* (1992) (G.S. 1019) together with proposals for reform.

[8] Ecclesiastical Commissioners Act 1840, s.27; Canon C22(1).

[9] See Chap. 7.

[10] Ecclesiastical Offices (Age Limit) Measure 1975, s.1, Sched.

[11] *ibid.*, s.3(1)(b). The diocesan bishop may confer the designation of archdeacon emeritus upon a person who retires immediately after holding the office of archdeacon: Church of England (Miscellaneous Provisions) Measure 1995, s.3. When an archdeacon wishes to resign it is no longer necessary for them to proceed by way of deed, but any such resignation must be in writing, signed and witnessed, and sent to the diocesan bishop: Church of England (Miscellaneous Provisions) Measure 1995, s.4.

[12] *Ballard v. Gerard* (1702) 12 Mod. Rep. 608.

[13] Ayliffe *Parergon Juris Canonici Anglicani* (2nd ed. 1734), p. 96.

[14] Ecclesiastical Commissioners Act 1836, Preamble, s.19; Godolphin *Repertorium Canonicum*, (3rd ed. 1687) p. 60.

[15] Godolphin *Repertorium Canonicum*, (*ante*) App. 5.

[16] Canon C22(2).

exercised either by the archdeacon themselves or by an official commissary to whom they have formally committed authority.[17] In cases where the archdeaconry is vacant or the archdeacon is unable by reason of illness or absence to carry out all or any of their functions the diocesan bishop may appoint one or more priests to perform the archdeacon's functions for such period as is specified in the instrument of appointment.[18]

Within the archdeaconry the archdeacon's function[19] is to assist the bishop in his office and in his pastoral care. In particular the archdeacon must see that all those who hold ecclesiastical office within the archdeaconry perform their duties with diligence, and must bring to the bishop's attention both that which calls for correction and that which merits praise.[20-21] Whether as a matter of strict law the archdeacon shares in the bishop's cure of souls is a difficult matter to determine, and one which is not ultimately of great practical importance.

Unless inhibited by a superior Ordinary, that is during the visitation of the bishop or archbishop when their own jurisdiction is suspended, the archdeacon is required to hold yearly visitations.[22] Episcopal visitations were considered earlier in this chapter. The purpose of an archdeacon's visit and their rights during such a visitation are the same as that of the bishop, and the reader is thus referred to that earlier discussion for the main principles involved.

In general the annual visitation is held shortly after the end of April at which time the churchwardens are to be admitted, and presentments (again discussed in relation to episcopal visitations) made. Although the visitation is for the benefit of the parish at large it may be held by grouping together a number of parishes and holding the visitation for all at one parish church.[23-24] The archdeacon has the power to cite the clergy to attend, but not the laity other than the churchwardens and possibly the sidesmen. At the visitation the archdeacon is expected to deliver an address known as a charge.[25]

3.22   The articles of inquiry which the archdeacon is authorised to deliver to the incumbent or priest-in-charge and to the churchwardens will relate to the administration of the parish, the state of church buildings, the arrangements made for services and the life and health of the parish generally. These must be answered in the presentments of the incumbent and churchwardens "advisedly and according to their consciences". These may contain sensitive information, such as complaints regarding each others conduct or that of a parishioner. The archdeacon may need to communicate that information to the bishop, DBF or other body, or take action such as calling a meeting of the PCC.

The Legal Advisory Board is of the view that whilst a person can seek an injunction to restrain a breach of a confidential relationship it would appear that presentments communicated to an archdeacon cannot give rise to such a remedy since those replying to the inquiries are under an obligation to do so. However, the archdeacon is under a duty to make proper use of the information received

---

[17] Canon C22(3).

[18] Church of England (Miscellaneous Provisions) Measure 1983, s.9.

[19] Jones, "Omnis Gallia . . . or the Roles of the Archdeacon" (1991) 2 Ecc. L.J. 236; Ravenscroft, "The Role of the Archdeacon Today" (1995) 3 Ecc. L.J. 379.

[20-21] Canon C22(4).

[22] Canon C22(5).

[23-24] *Shephard v. Payne* (1862) 12 C.B.N.S. 414 at 434, 435; affd, (1864) 16 C.B.N.S. 132, Ex. Ch.

[25] Ayliffe *Parergon Juris Canonici Anglicani* (2nd ed. 1734), p. 1515.

and not to communicate it improperly (such as to a newspaper) or maliciously, and could face proceedings in the consistory court for improper disclosure. Were an aggrieved party to commence an action for libel in respect of presentments or their subsequent disclosure the incumbent and churchwardens would have a defence of common interest in communicating the material and likewise the archdeacon unless there was express malice in their so doing.[26] The Legal Advisory Board has also expressed the view that information received from third parties, even in confidence, should be included in the presentments if it is information which could properly be so included, However, anyone who includes information which they have received from others would be advised to check the information for themselves and not to act upon hearsay.

The functions of the archdeacon in regard to pastoral breakdown and the procedure under the Incumbents (Vacation of Benefices) Measure 1977, the surveying of churches, and their role with regard to the faculty jurisdiction are discussed in Chapters 5, 8 and 11 respectively. In addition to those already described above the archdeacon has various other duties. They must examine and present candidates for ordination, either in person or by a deputy.[27] They must induct any priest who has been instituted into possession of the temporalities on receiving directions from the bishop so to do.[28] An archdeacon is an *ex officio* member of a number of bodies including the diocesan synod, pastoral committee and DAC, and may be a member of other diocesan boards or serve as a member of Convocation and of the General Synod.

Diocesan synods

As part of the system of synodical government introduced by the Synodical Government Measure 1969 diocesan conferences were dissolved and their functions transferred to newly-constituted diocesan synods for each diocese. However, the new system does not prevent the bishop of the diocese from summoning a conference of persons appearing to him to be representative of clergy and laity of the diocese on such occasions and for such purposes as he sees fit.[29]   **3.23**

The provisions relating to membership of, and the procedures for election to, diocesan synods are set out in the CRR. If it appears to a diocesan synod that these provisions ought to be varied to meet the special circumstances of the diocese and to secure better representation of either clergy, laity or both, then it may make a scheme for variation.[30] The assent of the house of bishops and a two-thirds majority of the houses of clergy and laity of the diocesan synod present and voting is required after which the scheme must be laid before a session of the General Synod. If a member of the General Synod gives notice that they wish the matter debated the scheme will not come into operation unless approved by the General Synod: otherwise it can come into operation on the day after the group

---

[26] *Legal Opinions*, pp. 8–9.
[27] Canon C7; *Ordinal*, Form and Manner of Ordering of Priests.
[28] *Phillimore, Ecclesiastical Law of the Church of England*, (2nd ed. 1895), Vol. 1, p. 382.
[29] SGM. s.4(7).
[30] CRR, r. 33(1).

of sessions during which it was laid, without the need for approval.[31] Once in operation the relevant provisions of the CRR will then have effect subject to the scheme.

It should be noted that where a diocese has been divided into areas or been subject to a re-organisation scheme, as discussed earlier in this chapter, provision is made for the constitution of an area synod for each such area.[32] The diocesan synod may delegate such of its functions in regard to the episcopal area for which the area synod is to act as it specifies by resolution. The CRR applicable to diocesan synods apply to these area synods with such modifications, adaptations and exceptions as the scheme bringing about the division of the diocese into areas provides for.

Composition

3.24   A diocesan synod consists of three houses, the House of Bishops, a House of Clergy and a House of Laity; membership of all three houses being set out in rule 30 of the CRR. The House of Bishops comprises the bishop of the diocese, suffragan bishops of the diocese, and any other person in episcopal orders working in the diocese whom the diocesan bishop nominates, with the concurrence of the archbishop. A suffragan bishop appointed as a provincial episcopal visitor may, in addition to being a member of the diocesan synod of which he is a suffragan, be invited by the bishop of the diocese where he resides to be a member of that diocesan synod.[33] The diocesan bishop is president of the diocesan synod.

The houses of clergy and laity consist of *ex officio*, selected and co-opted members together with the possible addition of up to 10 additional members, either clergy or laity, nominated by the diocesan bishop, who sit in the appropriate house. It should be noted that no person, other than the chancellor of a diocese and suffragans appointed provincial episcopal visitors, is entitled to be a member of more than one diocesan synod at the same time. The registrar of the diocese is the registrar of the diocesan synod and may appoint a deputy registrar of the diocesan synod. Both the registrar and any deputy are precluded from being elected, nominated, co-opted or *ex officio* members of the synod.

The *ex officio* members of the House of Clergy comprises any person in episcopal orders nominated by the bishop of the diocese, other than a suffragan bishop or a person nominated by him as a member of the House of Bishops; the dean or provost of the cathedral; the archdeacons; the proctors elected for the diocese, or from any university in the diocese, to the Lower House of the Convocation of the province; the person chosen by and from the clerical members of religious communities in the province to represent them in the Lower House of the Convocation, if they are resident in the diocese; the chancellor of the diocese and the chairmen of the DBF, DAC and the Diocesan Board of Education[34] if any of these are in holy orders. If they are not, they are

---

[31] *ibid.*, r. 26 (2)–(5).

[32] Dioceses Measure 1978, s.17.

[33] He is restricted from exercising his vote in the diocesan synod of which he is resident on matters referred to it by the General Synod.

[34] Diocesan Boards of Education Measure 1991, Sched., para. 4.

members of the House of Laity. To these are added the members elected by the Houses of Clergy of the deanery synods of the diocese, up to five members co-opted by the House of Clergy of the diocesan synod, and any members nominated by the bishop.

The House of Laity comprises members elected by the House of Laity of the deanery synods of the diocese. These sit with the *ex officio* members, who in addition to those specified above consist of all those elected from the diocese to the House of Laity of the General Synod and any other member of that House who is resident in the diocese. In addition the house may co-opt up to five members, who are actual communicants of at least 18 years of age.

Electors and candidates

Elections to the Houses of Clergy and Laity are governed by rule 32 of the CRR. **3.25** Elections to the diocesan synod must take place every three years, the election being held during a period and on dates fixed by the diocesan bishop, although elections must be completed by July 15 of the relevant year. Members of the diocesan synod are elected by the houses of the deanery synods, and the diocesan synod must determine the number of members to be elected by each house of every deanery synod not later than December 31 of the year preceding an election, subject to the proviso that at least two members must be elected by each house of every deanery synod. In the case of elections to the House of Clergy the numbers must be related, subject to the above requirement, to the number of members of those houses in their respective deanery synods. In the case of elections to the House of Laity numbers are related to the total number of names on the rolls of the parishes in the respective deaneries. The diocesan synod must exercise its powers to ensure that the total number of members for the two houses must not be less than 150 and must not exceed 270 including co-opted members. It is also incumbent upon the diocesan synod to ensure that the numbers in each house are approximately equal.

As we saw in Chapter 2 a register of lay electors is maintained by the diocesan electoral registration officer. The electors to the House of Laity are all the lay members of the deanery synods, excluding co-opted members, entered on the register, the qualifying date (including elections to casual vacancies) being 6.00 a.m. on the date on which nomination papers are issued.

Any lay person who is an actual communicant aged at least 18, whose name is entered on the roll of any parish in the deanery, or who is a lay person declared by the dean to be a habitual worshipper at the cathedral church of the diocese and to be associated with the deanery is qualified to be elected by the house of laity of a deanery synod.

Register of clerical electors

A register is also maintained of the members of the House of Clergy in the **3.26** deanery synods.[35] The same provisions regarding inspection and correction of the register, and in regard to appeals in respect of enrolment or removal of names,

---

[35] CRR, r. 29 (1). The co-opted members are listed separately.

apply to this register as to the register of lay electors described in Chapter 2. The only difference between the two registers is that in this case notice of any such appeal is given to the chairman of the house of clergy of the diocesan synod, and the bishop council appoints three or more of its clerical, rather than lay members to consider and determine the appeal.

Any clerical member of the deanery synod is qualified to be elected by the House of Clergy of a deanery synod to be a member of the diocesan synod, although they may not stand for election by more than one such synod. The provision[36] is unclear as to whether a clerk may stand for election by a deanery synod of which they are not a member. The fact that this proviso was considered necessary suggests that they can, but this would be in contrast to the requirement for lay candidates, who it would appear can only be elected by the deanery synod of the deanery with which they are associated. The electors of the clerical members are those entered in the register of clerical electors, other than co-opted members, the qualifying date being the same as for lay electors.

Elections

3.27 The presiding officers for the deaneries are appointed by the bishop and must not be members of the house of the deanery synod for which they are appointed. Candidates must be nominated by a qualified elector. Nominations, which must be in the specified form, are sent to the presiding officer[37] within the period specified by that officer. This date must be not less than 14 days prior to the date of the election. The nominations must be accompanied by a statement, signed by the candidate, stating their willingness to serve if elected. If they wish, the candidate may set out in not more than 100 words a factual statement for circulation with the voting papers, setting out their professional qualifications, present office and any relevant past experience. The provisions regarding the scrutiny of nominations and the supply of details of electors to candidates are identical to those applicable to the election of lay members to the House of Laity of the General Synod.[38]

Prior to December 31 in the year preceding an election diocesan synods are required to decide which form of voting papers are to be used in the election. Under one form the elections are conducted by the method of the single transferable vote. The alternative scheme allows for the presiding officer to decide as between persons who have received an equal number of votes. Voting papers must be returned within such period as the presiding officer specifies, this being not less than 14 days after issue. Each candidate must be notified of the result of the election by August 31 of that year.

Appeals

3.28 Provision is made for appeals by an elector or candidate in an election, or by the chairman of either the House of Clergy or the House of Laity. The relevant provisions[39] are essentially the same as those already described in relation to

---

[36] *ibid.*, r. 31(2).
[37] This may be by post, in person or by facsimilie transmission, but in the last case the original nomination paper must be sent to the presiding officer within three days of the closing date for nominations.
[38] See Chap. 2.
[39] CRR, rr. 44, 45.

elections to the House of Laity of the General Synod,[40] and are only discussed here to the extent that they differ from those provisions.

Notices of appeal arising out of an election to the House of Laity must again be given to the chairman of that house within the same time limits. In the case of an appeal arising out of an election to the House of Clergy the rules are not entirely clear.[41] However, the better construction would appear to be that notice must be given to the chairman of the House of Clergy within the same time limits as appeals relating to the House of Laity, but an appellant would be advised to serve notice on the chairman of both houses.

All appeals are referred to the bishop's council and the standing committee of the diocese. It appoints three or more (so long as there is an odd number) of either its lay or clerical members, as appropriate, to consider and determine the appeal.

Term of office

Elected members of the Houses of Clergy and Laity normally hold office for a **3.29** term of three years beginning, on August 1 following their election, although a person elected to fill a casual vacancy only holds their office for the unexpired period of the term of the person whose place they are elected to fill. Where a member elected by the House of Clergy of a deanery synod ceases to be qualified for election their seat will be vacated forthwith, unless they continue to work or reside in the diocese and the clerical members of the standing committee resolve, before the vacancy occurs, that the seat will not be vacated.[42] Where a member elected by the House of Laity of a deanery synod ceases to have the qualification of entry on the electoral roll of a parish in that deanery or to be an habitual worshipper at the cathedral church their seat is vacated forthwith.[43] This provision does not apply where that person is entered on the electoral roll of any other parish in the diocese or if previously on a parish roll is declared a habitual worshipper at the cathedral, and the lay members of the standing committee resolve, before the vacancy occurs, that the seat will not be vacated.

Casual vacancies

Where a casual vacancy occurs this may be filled by an election by the relevant **3.30** house of the deanery synod at a meeting held for that purpose. Otherwise an election is conducted in the same manner as an ordinary election.[44] An election must be held within six months from the occurrence of the vacancy, save that where the vacancy occurs within nine months of the period for holding a general

---

[40] See Chap. 2.
[41] Either that notice is to be given to the chairman of the House of Laity under the same time constraints, and the appeal then referred on by the chairman of the House of Clergy, or it is to be given to the chairman of the House of Clergy with no time constraint set out: *ibid*., r. 44(4), (11).
[42] *ibid*., r. 46.
[43] *ibid*., r. 46.
[44] *ibid*., r. 48.

election the vacancy is not to be filled unless the members of the bishop's council and the standing committee who are from the relevant house direct that it should.

Functions of the diocesan synod

3.31   It is the function of the diocesan synod to consider matters concerning the Church of England, to make provision for such matters in relation to its diocese, and to consider and express its opinion on any other matters of religious or public interest, although it may not issue any statements concerning the doctrine of the Church on any question.[45] The synod is to consider and express its opinion on any matters referred to it by the General Synod, and in particular to approve or disapprove provisions referred to it relating to forms of worship or union with another Christian body. It is also to advise the bishop on any matters upon which he may consult the synod,[46] it being the bishop's duty to consult with the synod on matters of general importance to the diocese.[47]

The diocesan synod must keep the deanery synods of the diocese informed of the policies and problems of the diocese and of the business which is to come before meetings of the diocesan synod. It must also keep itself informed, through the deanery synods, of events and opinion in the parishes, and must give opportunities for discussing at meetings of the diocesan synod matters raised by the deanery synods and by PCCs.[48] It may also delegate executive functions to the deanery synods.[49] In addition to these general functions the diocesan synod has various specific functions assigned to it by a number of enactments, many of which are considered under the relevant headings throughout this work. Whether any matters fall within the functions of the diocesan synod is a matter for the diocesan bishop to determine.[50]

Procedure

3.32   The diocesan synod is required to make standing orders which must include certain specified provisions so that various requirements set out in rule 34 of the CRR have effect.[51] In general such standing orders are based upon a model set of orders and do not differ widely from one diocese to another. A bishop's council and standing committee of the synod must be appointed. This may, subject to the standing orders, discharge the synod's function of advising the bishop on matters upon which he consults it. No person is entitled to serve as a member of more than one such council or standing committee.

A secretary to the synod must be appointed and the diocesan registrar is the registrar of the synod. A specified minimum of not less than two meetings a year

---

[45] SGM, s.4(2).
[46] SGM, s.4(2).
[47] *ibid.*, s.4(3).
[48] *ibid.*, s.4(5).
[49] *ibid.*, s.4(5).
[50] *ibid.*, s.4(6).
[51] CRR, r. 34(1).

must be held.[52] A meeting must also be held if a specified number of members request this. The bishop need not be chairman of the synod's meetings to the extent that the standing orders otherwise provide.

Rule 34 provides that in general nothing is deemed to have the assent of the synod unless the three houses of which it is comprised have each assented to it. However, questions relating only to the conduct of business may be decided by a majority of all members of the synod present and voting. All other questions shall be decided in the same way, and the assent of all three houses presumed, unless either the diocesan bishop or any ten members require that a separate vote of each house be taken. Where the House of Bishops is equally divided the diocesan bishop has the casting or second vote. In the case of a particular question, except a matter referred to the synod by the General Synod relating to forms of worship or union with another Christian body, the diocesan bishop has the power to direct that the said question shall only be deemed to have the assent of the House of Bishops if the majority who assent include the diocesan bishop. Questions relating to forms of worship or union with another Christian body referred to the synod by the General Synod are however deemed to have been approved if the Houses of Clergy and Laity are in favour. The diocesan bishop has the right to require that his opinion on any question be recorded in the minutes.

Diocesan boards and committees

In each diocese there are various boards and committees. In addition to the   **3.33** bishops's council and standing committee and the DBF[53] each diocese must establish a Pastoral Committee,[54] a Parsonages Board,[55] a Redundant Churches Uses Committee,[56] a DAC[57] and a Board of Education. There are also a number of non-statutory bodies in each diocese dealing with such matters as training, ordination, readers, the ministry of women, ecumenical matters, youth work, family welfare, social responsibility and missionary work, consideration of which are beyond the scope of a book such as this.

Diocesan Board of Education

Every diocese is required to have a board of education which is responsible to   **3.34** the diocesan synod,[58] to whom it reports. The board comprises the bishop and two persons nominated by him, who must be either a suffragan or full-time

---

[52] Other than in dioceses where area synods have been constituted, in which case only one meeting a year need be specified.
[53] See Chap. 8.
[54] See Chap. 5.
[55] See Chap. 8.
[56] See Chap. 8.
[57] See Chap. 11.
[58] Diocesan Boards of Education Measure 1991, s.1. The Board may be corporate or unincorporate: *ibid.*

assistant bishop or archdeacon, together with between 14 and 18 members elected by the diocesan synod of whom at least two must come from each archdeaconry in the dicocese.[59] The provisions ensure that at least two of these members must be clerical and six lay, and that some members are also members of the diocesan synod. Persons with relevant experience may also be co-opted. Either the bishop is chairman or he may appoint some other person after consulting with the board.

The main functions of the board are to promote, or assist in the promotion, within the diocese of education consistent with the faith and practice of the Church of England. They are charged with promoting religious education and worship in all schools within the diocese, and the promotion of church schools. They are required to advise the governors of church schools together with the trustees of church educational endowments, or any other person, on any matter affecting church schools within the diocese, and to promote co-operation between the Board and any person or body connected with education in the diocese.[60]

Church schools may be either voluntary or grant maintained,[61] voluntary schools being controlled, aided or special agreement schools pursuant to the Education Act 1944. Of these controlled and aided schools are by far the most common, control and aided being from the perspective of the local education authority not the church, with the consequence that church appointed governors only dominate in aided not controlled schools. No church school belongs to the parish or deanery in which it is situated, but each has its own trust under which it was established and its own governing bodies.

The law relating to education and in particular to church schools is complex. The spate of legislation concerning education over the last decade has only compounded these difficulties. In addition the complications arising from the terms of the trusts relating to any particular school or educational endowment must be borne in mind. It is therefore impossible in a work such as this to summarise the position, and much will in any event be dependent upon the individual trust.[62]

Religious education and worship in schools

3.35   The Education Reform Act 1988 requires all state funded schools known as maintained schools (which are either county, voluntary, special or grant maintained schools) to provide non-denominational, religious education as part of the curriculum for all maintained schools. The syllabus reflecting the fact that the religious traditions of Britain are in the main Christian, whilst taking into

---

[59] *ibid.*, Sched., Pt 1.

[60] *ibid.*, s.2.

[61] *ibid.*, s.10.

[62] See Duncan and Lankshear, *Church Schools, A Guide for Governors* (1996); Lankshear, *Preparing for Inspection in a Church School* (1996); Harris, *The Law Relating to Schools* (2nd ed., 1995); Lankshear, "The Role of the Church in Education in England and Wales—An Anglican Perspective" (1995) 124/5 *Law & Justice*; Francis and Lankshear (eds), *Christian Perspectives on Church Schools* (1993); Lankshear, *A Shared Vision, Education in Church Schools* (1992).

account the other principal religions.[63] A leading role in the provision of religious education and worship is played by the Standing Advisory Council on Religious Education (SACRE) which is constituted by the local education authority under the 1998 Act and comprises representatives of the principal Christian denominations and other religious traditions in the area.[64] Each SACRE must have within its ranks a representative of the Church of England and in appointing such a member the local education authority consults the Diocesan Board of Education.

The 1988 Act also require all state funded schools to provide a daily act of collective worship.[65] In county and most grant maintained schools that act of worship is to be wholly or mainly of a broadly Christian character without being distinctive of any particular Christian denomination.[66] In voluntary schools the content of the act of worship is to be determined by the governing bodies or by the trust deed.

Deaneries and rural deans

Every parish is within a rural deanery or, as it is often referred to today, particularly in urban areas, a deanery.[67] Despite its ancient origins the office of rural dean, or area dean as they are now often called, had by the Middle Ages suffered a decline, and had virtually ceased to exist in the centuries which followed the Reformation, until its revival in the nineteenth century. However, **3.36**

---

[63] Education Reform Act 1988, ss.2(1), 8(2), (3). The syllabus (which may be different for different schools or different classes or descriptions of pupils) is to be agreed locally by a "conference" appointed by the local education authority consisting of essentially the same persons as the SACRE: Education Act 1944, s.26(1), Sched. 5. In a voluntary school religious education is (depending upon whether the school is controlled, aided or a special agreement school) in accordance with either the agreed syllabus or the practice which applied before the school acquired its voluntary status, or which the trust deeds establish: Education Act 1944, ss.27, 28. The position of grant maintained schools is the same as that of county schools unless they are a denominational school or were a voluntary school immediately before acquiring grant maintained status: Education Act 1993, ss.138–141. Parents have the right to exclude their children from religious education: Education Reform Act 1988, s.9(3).

[64] Education Reform Act 1988, s.11.

[65] The Education Reform Act 1988, s.6. The act of worship need no longer be at the beginning of the day and separate acts may be provided for pupils in different age or school groups: *ibid*. Parents have the right to withdraw their children from acts of collective worship without giving reasons: *ibid*, s.9(3).

[66] Education Reform Act 1988, s.7. This provision allows for some acts of worship not to comply provided most do. The position of grant maintained schools is the same as that of county schools unless they are a denominational school or were a voluntary school immediately before acquiring grant maintained status: Education Act 1993, s.138. The head teacher of a county school may apply to SACRE to lift the restriction on Christian worship if they consider alternative collective worship appropriate in respect of the whole school or any class or description of pupils: Education Reform Act 1988, s.12. See *R. v. The Secretary of State for Education, ex p. Ruscoe and Dando* [1994] E.L.R. 495 on the question of a failure to provide collective worship contrary to ss.6, 7 of the Education Reform Act 1988.

[67] "Deanery" means rural deanery: SGM, s.9(2).

with the introduction of synodical government the rural dean has an important role to play in the deanery synods, which are the final tier of that system.

There is no statutory qualification for the office of rural dean although the CRR contemplates that the rural deal will be both a member of, and joint chairman of, the deanery synod,[68] implying that they should be qualified for membership of that synod and of its House of Clergy. In practice a clerk in holy orders within the deanery is generally appointed. The appointment is in the hands of the bishop of the diocese and the relevant archdeacon.[69] The office carries no remuneration, and there is no objection to any deacon nor to a female priest being appointed.[70] The office is not permanent, and a rural dean may be removed at will by their superior, whose minister they are.[71]

The statutory duties of the rural dean are few, but in practice they assist the archdeacon and advise parochial clergy in various matters. It is for the rural dean to report to the bishop any matter in any parish within the deanery which it may be necessary or useful for the bishop to know.[72] This is particularly so in the case of serious illness or other form of distress amongst the clergy or in any instance of a minister from another diocese officiating in any place otherwise than as provided for by canon.

The rural dean has specific duties to the archdeacon as well as to the bishop. If they have reason to believe that there is any serious defect in the fabric, ornaments and furniture of any church or chapel, or that the buildings of any benefice are in a state of disrepair they should report the matter to the archdeacon.[73] It is said that the rural dean may also give induction in the absence of the archdeacon, but in practice the rural dean now only does so on the archdeacon's mandate.

In addition to their role in respect of the deanery synod, discussed below, the rural dean has certain other roles within both the deanery and the diocese. They are a member of the diocesan board of patronage when that board is transacting business in respect of any business within the deanery, frequently act as sequestrators of a vacant benefice within the diocese, and are interested parties for the purposes of representations to the pastoral committee of the diocese.

Deanery synods

3.37   Deanery synods are the third tier of synodical government. They replaced ruridecanal conferences which were dissolved, although the functions of the deanery synod are much wider than the former conferences. In contrast to ruridecanal conferences, which did not exist in every area, a deanery synod is required to be constituted for each deanery.[74] Rule 24 of the CRR sets out the membership of the deanery synod, which consists of a House of Clergy and a House of Laity.

---

[68] CRR, r. 28(1)(a).
[69] Godolphin *Repertorium Canonicum*, (3rd ed. 1687) App. P. 6.
[70] See Chap. 7.
[71] Godolphin *Repertorium Canonicum*, (3rd ed. 1687) App. P. 6.
[72] Canon C23.
[73] Canon C23.
[74] SGM, s.5(1).

The House of Clergy consists of all the clerks in holy orders beneficed in or licensed to any parish in the deanery; any clerks in holy orders licensed to any institutions in the deanery under the Extra-Parochial Ministry Measure 1967; clerical members of the General Synod or diocesan synod resident in the deanery; other clerks in holy orders holding the bishop's licence throughout the diocese or in more than one deanery who are resident in the deanery[75]; one or more retired clerks in holy orders, one being elected or chosen by and from every ten such clerks resident in the deanery, in a manner approved by the bishop.[76]

The House of Laity consists of parochial representatives elected by the annual meetings of the parishes of the deanery and any lay members of the General Synod or diocesan synod or area synod whose names are entered on the roll of any parish in the deanery. In addition, if in the bishop's opinion any community of persons in the deanery who are in the spiritual care of a chaplain licensed by the bishop should be represented in that house, one lay person may be chosen by and from the members of that community and the house also includes[77] such other lay persons being deaconesses or lay workers licensed by the bishop to work throughout the diocese or in more than one deanery who are resident in the deanery.[78]

Both houses have the power to co-opt members who must be clerks in holy orders or lay persons who are actual communicants aged at least 18 years, respectively. However, co-opted members must not exceed five per cent of the total number of members of that house or three in number, whichever is the greater.

The diocesan synod must exercise its powers to ensure that the total number of members (including co-opted members) of any deanery synod does not exceed 150, and so far as is practicable does not number less than 50.[79] However, the total number may be exceeded in order to secure that the House of Laity is not fewer in number than the House of Clergy.

As with diocesan synods if it appears that the provisions relating to membership of deanery synods ought to be varied to meet the special circumstances of the diocese or deaneries and to secure better representation of clergy or laity, the diocesan synod may make a scheme to effect such variation.[80] The means by

---

[75] This is subject to a direction by the members of the House of Clergy of the bishop's council that, having regard to a number of parochial and non-parochial clergy in the deanery, that clerk is to have membership of a different, specified deanery, provided that such a clerk cannot be a member of more than one deanery synod in the diocese.

[76] Such clerks must be in receipt of a pension in accordance with the provisions of the Clergy Pensions Measure 1961 and not hold the licence of the bishop.

[77] That person must be an actual communicant member of the Church of England and is chosen in such manner as the bishop approves.

[78] This is subject to a direction by the members of the House of Laity of the bishop's council that, having regard to number of such deaconesses and lay workers in the deanery, they are to have membership of a different, specified deanery, provided that such persons cannot be a member of more than one deanery synod in the diocese.

[79] CRR, r. 25. The number of parochial representatives of the laity to be elected from parishes is to be determined by resolution of the diocesan synod not later than December 31 in the year preceding any such election, and the numbers are to be elected related to the numbers of names on the rolls of parishes, but so that the resolution must not make it possible for a parish with fewer than 26 names on the roll to have more than one representative: *ibid*.

[80] *ibid*., r. 26.

which such a scheme is made and brought into effect is the same as a scheme in respect of diocesan synods which has already been discussed above.

3.38   In addition the diocesan synod may also make provision by a scheme for representation on a deanery synod of the dean or provost, the residentiary canons and other ministers of the cathedral church of the diocese or any of them.[81] A scheme may also provide for representation of lay persons who in a parish church cathedral are on the electoral roll of the parish, or who in any other cathedral are declared by the dean to be habitual worshippers and whose names are not entered on the roll of any parish.[82] In either case such schemes require the assent of the House of Bishops and a two-thirds majority of the members of each of the other houses of the diocesan synod present and voting, copies of the scheme being required to be sent to members of the synod at least 14 days before the session at which it is to be considered.

Parochial representatives to deanery synods are elected by annual parochial church meetings every three years, the representatives then holding office for a term of three years from June 1 next following their election.[83] The conduct of the elections is considered in Chapter 4. Appeals against matters arising out of such elections are identical to those discussed in relation to elections to the House of Laity of diocesan synods, save that notices of appeal are given to the lay chairman of the deanery synod.[84]

Casual vacancies are to be filled as soon as practicable after the vacancy occurs. When the annual parochial church meeting is not due to be held within the next two months after the occurrence of the vacancy the vacancy must be filled by the election of a qualified person by the PCC.[85] That person then holds office for the unexpired portion of the term of office of the members whom they replace.

Vacation of seat

3.39   Where a lay member of the deanery synod who is either a parochial or cathedral representative ceases to have the qualification of entry on the electoral roll of a parish by which they were elected, or to be an habitual worshipper at the cathedral church, their seat is vacated forthwith.[86] The provision does not however apply where that person is entered on the electoral roll of any other parish in the diocese or if a parochial representative is declared a habitual worshipper at the cathedral, and the PCC so resolve before the vacancy occurs that the seat will not be vacated. By implication the PCC which must pass this resolution is that of the parish by whom the representative was elected.[87] The rules do not provide expressly for the vacation of their seat by members of the House of Clergy who cease to be qualified for membership of that house, since

---

[81] *ibid.*, r. 27.
[82] *ibid.*, r. 27.
[83] CRR, r. 25.
[84] *ibid.*, r. 43.
[85] *ibid.*, r. 48(1).
[86] *ibid.*, r. 46(1)(a), (2).
[87] However, the rule does not provide for a non parish church cathedral to pass such a resolution.

the vast majority are *ex officio* members. However, it would appear to be implicitly understood that those members who are elected should vacate their seat upon ceasing to be qualified.

Functions of deanery synods

The functions of a deanery synod are to consider matters concerning the Church **3.40** of England and to make provisions for such matters in relation to its, deanery, and to consider and express their opinion on any other matters of religious or public interest, although it is prohibited from issuing any statement purporting to declare the doctrine of the Church on any question. It must bring together the views of the parishes of the deanery on common problems, discuss and formulate common policies on those problems, and foster a sense of community and interdependence among those parishes, and generally should promote in the deanery the whole mission of the Church, pastoral, evangelistic, social and ecumenical. In addition it should make known, and so far as appropriate put into effect, any provision made by the diocesan synod, and also consider the business of the diocesan synod, particularly any matters referred to that synod by the General Synod. It should sound out parochial opinion whenever it is required to do so, or whenever it considers it appropriate so to do. Finally it should raise such matters as it considers appropriate within the diocesan synod.[88]

Where the diocesan synod delegates functions to the deanery synods in relation to the parishes within the deanery, the deanery synod must exercise those functions.[89] This is particularly so in the case where the determination of parochial shares or "quotas",[90] that is the amount to be subscribed to the expenditure authorised by diocesan synods, is delegated.

Meetings and procedure

The diocesan synod must make rules for deanery synods which must include **3.41** certain provisions, but subject to these provisions the deanery synod has the power to regulate its own procedure.[91] The rural dean and a member of the House of Laity are to be joint chairmen of the deanery synod, and they must agree between them who is to chair each meeting or particular items of business on the agenda. A secretary of the synod must be appointed and there must be a standing committee of the synod. A specified number of meetings must be held in each year. On those matters and circumstances which the rules specify, voting must be by Houses, otherwise decisions are to be taken by a majority of members present and voting. A report of the synod's proceedings must be prepared and circulated to all PCCs in the deanery.

---

[88] SGM, s.5(3).
[89] *ibid.*, s.5(4).
[90] See Chap. 8.
[91] CRR, r. 28.

Chapter Four: The Parish

A parish is a geographical area entrusted by the bishop to a minister who has the **4.1** cure or care of the souls within it. It is regarded by most members of the Church of England as the fundamental unit of the Church. It is to their local church that most active members of the Church of England go to worship and to which many more resort for the occasional offices of baptism, marriage and burial. Each parish has a parochial church council (PCC) responsible for much of the day to day administration of the parish, as well as churchwardens. Each parish also has a church electoral roll and those enrolled upon it are able to take an active part in the synodical government of the Church by standing as representatives of the laity in elections to the PCC, deanery and diocesan synods and to the General Synod.

Usually the minister who has the cure of souls will be the incumbent of a benefice, although increasingly such a minister may merely be a priest-in-charge who thus has no security of tenure. However, it is important to distinguish between the parish which is a geographical area and a benefice which is a freehold office. Whilst it often remains the case that a benefice is comprised of a single parish this is often no longer so. The benefice and various matters connected with this such as the establishment of team and group ministries are considered in the next chapter.

In this chapter we consider the nature of a parish and examine what it means to be a parishioner. We also look at the means by which various officers of the parish are appointed and their duties. Every parish must have churchwardens but we also look at the role of sidesmen, sextons or vergers, parish clerks and organists and other musicians. The requirements for the annual parochial church meeting and the business which must be transacted at it are considered together with elections to the PCC. The functions of the PCC and the duties of its members are also examined. Finally we discuss the creation of the church electoral roll and the qualifications for enrolment upon it.

Parishes[1]

Ancient parishes

The localisation of the cure of souls which occurred as more and more churches **4.2** were founded, has already been considered briefly in Chapter 3. This together with the allocation by the monastries of districts to be served by their members,

---

[1] See further MacMorran and Briden, *A Handbook for Churchwardens and Parochial Church Councils* (10th ed., 1996).

and the agreement between nobles and the ecclesiastical authorities regarding the foundation of churches by private individuals, led to the development of the parish system between the seventh and twelfth or thirteenth centuries. The boundaries of these ancient parishes were generally identical to or determined by those of the manors into which England was divided, although for reasons which remain unclear certain areas were left extra-parochial.[2] However, in many cases these extra-parochial places have now been united for ecclesiastical purposes with an adjoining parish. As well as forming ecclesiastical units the ancient parishes have been, and still are, administrative areas for secular purposes such as local government, and again extra-parochial places have in many instances been united to adjoining parishes for these purposes as well.

New parishes

4.3   In the nineteenth century population growth and increasing urbanisation led to the creation of new ecclesiastical parishes. This was effected initially by a local or special Acts of Parliament. Later, after the passing of the Church Building Act 1818 and the New Parishes Act 1843 (together with various amending Acts) the process was generally carried out by an order in Council ratifying schemes of the Church Building Commissioners. This entire body of legislation was largely replaced by the New Parishes Measure 1943, which was itself replaced by the Pastoral Measure 1968. Subsequently the 1968 Measure was repealed and replaced by the Pastoral Measure 1983 which enables new parishes to be created by means of a pastoral scheme, a subject which is considered in Chapter 5.

The general definition of an ecclesiastical "parish" is a district committed to the charge of the minister who has the cure of souls within it,[3] although the term may have particular statutory definitions in certain contexts, such as the CRR.[4] Minister in relation to a parish means either the incumbent, a curate licensed to the charge of a parish or a minister licensed as priest-in-charge where the rights of presentation are suspended, and a vicar in a team ministry to the extent that the duties of a minister are assigned to them.[5]

Conventional districts

4.4   Conventional districts are putative parishes which are usually formed with a veiw to their becoming parishes in due course. They are areas, often within new housing developments, which belong to one or more parishes.[6] With the

---

[2] *Blackstone's Commentary on the Laws of England* (14th ed. 1803), pp. 110–113.

[3] *ibid*.

[4] Parish is there defined as including a district which is constituted a conventional district and a chaplaincy within the diocese of Europe: CRR, r. 54(1).

[5] CRR, r. 54(1). The PCCPM also applies this definition: *ibid*, s.1.

[6] *Legal Opinions*, pp. 70–71. The rights of parishioners in regard to the occasional offices at the parish church remain unaltered. Furthermore, whilst those who reside or attend worship within the district may be enrolled on its church electoral roll it would appear that such persons are also entitled to be enrolled on the church roll of the parish of which the district forms part: *ibid*.

agreement of the relevant incumbent or incumbents the area is placed under the care of a curate in charge.[7] Any such agreement has to be renewed on a change of incumbent. The arrangement also requires the agreement of the bishop who licences the curate. All parishioners remain parishioners of the original parish or parishes to which the area belongs.[8]

For the purposes of the CRR a "parish" includes a conventional district.[9] Consequently the district may have its own churchwardens,[10] and PCC. As an alternative to a PCC for the district the annual parochial church meeting or meetings of the relevant parishes may make a scheme for the election of a district church council for the area.[11]

Parish place of worhsip

Where a parish does not have a parish church the bishop must make provision **4.5** for public worship according to the rites and ceremonies of the Church of England by licensing one or more buildings or parts of buildings for such worship and he may designate any such building or part building so licensed as a parish centre of worship.[12] For the purposes of legal requirements affecting parish churches any building so designated is deemed to be the parish church.[13] However, notwithstanding the fact that the building is deemed to be a parish church persons wishing to be married may elect to proceed as if there were no deemed parish church with the effect that their parish is instead deemed to belong to the adjoining parish and they can thus marry in its parish church.[14]

Churchwardens

The office of churchwarden dates from the thirteenth century. Until recent times **4.6** the ecclesiastical parish and the secular parish for local government were identical and churchwardens had various local government duties in addition to their ecclesiastical duties. The close connection between the ecclesiastical and secular administration was reflected in the fact that in ancient parishes any householder who was not exempt or disqualified was under a legal duty to serve as a churchwarden if appointed. Today, however, a churchwarden must normally be a communicant member of the Church of England or a church in communion with it and must consent to being appointed.

[7] The bishop may also licence a chapel within the district for the marriage of those persons who reside within that area: Marriage Act 1949, s.20.
[8] See n. 6 *ante*.
[9] CRR, r. 54(1). The PCCPM also applies this definition: *ibid.*, s.1.
[10] Churchwardens (Appointment and Resignation) Measure 1964, s.1, since by s.13 of this Measure "parish" has the same meaning as in the Representation of the Laity Rules which the CRR replace.
[11] CRR, r. 18(1)(b). District church councils are discussed below.
[12] Pastoral Measure 1983, s.29.
[13] *ibid.*
[14] Pursuant to the Marriage Act 1949, ss.6, 15.

The provisions relating to the numbers, qualifications, appointment and tenure of office are largely set out in the Churchwardens (Appointment and Resignation) Measure 1964. The 1964 Measure, however, contains saving provisions, the effect of which is that "existing custom" in relation to either the number of churchwardens for a particular parish, or as to the manner in which they are chosen, is preserved.[15] An existing custom is one in existence at the date of the commencement of the Measure in 1964 and which has continued for a period including the last 40 years before that date.[16] Such customs are special in each case and must be proved. It should be noted that the 1964 Measure does not generally apply to churchwardens of Guild Churches in the City of London.[17]

Generally there must be two churchwardens for every parish, whose functions are identical. The exception to there being two are where there is an existing custom to the contrary,[18] or where as the result of a pastoral scheme a parish has more than one parish church in which case there must be two churchwardens for each of the parish churches.[19] In this second case the 1964 Measure applies separately to each pair of churchwardens although all are churchwardens of the parish except in so far as they may arrange to perform separate duties in relation to each of the parish churches.[20]

Churchwardens must be chosen from persons who are resident[21] in the parish or whose names are on the church electoral roll of the parish.[22] They must be actual communicant members of the Church of England,[23] except where the bishop otherwise permits, and be aged 21 years or more.[24] They must also consent to serve,[25] with the consequence that ascertaining those persons who were exempt from service (that is clerks in holy orders and barristers) is now irrelevant. Certain persons were also disqualified from service and the 1964 Measure provides that nothing within it authorises the choice of a person who was disqualified under the existing law.[26] Therefore it

---

[15] Churchwardens (Appointment and Resignation) Measure 1964, s.12. Provided that where such custom requires the churchwarden to be chosen by the vestry and others a meeting of the parishioners is substituted for the vestry: *ibid.*, s.12(2). Nothing in the 1964 Measure amends, repeals or affects any local act or scheme affecting the churchwardens of a parish: *ibid.*, s.12(1).

[16] *ibid.*, s.13.

[17] *ibid.*, s.10. The only provision which is applicable is a requirement that the churchwardens be actual communicant members of the Church of England: *ibid.*, s.10(1).

[18] *R. v. Hinkley (Inhabitants)* (1810) 12 East 361; *R. v. Earl Shilton (Inhabitants)* (1818) 1 B. & A. 275.

[19] Pastoral Measure 1983, s.27(5)(e).

[20] *ibid.*

[21] Residence for these purposes is not defined but would seem to include residence of a regular but not a casual nature, which need not be the person's only residence.

[22] Churchwardens (Appointment and Resignation) Measure 1964, s.1(2).

[23] "Actual communicant" is to have the same meaning as in the Rules for the Representation of the Laity: *ibid.*, s.13. These rules are now repealed and replaced by CRR, r. 54, which gives a wider definition. As to the meaning of this definition see Chap. 2.

[24] Churchwardens (Appointment and Resignation) Measure 1964, s.1(3).

[25] *ibid.*, s.1(4).

[26] *ibid.*, s.12(4).

seems that aliens,[27] persons convicted of certain offences[28] and probably Jews[29] remain disqualified.

Choosing churchwardens

No parish may be legally without churchwardens and their appointment can be **4.7** compelled by mandamus.[30] Churchwardens must be chosen annually, not later than April 30 in each year,[31] in accordance with the 1964 Measure.[32] It is important to note that the term choice is used instead of elected. Existing customs may prescrbe a different method[33] but the primary method of choice in the 1964 Measure is by the joint consent of the minister of the parish and a meeting of the parishioners.[34] Joint consent is deemed to have been given where any motion putting forward a person for the office of churchwarden is declared carried by the person presiding over the meeting of the parishioners and the minister has signified their consent to the choice of that person either before the motion is put or immediately after it is carried.[35] However, a person is only deemed chosen by this method if both churchwardens are chosen in this way.[36] If the minister and parishioners cannot agree on the choice of both churchwardens, or no motions or insufficient motions are moved in accordance with the procedure laid down then, one churchwarden is to be appointed by the minister and the other elected by the meeting, of parishioners.[37] Where there is no minister the parishioners elect both churchwardens at their meeting.[38] A casual vacancy may be filled at any time by a person chosen in the same manner as the churchwarden whom they replace.[39]

---

[27] *Anthony v. Serger* (1789) 1 Hag. Con. 9 at 10.

[28] *ibid.*, in which it was held that persons convicted of a felony were excluded. See also Phillimore, *Ecclesiastical Law of the Church of England* (2nd ed. 1895), p. 1469. It is not clear what offences would bar an individual. Previously under the Parochial Church Councils (Powers) Measure 1921, s.15(2) (repealed) a conviction which would render a clergyman incapable of holding preferment under the Clergy Discipline Act 1892, s.1 (repealed) would disqualify a person from being elected or remaining a churchwarden. Today there is no similar provision. However, it should be noted that with certain exceptions a person is treated, after a period of rehabilitation, for all purposes as if they had not committed the offence for which they were convicted: Rehabilitation of Offenders Act 1974.

[29] *Anthony v. Serger ante; R. v. Bishop of Sarum* [1916] 1 K.B.

[30] *R. v. Wix Inhabitants* (1832) 2 B. & A. 197.

[31] Churchwardens (Appointment and Resignation) Measure 1964, s.2(1).

[32] And in accordance with any other Measure, Act or scheme affecting churchwardens: Canon E1(1).

[33] The fact that it has been the practice for many years for the minister to nominate one churchwarden may not be evidence of existing custom but of assumed disagreement between minister and parishioners: *Legal Opinions*, p. 46.

[34] Churchwardens (Appointment and Resignation) Measure 1964, s.2(2).

[35] Churchwardens (Appointment and Resignation) Measure 1964, s.2(2).

[36] *ibid.*

[37] *ibid.*, s.2(3).

[38] *ibid.*, s.2(4).

[39] *ibid.*, s.2(5), (6).

Meeting of parishioners

4.8   A meeting of the parishioners to choose the churchwardens is a joint meeting of the persons whose names are entered on the electoral roll of the parish and persons resident in the parish whose names are entered on a register of local government electors by reason of that residence.[40] The fact that the church-wardens are chosen by this latter group is the final vestage of the churchwarden's role as representatives of the general body of parishioners. In practice the meeting is usually held on the same occasion, and immediately before, the annual parochial church meeting, but legally the two meetings are separate not least because different persons are entitled to attend each.

   The meeting of parishioners must be convened by the minister or the churchwardens of the parish who must place a notice stating the place, date and time of the meeting at or near the principal door of the parish church and of every other building licensed for public worship in the parish for a period including the last two Sundays before the meeting.[41]

   If present the minister is chairman and if not a person chosen by the meeting presides.[42] The meeting must also appoint a person to act as clerk and record the minutes of the meeting.[43] The meeting has the power to adjourn and to determine its own rules of procedure.[44] Where Churchwardens cannot be chosen by joint consent the minister must not nominate a person or vote in the election of a churchwarden by the meeting, but may exercise a vote in respect of all other matters such as procedural issues.[45]

   Where the meeting elects a churchwarden the election must be conducted, announced and notified in the same manner as elections at annual parochial church meetings,[46] except that all persons entitled to attend the meeting other than the minister are entitled to nominate candidates and vote in the election.[47] Any elector or candidate in such an election has a right of appeal against the allowance or disallowance of a vote or against the result,[48] the procedure being basically the same as an appeal in respect of elections to the deanery or diocesan synod as discussed in chapter 3.

Admission

4.9   As soon as may be after April 30 each year, at a time and place chosen by the Ordinary, each churchwarden must appear before the Ordinary or his substitute to be admitted to office.[49] In years where an episcopal visitation is to take place it

---

[40] *ibid.*, s.3(1).
[41] *ibid.*, s.3(2), (3), (4).
[42] *ibid.*, s.3(5).
[43] *ibid.*, s.3(8).
[44] *ibid.*, s.3(7).
[45] CRR, r. 13(1).
[46] The election is under the procedure set out in CRR, r. 11, and not under the alternative schemes which permit voting by a single transferable vote to pursuant to CRR, r. 12, nor under a scheme which permits postal voting.
[47] CRR, r. 13(1).
[48] *ibid.*, r. 44(1)(a).
[49] Churchwardens (Appointment and Resignation) Measure 1964, s.7(1); Canon E1(2).

is conducted by the bishop or chancellor or a surrogate,[50] and in other years by the archdeacon, generally during their visitation. Appointment takes place after the churchwarden subscribes in the presence of the Ordinary the declaration that they will faithfully and diligently carry out the duties of their office.[51] The usual practice is that the churchwardens make their declaration *en bloc*.[52] Although chosen by the parish a churchwarden does not actually become such until their admission by the Ordinary.[53] It would appear that the act of admission is ministerial not judicial with the consequence that the Ordinary has no discretion to judge the fitness of a candidate[54] although they would presumably be justified in refusing to admit a person not legally qualified.[55] Once admitted a churchwarden remains in office until the appointment of their successors, unless they resign or vacate their office.[56] Where a churchwarden is chosen or elected again the following year reappointment and a renewal of the declaration are required.[57] Strictly speaking sidesmen ought to be admitted with the churchwardens but in practice this rarely happens.[58]

Deputy Churchwardens

In two instances provision may be made for the election of deputy churchwardens. The first is where a pastoral scheme establishes a team ministry and the scheme provides for the election or choice of one or two deputy churchwardens for the church, or any place of worship of any district within the area of the team ministry and for the functions of the churchwardens which may or must be delegated to such a deputy.[59] The second is where, in a parish with two or more churches or buildings licensed for public worship, the annual parochial church meeting makes a scheme providing for the election of a district church council for the district in which one of these is situated and that scheme provides for the election or choice of one or two deputy churchwardens for that church or building and the delegation to them of such functions of the churchwardens relating to it as the scheme provides, or as the churchwardens themselves delegate.[60]

Resignation

With the written consent of the minister and any other churchwarden of the parish, a churchwarden may resign their office by written instrument addressed to the bishop.[61] If this is accepted by the bishop the resignation takes effect

4.10

---

[50] *R. v. Sowter* [1901] 1 K.B. 396, C.A.

[51] Churchwardens (Appointment and Resignation) Measure 1964, s.7(1); Canon E1(2).

[52] The practice appears to have been unaffected by the 1964 Measure.

[53] Churchwardens (Appointment and Resignation) Measure 1964, s.9(1); Canon E1(2).

[54] *R. v. Rice* (1697) 5 Mod. Rep. 325; *R. v. Bishop of Sarum* [1916] 1 K.B. 466.

[55] The remedy for refusal to admit would appear to be an application for an order of mandamus: *R. v. Bishop of Sarum ante.*

[56] Churchwardens (Appointment and Resignation) Measure 1964, s.7(2); Canon E1(3).

[57] *Legal Opinions*, pp. 46–47.

[58] *ibid.*

[59] Pastoral Measure 1983, Sched. 3, para. 4(2).

[60] CRR, r. 18(4). The provision in regard to the making of such a scheme and its coming into operation are identical to those described below in relation to district councils.

[61] Churchwardens (Appointment and Resignation) Measure 1964, s.8(1).

forthwith.[62] A churchwarden is not otherwise entitled to resign.[63] The office is vacated if the churchwarden is not resident in the parish or their name is not on the electoral roll.[64] Curiously the 1964 Measure contains no provisions concerning vacation of office on death, incapacity or misconduct. Vacation by reason of death could be dealt with under the provisions in respect of casual vacancies. The bishop has the power to make provision for any matter not provided for in the 1964 Measure[65] but it is uncertain whether this power would extend to the declaration of a vacancy by reason of mental or physical incapacity or to the appointment of an additional churchwarden. From older authorities it is apparent that in the case of misconduct a churchwarden could be removed from office by the ecclesiastical courts, but this remedy is no longer available since proceedings against lay officers under the Ecclesiastical Jurisdiction Measure 1963 (EJM) have been abolished.[66] It is doubtful if a churchwarden could be removed by extra-judicial proceedings at a visitation or by an extraordinary meeting of parishioners, although there is authority for this remedy prior to the 1964 Measure.[67] The Incumbents (Vacation of Benefices) Measure 1977 empowers the bishop to disqualify a person from being a churchwarden for up to five years following an enquiry into a case of pastoral breakdown,[68] but the procedure is lengthy and cumbersome and not aimed specifically at the misconduct of a churchwarden.

In addition to his powers to make provision for any matter not provided for by the 1964 Measure, the diocesan bishop also has the power to appoint a person to do any act in respect of which there has been neglect or default on the part of any person or body charged with any duty under the Measure.[69] The bishop has the further power, in order to give effect to the intentions of the 1964 Measure, to extend or alter any time for holding a meeting or election, or to modify the procedure relating to it.[70] He also has the power, in cases where no valid choice of churchwardens has been made, to direct a fresh choice and in any case where difficulty arises, to give any directions which he considers expedient for the purpose of removing the difficulty.[71] However, none of these powers enables the bishop to validate anything which at the time that it was done was invalid.[72]

---

[62] *ibid.*

[63] Churchwardens (Appointment and Resignation) Measure 1964, s.8(2).

[64] *ibid.*, s.9.

[65] *ibid.*, s.11(1).

[66] EJM, s.82(2)(c). Even if some residual jurisdiction does lie (as to which see Chap. 11) it is not clear how proceedings would be brought.

[67] Ayliffe, *Parergon Juris Canonici Anglicani* (2nd ed. 1734), p. 171; Phillimore *Ecclesiastical Law of the Church of England* (2nd ed. 1895), p. 1479. These eminent writers state that if the churchwardens waste the church goods they are to be removed from office and new churchwardens chosen so that they can pursue an action in common law against their predecessors, the parishioners having no right to bring such an action for account.

[68] See Chap. 5.

[69] Churchwardens (Appointment and Resignation) Measure 1964, s.11(1).

[70] Churchwardens (Appointment and Resignation) Measure 1964, s.11(1).

[71] *ibid.*

[72] *ibid.*, s.11(2).

Proposed Churchwardens Measure

It is currently proposed to replace the Churchwardens (Appointment and **4.11** Resignation) Measure 1964 with a new Churchwardens Measure.[73] The draft of this new Measure provides that, as at present, there will be two churchwardens for each parish, or where a parish has more than one parish church two churchwardens for each church who will be churchwardens of the entire parish. However, where in any parish there is an existing custom regulating the number of churchwardens or the manner in which they are chosen that custom would be preserved, unless the meeting of parishioners resolved (subject to the consent of any person affected) to abolish it.

Provisions which currently enable the election of deputy churchwardens appear to be unaffected by the draft Measure.

As is currently the case a person will be required to have their name on the church electoral roll, be an actual communicant and at least 21 years of age. However, residence in the parish without enrolment on the church electoral roll will no longer be sufficient, although the diocesan bishop will have the right to waive other requirements in exceptional circumstances. In addition a person will be disqualified from being chosen under the new Measure if they are disqualified from being a charity trustee (under section 72(1) of the Charities Act 1993), or convicted of any offence mentioned in Schedule 1 to the Children and Young Persons Act 1993, or (as now) if disqualified under the Incumbents (Vacation of Benefices) Measure 1977. A person may also be disqualified for two years if they have served as churchwarden for six successive years unless the meeting of parishioners decide that this restriction is not to apply. However, any other rule of law which currently prevents certain persons from being a churchwarden is to cease to have effect.

As is now the case a person will be required to signify their consent to serve as a churchwarden, but will be restricted to doing so in respect of only one parish unless the parishes are related (because they belong to the same benefice, have the same minister or are held in plurality). The Measure provides for election of churchwardens by a meeting of parishioners and for the filling of casual vacancies, and sets out provisions to enable calculation of the exact term of office prior to the admission of new or the same churchwardens the following year. Where they were of the view that the election of a particular nominated person might give rise to serious difficulties between themselves and that person in carrying out their respective functions, the new Measure would give the minister of the parish power to make a statement that only one churchwarden is to be elected by the meeting, with the consequence that the other is chosen by the minister.

The procedure for admission to the office of churchwarden would remain the **4.12** same, but in order to resign the consent of the minister and any other churchwarden would no longer be required. In addition to the office being vacated if the churchwarden's name was removed from the church electoral roll or was not placed upon a new roll, it would also be vacated if the holder became disqualified from being chosen by reason of the disqualifications or convictions described above. Furthermore the new Measure would enable the bishop to

---

[73] The Measure is likely to come into force in 1997 or early 1998.

suspend a churchwarden for any cause which appeared to them good or reasonable, and would thus enable them to suspend for reasons of incapacity or misconduct, although suspension would not create a casual vacancy. The Measure makes no provision for an appeal against such a suspension.

Legal status of churchwardens

4.13 For the purpose of holding the church's goods (and in the City of London also land for ecclesiastical or parochial purposes) in perpetual succession churchwardens are a quasi-corporation.[74] However, they do not have any other legal incidents of a corporation and must be sued in their individual names and not by a corporate or official title.[75] Churchwardens may bring an action in their own names in respect of a matter which occurred during their predecessors' term of office.[76] However, an action in respect of the discharge or failure to discharge their own duties as churchwardens cannot be brought against them by their successors,[77] although in an appropriate case the court may order the intervention of the succeeding churchwardens to pursue an action on behalf of the PCC against a third party.[78] The general rule is that both churchwardens must concur in bringing an action[79] and in doing any other official act,[80] but there are exceptions to this. For example one churchwarden may apply for a faculty for alterations to a church.[81]

Functions of the churchwardens

4.14 The majority of the functions previously entrusted to the churchwardens were transferred to the PCC whose role is considered later in this chapter. A person chosen, appointed or elected as a churchwarden who is an actual communicant is made a member of the PCC until admitted to the office.[82] Once admitted as a churchwarden they become an *ex officio* member of the PCC.[83] Churchwardens

---

[74] *Blackstone's Commentaries on the Laws of England* (14th ed. 1803), p. 394; Gibson, *Codex Juris Ecclesiastici Anglicani*, (2nd ed. 1761) p. 215; *Withnell v. Gartham* (1795) 6 Term Rep. 388 at 396; *Fell v. Charity Lands Official Trustee* [1898] 2 Ch. 44 at 51, 59, C.A.

[75] *Fell v. Charity Lands Official Trustee (ante).*

[76] *Hadman v. Ringwood* (1589) Cro. Eliz. 145 at 179; *Com. Dig. Esglise* (F3); *Perkins v. Enraght* (1881) 7 P.D. 31 affd *sub nom. Harris v. Perkins* (1882) 7 P.D. 161, P.C. But the courts have in the past declined to substitute succeeding churchwardens to continue a predecessor's action. *ibid.*

[77] *Withnell v. Gartham ante; Att.-Gen. v. Salkend* (1853) 16 Bea. 554.

[78] *Halsbury's Laws of England* (4th ed.) Vol. 14, para. 550, n. 4.

[79] *Fry and Greata v. Treasure* (1865) 2 Moo. PCCNS. 539; *Fowke v. Berington* [1914] 2 Ch. 308, in which it was held that a churchwarden cannot sue alone.

[80] *Starkey v. Berton* (1610) Cro. Jac. 234; *Ritchings v. Cordingley* (1868) L.R. 3 A. & E. 113. There is some authority to suggest that different considerations apply where parishes are divided up into townships: *Astle v. Thomas* (1823) 2 B. & C. 271, where there were four churchwardens.

[81] *Bradford v. Fry* (1878) 4 P.D. 93 at 99, 100.

[82] CRR, r. 14(2).

[83] *ibid.*, r. 14(1)(d).

still, retain a number of functions being both officers of the Ordinary and guardians of the parish church.

Once admitted to their office churchwardens become officers of the Ordinary.[84] In former times when visitations took the form of court proceedings they had the duty to present all those guilty of an ecclesiastical offence to the Ordinary. Today their role in visitations is limited to the answering of presentments, which was considered in Chapter 3. In addition churchwardens must answer any enquiry the Ordinary may make at any time concerning parochial matters, and they may also inform the Ordinary of any matter requiring their intervention. The churchwardens are also under a duty to ensure that when any alterations, additions, removals or repairs are proposed to the fabric, ornaments or furniture of the church a faculty is obtained,[85] a matter considered further in Chapter 11.

As guardians of the parish church the churchwardens' responsibility extends to every consecrated church and chapel within the parish which does not have separate churchwardens and to the churchyard and curtilage.[86] Although the incumbent is the lawful custodian of the keys to the church the churchwardens have a right of free access in order to perform their duties.[87] The churchwardens are the legal owners of the moveables in the church such as the plate and ornaments, a matter considered further in Chapter 8, and may also act as trustees of parochial property. When a benefice becomes vacant and a sequestration occurs they frequently act as the sequestrators along with the rural dean.[88] During a vacancy in the benefice the register books are in their custody.[89]

Maintenance of order

The churchwardens have responsibility for the maintenance of order and decency **4.15** in the church and churchyard, especially during the time of divine service,[90] assisted by the sidesmen.[91] Their role is paramount to that of a constable and they are protected from charges of assault in the discharge of their duties if only reasonable force is used.[92] Neither they nor their assistants must permit any church or chapel to be profaned by any meeting in it for temporal objects inconsistent with the sanctity of the place,[93] It is their duty to ensure that the bells are only rung in accordance with the minister's direction.[94]

---

[84] Canon E1(4).
[85] Canon E1(4).
[86] Canon F13(3).
[87] *Moysey v. Hillcoat* (1828) 2 Hag. Ecc. 30 at 56, 57.
[88] See Chap. 5.
[89] *R. v. Cumley, ex p. Holloway* (1855) 3 W.R. 247; *Legal Opinions*, p. 48. See also Chap. 8.
[90] Canon E1(4); Ayliffe, *Parergon Juris Canonici Anglicani* (2nd ed. 1734), p. 171; *Haw v. Planner* (1666) 2 Keb. 124; *Cox v. Goodday* (1811) 2 Hag. Con. 138 at 141; *Palmer v. Tijou* (1824) 2 Add. 196 at 200, 201; *Burton v. Henson* (1842) 10 M. & W. 105 at 108. Barber, "Outrageous Behaviour" 4 Ecc. L.J. 584.
[91] Canon E2(3); *Palmer v. Tijou (ante)*.
[92] See n. 90 *ante*.
[93] Canon F15(1). See Chap. 8 as to uses of a church for public performances and exhibitions and the restrictions on the secular use of consecrated property.
[94] Canon F8 (2); *Harrison v. Forbes & Sisson* (1860) 6 Jur. N.S. 1353; *Redhead v. Wait* (1862) 6 L.T. 580. See also Chap. 9 regarding the possibility of an action for nuisance or under the Environment Protection Act 1990 as the result of ringing church bells.

The churchwardens must not allow any person to behave in the church, church porch or churchyard in such a way as to create a disturbance during the time of divine service.[95] They must also take care that nothing is done in the church which is contrary to the laws of both the Church and the Realm.[96] To prevent a disturbance they are entitled to remove any person from the church who disturbs the service[97] or who, before it has begun, indicates that they intend to create a disturbance,[98] and are not bound to enquire into the circumstances of the breach.

If any person is guilty of riotous, violent or indecent behaviour, whether or not it takes places at the time of divine service, or of disturbing, vexing, troubling or misusing any minister officiating there, the churchwardens must restrain the offender and if necessary take legal action against them.[99] However, churchwardens cannot interfere with the conduct of the service by the minister on the ground that there is any impropriety in its performance unless the minister's behaviour is actually riotous, violent or indecent, or their intervention is required to preserve the decorum of public worship.[1] During the service the churchwarden's role is to collect alms although they may turn out an unauthorised preacher.[2] The proper course if they are dissatisfied with the minister's conduct during the service is for them to complain to the Ordinary.[3]

It should be noted that "indecent" in this context has no sexual connotations. The purpose is to protect the sacredness of the place and this can be violated by interruptions.[4] In such cases the churchwardens have a statutory power is arrest the offender.[5] It would appear that the churchwardens do not have the authority to turn out a person from the church who commits a trespass when there is no divine service.[6] Therefore unless the trespasser is causing harm to church property it is suggested that the incumbent is consulted.

Allocation of seating

4.16 Seats must be provided in every church and chapel for the use of parishioners and others who attend divine service,[7] and it is for the churchwardens (acting on behalf and subject to any directions given by the Ordinary[8]) to allocate

[95] Canon F15, para. 2.
[96] Canon F15, para. 2.
[97] *Glever v. Hynde* (1673) 1 Mod. Rep. 168; *Reynolds v. Monckton* (1841) 2 Mood & R. 384. Indeed anyone has a common law right to remove anyone who is disturbing divine service: *Gleaver v. Hynde (ante)*; *Burton v. Henson (ante)*, although the primary duty is that of the churchwardens: *Cox v. Goodday (ante)*.
[98] *Hartley v. Cook* (1833) 9 Bing. 718 at 735; *Burton v. Henson ante.*
[99] Canon F15(3).
[1] *Hutchins v. Denziloe and Loveland* (1792) 1 Hag. Con. 170 at 173, 174.
[2] *Hutchins v. Denziloe and Loveland* (1792) 1 Hag. Con. 170 at 173, 174.
[3] *ibid.*
[4] *Palmer v. Roffrey* (1842) 2 Add. 141; *Worth v. Terrington* (1845) 13 M. & W. 781. See also *Abrahams v. Cavey* [1968] 1 Q.B. 479.
[5] Ecclesiastical Courts Jurisdiction Act 1860, s.3.
[6] *Worth v. Terrington (ante)*; *Taylor v. Timson* (1888) 20 Q.B.D. 671. See also Bursell, *Liturgy, Order and the Law*, (1996), p. 255.
[7] Canon F7(1).
[8] *Corvern's Case* (1612) 12 Co. Rep. 105; *Vicar, etc., of Claverley v. Parishioners, etc., of Claverley* [1909] P. 195 at 212.

seats.[9] The seats are to be allocated in such a manner as to allow for the service of God to be duly celebrated.[10] The allocation does not affect the right of any person to a seat or pew or to allocate seats conferred by faculty or prescription or statutory authority, nor the rights of ownership in a private chapel or aisle.[11] Nor does it affect any right of the minister to allocate seats in the chancel.[12] It should be noted that apart from statutory pew rents[13] the churchwardens have no right to demand rent or any other payment for a seat or pew.[14]

Parishioners have a right to seats in the main body of the church and the allocation of seats must not interfere with this,[15] but the churchwarden can give priority to those who pay a voluntary church rate or similar sum.[16] Although not clear it would appear that persons who have their name on the electoral roll of the church may be regarded as having the rights of parishioners for this purpose. Although as we shall see the right to attend divine service depends upon there being sufficient accommodation, the churchwardens cannot prevent a parishioner from standing if there are not enough seats.[17]

In allocating seats the churchwardens can direct individuals as to where they should sit and can allocate seats before or at the time of a particular service. A seat may also be allotted to an individual indefinitely and gives them a general right, against everyone except the churchwardens and the Ordinary,[18] to occupy it at all ordinary services if they claim it before the service begins.[19] However, the churchwardens cannot make an irrevocable assignment or divest themselves or their successors of the power to make a new allocation when this is desirable.[20] If it is necessary to dispossess the person to whom the seat is usually allocated they should be given notice.[21] The churchwardens may remove a parishioner and anyone else who sits in a seat assigned to another provided this is done without using unnecessary force and without causing public scandal or disturbing divine service[22] but the consistory court no longer has any jurisdiction in suits for the perturbation of seats.[23]

---

[9] Canon F7(2); *Coke's Institutes*, (1680) Vol. 3, p. 202; *Pettman v. Bridger* (1811) 1 Phil. Ecc. R. 312 at 323.

[10] Canon F7(2).

[11] *ibid.* As to which, see Chap. 8.

[12] The general existence of such a right is doubtful. There is a conflict of opinion in the authorities although most commentators assume these seats are at the disposal of the Ordinary. It is unlikely that the saving provision in Canon F7(2), would be sufficient to create such a right when none existed already.

[13] As to which, see Chap. 8.

[14] *Walter v. Gunner and Drury* (1798) 1 Hag. Con. 314.

[15] Canon F7(3).

[16] *Vicar of St Saviour, Westgate-on-Sea v. Parishioners of Same* [1898] P. 217 at 221.

[17] *Taylor v. Timson* (1888) 20 Q.B.D. 671.

[18] *Pettman v. Bridger* (above) at 324; *Re St Mary's, Banbury* [1987] Fam. 136.

[19] *Vicar, etc., of Claverley v. Parishioners, etc., of Claverley (ante).*

[20] *Corvern's Case (ante); Pettman v. Bridger (ante)* at 323, 324; *Asher v. Calcraft* (1887) 18 Q.B.D. 607.

[21] *Horsfall v. Holland and Woolley* (1859) 6 Jur. N.S. 278.

[22] *Reynolds v. Monckton* (1841) 2 Mood. & R. 384.

[23] EJM, s.82(2)(c).

Other responsibilities

4.17 Responsibility for providing sufficient bread and wine for Holy Communion rests with the churchwardens, who must act on the advice and direction of the minister.[24] The expenses of this are in practice (and probably in law) payable by the PCC.[25] The responsibility for providing all the other requisites for divine service such as books, linen and plate is now transferred from the churchwardens to the PCC. However, in practice it is often still left to the churchwardens, acting on behalf of the council. The churchwardens also take part in the collection of alms and other offerings given at the offertory in the communion service.[26]

In addition to discharging those duties assigned to them by law and custom churchwardens are enjoined to be foremost in representing the laity and in co-operating with the incumbent. They are also to use their best endeavours by example and precept, to encourage the parishioners in the practice of true religion and to promote unity and peace among them.[27]

Other parochial officers

Sidesmen

4.18 Sidesmen may be appointed by the annual parochial church meeting, although there is no obligation to do so.[28] If need arises sidesmen may also be appointed by the PCC between annual parochial church meetings.[29] All persons whose names are on the church electoral roll of the parish are eligible to serve as sidesmen.[30] Sidesmen are under a duty to promote the true cause of religion and to assist the churchwardens in the discharge of their duties in maintaining order and decency in the church and churchyards especially during times of divine service.[31]

Sextons, vergers and sacristans

4.19 The duties of a sexton (now often called a verger) vary from parish to parish.[32-33] They may include the care of the church, its furnishings, sacred vestments, ringing the bells, the care of the churchyard and digging graves. The term

---

[24] Canon B17(1).

[25] Canon F14.

[26] See Chap. 10.

[27] Canon E1(4).

[28] CRR, r. 9(4)(c); Canon E2(1).

[29] *ibid*.

[30] CRR, r. 10(2); Canon E2(2). Curiously there is no longer any provision to the effect that any person must signify their consent to act as sidesman or that there must be, in the opinion of the meeting, sufficient evidence of their willingness, as was required when sidesmen were elected. However, "appointment" must connote a willingness to be appointed.

[31] Canon E2(3).

[32-33] *Cansfield v. Blenkinsop* (1849) 4 Exch. 234.

"sacristan" which was once used synonymously with sexton now appears to be confined to a person who has no grave-digging duties. A sacristan's duties are in general concerned with the care of the sacred vessels and vestments and are often carried out by a voluntary worker. Occasionally, the term "beadle" is still used but it has lost its original meaning of a person who was the messenger and servant of the vestry and who carried out its orders.

A sexton (or any person who performs the duties of that office or assists in performing them) may be appointed and dismissed by the PCC acting jointly with the minister. It is they acting jointly who determine the salary and the conditions of tenure of the office or employment,[34] and also it would appear to be their responsibility to determine the functions to be performed. If the minister and PCC cannot agree the bishop may give such directions as appear necessary.[35] The office may be held by a woman.[36]

Parish clerks

The PCC and minister acting jointly have the same rights to appoint, dismiss and determine the conditions of tenure and the salary of a parish clerk.[37] The traditional role of a parish clerk was to lead the laity in its part in divine service, but today the clerk has a broader role. The office may be held by a man or woman including a clerk in holy orders. If such a clerk is appointed they must be licensed by the bishop in the same manner as a stipendary curate and are then entitled to perform all spiritual and ecclesiastical duties within the parish as the incumbent (with the bishop's sanction) from time to time requires.[38] They may be suspended or removed from office in the same manner and for the same causes and are subject to the same rights of appeal as any stipendary curate.[39]

Employees of the PCC

Where the minister and PCC are jointly responsible for the salary of a sexton, **4.20** parish clerk or any other employee, they are also responsible for compliance with provisions relating to the deduction of income tax at source (PAYE) and National Insurance Contributions.[40] All employers are requried to insure against liability for injury or illness of their employees.[41] They are also subject to the general law regarding redundancy payments, unfair dismissal, and health and safety regulations.

It is advisable to draw up contracts of employment for all employees. These should provide that the contract may be terminated by either party upon a

---

[34] PPCPM, s.7(iii); Canon E3.

[35] PPCPM, s.9(3).

[36] *Olive v. Ingram* (1739) 7 Mod. Rep. 263.

[37] *cf.* nn. 34, 35, above.

[38] Parish Clerks 1844, s.2. *ibid.*, s.3, which governs the appointment of such clerks is rendered obsolete by the PCCPM.

[39] Parish Clerks Act 1844. s.4.

[40] Further information and details can be obtained from the local offices of the Inland Revenue and Department of Social Security.

[41] See Chap. 8 where insurance in regard to various matters is considered.

specified period of notice, and set out the duties to be performed by the employee and the remuneration which is to be paid.[42]

Organists, choirmasters and other musicians

4.21 With the agreement of the PCC the minister may appoint an organist, a choirmaster (by whatever name called), or director of music.[43] Unlike other joint appointments in the case of termination of the employment the consent of the PCC may be dispensed with by the archdeacon.[44] The minister might ask for such a dispensation where it was felt that they could not obtain a fair hearing with the PCC, which might arise where many of the PCC were also members of the choir and supported the organist.[45]

An agreement should be drawn up setting out the terms upon which the organist is engaged, their duties, holidays and arrangements for a deputy.[46] These duties will include using their best endeavours to secure a devout and appropriate rendering of the musical portions of the church services, recognising the authority of the incumbent relating to the conduct of services, playing the organ at all the chief services on Sundays and great festivals and such lesser festivals and other weekdays as the agreement requires and to assist the choirmaster if this is a distinct role.[47]

Generally the organist will have a right to play at weddings, funerals and other services and to receive the customary fee, but if they do not wish to do so the incumbent may arrange for another organist. If those for whom the service is held wish a friend or relative to play then the organist would nonetheless be entitled to the customary fee.[48]

If a separate choirmaster is appointed their duties would include training the choir, arranging suitable practices at least once a week and the advancement of the interests of the choir as a whole.[49] It should be noted that a child chorister taking part in a religious service or a choir practice for such a service, whether or not they receive a reward, is not deemed to be employed for the purposes of the Children and Young Persons Acts 1933 to 1963 or any byelaws made under them.[50]

In Chapter 9 the rights of the minister to determine the music for the service are considered. The organist must not play against the minister's wishes but if forbidden to play arbitrarily may appeal to the Ordinary whilst continuing to obey the minister until the Ordinary prescribes the correct course.[51] In a dispute

[42] Model contracts are available from the Central Board of Finance.
[43] Canon B20(1). This applies to all churches and chapels excluding cathedral or collegiate churches or chapels where the matter is governed by statutes or customs: *ibid.*
[44] The function of the archdeacon is exercisable by the diocesan bishop where the archdeacon is also the minister: Canon B20(1).
[45] *Legal Opinions*, pp. 188–191.
[46] A model agreement is available from the Royal School of Church Music, which also gives advice on appropriate salary levels.
[47] See n. 45 *ante.*
[48] *ibid.*
[49] See n. 45 *ante.*
[50] Children and Young Persons Act 1933, s.30(1).
[51] *Wyndham v. Cole* (1875) 1 P.D. 130.

between themselves and the minister an organist must not use the organ so as to make the minister inaudible, and an organist who does so is in breach of the law.[52]

Parishioners

In Chapter 2 the question as to who were the members of the Church of England **4.22** was considered. A similar difficulty applies to identifying who are parishioners because the answer depends, in part at least, upon the context of the question. In older authorities parishioners tended to be identified as those householders of the parish together with persons, who although not actually resident, occupied land and tenements in the parish and paid rents upon them.[53] Parishioners in this sense took part in the busines of the vestry, including choosing the church-wardens, could be allotted seats in the church and shared the liability for repairs to the church.

The former obligation of parishioners to attend the parish church on all Sundays and other Holy days unless they had a reasonable excuse for absence or were a dissenter have been repealed. In regard to the right to attend church for divine service, to have children baptised there, or (provided all other lawful criteria are fulfilled) to be married there, residence alone in the parish is sufficient and all those who die in the parish are entitled to burial within the churchyard if space remains. As discussed in Chapters 10 and 11 these rights of parishioners in regard to the offices of the church are not dependent upon the person being a member of the Church of England.

The right of parishioners to attend church for divine service is a common law right which is subject to there being accommodation available for them to so do.[54] The right only extends to parishioners but if a person is prevented from attending their own parish church for example because they are on holiday they may present themselves for admission to some other church.[55] A parishioner's right to a seat was considered earlier in this chapter. A parishioner is entitled to receive the ministration of the church and of the parish clergy in the parish church and other proper places.[56] This is so whatever their religion (or if they profess none whatsover) as far as appropriate. Thus, for example, a person could be visited if sick but could not if unbaptised receive the Communion of the Sick even if in immediate danger of death.

Annual parochial church meeting

An annual parochial church meeting (annual meeting) must be held in each **4.23** parish not later than April 30 in each year.[57] All lay persons whose names are

[52] *Matthews v. King* [1934] 1 K.B. 505 at 507.
[53] See, *Att.-Gen. v. Parker* (1747) 3 Atk. 576.
[54] *Cole v. Police Constable 443A* [1937] 1 K.B. 316.
[55] *ibid.*
[56] *William's Case* (1592) 5 Co. Rep. 72b; *Henley v. Burstow* (1666) 1 Keb. 947; *Banister v. Thompson* [1908] P. 362; *R. v. Diddin* [1910] P. 57, C.A.; affd *sub nom. Thompson v. Dibdin* [1912] A.C. 533, H.L.
[57] CRR, r. 6(1). Where there is no meeting within the year the rural dean once the omission is brought to their notice must ascertain the cause, and report this to the bishop: *ibid.*, r. 53(5).

entered on the electoral roll of the parish are entitled to attend and take part in its proceedings.[58] A clerk in holy orders is entitled to attend and take part if beneficed or licensed to the parish or any other parish in the area of the benefice to which the parish belongs.[59]

All members of a team ministry are entitled to attend and take part in the meetings of the parish or parishes in the area of the benefice for which the team ministry is established.[60] If the parish is in an area of a group ministry all incumbents and priests in charge in the group ministry are entitled to attend and take part, and where the area of a group ministry includes the area of a benefice for which a team ministry has been established all vicars in the team ministry are entitled to attend and take part in the meetings of each of the other parishes in the area for which the group ministry is established.[61] A clerk in holy orders not beneficed or licensed to any other parish is also entitled to attend if resident in the parish,[62] or if the PCC has with the concurrence of the minister declared that clerk to be an habitual worshipper, or if they are a co-opted member of the PCC.[63]

The meeting must be convened by the minister of the parish by dint of a notice in the prescribed form affixed at or near the principal door of every church and every building licensed for public worship in the parish for a period including the last two Sundays before the day of the meeting.[64] It should be noted that if there is no minister or the minister is incapacitated the vice-chairman of the PCC (or if they are unwilling or unable to act the secretary or some other person appointed by the council, has the power to act) to convene the meeting.[65]

The directions governing the meeting and the day and time on which it is to be held are determined by the decision taken at the previous annual meeting, or by the PCC which has the power to vary directions of the annual meeting, or in the absence of such direction when the minister determines.[66] If present the minister is chairman of the meeting: otherwise it is chaired by the vice-chairman of the PCC if present, or failing that by a person chosen by the meeting.[67] The secretary of the PCC or some other person chosen by the meeting must act as clerk and record the minutes of the meeting.[68] The meeting has the power to adjourn and to determine its own rules of procedure.[69]

[58] *ibid.*, r. 6(2). Lay persons being all those who are not clerks in holy orders: *ibid.*, r. 54(2).
[59] *ibid.*, r. 6(3)(a).
[60] *ibid.*, r. 6(4), (5).
[61] *ibid.*, r. 6(4), (5).
[62] Residence must be more than casual: *ibid.*, r. 54(6). Such clerks cannot vote in the election of any parochial representative of the laity: *ibid.*, r. 11(5).
[63] *ibid.*, r. 6(3)(b), (c), (d).
[64] *ibid.*, r. 7(1). The prescribed form is set out in *ibid.*, App. 1, s.4.
[65] *ibid.*, r. 7(3).
[66] *ibid.*, r. 7(2).
[67] *ibid.*, r. 8(1). In the case of a team ministry the right to chair the meeting may be set out in the pastoral scheme and is also subject to *ibid.*, s.8(2) which enables the team rector to preside if neither the team vicar or vice-chairman of the PCC are present.
[68] *ibid.*, r. 9(8).
[69] *ibid.*, r. 9(7).

Business of the meeting

The PCC lays before the annual parochial meeting the following items which the **4.24** annual meeting is then free to discuss and to make recommendations to the PCC upon: a report on change in the church electoral roll since the last annual meeting, or in a year in which a new roll is prepared a report on the numbers entered on the new roll; an annual report on the PCC's proceedings (and from May 1, 1997 on the activities of the parish generally); an annual report on the financial affairs of the parish; the PCC's audited accounts for the year ending on the previous December 31; an audited statement of the funds and property, if any, remaining in the PCC's hands at the previous December 31; a report upon the fabric, goods and ornaments of the church or churches of the parish[70]; a report on the proceedings of the deanery synod.[71]

A copy of the electoral roll is to be available for inspection at the annual meeting whilst the audited accounts and statement must be affixed at or near the principal door of every church and every building licensed for public worship in the parish at least seven days before the annual meeting.[72] The accounts must be submitted to the annual meeting for approval (which can be withheld), and if approved must be signed by the chairman and then delivered to the PCC for publication (by affixing them in the same way as the unapproved versions before the meeting and at such other conspicuous places as the council thinks appropriate for at least 14 days).[73] A copy must also be sent to the secretary of the DBF.

From May 1, 1997 the requirement will be for the financial statements of the PCC for the year ending December 31 immediately proceeding the meeting, to have been independently examined or audited prior to their reception by the meeting.[74] The statements are to be considered by the PCC and if it thinks them fit, approved by it and signed by the chairman presiding at that meeting. They are then to be displayed for a continuous period of at least seven days before the annual meeting, including at least one Sunday when the church is used for worship, on a notice board either inside or outside the church.[75] The annual report on the proceedings of the PCC and activities of parish together with the financial statements are then considered by the annual meeting, and following this the PCC must publish and display them as well as sending copies to the secretary of the DBF.[76].

The annual meeting must in every third year elect parochial representatives of the laity to the deanery synod, and every year elect parochial representatives of the laity to the PCC.[77] They must also appoint the sidesmen (if any), together

---

[70] Under the CCEJM, s.5, as to which see Chap. 8.
[71] CRR, r. 9(1).
[72] *ibid.*, r. 9(2).
[73] *ibid.*, r. 9(3).
[74] CRR, r. 9(3)(a). In accordance with CRR, r. 54(8), which enables the General Synod to make regulations relating to the examination or audit.
[75] CRR, r. 9(3)(b), (c).
[76] CRR, r. 9(4). Publication and display is to be in the form prescribed by the General Synod pursuant to CRR, r. 54(8). In the absence of any regulations display should at the very least be in the same terms as display prior to the meeting.
[77] *ibid.*, r. 9(4).

with an independent examiner or auditor to the PCC for a term of office ending at the close of the next annual meeting. This examiner or auditor may not be a member of the PCC.[78] The elections and appointments are to take place in the order set out above.[79]

Any person entitled to attend the annual meeting may ask any question about parochial church matters or bring about a discussion of any matter of parochial or general church interest, by moving a resolution or by giving any particular recommendation to the council in relation to its duties.[80]

In exercising its functions the PCC must take into consideration any expression of opinion by any parochial church meeting.[81] However, an annual parochial church meeting cannot bind a future parochial church meeting and cannot refuse to allow a matter to be raised on the ground that insufficient or no notice has been given. If, however, after preliminary consideration the matter cannot be satisfactorily disposed of the meeting would be justified in adjourning or closing the meeting with a view to having recourse to a special or extraordinary meeting or to close the meeting and place the matter on the agenda for the next annual meeting, possibly with the recommendation that it be considered by the PCC in the meantime.[82]

Special arrangements exist for the first meeting of the parochial church council of a new parish created under a pastoral scheme.[83]

Special and extraordinary meetings

4.25   In addition to the annual meeting the minister may convene a special parochial church meeting and must do so on the written representation of not less than one-third of the lay members of the PCC.[84] The archdeacon may convene an extraordinary parochial church meeting on the same written representation by the PCC or on the written representation of one-tenth of those whose names are on the church electoral roll, in either case where the archdeacon considers these to have been made with sufficient cause.[85] Where they convene such a meeting the archdeacon must chair the meeting themselves or appoint a chairman, but otherwise the rules applying to special meetings are applicable.[86] Essentially the same persons are entitled to attend special and extraordinary meetings as would be entitled to attend were it an annual meeting being held on that date.[87] The only exception is that lay persons are required to have had their name on the electoral roll for 21 days before the date of the meeting.[88]

---

[78] n. 78, *ibid.*, r. 9(4). The rules do not require the auditor or examiner to be professionally qualified: whether they should be or not will be a matter for the parish depending upon the complexity of the accounts and the amount of funds as well as the suitablility of any volunteer.

[79] *ibid.*

[80] *ibid.*, r. 9(6).

[81] PPCPM, s.2(3).

[82] *Legal Opinions*, p. 7.

[83] CRR, rr. 7(5), (6), 9(5).

[84] CRR, r. 22.

[85] *ibid.*, r. 23. Where the archdeaon is also the minister of the parish any representation is made to the bishop who acts in the archdeaon's stead: *ibid.*, r. 22(2).

[86] *ibid.*

[87] CRR, r. 22.

[88] CRR, r. 22.

Elections

To be elected to the PCC or the deanery synod a person's name must be entered **4.26** on the electoral roll of the parish and they must be an actual communicant.[89] For membership of the PCC they must be at least 16 years of age and for the deanery synod 18.[90] A person cannot be nominated unless they have signified their consent to serve, or there is in the opinion of the meeting sufficient evidence of their willingness to do so.[91] They must also not have been disqualified by the bishop from serving under the Incumbents (Vacation of Benefices) Measure 1977,[92] nor be disqualified from being a charity trustee under the Charities Act 1993.[93]

Occasionally a parish officer, such as the parish clerk, may seek election to the PCC. Whilst their election is not unlawful the disadvantages of a paid employee sitting on the body which employs them is obvious and thus should if at all possible to be avoided.[94] A person cannot be elected by reference to their office. Therefore, if for example the meeting purports to elect the churchwardens as members of the deanery synod by reference only to their office, those persons should be considered elected in their personal capacity and will remain members of the synod even if they cease to be churchwardens.[95]

All candidates must for the purposes of the election be nominated and seconded by persons entitled to attend the meeting, and in the case of election to the PCC, by persons on the church roll.[96] This may be either prior to the meeting, in writing, or at the meeting (which may since the rules are silent be presumed to be either orally or in writing). If the number of candidates nominated is not greater than the number of seats to be filled the candidates may be declared elected forthwith.

Otherwise an election takes place. This is either under the procedure described below,[97] or pursuant to a scheme permitting voting by means of a single transferable vote,[98] at the annual meeting.[99] Alternatively if there is a scheme to permit postal votes (under either voting system) then voting is pursuant to that scheme.[1] Both such schemes are made by resolutions at the annual meeting, and are invalid unless approved by two-thirds of those present and voting.[2] If approved they do not become operative until the next annual meeting and may be rescinded by a subsequent resolution.

---

[89] *ibid.*, r. 10(1). A person who has their name on more than one electoral roll must choose one of those parishes for the purposes of election: *ibid.*, r. 1(4). The meaning of "actual communicant" was discussed in Chap. 2.

[90] *ibid.*

[91] *ibid.*, r. 10(3).

[92] s.10(6). As to which, see Chap. 5.

[93] CRR, r. 10(3).

[94] *Legal Opinions*, p. 104.

[95] *ibid.*, p. 6.

[96] CRR, r. 11(1).

[97] Pursuant to CRR, r. 11.

[98] The method is the same as that used in regard to elections to the House of Laity of the General Synod under rules made by the Synod with any necessary modifications: *ibid.*, r. 12. As to this system see Chap. 2.

[99] CRR, r. 12(1).

[1] CRR, r. 12(12).

[2] CRR, r. 12.

4.27   Where there is no scheme in force each person entitled to vote has as many votes as there are seats to be filled, but cannot give more than one vote to each candidate.[3] Votes may be given on voting papers signed on the reverse by the voter, or if no-one present at the meeting objects, by a show of hands. Where an election is not decided due to an equality of votes the decision between those who have received the equal number is to be decided by lot[4] In cases where there is a recount and the original count and recount are identical the original lot is to be used to make the determination.

Where the scheme provides for postal voting a presiding officer (who may not be a candidate) is appointed. Voting papers are distributed to all those present at the meeting entitled to vote and completed papers returned into the custody of the presiding officer before the close of the meeting. Anyone entitled to vote may make an application[5] for a postal vote. Those whose applications were received by the date specified in the notice convening the annual meeting must have sent or delivered to them within 48 hours of the close of the meeting a paper, which is to be returned to the presiding officer within a period of not less than seven and not more than 14 days as the presiding officer shall specify.[6]

Under either system of election the result must be announced as soon as is practicable.[7] The results must be affixed at or near the principal door of every church and every place licensed for public worship in the parish for not less than 14 days, and must state the date on which the result was announced.[8] Thereafter the secretay of the PCC is to hold a list of the names and addresses of the members of the council, this list being available for inspection on reasonable notice by any person resident in the parish or whose name is on the electoral roll, although there is no obligation to provide a copy of this list.[9] The names and addresses of the parochial representatives of the laity to the deanery synod must be sent, by the secretary of the PCC, to the dioccsan electoral registation officer and to the secretary of the deanery synod.[10]

Any candidate or elector in either election has a right of appeal against the allowance or disallowance of any vote given or tendered or against the result of such an election.[11] The procedure is identical to that discussed in Chapter 3 in relation to appeals in respect of elections to the deanery synod.

Parochial church councils

4.28   Until changes were made in the twentieth century the body which was in effect the ecclesiastical parish council was the vestry. That term comes from the room in the church were the priest put on his vestments. The vestry comprised the incumbent or curate-in-charge, persons (of either sex) who were rated to the

---

[3] CRR, r. 11(3).
[4] CRR, r. 11(8).
[5] The form for application for a postal vote is set out in *ibid.*, App. 1, s.4A.
[6] CRR, r. 12.
[7] CRR, r. 11(9).
[8] CRR, r. 11(9).
[9] CRR, r. 11(9).
[10] CRR, r. 11(10).
[11] *ibid.*, r. 44.

general rate in respect of the parish whether or not they resided there, together with those occupiers of rated heriditaments. The civil functions which the vestry exercised were transferred to local government bodies. Following provisions being made for the establishment of PCC's by the Church of England Assembly (Powers) Act 1919, the ecclesiastical functions of the vestry were largely transferred to the PCC in 1921. Vestries retained their power to choose the churchwardens until they were superceded by meetings of parishioners in accordance with the Churchwardens (Appointments and Resignation) Measure 1964, and with the coming into force of that Measure vestries became obsolete.[12]

The Parochial Church Councils (Powers) Measure 1921 defined the powers, duties and liabilities of PCCs making them to a large extent not just the successors of the vestry but also of the churchwardens and church trustees. Subsequent legislation has extended the powers of the PCC. The 1921 Measure was repealed and replaced by the Parochial Church Councils (Powers) Measure 1956 (PCCPM), whilst the provisions governing the constitution of the PCCs are contained in the CRR. Each council is a body corporate by the name of the PCC for which it is appointed, and has perpetual succession.[13]

Composition

The PCC includes all clerks in holy orders beneficed in or licensed to the parish. **4.29** In the case of a parish in the area of a benefice for which a team ministry is established this includes all the members of that team ministry. It also comprises any deaconesses or lay workers licensed to the parish,[14] and such a number of representatives of the laity as the annual meeting decides.[15] Any alteration in the number of representatives requires a resolution of the annual meeting which if passed does not take effect until the next annual meeting.[16]

All persons are members whose names are on the electoral roll of the parish and who are lay members of the General Synod or of any diocesan or deanery synod, excluding *ex officio* or co-opted members of these bodies.[17] As discussed previously churchwardens who are actual communicant members of the Church of England and whose names are on the roll of the parish are *ex officio* members. Any readers who are licensed to the parish or area which includes the parish and whose names are on the church roll may be members if the annual meeting so determines,[18] the apparent intention being that they should be individually selected rather than that the meeting should decide that all readers should or should not be *ex officio* members. It would appear that any readers' term of office should therefore be until the next annual meeting.

The PCC may also decide to co-opt members, who must not exceed one-fifth of the elected representatives of the laity or two persons whichever is the greater.

---

[12] The remaining provisions applying to them were repealed by the Church of England (Miscellaneous Provisions) Measure 1992, Sched. 4, Pt. I
[13] PCCPM, s.3.
[14] CRR, r. 14(1).
[15] CRR, r. 14(1).
[16] CRR, r. 14(1).
[17] Where they are on more than one electoral roll they must choose the PCC of which they are to be a member: *ibid.*, r. 1.
[18] CRR, r. 14(1).

These members may be either clerks in holy orders or actual lay communicants aged 16 years upwards,[19] whom it would appear need not have their names entered on the church electoral roll.

In the case of a group ministry, all the incumbents of all benefices, all priests-in-charge of any benefice in the group, (and where the area of the group ministry includes an area for which a team ministry is established all the vicars in that ministry) are entitled to attend meetings of the PCCs of all the parishes in the area for which the group is established although they are not members. They are also entitled to receive documents circulated to members of councils of which they are not themselves members and to speak but not vote at the meetings of such councils.[20]

Term of membership

4.30   Generally representatives of the laity hold office from the conclusion of one annual meeting until the conclusion of the next.[21] However, it is open to the annual meeting to decide that only one-third (or the number nearest to one-third) of the laity elected to the council are to retire each year. In this case the representatives who retire are those who have been the longest in office since they were last elected. As between those elected on the same day, if they cannot agree amongst themselves who should retire the decision is to be taken by lot. All representatives must retire at the conclusion of the third annual meeting after that at which they were elected.[22]

The annual meeting may decide that no representative of the laity may hold office for more than a specified number of years continuously.[23] It may also decide that, after a specified interval, a person who has ceased to be eligible because of this may stand for election again.[24]

If the name of any elected representative is removed from the parish roll or they refuse or fail to apply for enrolment when a new roll is being prepared (on the date when the new roll is completed), they will cease to be a member of the PCC on the date when their name is removed or the new roll is completed.[25] However, this removal is without prejudice to the right of the council to make that person a co-opted member.[26] A person is also disqualified from being a member of the PCC if they are disqualified from being a charity trustee under the Charities Act 1993 or are disqualified from serving as a member of the PCC by the bishop under the Incumbents (Vacation of Benefices) Measure 1977[27]; disqualification from the PCC taking effect on the same date as the other disqualification.[28]

---

[19] CRR, r. 14(1).
[20] *ibid.*, r. 14(4).
[21] *ibid.*, r. 16.
[22] *ibid.*, r. 16.
[23] *ibid.*, r. 17.
[24] *ibid.*, r. 17.
[25] *ibid.*, r. 14(3).
[26] *ibid.*, r. 14(3).
[27] s.10(6), as to which, see Chap. 5.
[28] *ibid.*, r. 14(3).

Co-opted members hold office until the conclusion of the next annual meeting, although this is without prejudice to their being co-opted on subsequent occasions for a similar term.[29] Readers were discussed above.

Those who are members of the council by reason of their election as lay members of a deanery synod hold office for a period beginning with the date of their election and ending with May 31 next following the election of their successors.[30] The presumption must be that all other *ex officio* members are members of the PCC until they cease to hold the qualifying office.

Before their term of office comes to an end a member of the council may resign their membership by notice in writing, signed by them, sent or given to the secretary of the PCC.[31] The resignation takes effect from the date specified in the notice, or if no date is specified the date the notice is received by the secretary.

General provisions relating to PCCs

The rules relating to the officers, meetings and procedure of PCCs are set out in Appendix II to the CRR.[32] A PCC may vary these rules with the consent of the diocesan synod, but otherwise the general rules apply.[33] Any question as to the interpretation of the provisions set out in Appendix II is to be referred to the diocesan bishop and any decision given by him or by a person appointed by him is final.[34] **4.31**

Officers of the PCC

The minister of the parish is chairman of the PCC and a lay member of the council must be elected as vice-chairman.[35] During a vacancy in the benefice, or when the chairman is incapacitated by absence, illness or any other cause, or when the minister invites them to do so, the vice-chairman acts, and has all the powers vested in the chairman.[36] **4.32**

The council may appoint one of its members to act as secretary, or if no member is appointed, must appoint instead some other fit person with such remuneration (if any) as it considers fit.[37] The secretary is to have charge of all documents relating to the current business of the council and is responsible for keeping the minutes and must record all resolutions passed.[38]

The PCC may appoint one of more of its members to act as treasurer solely or jointly, and failing such appointment, the office of treasurer must be discharged

---

[29] CRR, r. 14(1)(h).
[30] *ibid.*, r. 16.
[31] *ibid.*, r. 49.
[32] *ibid.*, r. 15.
[33] CRR, r. 15.
[34] *ibid.*, App. II, para. 18.
[35] *ibid.*, App. II, para. 1(a), (b).
[36] CRR, App. II, para. 1(c).
[37] *ibid.*, App. II, para. 1(d).
[38] *ibid.*, App. II, para. 1. They must also keep the secretary of the diocesan and deanery synods informed of their name and address.

jointly by those of the churchwardens who are members of the PCC, or if there is only one such churchwarden by them alone.[39] No remuneration is to be paid to any treasurer.[40]

A church electoral roll officer must be apppointed but this person need not be a member of the council and may be the secretary.[41] If not a member of the council they may receive remuneration.

If an independent examiner or auditor is not appointed by the annual meeting (or if such a person is appointed but unwilling to act) the PCC must make the appointment.[42] The examiner or auditor must not be a member of the council, and their remuneration (if any) is to be paid by the PCC.

Express provision is made for the term of the examiner or auditor's appointemnt, this being until the close of the next annual meeting.[43] In all other cases officers can be appointed for such term as the PCC considers fit, or in the absence of an express term, the appointment will terminate at the end of the first meeting of the PCC after the annual meeting following the officer's appointment.[44]

Although the office of secretary and treasurer could be held by the same person the Legal Advisory Commission is of the view that this is undesirable.[45] And although the rules do not forbid the minister being appointed as the treasurer or secretary this would also be undesirable. It would be possible for a PCC to co-opt a person to the council for the express purpose of their becoming treasurer or secretary were they suitably qualified.

Committees

4.33 The PCC has a standing committee which must consist of not less than five persons.[46] The minister and such churchwardens as are members of the council are *ex officio* members of the committee. In addition the council must appoint by resolution at least two (and sufficient to make five members in all) other members from amongst council members.[47] The purpose of the committee is to carry on the routine work of the PCC, and for this reason it is desirable that the treasurer and secretary be members.

The PCC has the power to remove these appointed members from the committee, but unless removed they hold office until the next annual meeting. The standing committee has the power to transact the council's business between council meetings. In theory therefore it could transact virtually any of the PCC's business in appropriate circumstances, subject to any limitations set by the PCC. However, the purpose of the standing committee must be borne in mind and frequent use of its extensive powers rather than confining them to emergency situations, would amount to an abuse of power.[48]

---

[39] *ibid.*, App. II, para. 1(e).
[40] *ibid.*, App. II, para. 1(e).
[41] *ibid.*, App. II, para. 1(f).
[42] *ibid.*, App. II, para. 1(g).
[43] *ibid.*, App. II, para. 1(g).
[44] *Legal Opinions*, p. 198.
[45] *ibid*.
[46] CRR, App. II, para. 14.
[47] CRR, App. II, para. 14.
[48] *Legal Opinions*, p. 201.

The PCC also has the power to appoint other committees for the purpose of undertaking or overseeing various branches of church work in the parish.[49] The minister is an *ex officio* member of all such committees, which may include members who are not members of the PCC,[50] and, it would appear, persons who are not on the church electoral roll.[51] It is also suggested that such committees may be given the power to co-opt persons themselves.[52]

Joint, district, team and group councils

In certain circumstances the annual meeting of a parish, acting either alone or jointly with other parishes has the power to make schemes to ensure due representation of the congregations of two places of worship and to establish district, joint, team or group councils. All these powers are set in CRR, rules 18 to 21. **4.34**

In each case for a scheme to be valid it must be approved by at least two-thirds of the persons present and voting at the annual meeting. It must also be approved by the bishop's council and standing committee which also determines when it may come into operation (this date being not later than the next ensuing annual meeting). If that council and committee gives approval subject to specified amendments those amendments must also be approved by a majority of two-thirds of those present and voting, either at the next annual or at a special parochial church meeting. In each case a special meeting may also be held for the purposes of deciding whether to make or join in such a scheme.

Schemes to the same effect as those made under the CCR may also be made pursuant to a pastoral scheme or order under the Pastoral Measure 1983.[52a]

Thus where a pastoral scheme establishes a team ministry for the area of a benefice comprising a parish with two or more churches or places of worship, the scheme may make (or authorise the bishop by instrument under his hand with the concurrence of the team rector to make) provisions to ensure due representation of each church or place of worship on the PCC of the parish, or for the election of a district church council. Similarly where a scheme establishes a team ministry for the area of a benefice which comprises more than one parish provision may be made for the establishment of a team council. Where a scheme establishes a group ministry the scheme may make (or authorise the bishop by instrument under his hand with the concurrence of all incumbents within the group to make) provision for the establishment of a group council.

In all such cases the provisions operate for the period specified in the scheme or instrument, not being a period exceeding five years from the date of the establishment of the team or group ministry, that period not being renewable. It would appear that as a matter of policy the General Synod decided that these arrangements should not be established on a permanent basis without a positive

---

[49] CRR, App. II, para. 15.

[50] *ibid*.

[51] CRR, App. II, para. 14. Indeed there is no qualification what so ever specified for persons who are not members of the PCC.

[52] See n. 48 *ante*.

[52a] Pastoral Measure 1983, Sched. 3, para. 4. Pastoral schemes and orders are considered further in Chap. 5.

decision by those in the parishes concerned being taken. However, at the end of the expiry period during which they remain operative the annual parish meeting of a parish or parishes has the power to make a scheme as described below to establish any such arrangements, or make alternative arrangements, on a permanent basis.

In any parish where there are two or more churches or places licensed for public worship the annual meeting may make a scheme for either or both of two purposes: first, for the election of representatives to the laity of the PCC in such a manner as to ensure due representation of the congregation of each church or place; secondly, the election of a district church council for any district in the parish in which such a church or place is situated.

In the case of a scheme for the election of a district council this must provide for the election of the lay representatives, the *ex officio* members, and the chairmanship, and may contain other provisions which the annual meeting considers appropriate. The scheme may also provide for the delegation of functions of the PCC and, subject to the particular scheme involved, the PCC itself may also delegate such of its functions as it considers appropriate. However, the functions of a PCC as an interested party under the Pastoral Measure 1983,[53] the Priests (Ordination of Women) Measure 1993,[54] or the Patronage (Benefices) Measure 1986,[55] where the parish must act as one, cannot be delegated. The scheme may also provide for deputy churchwardens and the delegation to them of functions of the churchwardens as discussed earlier. In the case of a team ministry every member of the team has a right to attend the meeting of any district church council in a parish in the area of the benefice for which the team ministry is established.

4.35   Where there are two or more parishes within the area of a single benefice or two or more benefices are held in plurality the annual meetings of all or some of the parishes in the benefice or benefices may make a joint scheme to provide for a joint parochial parish council. Such a joint council will comprise the ministers of the parishes and such number of representatives of each of those parishes elected by and from among the other members of the PCC of the parish as the scheme provides for. The scheme must also provide for the chairmanship, meetings and procedure of the joint council.

Where there is a joint council established for all the parishes of a benefice the functions of the PCC in respect of the selection of a new incumbent pursuant to the Patronage (Benefices) Measure 1986 will be exercised by that joint council.[56] Otherwise the scheme may specify which of the functions of the PCCs of each parish are to be delegated to the joint council, save that the fucntions of a PCC as an interested party under the Pastoral Measure 1983[57] or the Priests (Ordination of Women) Measure 1993[58] cannot be delegated. Subject to the same constraints as the scheme for the joint council and any pastoral scheme or order a PCC may also decide to delegate any of its functions to the joint council.

---

[53] Pt. I. As to which, see Chap. 5.
[54] s.3. As to which, see Chap. 7.
[55] Pt. II. As to which, see Chap. 5.
[56] Patronage (Benefices) Measure 1986, Sched. 2, para. 20.
[57] Pt. I. As to which, see Chap. 5.
[58] s.3. As to which, see Chap. 7.

A joint council meets from time to time for the purpose of consulting together on matters of common concern.[59] So too does a team or group council. In all these cases, as with the creation of district councils, the PCC's of each parish remain and continue to exercise all powers which have not been delegated. In particular a joint or group council is not a body corporate and there is no property vested in it.

Where a team ministry is established for the area of a benefice which comprises more than one parish the annual meetings in that area may make a joint scheme to provide for establishing a team council. Where a pastoral scheme establishes a group ministry the annual meetings of the parishes for the area for which the group ministry is established may make a joint scheme to provide for a group council.

The team council must comprise the team rector and all the members of the team other than the rector, together with every assistant curate, deaconess and lay worker licensed to a parish within the team who are not members of the team. This is subject to the proviso that where all these persons (excluding the team rector) would otherwise number more than a quarter of the total membership of the team council they may, and where they would number more than one-third must, select amongst themselves who will be members so that their total does not exceed one-third.

A group council must comprise all the members of the group ministry together **4.36** with every assistant curate, deaconess and lay worker licensed to any parish within the group. In addition both team and group councils will comprise such number of lay representatives elected by and from amongst the lay representatives of the PCC of each parish as may be specified in the scheme. If the area of a group ministry includes the area of a benefice for which a team ministry is established the scheme must also provide that the vicars in that ministry, as well as the rector and all other members of the team, are to be members of the group council. The scheme must also provide for the chairmanship, meetings and procedure of any team or group councils.

Where a team council is established in respect of a benefice comprising more than one parish the functions of each PCC in respect of the selection of a new incumbent pursuant to the Patronage (Benefices) Measure 1986 will be exercised by that team council.[60-61] Otherwise, as with a joint council and subject to the same constraints, the scheme may specify which of the functions of the PCCs of each parish are to be delegated to the team council, or a PCC may decide to delegate any of its functions. Likewise with a group council the scheme may specify which of the functions of the PCCs may be delegated and the PCCs may themselves delegate functions to the group council. However, in this case the constraints upon which powers may be delegated are identical to those in respect of district councils.

Functions of the PCC

The general functions of the PCC are set out in the PCCPM.[62] Their first duty is **4.37** to consult together with the minister on matters of general concern and importance to the parish. It would appear that whilst this means that the PCC

[59] For a fuller discussion of the legal status of joint councils see *Legal Opinions*, pp. 157–160.
[60-61] Patronage (Benefices) Measure 1986, Sched. 2, para. 19.
[62] s.2.

should have proper regard to the minister's wishes or suggestions it is free to differ from these if it believes it must do so in order to discharge any particular duty.[63] It was said in *Re St Peter's Roydon* that in a true spirit of charity a clash between incumbent and a council becomes unthinkable, although it was also said that the agreement between the minister and the PCC must signify genuine and informed consent since otherwise the requirement becomes a solemn farce. But as the facts of that case show such a breakdown can occur.

The other functions of the PCC include: co-operating with the minister in promoting the whole mission of the Church, pastoral, evangelistic, social and ecumenical; the consideration and discussion of matters concerning the Church of England or any other matters of religious or public interest, but not the declaration of doctrine of the Church on any question; the making and putting into effect of any provision made by the diocesan synod, but without prejudice to the powers of the council on any particular matter; and the giving of advice to the diocesan or deanery synod on any matter referred to the council and raising such matters as the PCC consider appropriate with either the deanery or diocesan synods. In the exercise of its functions the PCC is to take into consideration any expression of opinion by any parochial church meeting.

The majority of the power and duties of the vestry, churchwardens and church trustees (if any)[64] were transferred to the PCC in 1921.[65] In each case (subject to specified exceptions) the PCC acquired the like powers, duties and liabilities as the vestry, churchwardens and church trustees had on July 1, 1921.[66] In the case of the vestry the transfer excluded the right to elect churchwardens and sidesmen and the administration of ecclesiastical charities, but included the power of presentation to the benefice if that right was vested in or was in trust for the parishioners, and the power to make a voluntary church rate. The PCC acquired the functions of the churchwardens with respect to the financial affairs of the church including the collection (other than of alms received at Holy Communion) and administration of all money raised for church purposes and the keeping of accounts. The care, maintenance, preservation and insurance of the fabric of the church and its goods and ornaments and the care and maintenance of any churchyard (whether open or closed) also passed to the PCC, including the power to recover the cost of maintaining a closed churchyard.[67] However, the

---

[63] *Re St Peter Roydon* [1969] 1 W.L.R. 1849 at 1852. A decision on earlier wording where the primary duty was to consult in the initiation, conduct and development of church work. However, it is suggested that the same principles apply.

[64] Appointed under the Compulsory Church Rate Abolition Act 1868, s.9 (repealed by the Church of England (Miscellaneous Provisions) Measure 1992, Sched. 4, Pt I) for the purposes of accepting and holding any contributions for ecclesiastical purposes in the parish.

[65] Pursuant to the Parochial Church Councils (Powers) Measure 1921 which was repealed and replaced by the PCCPM: PCCPM, s.4. All enactments in any Act, whether general, local or personal, relating to any transfererred powers, duties or liabilities are to be subject to this Measure and are, so far as circumstances permit, to be construed as if any reference to the vestry, churchwardens or church trustees referred to the PCC and these Acts are to be construed with such modifications as may be necessary to carrying the PCCPM into effect: *ibid.*, s.4(2).

[66] See n. 65 *ante*. The power to issue burial certificates pursuant to the Burial Act 1855 was repealed except in relation to the City of London by the Local Government Act 1972, s.272(1).

[67] See n. 65 *ante*.

churchwardens retain their powers with respect to visitations, and the transfer of powers to the PCC does not affect their property in the goods and ornaments of the church.[68] It should be noted that where by virtue of a pastoral scheme or otherwise a parish has more than one parish church the powers, duties and liabilities of the PCC so extend.[69]

The functions of the PCC in regard to the selection of a new incumbent and **4.38** the requirement that it consent the extension of tenure of an incumbent beyond normal retiring age are described in Chapter 5. The resolution which a PCC may pass concerning women priests in the parish are considered in Chapter 7. The role of the PCC in providing various items required for divine service, its functions in relation to the selection of the forms of church services and the versions of scripture, together with the necessity to consult it regarding the vestments of the minister, are discussed in Chapter 9. It may also give general guidelines to the minister with respect to the burial in the churchyard or other parish burial ground of persons not having a right of burial there.[70] The PCC has various responsibilities in regard to the property of the church and its care and maintenance which are considered in Chapter 8.

In addition the PCC has a number of miscellaneous functions. It must be consulted in regard to matters such as proposed recommendations by the pastoral committee of the diocese affecting the parish, and in regard to action taken by the DBF in regard to the parsonage house and other relevant property.[71] It must also be a party to any agreement for the sharing of church buildings between the Church of England and another church.[72] The PCC is an interested party in faculty proceedings and frequently has a significant role to play in the conduct of such.[73] Finally the PCC has the power to make representations to the bishop with regard to any matter affecting the welfare of the parish.[74]

Conduct of financial affairs by PCC[75]

The PCC has the power to frame an annual budget of the amount required for **4.39** the maintenance of the work of the Church in the parish and otherwise to take such steps as it thinks necessary for the raising collecting and allocating of such sums.[76] Thus there is an implied power to borrow money,[77] but the question of whether the PCC may give security for a loan is more difficult. Unless the PCC had property which it could mortgage (which would almost certainly be held on trust by the DBF and thus require the consent of both the DBF and the Charity Commissioners) or one or more of its members could give a personal guarantee

---

[68] As to which, see Chap. 8.
[69] Pastoral Measure 1983, s.27(5)(d).
[70] See Chap. 11.
[71] See Chap. 5.
[72] See Chap. 12
[73] See Chap. 11.
[74] PCCPM, s.7(v).
[75] See also Carter and Perry, *A Handbook of Parish Finance* (1992).
[76] PCCPM, s.7(i).
[77] *Re St Peter Roydon* [1969] 1 W.L.R. 1849 at 1855, 1856.

most PCCs are unlikely to possess the means by which they could offer security in any event.

A PCC is a corporation with perpetual succession with the consequence that a change in membership cannot affect its liability for debts. The debt is that of the PCC and no individual member of it can be individually liable for any debt or other liability which has been lawfully incurred.[78] However, if a member acts without the authority of the PCC that protection is lost and they may be individually and alone liable for the debt. A member can of course also be individually liable for a debt where they have given a personal guarantee, for example to secure the PCC's overdraft at the bank.

Care should be taken where a contract between the PCC and one of its members is being contemplated. Unless the member involved fully explains the nature of the contract and their interest in it and take no part in the meeting at which the contract is debated and voted upon they could be held accountable as a trustee to hand over any profits made to the PCC.[79]

The PCC has the power to determine jointly with the minister the objects to which all money to be given or collected in church shall be allocated.[80] This power is no longer subject to the directions contained in the Book of Common Prayer as to the disposal of money given at the offertory. However, it should be noted that money collected by the incumbent at services which are not held in church is at the incumbent's disposal unless the money was raised for church purposes.[81]

4.40   Although the PCC is a trustee of the money in its hands it may subscribe a reasonable part of its general funds to any charity whose general objects are to further any part of the whole mission of the Church, so that the charity need not be one under which the parish or individual parishioners will benefit.[82]

One of the major claims upon the funds of the PCC will be the parish quota or share towards diocesan funds.[83] Another major claim will be the expenses involved in the upkeep and repair of the church, churchyard and other buildings such as the church hall. The diocesan synod may also require annual payments by the PCC towards the expenditure of the diocesan parsonages board or direct payments in respect of the upkeep of the parsonage house of the particular parish.[84]

The PCC should also pay the working expenses of all clergy and lay workers in the parish, although most PCCs fall short in this regard and many clergy and workers subsidise the parish by meeting some expenses themselves. Working expenses will include such items as running a car and its depreciation, public transport, office equipment, secretarial assistance, telephone, postage, stationery, hospitality, maintenance of robes, and the cost of providing a *locum tenens* to stand in on a short term basis, for example during holidays.[85]

---

[78] *Re St Thomas a Becket, Framfield* [1989] 1 All E.R. 170.

[79] *Legal Opionion*, p. 200.

[80] PCCPM (iv).

[81] *Marson v. Unmack* [1923] P. 163.

[82] *Legal Opinions*, p. 200.

[83] See Chap. 8.

[84] See Chap. 8.

[85] The Church Commissioners in their role as the Central Stipends Authority have published *The Parochial Expenses of the Clergy* (1986 revised edition) which is available free on request from 1 Millbank, London, SW1.

The power to levy a voluntary church rate belonged to vestries from 1868 when the Compulsory Church Rate Abolition Act 1868 came into force and was transferred to the PCC in 1921. By a separate provision of the PCCPM the PCC has the power to levy a voluntary church rate for specified purposes.[86] These include any purpose connected with the affairs of the church including the administrative expenses of the council and the costs of any legal proceedings. It is possible that compulsory church rates may in very limited cases still be enforceable under certain private or local Acts,[87] but the voluntary rate is not legally enforceable. In practice the power to levy it has not been widely used. Although however, notwithstanding this some parishes have sought to do so as a means of raising funds on a voluntary basis. Where a parish does seek to raise such a levy it would appear that it is to be assessed upon those members of the parish or district who are members of the Church of England in proportion to the rateable value of their property.[88]

The various reports and the audited accounts and statements which the PCC must lay before the annual meeting have already been described. In addition accounts of all trusts administered by the PCC must be laid before the DBF annually.[89] The PCC's audited accounts should be made up for the calendar year ending December 31.[90] They should be made up on income and expenditure, showing not only receipts and payments but also money due but not received, or owing but not paid, and any money prepared on account of or received but not due until the following year. A balance sheet is not required but is desirable. It should be noted that with effect from May 1, 1997 the independent examiner or auditor of the PCC's financial statements shall have a right of access to books, documents or other records (however kept) which relate to the financial statements.[91] They will also have a right to require information and explanations from past or present treasurers or members of the PCC, and in default of compliance with their request they may apply to the Charity Commissioners for an order or directions to be made to secure compliance.[92]

Meetings and proceedings

A PCC must hold at least four meetings a year and if no more than four are to be held these should as far as possible be at quarterly intervals.[93] Meetings must be convened by the chairman, which they may do at any time. However, if the chairman refuses or neglects to do so within seven days of their being presented with a resolution signed by at least one-third of the members of the PCC, those members may themselves convene a meeting.[94] **4.41**

As with parochial church meetings an extraordinary meeting of the PCC may be convened by the archdeacon upon the same terms as to written representations and under the same provisions as to chairing such a meeting and voting.[95]

---

[86] PCCPM, s.7(ii).
[87] Phillimore, *Ecclesiastical Law of The Church of England* (2nd ed. 1895), p. 1446.
[88] See *Gosling v. Veley* (1853) 4 H.L. Cas 679.
[89] PCCPM, s.8(4). See Chap. 8 regarding trusts generally.
[90] *ibid.*, s.8(1). See also regulations made pursuant to the Charities Act 1993, Pt VI.
[91] CRR, r. 15, App. II, para. 16.
[92] Pursuant to section 44(2) of the Charities Act 1993.
[93] CRR, App. II, para. 2.
[94] *ibid.*, para. 3.
[95] CRR, r. 23.

It is for the PCC to decide whether or not to open up its meetings to non-members and if so whether to restrict this to those on the church electoral roll. In either case it should be made clear that those non-members who are permitted to attend have no right to speak or vote. If a general policy of admittance was desired the PCC could nonetheless resolve to exclude non-members for certain business. Neither PCCs nor deanery nor diocesan synods are included within the list of bodies specified in the Public Bodies (Admission to Meetings Act) 1960 and consequently the press has no right to attend unless expressly authorised by the council or synod. In contrast debates of the General Synod are usually open to the public. In the case of the annual parochial church meeting only those entitled to attend may do so. If a journalist fell within that group they could attend but would not be entitled to report the proceedings without the consent of the meeting.[96]

Notices of all meetings except emergency meetings must be placed at or near the principal door of every church or place licensed for public worship in the parish at least 10 clear days before the meeting. The notice must specify the time and place of the intended meeting and be signed on behalf of the chairman or the persons convening the meeting.[97] Not less than seven days before the meeting a notice, including the times and place of the meeting, signed by or on behalf of the secretary, containing the agenda of the meeting including any motion or other business proposed by any member of the council of which notice has been received by the secretary, must be sent by post or delivered to every member of the council.[98]

4.42   The exception to the requirement for this second notice to the members is a meeting of the PCC which immediately follows the annual parochial church meetings and which is called solely for the purpose of appointing or electing officers and members of the standing committee. However, public notice must still be given at least 10 days before, as described above.[99] If for some good and sufficient reason the chairman, vice-chairman and secretary, or any two of them, consider that a meeting which has been convened should be postponed notice must be given to every member specifying a reconvened time and place within 14 days of the postponed meeting.[1]

Where an emergency arises, or other special circumstances which require immediate action warrant it, a meeting may be convened by the chairman, on not less than three clear days notice, which must be given in writing to the members of the PCC.[2]

The chair is normally taken by the chairman[3] but if they are not present or (subject to certain provisos) their office is vacant, then the vice-chairman takes

---

[96] *Legal Opinions*, pp. 216–217
[97] CRR App. II, para. 4.
[98] *ibid.*, App. II, para. 4.
[99] *ibid.*, App. II, para. 4.
[1] *ibid.*, App. II, para. 4.
[2] *ibid.*, para. 8.
[3] Where a pastoral scheme creates a team ministry the scheme or the bishop's licence may assign to the team vicar-chairmanship, or a share in the duties of the chairmanship of the PCC (and parochial church meeting). If the duties are to be shared the arrangements must ensure that the chairman on any occasion is determined in advance: Pastoral Measure 1983, Sched. 3, para. 4(1). Where the benefice is vacant and the rights of presentation are suspended the priest-in-charge is the chairman of the PCC: CRR, App. II, r. 5.

the chair. If neither the chairman nor vice-chairman is available.[4] to take the chair for any meeting or any particular business, a chairman must be chosen by the members present from amongst themselves.[5] If the person chairing the meeting thinks it expedient, or the meeting so resolves, they can vacate the chair either for the entire meeting or for the purposes of any business in which they have a personal interest or any other particular business.[6]

In order to transact any business a quorum of one-third of the members is normally required.[7] Furthermore no business other than that on the agenda may be transacted except by the consent of three-quarters of the members present.[8] The order of the business is to be that set out in the agenda, unless the PCC determines otherwise by a resolution.[9] The exception to the usual quorum to transact business is in the case of an emergency meeting when a majority of the existing members is required, but in such a case only the business specified in the notice convening the meeting may be transacted.[10] All business must be decided by a majority of the members present and voting, and if the votes are equal the chairman has a casting vote.[11] A meeting may adjourn its proceedings to such time and place as may be determined at that meeting.[12]

The minutes must record the names of members present at the meeting, and if one-fifth of those present and voting so require, the names of the members voting for and against any resolution. In addition any member is entitled to require that the way in which they cast their vote is recorded.[13] The minutes are to be available to all members of the PCC, who are also to have access to past minutes which the chairman and vice-chairman jointly determine to be relevant to current business.[14] The independent examiner or auditor of the PCC's financial statements, the bishop, the archdeacon and any person authorised by one of these in writing, is entitled to gain access to the approved minutes of meetings of the PCC without its authority.[15] Those persons whose name is on the church electoral roll may have access to the minutes of meetings of the PCC which were held after the annual parochial meeting in 1995, with the exception of minutes deemed by the PCC to be confidential,[16] with these exceptions no-one else may have access to the minutes other than in accordance with the specific authorisation of the PCC unless these minutes have been deposited in the diocesan record office.[17]

---

[4] In the case of a parish in the area of a benefice for which a team ministry is established if the vicar entitled to chair the meeting and the vice-chairman are not present the meeting is to be chaired by the rector of that team ministry: CRR, App. II, r. 5.
[5] CRR, App. II, para. 5.
[6] CRR, App. II, para. 6.
[7] CRR, App. II, para. 6.
[8] CRR, App. II, para. 6.
[9] *ibid.*, para. 7.
[10] *ibid.*, para. 8.
[11] *ibid.*, paras. 10, 11.
[12] *ibid.*, para. 13.
[13] *ibid.*, para. 12.
[14] *ibid.*, para. 12.
[15] *ibid.*, para. 12.
[16] *ibid.*, para. 12.
[17] Pursuant to the Parochial Registers and Records Measure 1978.

4.43   It should be borne in mind that the diocesan bishop may make rules for the carrying into effect of the PCCPM within the diocese.[18] If any act required to be undertaken by the terms of that Measure is not so performed by the person required to carry out the function within such time as the bishop may consider reasonable it may be done by or under the authority of the bishop.[19] In the event of the PCC and the minister being unable to agree upon any matter upon which their agreement or joint action is required under the Measure the matter must be dealt with or determined in such manner as the bishop may direct.[20] This could take the form of mediation, arbitration or conciliation involving the bishop or a person nominated by him or even in extreme cases by an *ex cathedra* statement issued by the bishop. If a serious pastoral breakdown occurs the provisions of the 1977 Incumbents (Vacation of Benefices Measure)[21] may become relevant. It should be remembered that the fault may lie as much with the PCC as with the incumbent. In the case of an omission by a parish to form or maintain a PCC the rural dean, upon the omission being brought to their notice, must ascertain and report the cause to the bishop,[22] who would presumably exercise his general powers pursuant to the CRR to appoint a person to remedy the default.[23]

The church electoral roll

4.44   There must be a church electoral roll for each parish on which the names of lay persons are entered,[24] the roll being available for inspection by bona fide inquirers.[25] As we have seen entry on the roll is a necessary qualification for the participation of a lay person in parochial church meetings and for election as a representative of the laity to the PCC, deanery and diocesan synods and to the House of Laity of the General Synod.

Until a PCC has been constituted for a parish the roll must be formed and revised by the minister and churchwardens. Thereafter it must be kept revised by or under the direction of the PCC which must appoint a church electoral roll officer, who is to have charge of the roll, to act under its directions.[26] If there is an omission to either prepare or maintain an electoral roll the rural dean, upon

---

[18] PCCPM, s.9. This does not apply where the functions of the PCC have been transferred to the administrative body of a cathedral: Cathedrals Measure 1963, s.12(4)(b).

[19] *ibid.*

[20] See n. 18 *ante.*

[21] See Chap. 5.

[22] CRR, r. 53(5).

[23] *ibid.*, r.53(2).

[24] *ibid.*, r.1(1).

[25] *ibid.* The PCC may charge for providing a copy of the roll. Because the roll is required by statute and made available to the public it gains exemption from the Data Protection Act 1984 (see s.34(1)) when kept in longhand. Where it is kept on a word processor or any machine with a memory (such as a typewriter) the Act will apply (*ibid.*, s.1(2)). If the PCC keeps only names and addresses (as required by the CRR) as a computer record it need not register as a data user under the terms of the Act, but should it keep further information, such as telephone numbers, it should register: *Legal Opinions*, pp. 118–119.

[26] CRR, r.1(5). The provisions relating to the formation of rolls for parishes created by pastoral schemes are set out in *ibid.*, r. 1(6).

the omission being brought to their notice, must ascertain and report the cause to the bishop,[27] who would presumably exercise his general powers under the CRR to appoint a person to remedy the default.[28]

All lay[29] persons of either sex who are aged 16 years or upwards[30] and who are baptised are entitled to have their names entered upon the electoral roll provided they sign an application form[31] for enrolment making one of several declarations.[32] They must declare themselves to be a member of the Church of England, or of a church in communion with it,[33] resident[34] in the parish; or they must declare themselves to be such a member who, although not resident in the parish, has habitually[35] attended public worship in the parish during a period of six months prior to enrolment; or they must declare themselves to be a member in good standing of a church which subscribes to the doctrine of the Holy Trinity (not being a church in communion with the Church of England)[36] and also declare themselves to be a member of the Church of England who has habitually attended public worship in the parish during a period of six months prior to enrolment.

It should be noted that a person is entitled to have their name on the roll of any number of parishes if qualified to have their name entered on the relevant rolls.[37] Addresses must be recorded where practicable although the omission of an address does not affect the validity of enrolment.[38]

As we saw the PCC must appoint a church electoral roll officer to act under its **4.45** directions.[39] It is the duty of this officer to ensure that the roll is kept constantly

---

[27] *ibid.*, r. 53(5).

[28] *ibid.*, r. 53(2).

[29] References in the CRR to lay persons must be construed as references to persons other than clerks in holy orders. *ibid.*, r. 54(2) A person who has executed a deed of relinquishment which has been enrolled in the High Court and is recorded in the diocesan registry is deemed not to be a clerk for these purposes or any other purposes of the CRR: *ibid.*, r. 54(3).

[30] A person who will have their sixteenth birthday after the intended revision of the roll or the preparation of a new roll but on or before the date of the annual parochial church meeting may complete an application form and be enrolled with effect from the date of their birthday: CRR, r. 1(2).

[31] Set out in CRR, App. 1.

[32] *ibid.*, r. 1(2).

[33] For membership of the Church of England see Chap. 2, and for churches which are in communion with the Church of England see Chap. 12. It is for the Archbishops of Canterbury and York to determine whether or not a church is in communion or not for the purposes of the CRR: *ibid.*, r. 54(5).

[34] Residence must be regular and not of a casual nature: CRR, r. 54(6). Where a person resides in an extra-parochial place they are deemed to reside in the parish in which it abuts, and if there is any doubt in the matter a determination is to be made by the bishop's council and standing committee: *ibid.*, r. 1(3).

[35] Habitual is not defined. It would not appear to exclude the possibility of frequent attendance at two places of worship.

[36] As to churches which subscribe to the doctrine of the Holy Trinity, see Chap. 12.

[37] CRR, r. 1(4). When a person who wishes to be enrolled also states their desire to be removed from the roll of any other parish, notice of this fact must be sent by the enrolling council to the council of that other parish: *ibid.*, r. 3(1).

[38] *ibid.*, r. 1(10). However, failure to comply does not affect the validity of an entry on the roll: *ibid.*

[39] *ibid.*, r. 1(7).

up to date by the addition and removal of names as from time to time required by the CRR, and they must report any such amendments to the roll to the PCC at its next meeting.[40] Anyone entitled to have their name entered on the roll must be added from time to time.[41] A person's name must be removed from the roll as the occasion arises under a number of circumstances: if they signify their wish to be removed; if they die; if they become a clerk in holy orders; if they were not entitled to have their name entered on the roll at the time when it was entered.[42] They must also have their name removed if they are no longer resident in the parish,[43] unless after ceasing to be resident they continue to attend public worship in the parish habitually or are prevented from doing so by illness or other sufficient cause.[44] Similarly a person who was not a resident of the parish who ceases to attend public worship habitually in the parish unless prevented from doing so by illness or other sufficient cause must have their name removed.[45] Removal is without prejudice to the right to be enrolled again if the person becomes so entitled.[46] Special provisions apply on the alteration of parish boundaries for the transfer of names from one parish roll to another.[47]

Except in the years when a new roll must be prepared the roll must be revised annually. The revision must be completed not less than 15 days or more than 28 days before the annual parochial church meeting, after due notice has been given by or under directions of the PCC.[48] Notice in the prescribed form[49] must be published by being affixed by the minister (or under their direction) on or near the principal door of every church and building licensed for public worship in the parish and remain there for a period of not less than 14 days before the revision.[50]

Upon revision all enrolments and removals which have been effected since the last revision must be reviewed and any further enrolments or removals effected.[51] Once revision has taken place the revised roll together with a list of names removed since the last revision must be published, by being exhibited for not less than 14 days before the annual parochial church meeting on or near the principal door of the parish church in such manner as the PCC appoints.[52] During the period when the copy is exhibited any errors or omissions in the roll may be corrected but, subject to this and to enrolment of any person entitled to be enrolled who signs an application for enrolment, no names are to be added or removed from the roll during the period between completion of the revision and the annual parochial church meeting.[53]

---

[40] ibid., r. 1(8).
[41] ibid., r. 1(8).
[42] ibid., r. 1(9).
[43] Where a person's name is removed because they have become resident in another parish notice should whenever possible be sent by the removing council to the council of that other parish: CRR, r. 3(2).
[44] ibid., r. 1(9).
[45] ibid., r. 1(9).
[46] ibid., r. 1(10).
[47] ibid., r. 2(8). Those persons resident in the area which is transferred to another parish must be asked if they wish their names transferred to that other parish: ibid.
[48] ibid., r. 2(1).
[49] ibid., App. I, s.2.
[50] ibid., r. 2(1).
[51] ibid., r. 2(2).
[52] ibid., r. 2(3).
[53] ibid., r. 2(3).

In the year 1996 and every sixth succeeding year (2002 being the next occasion) a new roll must be prepared.[54] Public notice of not less than two months before the annual parochial church meeting must be given in the prescibed manner,[55] the notice being affixed in the same manner as the revised roll. In addition at every service on the two Sundays during those 14 days the congregation must be informed of the preparation of the new roll.[56] The PCC must also take reasonable steps to inform every person whose name is on the previous roll that if they wish their name to be entered on the new roll they must apply for enrolment.[57]

The new roll must be prepared in the same timescale, and a copy of it **4.46** published in the same manner as the revised roll.[58] Again during this period when the copy is exhibited any errors or omissions in the roll may be corrected, but subject to this and to enrolment of any person entitled to be enrolled who signs an application for enrolment, no names are to be added or removed from the roll during the period between completion of the new roll and the annual parochial church meeting.[59]

The new roll is prepared by enrolling those who apply and are entitled to enrolment, (no person being excluded because they have not habitually attended public worship in the last six months when prevented by illness or other sufficient cause) and those whose sixteenth birthday falls between the date of preparation and the annual meeting.[60] A fresh application is required from all those whose names were entered on the previous roll.[61] On publication of the new roll the previous roll ceases to have effect.[62]

Not later than June 1 the chairman, vice-chairman, secretary or church electoral roll officer of the PCC must notify the secretary of the diocesan synod of the number of names on the roll of the parish at the date of the annual meeting.[63] When the notice is sent a copy of it must be affixed at or near the principal door of every church and building licensed for public worship in the parish and remain there for a period of not less than 14 days.[64]

An appeal lies in respect of any enrolment or refusal of enrolment on the roll of a parish or against the removal or refusal to remove any name from such a roll.[65] The appeal may be made by a person who is refused enrolment or whose name is removed from the roll or any person whose name is entered on the roll who wishes to object to the enrolment or removal of someone else's name.[66]

Notice of an appeal must be given in writing to the lay chairman of the deanery synod, not later than 14 days after the date of the enrolment, removal or

---

[54] *ibid.*, r. 2(4).

[55] *ibid.*, App. I, s.3.

[56] Or in the case of a church at which no service is held on either of those Sundays, at every service on the first Sunday after the notice is affixed: CRR, r. 2(4).

[57] *ibid.*, r. 2(5). No such efforts need be made in the case of a person whose name could be removed from the previous roll.

[58] *ibid.*, r. 2(6)(7).

[59] *ibid.*, r. 2(6)(7).

[60] *ibid.*, r. 2(6)(7).

[61] *ibid.*, r. 2(6)(7).

[62] *ibid.*, r. 2(6)(7).

[63] *ibid.*, r. 4.

[64] *ibid.*, r. 4.

[65] *ibid.*, r. 43(1).

[66] *ibid.*, r. 43(2).

refusal, or if the appeal arises on the revision or preparation of a new roll, not later than 14 days after publication of the same.[67] In any appeal the lay chairman of the deanery synod shall refer the appeal to the bishop's council and standing committee of the diocese unless within that time the appellant withdraws their appeal. The bishop's council shall then appoint three (or a greater but odd number) of their lay members to consider and decide the appeal.[68] The procedure for hearing such appeals, extending time limits, and the means of determining an appeal are the same as those set out in Chapter 2 in regard to appeals in respect of elections to the House of Laity of the General Synod.

4.47   It should be noted that an error in the electoral roll is not a ground of appeal against the result of any election unless it has either been determined that there is such an error or the question is awaiting determination and the error would or might be material to the result of the election.[69]

---

[67] *ibid.*, r. 43(3).
[68] *ibid.*, r. 43(4).
[69] *ibid.*, r. 43(3).

Chapter Five: The Benefice

As we saw in the previous chapter a parish differs from a benefice by being a **5.1** geographical area, whereas the latter is a freehold office. However, the rights of the incumbent who holds the benefice are now so limited that to describe them as being in possession of a freehold living is to suggest an arrangement which departs somewhat from the actual state of affairs. As the rights of the holder of the office have been curtailed so too have the rights of patrons to present an incumbent to a living. Advowsons or the right of patronage are no longer saleable and the exercise of patronage itself has been restricted by modern statutes.

Although it was in general the case that the incumbent of a benefice had the cure of the souls of a single parish, as we shall see this is frequently no longer so. Pastoral schemes and orders now make provision for the holding of benefices in plurality, for the union of benefices and for the establishment of team and group ministries.

In this chapter we look at the nature of a benefice and the rights and duties attached to it. We also look at the system of patronage and the restrictions upon the rights of the patron, together with the presentation and institution or collation of an incumbent to a benefice, and the restrictions upon the holding of benefices in plurality. We also consider the sequestration of benefices and their avoidance, examining in particular the procedure under the Incumbents (Vacation of Benefices) Measure 1977. We look at the potential for pastoral reorganisation under the provisions of the Pastoral Measure 1983, examining the scope of schemes and orders made pursuant to it and especially the creation of team and group ministries. Finally, we consider the operation of such team and group ministries.

Benefices

Between the seventh and thirteenth centuries when the parish structure first **5.2** came into being, churches were gradually established for most populated districts either by local nobles or by religious communities. In the case of the former these private individuals had effective control over the priest who was given the cure of souls of those in the area. In this way the system of private patronage arose. In the case of religious houses, collegiate churches or other religious corporations which could not perform the cure of souls themselves a priest was put in to the church to act in substitution and to fulfil the duties required, that priest being known as the vicar from the latin *vicarius* meaning substitute.

Churches received endowments and thus acquired property for the maintenance of the priest, glebe land from which the priest obtained a living being a common form of endowment. As the division into parishes developed the law recognised the *parochianus* or parson of the parish as a corporation sole, who in their representative capacity was capable of preserving for their successors in perpetuity the original endowments of the church.

The parishioners of each parish were subject to tithes; a tenth of their produce being given to the Church. Where the parish church was founded by a layman the priest appointed to the church was known as the rector and had the right to receive those tithes. However, where the church was founded by a religious community the priest appointed was the vicar and that community was the rector entitled to receive the tithes; provision being made for the vicar's endowment in perpetuity, initially by ecclesiastical constitutions and ordinances and later by statute.

A rectory is a benefice to which the whole of the tithe and any glebe land of the parish has always been attached for the maintenance of the priest. It is an essential feature of a rectory that some land is attached to it, although the church and churchyard will suffice.[1] Other benefices have been made rectories by statute.[2] Where a religious community or other religious corporation was the rector the rectory was said to be appropriated, the benefice occupied by the priest being termed a vicarage.[3] Following the Reformation and the dissolution of the monasteries many of these appropriated rectories passed into lay hands, and in such cases are known as impropriate rectories, the impropriator being referred to as the lay rector.

In addition to rectories[4] and vicarages (some of which were created by statute in the nineteenth century) a benefice might also have consisted of a perpetual curacy.[5] However, the holders of a perpetual curacy or any other benefice

---

[1] *Berry v. Wheeler* (1662) 1 Sid. 91.

[2] A benefice for which a team ministry is established under a pastoral schemes becomes a rectory if it is not one already; where a pastoral scheme provides for the union of two benefices one of which is a rectory; the new united benefice is a rectory; and where a pastoral scheme provides for the dissolution of a rectory; any new benefice created in consequence is a rectory if the scheme so provides: Pastoral Measure 1983, s.23.

[3] An incumbent who is not a rector but is authorised to solemnise marriages, churchings and baptisms and is entitled to receive for their own use the entire fees for the performance of these offices is designated the vicar of the parish, and their benefice the vicarage: Incumbents Act 1868, s.2 (repealed).

[4] This includes sinecure rectories which arose in some parishes where the rector acquired the right to obtain institution of both themselves and a vicar to the benefice so that together they had the cure of souls and the duty of officiating, but where over time these functions devolved upon the vicar alone so that rectory became a sinecure: Gibson, *Codex Juris Ecclesiastici Anglicani*, (2nd ed. 1761) p. 719.

[5] These curacies arose in cases where a religious community was exempt from appointing a vicar and could instead appoint a curate who had no endowment or possession of the church's endowments beyond that necessary to carry out their duties. Where the living later fell into the hands of lay impropriators they were bound to nominate a curate to serve the parish who was called a "perpetual curate" in recognition of the fact that the nominator had no power to remove them, once licensed by the bishop. A chapel which from time immemorial has had a district or chapelry attached to it, and whose inhabitants have had rights of baptism and burial and other spiritual services in it and not in the parish church and the fees for such services have been received by the minister of the chapel of right and custom is a parochial chapelry and was also a perpetual curacy whether or not it had endowments attached.

comprising a parish or parishes with full parochial status which is not a rectory or vicarage, are now vicars and their benefices vicarages.[6]

Although rare a church or chapel without a district may also in some instances be a benefice independent of the incumbent of the parish in which it is situated, since all churches, curacies or chapels which were augumented by the Queen Anne's Bounty (now the general fund of the Church Commissioners) thereupon became benefices or perpetual curacies.[7] The cure of souls in the parish in which they are situated remains in the incumbent of the parish church.[8] There may also be two or more benefices in the same church[9] and parish, held by different incumbents.[10]

Whether a benefice is a rectory or vicarage by reason of its historical origins or as the result of the application of statutory provisions will determine whether the incumbent should correctly be styled rector or vicar. However, beyond this the distinction is of little practical importance today.

Rights and duties of the incumbent

As we have already noted a benefice is a freehold office,[11] the holder of which is **5.3** usually styled the incumbent. The incumbent is a corporation sole[12] and has a freehold interest in the benefice until their death or until the benefice is otherwise legally vacated,[13] which now includes compulsory retirement at a specified age and removal under the procedures of the Incumbents (Vacation of Benefices) Measure 1977.

The subject of the incumbent's freehold and proposals for its abolition in favour of a "renewable term of years" has been debated by the General Synod on a number of occasions, most recently in 1995 when it accepted the recommendations of the Steering Group on Clergy Conditions not to proceed with reform of the system of freeholds, but no action has been taken.

The rights and duties of the incumbent in regard to the property of the church, its contents and the churchyard are explained in Chapter 8. The property of the benefice, namely the glebe land and parsonage house are also considered in that Chapter, as is the incumbent's entitlement to fees for the performance of certain offices and to a stipend. Here we examine the rights and duties of the incumbent in regard to the office itself rather than in respect of the property attached to it.

---

[6] As the result of the operation of the Pastoral Measure 1968, s.87 (repealed), although this section is not reproduced in the Pastoral Measure 1983.

[7] Queen Ann's Bounty Act 1714, s.4; *R. v. Bishop of Chester* (1786) 1 Term 396.

[8] Queen Ann's Bounty Act 1714, s.5.

[9] See, *e.g. Welch v. Bishop of Peterborough* (1885) 15 Q.B.D. 432.

[10] In such cases each benefice or portion of the whole benefice is called a mediety. After formal inquiry the bishop may apportion the spiritual duties between the incumbents, although there is no longer a statutory authority for so doing since the repeal of the Spiritual Duties Act 1839, s.1.

[11] *Kirton v. Dear* (1869) L.R. 5 C.P. 217 at 220.

[12] See Chap. 8.

[13] *Att.-Gen. v. Bereton* (1752) 2 Ves. Sen. 425 at 428; *Att.-Gen. v. Pearson* (1817) 3 Mer. 353 at 403; *Mason v. Lambert* (1848) 12 Q.B. 795 at 807.

The cure of souls

5.4   The bishop has the general cure of souls throughout the whole of his diocese[14] and therefore has the right to officiate personally at pleasure in any church within the diocese.[15] However, subject to the bishop's right the incumbent has the exclusive cure of souls within the parish and subject to the exceptions considered below no other clergy have any right to officiate publicly or perform clerical ministration without the incumbent's consent.[16] The incumbent is therefore the curate, although that term is now commonly used to refer to an assistant curate who serves under the incumbent.

The incumbent's exclusive right to the cure of souls is subject to the performance of offices and services, and in limited circumstances the solemnisation of matrimony, at any university, college, school, hospital, public or charitable institution within their parish by a minister licensed by the bishop to perform these.[17] It is also subject to the right of another minister to perform funeral services in certain circumstances.[18]

Furthermore, notwithstanding the incumbent's exclusive rights the minister of another parish may perform offices and services at the home of any person whose name is on the electoral roll of that minister's parish but who is resident in the incumbent's parish, provided that those present only include members of the family and household of that person.[19]

The incumbent's rights may also be forfeited by default, that is by a failure to perform duties,[20] although such a case would now be highly unusual. Finally, the exclusive right to the cure is subject to those instances where the ministry of another cleric is necessitated by urgent or weighty cause, for example exercising the ministry of absolution in respect of a person in danger of death.[21]

The incumbent may also consent to another member of the clergy exercising their ministry within the benefice, although in order to officiate such a minister will usually also require the authority of the bishop. The exception to the need to obtain the bishop's authority are cases when that cleric is minister for not more than seven days within a three-month period, or where they hold a licence to preach throughout the province or throughout England.[22]

All parochial duties are committed to and imposed upon the incumbent.[23] The rector (whether spiritual or lay) has the freehold of the church and churchyard,[24]

---

[14] *Duke of Portland v. Bingham* (1792) 1 Hag. Con. 157 at 161.
[15] However the bishop's right cannot be exercised by a deputy. Whether it may be exercised by a suffragan is unclear: *Halsbury's Laws of England* (4th ed.), Vol. 14, para. 690.
[16] *Clerke v. D, Prin v. Heath* (1669) 1 Mod. Rep. 11; *Duke of Portland v. Bingham (ante)*; *Carr v. Marsh* (1814) 2 Phil. Ecc. R. 198 at 206; *Farnworth v. Bishop of Chester* (1825) 4 B. & C. 555 at 568; *Nesbitt v. Wallace* [1901] P. 354.
[17] See further Chap. 6.
[18] See Chap. 10.
[19] Extra-parochial Ministry Measure 1967, s.1; Canon C8(4).
[20] *MacAllister v. Bishop of Rochester* (1880) 5 C.P.D. 194 at 203.
[21] Canon B29(4).
[22] See Chap. 7.
[23] *Moysey v. Hillcoat* (1828) 2 Hag. Ecc. 30 at 48. And all fees and emoluments arising from the performance of those duties belong to them: *ibid.* As to fees and stipends see Chap. 8.
[24] *Jones v. Ellis* (1828) 2 Y. & J. 265 at 275. And see Chap. 8.

but unless the rector and the incumbent are one does not have control over the cure of souls or performance of ministerial duties within the parish.[25] Since the incumbent has the exclusive cure of souls no church or chapel of ease or other public chapel may be consecrated by the bishop or a person licensed by the bishop to officiate in it without the consent of the incumbent.[26]

Duties of the incumbent

Canon C24 sets out the duties of those who have the cure of souls. An incumbent **5.5** must in the absence of reasonable hindrance, provide that Morning and Evening Prayer is said daily and that the Litany is said on appointed days in the church, or one of the churches, of which they are the minister.[27] Except for reasonable cause approved by the bishop of the diocese, they must celebrate or cause to be celebrated Holy Communion every Sunday and other great feast days and on Ash Wednesday,[28] and diligently administer the sacraments and other rites of the Church.[29] They must preach, or cause to be preached, a sermon in their church at least once each Sunday.[30] The incumbent must instruct, or cause the children to be instructed, in the Christian faith, and to use such opportunities of teaching or of visiting in the schools within their cure as are open to them. They must prepare carefully, or cause to be prepared, all such as desire to be confirmed and, if satisfied of their fitness, to present them to the bishop for confirmation. The incumbent is required diligently to visit their parishioners, particularly those who are sick and infirm, and to provide opportunities for any of their parishioners to resort to them for spiritual counsel and advice. They must also consult with the PCC on matters of general concern and importance to the parish.[31] If at any time the incumbent is unable to discharge their duties they must provide for the cure to be supplied by a priest, licensed or otherwise approved by the bishop of the diocese. It should be noted that these duties apply equally to a priest-in-charge during a vacancy in the benefice although they are not the incumbent.

Rights and duties in regard to performance of divine service

As well as the *duty* to provide for the conduct of divine service in all consecrated **5.6** places of worship within the benefice, the incumbent has the *right* to so provide,[32] and may, subject to complying with their duties, do so as they see fit for example, by authorising another minister to officiate.

[25] *Herbert v. Dean and Chapter of Westminster* (1721) 1 P.W. 773; *Att.-Gen. v. Bereton* (1752) 2 Ves. Sen. 425 at 428; *Duke of Portland v. Bingham* (1792) 1 Hag. Con. 157.

[26] *Carr v. Marsh* (1814) 2 Phil. Ecc. R. 198.

[27] As to the regular provision of statutory services and requirements relating thereto, see Chap. 9. Where the benefice comprises two or more parishes or chaplries the bishop may (in certain circumstances) direct that additional services be conducted on Sundays: Pluralities Act 1838, s.80.

[28] *ibid.*

[29] See also *Agar v. Holdsworth* (1758) 2 Lee. 515; *Kemp v. Wickes* (1809) 3 Phil. Ecc. R. 264 at 274; *R. v. James* (1850) 3 Car. & K. 167, C.C.R.

[30] See n. 27 *ante.*

[31] Canon C24(7); PCCPM, s.2(1).

[32] *Williams' Case* (1592) 5 Co. Rep. 72b; *Jones v. Stone* (1700) 1 Raym. 578; *Moysey v. Hillcoat* (1828) 2 Hag. Ecc. 30 at 46; *Rugg v. Bishop of Winchester* (1868) L.R. 2 P.C. 223

Where the benefice has more than one consecrated place of worship the incumbent commits an ecclesiastical offence of neglect of duty if they fail to provide for the performance of divine service in each,[33] or if they close one and disobey the bishop's order to perform a duty in it.[34] However, it appears that there is no obligation to perform all the services required of the incumbent in all places within the benefice if, for example, there are two or more parish churches.

The incumbent is bound to observe the legal requirements with reference to the performance of divine service,[35] but subject to this has control of the performance of divine service throughout the benefice.[36] Accordingly, save for the exceptions referred to above in regard to the cure of souls, no minister can perform divine service without the consent of a resident incumbent.[37]

In general the incumbent has the right to perform divine service in any consecrated building within their benefice without the licence of the bishop.[38] The exceptions are chapels of schools, hospitals and other institutions to which another minister is licensed by the bishop.[39] The incumbent also has no jurisdiction in respect of any other extra-parochial places.[40] It is doubtful that the incumbent has an absolute right to perform divine service in a private or proprietary chapel given that both constitute private property.

Holy Communion must not be celebrated in a building not consecrated or licensed for the purpose without permission from the bishop.[41] It would appear that technically the incumbent requires the bishop's licence to officiate at other services in unconsecrated or unlicensed buildings, but not it would seem for a service in the open air.[42-43]

Residential requirements

5.7 The term incumbent derives from the latin *incumbo*, in the sense of being diligently resident on the benefice, and residence requirements still apply to an incumbent today. An incumbent must reside on the benefice (or if they hold two

---

[33] *Bishop of Llandaff v. Belcher* (1687) *Rothery's Precedents*, no. 19, p. 42; *Hancock v. Bomer* (1692) *Rothery's Precedents*, no. 99, p. 47; *Jones v. Curtis* (1715) *Rothery's Precedents*, no. 119, p. 58; *Rugg v. Bishop of Winchester* (1868) L.R. 2 P.C. 223 at 234, 236, 237.

[34] *Rugg v. Bishop of Winchester* (1868) L.R. 2 P.C. 223 and see Chap. 11 regarding neglect of duty.

[35] *Parnell v. Roughton* (1874) L.R. 6 P.C. 46.

[36] *Hutchins v. Denziloe and Loveland* (1792) 1 Hag. Con. 170; *Wood v. Headingley-cum-Burley Burial Board* [1892] 1 Q.B. 713 at 729.

[37] *Carr v. Marsh* (1814) 2 Phil. Ecc. R. 198; *Farnworth v. Bishop of Chester* (1825) 4 B. & C. 555 at 568; *Hodgson v. Dillon* (1840) 2 Curt. 388 at 392; *Jones v. Jelf* (1863) 8 L.T. 399 at 401; *Richards v. Fincher* (1873) L.R. 4 A. & E. 107.

[38] *Moysey v. Hillcoat* (1828) 2 Hag. Ecc. 30 at 48. It is not for the incumbent to alienate this right since they have only a life interest and cannot injure their successors nor reduce the value of the advowson by diminishing the income of the benefice: *ibid.*

[39] As to which see Chap. 6.

[40] See Chap. 6.

[41] See Chap. 10.

[42-43] *Halsbury's Laws of England* (4th ed.), Vol. 14, para. 690 citing *Moysey v. Hillcoat (ante)*; *Finch v. Harris* (1702) 12 Mod. Rep. 640; *Bishop of Down v. Miller* (1861) 11 I. Ch. R. App. 1; *Kitson v. Drury* (1865) 29 J.P. 643; *Richard v. Fincher* (1874) L.R. 4 A. & E. 255 at 262; Canon C8(2).

benefices on one of them) and in the house of residence belonging to the benefice if there is such a house.[44] An incumbent who is also a member of a cathedral or collegiate body may include residence at these as equivalent to residence in the benefice if they are not absent from the benefice for more than five months in a calendar year.[45] Otherwise an incumbent must not be absent from their benefice for more than a total of three months in any one year unless they have a licence permitting non-residence or a legal exemption.[46] If an incumbent fails to reside monition may be issued requiring them to do so and failing this, if the non-residence persists (and subject to rights of appeal), part or all of the emoluments of the benefice may be forfeited.[47] The incumbent may petition the bishop for a licence to reside out of the house of residence, or outside the benefice, or outside the geographical limits normally permissable in such cases.[48] A licence may be granted by the bishop if he considers it appropriate after being satisfied of the facts on the following grounds: that the incumbent is incapable in mind or body[49]; that the parsonage house is unfit for residence (other than through negligence or default of the incumbent) and no fit house can be obtained; that the incumbent wishes to reside within their own house within the parish (provided the house of residence is kept in good repair); on account of the dangerous illness of the incumbent's spouse or a child of the family residing with them (for a period not exceeding six months, such permission only being renewable with the archbishop's permission).[50]

If the bishop refuses to grant such a licence an appeal may be made to the **5.8** archbishop within one month of that refusal, the archbishop either confirming the refusal or ordering the bishop to grant the licence, as he considers just.[51] The bishop may also grant a licence in other suitable cases to the extent allowed by the archbishop to whom the matter must be referred for approval or for disallowance of the licence in whole or part.[52]

Any licence granted only continues in force until the end of the calendar year in which it was issued,[53] or for a shorter period specified within it. An incumbent who is non-resident with the bishop's licence may not resume the duties of the benefice before the expiration of the period set out in the licence and, if non-

---

[44] Canon C25(1); *Butler & Goodale's Case* (1598) 6 Co. Rep. 21b; *Wilkinson v. Allot* (1776) 2 Cowp. 429; *Wright v. Legge* (1815) 6 Taun. 48; *Wright v. Flamank* (1815) 6 Taun. 52.

[45] Pluralities Act 1838, s.39. Certain other persons such as deans of cathedrals or collegiate churches, those holding readerships in the universities or serving as a chaplain to the Sovereign or certain other Royal persons or as chaplain to a bishop or archbishop are also permitted temporary non-residence whilst engaged on those duties: *ibid.*, s.38.

[46] *ibid.*, s.32; Canon C25(2).

[47] Pluralities Act 1838, ss.54–56. As an alternative to a monition to reside the bishop may seek penalties: *ibid.* The forfeiture is recoverable in the consistory court with payment enforceable by monition and sequestration: *ibid.*, ss.113, 114.

[48] These limits are set out in the Pluralities Act 1838 and are the limits for which a bishop would otherwise grant a licence on the grounds that there is no fit house of residence: Pluralities Act 1838, s.43.

[49] It should also be noted that pursuant to the provisions of the Incumbents (Vacation of Benefices) Measure 1977 the bishop may also grant leave of absence for up to two years to an incumbent unable to discharge his duties, as to which see below.

[50] *ibid.*, s.43; Canon C25(3), (4).

[51] *ibid.*, s.43; Canon C25(3), (4).

[52] Pluralities Act 1838, s.44.

[53] *ibid.*, s.46.

resident for more than 12 months cannot interfere with the duties of the benefice entrusted to a curate or curates by the bishop.[54]

Any licence permitting non-residence may be revoked by either the bishop or archbishop for good cause provided that the incumbent has been given an opportunity to show why it should not be revoked. If the revocation is by the bishop an appeal lies to the archbishop within one month of the revocation.[55]

Patronage

Advowsons

5.9   A minister's right to hold a benefice is acquired by their being presented to the benefice, that right of presentation being known as an advowson or right of patronage, and the holder of the right being called the patron. An advowson is a temporal right[56] which used to be regarded as a valuable property right, although now it can no longer be sold or transferred for valuable consideration.[57] Although an advowson no longer has a financial value it is still an important right. The law in regard to rights of patronage and the exercise of rights of presentation was modernised and simplified to a large extent by the Patronage (Benefices) Measure 1986.[57a]

---

[54] Pluralities Acts Amendment Act 1885, s.12.

[55] Pluralities Act 1838, s.49. No right of appeal is provided for where revocation is by the archbishop.

[56] It is an incorporeal hereditament: *Mirehouse v. Rennell* (1833) 1 Cl. & Fin 527 at 604, H.L.

[57] Patronage (Benefices) Measure 1986, s.3(1). The section applies to a transfer *inter vivos* but not to transfers by operation of law, upon the appointment of a new trustee or a transfer by the personal representatives of a deceased person: *ibid.*, s.3(9). Even when a transfer is not for valuable consideration special provisions apply. A pastoral scheme or order may make provision, with the consent of the registered patron or patrons and the person to whom the right is to be transferred, for a transfer. In cases where a right is to be transferred other than by a pastoral scheme or order the consents of the registered patron and the person to whom the right is being transferred are again required and the potential transferor must send to the bishop (or archbishop where the bishop is patron) and diocesan registrar a notice in the prescribed form stating specified particulars. The registrar must send the notice to the secretary of the relevant PCC giving an opportunity for the council to make representations within one month of the date the notice was sent. Any representations must be copied to the proposed transferor and be considered by the bishop, who may request the proposed transferor to consult with him whether or not any representations have been made. However, it would appear that the bishop's consent is only required in the case of a transfer by an ecclesiastical corporation: *ibid.* s.3. Where any advowson is held on trust for sale (or would be if the advowson were capable of sale), the trustees may transfer the advowson gratuitously to certain specified persons and bodies, and similarly the tenant for life of settled land may make a grant in fee simple of an advowson gratuitously to such bodies or persons: *ibid.*, ss.3, 33.

[57a] The Measure has been supplemented by the *Code of Practice on the Exercise of Rights of Presentation under the Patronage (Benefices) Measure 1986*, (1988), published on the authority of the Standing Committee of the General Synod of the Church of England.

Registration of patrons and their rights

By virtue of the Patronage (Benefices) Measure 1986 the functions of a patron **5.10** may only be exercised if the patron is registered.[58] The registrar of each diocese is required by the 1986 Measure to compile and keep a register of the patron or patrons of each benefice in the diocese and the nature of their interest.[59] That register is open to inspection by the public.[60] Any person to whom a right of patronage is transferred must now apply for registration within 12 months from the date of transfer.[61] In cases where there is no registered patron the diocesan board of patronage becomes the patron.[62] Registration is conclusive evidence of the matters registered,[63] In cases where a person is either already registered as a patron or applies for registration and the registrar decides that they should not be registered, procedures exist for the determination of the dispute between them.[64] A procedure also exists for determination of disputes where the registrar decides that information registered, or which a patron wishes to be registered, as to the exercise of a right ought not to be registered.[65] In the case of any such dispute the registrar is required to serve notice upon the person informing them of the decision and of their rights of appeal. That person may then appeal against the decision within 28 days of the date of the registrar's notice. Any appeal is referred to the chancellor of the diocese who decides whether to uphold the appeal or dismiss it. Appeal proceedings before the chancellor are to held in public and any party to the proceedings may be represented by a barrister or solicitor.[66] A procedure exists for the rectification of the register.[67]

Diocesan board of patronage

In each diocese there is a diocesan board of patronage consisting of the diocesan **5.11** bishop (who may not be elected chairman), three members elected by the House of Clergy of the diocesan synod and five laymen elected by the House of Laity of the diocesan synod. To these are added the archdeacon and both chairmen of the deanery synod in whose jurisdiction any benefice in respect of which business is to be transacted is situated.[68] The board may acquire, hold and transfer rights of patronage,[69] and may exercise any rights of patronage held.[70] As we have seen the board becomes the patron of any benefice where there is no registered patron.

---

[58] Patronage (Benefices) Measure 1986, s.1(2).

[59] *ibid.*, s.1(1); Patronage (Benefices) Rules 1987, S.I. 1987 No. 773, r. 2.

[60] Patronage (Benefices) Measure 1986, s.1(5).

[61] *ibid.*, Sched. 1, para. 4.

[62] *ibid.*, s.25.

[63] Patronage (Benefices) Measure 1986, ss.1(4), 2. The register is in a prescribed form as set forth in the Patronage (Benefices) Rules 1987, S.I. 1987 No. 773.

[64] Patronage (Benefices) Measure 1986, Sched. 1, paras. 7–9.

[65] *ibid.*

[66] The practice or procedure in connection with proceedings on such an appeal is contained in the Patronage (Appeals) Rules 1988, S.I. 1988 No. 1980.

[67] Patronage (Benefices) Measure 1986, s. 4, Sched. 1, para. 5. Save that no rectification may be made where the entry has been adverse to the claim of any person for more than 30 years or the benefice has been adversely held to a claim for the same period.

[68] Patronage (Benefices) Measure 1986, ss.26, 27, Sched. 3.

[69] However, no transfer may be made without the consent of the relevant PCC except where transfer is incidental to a transfer of the parish as between dioceses: *ibid.*

[70] Patronage (Benefices) Measure 1986, ss.26, 27, Sched. 3.

Particular patrons and their rights

5.12 A patron may be an individual or the right may belong to an office,[71] the most common being cases where the diocesan bishop is patron in which case he collates rather than presents his nominee. Both Her Majesty and the Duke of Cornwall possess the patronage or a share in the patronage of certain benefices. The extent to which their rights are affected by the Patronage (Benefices) Measure 1986 and special provisions relating to such benefices are set out in section 35 of that Measure, whilst section 36 applies those provisions to benefices in the patronage of the Lord Chancellor.[72]

The Sovereign is also the patron paramount of all other benefices. Although the Sovereign's right to fill benefices upon lapse has now been abolished (that right vesting in the diocesan board of patronage) the right to fill continues in two cases: first, where a benefice becomes vacant due to the promotion of its holder to a bishopric, and secondly, where a vacancy in a benefice of which the diocesan bishop is the registered patron occurs during a vacancy in the see.[73]

Certain patrons are under a disability. Thus where the patron is a minor the presentation is made by trustees since the legal estate vests in them. Where the patron is a patient under the Mental Health Act the right to present vests in the Lord Chancellor.[74] The 1986 Measure contains provisions for the exercise of patronage by the personal representatives of a deceased patron.[75]

Where patronage previously vested in the vestry of a parish (including cases where it vested in, or in trust for, parishioners) it now vests in the PCC.[76] Where the PCC is the registered patron the 1986 Measure makes modifications to the usual provisions regarding the procedure for presentation.[77]

Where the incumbent of another benefice is the registered patron and that other benefice is vacant or sequestered or the incumbent suspended or disqualified the bishop exercises the right of patronage.[78] In all other cases where as a result of censure a clerk in holy orders is suspended or inhibited from carrying out any of the duties attached to their preferment, any right of patronage which vests in them by reason of that preferment vests in the person entitled to appoint to the preferment during the period of suspension or inhibition.[79] It should also

---

[71] *ibid.*, s.2.

[72] Most of the provisions of the 1986 Measure do not apply to Crown benefices or those in the patronage of the Lord Chancellor. In particular there is no obligation to consult parish representatives although it has been stated, in answer to a question at the July 1994 group of sessions of the General Synod, that in practice the Crown or Lord Chancellor does consult them without being bound by their views. The provisions of the Priests (Ordination of Women) Measure 1993, ss.2, 3, are applied to Crown benefices and those in the patronage of the Lord Chancellor by s.7(1) of the 1993 Measure.

[73] Patronage (Benefices) Measure 1986, s.31.

[74] Mental Health Act 1983, ss.94, 96(5).

[75] Patronage (Benefices) Measure 1986, s.21.

[76] PCCPM 1956, s.4(1)(i); *Re Litchfield Cathedral Grant, Chapel-en-le-Firth PCC v. Bagshaw* (1929) 45 T.L.R. 583. And where the right vests in the inhabitants or parishioners the majority of electors are entitled to nominate: *Att.-Gen. v. Parker* (1747) 3 Atk. 576; *Edenborough v. Archbishop of Canterbury* (1826) 2 Russ. 93; *Att.-Gen. v. Cuming* (1843) 2 Y. & C. 139.

[77] Patronage (Benefices) Measure 1986, s.23, Sched. 2.

[78] *ibid.*, s.20.

[79] *ibid.*, s.22.

be noted that the 1986 Measure permits the exchange of benefices by incumbents subject to the agreement of the bishop of the diocese of each benefice, the registered patron whose turn it is to present to either benefice and the PCC of each benefice.[80]

The right of presentation or legal patronage, may be vested in one person, whilst the right of nomination is vested in another. In such a case the legal patron is trustee for the nominator and is bound to present their nominee to the bishop.[81] Similarly, where the legal estate vests in trustees they are bound to present the nominee of the persons equitably interested.[82]

Generally where the right of patronage is vested in co-owners the bishop may accept the presentation of one[83] but is not bound to act on a presentation in which they do not all concur.[84] The right of patronage may also be exercised by several persons in turn. If one of several part-patrons presents out of turn and the presentee is instituted or admitted this is a usurption and the patron entitled to the turn loses it for that cycle.[85] The turn is complete when the presentee is instituted or admitted.

Provision for rights of patronage purusuant to a pastoral scheme

Pastoral schemes may provide for vesting the patronage of the benefice in a **5.13** patron or patrons and where necessary, for determining the manner in which the right of patronage may be exercised.[86] Unless the scheme provides otherwise the patron of any new benefice is the diocesan board of patronage.[87] Regard must be had to the interests of those persons whose right of patronage will cease to exist by virtue of any scheme and to the interests of patrons of benefices to be held in plurality.[88] Where there are pastoral or practical objections a scheme need not provide for new rights of patronage to be conferred on any or all such patrons, nor for sharing the exercise of rights where benefices are to be held in plurality.[89]

Sequestration and other restrictions on the exercise of patronage

In certain cases, most notably under provisions contained within the Pastoral **5.14** Measure 1983, the patron's rights of patronage may be restricted.

---

[80] EJM, s.76.
[81] Gibson *Codex Juris Ecclesiastici Anglicani*, (2nd ed. 1761) p. 794.
[82] *Burn's Ecclesiastical Law* (4th ed., 1842), Vol. 1, p. 15.
[83] *Fuliambe's Case* (1539) Moore K.B. 4.
[84] And he may in due course collate if the right lapses before the co-owners can reach agreement: *Coke on Littleton, Institutes*, (4th ed. 1639), Vol. 1, p. 186b; Gibson, *Codex Juris Ecclesiastici Anglicani*, (2nd ed. 1761), p. 94. If the bishop does act on a presentation in which they do not concur, the common title is not disturbed since the advowson is not severable: *Coke on Littleton, Institutes*, (4th ed. 1639), Vol. 1, p. 186b; *Coke's Institutes*, Vol. x, p. 243a; *Barker v. Bishop of London* (1752) 1 Hyde 412n at 417.
[85] *Richards v. Earl of Macclesfield* (1835) 7 Sim. 257; *Keen v. Denny* [1894] 3 Ch. 169.
[86] Pastoral Measure 1983, s.32.
[87] Pastoral Measure 1983, s.32.
[88] *ibid*.
[89] *ibid*.

The diocesan bishop may suspend presentation during a vacancy in the benefice or within three months before the benefice is due to become vacant.[90] Before so doing he is required to obtain the consent of the pastoral committee, which suggests that such suspension may only occur pending the making of a pastoral scheme or order.[91] The bishop is also required to consult with the registered patron or patrons (unless the patron is the bishop himself or the patron's rights have lapsed) and the PCC of the relevant parish or parishes and both chairmen of the deanery synod of the deanery concerned.[92]

After consultation the bishop gives notice that during a specified period (not exceeding five years) the patron must not exercise the right of presentation without the consent of the pastoral committee and the bishop.[93] Notice must be given to the Church Commissioners, the registered patron or patrons (unless he is the bishop), both chairmen of the relevant deanery synod, the churchwardens of the relevant parish, and the sequestrators if these have been appointed, and a copy must be filed in the diocesan registry.[94] The churchwardens must affix the notice at or near the door of the parish church or (if there is none) the principal place of worship in the parish.[95] The bishop may suspend the right of presentation, even though that right is already restricted, pending the making of a pastoral scheme or order.[96] The suspension period may be extended for further periods, each not exceeding five years, by further notice.[97] The period of suspension ends if consent is given to presentation by the patron, or if the bishop gives notice (with the consent of the pastoral committee) terminating the period, or if a pastoral scheme or order provides for the holding of the benefice in plurality or otherwise provides for the suspension period to be terminated.[98] Where the right of presentation is suspended time does not run for the purposes of lapse.[99]

Where a suspension period has been declared by the bishop he must sequester the profits of the benefice during that period and must ensure that in appointing sequestrators one of those appointed is specially qualified by training or experience to discharge efficiently the duties of the office.[1] The sequestrators must make provision for the performance during the suspension period of the ecclesiastical duties of the benefice acting in accordance with directions from the bishop.[2] Before he gives any such directions, or if he proposes to appoint a priest-

---

[90] *ibid.*, s.67(1), (2).
[91] *ibid.* This question was raised in the case of the suspension of presentation of St Lukes, Kingston by the Bishop of Southwark in which leave to judicially review the actions of the bishop was granted by the High Court in 1996, but the case was settled before coming on for hearing. As to the functions of the pastoral committee see below.
[92] Pastoral Measure 1983, s.67(1), (2).
[93] *ibid.*
[94] Pastoral Measure 1983, s.67(6).
[95] *ibid.*, s.67(7).
[96] *ibid.*, s.69(4).
[97] *ibid.*, s.67(5).
[98] *ibid.*, s.67(4).
[99] *ibid.*, s.72.
[1] *ibid.*, s.68(1). The provisions of *ibid.*, Sched. 7 have effect with regard to the management of the property of the benefice and application of the profits: *ibid.*, s.68(5). As to sequestration generally see below.
[2] *ibid.*, s.68(2), (3).

in-charge, the bishop must consult the PCC of any relevant parish and also, so far as practicable, the patron.[3]

Where the pastoral committee of the diocese is considering certain matters which may lead to a pastoral scheme or order being made, the diocesan bishop may, upon receiving notice of a vacancy or impending vacancy in a benefice, give notice of this fact.[4] Notice must be given to the registered patron or patrons, the PCC and both chairmen of the deanery synod of the deanery concerned.[5] The notice prevents the exercise of the right of presentation without the consent of the pastoral committee or the bishop,[6] although it cannot restrict Crown and certain other rights of patronage without the consent of the Sovereign.[7] The restriction lasts for a year from notification unless proposals are submitted within that period to the Church Commissioners by the pastoral committee containing recommendations which would affect the benefice concerned.[8] Where the right of presentation is suspended time does not run for the purposes of lapse.[9]

Where a benefice is vacant when a registered patron receives a copy of **5.15** proposals for a pastoral scheme or order submitted to the Church Commissioners, or becomes vacant thereafter, the patron may not exercise the right of presentation without the consent of pastoral committee or bishop until occurrence of certain specified events.[10] Those events are the implementation of the scheme or order (in which case the rights of presentation are subject to that scheme or order); withdrawal or the disallowance of the proposals, scheme or order; the ommission of the relevant provisions from the scheme or order; and the expiry of a period of three years from the date the patron is sent the proposals. Again under such suspension time does not run for the purposes of lapse.[11]

One further restriction exists upon the exercise of the right of patronage, which prevents self presentation. If the registered patron or their representative is a clerk in holy orders or the spouse of such a clerk, that clerk is disqualified from being presented to that benefice, and such presentation is void.[12]

Procedure relating to presentation

The Patronage (Benefices) Measure 1986 sets out the procedure to be followed **5.16** in regard to the exercise of rights of presentation to a benefice. Once a benefice becomes vacant by reason of the death of the incumbent, or is likely to become vacant because of retirement, cessation (when the holder of the benefice is appointed to another ecclesiastical office) or resignation, the bishop must give

---

[3] Pastoral Measure 1983, s.68(2), (3).
[4] *ibid.*, s.69(2).
[5] *ibid.*, s.69(2).
[6] *ibid.*, s.69(2).
[7] *ibid.*, s.81(1).
[8] *ibid.*, s.69(3).
[9] *ibid.* s.72.
[10] *ibid.*, s.32.
[11] *ibid.* s.72.
[12] Benefices Act 1898 (Amendment) Measure 1923, s.3; Patronage (Benefices) Measure 1986, s.10.

notice of the vacancy to the registered patron (or patrons) and the secretary of the relevant PCC.[13] In cases where a suspension period has been declared or any restriction comes into force the bishop may not issue such a notice, and any notice which was given before the suspension or restriction came into force is deemed to be revoked with the consequence that anything done in pursuance of it has no effect.[14]

On receipt of the bishop's notice of the vacancy a patron who is an individual and who is not a clerk in holy orders must (if they are able) make a written declaration that they are an actual communicant member of the Church of England or of a Church in communion with it.[15] If the patron is unable to make the declaration of membership, or they are is able to make the declaration but are unable to discharge their functions as patron for any other reason, they may appoint a representative to act in their stead.[16] That representative may be either an individual who is able and willing to make the declaration of membership, or a clerk in holy orders, or certain specified bodies.[17]

Where the patron is a body of persons (whether corporate or unincorporate), an individual able and willing to make the declaration of membership or a clerk in holy orders must be appointed to discharge the functions of patron.[18] Where the right to present belongs to a non-ecclesiastical office the office-holder must likewise make the declaration of membership or appoint some other person to act as their representative, as must anyone who possesses the power of attorney with the consequence that the right of presentation is exercisable by them.[19]

In all cases the declaration of membership and the details of any individual who is to act as representative must be sent to the designated officer of the diocese within a specified time.[20] Failure to do so results in the loss of certain rights of the patron including a meeting with the PCC and the bishop and the right to offer to present a priest to the benefice.[21]

Within four weeks of the date on which notice of the vacancy is sent to its secretary the PCC must hold a meeting or meetings,[22] at which neither the outgoing incumbent, their spouse, the patron or the patron's representative are entitled to attend,[23] regardless of whether or not they would normally be entitled to attend as members of the PCC.

---

[13] Patronage (Benefices) Measure 1986, s.7; Canon C9(1).

[14] Pastoral Measure 1983, s.70. The benefice is deemed vacant upon the suspension period or restriction coming to an end: *ibid.*

[15] Patronage (Benefices) Measure 1986, s.8. An "actual communicant member" means either a member of the Church of England who is confirmed or ready and desirous of being confirmed, or a communicant member of a Church in communion with the Church of England, who has received Communion according to the use of the Church of England, or of a Church in communion with it at least three times during the twelve months preceding the date on which they make the declaration of membership: *ibid.*, s.39(1). As to churches in communion with the Church of England see Chap. 12.

[16] Patronage (Benefices) Measure 1986, s.8.

[17] *ibid.*

[18] Patronage (Benefices) Measure 1986, s.8.

[19] *ibid.*

[20] *ibid.*, s. 9.

[21] *ibid.*, s.14.

[22] *ibid.*, s.11(1).

[23] *ibid.*, s.11(2). Provision is made for the replacement of such a representative should they die or be unable to act for any reason: *ibid.*, s.11(4).

At such a meeting the PCC is to appoint two of its lay members to act as its representatives in selecting an incumbent.[24] A deaconess or lay worker licensed to the parish is disqualified from acting as such a lay parish representative of the parish, as are the spouse of the outgoing incumbent or the patron or patron's registered representatives if they are members of the PCC.[25] In the absence of appointment of two parish representatives by a meeting of the PCC two churchwardens who are members of the PCC are to act.[26] However, a church-warden who is the registered patron cannot act as a parish representative nor choose a churchwarden to act as such, and in any case where only one churchwarden is qualified to act for whatever reason they may be the sole parish representative.[27] Curiously any representative of the patron or spouse of the outgoing incumbent is not excluded, and if such a person were the only churchwarden qualified to act it seems that they must do so, and where there is only one churchwarden qualified who could do so.[27a]

At one such meeting the PCC is also required to prepare a statement **5.17** describing the conditions, needs and traditions of the parish and must decide whether to request a written statement from the bishop as to the needs of the diocese and the wider interests of the Church in relation to the benefice.[28] It must also decide whether to request a joint meeting with the patron and the bishop and whether to request the patron to consider advertising the vacancy.[29] The PCC as a whole must consider whether to pass a resolution that it will not accept a woman as the minister who presides at or celebrates Holy Communion or pronounces the Absolution in the parish, or a resolution rescinding an earlier resolution which was to this effect.[30] It should be noted that where the benefice comprises two or more parishes or the benefice is held in plurality or where a team council or joint PCC is established these provisions and those relating to meetings of the PCC are modified.[31]

In any case where the PCC fails to prepare a statement or does not request a joint meeting and the patron is the bishop, he may make an offer to collate any

---

[24] Patronage (Benefices) Measure 1986, s.11(1).

[25] *ibid.*, s.11(3).

[26] *ibid.*, s.11(5), (6).

[27] *ibid.*, s.11(5), (6).

[27a] Even though they would not be entitled to attend certain meetings of the PCC at which various decisions in regard to the selection of a new incumbent are taken, nor in the case of the outgoing incumbent's spouse could they attend a joint meeting of the patron, bishop and PCC: *ibid.*, s.11(1). The position would be curious, to say the least and for the representative of the patron would involve an inevitable conflict of interest. It is recommended that any parish in such a position should seek legal advice.

[28] Patronage (Benefices) Measure 1986, s.11(1).

[29] Patronage (Benefices) Measure 1986, s.11(1)

[30] Pursuant to the Priests (Ordination of Women) Measure 1993, s.3(1): *ibid.*, s.3(7). As to the issue of women priests generally, see Chap. 7.

[31] Patronage (Benefices) Measure 1986, s.23, Sched. 2. Thus each parish must be notified of a vacancy and must hold one or more joint meetings of their PCCs to appoint at least four persons (so as to enable each PCC to have at least one representative) to act as representatives in the selection of an incumbent and to perform other functions required by the 1986 Measure. In particular, at such a meeting or first meeting the PCCs must decide whether to prepare a joint statement of the conditions, needs and traditions of each parish in the benefice or whether each parish should prepare such a statement: *ibid.*

priest whom he sees fit to the benefice (in other words, place them in the office) without making any request for approval of the parish representatives.[32] In all other cases the patron is entitled to proceed to make an offer to any priest without the consent of the parish representatives, but still requires the consent of the bishop.[33] Should the bishop refuse to consent the patron is entitled to be given reasons for that refusal and seek review by the archbishop as described below.

As we have seen the PCC must decide whether to request a joint meeting with the patron and bishop. Similarly both the patron and the bishop have a right to request such a meeting by sending notice to the secretary of the PCC.[34] If any of these so requests a joint meeting then a meeting of the PCC, the patron (and if the patron is not the bishop) the bishop, must be held to exchange views on the statements of the needs of the parish and diocese.[35] The statement as to the needs of the diocese may be presented orally by the bishop unles either the PCC or the patron have requested that this be put in writing.[36] This joint meeting must be held within a period of six weeks beginning on the date when the meeting was first requested, at least 14 days' notice being given of the time and place unless all concerned agree a shorter period. The meeting is only treated as having been held if the bishop and the patron (or the persons appointed to attend on their respective behalfs) are present, together with one-third of the members of the PCC entitled to attend.[37] Once again the outgoing incumbent and their spouse are not so entitled. Both the rural dean of the relevant deanery (unless they are the outgoing incumbent) and the lay chairman of the relevant deanery synod must be invited to attend,[38] but their attendance is not compulsory.

5.18   Where a joint meeting was requested no offer may be made to a prospective incumbent by the patron unless such a meeting has been held, or it was agreed by all parties that it should not be held, or the prescribed period of time for holding it has expired.[39] The making of an offer must be approved by the parish representatives and (unless he is the patron) the bishop.[40] If the parish representatives do not respond within two weeks from the date on which the patron sends them a request to approve an offer to a prospective incumbent, they are deemed to have given their approval.[41]

If either the parish representatives or bishop refuses to approve the making of an offer they must notify the patron of the grounds of their refusal.[42] The patron is then entitled to request the archbishop to review the matter. The archbishop may authorise such an offer, save that he cannot approve an offer where refusal was purely on grounds of gender and a relevant declaration or resolution under

---

[32] *ibid.*, s.15.
[33] *ibid.*, s.15.
[34] *ibid.*, s.12.
[35] *ibid.*, s.12.
[36] *ibid.*, s.12.
[37] *ibid.*, s.12.
[38] *ibid.*, s.12.
[39] *ibid.*, s.13(1), (2).
[40] *ibid.*, s.13(1), (2).
[41] *ibid.*, s.13(3).
[42] *ibid.*, s.13(4), (5).

the Priests (Ordination of Women) Measure 1993 is in force which would be contravened by such an offer.[43]

Presentation to benefices remaining vacant for nine months

Where a priest accepts an offer which has been made to them by the patron in **5.19** accordance with the terms of the 1986 Measure the patron must (unless they are bishop) send a notice to the bishop presenting that priest for institution to the benefice.[44] If the bishop does not receive a notice of presentation, or where he is the patron no acceptance of his offer to collate a priest has been received, within nine months[45] of the benefice becoming vacant, the right of presentation becomes exercisable by the archbishop of the province.[46]

Nothing in the 1986 Measure affects the power of a bishop to refuse to institute or admit a presentee,[47] a matter considered below. A bishop may not institute or collate any person to a benefice unless the relevant notice is served upon the secretary of the PCC, and a period of three weeks has expired from the date the notice was served.[48] The secretary of the PCC must cause the notice or a copy of it to be affixed (and remain for two weeks) at or near the principal door of every church in the parish and every building licensed for public worship, and take such other steps as they consider expedient for publicising the notice, and must sign an endorsement that these requirements have been complied with at the expiry of the period.[49] Thereafter the bishop should proceed to institution as speedily as possible, preferably in the parish church of the benefice,[50] a procedure described below.

Disturbance of patronage

Now that a patron is required to be registered pursuant to the 1986 Measure the **5.20** possibility of the patron's right being disturbed must in most cases be remote. Disturbance occurs when a pretending patron (that is a person not entitled to make the presentation) presents a minister to the benefice or when such a minister demands or obtains institution or admission to the benefice. It may also occur where the bishop institutes or admits a minister presented by a pretending patron or if he collates such a minister when he is not the patron, or refuses or unduly delays instituting or admitting a minister presented by the rightful

---

[43] *ibid.*, As to such declarations and resolutions, see Chap. 7.

[44] *ibid.*, s.13(6).

[45] Subject to certain exclusion periods where the rights of presentation are suspended, restricted or where the refusal of the bishop to approve an offer is the subject of a review by the archbishop: *ibid.*, s.16(2).

[46] *ibid.*, s.16. This right is subject to certain provisions as to the procedure to be adopted: *ibid.*

[47] *ibid.*, s.17(1).

[48] *ibid.*, s.19(1); Patronage (Benefice) Rules 1987, S.I. 1987 No. 773, r. 12.

[49] Patronage (Benefices) Measure 1986, s.19(2); Patronage (Benefice) Rules 1987, S.I. 1987 No. 773, r. 13.

[50] Canon C10(4).

patron.[51] It is suggested that now only in this final case is disturbance now likely to occur. The grounds on which a bishop may refuse to admit or institute are considered later in this chapter.

There are four remedies for disturbance, an appeal to the archbishop and the Dean of Arches and Auditor; an action of *quare impedit*; a suit of *duplex querela*; or a *jus patronus*. In particular this latter remedy, the purpose of which is to establish in the consistory court who is the true patron, must be in effect obsolete in view of the 1986 Measure and its procedure for resolving disputes as to the person entitled to be registered as patron, and is thus not considered further.

An amended procedure now exists for cases where a bishop refuses to institute or admit a presentee on a ground of unfitness or disqualification which is sufficient in law to justify that refusal, but which is a ground other than one of doctrine or ritual. The bishop must set out the grounds of refusal in writing to both the patron and the presentee,[52] either of whom may appeal within one month thereafter to a tribunal consisting of the archbishop of the relevant province and the Dean of the Arches and Auditor.[53] Such appeals must be held in public and any party is entitled to be represented by either a barrister or solicitor.[54] After hearing the appeal the archbishop and the Dean of the Arches and Auditor may either direct institution or admission or uphold the decision of the bishop, their judgment in the matter being final.[55]

Where the bishop refuses to institute or admit on the ground of unfitness on a ground of doctrine or ritual an action in the nature of a *quare impedit*[56] can be brought in the secular courts, the procedure being begun by writ of summons as in a normal action in the High Court.[57] Such an action can also be brought where the refusal is on any other ground but the bishop fails to signify this ground to the patron and presentee in writing, or on certain other grounds which are now almost certainly obsolete.[58]

Alternatively where the bishop refuses to institute or admit on the ground of unfitness in respect of doctrine or ritual, or refuses on some other ground sufficient in law but fails to signify it to the patron and presentee in writing, or where he refuses on some ground which appears insufficient in law, the presentee (but not the patron) may bring a suit of *duplex querela* (double complaint) before the Court of Ecclesiastical Causes Reserved, from which an appeal lies to the Commission of Review.[59] However, where another priest has been inducted the suit can no longer be brought, since that priest has acquired a temporal right which can only be challenged before a secular court,[60] by an action in the nature of a *quare impedit*.

---

[51] *Rolle's Abridgement of the Common Law*, Vol. 2, p. 366.

[52] Benefices Act 1898, ss.3, 11.

[53] *ibid*.

[54] *ibid.*, s.3(2). The procedure is governed by the Benefices (Institution Appeals) Rules 1988, S.I. 1988 No. 1996.

[55] Benefices Act 1898, ss.3, 11.

[56] As to which see *Halsbury's Laws of England* (4th ed.), Vol. 14, para. 822.

[57] Benefices Act 1898, s.3(1), (5).

[58] *e.g.* where a patron lacks title.

[59] Benefices Act 1898, s.3(1), (5); EJM, ss.10(1)(b), 11(2). See also *Halsbury's Laws of England* (4th ed.), Vol. 14, para. 823.

[60] *Burn's Ecclesiastical Law* (14th ed. 1842), Vol. 1, p. 161.

Filling of benefices

Simony

The full extent of the offence of simony[61] has not been settled in English law. It **5.21**
includes the buying or selling of holy orders or of an ecclesiastical benefice or
admission to a benefice, and may extend to all trafficking in spiritual things. The
procuring or acceptance of the presentation, institution, collation, induction or
admission to a benefice in consideration of money, profit or benefit, whether
direct or indirect is simonical and void.[62] Where simony occurs and the benefice
becomes void as a consequence, presentation on the vacancy must be made by
the diocesan patronages board.[63] Any person guilty of simony is liable to a fine
not exceeding £100 on summary conviction, and a priest who corruptly procures
or accepts the benefice becomes disabled from holding it.[64] Although the offence
remains on the statute book simony has not been a problem in the late twentieth
century.

Presentation

Presentation by the patron or their representative is the first legal step towards **5.22**
filling a benefice. A presentation is made when it is exhibited to the bishop,[65] this
as we have seen now being undertaken by means of a notice pursuant to the 1986
Measure. Presentation is not complete until institution or admission of the
presentee, (and in the cases where the Sovereign is patron) until induction. Thus,
although the patron has the legal right to make a presentation to the benefice the
spiritual rights of the church are protected by subjecting the person nominated to
the judgement of the bishop.[66]

The presentee must be a fit person[67] in that they must be of canonical age (that
is under 70 years of age),[68] and in priest's orders by episcopal ordination (or able
to obtain such ordination before institution or admission),[69] of sufficient learning[70] and a person against whose orthodoxy and morals no charge can be
established.[71] The bishop has 28 days to make inquiries and to inform himself of
the sufficiency of the presentee's qualifications.[72] If the bishop so requires a

---

[61] From Simon Magnus, see Acts 9:18–19.
[62] Simony Act 1588, s.4.
[63] Patronage (Benefices) Measure 1986, s.28.
[64] Simony Act 1588, s.4.
[65] *Rudd v. Bishop of Lincoln* (1623) Hut. 66.
[66] *Mirehouse v. Rennell* (1833) 1 Cl. & Fin 527 at 530, H.L.
[67] *Bishop of Exeter v. Marshall* (1868) 3 L.R. H.I.. 17.
[68] Ecclesiastical Offices (Age Limit) Measure 1975, s.1.
[69] Act of Uniformity 1662, s.10; Canon C10(1).
[70] Canon C10(2).
[71] *ibid.* See also *Bishop of Exeter v. Marshall* (1868) 3 L.R. H.L. 17 at 39; *Heywood v. Bishop of Manchester* (1884) 12 Q.B.D. 404 at 418, *per* Pollock B. that this could not be considered an exhaustive list of the ecclesiastical impediments to justify refusal of a presentee.
[72] Canon C9(2).

presentee must produce testimony as to their moral life.[73] No bishop can admit or institute a woman priest to a benefice where a relevant resolution under the Priests (Ordination of Women) Measure 1993 is in force in any parish comprised in the benefice.[74]

Refusal to admit or institute presentee

5.23   Nothing in the Patronage (Benefices) Measure 1986 affects the power of a bishop to refuse to institute or admit a presentee.[75] In particular the bishop may refuse a presentee where not more than three years have elapsed since that priest was ordained a deacon.[76] A presentee may also be refused on the grounds that they are unfit to discharge the duties of the benefice by reason of physical or mental infirmity or incapacity, pecuniary embarrassment of a serious character, grave misconduct, neglect of duty in an ecclesiastical office, evil life, having by their conduct caused grave scandal concerning their moral character since their ordination, or having with reference to the presentation knowingly been a party or privy to any invalid transaction or agreement which is invalid under the Benefices Act 1898.[77] Refusal by the bishop to institute or admit may constitute a disturbance of patronage. The procedure to be followed should the bishop refuse and the rights of appeal available to the patron and presentee in such circumstances have already been considered.

The bishop may also refuse a presentee who has not previously held a benefice or the office of vicar in a team ministry on the ground that they have had either no, or less than three years' experience as a full-time parochial minister.[78] Where the refusal is on this ground a slightly different appeal procedure applies. Again the bishop must signify his refusal and the ground for it in writing to the patron and the presentee, either of whom then has the right to appeal within one month thereafter to the archbishop of the province, who in this case sits alone without the Dean of the Arches and Auditor.[79]

In addition to the two grounds of refusal relating to the length of experience of the presentee as a minister the House of Bishops of the General Synod stated in 1990 that clergy should not be appointed as incumbents if they had been in holy orders for less than four years, subject to the diocesan bishop's discretion to appoint a person aged 40 years or over after a shorter period. This goes beyond

---

[73] Canon C10(2). As to the form established by custom see *Bishop of Exeter v. Marshall* (1868) 3 L.R. 17 at 48, H.L.

[74] Priests (Ordination of Women) Measure 1993, s.5; Canon C10(2A). As to various issues concerning the institution and admission of women priests to benefices, see Chap. 7.

[75] Patronage (Benefices) Measure 1986, s.17(1).

[76] Benefices Act 1898, s.2(1)(b); Canon C10(3a). The bishop may also refuse if at the date when the vacancy arises not more than one year has elapsed since a transfer of the right of patronage unless it can be proved that the transfer was not effected in view of the probability of the vacancy arising within the year: Benefices Act 1898, s.2(1)(a).

[77] *ibid.*

[78] Benefices Measure 1972, s.1(1); Canon C10(3b).

[79] Benefices Measure 1972, s.1(2). The procedure is governed by the Benefices (Institution Appeals) Rules 1988, S.I. 1988 No. 1996: Benefices Measure 1972, s.1(2A); Benefice Act 1898, s.11. There is no provision for the proceedings to be in public nor for the parties to be legally represented.

the strict legal requirements of both the Benefices Act 1898 and the Benefices Measure 1972 and would not therefore be a ground for refusal to admit or institute. However, a bishop can be expected to apply this criteria in cases where he is the patron or in exercising his right of veto under the Patronage (Benefices) Measure 1986 in respect of the patron's proposal to make an offer to a nominee.

Admission

Strictly speaking admission simply meant the bishop's declaration of approval of **5.24** the presentee, but the term is now generally used to mean the actual transfer of the cure of souls and spiritualities to the new incumbent. Admission occurs either by institution or, where the bishop is the patron or acquires the right to present, by collation. Where collation occurs there is no presentation, but the act of admission is in the same form as institution. Before admission the priest must subscribe a declaration of assent and take the oaths of allegiance and canonical obedience in the presence of the bishop of his commissary.[80] The declaration against simony is no longer required.[81]

Institution or collation

Institution or collation is by the bishop or in grave and urgent cases by his **5.25** commissary.[82] The priest kneels before the bishop who reads the words of institution from a written instrument, whilst the presentee holds in both hands the episcopal seal which is appended to this document.[83] The bishop then delivers the instrument of institution to the presentee.

In general institution, or collation and induction occurs at the same time, and are held at a service at the parish church of the benefice, although this is not necessary. Where these do take place at a service the bishop presents the new incumbent to the congregation on whose behalf the incumbent is welcomed by the churchwardens. It is customary for the incumbent to be led to the font, prayer desk, lectern, pulpit and sanctuary where they are reminded of their duties in regard to the conduct of public worship and the ministry of the Word and sacraments. It is no longer necessary for the priest to read publically the Thirty-Nine Articles and make the declaration of assent on the first Sunday on which they officiate.

By institution or collation the cure of souls of the benefice is committed to the priest. They are admitted to the office to pray and preach and are bound to discharge all the duties of an incumbent. They may enter into the property of the benefice and may receive the profits of it, but until induction have no title to sue or deal with them.

---

[80] As to which see Chap. 7.
[81] Church of England (Miscellaneous Provisions) Measure 1976, s.1. Amending Canon no. 5 revoking Canon C16.
[82] Canon C10(5)–(10).
[83] Canon C10(5)–(10).

Induction

5.26   Induction of an instituted or collated priest into the temporalities of the benefice is performed by the archdeacon[84] to whom the bishop issues directions for induction, or a person to whom the archdeacon delegates that duty by precept.[85] The person who carries out the induction takes the priest's hand and lays it upon the key or ring of the church door (or in the absence of these the wall) whilst they pronounce the words of induction, following which the priest who is inducted tolls the bells to make the induction public.[86] The bishop's directions are then returned with a certificate of the induction endorsed upon it.[87] Where the appointment is to a benefice in the area of which there are two or more parish churches the bishop may direct in which the induction is to take place.[88] By induction the priest is put into complete possession of the church and benefice,[89] and thus becomes the holder of the freehold office.

Pluralities

5.27   Prior to the Pastoral Measure 1968 coming into force[90] in general no incumbent could hold more than one benefice at a time. Certain exceptions were permitted and thus more than one benefice, known as a plurality, could be held by licence or dispensation from the Archbishop of Canterbury or could be authorised by bishop's orders, whilst certain cathedral preferments could be held in addition to benefices without the need for a licence or dispensation.

   Today no person may hold benefices in plurality except in pursuance of a pastoral scheme or order or under the provisions of the Pastoral Measure 1983.[91] This Measure enables a person to hold a cathedral preferment with a benefice, or with two or more benefices authorised to be held in plurality, so long as the cathedral statutes provide or allow for this, but any such cathedral preferment may only be held in one cathedral.[92]

   A pastoral scheme or order may provide for two or more benefices to be held in plurality subject to any conditions which may be specified.[93] Except with the leave of the bishop the incumbent of such benefices held in plurality may not resign one without resigning the others.[94] Unless the provisions of a scheme or order provides otherwise the provisions for holding benefices in plurality

---

[84] Unless by prescription or composition others have that right: Gibson's *Codex Juris Ecclesiastici Anglicani*, (2nd ed. 1761) p. 815; *Burn's Ecclesiastical Law* (14th ed. 1842), Vol. 1, p. 172.

[85] Canon C11(1), (3).

[86] Canon C11(2).

[87] Canon C11(2).

[88] Pastoral Measure 1983, s.75.

[89] *Hare v. Bickley* (1577) 2 Pl. 526 at 528; *Burn's Ecclesiastical Law* (4th ed.), Vol. 1, p. 176.

[90] On April 1, 1969 (now repealed and consolidated in the Pastoral Measure 1983).

[91] Pastoral Measure 1983, s.85.

[92] *ibid.*

[93] *ibid.*, s.18.

[94] Pastoral Measure 1983, s.18.

continue during a vacancy in them.[95] However, the provisions may be terminated when the bishop gives notice of a vacancy or impending vacancy.

Termination occurs either by the bishop giving notice of termination to the patrons and those who will become patrons on termination of the plurality and the Church Commissioners, or by an interested PCC. Such a PCC may, within 28 days of notice of the vacancy, pass a resolution that the provisions are to be terminated, and must then notify the bishop of this, who must in turn notify other interested PCCs, relevant patrons and the Commissioners.[96] Termination is without prejudice to any provisions relating to the future exercise of rights of patronage of the benefices concerned in the event of a renewal of the plurality.[97]

Sequestration

Sequestration of a benefice may occur during a vacancy in the benefice, or in the course of proceedings in an ecclesiastical court against the incumbent and in certain limited cases of default by the incumbent.[98] The churchwardens of every parish comprised in the benefice and the rural dean are to be the sequestrators, together with any other person whom the bishop considers it desirable to appoint.[99]   **5.28**

Under the process of sequestration the profits and income of the benefice are taken and held by the sequestrators to be applied in the appropriate manner as required. The sequestrators are the bailiffs or agents of the bishop. If there is an assistant curate licensed to any parish within the benefice they continue in office. In cases where they cannot cope alone or where there is no assistant curate, the bishop may appoint a priest-in-charge. If he does not do so the sequestrators may make provision for the cure of souls.

In practice since the coming into force of the Endowments and Glebe Measure 1976[1] the income which is receivable by the sequestrators will, save in exceptional cases, only consist of fees which would otherwise have been payable to the incumbent such as for marriages and burials.[2] Thus although the sequestrators receive the profits of the benefice and should pay out of these the costs of serving the cure during the vacancy as determined by the bishop.[3] in practice the funds

[95] Pastoral Measure 1983, s.18.
[96] Pastoral Measure 1983, s.18.
[97] Pastoral Measure 1983, s.18.
[98] Sequestration may no longer be issued by any court (secular or ecclesiastical) in order to obtain satisfaction of a debt owed by the incumbent, by reason of the bankruptcy of the incumbent, or in order to apply the profits of the benefice where the incumbent is unable by reason of old age or infirmity to discharge their duties: Church of England (Miscellaneous Provisions) Measure 1992, s.1(2).
[99] Church of England (Miscellaneous Provisions) Measure 1992, s.1(1). In the case of a team ministry the team vicars or other team members may take the place of the rural dean: *ibid.*, ss.1A, 1B.
[1] The Measure had the effect of substituting the endowments of the benefice and any glebe land for a fixed annuity which is not payable on a vacancy in the benefice (see Chap. 8).
[2] See Chap. 8.
[3] Benefices (Sequestrations) Measure 1933, s.1.

available to them are unlikely to be sufficient thus the balance will need to be defrayed out of the diocesan stipends fund.

With the approval of the bishop, the sequestrators may make provision for care and upkeep of the house of residence and may in certain circumstances be authorised to grant a lease of parsonage land.[4] With the bishop's consent they may also make provision for the cost of professional assistance required by them and for the payment of interest borrowed by them in the course of their duties.[5] The sequestrators may bring any action or proceedings to recover profits of the benefice.[6] Save in limited circumstances at the close of sequestration the sequestrators must pay the balance of any profits in their hands to the Church Commissioners for allocation to the income account of the diocesan stipends fund.[7]

5.29   As we have already seen where the right of presentation to a benefice is suspended a period of sequestration must issue to cover the whole of the period of suspension, and the bishop must ensure that one of the sequestrators appointed is a person specially qualified by training or experience to discharge the function of sequestrator efficiently. In such circumstances in addition to the usual powers the sequestrators may exercise all such powers in relation to the property of the benefice as an incumbent has provided they have the consent of the bishop so to do.[8]

Where an incumbent is censured with suspension or inhibited from exercising or performing the rights and duties of their office the court will direct sequestration of the profits of the benefice. The bishop may then appoint some other person or persons to perform the duties, and he may assign any part of the incumbent's guaranteed annuity or personal grant if any and the profits of the benefice, to such person or persons so appointed.[9] As we have seen sequestration may also issue in cases of default for non-compliance with an order to reside on the benefice.[10] In the latter case sequestration does not of itself interfere with provision of the cure by the incumbent nor with their duty to reside on the benefice, but if the sequestration remains in force for more than six months and the bishop is of the opinion that scandal or inconvenience will arise from the incumbent continuing to perform the services the bishop may inhibit them from doing so.[11]

Avoidance of benefices

5.30   A benefice is avoided by the death or resignation of the incumbent. A benefice will become void by cessation where the incumbent is created a bishop or takes another benefice or ecclesiastical dignity or preferment which cannot be held

[4] *ibid.*, s.2; Endowments and Glebe Measure 1976, s.38(2).
[5] Benefices (Sequestrations) Measure 1933, s.2; Endowments and Glebe Measure 1976, s.38(2).
[6] Sequestration Act 1849, s.1.
[7] Endowments and Glebe Measures 1976, s.38.
[8] Pastoral Measure 1983, Sched. 7. This Schedule sets out detailed provisions regarding the application of the profits of the benefice and payment of the balance at the close of sequestration, and also provides for the sequestrators to render income and expenditure accounts to the bishop annually and at the close of sequestration.
[9] EJM, s.71.
[10] For the procedure to be followed in regard to such sequestration see the Pluralities Act 1838, ss.112, 113.
[11] Sequestration Act 1871, s.5.

lawfully with the benefice.[12] A benefice is also avoided by a declaration of such by the bishop, by deprivation, in certain cases on the coming into operation of a pastoral scheme, and may also be avoided on the exchange of benefices by two incumbents.

An incumbent of a benefice and certain other holders of offices such as a vicar in a team ministry are required to retire when they reach 70 years of age.[13] However, in cases where the bishop considers that the pastoral needs of the parish make this desirable and he obtains the consent of the PCC of every parish comprised in the benefice he may authorise the incumbent to continue in office for a further period or periods until they reach the age of 72.[14]

In cases where the incumbent dies in office and was residing in a house of residence annexed to the benefice the widowed spouse is legally entitled to occupy the house for a period not exceeding two calendar months.[15]

Resignation (other than pursuant to the Incumbents (Vacation of Benefices) Measure 1977) must be made to the diocesan bishop, by the incumbent either in person or in writing tendered in the prescribed form and signed by them.[16] Save on exchange of benefices resignation must be unconditional, although it may specify that it takes effect at a future date.[17] The bishop is not obliged to accept,[18] and his acceptance is not in any specified form nor is it required to be in writing.[19] Once accepted resignation takes effect and cannot be revoked.[20] On occasion resignation may be at the bishop's request (although he cannot compel resignation) to avoid scandal or legal proceedings, and he may agree to postpone the declaration of vacancy until a later date.[21] In such cases the bishop's acceptance of the resignation is implied. Corrupt resignation, that is obtaining directly or indirectly any benefit for resigning, renders the incumbent and the provider of the benefit liable on summary conviction to a fine not exceeding £100.[22]

A benefice is avoided and becomes vacant on the deprivation of the incumbent. The incumbent may be deprived of the benefice by law of definitive sentence where they are guilty of certain offences or conduct, or where they are disqualified in law from holding it, or where there has been simony in connection with their presentation institution, collation or admission whether or not they

---

[12] *Edes v. Bishop of Oxford* (1667) Vaug. 18; *Burder v. Mavor* (1848) 1 Rob. 614; Pastoral Measure 1983, s.85(4).

[13] Ecclesiastical Offices (Age Limit) Measure 1975, s.1(3). The Measure does not apply to those in office on January 1, 1976: *ibid*. s.1(4)(d).

[14] *ibid.*, s.3(2).

[15] Pluralities Act 1838, s.36. This section was specifically amended by the Priests (Ordination of Women) Measure 1993, Sched. 3, to include the widower of a female incumbent.

[16] Church of England (Miscellaneous Provisions) Measure 1992, s.11, Sched. 2; *Reichel v. Bishop of Oxford* (1887) 35 Ch.D. 48 at 74, 75, C.A., affd (1889) 14 App.Cas. 259 at 265, H.L.

[17] *Reichel v. Bishop of Oxford* (1889) 14 App.Cas. 259 at 265, H.L.

[18] *Burn's Ecclesiastical Law* (14th ed. 1842), Vol. 3, p. 543; *Marchioness of Rockingham v. Griffith* (1755) 7 Bac. Abr. 472; *Fletcher v. Lord Sondes* (1827) 3 Bing. 510 at 544, H.L.

[19] *Reichel v. Bishop of Oxford (ante).*

[20] *ibid.* Whether it may be revoked before acceptance is not clear: *ibid.*, at 14 App.Cas. 271.

[21] *Reichel v. Bishop of Oxford (ante).*

[22] Simony Act 1588, s.7.

were a party to it. If the incumbent's ordination was corruptly procured and they are admitted to a benefice within seven years of such ordination it becomes void on their admission as if they were dead.[23] A person not admitted to priest's orders who is instituted or admitted to a benefice cannot retain possession of it but whilst they hold it their spiritual and temporal acts are valid.[24]

The Incumbents (Vacation of Benefices) Measure 1977

5.31   Provision is made by the Incumbents (Vacation of Benefices) Measure 1977 (as amended by the Incumbents (Vacation of Benefices) (Amendment) Measure 1993) for the vacation of a benefice by an incumbent where there has been a serious breakdown in the pastoral relationship between incumbent and parishioners or where the incumbent is too old or infirm to discharge the duties of the benefice adequately. The Measure applies to the office of rector or vicar with the cure of souls, including a vicar in a team ministry established pursuant to a pastoral scheme or order, but not an office in a Royal Peculiar or dean or provost of a parish church cathedral.[25]

The 1977 Measure (as amended) imposed a duty upon the House of Bishops of the General Synod to draw up a Code of Practice containing rules of guidance in order to promote better relations between incumbent and parishioners and to remove their causes of estrangement.[26] Accordingly pursuant to that Measure the Incumbents (Vacation of Benefices) Measures 1977 and 1993 Code of Practice was issued in January 1994. However, the Code states that the rules of guidance contained within it in no way qualify or detract from the provisions of the 1977 Measure or rules made under it.[27] The Code also draws attention to the purpose of the 1977 Measure, making clear that its provisions should not be used as a substitute for disciplinary proceedings under the EJM nor as a substitute for pastoral reorganisation.[28] The Code also warns that because of the discretionary powers given to the diocesan bishop in cases of inquiry into a pastoral situation under Part I of the 1977 Measure the bishop should avoid close personal involvement during the preliminary stages of any case or potential case.[29]

Enquiry into pastoral situation

5.32   A request for an enquiry into the pastoral situation of a parish may be made on the ground that there has been a serious breakdown of the pastoral relationship between incumbent and parishioners, to which the conduct of incumbent,

[23] *ibid.*, s.9. See also Chap. 7.
[24] *Costard v. Winder* (1600) Cro. Eliz. (1) 775; *Hawle v. Corri* (1820) 2 Hag. Con. 280 at 288.
[25] Incumbents (Vacation of Benefices) Measure 1977, s.19. A working party of the General Synod has recommended the extension of the procedures to infirm cathedral clergy and archdeacons and to ineffective clergy holding any office: *Under Authority*, the report of the General Synod Working Party Reviewing Clergy Discipline and the Working of the Ecclesiastical Courts (1996) (GS 1217).
[26] *ibid.*, s.1.
[27] para. 1.
[28] para. 3.
[29] para. 18.

parishioners or both, has contributed over a substantial period.[30] Serious breakdown occurs where the relationship is such as to impede the promotion in the parish of the whole mission of the Church of England, pastoral, evangelistic, social and ecumenical.[31] The request may be made by the incumbent of the benefice to which the parish belongs, the relevant archdeacon, or by a majority of not less than two-thirds of the lay members of the PCC present and voting on a resolution that such a request be made.[32] Where the incumbent is also the archdeacon a request may be made by a majority of the bishop's council and standing committee of the relevant diocesan synod.[33] Where these bodies or the PCC make such a request or notify the bishop of their intention to make one this must be signed by all persons making it and they must specify two persons from amongst them who are willing to act as representatives.[34]

An enquiry can only take place after the persons concerned have had an opportunity to resolve the pastoral situation. Accordingly a request for an enquiry cannot be made until notice of their intentions has been given by the person intending to make it to the relevant bishop at least six months and not more than 12 months before such a request is actually made.[35] Both the request and a notice of intention to make it should be in writing to the relevant bishop and, in the case of a request, also to the secretary of the relevant diocesan synod, and should contain the particulars as to why such an enquiry is justified.[36] The secretary must then notify the incumbent unless they made the request, and similarly the archdeacon and secretary of the PCC.[37]

The request may be withdrawn by notice in writing given to the bishop by either the person who made it, or, where the request was made by the PCC, by a majority of its lay members present and voting at a duly convened meeting on a resolution that it be withdrawn, or, where the request was by the bishop's council and standing committee of the diocesan synod, by a majority of their members.[38]

The Code of Practice provides that when the bishop receives a notice of **5.33** intention to request an enquiry he should as soon as possible interview the parties, that is the incumbent and representatives of the lay members of the PCC, at least once together and once separately.[39] If these interviews fail to effect a reconciliation the bishop is then recommended by the Code to appoint a person (other than the archdeacon) whom he considers suitable, to explain the implications and possible consequences of invoking the 1977 Measure.[40] That person should also seek to appoint a conciliator (other than the archdeacon, who is acceptable to the parties and if unable to do so report to the bishop.[41] Any conciliator should then use their best endeavours to interview incumbent and parishioners and bring them into dialogue with each other, this process of

---

[30] *ibid.*, s.1A(1).
[31] *ibid.*, s.19A.
[32] *ibid.*, s.1A(1).
[33] *ibid.*, s.1A(1).
[34] *ibid.*, s.1A(3).
[35] *ibid.*, s.1A(1A).
[36] *ibid.*, s.1A(1A).
[37] *ibid.*, s.1A(6).
[38] *ibid.*, s.1(7).
[39] para. 6.
[40] para. 7.
[41] para. 7.

reconciliation being completed if possible within six months of the notice of intention to request an enquiry.[42] The conciliator should make a factual report once the reconciliation or attempted reconciliation process has been completed, it being a matter for the bishop whether he makes further attempts at reconciliation before a formal request for an enquiry is received.[43]

Where the bishop receives a request for an enquiry and neither the archdeacon nor the incumbent of the benefice is the person making the request he must direct the relevant archdeacon to seek to remove the cause of the estrangement.[44] The bishop may appoint another archdeacon where the archdeacon to whom the direction is made informs him that it would not be right or expedient for them to act.[45] Not more than six weeks after receiving the bishop's direction the archdeacon must report to the bishop whether in their opinion such an enquiry would be in the best interests of the incumbent and parishioners, and should accordingly be instituted. One of the factors which the archdeacon will have regard to is the extent to which the Code of Practice has been complied with.[46]

If he considers it appropriate the bishop may institute an enquiry in a number of circumstances: where the archdeacon making the preliminary report recommends it is required, or where within six months of reporting to the contrary the archdeacon informs the bishop that it is now required; where within six months of the archdeacon recommending that an enquiry is not required the incumbent, or secretary or designated representative of the PCC informs the bishop that such is required.[47] The bishop may also institute an enquiry where the request for it was made by the relevant archdeacon, or the archdeacon is the incumbent of the benefice to which the parish belongs (there having been no report by the archdeacon in either of these circumstances).[48] The decision whether or not to institute an inquiry is, subject to one of these conditions being satisfied, at the discretion of the bishop.

An enquiry is instituted by the bishop giving the secretary of the diocesan synod a direction.[49] If within six months of any of the above occuring the bishop neither gives a direction nor notifies the secretary that he proposes not to, a direction is deemed to have been given.[50]

Where a request for an enquiry has been made the incumbent may ask the bishop to accept their resignation at any time before the bishop notifies them of the action he proposes to take following the report of the enquiry.[51] The bishop may accept the resignation if he considers it in the best interests of the Church, and if the resignation is accepted no further steps are taken in connection with the enquiry.[52]

---

[42] paras. 8, 9.
[43] paras. 10, 11.
[44] *ibid.*, s.2(1), (2), (4).
[45] *ibid.*, s.2(3).
[46] *ibid.*, s.2(5).
[47] *ibid.*, s.3(1).
[48] *ibid.*, s.3(1).
[49] *ibid.*, s.3(1A).
[50] *ibid.*, s.3(1A), (1B).
[51] *ibid.*, s.4(1).
[52] *ibid.*, s.4(1), (3).

Institution of enquiry on grounds of disability

The bishop may also instruct the secretary of the diocesan synod in writing to **5.34** institute an enquiry as to whether an incumbent is unable to discharge adequately the duties of the benefice through disability arising from age or infirmity of mind or body.[53] Such an enquiry must consider whether the incumbent should resign the benefice or be given assistance in discharging their duties.[54] This provision does not apply to a suffragan bishop to whom the Bishops (Retirement) Measure 1986 applies or to a dean, provost or archdeacon to whom the Church Dignitaries (Retirement) Measure 1949 applies.[55]

Enquiry by provincial tribunal

An enquiry must be conducted by a provincial tribunal for the province in which **5.35** the benefice is situated.[56] A tribunal consists of five persons appointed by the vicar-general of the province.[57] The chairman is either the chancellor of a diocese in the province other than the diocese in which the parish is situated, or Queen's Counsel who is a communicant member of the Church of England.[58] Two members are clerks in holy orders from the panel appointed[59] from members of the Lower House of the Convocation of the province and the remaining members are lay persons from the panel appointed[60] from the members of the House of Laity of the General Synod.[61] No person who is ordinarily resident or whose name is entered on the electoral roll of any parish in the diocese, or a clerk in holy orders authorised to exercise their ministry in the relevant diocese, may be appointed.[62]

The list of names and addresses of proposed members is sent by the secretary of the diocesan synod to the incumbent, informing them of their rights of objection.[63] Within three weeks of the list being sent the incumbent may object to any proposed member or members by sending notice in writing to the secretary of the diocesan synod, setting out the name, and specifying the grounds of objection.[64] Any such objection is referred to the vicar-general of a province other than the province for which the tribunal is to be constituted, to determine if the objections are reasonable.[65] If the objections are upheld and a new member appointed the incumbent has the same rights of notification and objection to that

---

[53] *ibid.*, s.6(1).
[54] *ibid.*, s.6(2).
[55] As to which see Chap. 3.
[56] Incumbents (Vacation of Benefices) Measure 1977, ss.5, 6(1A).
[57] *ibid.*, s.7, Sched. 1, para. 1.
[58] *ibid.*, s.7, Sched. 1, para. 1.
[59] Under the Pastoral Measure 1983, Sched. 4, para. 15(1), Appeal Tribunal for compensation of clergy.
[60] *ibid.*
[61] Incumbents (Vacation of Benefices) Measure 1977, s.7, Sched. 1, para. 1.
[62] *ibid.*
[63] Incumbents (Vacation of Benefices) Measure 1977, Sched. 1, paras. 2(3), 3.
[64] *ibid.*
[65] Incumbents (Vacation of Benefices) Measure 1977, Sched. 1, paras. 2(3), 3.

person, unless if the objection were allowed the tribunal could not be constituted there being no other person to serve.[66] Any person appointed to serve may refuse to accept if in their opinion it would not be right to serve as a member.[67]

Where the enquiry is into the pastoral situation the secretary of the PCC of the parish to which the enquiry relates and of any other parish of the benefice is notified and asked if they wish to make representations to the tribunal.[68]

On an enquiry into the pastoral situation the incumbent may be assisted, or be represented in their absence, by some other person, whether professionally qualified or not, at any meeting of the tribunal to which they are invited or entitled to attend.[69] At such an enquiry all the parties, that is the incumbent, archdeacon, PCC, or persons specified in the request for an einquiry as willing to act as their representatives, may also be represented by a solicitor or barrister.[70]

The tribunal may direct that the incumbent undergo a medical examination to obtain a report on their mental or physical condition.[71] Such an examination may be directed whether the enquiry is into a pastoral breakdown or into the disability of the incumbent. Where the incumbent fails to take the steps required to give effect to such a direction the tribunal may draw such inferences, if any, as appear proper in the circumstances, without prejudice to the drawing of other inferences which may be drawn in the course of the enquiry.[72]

The practice and procedure of provincial tribunals in relation to enquiries is set out in Rules drawn up by the Vacation of Benefices Rules Committee.[73]

Report of tribunal

5.36   Where the enquiry is into the pastoral situation the tribunal must report to the bishop whether there has been a serious breakdown and whether the conduct of the incumbent or parishioners or both has contributed to the breakdown over a substantial period.[74] Alternatively, instead of reporting in this way, where the tribunal considers that the incumbent is unable to discharge their duties because of age or infirmity of mind or body, they may instead make a report to the bishop to this effect.[75] Where the enquiry was into the disability of an incumbent the report must be made to the bishop as to whether the incumbent is unable to discharge adequately their duties because of age or infirmity of either mind or body.[76] The reports should contain recommendations as to the action to be taken by the bishop, save that no recommendation that the bishop execute a declaration of avoidance or that the incumbent should resign are to be made unless at least four members of the tribunal are agreed upon this.[77]

[66] *ibid.*, Sched. 1, paras. 5, 6.
[67] *ibid.*, Sched. 1, para. 2(2).
[68] *ibid.*, s.8(1).
[69] *ibid.*, s.7(4).
[70] *ibid.*, s.7(5), (6).
[71] *ibid.*, s.7A(1).
[72] *ibid.*, s.7A(2).
[73] *ibid.*, s.18; Incumbents (Vacation of Benefices) Rules 1994, S.I. 1994 No. 703.
[74] Incumbents (Vacation of Benefices) Measure 1977, s.9(1).
[75] Incumbents (Vacation of Benefices) Measure 1977, s.9(2).
[76] Incumbents (Vacation of Benefices) Measure 1977, s.9(3).
[77] *ibid.*, s.9(4), (5).

Inhibition in cases of disability

Where an enquiry has been instituted into the disability of the incumbent or **5.37** where the tribunal has reported that the incumbent is unable to discharge their duties because of age or infirmity, and it appears to the bishop desirable in the interests of the Church of England that he should act, he may serve a notice on the incumbent inhibiting them from executing or performing any right or duty of or incidental to their office (as specified by the bishop) without the bishop's consent.[78]

Where the tribunal reports that the incumbent is unable to discharge adequately their duties by reason of disability a notice of inhibition must not be served after the expiry of three months from the making of the report unless the bishop has notified the incumbent that it is desirable that they should resign or the bishop has given the incumbent leave of absence.[79] A notice issued before the tribunal reports ceases to have effect unless the tribunal reports that the incumbent is unable to discharge their duties adequately.[80] A notice issued after the making of the report also ceases to have effect three months after the making of the report unless the bishop has notified the incumbent that they should resign or has given them leave of absence.[81]

Powers of the bishop in case of pastoral breakdown

If the tribunal so recommends the bishop may execute a declaration of **5.38** avoidance, declaring the benefice vacant as from a specified date.[82] At the same time he must disqualify the incumbent from executing or performing any right or duty of or incidental to their office without the bishop's consent, from the date the declaration is executed until the date it takes effect.[83]

Where the tribunal reports that the breakdown has been contributed to by the conduct of the incumbent over a substantial period of time the bishop may rebuke the incumbent.[84] He may also disqualify any of them from executing or performing any right or duty of or incidental to their office for a specified period, although he must make alternative provision for the discharge of those duties.[85]

Where the tribunal reports that the breakdown has been contributed to by the conduct of the parishioners over a substantial period of time the bishop may rebuke any of the parishioners.[86] He may also if he thinks fit disqualify any of them from being a churchwarden or a member or officer of the PCC of the parish in question and such other parishes in his diocese as he may specify, for such period as he may specify not exceeding five years.[87] A person so disqualified

[78] *ibid.*, s.9A(1), (2).
[79] *ibid.*, s.9A(3).
[80] *ibid.*, s.9A(4).
[81] *ibid.*, s.9A(4).
[82] *ibid.*, s.10(2)), (3), (4).
[83] *ibid.*, s.10(5), (8).
[84] *ibid.*, s.10(5), (8).
[85] *ibid.*, s.10(5), (8).
[86] *ibid.*, s.10(6).
[87] *ibid.*, s.10(6).

cannot become a member of the relevant PCC by virtue of lay membership of a deanery or diocesan synod or the General Synod.[88]

The bishop may subsequently revoke the disqualification of either the incumbent or parishioners before the time specified has expired.[89] He may also give pastoral advice and guidance to the incumbent and parishioenrs.[90]

Powers of bishop in case of disability

5.39   Where the tribunal reports that the incumbent is unable to discharge their duties adequately because of disability the bishop may, if the tribunal has so recommended, notify the incumbent that they should resign.[91] An incumbent who is to resign must execute a deed, resigning from the date specified in that deed. If the incumbent fails or refuses to resign within one month of the notification that they should resign the bishop must execute a declaration of avoidance, declaring the benefice vacant from the date specified therein.[92]

Alternatively the bishop may, with the incumbent's consent, appoint and license an assistant curate to assist the incumbent.[93] If the incumbent refuses or fails to comply with a request to consent to such an appointment the bishop must execute a declaration of avoidance, declaring the benefice vacant from the date specified therein.[94] The bishop may also give the incumbent leave of absence for a maximum of two years, and must make provision for the discharge of their duties during that period, or make any other temporary provision for discharge of the incumbent's duties.[95]

Implementation of recommendations or other action

5.40   As soon as practicable after receiving the tribunal's report the bishop must notify the incumbent of the action he proposes to take or that no action is required.[96] He must also notify the archdeacon, the secretary of the PCC and any delegated representative.[97] The bishop has a discretion as to whether or not he implements the tribunal's recommendations and also whether or not to publish the tribunals's report. In deciding whether or not to publish all or part of the report the Code of Practice states that regard should be had to whether or not the enquiry or any part took place in public. If part of the hearing took place in public this suggests a strong case for at least publishing the basic facts and recommendations.

---

[88] *ibid.*, s.10(6A). CRR, rr. 10(3)(b), 14(3)(c).
[89] Incumbents (Vacation of Benefices) Measure 1977, s.10(9).
[90] *ibid.*, s.10(7).
[91] *ibid.*, s.11(1), (2), (a), (5), (6). The resignation may apply to all benefices held in plurality, notwithstanding that the recommendation of the tribunal applied to only one of them: *ibid.*, s.11(4).
[92] *ibid.*, s.11(1), (2), (6).
[93] *ibid.*, s.11(1), (2), (c), (d).
[94] *ibid.*
[95] *ibid.*, s.11.
[96] *ibid.*, s.12(1).
[97] *ibid.*, s.12(1).

However, in the interest of justice and of justice being seen to be done, the interests of the incumbent, parishioners and anyone else involved and pastoral considerations (such as whether the incumbent is to continue in the parish) must be borne in mind together with the bishop's own position.[98]

An incumbent of any benefice which he has resigned or which has been declared vacant must vacate their official residence within three months after the date specified in the deed of resignation or declaration of avoidance.[99]

Compensation and pension provisions

Where the incumbent resigns with the agreement of the bishop, or after an   **5.41** enquiry into the pastoral situation the bishop has declared the benefice vacant, the incumbent is entitled to compensation for loss suffered, on making an application in writing to the DBF.[1] The amount and the circumstances in which such compensation may be altered, terminated, suspended or reduced are set out in detailed provisions.[2] Where the tribunal has reported that the incumbent is unable to discharge their duties by reason of infirmity, or where after an enquiry into the incumbent's disability the incumbent has resigned or the bishop declares the benefice vacant, the incumbent is deemed to have become so incapable on the date the resignation or declaration took effect.[3] Unless they have already reached retiring age at the relevant date they are also deemed to have satisfied the Church of England Pensions Board of the fact that they have become incapacitated and that the infirmity is likely to be permanent, in order to qualify for a pension.[4]

The Pastoral Measure 1983

The Pastoral Measure 1983[5] provides for changes in benefices, the creation of   **5.42** new parishes, the establishment of team and group ministries, pastoral reorganisation and incidental matters which are considered here, as well as the holding of benefices in plurality which we have already looked at. In addition the Measure contains provisions for dealing with redundant churches, a subject considered more fully in Chapter 8.

The Measure applies to churches, burial grounds and land provided under private and local Acts.[6]

---

[98] para. 17.
[99] Incumbents (Vacation of Benefices) Measure 1977, s.12(2).
[1] *ibid.*, s.13.
[2] See *ibid.*, Sched. 2.
[3] For the purposes of the Church of England (Pensions) Measures and Regulations.
[4] Incumbents (Vacation of Benefices) Measure 1977, s.14.
[5] The 1983 Measure consolidated the provisions of the Pastoral Measure 1968 and the Pastoral (Amendment) Measure 1982. A Code of Practice has also been produced: *Pastoral Measure 1983, Code of Recommended Practice* (1983).
[6] Pastoral Measure 1983, s.90. Any Act providing such land may be revoked by a pastoral scheme under the Measure if it appears to the Church Commissioners to be a provision inconsistent with or rendered unnecessary by that scheme or by the applicable provisions of the Measure: *ibid.*

Pastoral committee

5.43   There is a pastoral committee for every diocese in England,[7] whose constitution is set out in the first Schedule to that Measure. If he so wishes the diocesan bishop may, and invariably is, a member of the committee, whilst all suffragan bishops and archdeacons in the diocese are *ex officio* members.[7a] The DBF, the diocesan parsonages board and the DAC must each appoint a member of the pastoral committee (who must be a member of the body which appoints them). The remaining members may be appointed or elected in such manner as the diocesan synod determines, provided that at least one half of all the members are elected, not more than one-third are *ex officio* members, and the number of members who are clergy and laity are as near the same as possible. All members other than *ex officio* members hold office for five years (or less if the synod so determines) but are eligible for re-appointment.

Not less than one-third of the committee's members form a quorum and every question submitted to it is to be decided by a majority of those present and voting. The committee may delegate certain of its functions to sub-committees which may include persons who are not members of the pastoral committee. If however any person is to meet a sub-committee not less than two persons of that sub-committee must be members of the committee. The committee must present an annual report to the diocesan synod. Subject to these provisions and any directions given by the diocesan synod the pastoral committee may regulate its own procedure. Although the diocesan synod has a large measure of control over the composition and procedure of the pastoral committee it is subject to the directions of the bishop and must submit its recommendations to him.

The pastoral committee of a diocese must review the arrangements for pastoral supervision in the diocese and, where it considers it necessary or the bishop so directs, make recommendations to the bishop covering any of the matters (including matters affecting other dioceses) which may be provided for under the 1983 Measure, other than the alteration of diocesan boundaries.[8] Where the committee decides on its own initiative to review arrangements it must consult the bishop and give him particulars of the matters which it intends to consider and the benefices which will be affected.[9] The committee must at all times have regard to the making of provision for the cure of souls within the diocese as a whole, and to the traditions, needs and characteristics of individual parishes.[10] The diocesan synod may also indicate any matters of diocesan policy to which the committee should have regard.[11] In order to carry out its functions the committee may make such enquiries and hold such consultations and interviews as it sees fit and consider representations made to it by any person.[12]

Where it appears to the bishops of two or more dioceses that is desirable to consider diocesan boundaries (which requires the exercise of powers subject to

---

[7] *ibid.*, s.1.
[7a] Save that a suffragan bishop appointed to act as a provincial episcopal visitor for the purposes of the Episcopal Ministry Act of Synod 1993 is not an *ex officio* member.
[8] *ibid.*, s.2(1).
[9] *ibid.*, s.2(2).
[10] *ibid.*, s.2(3).
[11] *ibid.*, s.2(4).
[12] *ibid.*, s.16(2).

the consent of the Diocese Commission) and pastoral arrangements in adjacent areas a joint pastoral committee may be constituted with the consent of the Dioceses Commission which nominates a member to that committee.[13] All the provisions set out below apply in regard to the recommendations of such a committee and the formulation and submission of draft proposals by it as they do to a diocesan committee, save that the bishops and registrars of each diocese act instead of the bishop or registrar of a single diocese.[14]

Consultation and preparation of draft proposals

So far as practicable the pastoral committee must obtain the views of interested parties,[15] before deciding to make recommendations to the bishop.[16] Where those interested parties are local planning authorities they should be invited to express a view[17] and where they are the incumbent, vicars in a team ministry or the PCC they, or in the case of a PCC its representatives, should be afforded an opportunity if desired of meeting either the pastoral committee, a sub-committee of it or its representatives.[18] Where the proposal is to recommend union of or dissolution of any benefice, or their holding in plurality, or the establishment of a team or group ministry, or the abolition of any office of vicar in a team ministry, the incumbent of each benefice affected or the holder of the office of vicar must be given an opportunity to meet the pastoral committee itself.[19]

5.44

In the case of a church which it is proposed to make redundant the pastoral committee should ascertain the views of any local planning authorities concerned.[20] It must also notify the Council for the Care of Churches, which is obliged to prepare a report for the committee relating to the historic and architectural qualities of each church mentioned in the notice and of other churches in the area, and the historic and aesthetic qualities of their contents, and any special features of any churchyard or burial ground annexed to them.[21] Although a pastoral scheme may make a declaration of redundancy it can only make further provision for that church in limited circumstances. These circumstances and the procedure to be followed in regard to redundant churches including the making and effect of redundancy schemes are all matters considered in Chapter 8.

Any recommendations which the pastoral committee wishes to make should be submitted to the bishop in the form of draft proposals.[22] A copy of the report of the Council for the Care of Churches must be annexed where a declaration of redundancy is proposed, and, in all cases a statement of the views of interested parties may be annexed.[23] The bishop may make any amendments to the

---

[13] *ibid.*, s.13.
[14] *ibid.*, s.13.
[15] Defined according to the nature of the proposals in *ibid.*, s.3.
[16] As to which see *Elphick v. Church Commissioners* [1974] A.C. 562.
[17] Pastoral Measure 1983, s.3(1).
[18] *ibid.*, s.3(5).
[19] *ibid.*, s.3(5).
[20] *ibid.*, s.3(7).
[21] *ibid.*, s.3(8).
[22] *ibid.*, s.3(10).
[23] *ibid.*, s.3(10).

proposals which appear to him to be desirable,[24] and if he approves of the draft proposals he submits them to the Church Commissioners.[25] The pastoral committee must send a copy of the proposals submitted by the bishop to all interested parties, notifying them that if the Commissioners prepare a draft scheme or order they will be given an opportunity to make representations.[26]

Powers exercisable by pastoral scheme or order

5.45   Many of the powers under the 1983 Measure may be exercised by either a pastoral scheme or a pastoral order.[27] In both instances proposals are considered by the Chuch Commissioners, but with slightly differing procedures. Thereafter an order may be made by the bishop whereas a scheme requires the confirmation of an Order in Council.

Pastoral schemes may provide for the creation of new benefices and parishes (by union or otherwise), for the alteration of the boundaries of benefices and parishes, (including the transfer of a parish from one benefice to another), and for the dissolution of existing benefices and parishes.[28] Similar provisions may also be made in respect of archdeaconries and rural deaneries.[29] A scheme or order may provide for the creation of extra-parochial places, the incorporation of existing extra-parochial places in parishes, or the definition of the boundaries of a benefice, parish or extra-parochial place, or the alteration of the area of an existing extra-parochial place.[30] A scheme must name any new benefice or parish created by it, and a scheme or order may alter the name of existing benefices and parishes.[31] A scheme which provides for creation of a new benefice may also provide for the designation or selection of the first incumbent and associated matters.[32] Special provisions apply in the case of to the first rector in a team ministry or first incumbent of a benefice in a group ministry.[33]

A new parish may be created with full parochial status notwithstanding that the parish will have no parish church when the provision comes into operation,[34] but the bishop must then license one or more buildings for public worship.[35] When benefices are united all or some of the parishes within may be united or may remain separate.[36] Pastoral schemes may provide for a new church, and for it to become, after approval by the Church Commissioners and following consecration, a parish church, and for the designation of any church in a parish affected

[24] *ibid.*, s.3(9).
[25] *ibid.*, s.4(1).
[26] *ibid.*, s.4(2).
[27] The powers to be exercised by order are set out in *ibid.*, s.37. All other powers must be exercised by a scheme.
[28] *ibid.*, ss.17, 37. It may also provide for the merger of any benefice with a sinecure rectory or any office of minister of a church or chapel without the cure of souls: *ibid.*, s.35.
[29] *ibid.*, ss.19, 37.
[30] *ibid.*, save that a scheme is required to effect the transfer from a benefice or parish of any church used for public worship.
[31] See n. 28 *ante*.
[32] *ibid.*, s.24.
[33] See below.
[34] See n. 28 *ante*.
[35] *ibid.*, s.29(1).
[36] See n. 28 *ante*.

by the scheme as a parish church, or that a parish church cease to be such.[37] A scheme may also authorise the making of sharing agreements on behalf of the Church of England in respect of specified consecrated churches and parsonage houses, which will place such property in joint ownership with that church and any other church.[38] Such provision may specify terms and conditions under which authorisation is given.

Where a parish has more than one parish church by virtue of designation in a pastoral scheme the parishioners have the same rights of worship in each of the parish churches.[39] Thus marriages may be solemnised in any of the parish churches and burial rights are not affected by the designation.[40] The powers, duties and liabilities of the PCC extend to each of the parish churches and although two churchwardens are to be appointed for each of the churches all will be churchwardens of the whole parish except in so far as they arrange to perform separate duties in relation to the separate churches.[41]

The provisions in respect of patronage have beem considered earlier. A pastoral scheme may, subject to certain conditions, make provision in respect of the income of the endowments of a benefice other than one which will cease to exist by virtue of that scheme.[42] A scheme or order may also make provision for the designation of the house of residence of the incumbent of any benefice created or affected by a scheme or to be held in plurality, or of a vicar in a team ministry established by the scheme.[43] It may also provide for the transfer to the incumbent of any benefice for their official residence a parsonage house, or part thereof, or a site for such house, or a house situated on diocesan glebe land, and for the transfer to them of any parsonage and diocesan glebe land.[44] A scheme may in addition provide for the transfer of a parsonage house, or part thereof, and parsonage land to the DBF to be held as part of the diocesan glebe land.[45]

5.46   A scheme or order may contain such supplementary or consequential provisions as apear to the Church Commissioners, with the agreement of the bishop or bishops concerned (given after consultation with any pastoral committee concerned), to be necessary or expedient.[46] A scheme or order may also provide that it, or any of its provisions, come into operation on a specified date or date or upon the happening of a specified event or events or contingency.[47]

Where a scheme creates a new benefice by the union of benefices any property previously vested in the incumbent in right of the benefice vests in the new incumbent,[48] subject to express provision in the scheme and provisions relating to property held on charitable trusts.[49] Similarly where such property becomes

---

[37] *ibid.*, ss.17, 27.
[38] *ibid.* As to sharing agreements, see Chap. 8.
[39] *ibid.*, s.27(5).
[40] *ibid.*, s.27(5).
[41] *ibid.*, see also Chap. 4.
[42] *ibid.*, s.33. As to the endowments and income of benefices, see Chap. 8.
[43] *ibid.*, s.31. As to property of a benefice, parsonage houses, diocesan glebe land, and the role of the DBF, see Chap. 8.
[44] *ibid.*
[45] See n. 43 *ante.*
[46] Pastoral Measure 1983, s.38(1).
[47] *ibid.*, s.38(2), (3).
[48] *ibid.*, s.40, Sched. 3, para. 7.
[49] *ibid.*, Sched. 3, para. 11.

situated in a parish belonging to another benefice it vests in the incumbent of the benefice in which it is situated.[50] Where property vests in a person by virtue of general vesting provisions or is transferred by a pastoral scheme or order it vests without a conveyance and free from all previously existing trusts and charges in favour of any benefice.[51] Provision is also made for the application of the net proceeds of property transferred to the DBF for disposal.[52] Any transfer of property to the DBF for diocesan or parochial purposes is without consideration, unless the scheme provides otherwise.[53]

Making a pastoral scheme or order

5.47   The Church Commissioners must consider all draft proposals submitted to them, and make any comments upon them,[54] their comments then being considered by the bishop in consultation with the pastoral committee.[55] The Commissioners may subsequently make any amendments to the proposals which appear to them to be desirable provided they have the agreement of the bishop, his agreement only being given after consultation with the pastoral committee.[56]

Following this consultation procedure the Commissioners prepare a draft scheme or order.[57] If the draft proposals could be implemented by an order the Commissioners must prepare a draft order. They may also prepare such an order if part only of the proposals could be implemented by order, so as to give effect to those proposals or part thereof.[58] Otherwise a draft scheme is prepared.

The draft scheme or order must be served on all interested parties, together with a notice stating that written representations may be made to the Commissioners by a specified date,[59] (which may be extended[60]) In the case of a draft scheme a copy must be sent to the secretary of the PCC of every parish affected, who is required to affix a copy on or near the principal door of every church and place of worship within the parish.[61]

The Commissioners must consider all representations made to them and may if they think fit afford an opportunity to any person (whether or not they have made written representations) to make oral representations to them.[62] However, as we shall see, only those who make written representations regarding a scheme have a subsequent right of appeal. As a result of any representations, or at the request of the bishop who acts after consultation with the pastoral committee, the Commissioners may make amendments to a scheme or order.[63] However, any

[50] *ibid.*, s.40, Sched. 3, para. 7.
[51] *ibid.*, s.40, Sched. 3, para. 7.
[52] *ibid.*, Sched. 3, para. 9. See also Chap. 8.
[53] *ibid.*, s.40, Sched. 3, para. 9. See also Chap. 8.
[54] *ibid.*, s.5(1).
[55] *ibid.*, s.5(1).
[56] *ibid.*, s.5(3).
[57] *ibid.*, s.6(1).
[58] *ibid.*, s.5(4).
[59] *ibid.*, s.6(1).
[60] *ibid.*, s.6(6).
[61] *ibid.*, s.6(4).
[62] *ibid.*, s.6(5).
[63] *ibid.*, s.7(1).

such amendments may only be made with the agreement of the bishop, his agreement only being given after consultation with the pastoral committee.[64] An amended draft scheme or order is treated in the same manner as an original draft; and thus the same procedures regarding notice of the proposals and the opportunity to make representations and for further amendments to the scheme or order apply.[65]

If at any stage the bishop (after consultation with the pastoral committee) requests the Church Commissioners not to proceed with any proposals or withdraw a draft scheme or order the Commissioners must comply.[66] It should also be noted that a pastoral scheme may be revoked or amended by a subsequent scheme or amended by a subsequent order.[67] Similarly an order may be revoked or amended by a subsequent scheme or order.[68]

In cases where a pastoral order is to be made a draft copy is sealed by the Commissioners and submitted to the bishop who may then make the order by applying his seal.[69] In the case of a draft scheme the Commissioners must obtain the bishop's consent before sealing it, and then submit it for confirmation by Order in Council.[70] Once an order is made its validity cannot be questioned in legal proceedings. Similarly, a scheme may not be questioned in legal proceedings once made and confirmed, but a right of appeal exists in relation to a scheme following its submission to Her Majesty in Council for confirmation.[71]

Appeal against pastoral scheme

As soon as possible after submission of a pastoral scheme to Her Majesty in Council for confirmation the Church Commissioners, must so far as its practicable, serve on those who made written representations notice informing them of the fact of submission.[72] This notice must be accompanied by a written statement of the Commissioners' decision with respect to the representations made and the reasons therefore. It must also set out the right of those who made the written representations to the Commissioners to appeal to Her Majesty in Council (including specifying on what date notice of intention to apply for such leave must be given), subject to their obtaining leave from the Judicial Committee of the Privy Council.[73] The procedure for an application to obtain leave of the Judicial Committee to appeal and for an appeal are set out in Schedule 2 to the Pastoral Measure 1983. At the hearing of the appeal the onus is on the appellant to satisfy the Judicial Committee that the scheme is open to objections on the merits of it which would justify its being upset[74]: It should be noted that the

5.48

---

[64] *ibid.*, s.7(1).
[65] *ibid.*, s.7(2).
[66] *ibid.*, s.15.
[67] *ibid.*, s.39. Any amending scheme or order may provide for any matters which the original scheme or order could have provided for: *ibid.*
[68] *ibid.*
[69] *ibid.*, ss.8, 9, 11(2).
[70] *ibid.*, ss.8, 9, 11(2).
[71] *ibid.*, s.11(1).
[72] *ibid.*, s.9(1).
[73] *ibid.*, s.9(1).
[74] *Elphick v. Church Commissioners* [1974] A.C. 562, P.C.

Committee will be slow to dissent from the recommendations embodied in the scheme except for the most cogent reasons.[75] After hearing the appeal the Committee reports to Her Majesty in Council and makes a recommendation.[76] Her Majesty in Council may then either allow the appeal (in which case the scheme is of no effect but without prejudice to the making or submission of a further scheme), dismiss the appeal and confirm the scheme, or return the scheme to the Church Commissioners for reconsideration.[77] In the latter case the Commissioners may then withdraw the scheme, re-submit it without amendment, or amend it with the agreement of the bishop (given after consultation with the pastoral committee).[78]

Compensation of clergy

5.49   A pastoral scheme which dissolves a benefice, archdeaconry or rural deanery or abolishes or results in the abolition of the office of vicar in a team ministry may be brought into operation without the consent of the relevant holder of the office and without waiting for a vacancy in that office to occur.[79] Clergy who thus lose their office as the result of such a scheme, together with any incumbent, archdeacon or vicar in a team ministry who agrees with the pastoral committee that they will resign to enable or facilitate a scheme coming into operation, is entitled to compensation for the consequential loss of their office.[80] So too is any incumbent of a benefice deemed by a scheme to be vacated,[81] or for which a team ministry is established in circumstances where they are required to vacate the office of first rector or team vicar at the expiration of any term for which that office is to be held.[82]

Compensation consists of periodical payments or a lump sum or a combination of the two, and pending final determination of the sums payable payment may be made on account.[83] Special provisions apply to pensions payable pursuant to the Clergy Pensions Measure 1961.[84]

A claim for compensation must be in writing and sent to the secretary of the pastoral committee, either before the date the relevant provision of the pastoral scheme or order comes into effect or not later than 13 weeks after that date.[85] Particulars must be given of the loss suffered and the amount claimed, and

[75] *ibid., Hargreaves v. Church Commissioners* [1983] 2 A.C. 457, P.C.
[76] *ibid.*
[77] Pastoral Measure 1983, s.9(5).
[78] *ibid.*, s.9(6).
[79] *ibid.*, s.25(1).
[80] *ibid.*, s.26, Sched. 4, paras. 1–4.
[81] Which occurs where a benefice is not vacant on the coming into operation of a provision in a pastoral scheme for the holding of the benefice in plurality, or the establishment of a team or group ministry, where the incumbent is not to continue to hold office by virtue of a designation under the scheme or an appointment pursuant to it: *ibid.*, s.25(2).
[82] Pastoral Measure 1983, s.26, Sched. 4, paras. 1–4.
[83] *ibid.*, Sched. 4, para. 7.
[84] *ibid.*, Sched. 4, para. 13.
[85] Compensation of Clergy Rules 1970, S.I. 1970 No. 1009 (which in the absence of new rules made pursuant to the Pastoral Measure 1983, Sched. 4, para. 16, still applies by virtue of the Interpretation Act 1978, ss.17(2)(b), 22(3)).

whether periodic payments or a lump sum or both are sought.[86] The claimant has a right to an interview with the committee before determination of the claim, and may be represented at this by a barrister or solicitor or assisted by a friend.[87] Any costs reasonably incurred by the claimant in connection with such an interview are refunded to them out of the legal aid fund.[88] The committee must give its reasoned decision within 28 days of the making of the claim or the holding of an interview, and explain how any amount determined is calculated.[89] A claimant initially refused compensation or already receiving compensation may apply for a grant, renewal of increase on the ground that their circumstances have materially altered to their disadvantage.[90]

The right to compensation and amount payable is determined in the first instance by the pastoral committee.[91] In meeting to determine the amount of compensation, or when interviewing the claimant, the bishop or suffragan bishop and a member representing the DBF must be present and the committee's functions may not be delegated to a sub-committee.[92] The committee must take into account emoluments of any ecclesiastical office which the claimant has been or is to be appointed to, and any other regular remunerated employment in which they are, or are to be, engaged, and the claimant must disclose any such office or employment.[93] Account may also be taken of any ecclesiastical office which the claimant has refused to accept without good reason, provided the committee considers that office reasonably comparable to the office in respect of which compensation is sought.[94]

If any claimant executes a deed of relinquishment, becomes a member of a **5.50** religious body not in communion with the Church of England, or becomes disqualified from holding preferment in the Church of England, the committee may refuse the claim.[95] Similarly, if any clergy receiving, or having received compensation, falls under such heads, the committee may order that no further payments be made.[96] If the claimant fails to disclose any ecclesiastical office held or offered to them, or remunerated employment held or to be held, and as a result the committee is of the view that it has made payments in excess of or which it would otherwise not have made, it may direct repayment of the relevant amount.[97] Before the committee exercises its powers to suspend, reduce or terminate compensation or recover payments it must give written notice to the relevant person that it is considering exercising such powers.[98] Any person so affected may send written representations to the secretary of the committee within 14 days of receiving such notice and the committee must give a reasoned decision in writing.[99]

[86] *ibid.*
[87] See n. 85 *ante.*
[88] Church of England (Legal Aid) Measure 1994, Sched. 1.
[89] See n. 85 *ante.*
[90] Church of England (Legal Aid) Measure 1994, Sched. 1. Sched. 4, para. 10.
[91] Pastoral Measure 1983, Sched. 4, para. 6.
[92] *ibid.*, Sched. 4, para. 14.
[93] *ibid.*, Sched. 4, paras. 8, 12.
[94] *ibid.*, Sched. 4, paras. 8, 12.
[95] *ibid.*, Sched. 4, para. 11.
[96] *ibid.*, Sched. 4, para. 11.
[97] *ibid.*, Sched. 4, para. 12.
[98] See n. 85 *ante.*
[99] See n. 85 *ante.*

A right of appeal exists from the decision of the pastoral committee on a claim for compensation, or against the exercise of the committee's powers to suspend or reduce the amount of compensation, or terminate or recover payments, or against a refusal to make a grant, or renew or increase compensation.[1]

The appeal is to the appeal tribunal of the relevant province[2] and must be made by sending notice of appeal to the secretary of the appeal tribunal within 28 days of the committee's decision being sent to the claimant (together with a copy sent to the secretary of the committee).[3] The appellant must be given at least 14 days notice of an appeal hearing and may be represented by a barrister or solicitor or assisted by a friend.[4] The appeal tribunal may if it thinks fit receive oral or written evidence and is not bound to observe strict rules of admissibility of evidence.[5] It may confirm the committee's decision, substitute such decision as it thinks fit, or send the case back to the committee to reconsider together with such directions as it considers fit.[6] Any costs reasonably incurred by the claimant are refunded to them out of the legal aid fund.[7] Whether such costs have been incurred and the amount payable is determined on application to the diocesan registrar, with a right of appeal from their decision to the chancellor.[8]

Team and group ministries

5.51 Team and group ministries provide a legal framework for collaborative ministry. These model structures which were first set out in the Pastoral Measure 1968, developed as a result of certain instances of informal collaboration in both rural and urban areas. Some amendments were made to the structure for team ministries in the Pastoral Measure 1983 to enable additional clerical and lay persons to become members of a team.[9] Further amendments, mainly to team structures, have been made with the enactment of the Team and Group

---

[1] *ibid.*, Sched. 4, paras. 6, 9, 10, 11, 12.

[2] As to the constitution of which see *ibid.*, Sched. 4, para. 15.

[3] Compensation of Clergy Rules 1970, S.I. 1970 No. 1009 (which in the absence of new rules made pursuant to the Pastoral Measure 1983, Sched. 4, para. 16, still applies by virtue of the Interpretation Act 1978, ss.17(2)(b), 22(3).

[4] *ibid.*

[5] See n. 3 *ante.*

[6] See n. 3 *ante.*

[7] See n. 3 *ante.*

[8] See n. 3 *ante.*

[9] Some team ministries set up under a scheme pursuant to the Pastoral Measure 1986 were not amended in line with the Pastoral Measure 1983 to provide for the appointment of other team members. The Team and Group Ministries Measure 1995 automatically adds such provisions to those schemes: Pastoral Measure 1983, s.20A (1), (2). A procedure by which writtten representations opposing the coming into force of these automatic changes could be made by a PCC to the pastoral committee of the diocese. If representations were made the committee was to refer the matter to the Church Commissioners for their determination as to whether or not the provisions should apply: Pastoral Measure 1983, s.20A (3), (4). The time limit for making such representations has expired, but the new provisions may not apply to some schemes by reason of the Commissioners' determination.

Ministries Measure 1995.[10] A Code of Practice which deals with the implementation of the new Measure and with team and group ministries generally, has also been produced.[11] It should be noted that the Code of Practice emphasises that the establishment of a team or group ministry should not be motivated solely by a desire for pastoral reorganisation or as a response to a reduction in clergy numbers but out of genuine commitment to collaborative ministry.[12]

In this section we examine the provisions relating to team and group ministries, other than those in respect of district, team and group councils which we have already considered in Chapter 4.

Team ministries

A pastoral scheme may provide for the establishment of a team ministry for the **5.52** area of any benefice.[13] Whilst such a ministry is usually restricted to one benefice it may extend into the area of any other benefice held in plurality.[14] The cure of souls in the area is shared by a team of priests consisting of the incumbent of the benefice who is the team rector,[15] together with one or more additional priests each with the title of vicar who have equal status with the incumbent, and who together with the rector constitute the team chapter.[16]

Pastoral care of persons in the area is undertaken by the team chapter which shares the cure of souls, together with all other persons who are from time to time authorised by licence or permission of the bishop to serve in the area as members of the team; these further persons together with the team chapter constituting the team.[17] It is possible for a team ministry to consist of a rector and one team vicar but the Code of Practice recommends that the team consists of at least three and not more than eight to ten members.[18]

Team rector

Until the enactment of the 1995 Measure the office of rector was, depending **5.53** upon the terms of the scheme, either a freehold office or an office to be held for

---

[10] The 1995 Measure was based upon two reports: *Report of the Working Party on Team and Group Ministries* (1991) (G.S. 933) and *Team and Group Ministries: A Report of the Ministry Co-Ordinating Group* (1985) (G.S. 660).

[11] *Team and Group Ministries: Code of Recommended Practice* (1996). This Code supplements and in part replaces the material on team and group ministries in the *Pastoral Measure 1983: Code of Recommended Practice*. See also *Good Practice in Group and Team Ministry* (A.C.C.M. Occasional Paper No. 39 1991) and *The Sign We Give*, Report of the Working Party on Collaborative Ministry, Bishops' Conference of England and Wales (1995).

[12] Para. 18.

[13] Pastoral Measure 1983, s.20(1).

[14] *ibid.*, s.20(12).

[15] If the benefice is not a rectory already it becomes one under the pastoral scheme and its incumbent becomes the rector: *ibid.*, s.20(1).

[16] *ibid.*

[17] *ibid.*, s.20(1).

[18] Para. 32.

a term of years, as specified, that term being extendible.[19] All schemes made after May 1, 1996 must now provide that the office of rector is for a specified term of years[20] not a freehold office,[21] and all future appointments must be for a "specified term of years".[22] The fact that the office of rector may be held for a term of years does not affect its attributes as a benefice; the rector is a corporation sole, and has all the legal rights, powers and duties of an incumbent, including those in regard to the holding of property.[23]

5.54   The pastoral scheme may designate the first rector,[24] and must, unless the bishop is the sole patron, provide for the presentation of subsequent (and if necessary the first) rector. Presentation where the bishop is not sole patron[25] will usually be either by a special patronage board constituted by the scheme or by the diocesan board of patronage.[26] A special patronage board consists of the bishop as chairman and such other members as the scheme may provide for, or whom the bishop is empowered by the scheme to appoint.[27] Where presentation is to be made by the diocesan patronage board rights are given to persons specified in the pastoral scheme to attend and vote at relevant meetings of the board.[28]

Where the bishop or the diocesan board of patronage or special patronage board are to make the presentation they must consult the other members of the

[19] Pastoral Measure 1983, s.20(2). The restrictions in the Ecclesiastical Offices (Age Limit) Measure 1975, s.1 do not prohibit such extension where the rector was, until the coming into force of the pastoral scheme or order designating them rector, the incumbent of a benefice affected by the pastoral scheme or order, provided he held that benefice on January 1, 1976: Church of England (Miscellaneous Provisions) Measure 1978, s.2.

[20] The "specified term of years" is the term laid down by pastoral scheme or order specifically in relation to the relevant sub-sections of the Pastoral Measure 1983 as amended by the Team and Group Ministries Measure 1995. Where no term of years is laid down in this way the "specified term of years" is to be seven years unless and until it is altered pursuant to the Pastoral Measure: Pastoral Measure 1983, s.20(15).

[21] Pastoral Measure 1983, s.20(2), (7).

[22] The "specified term only applies to a rector who takes office after May 1, 1996. Thus if a scheme provides for the rector to hold for a particular term of years other than seven years that term will apply to a rector in office on May 1, 1996, but the "specified term" will apply to a rector appointed subsequently.

[23] Pastoral Measure 1983, s.20(2), (7).

[24] *ibid.*, s.20(4).

[25] The Code of Practice considers it undesirable that the bishop should be sole patron and recommends that where the bishop is sole patron of an existing team consideration is given to changing that arrangement by pastoral order: para. 48.

[26] *ibid.* Sched. 3, para. 1(1), (2). Where the Crown or Lord Chancellor held rights of patronage to the benefice those rights are preserved. Although in such a case the team vicars have no legal right to be consulted and it was stated in answer to a Synod Question at the July 1994 Group of Sessions that in practice they are: Code of Practice, para. 52.

[27] Pastoral Measure 1983, Sched. 3, para. 1(4), (5). In framing the scheme regard must be had for the interests of persons who previously held patronage rights but it is not essential that they be members where there are pastoral or practical objections: *ibid.* It is possible for the scheme to provide for representatives of the laity of the parishes concerned to be members: *ibid.* A right to be a member of the board is (except where vested in a person in right of their office or for life of a term of years) transferable both *inter vivos* and on death, but is not saleable and is not deemed to be a right in land: *ibid.*, Sched. 3, para. 1(10).

[28] *ibid.*, Sched. 3, para. 1(9).

team before choosing a new rector.[29] In addition where presentation is to be made by either the diocesan board of patronage or special patronage board, every team vicar, deacon with equivalent functions or any other team member with special responsibility for the pastoral care of a particular area has the right to attend meetings of the board.[30] These persons are entitled to one vote between them, exercised in accordance with the decision of the majority present at the meeting if there is disagreement.[31]

The exercise of rights of patronage in the case of a benefice in a team ministry are subject, as with the appointment of all incumbents, to the Patronage (Benefices) Measure 1986, which we considered earlier in this chapter. In choosing representatives of the PCC's, or team council concerned it is recommended that at least one of them is the representative of any particular area, church or sector for which the team rector is to have informal special responsibility.[32]

The statement of the House of Bishops of the General Synod regarding the appointment of clergy to posts of incumbent status applies to a team rector, as do the provisions of the Benefices Act 1898 and the Benefices Act 1972, all of which were discussed earlier in this chapter. The Ecclesiastical Offices (Age Limit) Measure 1975 also applies so as to limit appointments to those aged under 70 years.[33] In addition a team rector should be able to exercise leadership, but also be able to share power, authority and information with other team members, all of whom should possess maturity and a personality suited to collaborative ministry.[34]

Vicar in a team ministry

The office of vicar in a team ministry is an ecclesiastical office which was held for a term of years specified in the scheme or fixed in accordance with the bishop's licence.[35] A person appointed to the office must be a priest.[36] In regard to appointments made after May 1, 1996 the appointment is for a "specified term of years."[37] Although not as a matter of law an incumbent, a team vicar has equivalent status and the same security of tenure as the incumbent of a benefice.[38] Accordingly, their appointment is unaffected by a vacancy arising in the office of team rector.[39]   **5.55**

---

[29] *ibid.*, Sched. 3, para. 1(3). Where the bishop is the sole patron it is recommended that he considers how best to ensure that team members who would have the right to attend and vote in the case of a patronage board are particularly closely involved in the appointment: Code of Practice, para. 51(b).
[30] Pastoral Measure 1983, Sched. 3, para. 1(7A).
[31] *ibid.*
[32] Code of Practice, para. 53(e).
[33] Ecclesiastical Offices (Age Limit) Measure 1975, s.1, Sched.
[34] Code of Practice, paras 41, 57.
[35] Pastoral Measure 1983, s.20(3) (prior to amendment). Such term is extendable, see n. 19 *ante*; the provisions described therein apply equally to team vicars as to rectors.
[36] Pastoral Measure 1983, s.20(1), (3A).
[37] See n. 20 *ante*.
[38] Pastoral Measure 1983, s.20(1), (3), (8).
[39] *ibid.*

If the pastoral scheme so provides vicars may be chosen by the same body as the rector; otherwise they are chosen by the bishop and rector jointly.[40] Before the body, or persons entitled to choose a vicar do so, they must consult other members of the team, the PCC of every parish belonging to the benefice for the relevant area, and if a special cure is to be assigned to the vicar, any district church council concerned.[41]

Where the appointment is to be made by either the diocesan patronage board or a special patronage board the rector, team vicars, and any deacon with equivalent status, or any other team members with special responsibility for the pastoral care of a particular area have the right to attend and vote at such meetings.[42] The team rector has one vote and the other team members share one vote, exercised in accordance with the decision of the majority present at the meeting if there is disagreement.[43]

In all cases the parish representatives appointed by the PCC or PCCs concerned or by the team council now have substantially the same rights of appointment of a team vicar as they do under the Patronage (Benefices) Measure 1986 in regard to the appointment of the team rector.[44] Accordingly no offer of appointment is to be made to a team vicar unless the making of the offer has been approved by the parish representatives.[45] In cases where the representatives refuse to approve the making of the offer they must notify the person or body entitled to choose the team vicar of the reasons for so doing in writing.[46] That person or body may then request the archbishop of the relevant province to review the matter, and the archbishop may after review authorise the making of the offer.[47]

In all cases the statement of the House of Bishops regarding appointments to posts of incumbent status should be born in mind; however the provision discussed earlier in this chapter in respect of the Benefices Act 1898 and the Benefices Measure 1972 do not apply. The Ecclesiastical Offices (Age Limit) Measure 1975 applies so as to limit appointments to those aged under 70 years.[48] In addition the person appointed should have appropriate experience and maturity and it is recommended that the post should not be treated as equivalent to a second assistant curacy.[49]

Vicars are appointed by licence under seal, and unless the bishop otherwise directs, publicly admitted to a church in the area.[50] By virtue of their office a team vicar has (subject to their licence) authority to perform in the area of the benefice all such offices and services as may be performed by the incumbent.[51] However, this is subject to the proviso that a woman vicar does not have

---

[40] Pastoral Measure 1983, s.20(4)(b); Sched. 3, para. 2(1), (4).
[41] *ibid.*
[42] Pastoral Measure 1983, Sched. 3, para. 2(2), (3).
[43] *ibid.*
[44] And the same recommendations regarding the appointment of such representatives applies as in the case of a team rector discussed above: Code of Practice, para. 61.
[45] Pastoral Measure 1983, Sched. 3, para. 2, (6).
[46] *ibid.*
[47] Pastoral Measure 1983, Sched. 3, para. 2, (6).
[48] Ecclesiastical Offices (Age Limit) Measure 1975, s.1, Sched.
[49] Code of Practice, para. 62.
[50] Pastoral Measure 1983, s.20(4)(b), Sched. 3, para. 2(1), (4).
[51] *ibid.*, s.20(8).

authority to preside at or celebrate Holy Communion or pronounce the Absolution in a parish to which a resolution in the form set out in Resolution A of Schedule 1 to the Priests (Ordination of Women) Measure 1993 applies.[52]

Deacons within a team ministry

A deacon (who cannot hold office as a team rector or vicar) may be licensed to **5.56** serve in a team ministry as part of the team and perform, so far as is consistent with their office, all such offices and services as may be performed by an incumbent.[53] The appointment is for a "specified term of years".[54] Such deacons have the same security of tenure as an incumbent of a benefice and are not affected by a vacancy in the benefice of the rector,[55] but are not members of the team chapter. The Ecclesiastical Offices (Age Limit) Measure 1975 applies so as to limit appointments to those aged under 70 years.[56] It should be noted that these provisions were intended for cases where a mature and experienced deacon does not wish to seek ordination to the priesthood not where a newly ordained deacon is serving their first assistant curacy.[57]

Where a deacon has been so licensed the licence shall not be revoked by the bishop unless he is satisfied that there has been a serious breakdown of the pastoral relationship between the deacon and the parishioners concerned or because the deacon is unable to discharge their pastoral duties adequately by reason of age or infirmity.[58]

Other team members

A team ministry may also include various clerical and lay persons who are not of **5.57** incumbent status. A distinction must be drawn between those persons who are licensed or have permission to officiate within the benefice but who are not members of the team, and those who are specifically licensed as a member of the

---

[52] Pastoral Measure 1983, s.20(8). The proviso was added to section 20(8) of the Pastoral Measure 1983 by the Priests (Ordination of Women) Measure 1993, Sched. 3, para. 6. Curiously Sched. 1 to the Team and Group Ministries Measure 1995 sets out s.20 of the Pastoral Measure 1983 as amended by s.1 of the 1995 Measure without including the proviso. References to other enactments, unless the contrary intention appears, is a reference to that enactment as amended: Interpretation Act 1978, s.20(2). Thus the reference in s.1(13) and the text of the amended s.20(8) Pastoral Measure 1983 in the 1995 Measure should include the proviso. However, although the position is not entirely clear, it is to be presumed that no repeal of the proviso is implied and that the 1993 amendment remains.

[53] Pastoral Measure 1983, s.20(9A).

[54] See n. 20 *ante.*

[55] Pastoral Measure 1983, s.20(3A).

[56] *ibid.*, s.20(9A).

[57] Code of Practice, para. 72.

[58] Church of England (Legal Aid and Miscellaneous Provisions) Measure 1988, s.7(1A). A serious breakdown of the pastoral relationship is to be construed in accordance with s.19A of the Incumbents (Vacation of Benefices) Measure 1977: Church of England (Legal Aid and Miscellaneous Provisions) Measure 1988, s.7(1A).

team. Persons licensed to serve as members of the team are to serve for the period specified in the licence.[59] However, no one is to be so licensed unless nominated for that purpose by the team rector with the consent of a majority of the other team members and the consent of each PCC concerned, except in the case of a person whose licence to serve in the team ministry is being renewed when nomination is not required.[60]

Assignment of special cure or special pastoral responsibility

5.58 Either the pastoral scheme or the bishop's licence may assign to a team vicar a special cure of souls in respect of a part of the benefice and if appropriate the title of vicar of a particular church, or special responsibility for a particular pastoral function, either of which may be independent of the team rector's general responsibility.[61]

Similarly either the pastoral scheme or bishop's licence may assign any team member (clerical or lay) who is not a member of the team chapter special responsibility for pastoral care in respect of a part of the area of a benefice, so far as is consistent with that member's office.[62] Such assignment may, if by licence, be subsequently varied or revoked.

In addition to the formal delegation of special responsibilities informal arrangements for the division of responsibilities may be advisable.[63] However, where a body or organisation has a formal constitution providing that the incumbent holds a particular office, such as governor of a church school the team rector should take advice as to whether the functions can be properly delegated to another team member.[64]

Extended meaning of minister in cases where special cure or responsibility has been assigned

5.59 Given the possibility of assignment of either a special cure or special responsibility the Team and Group Ministries Measure 1995 has amended certain enactments so that the definition of minister, ordinarily applicable only to an incumbent or priest-in-charge is thereby extended.

Accordingly "minister" for the purposes of the CRR may include a team vicar to the extent that the duties of a minister are assigned to them by a pastoral scheme or order or by the bishop's licence.[65] In addition, in regard to the special

[59] Pastoral Measure 1983, s.20(3B).
[60] *ibid.*
[61] *ibid.*, s.20(8).
[62] *ibid.*, s.20(8A).
[63] Code of Practice, para. 73.
[64] *ibid.*, para. 75. In the case of a trustee of a charitable trust established for the ecclesiastical purposes of the Church of England which provides for the incumbent of the benefice to be a trustee, it is suggested that a team vicar with special cure of souls for the area or a major part of the area covered by the trust could take the incumbent's place but the point is not without doubt, and legal advice should be sought. The position is more doubtful still in regard to other team members taking the incumbent's place.
[65] CRR, r. 54.

provisions of the CRR regarding the minister's chairmanship of the PCC, where a special cure of souls in respect of the parish has been assigned to a vicar in a team ministry or where there has been no such assignment but a special responsibility for pastoral care in respect of the parish has been assigned to a member of the team under section 20(8A) of the Pastoral Measure 1983, that vicar or member shall be deemed to be the minister.[66]

Similarly for the purpose of the Churchwardens (Appointment and Resignation) Measure 1964[67] and the CCEJM[68] "minister" now includes a team vicar where a special cure of souls in respect of the parish has been assigned to them. Where there has been no such assignment but a special responsibility for pastoral care in respect of the parish has been assigned to a member of the team under section 20(8A) of the Pastoral Measure 1983 "minister" includes that vicar or other team member.[69]

Special provisions in regard to parsonage houses, glebe land and other property

The main provisions relating to parsonage houses and glebe property are discussed in Chapter 8. However, it should be noted that the Team and Group Ministries Measure 1995 introduced various provisions to ensure that team members are consulted in regard to their houses and in respect of other property matters affecting the benefice. **5.60**

Usually each team ministry has a benefice owned parsonage house owned by the team rector in their capacity as the incumbent, and one or more other houses owned by the diocese. However, it is not necessary for the team rector to occupy the official parsonage house.[70]

A parsonage house may not be disposed of without the consent of the team member occupying it.[71] Nor may the team rector or bishop exercise any powers in relation to the house if it is to be occupied by the rector, such as sale or improvements, without keeping the member informed of matters arising from the proposal and giving them an opportunity to express their views before proceeding.[72] Similarly the DBF may not alter or dispose of any house occupied by a member of a team ministry without keeping the member informed of matters arising from the proposal and giving them an opportunity to express their views before proceeding.[73] In relation to the disposal of glebe property all team vicars

---

[66] *ibid.*, App. II, r. 1. Save where that vicar or team member is incapacitated by absence or illness in which case the team rector is deemed to be the minister: *ibid.*

[67] s.13.

[68] s.31.

[69] Such team vicars or other team members must now be a party to any sharing agreement relating to any church building pursuant to the Sharing of Church Buildings Act 1969: *ibid.*, s.1(3).

[70] Code of Practice, para. 76. Ideally all team clergy should occupy houses of parsonage standard: *ibid.*

[71] Parsonages Measure 1938, s.1. Nor may sequestrators make improvements to a parsonage house without the consent of a team member occupying it during a vacancy in the benefice: *ibid.*, s.2A.

[72] *ibid.*, s.3.

[73] Diocesan Boards of Finance Measure 1925, s.3; PCCPM, s.6.

and any team member occupying the property now have a right to be informed of the proposals and to make representations which must be passed to the Church Commissioenrs by the DBF.[74]

A team rector who receives any statutory notice concerning ecclesiastical property in the benefice must also now keep all other members of the team informed. They must also give team members an opportunity to express their views and take account of those views before taking any action in regard to the notice.[75]

Team meetings

5.61 The rector in a team ministry must convene meetings of the team at regular intervals for the purpose of discussing and reaching a common mind on all matters of general concern or special interest to the team ministry.[76] In addition if any team member makes a written request to the team rector to convene a meeting to take place within 28 days and the rector fails to do so that team member may convene a meeting.[77]

The rector may preside at all team meetings if present, but may ask not to take the chair. In cases where the rector is not present or asks not to chair the meeting a deputy chairman appointed by the meeting presides.[78]

Role of team members during vacancy in the benefice

5.62 During a vacancy in the benefice the bishop may appoint a person holding the office of team vicar to act as rector for the purpose of having general responsibility for the cure of souls and leadership of the team, convening team meetings and nominating persons to be licensed as team members.[79] The bishop has complete discretion as to whether or not to make such an appointment and as to which team vicar is chosen.[80] The functions of such an acting team rector are not equivalent to a priest-in-charge, and they do not displace the functions of either the sequestrators or the lay chairman of the PCC.

As with every other vacancy in a benefice sequestrators are automatically appointed. However, whereas normally the sequestrators are the churchwardens, the rural dean and any other person the bishop considers it desirable to appoint, the place of the rural dean is normally taken by the team vicars and by any other team member who has special responsibility for the pastoral care of an area which is not within the area of a team vicar's special cure of souls.[81] However, the

---

[74] Endowments and Glebe Measure 1976, s.20. All team members must be consulted before parsonage land not required for occupation by the incumbent can be transferred to the DBF by the Church commissioners: *ibid.*, s.32.

[75] Pastoral Measure 1983, s.20(13),

[76] *ibid.*, s.20(10).

[77] *ibid.*, s.20(10A).

[78] *ibid.*, s.20(10).

[79] *ibid.*, s.20(14).

[80] Code of Practice, para. 102.

[81] Church of England (Miscellaneous Provisions) Measure 1992, s.1A, 1B.

appointment of the team vicars and other members is subject to the discretion of the bishop to decide not to appoint them.[82]

Reviews

The Code of Practice recommends regular reviews of the working of the team as **5.63** a whole as well as regular ministerial appraisals for each team member. In the case of team members holding office for a term of years a procedure for review is recommended in order to assist in deciding whether to continue the minister's team membership, involving the bishop, other team members, and representatives of all PCCs and of any congregation or sector for which that member has special responsibility and of any ecumenical partner churches.[83]

Termination or variation of team ministry

As the Code of Practice states, collaborative ministries tend to have a "life cycle" **5.64** during which a time may be right for them to be both restructured or disbanded.[84] A pastoral scheme may terminate a team ministry by abolishing the offices of team vicars and restoring the rectory where it is held on a term of years to a freehold office.[85] It may also make alterations to the structure of such a ministry by, for example, changing the number of offices of team vicar.[86]

Group ministries

A pastoral scheme may provide for the establishment of a group ministry for a **5.65** specified group of benefices.[87] The arrangement is a permanent one[88] and is thus not to be used as a temporary expedient. Nor is it an arrangement which is personal to the clergy who are incumbents within the group at the time when the original scheme comes into operation.

The main difference between a team and group ministry is that a group ministry is a collaborative ministry between incumbents who have all the rights and duties of an incumbent within their own benefice, whereas a team ministry is normally confined to a single benefice and involves sharing the incumbent's

---

[82] *ibid.*

[83] Paras. 95–97. In cases where there is a formal ecumenical partnership with other churches the Code recommends that the procedures for review are compatible with those existing for non-Anglican colleagues.

[84] Para. 14.

[85] Pastoral Measure 1983, s.22.

[86] *ibid.* A scheme may also, with the consent of the rector or vicar concerned, change the office of rector from a freehold to one held for the specified term of years or alter the term of years for which either such office is held to accord with the specified term, or make provision for the right of presentation of the rector to be transferred to the diocesan patronage board or a special patronage board.

[87] *ibid.*, ss.21(1), 35(4).

[88] Subject to alteration or termination by a pastoral scheme.

normal authority. A benefice with a team ministry may however be one of the benefices within a group ministry. In that case the team rector and all team vicars are treated as incumbents for the purposes of the group ministry.[89] It should also be noted that, save in relation to those provisions dealing with the rights and duties attaching to the office of incumbent, all provisions apply to a priest-in-charge of a benefice within the group as they do to an incumbent.[90]

The first person (who may be the existing incumbent) to hold any benefice as a benefice in the group may be designated by the pastoral scheme under which that group ministry is established.[91] Otherwise the incumbent is presented or collated to the benefice by the patron in the normal way, save for one exception. In cases where the bishop is not the patron he is required to give his approval to the choice, and must consult all other incumbents and any priests-in-charge within the group before making his decision.[92] In cases where the bishop withholds his approval the patron may bring the decision before the archbishop of the relevant province for review, and may present the person concerned if the archbishop authorises them to do so.[93]

The relationship between incumbents and any priest-in-charge in a group ministry is in the nature of a partnership. On a vacancy in any benefice in the group the incumbent is admitted to the relevant benefice as an office in the group ministry.[94] All the rights and duties of the group ministry are attached to that benefice, and so long as the group continues and the benefice is included within it the incumbent may not withdraw or resign from those rights and duties other than by resigning the benefice.[95]

It is the duty of all incumbents within the group to assist each other to make the best possible provision for the cure of souls throughout the area of the group ministry.[96] Each incumbent has the authority to perform offices and services in each benefice within the group,[97] except that a woman incumbent does not have authority to preside at or celebrate Holy Communion or pronounce the Absolution in a parish to which a resolution in the form prescribed in the Priests (Ordination of Women) Measure 1993, section 3(1) applies.[98] In performing such offices and services in the area of another benefice the incumbent concerned must act in accordance with directions of the incumbent of that benefice.[99]

The incumbents (including any team vicars) or priests-in-charge of the benefices constitute the group chapter. The group chapter must meet for the purpose of discussing and reaching a common mind on all matters of general concern or special interest to the group ministry.[1] The pastoral scheme setting up

[89] Pastoral Measure 1983, s.21(6).
[90] *ibid*., s.21(7), which applies to all the provisions in s.21 save for subss. (2), (3).
[91] *ibid*., s.21(3), Sched. 3, para. 3. The Code of Practice, para. 127 however recommends wide consultation, and that when the PCC prepares its statement under the Patronage (Benefices) Measure 1986 on the conditions, needs and traditions of the parish it stresses the importance of seeing the benefice in the context of the group ministry.
[92] Pastoral Measure 1983, s.21(3), Sched. 3, para. 3.
[93] *ibid*.
[94] *ibid*., s.21(1).
[95] *ibid*.
[96] *ibid*., s.21(1).
[97] *ibid*.
[98] *ibid*., s.20(1). See also Chap. 7.
[99] Pastoral Measure 1983, s.20(1).
[1] *ibid*., s.21(4).

the chapter may provide for the chairmanship of it. Subject to this the members elect their own chairman, normally for a period of three years.[2] The chairman convenes meetings and presides at them. When the chairman is absent a deputy chairman is appointed by the meeting.[3]

Assistant clergy and lay ministers are not part of the group chapter, although it is likely that they will be authorised to serve in the parishes covered by the group. The Code of Practice recommends that these ministers are given the opportunity to participate in meetings of the "greater chapter" from time to time, convened by the chairman of the group chapter.[4] The Code of Practice also recommends that regular reviews of the group ministry take place.

It is for the group chapter and any group council to identify areas for joint action and co-operation. However, the Code of Practice recommends that a regular interchange of ministry take place across the group as a matter of course, not only to provide cover for holidays and illness. Thus the group identity can be fostered without the special relationship between the incumbent and their parish or parishes being prejudiced.[5]

Termination or variation of group ministry

A pastoral scheme may terminate a group ministry by abolishing the rights and duties attaching to the benefices in the group.[6] A scheme or order may also alter such a ministry by reducing, increasing or changing the benefices within the group.[7]

5.66

[2] *ibid.*
[3] *ibid.*, s.21(4).
[4] Code of Practice, para. 136.
[5] *ibid.*
[6] Pastoral Measure 1983, s.22.
[7] *ibid.*

Chapter Six: Non-Parochial Units

In Chapter 4 we considered the parish, which can be regarded as the basic unit of **6.1** organisation within the Church of England. However, despite the importance of the parish structure there are some ecclesiastical places which are not within a parish, nor even within a diocese, and it is with these places that this chapter is concerned.

Of these non-parochial places the most significant are cathedrals, but we shall also be examining the position of peculiars, which are places where the bishop does not possess Ordinary jurisdiction, and guild churches of the City of London. Finally we will consider the position of the various types of chapel, including those of institutions and of the armed forces, and explore the extent to which their chaplains may minister free from the control of the incumbent of the parish in which the chapel is situated.

Cathedrals

Originally the cathedral, or more accurately the cathedral church was the only **6.2** church in the diocese or *parochia*. Containing the throne or *cathedra* of the bishop from which it derives its name, the cathedral remains, and is often described as, the mother church of the diocese.[1] Cathedrals are categorised as either dean and chapter cathedrals, or parish church cathedrals, which are of more recent origin, having been thus designated under the Cathedrals Measure 1963.

The dean and chapter cathedrals can be further divided—although this is now only a matter of historic interest—into those of the old foundation (York, St Paul's, Hereford, Lincoln, Lichfield, Chichester, Exeter, Salisbury and Wells) which before the Reformation had been in the charge of secular priests, and those of the new foundation (Canterbury, Winchester, Worcester, Ely, Carlisle, Durham, Rochester and Norwich) which had been monastic but which after the Reformation were put in the charge of secular canons. The five cathedrals (Chester, Peterborough, Oxford, Gloucester and Bristol) founded *de novo* by Henry VIII have also been categorised as being of the new foundation, but the description is not strictly accurate.[2]

When a new diocese was created an existing parish church was generally designated the cathedral church and its incumbent styled provost. Such a church's

---

[1] *e.g.* Cathedrals Measure 1963, s.9(2).
[2] *Halsbury's Laws of England* (4th ed.), Vol. 14, para. 610.

dual role is recognised in its constitution and statutes which provide for its administration as a cathedral and for the continuation of the ministry to its own parish. Provision does exist for a parish church cathedral to become a dean and chapter cathedral.[3]

Each cathedral has its own constitutions and statutes which provide for its governing body, the appointment and functions of a dean or provost and other clergy and officers and for other matters concerning its organisation. Despite its close connection with the bishop and the fact that it is subject to his visitation, the cathedral has considerable autonomy; in particular it is not subject to either diocesan administrative control nor, since the bishop is not the Ordinary, to the jurisdiction of the consistory court.

6.3   The role of cathedrals was considered recently in the Archbishops' Commission on Cathedrals. Whilst that Commission recognised the importance of the independence of cathedrals, it also stated that they should not be so independent as to stand against the authority of the Church as a whole, and that in particular the cathedral should not offer a scrutiny of episcopal stewardship, nor an alternative reference point in the diocese, the episcopal and diocesan strategy being of primary importance in the administration of the Church.[4] That Commission also concluded that there were as many different types of cathedrals as there were cathedrals, recommending the abolition of the distinctions between dean and chapter and parish church cathedrals in favour of a new uniform model of cathedral organisation. This would involve the creation of a greater Council for each cathedral, with the diocesan bishop as its chairman, together with an administrative council responsible for running the cathedral with a dean as its chairman, in much the same way as the current administrative bodies. The proposals also include greater involvement for the laity, both worshippers and employees of the cathedral, in its governance and suggest that the cathedral be given a recognised place in the structure of synodical government.[5]

Cathedrals Measure 1963

6.4   The 1963 Measure applies to all cathedrals in England which then existed,[6] other than Christ Church, Oxford,[7] to which it has only limited application. Whilst it is true that all the dean and chapter cathedrals are governed by their own constitutions and statutes, certain common factors apply to all of them. In the case of Christ Church, which is both a constituent college of the University of Oxford and a cathedral church and which lies almost wholly outside the scope of the 1963 Measure, few parallels exist with other cathedrals, and it must therefore be regarded as unique that further consideration of its position is beyond a work of this nature.

---

[3] Cathedrals Measure 1963, s.14.

[4] *Heritage and Renewal*, the Report of the Archbishops' Commission on Cathedrals, G.S. 1994 No. 1192, Chap. 2.

[5] *ibid.*, Chap. 6.

[6] Cathedrals Measure 1963, s.55. This Measure and the Cathedrals Measure 1976 also apply to a church which becomes the cathedral church of a new diocese created by a reorganisation scheme under the Dioceses Measure 1978: *ibid.*, s.22.

[7] *ibid.*, ss.52(1), 42, 54, 55 proviso (a).

The 1963 Measure established a Cathedrals Commission whose purpose was to prepare schemes for each cathedral in order to bring their constitutions and statutes into conformity with the Measure, thus ensuring a greater uniformity in the governance of cathedrals. The Commission, which was to cease in 1966, has been replaced by the Cathedrals Statutes Commission, whose function is to prepare schemes for revising a cathedral's constitution and statutes when an application is made to it by the consenting body of a cathedral.[8]

A scheme made pursuant to the 1963 Measure could either provide for a new constitution and statutes or amend those already existing, which were often of ancient origin.[9] The Measure specified certain obligatory provisions which were to be included within the new or amended constitution and statutes.[10] Thus provision was made for the diocesan bishop to be the visitor of the cathedral church and for the exercise of his functions as visitor, as well as setting out the occasions on which the bishop was to have the right to officiate in or use the cathedral and the conditions to which this right was subject.

The principal governing body of a cathedral is called the capitular body. In a dean and chapter cathedral the capitular body is the general chapter consisting of the dean and all the canons whether residentiary or not. In a parish church cathedral it is the cathedral chapter which consists of the provost, the canons of the cathedral and the archdeacons of the diocese, with the possible inclusion of the bishop for specified purposes. A dean and chapter are a corporation aggregate and it would appear that the chapter of a parish church cathedral has the same status.[11] In either case the constitution and statutes provide that the capitular body has a common seal which its administrative body must be empowered to affix to any document.

In the case of dean and chapter cathedrals provision was made for the continuance or establishment of a general chapter. Provision was also made for the administrative functions to be performed, either by the general chapter with delegation to an administrative committee, or by an administrative chapter, comprising the dean and residentiary canons and any other specified members of the general chapter. In either case this chapter was to be referred to as the administrative body.

The constitution and statutes of a parish church cathedral provide for the continuance of a cathedral chapter. The administrative functions of such cathedrals are performed either by the cathedral chapter, which must delegate determined functions to an administrative committee, or the cathedral council or administrative chapter, again in each case referred to as the administrative body. Thus in the case of these cathedrals membership of the administrative body is not necessarily confined to those who are members of the capitular body.

[8] Cathedrals Measure 1976, s.1. The procedure is set out in this Measure. The Commission prepares a draft scheme after consultation with the consenting body of the cathedral and submits it to the bishop, Church Commissioners and every other person likely to be affected, so far as is practicable, as well as publishing the scheme. Written representations are then considered and after further consultation the scheme (with any amendments) is laid before the General Synod. If Synod does not pass a resolution to prevent the scheme the Commissioners then make the scheme; all those who made written representations against it having a right of appeal to the Privy Council.

[9] Cathedrals Measure 1963, s.5 (repealed).

[10] *ibid.*, ss.6–10.

[11] *Halsbury's Laws of England* (14th ed.), Vol. 14, para. 638.

6.5 For all cathedrals provision is made for the holders of two residentiary canonries to be engaged exclusively on cathedral duties, but these provisions are not regarded as limiting the number of residentiary canons who may be engaged on such duties. Cathedral duties are those which are either undertaken in connection with the cathedral church, or pastoral duties within the diocese which in the opinion of its administrative body should be discharged from the cathedral as the mother church of the diocese.

Provision was also made in the case of all dean and chapter cathedrals for the appointment of a dean by the Sovereign, and in the case of a parish church cathedral for the appointment as provost of the incumbent of the benefice for which the cathedral is the parish church. The maximum number of both residentiary and non-residentiary canons was specified together with their manner of appointment. In respect of rights of patronage exerciseable by the capitular body, these are now exercised either by the dean and chapter or the dean and chapter's patronage committee, or, in the case of a parish church cathedral, by the cathedral or administrative chapter or a patronage committee of the cathedral chapter. Provision was also made in respect of certain other matters concerning the property and finances of cathedrals which are considered in Chapter 8.

In the case of parish church cathedrals the jurisdiction of the archdeacon and rural dean over the parish of the cathedral was abolished and their functions taken over by the administrative body of the cathedral. Any jurisdiction which the consistory court exercised over the cathedral was also abolished although, as we shall see in Chapter 8, that jurisdiction may now be restored if the administrative body and the diocesan synod so wish.

In cases where the constitution and statutes provided for the transfer to the administrative body of the cathedral those functions in relation to the parish previously exerciseable by the PCC, they must also provide that at least one-third of the lay persons appointed to the body responsible for those functions are elected at the annual parochial church meeting. Upon the transfer of functions the CRR have effect, subject to certain modifications, in relation to the parish concerned, as does the PCCPM.[12]

Despite the fact that these obligatory provisions have achieved some degree of uniformity, the inclusion of various additional and optional provisions means that the constitutions and statutes of the cathedrals do contain significant differences of which anyone concerned with, or wishing to understand, the administration of a cathedral should be aware.

Clergy

6.6 As we have already seen[13] no person may hold a cathedral preferment with a benefice unless the cathedral statutes provide for or allow this, and no person may hold preferment in more than one cathedral. In addition it should be noted that the administrative body of a cathedral, or in the case of certain parish church cathedrals the PCC, may pass resolutions pursuant to the Priests (Ordination of Women) Measure 1993 which would preclude a woman from being appointed

---

[12] Cathedrals Measure 1963, s.12.
[13] See Chap. 5.

dean or provost, and which would curtail the functions of a women priest subsequently appointed as a canon.[14] Although cathedrals enjoy considerable autonomy their clergy may be subject to the disciplinary proceedings under the EJM.

Deans and provosts

A dean, or cathedral dean as they are sometimes called to distinguish them from **6.7** other deans, is the head of the general chapter of a dean and chapter cathedral, and a cathedral provost the head of the chapter of a parish church cathedral. Both dean and provost are styled the "Very Reverend" and are said to be next in dignity to the bishop of the diocese, although this is also a position ascribed to the chancellor of the diocese and to the archdeacon. The dean is sometimes called the archpresbyter of the diocese although it is doubted whether the dean has the cure of souls of anyone other than the chapter.[15]

No person can be appointed as cathedral dean or provost who has not been in priest's orders for six years,[16] nor must the person appointed be more than 69 years old.[17] In either case the office must also be vacated when the holder reaches the age of 70, unless there are special circumstances which the diocesan bishop considers make it desirable that they should continue in office after that date, in which case the bishop may authorise them to continue in office for a further period not exceeding one year.[18] Should a dean wish to resign a deed is not required but the resignation should be in writing, signed and witnessed, and sent to the Sovereign.[19] A provost, as incumbent of the parish, follows the same procedures regarding resignation as would any incumbent.[20]

The constitution and statutes of the cathedral provide for the appointment of the dean by the Sovereign. The requirements for the post are first assessed by the Prime Minister's secretary for appointments who consults with the bishop, cathedral chapter, other staff and the retiring dean. A list of potential candidates is then drawn up and, after further consultation the person considered most suitable is asked if they would be willing for their name to be put forward. If they are willing the Prime Minister then recommends their appointment to the Sovereign.[21]

---

[14] See Chap. 7. Such a woman priest would be precluded from presiding at Holy Communion or pronouncing the Absolution at any service in the parish in the case of a parish church cathedral or at any service other than one held on the direction of the bishop in the case of a dean and chapter cathedral.

[15] *Halsbury's Laws of England* (14th ed.), Vol. 14, para. 640.

[16] Ecclesiastical Commissioners Act 1840, s.27; Church of England (Miscellaneous Provisions) Measure 1995, s.5; Canon C21(1).

[17] Ecclesiastical Offices (Age Limit) Measure 1975, s.1, Sched.

[18] *ibid.*, ss.1, 3. Thid does not apply to a person who held office on January 1, 1976.

[19] England (Miscellaneous Provisions) Measure 1995, s.4.

[20] See Chap. 5.

[21] The manner in which deans, provosts and residentiary canons are appointed is set out in *Senior Church Appointments*, the Report of the Working Party established by the Standing Committee of the General Synod (G.S. 1992 No. 1019), together with proposals for reform. See also *Heritage and Renewal*, the Report of the Archbishops' Commission on Cathedrals (G.S. 1994 No. 1192), Chap. 8, which broadly adopts the same approach as the Working Party regarding such appointments. The Commission also questions whether it is appropriate for such appointments to carry with them freehold tenure.

A provost of a parish church cathedral is usually appointed by the patron of the benefice, and the provisions of the Patronage (Benefices Measure) 1986 will apply.[22] In almost every case the bishop is patron of these churches.

The duties of deans and provosts are set out in Canon C21. They must ensure the observation of the statutes and laudable customs of their church so long as they are neither repugnant to the Word of God or contrary to the Royal prerogative. They must also ensure observance of the statutes of the Realm concerning ecclesiastical order, and obey the lawful directions of the bishop in his visitation. They are also required to be resident in the cathedral for the time prescribed by law and the statutes of the cathedral, and whilst there to preach the Word of God and perform all the duties of their office, unless hindered by weighty or urgent cause. Finally, they are under a duty to provide, as far as possible, that during the time of divine service all things are done with such reverance, care and solemnity as to set forth the honour and glory of God. Although the cathedral is not subject to diocesan administration the dean or provost is an *ex officio* member of the diocesan synod.

Canons

6.8 Originally the term canon applied only to those residentiary members of the cathedral chapter other than the dean. Now the term has a wider meaning, being also applied to non-residentiary canons or prebendaries, but not to minor canons or any person not in holy orders.[23] In some chapters canons were previously known as prebendaries,[24] and still in certain cathedrals non-residentiary canons are referred to as prebends. Non-residentiary canons are also identified with honorary canons, although strictly the terms should not be regarded as interchangeable since it is possible for a stipendiary canon not to be a residentiary canon whereas an honorary canon receives no emoluments.[25] Honorary canonries were founded in 1840 in any cathedral which did not already have non-residentiary prebends or dignities to be conferred as a distinction upon deserving clergy.[26]

Generally speaking a residentiary canon is required to reside within the diocese. However, provision may be made within the constitution and statutes of a cathedral for the appointment of canons not resident in the diocese, or for a canon who ceases to reside in the diocese to continue in office at the request of the bishop.[27] Some non-residentiary canons may be appointed in connection with a specific office or function and would continue as canons so long as they hold that office or perform the function, regardless of whether or not they cease to reside in the diocese.[28]

---

[22] See Chap. 5.

[23] Cathedrals Measure 1963, s.52(1).

[24] The term derives from endowments *in praebendam* for the maintenance of a secular priest or regular canon.

[25] Pastoral Measure 1983, s.85(5) refers to a residentiary or stipendiary canon.

[26] Ecclesiastical Commissioners Act 1840, s.2 (repealed). Similar provision was made on the founding of new bishoprics.

[27] Cathedrals Measure 1963, s.11(2)(e)(f).

[28] *ibid.*

A canon, or at least a canon of a dean and chapter cathedral, is a corporation sole. The canon has a stall in the choir and a voice in the cathedral.[29] As well as providing that two of the residentiary canons are to be engaged exclusively on cathedral duties the constitution and statutes of a cathedral may provide for a canonry to be annexed to a particular office.[30] Thus in some cathedrals one of the canons is known as chancellor, this office needing to be distinguished from the diocesan chancellor, and in others one is known as treasurer. There are also, in some cathedrals, canons theologian.[31]

No person can be appointed as a canon residentiary who has not been in holy orders for six years. A deacon may be appointed to this office, and to that of a non-residentiary canon, notwithstanding anything to the contrary in the cathedrals statutes and constitution.[32] An exception to the requirement of holy orders is made in the case of a canonry annexed to any professorship, headship or other office in any university.[33] The majority of canonries are in the gift of the diocesan bishop although the Sovereign has the right to appoint some residentiary canons in certain cathedrals and the Lord Chancellor in some others.[34]

The same requirements regarding the maximum age for appointment and retirement apply to residentiary canonries (other than those annexed to a professorship in a university) as to deans and provosts. The constitution and statutes of the cathedral provide for the number of canons and their manner of appointment, and subject to these a canonry is a freehold office. A residentiary canon is subject to the same duties as a dean or provost and the procedure for resignation is the same as that for a dean.

Other offices and appointments

The constitution and statutes of a cathedral may provide for the constitution of **6.9** any body or creation of any office for the performance of functions in relation to the cathedral or diocese.[35] In particular the constitution and statutes may provide for a college of lay canons, specifying their functions. They may also provide for the appointment and terms of service of those holding office in the cathedral or employed in connection with it, there being a large body of lay persons serving the cathedral who receive remuneration in addition to those who volunteer their services.[36] These include organists, lay clerks and choristers for the choir, vergers, those concerned with the upkeep of the fabric and the supervision of visitors and a registrar who is a solicitor and who often also acts as the chapter clerk. In Canterbury the office of seneschal or chief lay advisor to the dean and chapter, who acts as a link to the laity, has been revived.[37]

[29] *Halsbury's Laws of England* (4th ed.), Vol. 14, para. 644.
[30] Cathedrals Measure 1963, s.11(2)(g).
[31] *Halsbury's Laws of England* (4th ed.), Vol. 14, para. 644.
[32] See Chap. 7.
[33] Canon C21(1); Church of England (Miscellaneous Provisions) Measure 1995, s.2(3).
[34] See n. 21, *ante*.
[35] Cathedrals Measure 1963, s.11(1)(a), (b), (j).
[36] *Heritage and Renewal*, the Report of the Archbishops' Commission on Cathedrals, ((1994) G.S. No. 1192) Chap. 9, considers the position of these and makes various recommendations.
[37] *The Times*, May 18, 1974.

Those Clerks in holy orders who are assistants to the members of the cathedral chapter are usually described as minor canons, vicars choral or priest vicars. The office is one of ancient origin and was originally endowed. They do not have the cure of souls, nor is their office a benefice and it would appear that the office is no longer capable of conferring a freehold.[38] Usually the persons serving as sacristan (looking after the vergers and furnishings) and precentor (looking after the music in co-operation with the organist) are minor canons or vicars choral but in some cathedrals, especially those of the ancient foundation, the office of precentor is held by a canon. All minor canons have the same obligations regarding the proper conduct of divine service as the dean, provost and residentiary canons.

Incapacity of church dignitaries

6.10 The Church Dignitaries (Retirement) Measure 1949 makes provision for the removal of dignitaries on the grounds of age or infirmity. The Measure does not deal with situations where the dignitary proves unsuitable for the post, or where a breakdown of relations occurs, and its powers have hardly ever been evoked, if at all.[39] The Measure extends to deans provosts of cathedral churches, archdeacons, canons and prebendaries whether or not stipendiary and any clergy holding a freehold office other than the incumbent of a parish.[40]

Where the bishop is satisfied that such action is proper he may, by notice in writing, require a special meeting of the cathedral chapter to consider and report to him whether in their opinion the dignitary is incapable of performing their duties adequately through disability arising from age or infirmity, whether mental or physical, and if so if they should retire. If the position is other than an honorary office the chapter must also consider whether on retirement an additional pension should be granted in addition to that which would have been paid if the dignitary had retired voluntarily.[41] The chapter must consider the question and invite the dignitary concerned (who may be assisted or represented in their absence by a friend or advisor) and the bishop's representative (if the bishop appoints one) to confer with them, either separately or together.[42]

The dignitary must be served with a copy of the bishop's notice and the special meeting must not be summoned unless 21 days have elapsed. Within 15 days of receiving the notice the dignitary may require a medical examination and the meeting must not then be summoned until the medical report has been sent to the dean or provost. The dignitary is entitled to give oral evidence and call witnesses at the meetings of the chapter and to be present at any meeting at

---

[38] *Halsbury's Laws of England* (14th ed.), Vol. 14, para. 647.

[39] *Heritage and Renewal*, the Report of the Archbishops' Commission on Cathedrals, (1994) (G.S. No. 1192) Chap. 8, which proposes reform of the current procedures.

[40] Church Dignitaries (Retirement) Measure 1949, s.12. It excludes holders of offices in royal peculiars, members of the dean and chapter of Christ Church, Oxford and lay canons.

[41] *ibid.*, s.1. If the dignitary concerned is a member of the chapter they may not sit or vote at the special meeting, and where it is the dean or provost notice of the meeting must be sent to another member of the chapter: *ibid.*, s.13.

[42] *ibid.*

which any other person is to give evidence and put questions to that person as well as being able to require others to give evidence.[43] The chapter may also ask the bishop or his representative to make futher enquiry into the matter and report back to it.[44]

The chapter must then make a report in writing to the bishop, but should only report that it is desirable a dignitary retire if at least two-thirds of its members present and voting were in favour.[45] If they report in favour of retirement the bishop has the power, within six months of receipt of the report, depending upon the office in question either to petition the Sovereign, declare the office vacant or to execute an instrument himself (that matter being one for his discretion).[46]

Where the dignitary is also the incumbent of a parochial benefice the declaration of vacancy of the dignity has the effect of vacating the parochial benefice. However, the dignitary may be the the subject of proceedings under the Incumbents (Vacation of Benefices) Measure 1977 in respect of that parochial benefice. In cases where the incumbent resigns his parochial benefice as a result of a notification from the bishop or the bishop has declared the benefice vacant as a consequence of such proceedings, the bishop may treat the report of the diocesan committee or provincial tribunal under the 1977 Measure as if it had been a report of the cathedral chapter, and may then decide whether to declare or petition the Sovereign to declare the cathedral office vacant, there being no appeal from his decision to do so.[47]

Peculiars

Royal peculiars are subject only to the Crown. Two, Westminster Abbey and St George's Chapel, Windsor, resemble cathedrals in that they are governed by a dean and chapter, who are appointed by the Sovereign. In each case the dean is the Ordinary and the Sovereign the Visitor (through the Lord Chancellor). The chapels royal are also royal peculiars and subject only to the Crown.[48]   **6.11**

Few peculiars now survive in England, since most were abolished by statute, and the status of those which are alleged to remain has in many cases been challenged. In all cases although free of episcopal jurisdiction they are subject to the visitation of the Archbishop of Canterbury. Since all parish churches are now subject to the jurisdiction of the consistory court any peculiar which is a parish church has lost its independence in this respect.[49]

Bocking and Battle are peculiars with a dean but no canons. The Temple Church, Lincoln's Inn and Gray's Inn are probably peculiars with the Benchers of the respective Inns as the Ordinary, or at least extra-diocesan.[50] St Edward's, Cambridge was long thought to be a peculiar but its status has now been challenged and it would appear not to be.[51]

[43] Church Dignitaries (Retirement) Rules 1986, S.I. 1986 No. 1143. All relevant meetings of the chapter require a quorum of at least half the members entitled to attend and vote.
[44] See n. 41, *ante.*
[45] *ibid.*
[46] Church Dignitaries (Retirement) Measure 1949, s.2.
[47] *ibid.*, s.14.
[48] See *The Church of England Yearbook.*
[49] CCEJM, s.11(1).
[50] *Halsbury's Laws of England* (14th ed.), Vol. 14, para. 492.
[51] Briden and Hanson, *Moore's Introduction to English Canon Law* (3rd ed., 1992), p. 45.

College Chapels in the universities of Oxford and Cambridge, whilst not generally refered to as peculiars, do claim to be outside the respective jurisdictions of the Bishops of Oxford and Ely, and to have their own Ordinary who is generally the governing body of the college. It is far from clear whether the Ordinary is visitable by the visitor of the college, the Archbishop of Canterbury or both or neither. Whatever their true status in practice the colleges behave as though they are extra-diocesan and their claims have not been greatly contested.[52]

Guild churches

6.12 Guild churches exist only in the City of London. They were created by the City of London (Guild Churches) Act 1952 in response to the problem of the large number of parish churches in the City which had few resident parishioners, taking advantage of the need to reorganise following war damage. Sixteen churches were designated guild churches,[53] the term being of no particular significance and not implying any connection with any guild.

The main purpose of a guild church is to minister to the non-resident population of the City. A secondary function is to provide a reserve of clergy with special qualifications in scholarship, preaching and other skills which would render them suitable for specialised work elsewhere.[54]

The area which previously formed the parish of the guild church was transferred to another parish,[55] but the minister of the guild church, the church itself and its churchyard are free from the jurisdiction and control of the incumbent, churchwardens and PCC of the parish within which they are situated. They remain however within the relevant deanery, archdeaconry and within the Diocese of London diocese.[56]

The effect is to create a parish church without a territorial parish. Each church has a patron, a minister who is styled a vicar, stipendiary curates (if required), churchwardens, sidesmen (if required), a guild church council, church electoral roll and a guild church clerk.[57]

The minister appointed must be in priest's orders and has the cure of souls of those on the guild church electoral roll. In regard to the church and churchyard the vicar has all the rights and duties of an incumbent and is subject to ecclesiastical discipline in the same way. A vicar is initially appointed for five years. This may be extended for a further period of three years, and the vicar may resign at any time with the bishop's consent. In general such a vicar may not undertake other duties except with the approval of the Bishop of London.[58]

---

[52] *ibid.*, p. 46.

[53] City of London (Guild Churches) Act 1952, s.4(1), Sched. 1. These are: All Hallows London Wall, St Andrew's Holborn, St Benet Paul's Wharf, St Botolph without Aldersgate, St Dunstan in the West, St Ethelburga Bishopsgate, St Katherine's Cree, St Lawrence Jewry, St Margaret Pattens, St Martin Ludgate, St Mary Abchurch, St Mary Aldermanbury, St Mary Aldermary, St Mary Woolnoth, St Michael Paternoster Royal and St Nicholas Cole Abbey.

[54] *ibid.*, s.5.

[55] The parish of the guild church does not cease to exist for civil purposes: *ibid.*, s.34.

[56] *ibid.*, s.5.

[57] *ibid.*, s.6.

[58] *ibid.*, s.12.

Lay members of the Church of England who declare themselves to be such, aged at least 16, who are baptised and who also declare that they do not belong to any body which is not in communion with the Church of England and who make a written application to the vicar are entitled to have their names on the electoral roll.[59] However, no person may be on the roll of more than one guild church nor on a guild church roll if they are on the roll of a parish in the City of London. For the purposes of the CRR, which prescribe the qualifications for election or membership to a deanery or diocesan synod or the House of Laity of the General Synod, a person on the roll of a guild church is deemed to be on the roll of the parish in which that guild church is situated.[60]

The guild church council corresponds to the PCC of a parish, and it elects representatives to the deanery synod under a special scheme.[61] Churchwardens are appointed at the annual guild church meeting under a procedure similar to that for choosing churchwardens of a parish and they have similar powers, duties and liabilities as parish churchwardens.[62]

The vicar has control of all services held in the church but is not obliged to hold any public service on a Sunday.[63] The Bishop of London may licence guild churches for the solemnisation of marriages between persons at least one of whom is on the electoral roll.[64] Baptism may occur of those under 18 years if one of their parents is on the roll, of those over 18 who intend to apply for enrolment and of any other person with the written consent of the incumbent of the parish in which they reside.[65]

Chapels

As a matter of strict law the term chapel relates only to a building consecrated **6.13** for the purposes of divine worship according to the rites of the Church of England which is not a parish or cathedral church.[66] A chaplain is someone who is appointed to perform divine service in such a chapel. In addition to ministers of chapels of ease, proprietary and private chapels, there are chaplains in institutions such as universities, schools, hospitals, prisons, charitable institutions and cemeteries and chaplains of the armed forces.

Chapels of ease

A chapel designated a chapel of ease may have been built for the convenience of **6.14** those parishioners who live at some distance from the parish church for prayer and preaching, although the sacraments and burials should be performed in the

[59] *ibid.*, s.15. An appeal against refusal lies under the CRR as it would to an appeal against a refusal of enrolment on church electoral roll: *ibid.*

[60] CRR, r. 5.

[61] City of London (Guild Churches) Act 1952, ss.17, 18.

[62] *ibid.*, s.19.

[63] *ibid.*, s.12.

[64] *ibid.*, s.22, which applies the law relating to solemnisation and registration of marriages generally to these churches.

[65] *ibid.*, s.23, which applies the law relating to the registration of baptism to these churches.

[66] *Halsbury's Laws of England* (4th ed.), Vol. 14, para. 1225.

parish church.[67] Such a chapel is served either by the incumbent, or a stipendiary curate or by a minister specially appointed to it by the incumbent,[68] to whom they are subordinate.[69] A declaration of redundancy may be made in respect of a chapel of ease as it may in the case of a church.[70]

Where a chapel has an ancient division of a parish attached to it by immemorial custom, with parochial rights of baptising and burial, it is called a parochial chapel.[71] A chapel may be annexed to, or form part of, the structure of a parish or cathedral church, in which case the question of whether or not it forms part of that church is one of fact to be decided by reference to its history.[72] Chapels may have a district attached to them, referred to as chapelries.[73]

Private and proprietary chapels

6.15   A private chapel is one built by persons at or near their own house for themselves and their families. However, attendance at the chapel is not confined to members of the owner's family. A person or group of persons may provide a chapel (whether or not consecrated) to which those whom they are prepared to admit may attend, which is commonly known as a proprietary chapel. Those who own a private or proprietary chapel or have the right to make appointments to it may appoint whomsoever they wish to minister there,[74] provided that such a person is (unless the incumbent and unless the chapel is consecrated[75]) authorised by the Ordinary and the consent of the incumbent is obtained.[76] A chaplain ministering in a private chapel must seldom celebrate Holy Communion there on Sundays and other great feast days in order that the residents of the house may resort to their parish church to attend divine worship.[77] It should be noted that proprietary chapels are no longer encouraged and that the modern practice has been for private chapels not to be consecrated.[78]

---

[67] *Rolle's Abridgment of the Common Law*, Vol. 2, p. 340.

[68] Exceptionally the right of appointment may be vested in someone other than the incumbent and it may be in such circumstances that the appointed minister is not subordinate to the incumbent and on occasion such chapels have been made presentative by private Act of Parliament. See further *Halsbury's Laws of England* (4th ed.), Vol. 14, para. 1226.

[69] *Nesbitt v. Wallace* [1901] P. 354.

[70] Pastoral Measure 1983, s.28.

[71] See n. 65, *ante.*

[72] *Duke of Norfolk v. Arbuthnot* (1880) 5 C.P.O. 390, C.A.

[73] See n. 65, *ante.*

[74] *Moysey v. Hillcoat* (1828) 2 Hag. Ecc. 30.

[75] Holy Communion can only be celebrated in an unconsecrated building with the permission of the diocesan bishop: Canon B40.

[76] Canon C8(2), (4). A subsequent incumbent may refuse consent to a chaplain already officiating with the consent of the previous incumbent: *Richards v. Fincher* (1874) L.R. 4 A. & E. 255.

[77] Canon B41(1).

[78] *Halsbury's Laws of England* (4th ed.), Vol. 14, paras. 1225, 1227.

Chaplains to institutions

The bishop of the diocese in which any institution (including universities, **6.16**
colleges, schools,[79] hospitals,[80] prisons,[81] and cemeteries[82]) is situated, may license
a deacon or priest to perform such offices and services as the licence specifies[83]
on any part of the premises forming part of, or belonging to, the relevant
institution,[84] whether or not the institution possesses a chapel. Performance of
offices and services in accordance with such a licence does not require the
consent of the incumbent, and as we saw in Chapter 5 is free from their control.[85]
The licence cannot extend to the solemnisation of marriages, save that where the
solemnisation of the marriage of a person who is either house-bound or detained
in an institution is to be solemnised in accordance with the rites of the Church of
England pursuant to the Marriage Act 1949, s.26(1)(dd), the licence of the
chaplain of that institution will be treated as extending to the solemnisation of
that marriage.[86] Any alms collected in the course of, or in connection with, the
chaplain's performance of such offices and services may be disposed of as they
determine, subject to any directions given by the bishop.[87]

In the case of the proposed appointment of a women priest as chaplain the
bishop should consult with the appropriate authorities of the relevant institution.[88] The Hospitals Chaplaincies Council has produced guidelines on arrangements in hospitals,[89] and recommends that appropriate arrangements be made
with local clergy in the case of those patients who have a conscientious objection
to receiving Holy Communion from a celebration presided over by a women
priest. Similar arrangements would also need to be considered in other
institutions.

The Armed services

Army and air force station may be consituted extra-parochial places with the **6.17**
consent of the diocesan bishop, and declared by Order in Council to be under the
exclusive jurisidiciton of an archbishop or bishop.[90] At present the Bishop of

---

[79] Chaplains of certain public schools are free from the jurisdiction of the incumbent:
Public Schools Act 1868, s.31; Extra-Parochial Ministry Measure 1967, s.2(5); Education
Act 1973, s.1(4), Sched. 2, Pt. III.

[80] The Hospital Chaplaincies Council has produced a number of guides including
A Handbook of Hospital Chaplaincy (1994).

[81] The appointment is governed by the Prison Act 1952, ss.7, 9.

[82] A burial authority has the power to make an appointment A cemetery company
established by Act of Parliament prior to April 1, 1974 still retains the power to make an
appointment under the Cemeteries Clauses Act 1847.

[83] Extra-Parochial Ministry Measure 1967, s.2; Canons B41(2), (3), C8(4).

[84] Extra-Parochial Ministry Measure 1967, s.2(1). Premises for these purposes include
residential premises managed by the institution and occupied by members of staff of the
institution: *ibid.*

[85] *ibid.*, s.2(2).

[86] Extra-Parochial Ministry Measure 1967, s.2(1A): Canon B41(2). See also Chap. 10.

[87] Extra-Parochial Ministry Measure 1967, s.2(3).

[88] Code of Practice issued by the House of Bishop, January 1994, in respect of the Priests
(Ordination of Women) Measure 1993.

[89] See *ibid.*, App. D.

[90] Army Chaplains Act 1868; Air Force (Application of Enactments) (No. 2) Order 1918,
No. 158.

Croydon is bishop to the forces. The Secretary of State may appoint any army or air force chaplain to perform functions in that district, and in any chapel within it whether consecrated or not.[91]

Army chaplains (who are commissioned members of the forces) are under the supervison of the Chaplain General of the Forces who holds the ecclesiastical dignity of archdeacon under the Archbishop of Canterbury, as does the Chaplain-in-Chief who supervises all air force chaplains.[92] Chaplains in the Royal Navy hold no naval rank, although the Chaplain of the Fleet is likewise granted the ecclesiastical dignity of archdeacon under the Archbishop of Canterbury.

Royal and official chaplains

6.18   The Sovereign, peers of the Realm and certain other persons have the right to appoint chaplains to serve in their own private chapels and households.[93] The clergy of the Chapels Royal consist of a dean, sub-dean, clerk and deputy clerks of the closet, domestic chaplains, chaplains and priests in ordinary, honorary chaplains and priests and deputy priests.[94] The Speaker of the House of Commons appoints a chaplain to read prayers each day when the House meets for business and to attend them on State occasions.[95]

---

[91] *ibid.*

[92] *ibid.*

[93] Gibson *Codex Juris Ecclesiastici Anglicani (3rd ed. 1761) Canonici*, pp. 908, 909. The right exists in common law, see, *e.g. Drury's Case* (1601) 4 Co Rep 89b at 90a.

[94] *Halsbury's Laws of England* (4th ed.), Vol. 14, para. 732.

[95] Erskine May, *Parliamentary Practice* (18th ed.), p. 263.

Chapter Seven: Ecclesiastical Persons

Every member of the *laos* or people of God is an ecclesiastical person by virtue **7.1** of their having been admitted to the Church through their baptism. However, through the centuries a distinction has been drawn between the ministry of those who are ordained, that is the clergy, and the ministry of the remainder, known as the laity. Prior to the Reformation the distinction between the two groups became blurred, as a result of the existence of minor orders such as readers and acolytes, and the position of the male members of religious orders who might or might not be ordained. In an age when learning was in the main confined to those closely associated with the Church many secular posts were occupied by "clerks" who again might or might not be ordained. In time this led to the "benefit of clergy", which gave limited exemption from the criminal jurisdiction of the secular courts, and was available to all males (and female religious) who could demonstrate a basic ability to read. This privilege was not to be fully abolished until 1827.

After the Reformation when learning became more widespread and more secular posts began to be filled by laymen the distinction between clergy and laity gradually reasserted itself. Thus clergy tended to be set apart and most secular occupations, teaching being one notable exception, began to be regarded as unsuitable for them. As the twentieth century draws to a close this distinction has once again become blurred by the ordination of a new group of non-stipendiary clergy[1] who generally continue with their secular occupations, by the growth in numbers of readers and licensed lay workers, and by the consolidation of the Anglican religious orders.

In this chapter we will consider what is required of those ordained as ministers of the Church of England, their status and functions, and the obligations, duties, and rights relating to them. Since we have already considered the position of bishops in Chapter 3 we will be concentrating here upon priests and deacons, and upon the unbeneficed clergy, since those who are beneficed were the focus of Chapter 5. Finally we consider the requirements for admission to the orders of

---

[1] Their position is not considered in detail in this book since they are subject to the same legal rights and duties as all ministers save in regard to their right to receive a stipend. See further The Advisory Board of Ministry's *Non-Stipendiary Ministry in the Church* (1983) and *Regulations for Non-Stipendiary Ministry* (1994). Recently some dioceses have introduced schemes for local non-stipendiary ministers as a further development. Although the procedures and criteria for selection vary from scheme to scheme in all cases the ministers are in effect "self-selected" by the relevant parish or parishes of a benefice and are only ordained in the expectation that they will minister in a single parish or benefice.

deaconess, reader and licensed lay worker, and the duties of these offices together with the position of those in vowed religious communities.

Ordination

Qualifications

7.2   In the Church of England there are three orders of ordained ministers: bishop, priest and deacon,[2] and the term minister is used to refer to a person ordained to any of these three orders.[3] To enter the ordained ministry, and thereby become a clerk in holy orders, an entrant must be tried, examined and admitted according to the Ordinal,[4] or other form of approved or authorised service, or else previously obtained episcopal consecration or ordination in a church whose orders are recognised and accepted by the Church of England.[5] Strictly speaking deacons are made and priests ordained, but it is now usual to refer to the ordination of deacons as well as priests.

A bishop has absolute discretion as to whom he ordains,[6] provided that the candidates fulfil the legal requirements of the office. Each candidate must have been baptised and confirmed, possess a sufficient knowledge of holy scripture and of the doctrine, discipline and worship of the Church of England as set forth in the 39 Articles of Religion, the Book of Common Prayer and the Ordinal, and fulfil the requirements as to learning and other qualities which, subject to any directions given by the General Synod, the bishop deems necessary for the office of deacon.[7] They must also be of virtuous conversation, of good repute, such as to be a wholesome example to the pattern and flock of Christ,[8] and "without crime".[9] The Church does not commend homophile sexual relationships, but it is left to individual candidates' own consciences to act responsibly. In particular it is not considered appropriate to question candidates as to their sexual lives unless there are strong reasons for doing so.[10]

---

[2] Canon C1(1).

[3] As to the ministry generally see Russell, *The Clerical Profession* (1980); Tiller, *A Strategy for the Church's Ministry* (1985).

[4] *The Ordinal.*

[5] Canons A4, C1(1); Preface to the *Ordinal.* The alternative service must be approved by the General Synod under Canon B2, or authorised by the archbishops pursuant to Canon C4A; Canon C1(1).

[6] *R. v. Archbishop of Dublin* (1833) A1. & N. 244.

[7] Clergy (Ordination and Miscellaneous Provisions) Measure 1964, s.1(1); Canons C4(1), C7.

[8] Canon C4(1).

[9] Preface to *The Ordinal.* "Without crime" is taken as referring to "offences" which have been confessed and in respect of which absolution has been received, whether publicly (during general confession) or privately. It does not mean that a person who has been convicted of a criminal offence could not be ordained. As to "notable crime", which is a bar to ordination, see *Kensit v. Dean and Chapter of St Paul's* [1905] 2 K.B. 249 at 256, D.C.

[10] *Issues in Human Sexuality.* A statement by the House of Bishops (1991) (GS Misc. 382) Chap. 5.

In examining the candidates the bishop must be assisted by the archdeacons and other ministers appointed for the purpose.[11] It should be noted that, in the modern Church, candidates undergo a period of theological training prior to ordination. They are selected for such training at bishops' selection conferences organised by the Advisory Board of Ministry,[12] having been sponsored to that conference by a diocesan bishop who himself generally acts on the advice of the diocesan director of ordinands. Although it is possible for a bishop to ordain a candidate who is not selected by the Board nor receives such training, such cases are exceptional. It is of course open to a bishop, in the exercise of his discretion, to refuse to ordain a candidate, notwithstanding such training, and this does on occasion occur.

The minimum age for a deacon is 23 years and for a priest 24 years unless they **7.3** have a faculty from the Archbishop of Canterbury.[13] Although there is an upper age limit of 69 years for appointment to most ecclesiastical offices[14] this does not operate as a bar to ordination itself, but ordinations of persons over 70 years of age are rare.

No person can be admitted into holy orders who is suffering, or who has suffered, from any physical or mental infirmity which in the opinion of the bishop will prevent them from performing the duties of the office,[15] and a medical examination is generally included in the selection procedures. However, the traditional view that certain physical impediments, such as blindness, were a bar to ordination, no longer appears to have any application.[16] Another impediment which has also been removed is that of illegitimacy, which no longer prevents a candidate from being ordained.[17]

Anyone who has remarried and has a former spouse still living, or who is married to a person who has been previously married and whose former spouse is still living, cannot be admitted to holy orders, unless a faculty has been granted by the archbishop of the province.[18] The procedure for obtaining such a faculty must be in accordance with directions given by the Archbishops of Canterbury and York.[19] Essentially these directions require that all relevant persons (that is the candidate, their spouse, two referees and where possible the former spouse)

[11] See n. 7 *ante.*
[12] See The Advisory Board of Ministry, *A Review of Selection Procedures in the Church of England* (1995). The Turnbull Commission proposes the transfer of the Board's functions to the Resources for Ministry Department of the new Archbishops' Council, which would be responsible to the House of Bishops with respect to vocation, selection and training: *Working as One Body*, The Report of the Archbishops' Commission on the Organisation of the Church of England (1995).
[13] Clergy Ordination Act 1804, ss.1, 2; Clergy (Ordination and Miscellaneous Provisions) Measure 1964, s.2; Preface to *The Ordinal*; Canon C3(5), (6). The faculty only enables the priest or deacon to be ordained one year earlier than the generally permitted age.
[14] Ecclesiastical Offices (Age Limit) Measure 1975, s.1, Sched. 1.
[15] Canon C4(3).
[16] See, *e.g. Kensit v. Dean and Chapter of St Paul's (ante).*
[17] Clergy (Ordination and Miscellaneous Provisions) Measure 1964, s.8; Canon C4(4). Previously it was considered necessary to obtain a faculty from the Archbishop of Canterbury. Nor does illegitimacy act as a bar to the consecration of a bishop: *ibid.*
[18] Clergy (Ordination and Miscellaneous Provisions) Measure 1964, s.9(1), (2); Canon C4(3), (3A).
[19] The directions are published as a supplement to the Canons of the Church of England (5th ed. 1993).

must be interviewed by the diocesan bishop or his representative. In addition the matter is discussed with the incumbent or priest-in-charge of the parish where the candidate usually worships and any other persons considered appropriate. A report is then made, and after interviewing the candidate and their spouse, the bishop must decide whether to apply to the archbishop. If such an application is made the archbishop may then make such further enquiries as he considers appropriate before deciding whether to grant a faculty. The candidate has no right to make direct representations to the archbishop nor to appeal against his decision. A faculty is not required in the case of a person who is divorced but not remarried, but this does not mean that the fact of the divorce should not be taken into account in assessing the candidate's suitability.[20]

Preliminaries to ordination

7.4 A candidate to be ordained a deacon must exhibit to the bishop evidence of their birth, baptism and confirmation, and letters testifying to their former good life and behaviour from persons specified by the bishop.[21] To be ordained a priest a deacon must exhibit to the bishop their Letters of Orders (see below), together with letters on the same terms as a deacon.[22]

A deacon is not to be ordained to the priesthood for a least a year unless the bishop finds a good reason to the contrary, in order that their behaviour as a deacon may be assessed and in order that they may become experienced in ecclesiastical administration.[23] Such cases will be rare, and it should be noted that if a person is to be ordained as a deacon and priest on the same day a faculty is required from the Archbishop of Canterbury.[24]

Candidates for admission into holy orders must generally exhibit to the bishop of the diocese a certificate which demonstrates that they have an ecclesiastical office or "title", which the bishop considers sufficient,[25] and in which they may attend the cure of souls and execute their ministry. There are exceptions to this requirement including those holding office in a university, a fellowship in any college or hall within a university, or teaching in a school and those who are to be chaplains in any of these institutions. Members of the staff of theological colleges are also excepted as are those living under vows in the house of any religious order or community.[26]

Generally no person may be admitted by any bishop other than the bishop of the diocese in which they are to exercise their ministry. The main exception is where they bring with them Letters Dimissory from the bishop of that diocese.[27]

---

[20] *Legal Opinions*, p. 108. The same applies in a case where two marriages have ended in divorce.

[21] Canon C6(1).

[22] Canon C6(2).

[23] Canon C3(8); *The Ordinal*, Form and Manner of Making Deacons.

[24] Canon C3(7).

[25] Canon C5(1). It is doubtful whether the bishop's obligation to maintain any clerk in holy orders whom he ordained without a title survived the Reformation: *Halsbury's Laws of England* (4th ed.), Vol. 14, para. 656, n. 2.

[26] Canon C5(2). The relevant university, college, hall, school, theological college or house must be within the bishop's diocese.

[27] Canon C5(4); or are a fellow of any college or hall in the universities of Oxford or Cambridge: Canon C5(5). The other exception is ordination for service overseas (see Chap. 12).

Before ordination each candidate who is to be ordained priest or deacon must,[28] in the presence of the bishop by whom they are to be ordained or that bishop's commissary, make and subscribe to the declaration of assent to the Church's inheritance of faith as recorded in the holy scriptures and set forth in the catholic creeds and historic formularies of the Church of England,[29] and promise to use only those forms of service authorised or permitted by Canon.[30] They must also take and subscribe to the oath of allegiance[31] and take the oath of canonical obedience to the bishop.[32]

Ordination

Ordination to the office of priest or deacon should normally occur on a Sunday **7.5** immediately following the four Ember weeks,[33] or on the Feasts of Saint Michael and All Angels, Saint Peter and Saint Thomas the Apostle, or within the week immediately following either of these three days.[34] It is to be held in the cathedral or other church or chapel at the discretion of the bishop,[35] after Morning Prayer is ended,[36] any authorised form of Holy Communion being used.[37]

One of the archdeacons, their deputy, or any such person who by ancient custom has the right to do so, presents the candidates for ordination to the bishop.[38] In the case of a candidate receiving the order of the diaconate the bishop then lays his hands upon their head.[39] For a candidate receiving the order of priesthood, all the priests taking part in the ceremony lay their hands on their head, along with the bishop.[40]

The days when simony (see Chapter 5) was a common offence are past. Nonetheless it should be noted that any person who directly or indirectly receives

[28] The Clerical Subscription Act 1865, s.11 states that no oath shall be administered during the service. This prohibition does not apply to the oath of canonical obedience: *ibid.*, s.12.

[29] *i.e., The Thirty-nine Articles of Religion, Book of Common Prayer* and *The Ordinal.*

[30] Church of England (Worship and Doctrine) Measure 1974, s.2(1); Canon C15, (1) which sets out the form.

[31] Clerical Subscription Act 1865, s.4; Promissory Oaths Act 1868, s.9; Canon C13(1).

[32] Canon C14(3).

[33] *i.e.* The weeks containing the Wednesday, Friday and Saturday after the first Sunday in Lent, the Feast of Pentecost, September 14, and December 13.

[34] Preface to *The Ordinal*; Canon C3(1). On urgent occasion the bishop may appoint another Sunday, Holy Day or one of the Ember Days: *ibid.*

[35] Preface to *The Ordinal*; Canon C3(2). For a further discussion of the services of ordination and consecration see Bursell *Liturgy, Order and the Law* (1996), pp. 230–6. The Code of Practice in respect of the Priests (Ordination of Women) Measure 1993 issued by the House of Bishops considers the question of ordination. It states that in the case of ordinations to the diaconate it would be inappropriate to exclude candidates of one sex or to arrange a separate service for ordinands opposed to the ordination of women. However, in respect of ordinations to the priesthood appropriate sensitivity should be shown: *ibid.*, paras. 13–15.

[36] Rubrics at the beginning of *The Ordinal.*

[37] Canon C3(4A).

[38] Canon C3(3).

[39] *The Ordinal,* The Form and Manner of Making Deacons.

[40] Canon C3(4); *The Ordinal,* The Form and Manner of Ordering Priests.

or agrees to receive money (beyond the lawful fees), or profits by effecting or promising the ordination of any clerk in holy orders, is liable to a fine, as is the clerk who is corruptly ordained.[41]

Following ordination "Letters of Orders", under the bishop's seal, are issued to the person ordained. These are simply a record of the transaction[42] and confer nothing, since ordination is complete without them.[43]

Women priests

7.6   Since 1987 a woman has been able to be ordained a deacon, and since 1994 can be ordained as a priest. In either case the ordination is dependent upon the candidate satisfying the requirements of canon law regarding admission to those offices.[44] However, a woman may not be consecrated as a bishop.[45] The making of women deacons was relatively uncontroversial, but many within the Church of England regard the ordination of women to the priesthood as theologically unacceptable.[46] They see themselves as being in impaired communion with other members of the Church of England and the Church of England as having reduced itself to sectarian status within the Western Catholic Church.

In order to avert schism and to make provision for those of differing convictions within the Church, arrangements were put in place to respect the consciences of, and ensure suitable pastoral provision for, those opposed to the ordination of women. In addition to the Priests (Ordination of Women) Measure 1993 itself, the Epsicopal Ministry Act of Synod 1993 introduced extended episcopal care, for certain parishes, whilst a Code of Practice issued under the authority of the House of Bishops in January 1994[47] sets out matters not "easily or appropriately provided for in the legislation".

---

[41] Simony Act 1588, s.9.

[42] A clerk may be required to produce their Letters of Orders at the visitation of the bishop or archdeacon in whose diocese or archdeanery they are officiating: Canon C18(4).

[43] *R. v. Morton* (1873) L.R. 2 C.C.R. 22.

[44] Deacons (Ordination of Women) Measure 1986, s.1(1); Priests (Ordination of Women) Measure 1993, s.1(1); Canons C4A(1), C4B(1). A woman in a diocese where an episcopal declaration is not in force must apply to her diocesan bishop if she wishes to be put forward as a candidate for ordination. In dioceses where a declaration is in force she should apply to the bishop of a neighbouring diocese (and if she is already a deacon inform her diocesan bishop of this). The bishop of the neighbouring diocese may obtain observations from the woman's diocesan bishop before making a decision regarding her suitability. If accepted for training the candidate is sponsored by the bishop to whom the application is made not her diocesan bishop: Code of Practice, paras. 8–10.

[45] Priests (Ordination of Women) Measure 1993, s.1(2).

[46] For a detailed examination of the arguments see Watts (ed.), *Through a Glass Darkly: A Crisis Considered* (1993). See also Maclean "Women Priests, The Legal Background" (1989) 5 Ecc. L.J. 24.

[47] The Code of Practice is published by the General Synod (available from Church House Bookshop) and also contains the text of the Episcopal Ministry Act of Synod 1993, the Guidelines issued by the House of Bishops for the Testing and Discernment of Vocation and the Preparation for Ordination to the Priesthood of Women already in Deacons' Orders, and a pamphlet for PCCs.

The Code of Practice, which as we have already seen in Chapter 2 has no legal but great moral force, effectively sets out what may be termed the "spirit of the law". In particular it considers various situations which may arise where particular sensitivity is required to respect the opposing views and positions of both clerical and lay members of the Church.

For those clergy, deaconesses and licensed lay workers who nonetheless resigned from ecclesiastical service because of the ordination of women to the priesthood, special financial arrangments were made. The provisions relating to these were embodied in a further Measure.

Declarations by a diocesan bishop

A bishop of a diocese who was in office[48] on February 22, 1994,[49] may make any **7.7** one or more of three declarations, any or all of which may be subsequently withdrawn.[50] These declarations state that a woman is not, within the diocese, to be ordained to the office of priest; to be instituted or licensed to the offices of incumbent or priest-in-charge or team vicar; or to be given a licence or permission to officiate as a priest.[51] However, this final declaration does not prevent a woman from being allowed, under any Canon, to officiate as a priest in a church or chapel for one period of up to seven days in any period of three months, without reference to the bishop.[52]

Where a bishop who has made such a declaration ceases to hold office the declaration continues in force until six months after the date on which his successor takes office.[53] No suffragan or other bishop discharging any of the functions of the bishop of the diocese may act in contravention of a declaration.[54]

The Code of Practice states that, because of the effect of the declaration on his suffragans and on the diocese as a whole, the bishop should consult with other bishops in the diocese and the bishop's council. Nonetheless, as the Code recognises, the declaration is for the protection of the diocesan bishop. The Code also states that diocesan bishops who elect not to make all or any declarations will fully respect the views of suffragan, area and assistant bishops and will not expect or require them to act against their conscience.[55]

---

[48] The use of *a bishop of the diocese* is ambiguous. However, from the scheme of the legislation as a whole and the Code of Practice issued by the House of Bishops in January 1993, it is evident that the intention is that only *the diocesan bishop*, in office in that see at the relevant date, may make such declarations.

[49] *i.e.* the date on which the Canon enabling women to ordained to the office of priest was promulged: Priests (Ordination of Women) Measure 1993, s.2(8).

[50] *ibid.*, s.2(2), (3). Such notice or withdrawal must be in writing, signed by the bishop, and be sent to specified persons including the Sovereign and the archbishop of the relevant province: *ibid.*, s.2(4).

[51] *ibid.*, s.2(1)(a), (b), (c).

[52] *ibid.*, s.2(7).

[53] *ibid.*, s.2(5).

[54] *ibid.*, s.2(6). Acting in contravention constitutes an ecclesiastical offence for which proceedings may be taken under the EJM: *ibid.*, s.5(a).

[55] paras. 4, 5.

Discrimination

7.8   It is provided in the 1993 Measure that nothing in the Sex Discrimination Act 1975, Part II, shall render unlawful discrimination on the grounds of sex against a woman in respect of her ordination to the priesthood, the giving to her of a licence or permission to serve or officiate as a priest, her appointment as dean, incumbent, priest-in-charge or team vicar, or (in the case of a woman ordained as a priest),[56] as assistant curate.[57] In so far as women priests are held to be employees (as to which see below) the Church would presumably seek to rely upon the Sex Discrimination Act 1975, section 19.[58] However, this provision only excludes from the scope of the 1975 Act employment for the purposes of an organised religion where the employment is limited to one sex in order to comply with the doctrines of an organised religion, or to avoid offending the religious susceptibilities of a number of its members. Thus the Church could only gain protection if "the employment" which is excluded from the scope of the 1975 Act refers to specific posts not to employment within the Church as a whole, which is no longer restricted to one sex.[58a]

Except as provided for by the 1993 Measure and the Act of Synod, the Act of Synod states that there is not to be discrimination in respect ordination, nor of appointments to senior office, by any person or body on the grounds of a candidate's view or position taken on the question of the ordination of women.[59] However, the fact that the declarations pursuant to the 1993 Measure may only be made by those diocesan bishops in office in early 1994 means that in time no diocesan bishop will be able to prevent women priests being ordained, instituted or licensed to offices within the diocese, or given licences or permission to officiate within the diocese, with the consequence that some opponents will not feel able to accept such appointments.

Some limited protection is offered to bishops opposed to women's ordination to the priesthood, particularly to those who were not in office in February 1994. The Episcopal Ministry Act provides that where a diocesan bishop is opposed (including a bishop in office at the relevant date who could have issued declarations, but was unwilling to do so) the ordination of women to the priesthood and their licensing and institution is to be carried out by the archbishop or a bishop acting as his commissary.[60] Although the Act states that the archbishop will do so either at the bishop's request or in his exercise of metropolitan jurisdiction, that jurisdiction is restricted by the Act of Synod to

---

[56] This wording would appear intended to not exclude a claim by a woman deacon in respect of appointment as an assistant curate.

[57] Priests (Ordination of Women) Measure 1993, s.6.

[58] *ibid.*, is without prejudice to the Sex Discrimination Act 1975, s.19.

[58a] The Church of England may also be in breach of the E.C. Directive No. 76/207 (Equal Treatment for Men and Women as Regards Access to Employment, Vocational Training and Promotion and Working Conditions) in respect of its current legislation and practices surrounding the employment of women priests. Further, it is highly debatable that the powers of derogation under the E.C. Directive 76/206 extend to s.19 of the 1975 Act in any event, even if s.19 might otherwise provide the Church with an exemption, thus bringing the Church into conflict with European Community Law.

[59] Episcopal Ministry Act of Synod 1993, s.1.

[60] *ibid.*, s.11.

cases where the diocesan bishop has no objection. Alternatively the diocesan bishop may himself make arrangements for the ordination, licensing and institution of women by another bishop. The ability of a diocesan bishop not to make arrangements with another bishop or to raise objections to the archbishop exercising his metropolitan jurisdiction is presumably curtailed by the provison in the Act that there is to be no discrimination against candidates for ordination on the grounds of their views or position, a protection which must be intended to extend to women ordinands themselves.

Resolutions by a parish

Subject to some restrictions a PCC may pass either or both of two resolutions: **7.9** Resolution A, that it would not accept a woman as the minister who presides at or celebrates the Holy Communion or pronounces the Absolution in the parish; or, under Resolution B, that it would not accept a woman as the incumbent, priest-in-charge, or a team vicar of the benefice.[61] Such resolutions cannot be passed unless four weeks notice of the time and place of the meeting has been given, save where notice of a vacancy has been given under the Patronage Benefices Measure 1986 (see Chapter 5).[62] Nor can a resolution be passed unless the meeting is attended by at least one half of those entitled to attend.[63] Finally the PCC may not consider whether to pass Resolution A where the benefice has a woman priest as incumbent, priest-in-charge, team vicar or assistant curate.[64]

Curiously a PCC is not prohibited from considering or passing Resolution B in identical circumstances to those which prohibit them considering Resolution A. Since "accept" is not defined, the consequences of a PCC passing such a resolution are far from clear. A woman inducted into the benefice has security of tenure, and so to a lesser extent does a team vicar, and it is unlikely that such a resolution could operate to displace them. On the other hand it is unlawful for any bishop, priest or deacon to act in contravention of any resolution passed by a PCC,[65] so that were the situation to arise a stalemate would be likely to develop, not least because no other minister could officiate without the permission of the minister with the cure of souls. Whether such stalemate could constitute a pastoral breakdown for the purposes of the Incumbents (Vacation of Benefices) Measure 1977 (see Chapter 5) is a moot point.

The position of a parish within a team or group ministry may be especially difficult.[65a] Where a PCC within the team benefice or group has passed Resolution A, no woman incumbent within the group or female team vicar may preside at or celebrate Holy Communion or pronounce the Absolution.[66] However, nothing prevents such women priests from taking other services and

---

[61] Priests (Ordination of Women) Measure 1993, s.3(1), Sched. 1, which sets out the forms.
[62] *ibid.*, s.3(4).
[63] *ibid.*
[64] *ibid.*, s.3(3).
[65] *ibid.*, s.5(b). The offence being one in respect of which proceedings may be taken under the EJM: Priests (Ordination of Women) Measure 1993, s.5(b).
[65a] As to which see *Team and Group Ministries Measure: Code of Recommended Practice* (1996), paras. 65–68 and see Chap. 5.
[66] Pastoral Measure 1983, ss.21(1)(a), 20(8).

they are not for example prevented from celebrating Evening Prayer or conducting marriages within that parish.

Any resolution passed continues in force until it is rescinded, which the PCC may do by passing a resolution to rescind, after complying with the same provisions regarding notice of the meeting and its quorum as for the passing of the initial resolution.[67] On the passing of any resolution (including a resolution to rescind), copies must be sent to the bishop of the diocese, rural dean, lay chairman of the deanery synod, registrar of the diocese, the designated officer of the diocese for the purposes of the Patronage (Benefices) Measure 1986 and the registered patron.[68]

7.10   Special provisions cover guild churches and parish church cathedrals to enable them to consider, pass and rescind effectively the same resolutions.[69] The only difference is that in respect of a parish church cathedral a service may be held on the direction of the diocesan bishop which would otherwise contravene such resolutions.[70] Thus the bishop may, for example, direct a woman to preside at Holy Communion notwithstanding a resolution against this.

The administrative body of a dean and chapter cathedral may also pass or rescind similar resolutions to those which a PCC may pass; Resolution A being subject to the proviso that it does not apply to a service held on the direction of the bishop, and Resolution B being to the effect that it would not accept a woman as dean.[71] However, neither Resolution may be considered if the dean or any of the residentiary canons are a woman priest, thus avoiding some of the potential difficulties discussed in relation to a parish.

A parish (other than one in which there is a parish church cathedral) which has passed either or both Resolution A and B may decide to petiton the diocesan bishop for "extended episcopal care". The nature of this care and its attendant difficulties have been considered in Chapter 3.

Ordination of Women (Financial Provisons) Measure 1993

7.11   The aim of this Measure was to make financial provision for those stipendiary clerks in holy orders, deaconesses and licensed lay workers[72] who felt obliged to resign as the direct result of the promulgation of the Canon enabling women to be ordained priests. In order to qualify such persons must, on February 22, 1994 or within the six months preceding that date, have been in whole-time stipendiary ecclesiastical service which was pensionable,[73] in the provinces of Canterbury or York. They must have been in such service for at least five years (continuously or discontinously for an aggregate of that time) and not be either of retiring age nor already in receipt of a pension.[74] They must also resign between August 22, 1993

---

[67] Priests (Ordination of Women) Measure 1993, s.3(2).

[68] *ibid.*, s.3(5).

[69] *ibid.*, s.3(8)(9).

[70] *ibid.*, s.3(6).

[71] *ibid.*, s.4.

[72] Ordination of Women (Financial Provisions) Measure 1993, s.1(2).

[73] Pensionable service and a pension are both with reference to pension regulations for the time being in force under the Clergy Pensions (Amendment) Measure 1972, s.6.

[74] *ibid.*

(*i.e.* six months after the promulgation of the Canon) and February 22, 2004, and make a declaration[75] that they would not have resigned but for their opposition to the ordination of women priests[76]

Those who qualify have a right to participate in any church housing schemes, and subject to certain conditions are entitled to a resettlement grant and periodical payments for a minimum of 36 months. The Church of England Pensions Board which makes these also has a discretion to provide financial benefit by way of periodical payments, grant, loan or otherwise as it sees fit to such persons, and to those who have resigned from an office or employment or a religious community, who have suffered or will suffer financial hardship.[77]

Further consideration of the detailed provisions is beyond the scope of this book. However, it should be noted that a procedure exists for appeals against the determination of the Board to a tribunal, which has the power to affirm or to substitute any other determination which the Board could have made for the original determination.[78]

Application of certain legislation to women

Before leaving the subject of women priests the problems of the application of certain legislation to them and to women deacons needs to be considered. The two relevant Measures of 1986 and 1993 provide that, in any canon, order, rule or regulation relating to deacons or priests, words importing the masculine gender include the feminine, unless the contrary intention appears.[79] It will be noted immediately that there is no general provision that words importing the feminine gender should include the masculine. Thus, for example, where reference is made to a husband this can be read as a wife but the converse is not applicable.   **7.12**

The position of women clerks in holy orders is rendered all the more difficult because no general provision has been made for the application of relevant Acts of Parliament and Measures of the Church Assembly or General Synod to them. The Interpretation Act 1978 applies in full to all Acts and Measures passed after January 1, 1979 and in part to some earlier legislation.The consequence of this is that in all Acts and Measures passed after the year 1850 words importing the masculine gender include the feminine,[80] whilst in those passed after January 1, 1979 words importing the feminine include the masculine.[81]

Although certain legislation has been specifically amended there are a number of provisions which apply only to men and not to women in holy orders.[82]

---

[75] The form is set out in the Ordination of Women (Financial Provisions) Measure 1993, Sched.

[76] *ibid.*, ss.1(1), 2, 3, 4. Provision is also made for the augmentation of pensions: *ibid.*, s.9.

[77] *ibid.*, s.5.

[78] *ibid.*, s.10; Ordination of Women (Financial Provisions) (Appeals) Rules 1993, S.I. 1993 No. 2847.

[79] Deacons (Ordination of Women) Measure 1986, s.4; Priests (Ordination of Women) Measure 1993, s.9.

[80] Interpretation Act 1978, s.6(a), Sched. 2, Pt I.

[81] *ibid.*, s.22, Sched. 2, Pt I.

[82] Both the 1986 and 1993 Measures rely upon the implied repeal of section 10 of the Act of Uniformity, which states that no person is capable of being admitted as incumbent or to any other ecclesiastical promotion or dignity if *he* is not ordained priest, since the Interpretation Act does not assist.

One example of this is the restrictions on clerks engaging in trade discussed below.[83]

Canon C4B, which enabled women to be ordained as priests expressly provides that in the forms of service contained in the Book of Common Prayer or in the Ordinal words importing the masculine gender in relation to the priesthood shall be construed as including the feminine. The failure to extend this provision to other alternative or authorised services is curious. It is doubtful that they are covered by the provisions of the 1986 and 1993 Measures and it may therefore be that, as a matter of strict law, women priests are precluded from utilising such forms of service.

Duties, privileges and disabilities of ministers

Specific duties of deacons and priests

7.13   The duties of a deacon, in the church where they are appointed to serve, are to assist the priest in divine service, and especially in the administration of Holy Communion; to read the holy scriptures and homilies in the church and to preach, if so licensed; and to instruct the youth in the catechism and, in the absence of the priest, to baptise infants.[84] The provision that the priest must be absent is important; it is not the usual function of a deacon to baptise. A deacon is also to work with the members of the church in caring for the poor, the needy, the sick and all who are in trouble, and to strengthen the faithful and search out the careless and indifferent.[85] A deacon may perform the burial service and may also, as with baptism, solemnise a marriage in the absence of the priest.[86] The Archbishops of Canterbury and York have jointly issued guidelines for deacons conducting marriage services.[87]

Criticism has been made of the fact the too much emphasis has been placed upon the diaconate being a transitional office and one which is treated simply as an apprenticeship for the priesthood.[88] The ministry of deacons lacks a precise structure, and although deacons as ordained ministers are entitled to be members of, or represented in, the houses of clergy of deanery and diocesan synods and of

---

[83] Although their so doing may be *de minimis*, or alternatively a variation not of substantial importance permissible under Canon B5(1).

[84] *Book of Common Prayer*, Form and Manner of Making Deacons; Canon C8.

[85] *ibid*.

[86] The general view that deacons cannot pronounce the blessing has no canonical basis: *R. v. Millis* (1844) 10 Cl. & Fin. 534; *Cope v. Barber* (1872) L.R. 7 C.P. 393.

[87] These are published as an Appendix to the Canons of the Church of England (5th ed., 1993). Entitled "Solemnisation of Marriage by Deacons", these state that normally the minister officiating should be a priest or bishop and a deacon may only officiate with the consent of the incumbent or priest-in-charge. Consideration should be given to the wishes of the couple, but a significant factor in reaching a decision will be who prepared the couple. Since training to prepare couples for marriage is currently a post ordination task it will be rarely if ever that a deacon solemnises marriage in the year following their ordination to that order.

[88] *Deacons in the Ministry of the Church*, A Report to the House of Bishops of the General Synod (1988) (GS 802); Hall (ed.), *The Deacon's Ministry* (1992).

the House of Clergy of the General Synod, their functions in regard to liturgy and the sacraments may all, with the exception of solemnisation of matrimony, also as we shall see be performed by lay persons.

Upon ordination a priest receives authority to preach the Word of God and to administer the Holy Sacraments[89] in the congregation where they are lawfully appointed to discharge those functions.[90] Unless ordained priest no person is capable of being admitted to any benefice or other ecclesiastical preferment.[91]

This prohibition would thus appear to preclude a deacon from holding any ecclesiastical preferment. For this reason it was recently considered necessary, with the ordination of women deacons who were unable, until 1994, to progress to the priesthood, to make an express statutory declaration that a deacon could be appointed to the office of rural dean.[92] Provision was also made for deacons, who had been ordained for at least six years, to be appointed to the office of residentiary canon in any cathedral church with the appropriate style, title and dignity, notwithstanding anything in the constitution or statutes of the cathedral church to the contrary.[93] However, this is not to be construed as requiring such a person to preside at or to celebrate Holy Communion or to pronounce the Absolution. A similar provision was also enacted in respect of deacons' appointment as non-residentiary canons, but without the requirement that they must first be ordained for six years.[94]

Duties, disabilities and privileges of all ministers

Certain duties, privileges and disabilities relate to all ordained ministers, that is   **7.14**
to deacons, priests, and to bishops whose specific functions were considered in
Chapter 3. It must be remembered that when provisions appear to be only of
application to deacons and priests they will apply equally to a bishop, who is also
both a deacon and a priest just as a priest is also a deacon.

Every minister is under an obligation to say daily Morning and Evening Prayer, either privately or openly, and to celebrate or be present at Holy Communion every Sunday and other principal feast days, unless prevented by sickness or other urgent cause. They must also be diligent in daily prayer and intercession, in examination of their conscience and in the study of holy scripture and other studies relating to their ministerial duties.[95]

---

[89] *i.e.* baptism and the Lord's Supper: Thirty-nine Articles of Religion Art. XXV. See also Chap. 10.

[90] *Book of Common Prayer*, Form and Manner of Ordering Priests.

[91] Act of Uniformity 1662, s.10. "Preferment" is not defined in this Act. For the purposes of the Clerical Disabilities Act 1870, s.2 (which applies that given in the Church Discipline Act 1840 (repealed)) a wide definition is given. For the purposes of the EJM "preferment" includes an archbishopric, bishopric, archdeaconry, dignity or office in a cathedral or collegiate church, benefice, and every curacy, lectureship, readership, chaplaincy, office or place which requires the discharge of any spiritual duty: EJM, s.66(1).

[92] Church of England (Miscellaneous Provisions) Measure 1992, s.14.

[93] *ibid.*, s.15; Canon C21(1A); Ecclesiastical Commissioners Act 1840, s.27.

[94] Church of England (Miscellaneous Provisions) Measure 1992, s.16.

[95] Canon C26(1); *Book of Common Prayer*, rubric following the Preface, "Concerning the Service of the Church".

The Canons no longer specify in detail what a minister should wear when not conducting services, but they are required to dress in a way which is a sign and mark of their holy calling and ministry.[96] The only exceptions are during the times of recreation or for another justifiable reason and even then they must still dress in a manner suitable to the office. Although the clerical collar, which is often known as the dog or Roman collar, is still the most common outward symbol of a minister, it is in fact a nineteenth century innovation adopted by English ministers from the continent, and has no canonical or other authority. Accordingly no minister is under any compulsion to wear such a collar, and indeed its use is now somewhat less common.

A minister is required to live their own life and to guide that of their families, so far as they are able, according to the doctrines of Christ, and to make themselves and their family examples of the Christian life.[97] Although the House of Bishops has stated that clergy should not engage in sexually active homophile partnerships, intrusive interrogations to determine whether such is the case should not be undertaken.[98] Steps may be taken to protect the Church's teaching and to avoid public scandal, but clergy who give no occasion for public scandal are entitled to be treated with trust and respect.[99]

At the heart of every minister's vocation is the undertaking to serve God and not to devote their lives to any other inconsistent purpose. This is especially clear in the bishop's address to ordinands prior to their ordination to the priesthood, when they are enjoined to forsake and set aside, as much as they may, all worldly cares and studies, and to devote themselves entirely to this one thing.[1] To what extent this obligation conflicts with the recent trend to ordain non-stipendiary ministers, who whilst offering clerical assistance in a parish generally remain in their secular occupation following ordination, is a matter of some theological debate, consideration of which is outside the scope of this book.

The Canons state that ministers must not become involved in occupations or activities which are inappropriate to the sacred nature of the office and which are either detrimental to the performance of those duties or which might give just cause for offence to others.[2] Neither must they engage in any trade or other occupation in such a manner as to affect the performance of their duties, except to the extent authorised by statute or with the licence of the bishop.[3] Allied to these provisions are statutory restrictions imposed upon those holding ecclesiastical offices or licensed to perform such duties from engaging in certain occupations.

7.15   In order to take a farm of over 80 acres for his own use or occupation such a minister requires the written permission of the bishop.[4] A minister is prohibited

---

[96] Canon C27.

[97] Canon C26(2).

[98] *Issues in Human Sexuality*, A Statement of the House of Bishops (1991) (GS Misc. 382) Chap. 5.

[99] *ibid.*

[1] *The Ordinal*, The Form and Manner of Ordering of Priests.

[2] Canon (2612).

[3] Canon C28(1).

[4] Pluralities Act 1838, s.28. The bishop's consent must specify the number of years for which it is given and cannot exceed seven years: *ibid.* Although the statute does not require the minister to obtain a licence it is implicit in both the Clergy (Ordination and Miscellaneous Provisions) Measure 1964, s.11(1) and Canon C28(1) that such is required.

from engaging in trading activities either in person or indirectly, for example through an agent. There are limited exceptions to this general prohibition. First where the trade has been or is carried on by or on behalf of more than six partners. Secondly where the trade or any share of it has devolved upon him or for his benefit under a will or by virtue of any devise, bequest, inheritance, intestacy, settlement, marriage, bankruptcy or insolvency. However in these instances can the minister act as either director or managing partner nor trade in person.[5]

Certain activities are declared to be outside the scope of the general prohibition on trading. Teaching or keeping a school or seminary and activities related to running an education establishment, publishing books or other works, and being involved in the management of certain benefit and other societies are all exempted. So too are the buying and selling of household goods for himself or his family, or anything for the occupation of any glebe or other land which such a minister may lawfully hold or possess, although in the case of these last articles the minister must not buy or sell them in person from any market, fair or place of public sale.[6]

All such restrictions may be dispensed with by licence from the bishop.[7] Before granting a licence the bishop must consult with the PCC of any parish in which the minister holds office. If the bishop refuses a licence the minister may appeal to the archbishop within one month of the refusal, the archbishop having power to confirm or overrule the bishop's refusal. After the archbishop has made his decision no further right of appeal exists.[8]

Failure to obtain permission for farming renders the minister liable to payment of a penalty[9] whilst unlawful trading constitutes an offence which may lead to suspension from office temporarily, or for a third offence, permanently.[10] Proceedings in respect of penalties for unlawful farming may be brought against an incumbent,[11] and for unlawful trading against any minister, in the consistory court.[12]

It should be noted that none of these statutory prohibitions and thus none of the penalties nor offences in respect their breach apply to women ministers (see above). However, in view of the general canonical prohibition against such activities without a licence, a woman minister wishing to engage in such activities would be advised to obtain a licence from the bishop.

A minister cannot be elected to serve as a member of the House of Commons,[13] and a clerk in holy orders is ineligible to serve on a jury.[14] Generally speaking

---

[5] Pluralities Act 1838, s.29. A contract entered into by a clergyman trading or dealing illegally may be enforced against him: *ibid.*, s.31.

[6] *ibid.*, s.30.

[7] Clergy (Ordination and Miscellaneous Provisions) Measure 1964, s.11(1); Canon C28(1).

[8] Clergy (Ordination and Miscellaneous Provisions) Measure 1964, s.11(2); Canon C28(2).

[9] Pluralities Act 1838, s.28.

[10] *ibid.*, s.31.

[11] Penalties in respect of unbeneficed clergy may be recovered in the High Court: *ibid.*, s.117; Supreme Court Act 1981, s.151(5), Sched, 4, para. 1.

[12] EJM, s.6(1)(d); Pluralities Act 1838, s.112.

[13] House of Commons (Clergy Disqualification) Act 1801, s.1.

[14] Juries Act 1974, s.1, Sched. 1, Pt I, Group C.

ministers are exempt from the obligation to serve in any secular capacity,[15] although they are not disqualified from membership of a local authority.[16]

Finally mention should be made of the fact that it is a statutory criminal offence, punishable in the secular courts, to obstruct or prevent a minister from officiating in a church or elsewhere, or to strike, offer violence to, or arrest upon any civil (but not criminal) process, a minister engaged or about to be engaged upon such duties, or who is going to or returning from the performance of such duties.[17]

Relinquishment of holy orders

7.16   Once ordained no clerk in holy orders can be divested of the character of his order. However, they may voluntarily relinquish the exercise of their orders, the effect of which is that they are reduced to the status of a lay person. A clerk may also be deprived of the exercise of their orders, or be deposed from them, that is unfrocked, by legal and canonical process.[18] However, it should be noted that if a priest who is deposed continues to carry out priestly acts, for example to celebrate Holy Communion, it is the view of the Western Catholic Church that any such acts, although irregular, are valid.

To relinquish their orders a deacon or priest must first resign any ecclesiastical preferment[19] held by them, before executing a deed[20] relinquishing all rights, privileges, advantages and exemptions of their office. The deed must then be enrolled in the Central Office of the Supreme Court of Judicature, and an office copy of the enrolment, together with a statement of their place of residence, must be delivered to the bishop of the diocese in which the last preferment was held, or if no preferment was held at the time of resignation, to the bishop of the diocese in which they are resident. After delivery to the bishop of the copy of the

---

[15] *Coke on Littleton, Institutes*, (4th ed. 1639), Vol. 1, p. 94a; *Coke's Institutes*, (1680), Vol. 3, p. 114. By statute this generally includes exemption from conscription into the armed forces: National Service Act 1948, s.1, Sched. 1.

[16] Thus they are not referred to in the Local Government Act 1972, s.80.

[17] Offences against the Person Act 1861, s.36. Ministers also enjoy protection under the common law from such arrest whilst going to, attending and returning from episcopal visitations: *McGreath v. Geraghty* (1866) W.R. 127; *Blane v. Geraghty* (1866) W.R. 133, and going to and from and whilst at Convocation: *Coke's Institutes*, (1680), Vol. 4, p. 323. It also appears to be an offence at common law to disturb a priest of the Church of England in the performance of divine worship: *R. v. Parry* (1680) Trem. P.C. 239. Under the Ecclesiastical Courts Jurisdiction Act 1860 it is a criminal offence to molest, disturb, vex or trouble, disquiet or misuse by any other means, an authorised preacher or a clergyman in holy orders ministering or celebrating any sacrament or any divine service, office or rite: *ibid.*, s.2. The Act also makes it an offence to commit "riotous, violent or indecent behaviour" in the course of lawful liturgical action. The offence may be committed in any cathedral, church, or chapel of the Church of England or chapel of any other religious denomination as well as a certified place of worship and extends to acts committed at any time, not just during divine service, in any churchyard or burial ground: *ibid.*, s.2. See also Chap. 4.

[18] As to which see Chap. 11.

[19] For the meaning of "preferment" see n. 91, *ante*.

[20] Clerical Disabilities Act 1870, s.3; Supreme Court Act 1981, s.19(2)(a); Canon C1(2).

enrolment and statement notice of this must then be given to the archbishop of the province in which the bishop's diocese is situated.[21]

Six months after delivering the deed to the bishop the minister seeking to relinquish their orders may apply to the bishop to cause it to be recorded in the diocesan registry; a request with which the bishop is bound to comply.[22] However, a relinquishing minister may apply to have the deed registered earlier in a case where proceedings of which the bishop has noticed have been taken against them and where these proceedings are terminated by a definitive sentence, or interlocutory decree having the same effect as a definitive sentence being pronounced against them.[23] Again the bishop is bound to comply with the request.[24]

Once the deed is recorded the priest or deacon executing it becomes incapable **7.17** of officiating or acting as a minister of the Church of England and of holding preferment with it. They cease to enjoy all rights, privileges and exemptions attaching to the office of deacon or priest, and every licence and office held by them which must by law be held by a minister, is determined and becomes void. They are also free from all disabilities, disqualifications, restraints and prohibitions to which they were subject as a clerk in holy orders, and from all jurisdiction, penalties, censures and proceedings to which they might otherwise have been amenable or liable.[25]

A priest or deacon who relinquishes their legal status as a clerk in holy orders still retains the indelible character of their order.[26] Relinquishment carries with it various practical consequences which effectively reduce the minister's status to that of a lay person, but their status as a minister is in reality only suspended, since it may be revived without the necessity for reordination. Indeed reordination is not possible.

Should they wish to resume their legal status a deacon or priest may petition the archbishop of the province in which the diocese where the deed of relinquishment is recorded is situated, for enrolment of the deed to be vacated.[27] The petition must set out the reason for executing the deed of relinquishment, the nature of their work or employment and places where they have resided since its execution, and their reasons for wishing to resume the status of an officiating minister, together with a supporting statutory declaration. On receipt of the petition, and after such consultation as he deems necessary, which must if the deed is not enrolled in the archbishop's own diocese include consultation with

---

[21] Clerical Disabilities Act 1870, s.4. A copy of the record must be given to the priest or deacon on payment of a fee and the copy, certified by the registrar, is evidence of the due execution, enrolment and recording of the deed, and of the fulfilment of the requirements of the Act in relation to it: *ibid.*, s.7. Where the deed has been executed and enrolled at the Central Office it may be vacated, notwithstanding the lapse of six months: *Re Clerical Disabilities Act 1870, ex p. Cowan* (1927) 137 L.T. 515.

[22] Clerical Disabilities Act 1870, s.5.

[23] See Chap. 11.

[24] Clerical Disabilities Act 1870, s.4.

[25] *ibid.*, s.4. Neither the minister nor their estate is relieved from any liability in respect of dilapidations (see Chap, 5) or from any other debt or other pecuniary liability incurred or accruing before or after execution of the deed of relinquishment: Clerical Disabilities Act 1870, s.8.

[26] Canon C1(2).

[27] Clerical Disabilities Act 1870 (Amendment) Measure 1934, s.1.

the bishop of the diocese in which it is recorded, the archbishop may request[28] vacation of the enrolment.[29]

Upon vacation of the roll the minister may resume clerical functions to such extent as the bishop of the diocese in which they officiate determines. This is subject to the restriction that they are incapable of holding any benefice or other preferment, including that of a curate licensed under seal, for two years after the vacation is recorded, and thereafter may only hold such with the bishop's consent.[30] Otherwise they are in the same position as if they had never relinquished their status.[31]

Unbeneficed clergy

7.18 All ministers who are not the incumbent of a benefice are referred to as unbeneficed clergy. Included within this group are priests in charge of a parish, vicars in team ministries, assistant curates, lecturers and preachers, chaplains and ministers of proprietary chapels and chapels of ease. Also included are all those who have no definite parochial or other ministerial charge, for example, retired clergy, those in teaching and administrative posts and some non-stipendiary ministers.

As we saw in Chapters 5 and 6 it is generally the case that all unbeneficed clergy require the authority of the bishop of the diocese to enable them to officiate anywhere in the diocese, as well as the consent of the incumbent of the parish. Those cases where the incumbent's consent is not required were discussed in Chapter 5.

Bishop's authority to officiate

7.19 That authority is conferred by the bishop admitting the minister to serve in the diocese by licence, or by the bishop giving his written permission.[32] A licence takes either the form of a general licence to preach or otherwise to minister in any parish or ecclesiastical district (subject to the consent of the incumbent of the parish where this is required)[33] or a licence to perform a particular office.[34] In the case of a licence granted to an assistant curate or to a member of a team ministry this may specify the term of years for which it is to have effect.[35] Before the licence is granted the minister must take the oath of canonical obedience to the bishop of the diocese.[36]

[28] Upon production of the request the enrolment is vacated as if ordered by the High Court and the vacation is recorded in the diocesan registry: *ibid*. A copy of the record must be given to the clergyman on payment of a fee and the copy, certified by the registrar, is evidence of the vacation and its recording: *ibid*., s.3(1).

[29] Clerical Disabilities Act 1870 (Amendment) Measure 1934, s.1.

[30] *ibid*., s.2(1). The bishop's consent after two years may be general or in respect of a particular benefice or preferment: *ibid*., s.2(2).

[31] *ibid*., s.1(5).

[32] Canon C8(3); Act of Uniformity 1662, s.15.

[33] Canon C8(4).

[34] Canon C12(1).

[35] *ibid*.

[36] Canon C14(3). The oath is taken in the presence of the bishop or his commissary.

The bishop is not to grant such a licence to any minister who comes to him from another diocese unless they first show him their Letter of Orders or other proof that they are ordained, and bring testimony of their honesty, ability and conformity to the doctrine, discipline and worship of the Church of England, from the bishop in whose diocese they have previously resided.[37] A bishop does not have to grant a licence and need not give any reason for refusing either his licence or permission, even in cases where the minister is licensed or beneficed in another diocese.[38]

There are limited exceptions to the requirement that the bishop's authority is required. A minister having the cure of souls, or sequestrator when the cure is vacant, or the dean or provost and canons residentiary of any cathedral or collegiate church, may allow a minister of whose life, standing and qualfications they are satisfied, to minister for not more than seven days within three months without reference to the bishop of other Ordinary. That minister is required to sign the services register when he officiates.[39]

No member of a cathedral chapter is prevented from performing their duties and exercising their ministry by lack of authority from the bishop. A minister who has a licence to preach throughout the province from the archbishop, or throughout England from the University of Oxford or Cambridge, may do so without further authority. Finally a funeral service which may, under the Church of England (Miscellaneous Provisions) Measure 1992, be performed without the consent of the minister of the parish[40] does not require authority of the bishop.[41]

Revocation of licence[41a]

Where the bishop has given his licence this may be revoked summarily for any **7.20** cause which appears to him good and reasonable.[42] The power of revocation extends to licences granted to assistant curates or to members of team ministries for a term of years before the expiration of the term.[43] It would appear that in cases where the licence is not revoked summarily there is no necessity for the bishop to give reasons nor is there any right of appeal.[44] What constitutes

---

[37] Canon C12(2).

[38] *Bishop of Down v. Miller* (1861) 11 I. Ch. R. App. 1 at 9.

[39] Canon C8(2). Such ministry must not be in contravention of any resolution in either of the forms set out as Resolution A in Scheds 1 or 2 to the Priests (Ordination of Women) Measure 1993: *ibid*.

[40] As to which see Chap. 10.

[41] Canon C8(2).

[41a] Concern has been expressed at the manner in which the licence of unbeneficed clergy may be withdrawn and the lack of protection which they enjoy in contrast to those with a freehold. A working party has recently recommended changes to the position regarding the revocation of licences with a view to ensuring that the same disciplinary procedures could be followed for both unbeneficed and those with a freehold office: *Under Authority*, the report of the General Synod Working Party Reviewing Clergy Discipline and the Working of the Ecclesiastical Courts (1996) (GS 1217). As to which see Chap. 11.

[42] Church of England (Legal Aid and Miscellaneous Provisions) Measure 1988, s.7(1); Canon C12(5).

[43] Canon C12(6).

[44] *Legal Opinions, ante*, p. 230. However, the bishop's actions in such circumstances may be open to judicial review.

reasonable, as opposed to summary, notice would depend upon the circumstances and in particular the length of time during which the licence had been held.

In cases of summary revocation before giving notice the bishop must give the minister an opportunity to show reasons to the contrary. If the bishop proceeds he serves a notice of revocation, which must inform the minister that they can appeal to the archbishop of the province, provided they do so within 28 days of service of the notice.[45]

Where an appeal is made the archbishop must hear the appeal himself or appoint a diocesan or suffragan bishop, drav..1 from outside the diocese concerned, to hear the appeal. The appeal is to be conducted in accordance with rules approved by the Archbishops of Canterbury and York. After either hearing the appeal, or receiving a written report from the bishop who heard the appeal, the archbishop must decide whether to confirm, vary or cancel the revocation, his decision in the matter being final.[46]

It should be noted that the provisions in respect of the summary revocation of licences granted to deaconesses, readers and lay workers and in respect of their rights of appeal are identical to those set out above in respect of all unbeneficed ministers.[47]

Unbeneficed clergy in the parish

7.21 Many of the unbeneficed clergy who have no definite parochial or ministerial charge hold the bishop's licence or permission to officiate in the diocese in which they are resident and consequently may be invited to officiate in any church or chapel in the diocese where assistance is required. However, most unbeneficed clergy officiating within a parish fall under one of two heads. Either they are ministers who are in charge of a benefice which lacks an incumbent, or they are clergy appointed to assist an incumbent. Before considering these two groups in more detail it should noted that there is no age limit for such appointments, nor does age affect the tenure of office for any of these clergy.[48]

Curate, as we saw in Chapter 5, is the correct term for the minister who has the cure of souls within the parish. Strictly speaking therefore a minister who assists the curate is the assistant curate, but the practice of referring to such an assistant as the curate is so widespread that any other use of that term is confusing and may be misleading. It is incorrect to refer to such an assistant curate who is informally attached to a chapel of ease as a curate-in-charge, since the attachment will be no more than an informal arrangement of responsibilities within the parish.

---

[45] Church of England (Legal Aid and Miscellaneous Provisions) Measure 1988, s.7(1); Canon C12(5).

[46] *ibid*.

[47] Church of England (Legal Aid and Miscellaneous Provisions) Measure 1988, s.7(1); Canons D3(3A), E6(3), E8(5).

[48] The provisions of the Ecclesiastical Offices (Age Limit) Measure 1975 do not apply. However, in the case of a priest-in-charge the bishop may apply the guidelines laid down by the House of Bishops of the General Synod regarding the requirements that clergy who were incumbents or of incumbent status be in priest's orders for at least four years, save in the case of those aged over 40 years.

Curate-in-charge is the correct term for an unbeneficed minister who is formally appointed to be in charge of the benefice in the absence of an incumbent. However, priest-in-charge or minister-in-charge are equally correct terms for such a curate and, given that curate-in-charge is also the proper description of an assistant curate of a parish who has been given charge of a conventional district, either of these is to be preferred.

Priest-in-charge

Where a benefice is under sequestration[49] the bishop may licence a minister to be **7.22** priest-in-charge of the benefice for as long as the sequestration continues.[50] The most common reason for sequestration is due to the benefice becoming vacant, but it is not generally considered necessary to license a priest-in-charge for the period between the vacation of the benefice by one incumbent and the admission of another. The most usual case when a priest-in-charge is appointed is when the bishop has suspended presentations to the benefice in contemplation of a pastoral scheme.

A priest-in-charge takes the oath of canonical obedience to the diocesan bishop[51] and makes the declaration of assent[52] before being licensed. They also make the declaration of assent in front of the congregation which is assembled for divine service on the first Sunday on which they officiate, in the church or one of the churches in which they are licensed to serve.[53]

A priest-in-charge has the same rights and duties in respect of the services in the church and the cure of souls as an incumbent,[54] and many Acts, and Canons relating to the functions and duties of an incumbent specifically extend to them. In cases where the presentation to a benefice has been suspended the bishop may require the priest-in-charge to reside in the parsonage house,[55] but unless this power is specifically exercised they are not under any obligation to reside in any particular house or even within the area of the benefice.

The priest-in-charge's appointment lasts whilst the benefice continues to exist and remains under sequestration, or until the appointment is determined by the bishop. However, the bishop may revoke the licence at any time, the procedure for revocation and the priest's rights of appeal being the same as those already described above in relation to unbeneficed clergy generally. If they wish to resign the curacy the priest-in-charge must give the bishop three months notice, unless the bishop waives this requirement.[56] There is no longer any objection to a minister being licensed as priest-in-charge for more than one benefice, nor to an incumbent of one benefice being licensed as priest-in-charge of another.

Assistant curates

Normally an assistant curate (whether priest or deacon) is appointed to a parish **7.23** in cases where the workload is too great for the incumbent alone, and in such cases their appointment is at the discretion of the incumbent. An assistant may

---

[49] See Chap. 5.
[50] Pluralities Act 1838, s.99.
[51] Canon C14(3).
[52] Canon C15(1).
[53] Canon C15(4).
[54] *Pinder v. Barr* (1854) 4 E. & B. 105.
[55] Pastoral Measure 1983, s.68(4).
[56] Pluralities Act 1838, s.97.

also be appointed with the incumbent's consent when the incumbent is under a disability.[57] Unless the assistant is actually licensed to the curacy they have no security of tenure and may be dismissed at will by the incumbent.[58] A licence will only be granted by the bishop if the assistant is nominated by the incumbent and sometimes an assistant curate comes tu the parish on a trial period with the consent of the bishop.

Notwithstanding the role of the incumbent in the appointment, the bishop will only grant a licence if satisfied that the nominee is a fit and proper person, and he may revoke the licence at any time. Again the procedure for revocation by the bishop and the curate's rights of appeal are the same as those already described above. In addition the incumbent may determine the appointment on six months notice.[59]

As with a priest-in-charge a curate takes the oath of canonical obedience to the diocesan bishop and makes the declaration of assent before being licensed. They also make the declaration of assent in front of the congregation which is assembled for divine service on the first Sunday on which they officiate, in the church or one of the churches in which they are licensed to serve.

An assistant curate must act in accordance with directions from the incumbent,[60] who is responsible for what is done by the curate under their directions or with their consent.[61] If they wish to resign the curacy the assistant must give the incumbent and the bishop three months notice, unless the bishop waives this requirement.[62]

Lecturers and preachers

7.24 Lecturers or preachers are clerks in holy orders elected or otherwise appointed for the special purpose of lecturing or preaching. They must be licensed by the bishop or archbishop of the province,[63] but where there is a right to elect or appoint such a person the bishop is bound to license them if they are "orthodox, an honest liver and loyal".[64] Before being licensed they must take the oath of allegiance, must make and subscribe the declaration of assent, and must take an oath of obedience to the bishop or archbishop who licenses them.[65] Such appointments are now rare outside the universities, but some parishes do have endowed lectureships. With the consent of the incumbent the bishop may require

[57] Pursuant to the Incumbents (Vacation of Benefices) Measure 1977 as to which see Chap. 5.
[58] *Martyn v. Hind* (1779) 2 Cowp. 437 at 440.
[59] Pluralties Act 1838, s.95.
[60] *Martyn v. Hind*, (*ante*).
[61] *Parnell v. Roughton* (1874) L.R. 6 P.C. 46 at 53.
[62] Pluralities Act 1838, s.97.
[63] Act of Uniformity 1662, s.15; *R. v. Bishop of London* (1811) 13 East. 419; *R. v. Archbishop of Canterbury and Bishop of London* (1812) 15 East. 117.
[64] *Churchwardens of St Bartholomew's Case* (1700) 3 Salk. 51, Holt 418; *R. v. Bishop of London* (1743) 1 Wils. 11; *R. v. Archbishop of Canterbury and Bishop of London* (*ante*). Such a person cannot be elected, however, without the consent of the incumbent unless there is ancient custom to the contrary: *R. v. Bishop of London* (1743) 1 Wils. 11.
[65] Canons C13(1), C14(3), C15(1). In the presence of the bishop by whom they are to be licensed or his commissary.

a lecturer or preacher to perform other duties as assistant curate or otherwise within a benefice.[66]

Employment status of ministers[67]

The question of whether or not a person is an employee is important in **7.25** determing the rights which they may have under secular law. The Employment Protection (Consolidation) Act 1978 sets out various rights, and in particular the right not to be dismissed unfairly. An "employee" is defined as a person who enters into or works under a contract of employment, that contract being a contract of service.[68] Generally speaking clergy are not employees, but are office holders. However, being an office holder is not incompatible with being an employee, and what determines whether a person is an employee is not whether they hold an office but whether they have a contract of employment.

An incumbent is the holder of a freehold office from which they cannot be removed except by due legal process. The vocation of the priesthood together with the spiritual nature of their functions means that the office is incompatible with the existence of a contract of employment.[69] Such reasoning has been accepted in the case of Methodist and Presbyterian Church of Wales ministers,[70] and would seem to apply equally to incumbents of the Church of England, and to vicars of team ministries who have the same status as incumbents.[71] The same principle also applies to holders of other ecclesiastical offices such as bishops, deans and provosts of cathedrals, residentiary canons, and archdeacons.[72]

Unbeneficed clergy are licensed under seal by the bishop, the licence authorising a ministry which would not otherwise be permissible. It is not of itself an indication of a contract of employment. With regard to assistant curates engaged in parochial work the courts have accepted that they are holders of an ecclesiastical office whose rights are not defined by contract,[73] although recent cases before employment and industrial tribunals have doubted,[74] and in one case

---

[66] Lecturers and Parish Clerks Act 1844, s.1; EJM, s.87, Sched. 5.

[67] See generally, *Clergy Conditions of Service, A Consultative Paper*, G.S. 1994 No. 1126; *Legal Opinions*, pp. 120–129; Doe, *The Legal Framework of the Church of England* (1996), pp. 198–200.

[68] Employment Protection (Consolidation) Act 1978, s.153.

[69] In *Re Tyler* (Application No. 21283/93), the European Court of Human Rights stated that the functions of a priest of the Church of England were more in the nature of public service than they are of private professional practice.

[70] *President of the Methodist Conference President v. Parfitt* [1984] Q.B. 368, C.A.; *Davies v. Presbyterian Church of Wales* [1986] 1 W.L.R. 323, H.L.

[71] See *Legal Opinions*, p. 122, where it is also suggested that the same applies to priests-in-charge.

[72] *ibid.*

[73] *Re National Insurance Act 1911: Re Employment of Church of England Curates* [1911] 2 Ch. 563. The decision was followed in *President of the Methodist Conference President v. Parfitt* (*ante*) (although the view that in appropriate cases the spiritual nature of the work might not exclude the possibility of a contractual relationship was expressed by L.J. Dillon at p. 376) and *Davies v. Presbyterian Church of Wales* (*ante*).

[74] *Barthorpe v. Exeter DBF* [1979] I.C.R. 900, EAT; *Turns v. Smart, Carey and Bath and Wells DBF* (Employment Appeal Tribunal No. EAT 510–90, June 11, 1991); *Fane v. Bishop of Manchester* (Industrial Tribunal No. 8–229–232, February 27, 1990).

declined to follow, this decision, holding that an assistant curate may be employed.[75] The position is therefore uncertain, but current developments in employment law indicate a greater willingness to hold that such ministers are employees.

Other clergy such as deacons who are licensed to a parish would appear to be in the same uncertain position. However, those in sector ministry are in a different position, since most will be employees, as will most extra-parochial ministers in institutions. Some clergy are only involved in sector ministry part-time, receiving a salary as an employee in respect of their sector ministry and a stipend in respect of an ecclesiastical office in respect of which they have the cure of souls. Another common arrangement is for a minister to hold both an ecclesiastical office and be involved in sector ministry (a parochial minister who also holds a diocesan post) but receive only one source of income. Such cases will depend upon their particular facts, although the question of whether the intention was to confer an office or employment upon the minister will be of primary importance.[76]

The position of deaconesses and licensed lay readers and workers is not entirely clear; if in receipt of a salary they may be employees. An industrial tribunal was prepared to hold that a stipendiary reader was an employee.[77] Were such a lay minister to be an employee, and were their licence to minister revoked by the bishop, the contract of employment would not automatically terminate. However, the licence would be a prerequisite for performance of the contract of employment and were they subsequently dismissed it is likely that such dismissal would be fair.[78]

The ministry of the laity

7.26   As we have already noted every member of the *laos* is an ecclesiastical person and in the twentieth century the theological approach of the Church has once again been to refer to the ministry of the laity, evidenced in service to the Church and in worship and witness to the Gospel in their daily life. Although certain duties are imposed upon the laity by Canon, such as observance of the Lord's Day and other feasts,[79] receiving Holy Communion regularly,[80] examining their consciences[81] and avoiding schismatic conduct,[82] these duties are not enforceable.[83] The laity, but more particularly parishioners, have as we saw in Chapter 4 rights to the ministrations of the church, which are enforceable.

---

[75] *Coker v. Diocese of Southwark* [1995] I.C.R. 563: an industrial tribunal accepted jurisdiction to hear a claim for unfair dismissal by an assistant curate, thus accepting that a contract of employment was in existence.

[76] *Legal Opinions*, pp. 122–124, and 126–129 where model contracts are set out.

[77] *Barthorpe v. Exeter DBF* (*ante*). The case was remitted for the tribunal to decide who the employer was but settled before a decision was reached.

[78] *Legal Opinions*, p. 125. Presumably this would only be so if the revocation itself was justified. Whether this could be questioned by the industrial tribunal or only by the High Court upon a judicial review is far from clear.

[79] Canon B6.

[80] *ibid.*, B15(1).

[81] *ibid.*, B29(1).

[82] *ibid.*, A8.

[83] See Chap. 11.

An Act of Convocation[84] states that the duties of the Church's members are to pray daily and to read the Bible regularly, to join in the worship of the Church every Sunday, to observe holy days, after due preparation to receive Holy Communion regularly and particularly at the great festivals of the Church and on the great occasions of their own lives, to make Fridays and the season of Lent special by acts of devotion and self-denial, to contribute worthily to the work of the Church at home and abroad and for the relief of those in need, to uphold the marriage laws of the Church, and to bring up children to love and serve the Lord.

The Church has various lay officers including, as we saw in Chapter 4, churchwardens, sidesmen, parish clerks and other parish officers; it also has, as we shall see in Chapter 11, ecclesiastical judges who may be members of the laity. In addition certain members of the laity are licensed by the bishop to specific ministerial roles and it is with an examination of these that we are now concerned.

Deaconesses

Deaconess is not another term for a women deacon, but refers to a member of the order of deaconesses set up in the nineteenth century. A deaconess is not a clerk in holy orders and is not subject to the criminal jurisdiction of the ecclesiastical courts.[85] Women were admitted to the order by prayer and the laying on of hands by the bishop, but whilst the order still exists no new members have been admitted since the date when women were enabled to become deacons.[86]   **7.27**

It is the function of a deaconess, under the direction of the minister in the place where she is licensed by the bishop, to serve, to lead the people in public worship, to exercise pastoral care, to instruct the people in the Christian faith and to prepare them for the reception of the sacraments.[87] A deaconess may be authorised by the bishop and invited by the minister to say or sing Morning and Evening Prayer, save for the Absolution, to distribute the holy sacrament of the Lord's Supper to the people and to read the Epistle and Gospel at the celebration of the Holy Communion. The deaconess may also be authorised by the bishop, at the invitation of the minister of a parish or non-parochial minister, to preach at divine service, to church women, to baptise in the absence of the minister, with the goodwill of the persons responsible to bury the dead or read the burial service before or after a cremation, and to publish banns of marriage at Morning and Evening Prayer[88] on occasions where a lay person is permitted by statute to do so.[89] Any deaconess licensed to a parish is a member of the PCC.[90]

---

[84] Adopted by both Canterbury and York in 1953. Smethurst, Wilson and Riley (eds), *Acts of the Convocations of Canterbury and York* (revised ed., 1961), pp. 172–173. See also Doe, *The Legal Framework of the Church of England* (1996) 225–228).

[85] EJM, ss.14(1), 17, 69, 82(c).

[86] Deacons (Ordination of Women) Measure 1986, s.2; Canon D 2(2A). New members cannot be admitted unless they were accepted for training prior to February 16, 1987.

[87] D1(2), (3), (4); Deaconesses and Lay Ministry Measure 1972, s.1(5).

[88] *ibid*.

[89] For the circumstances in which a lay person may publish banns see the Marriage Act 1949, s.9 and Chap. 10.

[90] CRR, r.14(1)(b).

To exercise her office in any diocese a deaconess must be licensed by the diocesan bishop.[91] Identical provisions to those considered above in regard to unbeneficed clergy apply to both the revocation of the deaconess' licence and her rights of appeal against this.[92]

A deaconess who is licensed or holds a bishop's permission to officiate, and in either case satisfies the requirements as to the persons who may be ordained as deacons, may apply to that bishop for his consent to her ordination as a deacon. The bishop may give his consent notwithstanding that she has not been further examined in her knowledge of holy scripture or of the doctrine, discipline or worship of the Church of England nor exhibited any certificate or document.[93]

Readers[94]

7.28   Any baptised and confirmed lay person who satisfies the bishop of the diocese that they are a regular communicant of the Church of England may be admitted by that bishop to the office of reader.[95] Although a member of the laity the use of the term "lay reader" is not correct.

A candidate for admission in a parish or district must be nominated to the bishop by the minister, and a candidate for a wider area must be nominated by one of the rural deans or archdeacons in consultation with the minister of the candidate's parish.[96] Sometimes these are referred to as parish and diocesan readers respectively, although these terms tend not to be much used today.

The nominator must satisfy the bishop that the candidate is of good life, sound in faith, a regular communicant and well fitted for the work of reader and must provide all such other information about the candidate and the duties which they will be required to perform as the bishop may require.[97] No person can be admitted unless they are found on examination by the bishop or other competent persons to possess a sufficient knowledge of holy scripture and of the doctrine and worship of the Church of England as set forth in the Book of Common Prayer, that they are able to read the services of the Church plainly, distinctly,

---

[91] Canon D3(1). Where she is to be licensed to serve in a team ministry the licence may specify the term of years for which it is to have effect: *ibid.*, E6(1A). Where the deaconess is to exercise her office temporarily the bishop's written permission is sufficient: *ibid.* Before licensing a stipendiary deaconess the bishop must satisfy himself that adequate provision has been made for her salary, insurance against sickness or accident and a retirement pension: *ibid.*, D3(3). Every deaconess to be licensed in any place must make and subscribe to the declaration of assent and take an oath of canonical obedience: *ibid.*, D3(2).

[92] Canon D3(3A), (3B).

[93] Clergy (Ordination and Miscellaneous Provisions) Measure 1964, s.1; Deacons (Ordination of Women) Measure 1986, s.1(1), (2); Canon C4A(1), (2).

[94] The office dates in it present form from 1866 by resolution of all the bishops. The office of reader or "lector" was one of the five minor orders which lapsed (with a brief revival under Elizabeth I) at the Reformation.

[95] Canon E4(1).

[96] *ibid.*, E5(1).

[97] *ibid.*, E5(2).

audibly and reverently, and that they are capable of both preaching and teaching.[98]

Admission is by delivery of the New Testament to the candidate by the bishop.[99] There is no imposition of hands. Before admission the candidate must make and subscribe a declaration of assent together with a promise to use only the forms of service authorised or allowed, and an oath of obedience to the bishop.[1] The bishop must give the reader a certificate of their admission to the office, and if the reader moves to another diocese admission to the order is not to be repeated,[2] although they will need to be relicensed.

To exercise their office a reader must be licensed by the bishop.[3] Before being licensed they must first make the prescribed declarations of assent and obedience and a further declaration as to conduct.[4] The bishop must not license a stipendiary reader until he has satisfied himself that adequate provision has been made for a stipend, for their insurance against sickness or accident and for a retirement pension.[5] Licences held by those under 70 years of age should be kept under review, whilst readers over 70 should officiate on the basis of the bishop's written permisison rather than a licence.[6] Again, identical provisions to those considered above in regard to unbeneficed clergy apply to both the revocation of a reader's licence and their rights of appeal against this.[7]

A reader may lawfully visit the sick, read and pray with them, teach in Sunday **7.29**
school and elsewhere and generally undertake such pastoral and educational work and give such assistance to any minister as the bishop may direct. They may also during the time of divine service read Morning and Evening Prayer, save for the Absolution, publish banns of marriage at Morning or Evening Prayer on occasions on which a lay person is permitted by law to do so,[8] read the Word of God, preach, catechise the children, receive and present the offerings of the

---

[98] *ibid.*, E5(3). This is normally delegated to a diocesan readers' board, which also supervises the candidate's training. See also *Bishop's Regulations for Reader Ministry* (1991). The PCC or equivalent in the place where the reader is to serve should also express its approval.

[99] Canon E5(5), in the presence of the bishop by whom they are to be licensed or his commissary. An office for the Admission of Readers was approved by both Houses of the Convocations of Canterbury and York on May 23 and 24, 1939 and May 20, 1940 respectively.

[1] Canon E5(4), where the forms of the declarations are set out. These are made in the presence of the bishop by whom they are to be licensed or his commissary.

[2] *ibid.*, E5(6). The names of all persons admitted and licensed must be entered in a register kept by the diocesan registrar: *ibid.*, E4(3).

[3] *ibid.*, Canon E6, para. 1, proviso. Where the reader is to be licensed to serve in a team ministry the licence may specify the term of years for which it is to have effect: *ibid.*, E6(1A). A reader is usually licensed to serve in a particular parish and it is now unusual to grant a diocesan reader's licence. Where the reader is to exercise the office temporarily the bishop's written permission is sufficient.

[4] *ibid.*, E6(2), in the presence of the bishop by whom they are to be licensed or his commissary. The declarations of assent and obedience do not need to be made again if admission and licensing occur on the same day: *ibid.*

[5] *ibid.*, E6(4).

[6] *Bishop's Regulations for Reader Ministry* (1991).

[7] Canon E6(3), (3A).

[8] For the circumstances in which a lay person may publish banns see the Marriage Act 1949, s.9 and Chap. 10.

people and distribute the holy sacrament of the Lord's Supper to the people.[9] In addition they may be authorised, at the invitation of the minister of a parish or non-parochial minister, to bury the dead or read the burial service before or after a cremation with the goodwill of the persons responsible.[10]A reader who is licensed to and whose name is on the roll of the parish is a member of the PCC if the annual meeting so determines.[11]

A reader should act in accordance with a written agreement made between them and the minister to whom they are responsible, which clearly sets out their duties. They should also only act with the written permission of any other incumbent or priest-in-charge in a place where they are to minister. They should also submit an annual report to a warden or an appointed delegate.[12] Discipline of readers is dealt with at episcopal level, the bishop having as we have seen, the power of revocation of the licence.

Licensed lay workers

7.30   A lay person who satisfies the diocesan bishop that they are a baptised, confirmed and communicant member of the Church of England, has had the proper training and possesses the other necessary qualifications, which are undefined, may be admitted by the bishop to the office of evangelist and thereby as a lay worker.[13] The requirements for admission and licensing lay workers and for the revocation of that licence are essentially the same as those in respect of readers.[14]

They may, if authorised by licence or permission of the bishop, under the direction of the minister, lead the people in public worship, exercise pastoral care, evangelise, instruct the people in the Christian faith, and prepare them for the reception of the sacraments.[15] They may also be authorised and invited to say or sing Morning or Evening Prayer (save for the Absolution) and distribute the holy sacrament of the Lord's Supper to the people and read the epistle and the Gospel.[16] The bishop may also authorise them to perform, at the invitation of the minister of a parish or extra-parochial minister, the duties of preaching at divine service and churching women, with the goodwill of the persons responsible to bury the dead or read the burial service before or after a cremation and to publish the banns of marriage at Morning and Evening Prayer on occasions on

---

[9] Canon E4, (2). A table of duties was approved by both Houses of the Convocations of Canterbury and York on May 23 and 24, 1939 and May 20, 1940 respectively. See also the Book of Common Prayer rubric headed "The order for Morning and Evening Prayer".

[10] Deaconesses and Lay Ministry Measure 1972, s.1(1); Canon E4(2A).

[11] CRR, r. 14(1)(e).

[12] *Bishop's Regulations for Reader Ministry* (1991).

[13] Deaconesses and Lay Ministry Measure 1972, s.1(1); Canon E7(1), (2).

[14] Canon E8. However, a lay worker makes no declaration as to conduct on admission, and the register book containing their details must also specify the particular duties which they have been licensed to perform. There are no centralised guidelines or bishops' regulations supplementing the canonical provisions as there are for readers.

[15] Canon E7(3).

[16] *ibid.*, E7(4).

which a lay person is permitted by law to do so.[17] Any stipendiary lay worker licensed to a parish is a member of the PCC.[18]

Prior to the admission of lay persons to the order of evangelists a woman, whom the bishop was satisfied was baptised and confirmed and a regular communicant of the Church of England and possessed the necessary qualifications, could be commissioned by him as a woman worker, and was thereupon given a certificate of commission.[19] Identical provisions regarding admission, licensing and duties applied to women workers as now apply to lay workers and the provisions relating to lay workers now apply to such women workers.

Vowed members of religious communities[20]

The vowed members of religious communities live subject to the rules and discipline of their order and community. Unless they are ordained as a deacon, priest or bishop, they are not ecclesiastical persons and are therefore not subject to the criminal jurisdiction of the ecclesiastical courts.[21] Where a bishop does ordain a religious to the office of deacon or priest in practice he is ordaining them to the title of holy poverty, although there is no such title in law and as a matter of law they do not require a title.[22] Vowed members of religious communities enjoy no special privileges save that they are exempt from jury service.[23]

7.31

[17] *ibid.*, E7(5). For the circumstances in which a lay person may publish banns. See the Marriage Act 1949, s.9 and Chap. 10.

[18] CRR, r. 14(1)(b).

[19] See Canon E7(1), (2), prior to its substitution by Canon promulged February 25, 1976.

[20] See further the Advisory Council on the Relations of Bishops and Religious Communities, *A Directory of the Religious Life* (4th ed. 1990).

[21] EJM, ss.14(1), 17, 69, 82(c).

[22] Canon C5, (2)(e).

[23] Juries Act 1974, s.1, Sched. 1, Pt I, Group C.

Chapter Eight: Property and Finance of the Church of England

After centuries during which it has been the beneficary of countless endowments **8.1** the Church of England has great wealth. This wealth it holds either in the form of real property, essentially land, buildings and rights attaching to these, or personal property, which encompasses everything else, including articles belonging to a parish church and the Church's substantial investments. General secular law applies to Church property, but superimposed upon this, either adding to, modifying or nullifying that law, are the ecclesiastical laws. It is an examination of these laws ecclesiastical, and their effect upon the property of the Church with which this Chapter is primarily concerned.

The complex way in which the Church holds its property and the law relating to such propety has been the subject of some criticism. The various functions of the Church Commissioners, who as we shall see occupy a pivotal role in regard to the holding and management of Church property, were the subject of scrutiny by the Turnbull Commission.[1] Amongst its recommendations were proposals to transfer many of the Commissioners' functions to the proposed Archbishops' Council whilst placing responsibility for other financial matters in the hands of the dioceses. These proposals are considered in more detail below.

In addition the Commission proposed that a Church Heritage Board could be established as a supporting structure to the new Archbishops' Council. At present several different bodies are responsible for the Church's heritage in its buildings including the Council for the Care of Churches, the Cathedrals Fabric Commission, the Advisory Board for Redundant Churches, the Redundant Churches Committee and the Churches Conservation Trust. Although the Commission did not consider it appropriate to merge these bodies and notwithstanding the current co-operation between them by means of occasional meetings, a central point of contact and co-ordination was seen to be of value to support the work of preserving the Church's heritage.

In this chapter we consider the representative owners of Church property, the acquisition of property, consecration and its legal effects. We look at the rights of various persons in respect of churches, churchyards and moveables, and the duties of care, maintenance, and preservation of these and other parochial property, including register books and other records. The property of the benefice, trust property, and the relatively recent phenomena of church sharing

---

[1] *Working as One Body*, The Report of the Archbishops Commission on the Reorganisation of the Church of England (1995).

agreements are also considered, as are the removal of the legal effects of consecration and the redundancy schemes for churches which are no longer required. The status, care and maintenance of cathedral property is also examined. Finally we consider the finances of the Church, including its investments, entitlement to certain fees and the quota system by which much of its income is now obtained from parishes. In addition we will examine the role of the Church Commissioners and diocesan boards of finance, and the position in regard to stipends, remuneration and pensions of clergy and lay ministers and their dependents.

Representative owners of church property

8.2   English law always looks to find who the person is in whom property is vested. In other words it seeks to find the identity of the legal, as opposed to the beneficial owner. Frequently the person who as a matter of law owns the property derives no or only limited benefit from it, holding it for, or mainly for, the benefit of others. In other words such a person holds the property in trust.

As we have already seen the Church of England is not a corporation, but an aggregate of its members.[2] Therefore the Church as such does not hold property, rather it does so through representative owners. In order to ensure that it continues to be applied to its intended purpose, Church property is generally vested in ecclesiastical corporations rather than in an individual. These corporations are recognised by the law as having a permanent capacity, because of their office or function, to hold property, and are, within the limitations of their powers, as capable of so holding property as an individual or a body of persons. As a result, whilst the holder of a particular office may change, the corporation itself continues to hold its property unaffected by such a change. These corporations are specifically categorised as ecclesiastical because of the spiritual character of the office or function, or because of the spiritual purpose for which they were constituted.[3]

Archbishops,[4] bishops,[5] certain deans,[6] prebendaries and canons,[7] vicars choral,[8] and all archdeacons[9] are ecclesiastical corporations sole. So too are all incumbents (whether rectors or vicars).[10] An ecclesiastical corporation aggregate consists of two or more individuals or bodies which are themselves corporations combined. Chapters of cathedrals and colleges of vicars choral amongst others are corporations aggregate.[11] Other examples of ecclesiastical corporations are

---

[2] In Chap. 2.

[3] *Blackstone's Commentaries on the Laws of England* (14th. ed. 1803), p. 470.

[4] *Rolle's Abridgement of the Common Law*, Vol. 1, p. 512.

[5] *Coke on Littleton, Institutes*, (4th ed. 1639) Vol. 1, p. 250a.

[6] *Mirehouse v. Rennell* (1833) 1 Cl. & Fin. 527 at 538, H.L.; Cathedrals Measure 1963, s.15(1).

[7] *Gleaves v. Parfitt* (1860) 7 C.B.N.S. 838; Cathedrals Measure 1963, s.15(1).

[8] *Blackstone's Commentaries on the Laws of England*, (14th ed. 1803), p. 470.

[9] *Tufnell v. Constable* (1838) 7 Ad. & El. 798.

[10] n. 5 above. This includes rectors and vicars of new benefices created by pastoral schemes, and the rector of a team ministry: Pastoral Measure 1983, ss.23(5), 20(2). A lay rector is merely a corporation sole, not an ecclesiastical corporation.

[11] Ecclesiastical Leasing Act 1842, s.1 (part repealed).

PCCs which are bodies corporate,[12] as are churchwardens for some purposes. The Church Commissioners, who hold much of the the Church's property, are a body corporate[13] as are the Church of England Pensions Board[14] and all DBFs.[15]

Ecclesiastical property

Although references are often made to ecclesiastical property it should be noted **8.3** that ecclesiastical property is not a term confined to the property of the Church of England, nor is an ecclesiastical charity restricted to purposes connected with it. Property is generally regarded as ecclesiastical where the person in whom the legal right is vested is a representative of a church, or where the right itself relates to a church, or where the relationship between the right and the person in whom it is vested arises out of or relates to a church; church being used in the sense of an organism distinct from the individual members who comprise it.[16]

Property is therefore ecclesiastical property where it is appropriated for use in connection with, or for the benefit of, a church including any spiritual purpose, or for use by, or for the benefit of, the officers or members of a church, even though the benefit derived by the members may be of a temporal nature.[17] Any property owned by a person in the capacity of a representative of a church is also ecclesiastical property whether or not it is applied to an ecclesiastical purpose.[18]

Acquisition of land

Although anyone may convey land to the Church of England[19] the Church **8.4** Commissioners have special powers to acquire land of their own initiative by way of gift, devise or purchase for a new church.[20] The scope of these powers includes the acquisition of buildings or land intended to be used for the erection of a church, church hall or ecclesiastical residence. It also includes land or property purchased so as to enable the enlargment or improvment of any of these buildings as well as land to provide or extend a churchyard or burial ground. Gifts or bequests of money may also be accepted and then consequently used to assist in the purchase of such land. Once acquired by the Commissioners the land vests in the incumbent of the parish in which the property is situated.[21]

---

[12] PCCPM, s.3.

[13] Church Commissioners Measure 1947, s.1.

[14] Church of England Pensions Measure 1961, s.21.

[15] Diocesan Boards of Finance Measure 1925, s.1.

[16] A distinction evident in *Rector and Churchwardens of St George's Hanover Square v. Westminster Corporation* [1910] A.C. 225, H.L.

[17] *Re Perry Almshouses: Re Ross's Charity* [1899] 1 Ch. 21, C.A.

[18] Local Government Act 1894, s.75(2) applied by the Charities Act 1993, s.96.

[19] Gifts for Churches Acts 1803 and 1811; New Parishes Measure 1943, s.14; Pastoral Measure 1983, s.76. This includes grants of land to the Church Commissioners by the DBF or any other body holding diocesan land on trust, and subject to certain conditions, by the incumbent.

[20] New Parishes Measure 1943, ss.13(1), (2), 14(1), 15(1), (2).

[21] *ibid.*, s.16. Land for the extension of a churchyard may be conveyed directly to the incumbent: Consecration of Churchyards Act 1867.

The Church Commissioners also have the power to makes grants or loans to DBFs for the provision of church buildings in areas where, having regard to recent housing development, they are satisfied there is not currently adequate provision. This power is only exercisable on the written request of the diocesan pastoral committee and only then with the consent of the diocesan bishop.[22] This power to acquire land or buildings or to make grants and loans extends to land or buildings which are to be the subject of a sharing agreement.[23]

Disposal of unconsecrated land acquired

8.5   Where land or buildings remain unconsecrated and are no longer required for the purpose for which they were originally obtained the owner of the land may sell, exchange, appropriate, transfer or reconvey it or any part of it. If the Church Commissioners are the owners they will require the consent of the incumbent and the bishop before so doing, and if the owner is the incumbent the consent of the bishop and Commissioners is needed. These powers enable the property or the proceeds from its sale to be utilised for any ecclesiastical purpose or to benefit any educational charitable or public purpose relating to the ecclesiastical district in which it is situated or to be transferred to the DBF to be held as glebe land.[24]

Church planting

8.6   The establishment of a new congregation or centre of worship, generally known as church planting, has been the subject of a report and of guidance endorsed by the House of Bishops of the General Synod.[25] Church planting generally arises when a congregation grows to a size where its existing building can no longer adequately accommodate it, although it may also stem from a desire to better serve the needs of one district of the parish or indeed form part of its evangelistic mission.

Even when planting occurs within the parish boundaries it is recognised as having a potential effect on the ministry of other parishes and denominations. Careful long-term planning is advised, as is extensive consultation, with amongst others, the area dean, archdeacon, diocesan advisors on mission and evangelism, leaders of other denominations and local congregations and civic and community leaders.

Oversight remains the responsibility of the person who has or shares the cure of souls within the benefice, even if this is temporarily delegated by agreement,

---

[22] New Housing Areas (Church Buildings) Measure 1954, s.1.

[23] Sharing of Church Buildings Measure 1970, s.2.

[24] New Parishes Measure 1943, s.17. Consecrated land is expressly excluded. The section provides that in certain cases the property must be offered for resale or if gifted reconveyed to the original owner. Similar provisions regarding disposal apply to persons in whom any land granted under the Gifts for Churches Acts 1803 and 1811 or the Consecration of Churches Act 1867 is vested where that land was acquired by the Church Commissioners of their predecessors: *ibid.*

[25] *Breaking New Ground: Planting in the Church of England*, (1994) (G.S. No. 1099), a report commissioned by the House of Bishops, which contains guidance on this issue.

and the PCC of the parish remains responsible for legal and financial matters. The guidance from the House of Bishops recommends that agreements be drawn up between the planting and planted church and between the diocese and the planted church. Such an agreement should deal with matters including buildings, leadership, administration, decision making, liturgy and worship and ecumenical involvement.

Consecration

One of the most important distinctions in respect to church property is that **8.7** between consecrated and unconsecrated property. A church or chapel may be erected before the ground is consecrated, and may be used with the bishop's consent for divine service and the administration of the sacraments, but a building does not as a matter of law become a church or a parish church until it has been consecrated for the purpose of public worship.[26] Although there is no similar necessity for a churchyard to be consecrated the practice of so doing is widespread.[27]

In recent years some places of public worship have been inaugurated using a simple service of dedication rather than being consecrated but, strictly speaking, even after their dedication, cannot be termed churches. Consecration is not restricted to churches and churchyards. For example a private chapel may be consecrated, although should this occur the chapel is brought within the jurisdiction of the Ordinary and consequently limitations are placed upon the owners who no longer can act independently in matters pertaining to the chapel.[28]

Although exceptions have been permitted it is generally accepted that the freehold of the land must be secured prior to consecration. Once this has been achieved and the conveyance of the land executed, a petition is presented to the bishop. This recites the conveyance and requests him to separate the land, or land and buildings, from all profane and common uses and to dedicate the same to God and divine worship. Further it requests that the property be consecrated for the celebration of divine offices or such other ecclesiastical purposes as are desired, according to the doctrine and discipline of the Church of England. It is accepted that the bishop's right to withhold his sanction to the foundation of a church, or to refuse to consecrate a building erected for that purpose, is absolute.[29]

Consecration is effected by the decree of a competent ecclesiastical court. The act or sentence of consecration signed by the bishop setting aside the land or buildings in *sanctos usus* constitutes the legal act of consecration. When the

[26] Interpretation Measure 1925, s.3; Pastoral Measure 1983, s.87(1); *Sedgwick v. Bourne* [1920] 2 K.B. 267 at 275.
[27] *Newsom*, p. 147. It will depend upon the original sentence of consecration. Burial grounds may also be consecrated, even when in the ownership of the civil authorities: *Re Coleford Cemetery* [1984] 1 W.L.R. 1369. Additional ground adjacent to a churchyard may also be consecrated pursuant to the Consecration of Churchyards Act 1867.
[28] *Re Tonbridge School Chapel* [1993] 1 W.L.R. 1138; *Re Tonbridge School Chapel (No. 2)* [1993] Fam. 281.
[29] *Sedgwick v. Bourne* [1920] 2 K.B. 267, D.C. The right to consecrate belongs to the bishop: Canon C18(4).

preliminaries are complete the bishop, with such religious ceremonial as he sees fit, consecrates the land and buildings. He declares by sentence that he separates and sets them apart from all profane and common uses, and dedicates them to the service of God, consecrating them for the use intended. Furthermore he openly and publicly pronounces, decrees and declares them to be so separated, dedicated and consecrated, and states that such separation ought to remain so for ever.

The act of consecrating a church does not necessarily extend to all the ornaments and fittings within it, although generally it does. The petition for consecration presented to the bishop assures him that all things have been rightly done and he is entitled to act upon this assumption. If there are any ornaments which are not in accordance with ordinary usage the act of consecration does not of itself stamp them with the bishop's approval, unless the bishop's attention has been explicitly drawn to them so as to enable him to exercise his discretion, or unless the sentence of consecration expressly refers to them. Accordingly they may be removed by a decree of the consistory court.[30]

Effects of consecration

8.8 The effect of consecration is to set the property apart for all time, to be used solely for sacred purposes. In the case of real property the effects of consecration may only be removed by an Act of Parliament, a Measure or episcopal action pursuant to these. For personal property the position is somewhat different. The moveables or chattels of a church or chapel may be disposed of pursuant to a faculty granted by the consistory court.[31]

Once real property has been legally consecrated it retains its ecclesiastical character whosoever the actual owner or the nature of their tenure. If consecrated as a parish church the foundation of the church will include the cure of souls and all other rights attached to the district assigned to it. Should the building be destroyed in the eyes of the law the church continues to exist and the body corporate which was endowed in respect of it remains in possession of that endowment. It is doubtful that re-consecration is necessary when such a church is rebuilt.[32]

All consecrated property is subject to the jurisdiction of the Ordinary. Most parish churches and their churchyards and consecrated burial grounds are within the jurisdiction of the bishop as Ordinary, but as we saw in Chapter 6 other persons may have Ordinary jurisdiction. The Ordinary's permission is required before any act is undertaken relating to consecrated land or buildings or their contents. Episcopal sanction for such alterations is sought by petitioning the consistory court (where the chancellor is, by delegation, the Ordinary for these purposes) for a faculty. Faculty jurisdiction is considered in Chapter 11.

[30] *Markham v. Shirebrook Overseers* [1906] P. 239.
[31] *Wood v. Headingley-cum-Burley Burial Board* [1892] 1 Q.B. 713 at 725; CCEJM, s.22. For episcopal removal in the case of real property the bishop must be satisfied that it is not held or controlled by an ecclesiastical corporation or the DBF and no purpose would be served by its remaining consecrated. See also *Re St Martin-le-Grand York* [1990] Fam. 63. The removal of the legal effects of consecration in regard to both real property and moveables is considered below.
[32] *Parker v. Leach* (1866) L.R. 1 P.C. 312; *Newsom*, p. 3.

Unconsecrated property subject to the jurisdiction of the Ordinary

Where unconsecrated land forms or is part of the curtilage of a church **8.9** (curtilage being land occupied together with the church and which generally surrounds it)[33] and the church itself is within the jurisdiction of an ecclesiastical court, that court also has jurisdiction over the curtilage.[34] It is therefore the case that unconsecrated churchyards which are commonly found adjacent to churches erected in the nineteenth and twentieth century, are subject to the faculty jurisdiction.[35]

As stated previously dedication, although indicative of pious intent, does not of itself bring about the same legal effects as consecration.[36] Any building dedicated and licensed for public worship prior to March 1, 1993 may, by bishop's order (revocable at any time) be subject, together with its furnishings and contents, to the jurisdiction of the consistory court. Thus for the period specified in the order the position of the building is the same as if it has been consecrated.[37] For a building licensed for public worship after March 1, 1993, the reverse applies. The building and all articles appertaining to it are subject to the jurisdiction of the consistory court just as they would be if the building were consecrated unless removed from the jurisdiction by bishop's order, after consultation with the DAC.[38] Notwithstanding such removal the bishop may still direct that an article must remain within the faculty jurisdiction due to its outstanding architectural, historic, archaeological or monetary value or because it is at special risk of being stolen or damaged.[39] It has been suggested that the consistory court may grant faculties more freely in respect of these buildings, since they are only licensed temporarily for public worship, and are not set aside for all time.[40]

The jurisdiction of the Ordinary over consecrated places of burial extends to all acts necessary in the interests of justice or of the decent and respectful treatment of the dead. Except where a body is removed from one consecrated Church of England burial place to another, and subject to certain statutory exceptions, a body cannot be removed without a licence from the Secretary of State in addition to a faculty.[41] It is an indictable offence to remove a corpse from its place of burial without the requisite authorisation.[42]

---

[33] *Re St John's Church, Bishop Hatfield* [1967] P. 113 at 115. The titles of the land must not conflict.

[34] Faculty Jurisdiction Measure 1964, s.7(1); *Re St John's Church, Bishop Hatfield* (*ante*); *Re St Mary Magdalene, Paddington* [1980] 3 W.L.R. 243.

[35] CCEJM, s.11(3); *Re St George's, Oakdale* [1976] Fam. 210 at 241. See also *Newsom*, pp. 185–7.

[36] *Re Tonbridge School Chapel (no. 2)* (*ante*).

[37] Faculty Jurisdiction Measure 1964, s.6(1); CCEJM, s.11(1), Sched. 7.

[38] CCEJM, s.11(2), (3).

[39] *ibid.*, s.11(4), (5).

[40] *Newsom*, p. 184.

[41] Burial Act 1857, s.25. As to the granting of the faculty, see Chap. 11.

[42] *R. v. Sharpe* (1845) Dec. & Bell C.C. 160 cited *Williams v. Williams* (1882) 20 Ch. D. 659 at 663.

Restrictions on use of consecrated property for secular purposes

8.10   Since consecrated property is set aside for sacred purposes a faculty should not be granted to enable it to be used for secular purposes. It has been held[43] that unless the original purpose of consecration can no longer be carried out, the only secular purpose for which such a faculty may be granted is in order to allow part of a churchyard to be used as a highway or to enable other "rights of user" over the churchyard. However, in practice faculties are granted for limited secular purposes such as the use of a church crypt by a charity, the conversion of an area within the church for lavatories or a kitchen, or the placing of an aerial on a church tower.[44] In respect of churchyards faculties are often granted to allow cranes to oversail when this is necessitated by the need to carry out works on an adjacent site, or for a car park.

In regard to disused burial grounds, the grant of a faculty for the erection of buildings is also subject to section 3 of the Disused Burial Grounds Act 1884.[45] This prohibits all building save that for the purpose of enlarging (which means any such building must be structurally attached to the original) a church, chapel, meeting house or other place of worship. Given modern liturgical practices including family services, many church halls may now be regarded as places ancillary to worship rather than as a general meeting place.[46] The Act applies to all disused burial grounds no longer used for interments, whether partially or wholly closed under provisions of any statute or Order in Council.[47] One area where difficulties may arise in the application of the 1884 Act is over the question of what consitutes a "building" for the purposes of the statute. Even a shed for holding maintenance equipement will probably fall within the term and thus be prohibited.[48] Land may be freed from the restraints of the 1884 Act by a scheme pursuant to section 30 of the Pastoral Measure 1983, which could be made for the express purpose of building such an extension.

Rights in respect of churches, churchyards and moveables

Vesting of the freehold of the church and churchyard

8.11   As we have already seen in Chapter 4, by the fourteenth century the Realm had been divided into parishes and extra-parochial places. Accordingly at that time churches ceased to be founded in the ancient manner, and thus all churches

---

[43] *Re St John's Chelsea* [1962] 1 W.L.R. 706 at 708. See also *Re St Mary the Virgin, Woodkirk* [1969] 1 W.L.R. 1867; *Re St Martin le Grand York* [1990] Fam. 63.

[44] See, *e.g. Re All Saints, Harborough Magna* [1992] 1 W.L.R. 1235 which reviewed many of the relevant considerations. *Newsom* considers the subject in detail at pp. 110–113.

[45] See *Newsom*, pp. 164–166.

[46] *Re St Mary's, Luton* [1967] P. 151; [1968] P. 47 in which the question of the application of the Dissued Burial Ground Act 1884 was considered exhaustively.

[47] Open Spaces Act 1887, s.4.

[48] *Bermondsley B.C. v. Mortimer* [1926] P. 87. There a gardener's shed was permitted because the Open Spaces Act 1906 which also applied to the land legitimised it.

established after this time are described as being modern foundations. The distinction is of some relevance when considering in whom the freehold of a church and its churchyard are vested.

Where the incumbent of an ancient parish is the rector the freehold is generally vested in them,[49] but where there is both a rector and a vicar the better view is that the freehold vests in the rector.[50] In those now rare cases where there is still a lay rector the enjoyment of the property belongs to that rector only to the extent that this can be exercisable by a layman. Thus the incumbent retains possession to the extent necessary for the performance of their sacred duties.[51] By virtue of statutory provisions, where a church or churchyard was consecrated in modern times the freehold vests in the incumbent not the rector.[52]

Although the incumbent is generally spoken of as having the freehold, their rights and equally their liabilities in regard to the property are so severely limited that they cannot be described as the owner of the property in anything other than a strict legal sense. Even then, the incumbent has only a life interest, the fee simple being in abeyance,[53] and the incumbent's title being analogous to that of a tenant for life.[54]

Rights in regard to the church and churchyard

Whosoever the freehold is vested in, it is held for the use of the parishioners for the purposes of attending their church services[55] and for their burial in the churchyard, management on their behalf being vested in the incumbent, church-wardens and PCC.[56] Parishioners are also entitled to a right of way to the church[57] and have a right of access to it for divine service.[58] Although the keys to   **8.12**

[49] *Walter v. Montague and Lamprell* (1836) 1 Curt. 253 at 260.
[50] *ibid.*; *Jones v. Ellis* (1828) 2 Y. & J. 265 at 273; *Greenslade v. Darby* (1868) L.R. 3 Q.B. 431; *Griffin v. Dighton* (1864) 5 B. & S. 93 at 103, Ex. Ch.; *Batten v. Gedye* (1889) 41 Ch. D. 507; but see *Vicar and One Churchwarden of St Botolph without Aldgate v. Parishioners of St Botolph without Aldgate* [1892] P. 161 at 167 where the contrary view is expressed.
[51] *Winstanley v. North Manchester Overseers* [1910] A.C. 7, H.L.
[52] Church Buildings Acts 1818 to 1884, now mainly repealed; Church Building Act 1945, s.13 (repealed); New Parishes Act 1856, s.10 (repealed); New Parishes Measure 1943, s.29(4); Pastoral Measure 1968, s.76(3) (repealed). The incumbent or the PCC may take proceedings to obtain a faculty vesting privately owned parts of a church or building forming part of it in the person or body in whom the church is vested, where the petitioners satisfy the court that there has been no communication with those in whom the private part is vested and no works have been undertaken in respect of that part within seven years by any person or body claiming adverse possession: FJM, s.1.
[53] *Rector and Churchwardens of St Gabriel, Fenchurch Street v. City of London Real Property Co. Ltd* [1896] P. 95 at 101; *Re consecrated land in Camomile Street* [1990] 3 All E.R. 229.
[54] *The Ecclesiastical Commissioners for England & Wales v. Rowe* (1880) 5 App. Cases 736 at 744.
[55] *Griffin v. Dighton* (1864) 5 B. & S. 93; *Winstanley v. North Manchester Overseers* [1910] A.C. 7; See also *Re consecrated land in Camomile Street* [1990] 3 All E.R. 229.
[56] *Fryer v. Johnson* (1755) 2 Wils. 28; PCCPM, s.4(1)(ii)(c).
[57] *St Edmundsbury and Ipswich Diocesan Board of Finance v. Clark (No. 2)* [1973] 1 WLR 1572, affd [1975] 1 W.L.R. 468, C.A. When rectories and vicarages next to churches are sold care should be taken to ensure adequate rights of way are maintained.
[58] *Griffin v. Dighton* (*ante*); *Cole v. Police Constable 443A* [1937] 1 K.B. 316.

the church belong to the incumbent,[59] as we saw in Chapter 4 the churchwardens have a right of access to the church and churchyard in order to carry out their duties.

Likewise the PCC's right of access is limited to that necessary in order to carry out its duties. Should the incumbent improperly refuse access to anyone entitled to it such access will be granted by higher authorities.[60]

Fittings, but not moveables, placed in and devoted to the use of the church of a parish are under the control of the incumbent with regard to their use for divine service.[61] As we saw in Chapter 4 bells may only be rung at the direction of the incumbent.[62]

Notices

8.12A   The incumbent has the right to decide what notices may be exhibited on church notice boards inside and outside the church, save those subject to statutory direction. Section 2 of the Parish Notices Act 1837 requires notices which were previously given out in a church or chapel or at its doors during or after divine service to be displayed before divine service at or near the doors of all the churches or chapels concerned. An incumbent is recommended to provide a board for "public notices" and not to object to the affixing of notices to it by the local authority or other authority.[62a]

Third party rights over churchyard

8.13   The alleged rights of third parties, acquired by prescription, over a churchyard is a difficult area, and one not fully developed by authority. In general such rights are rights of way or lights, and where the question of their existence arises in relation to the grant of a faculty the consistory court has power to determine whether such a right exists.[63] Whether such rights (as opposed to licences of indefinite duration)[64] can arise in relation to consecrated churchyards had not been satisfactorily resolved, and involves questions of the general law of property.

Similar questions arise where a public, as opposed to a private, right of way over a churchyard is said to exist. It is unlikely such right could arise by 20 years of actual user giving rise to a presumption of dedication, since section 31 of the Highways Act 1980 expressly does not apply where no common law right of

---

[59] *Ritchings v. Cordingley* (1868) L.R. 3 A. & E. 113; *Lee v. Matthews* (1830) 3 Hag. Ecc. 169; *Redhead v. Wait* (1862) 6 L.T. 580.

[60] *Starky v. Watlington Sussex (Churchwardens)* (1692) 2 Salk. 547.

[61] *Harrison v. Forbes & Sisson* (1860) (*ante*); *Lee v. Matthews* (*ante*); *Daunt v. Crocker* (1867) L.R. 2 A. & E. 41.

[62] As to the ringing of bells generally see Chap. 9.

[62a] *Legal Opinions*, p. 185. It should be noted that new notice boards in the churchyard and possibly church porch are subject to control by the local planning authority who should be consulted before any new notice board is erected. In particular there are restrictions as to the size of any board and as to illuminated signs.

[63] *Re St Martin le Grand, York* [1990] Fam. 63.

[64] *ibid.*

presumed dedication could be obtained (and none could where, as in consecrated churchyards, the fee simple is in abeyance).[65] Nonetheless to prevent such a presumption arising where the public are permitted to use a footpath running through a churchyard as a matter of grace, the footpath should be closed for one day a year, a notice exhibited in the churchyard, or a plan deposited with the relevant authority after which a statutory declaration must be made every six years that no rights arise.[66]

Where part of a churchyard is given over to an adjacent highway it should be noted that the faculty does not dedicate it as a highway but permits its use as such for an indefinite period.[67]

Moveables or contents of a church

Moveables or the contents of a church fall into two categories, those which are **8.14** used in the performance of the service and rites of the church, which are often referred to as ornaments, and the remainder, referred to as decorations.[68] The moveables, or chattels as they are sometimes called, of a church or chapel of ease belong at law to the churchwardens who hold them, as a quasi-corporation,[69] for the benefit of the parish church and its congregation, not as beneficial owners.[70] However, the care, maintenance and preservation of such chattels is the responsibility of the PCC.[71] Both the churchwardens and the PCC must allow the moveables to be used in connection with divine service under the direction of the incumbent.

The churchwardens are also required to maintain an inventory of all moveables and to hand over to their successors all the goods of the church in their hands together with the inventory which the successors should check.[72] It should be remembered that a faculty is required to authorise the introduction of anything into the church, just as it is also required to authorise the disposal of anything. These are matters considered in more detail in Chapter 11.

Disposal of moveables

The moveables of a parish church may be diposed of by the churchwardens (with **8.15** joint assent). In order to do so they require the consent of the parish, which is signified by a resolution of the PCC and a faculty from the consistory court.[73] The

---

[65] See *Newsom*, p. 157 who recommends the taking of special advice where a right of way across consecrated land is set out in a map kept by a local authority pursuant to the National Parks and Access to the Countryside Act 1949, s.32.

[66] *Legal Opinions*, p. 53.

[67] *Re Bideford Parish Church* [1900] P. 134.

[68] As to which see Chap. 9.

[69] *Blackstone's Commentaries on the Laws of England* (14th ed.). Vol. 1, p. 394; *Jackson v. Adams* (1835) 2 Bing. N.C. 402.

[70] Canon E1 (5); *Jackson v, Adams* (*supra*); *Re St Gregory's Tredington* [1972] Fam. 236 at 240.

[71] PPCPM, s.4(1)(ii)(b).

[72] Canon E1(5).

[73] See Chap. 11 and *Newsom*, pp. 130–134.

circumstances which the court will take into account when considering whether to grant such a faculty are discussed in Chapter 11. The disposal may be by sale, whether or not at full value, bailment (gratuitous or for valuable consideration) or by gift. Once disposed of the contents lose their sacred character, unless for example they are disposed of to another church. It should be remembered that the fixtures and fittings of the church, that is things which are physically attached to it such as the font, and are thus categorised as real property, may not be disposed of in this way but are subject to the same restrictions as consecrated land and buildings.[74]

The churchwardens are not trustees, so if the contents are disposed of improperly they cannot give good title,[75] although in appropriate circumstances a confirmatory faculty may be subsequently obtained.[76] Where contents have been improperly removed the churchwardens are the proper plaintiffs in proceedings to recover them at common law.[77] Arguably the PCC is also a competent plaintiff, and has a statutory duty to sue, joining the churchwardens as defendants, if the churchwardens do not act themselves. If neither act then the archdeacon may be able to apply to the High Court for an order of mandamus, compelling the churchwardens or the PCC to sue.[78] Where the contents are improperly removed other than by theft the right of recovery is lost after the expiry of six years from the date of the disposal.[79]

Pews and pew rents

8.16   As we saw in Chapter 4 seats must be provided in every church for the use of parishioners and others attending divine service. A pew is simply an enclosed seat in a church,[80] and there is no personal property in pews erected for the inhabitants of the parish,[81] nor is there property in, nor right to sell or let, a pew or seat in the body of a parochial church or chapel at common law since these belong to the parishioners at large.[82] However, a right to use a particular pew or seat may have been acquired either by faculty, or, prescription on which a faculty may be presumed,[83] or by a private Act of Parliament by or under the Church Buildings Acts.[84] The right is in the nature of an easement, consisting of the right to occupy during divine service and other religious observances,[85] and carries with

---

[74] Pastoral Measure 1983, s.56(2).
[75] Save possibly in cases of sale in market overt. See *Legal Opinions*, p. 147, and Doe, *The Legal Framework of the Church of England* (1996), p. 427. Churchwardens who improperly dispose of moveables may be liable to a charge of theft under the Theft Act 1968, s.1(1).
[76] *Re St Mary's Barton-Upon-Humber* [1987] Fam. 41.
[77] *Legal Opinions*, pp. 148–149.
[78] *ibid*.
[79] Limitation Act 1980, s.2.
[80] *Brumfit v. Roberts* (1870) L.R. 5 C.P. 224 at 232.
[81] *Hawkins and Coleman v. Comeigne* (1818) 3 Phil. Ecc. R. 11.
[82] *Pettman v. Bridger* (1811) 1 Phil. Ecc. R. 316 at 323; *Brumfit v. Roberts* (*ante*).
[83] If a question as to the existence of such a right arises it must be dealt with by the temporal courts: *Philips v. Halliday* [1891] A.C. 228, H.L.
[84] This a complex area of law as to which see *Halsbury's Laws of England* (4th ed.), Vol. 14, paras 1086 *et seq*.
[85] *Brumfit v. Roberts* (*ante*) applied *Re St Mary's Banbury* [1987] Fam. 136.

it the burden of repairing the pew.[86] The right to use a pew cannot be removed by faculty,[87] which may present difficulties where a scheme for the re-ordering of a church is proposed.

Express power was given by statute to the Ecclesiastical Commissioners (now the Church Commissioners) and various bodies and persons to fix a scale of payment for seats or pews in certain churches or chapels, in order to raise funds for building expenses or maintaining ministrations of the church. Existing rights to recover pew rents in districts and parishes formed under the Church Buildings Acts 1818 to 1884 and the New Parishes Acts 1843 to 1884 remain unaffected by the repeal of the bulk of these Acts, but no provision was made for taking pew rents in the cases of districts and parishes formed under the New Parishes Measure 1943, nor the Pastoral Measures 1968 and 1983. Rents which are still payable are payable in advance[88] and in cases of non-payment the PCC may bring an action for non-payment.[89]

Monuments

Where a person sets up a monument in a church or churchyard it remains their **8.17** property, so that they may sustain an action for trespass against anyone who removes or defaces it.[90] Although it has been suggested that the modern legal position is that the monument passes after that person's death to the persons entitled under their will or intestacy, the better view is the older one, namely that it becomes the property of the heir of the deceased in whose honour it was erected,[91] although the task of identifying such heirs may not be an easy one. The rights of such owners are however limited and controlled by the faculty jurisdiction,[92] as is the introduction of new monuments.

Herbage and grazing rights

The rights to herbage and timber are vested in the incumbent,[93] although as we shall **8.18** see the latter is subject to the rights of the PCC. It would appear that the PCC has no duty or general power to cut grass, but the owner of the churchyard is bound to prevent herbage from being an obstruction to parishioners.[94] Although the church-yard cannot be turned into a field, grazing for sheep, horses or donkeys, for example, may not be inappropriate, and has, on occasion, been recommended.[95]

---

[86] *Crisp v. Martin* (1876) 2 P.D. 15; *Churton v. Frewen* (1866) L.R. 2 Eq. 634.

[87] *Re St Mary's Banbury* (*ante*).

[88] New Parishes Measure 1943, s.32(1)(c).

[89] *ibid.*; PCCPM, s.4(1)(ii)(a).

[90] *Lady De Wyche's Case* (1469) Y.B. 9 Edw. 4, Trin. 8; *Covern v. Pym* (1612) 12 Co. Rep. 105; *Spooner v. Brewster* (1825) 3 Bing. 136.

[91] *Lady De Wyche's Case* (*ante*); *Corven v. Pym* (*ante*); *Re St Andrew's, Thornhaugh* [1976] 1 All E.R. 154. The Faculty Jurisdiction Measure 1964, s.3(4) adopts the older view in its defintion of "owner".

[92] As to which see Chap. 11.

[93] *Cox v. Ricraft* (1757) 2 Lee. 373. Where the freehold is vested in a rector who is not the incumbent it is generally presumed that this forms part of the vicar's endowment: *Greenslade v. Darby* (1868) L.R. 3 Q.B. 421.

[94] *Legal Opinions*, pp. 50–51. *Moore's Introduction to English Canon Law*, p. 88.

[95] *ibid.*

Use of church or chapel for performance or exhibition

8.19 Consecration has the effect of setting aside the property for sacred use for all time. Accordingly there are restrictions on the uses to which it may be put. Canon F16 provides that where any church or chapel is to be used for a play, concert or exhibition of films or pictures, the minister must take care that the words, music and pictures are such as befit the House of God, are consonant with sound doctrine, and make for the edifying of the people. The minister must also obey the general directions of the bishop, refer to him in cases of doubt, and consult the relevant authorities regarding precautions against fire and other dangers. It should be remembered that no premises may be used for the public performance of any play except under a licence,[96] the licensing authority being either the district council or other council as appointed. Copyright considerations should also be borne in mind in regard to such performances and exhibitions.[97]

Duties of care, maintenance and preservation of churches, churchyards, other parochial buildings and moveables

8.20 The Care of Churches and Ecclesiastical Jurisdiction Measure (CCEJM) 1991 which was introduced following the recommendations of the Faculty Jurisdiction Commission[98] had a major impact upon the care and conservation of churches, their contents and churchyards.[99] The Measure is part of an agreement reached between the General Synod and the Department of the Environment in order to ensure the continuation of the ecclesiastical exemption.

Listed buildings and the ecclesiastical exemption

8.21 Certain ecclesiastical buildings which were for the time being used for ecclesiastical purposes were exempted from the planning controls ordinarily applicable to listed buildings.[1] However, there is no exemption for such buildings from general planning controls, and where permission is required this must be obtained from the relevant plannng authority before any works are carried out.

The scope of this ecclesiastical exemption, was subsequently restricted to ecclesiastical buildings subject to the faculty jurisdiction of the Church of England, or to its procedure under the Care of Cathedrals Measures, or to the buildings of other churches which have regimes similar to those of the Church of England,[2] provided that the building's primary use is as a place of worship.[3] The

---

[96] Theatres Act 1968, s.12.

[97] For advice in this regard see *Legal Opinions*, pp. 72–91.

[98] *The Continuing care of Churches and Cathedrals*, the Report of the Faculty Jurisdiction Commission (1994).

[99] The General Synod has published the *Care of Churches and Ecclesiastical Jurisdiction Measure: Code of Practice* (1993) which sets out framework of the legislation and gives advice on its application.

[1] Planning (Listed Buildings and Conservation Areas) Act 1990, s.60.

[2] These being the Church in Wales, the Roman Catholic Church, the Methodist Church, the Baptist Unions of Great Britain and Wales, and the United Reformed Church.

[3] Ecclesiastical Exemption (Listed Buildings and Conservation Areas) Order, S.I. 1994 No. 1771, art. 4.

exemption also applies to associated structures of these buildings, subject to certain qualifications and restrictions, and to additional specified categories. It is also extended to peculiars and other similar Church of England buildings.[4]

The listing of churches is well established. In recent years listing has extended to box tombs and other monuments within the churchyard, but these do not retain the ecclesiastical exemption if they are listed separately.[5]

Duties of churchwardens to inspect and keep records

The churchwardens of every parish are under a duty to record all land (known as a terrier) and all articles (known as an inventory) appertaining to their church. They must also keep, in a log book, a record of all alterations, additions and repairs and other events affecting this property, and of the location of any other documents relating to this which are not kept in the log book itself.[6] In preparing these records the churchwardens must act in consultation with the minister. A copy of the inventory is maintained by a person nominated by the bishop, and that person must be sent copies of the inventory and notified of any alterations to it.[7]

Churchwardens are also under a duty to inspect the fabric and articles of the church at least once a year on behalf of the PCC.[8] They must then produce an annual fabric report on the fabric and articles, including an account of all actions taken or proposed during the previous year for their protection and maintenance and in particular they must report on any recommendations contained in the inspection scheme (see below).[9] They must deliver this report to the PCC at its last meeting prior to the annual parochial church meeting and present it (with such ammendments as the PCC may make) to the annual meeting.[10] The churchwardens must also produce to the PCC the terrier, inventory and log book relating to events occuring in the previous year and all other records which will assist the council in discharging its duties in relation to the facric and articles of the church.[11]

8.22

---

[4] *ibid.*, art. 6. It is doubtful that these buildings will continue to enjoy an exemption if they fail voluntarily to bring themselves within the faculty jurisdiction: see the statement from the Dept of National Heritage, July 1994.

[5] Ecclesiastical Exemption (Listed Buildings and Conservation Areas) Order, S.I. 1994 No. 1771, art. 5. However, the ecclesiastical exemption does still apply to such monuments notwithstanding the fact that they are listed separately if they are subject to the Care of Cathedrals Measures rather than to the faculty jurisdiction: *ibid*. Ancient monuments in churchyards may also be listed pursuant to the Ancient Monuments and Archaeological Areas Act 1979. An ecclesiastical building in use for ecclesiastical purposes cannot be listed under this Act, but all structures in churchyards can be, as can the whole churchyard.

[6] CCEJM, s.4. The form of the terrier, inventory and log-book are to accord with recommendations made by the Council for the Care of Churches, and the Council publishes its own editions of these for use by parishes, entitled *The Church Register* (1995), and *The Church Log Book* (3rd ed., 1996). Canon F13(4).

[7] CCEJM, s.4.

[8] CCEJM, s.5.

[9] In pursuance of the Inspection of Churches Measure 1995, s.1.

[10] CCEJM, s.5.

[11] *ibid.*

Inspection of churches under diocesan scheme[12]

8.23 The CCEJM made considerable amendments to the Inspection of Churches Measure 1955 which had already established a regime for the inspection of churches within each diocese.

Through the DAC all diocesan synods are required to draw up a scheme providing for the inspection of every church within the diocese at least once every five years. The scheme must provide for the establishment of a fund for the cost of such inspections and the appointment of a qualified person to inspect and report on churches within the diocese, generally known as the church architect.[13] The report must be sent to the relevant archdeacon, the PCC, the incumbent of the benefice and the secretary of the DAC. The church architect is under a duty to ensure that a faculty is obtained when required.[14]

Inspection now extends to any moveable article in the church of outstanding architectural, artistic, historical, archaeological or significant monetary value, or at special risk of being stolen or damaged, and to any ruin in the churchyard which possesses one of these five qualities, and any tree in the churchyard in respect of which a tree preservation order is for the time being in force.[15]

Survey by archdeacon

8.24 At their annual visitation every archdeacon is under a duty to survey, either in person or by deputy, the churches, chancels and churchyards within their jurisdiction, and to give directions for the amendment of all defects in their walls, fabric, ornaments and furniture.[16] If these directions are not obeyed the archdeacon should apply for a faculty to do the work themselves. The archdeacon also has powers, if an inspection has not been carried out under the diocesan scheme for over five years, or if they are not satisfied with such an inspection, to arrange an inspection or further inspection with the consent of the bishop.[17]

Duties of PCC[18]

8.25 The PCC is under a duty to ensure that churches and chapels in the parish are decently kept and well and sufficiently repaired and that all things in them are maintained in an orderly and decent fashion. Furthermore they must ensure that

---

[12] See also The Council for the Care of Churches, *A Guide to Church Inspection and Repair* (2nd ed., 1995).

[13] Inspection of Churches Measure 1955, s.1(1).

[14] *Re St Thomas a Becket, Framfield* [1989] 1 W.L.R. 689 at 693.

[15] Inspection of Churches Measure 1955, s.1A.

[16] Canon C22(5).

[17] Inspection of Churches Measure 1955, s.2.

[18] The Council for the Care of Churches publishes a number of helpful books on particular aspects of church repair, maintenance and conservation including glass, bells, flooring, redecorating, heating, lighting, wiring and sound amplification. It also publishes a general guide entitled, *How to Look After your Church*.

the churchyards are duly fenced and kept in an orderly and decent manner.[19] The duty extends to the appertenant of the church and churchyard including rights of way,[20] and the PCC may sue for protection of the churchyard and these rights.[21]

Extent of liability of PCC to repair

Although the PCC is generally liable for the costs of repairs, exceptions may arise **8.26** in the case of repairs to the chancel or to a private aisle. However, it has to be said that generally the existence of such exceptions are now more a matter of historical interest than a practical issue.

Under canon law the rector of a parish was responsible for the repair of the whole church, but in England the liability was divided by common custom, with the parishioners responsible for repairs to the body of the church and the rector (whether spiritual or lay) for repairs to the chancel.[22] Although in certain parishes the rector's liability to repair remains, this situation is now something of a rarity and in general such responsibilities have been abolished or limited by statute.[23] In the rare cases where the liability of a rector to repair a chancel does remain it is enforceable in the county court.[24]

Occasionally the chancel of a parish church is also a chapel coeval with the church, that is it was built contemporaneously with the church, but was held and used exclusively as part of an estate. In such a case the person entitled to its use is also the person liable for its repair.[25] The same is also true of a private aisle built within a church,[26] although once again few such aisles remain private.

One further historical exception to the PCC's obligation arises in the case of certain parishes of ancient foundation, where by immemorial usage the incumbent or owner of a particular piece of land was bound to maintain the churchyard and its fences. Such duties were once held to be enforceable,[27] and if the tradition has carried on unabated may still be enforceable today.

However, in general the obligation to maintain and repair the church fell upon the churchwardens, and as we saw in Chapter 4, has now been transferred to the PCC. The voluntary church rate[28] which it may levy for any purpose connected

---

[19] PCCPM, s.4(1)(ii)(c); Canons F13(1), (2), F14.
[20] *St Edmundsbury and Ipswich Diocesan Board of Finance v. Clark (no. 2)* [1973] 1 W.L.R. 1572; affd [1975] 1 W.L.R. 468 C.A.
[21] *ibid.*, PCCPM, s.4(1)(ii)(c).
[22] *Pense v. Prouse* (1695) 1 Raym. 59; *Representative Body of the Church in Wales v. Tithe Redemption Commission* [1944] A.C. 228, H.L.
[23] Most incumbent rectors were freed of all liabilities and others could transfer the responsibility by payment of a capital sum to the DBF: Ecclesiastical Dilapidations Measure 1923, s.52; Ecclesiastical Dilapidations (Amendment) Measure 1929, s.18; Repair of Benefice Buildings Measure 1972, s.29. Save for certain exempted cases, with the extinguishment of tithe rentcharges created in 1836 (a common form of rectorial property in the nineteenth century) the owner of such a rentcharge ceased to be liable for the repair of the chancel: Tithe Act 1936, s.31. See also *Legal Opimons*, p. 39.
[24] Chancel Repairs Act 1932, ss.2, 3.
[25] *Churton v. Frewen* (1866) L.R. 2 Eq. 634.
[26] *Williams v. Bond* (1690) 2 Vent. 238.
[27] *Claydon v. Churchwardens of Dunscombe* (1638) 2 Roll. Abr. 287; *R. v. Reynell* (1805) 6 East 315.
[28] See Chap. 4.

with the affairs of the church may be used for repairs. Although the obligations of the churchwardens, now devolved upon the PCC, were previously enforceable in law, the abolition of the compulsory church rate[29] has meant that the PCC's liability for repairs now extends no further than the funds which it has in its hands.[30]

Maintenance of the churchyard[31]

8.27   As we have seen the PCC has a responsibility to ensure that the churchyard is fenced[32] and kept in an orderly and decent manner. What constitutes an adequately managed churchyard depends to a degree upon the prevailing local circumstances. What might be appropriate to a rural parish churchyard might well not be in the case in an urban environment.[32a]

The powers, duties and liabilities of the PCC in respect of the care and maintenance of churchyards extends to the trees within it (and to those which it is proposed to plant),[33] which also fall under the jurisdiction of the consistory court.[34] The chancellor of a diocese must, after consultation with the DAC, give written guidance to all PCCs in the diocese regarding the felling, lopping and topping of trees in churchyards.[35] The net proceeds from the sale of timber from such trees must be paid to the PCC and applied to the maintenance of the fabric of any church maintainable by that council.[36]

In general the planting of a new tree is not a *de minimis* matter and does therefore requires a faculty.[37] PCCs should have particular regard to trees protected by preservation orders.[38] In the case of churchyards which are situated within conservation areas they should also bear in mind that such trees are subject to statutory protection, and that acts in relation to such trees generally require prior notice to the local planning authority, as well as being within the chancellor's guidelines or require to be authorised by faculty.

The freeholder may maintain any action for trespass in the case of an unauthorised interference with the churchyard.[39] Where the freehold is vested in

---

[29] See Chap. 4.

[30] *Veley v. Pertwee* (1870) L.R. 5 Q.B. 573.

[31] Practical guidance is to be found on how to discharge the responsibility for maintenance of the churchyard in Burnham and Stapleton, *The Churchyards Handbook* (3rd ed., 1988) and The Council for the Care of Churches, *Wildlife in Church and Churchyard* (1995).

[32] Previously "sufficiently" or "properly" have been used, suggesting it is a question of degree according to local circumstances: *Legal Opinions*, p. 52.

[32a] A churchyard or part of it could be notified by the Nature Conservancy Council as a site of special scientific interest because of its flora or fauna or geological or physiological features: Wildlife and Countryside Act 1981, s.28. In such cases the agreement of the Nature Conservancy Council is required before an operation is carried out which the Council has warned could cause danger to the site.

[33] CCEJM, s.6.

[34] *ibid.*, s.11(1)

[35] CCEJM, s.6.

[36] *ibid.*

[37] *Newsom*, p. 181.

[38] Under Part VIII of the Town and Country Planning Act 1990.

[39] *Jones v. Ellis* (1828) 2 Y. & J. 265 at 274; *Walter v. Montague and Lamprell* (1836) 1 Curt. 253 at 260.

the incumbent, or falls into abeyance during a vacancy in the benefice,[40] the PCC may take proceedings to protect the church and churchyard.[41] Unauthorised interference with the churchyard, whether by the rector, incumbent or anyone else, is an offence against ecclesiastical law.[42] However, a civil court will grant an injunction to restrain interference on the application of the PCC.[43] Erection of a monument without permission constitutes a trespass[44] as does any work undertaken without a faculty.

Closed churchyards

Generally a churchyard is "closed" if it has been closed for burials by an Order in   **8.28** Council under the Burial Acts. Thus a churchyard where burials have merely ceased to take place, or one where further burials are prohibited by local Act of Parliament, is not for these purposes considered to be closed. Most Orders for the discontinuance of burials originate from the nineteenth century and were enacted for reasons of public health. Today public health considerations are in practice the sole ground under which ministers will make representations to Her Majesty in Council, and such an Order is not made for the purpose of relieving the ecclesiastical authorities of the burden of maintenance.

The procedure for transferring responsibility for closed churchyards to local authorities has now been simplified.[45] The functions and liabilities of the PCC in regard to maintenance and repair are transferred to the local authority, but the churchyard itself is not transferred and all other rights and powers remain unaffected including the subjection of the land to the faculty jurisdiction.[46] In particular a churchyard can only become an open space under the Open Spaces Act 1906 if agreement is forthcoming from the incumbent and PCC, as well as from the local authority, and even then it remains consecrated ground.[47]

It should be noted that the local authority's responsibility to keep the churchyard in decent order can be no greater than the PCCs. If they are dissatisfied with the standard of care being exercised, the incumbent and PCC can apply to the High Court for judicial review if they consider the local authority is failing in that duty.[48]

---

[40] *Re St Paul's Covent Garden* [1974] Fam. 1.
[41] *ibid*.; *St Edmundsbury and Ipswich Diocesan Board of Finance v. Clark (No. 2)* [1973] 1 W.L.R. 1572; affd [1975] 1 W.L.R. 468, C.A.
[42] *Bennett v. Bonaker* (1830) 3 Hag. Ecc. 17; *Burgoyne v. Free* (1829) 2 Hag. Ecc. 456; *Walter v. Montague & Lamprell* (1836) 1 Curt. 253; *Marriott v. Tarpley* (1838) 9 Sim. 279.
[43] *Marriott v. Tarpley (ante)* at 288; *Batten v. Gedye* (1889) 41 Ch. D. 507. But not to a parishioner: *ibid*.
[44] *Beckwith v. Harding* (1818) 1 Bl. & Ald. 508; *Re Woldingham Churchyard* [1957] 1 W.L.R. 811.
[45] Local Government Act 1972, s.215(2), (3); Burial Act 1855, s.18 (repealed except in its application to the City of London).
[46] See *Newsom*, pp. 163–164.
[47] Open Spaces Act 1906, ss.1, 6, 9, 10, 11.
[48] *Legal Opinions*, p. 68.

Insurance

8.29   The PCC is under a duty to insure the fabric of the church together with the goods and ornaments thereof.[49] This duty extends to the insurance of all other buildings and land of the parish, other than glebe property, all of which should be insured against all usual risks, including third party liability.[50] The PCC is not obliged to pay insurance premiums out of its members' own pockets, and accordingly when obtaining cover it must have regard to the income available taking account of other proper claims upon it. A further claim on its finances is the insurance of parish property which is vested in the DBF, since the PCC must also keep it indemnified in respect of premiums and the costs of insuring that property.[51]

Insurance against third party or public liability should be given priority by the PCC, although there is currently no obligation to take out such insurance. The civil law imposes an absolute liability for accidents or injuries caused to members of the public under the Occupiers Liability Act 1957, and for these purposes the occupier of the church and churchyard (unless closed) will include the incumbent and PCC, and in the case of monuments the owner. The duty extends to all those lawfully on the property but probably not to trespassers, the occupier being obliged to ensure that the property is reasonably safe for the purposes for which those persons on the property are present.[52]

If the PCC should employ a person or persons, and virtually every council does, the Employers' Liability (Compulsory Insurance) Act 1969 imposes an obligation to insure against its liability for injury or illness to its employees arising in the course of, or as a result of, their employment.

Since in the case of church property it is not always easy to state with confidence the identity of the owner, occupier or employer, the Legal Advisory Board recommends that the whole of the "church interest" should be covered. Thus the interests of bishop, incumbent, priest-in-charge, PCC and church-wardens are all adequately protected.[53]

Exemption from council tax

8.30   Places of public religious worship which are certified as such, whether or not they belong to the Church of England, as well as places used in connection with a place of worship, such as a church hall, are exempt from council tax. So too are any properties occupied (for carrying out administrative or other activities including use for office purposes) by an organisation responsible for the conduct of religious worship in a place of public worship.[54] Accordingly much parish property will be exempt.

---

[49] PCCPM, s.4(1)(ii)(b).
[50] *Legal Opinions* pp. 151–155, which also sets out further details and gives advice in regard to obtaining such insurance. Many dioceses operate a group scheme organised by the DBF.
[51] PCCPM. s.6(4).
[52] See n. 50 *ante*.
[53] See n. 50 *ante*.
[54] Local Government Finance Act 1992, s.117(1); Local Government Finance Act 1988, s.51, Sched. 5, para. 11.

Register books and other records[55]

Register books and other records are an important part of the property of the **8.31**
Church of England, and are governed by the Parochial Registers and Records
Measure 1978.[56] Although the Measure is primarily concerned with register
books, the term records extends to include a range of other material,[57] such as
grants of faculties and archdeacon's certificates, plans, specifications, terriers,
inventories, logbooks, reports by the churchwardens, the quennial survey reports
and any other material relating to the fabric of the church, and any title deeds to
property. Minutes and accounts relating to the PCC, minutes of the annual
parochial meeting, and material relating to the churchwardens should also be
included, as should Pastoral Orders and Schemes and Orders in Council. Trust
deeds where the trustees act in an official ecclesiastical capacity as well as
documents relating to charities and most correspondence should also be preserved. Finally consideration should be given to the inclusion of photographs,
maps, drawings and files of parish magazines.

A register book of public and private baptisms is to be provided for every
parish (or each parish church where there is more than one) and a register book
of burials (which includes the deposit of cremated remains[58]) for every parish
which has a burial ground in use (or for each ground if there is more than one).[59]
These books (which must be of durable material and have the headings for each
column of information required printed upon each page and each place of entry
numbered consecutively) must be provided by and are deemed to belong to the
PCC of the parish.

Register books for both the banns of marriage and marriage are supplied by
the Register General to the incumbent or priest-in-charge of every church or
chapel where marriages may be solemnised according to the rites of the Church
of England.[60] Ownership of these registers and registers of confirmation and
services vest in the incumbent.[61] In all cases there are detailed provisions as to
the entries which must be made in the registers. These are considered in
connection with the relevant sacrament or service in Chapter 10.

Custody of all the register books, including those of baptism and burial, is in
the hands of the incumbent, or where the bishop has appointed a priest-in-charge
during a period of suspension under the Pastoral Measure 1983, that priest, or
during a vacancy in the benefice, the churchwardens.[62] Whosoever has custody of
the registers is responsible for their safe-keeping, care and preservation.[63]
Schedule 2 to the 1978 Measure sets out the conditions under which they must be

---

[55] See also *A Guide to the Parochial Registers and Records Measure 1978* (2nd ed., 1992).
[56] As amended by the Church of England (Miscellaneous Provisions) Measure 1992. See
also Canons F11, 12.
[57] Parochial Registers and Records Measure 1978, s.25.
[58] *ibid.*
[59] *ibid.*, s.1. The main provisions regarding registers, but not inspections or deposits in the
records office, are applied, with necessary modifications, to cathedrals, collegiate
churches and to any other church or chapel which does not belong to a parish: *ibid.*, s.5.
[60] Marriage Act 1949, ss.7, 54.
[61] Parochial Registers and Records Measure 1978, s.1.
[62] *ibid.*, s.6.
[63] *ibid.*, s.11.

kept. These include specifications for locked steel cabinets or fire-proofed muminents rooms, and provisions as to checks on temperature and humidity and the keeping of records of checks carried out at least weekly of thermometer and hygrometer readings. In addition the bishop may issue directions with respect to safe-keeping, care and preservation, the costs of complying with these directions and with the terms of Schedule 2 being the responsibility of the PCC.[64]

8.32   In each diocese there is a diocesan record office into which most non-current records whose contents are over a hundred years old must be deposited. In addition other records, other than current registers, may also be deposited in this office if it is deemed appropriate or required.[65] In all cases where records are deposited and custody, but not ownership, passes to the Chief Officer of the diocesan record office.[66]

The archdeacon must arrange for periodic inspections of all registers and records, such inspection to be carried out by a person appointed after consultation with the Chief Officer of the diocesan record office.[67] Inspections take place within five years of the preceding inspection, and must include the making of a full list of current and completed registers together with a list describing all records of whatever date. A certificate of the continuing accuracy of any previous lists (apart from specified amendments) will also be made. A report on these lists and the certificate is then made to the archdeacon who is also sent a copy of the new certificate as are the incumbent or priest-in-charge and PCC.

Where the standard of care for records has not been satisfactorily complied with, episcopal directions ignored, or mandatory deposits in the record office have not taken place, the bishop must inform the custodians and the PCC of the facts and give them the opportunity to make written representations within a period of not less than 28 days. If after duly considering the representations the bishop is of the opinion that the matter is in need of urgent action he may order the records to be placed in the diocesan record office: otherwise he makes an order for compliance.[68] Ultimately the bishop has the power to resort to the county court as a final means for the enforcement of such an order, the statute providing a somewhat unusual means of enforcing his visiatorial authority through the temporal courts.

Provision is made for searches of the register books of baptism and burials upon payment of a fee.[69] A custodian must permit such searches (which may be of photographic copies instead of the originals), although these should be by appointment and at reasonable times. Due to security considerations and in order to prevent damage occuring the person searching should be supervised and

[64] *ibid*.
[65] *ibid*., ss.7, 10, 11. Provision also exists for the closure of old registers: *ibid*., s.9A. The diocesan records office may also act as a repository for manorial and tithe records.
[66] *ibid*., s.13. This includes temporary deposits for the purposes of exhibitions: *ibid*., s.16.
[67] *ibid*., s.9. Provision is also made for the inspection of ecclesiastical libraries: Parochial Libraries Act 1708.
[68] Parochial Registers and Records Measure 1978, s.12.
[69] *ibid*., s.20. Searches may also be made of the register books of marriages where the entry was made prior to July 1, 1937: Marriage Act 1949, s.63. For fees see the Registration of Births, Deaths and Marriages (Fees Order, S.I. 1994 No. 3257). The Parochial Register and Records Measure 1978, s.20 is applicable with any necessary modifications to cathedrals, collegiate churches and to any other church or chapel which does not belong to a parish.

where copying is likely to be extensive temporary deposit at the diocesan record office should be considered.

Property of the benefice

Glebe land

The term "manse" was previously applied to the total property of a benefice, **8.33** which comprised the parsonage house, glebe land and buildings. Glebe land encompasses all the land and buildings of the benefice except the parsonage house (unless the original parsonage house has been split so that part of it forms the current parsonage and part is now glebe). Glebe land and buildings are now vested, under the Endowments and Glebe Measure 1976, in the DBF, to be held, managed and dealt with by that board for the benefit of the diocesan stipends fund.[70] Providing it has the consent of the Church Commissioners the DBF also has the power to acquire land or approriate land vested in it for glebe,[71] and other parsonage land which is no longer required may be transferred to the DBF and held as glebe land.[72]

The DBF has various powers in relation to glebe land, which tends in the main to be agricultural or residential property. In particular it may permit clergy or a lay worker to reside in a dwelling house situated on glebe land without payment of rent.[73] It may sell, exchange, lease, mortgage or otherwise deal with any diocesan glebe land on terms authorised by the Church Commissioners.[74] The proceeds of such disposal and any capital moneys arising must be paid to the Commissioners and allocated to the diocesan stipends fund, whilst rents and other periodic payments in the nature of income must be paid to the Commissioners and be allocated to the income account of the stipends fund.[75] The DBF must keep diocesan glebe land income and minerals accounts, and keep the Commissioners informed of matters affecting diocesan glebe land.[76]

Parsonage houses[77]

The parsonage house, which is the official residence of the incumbent, is vested **8.34** in the incumbent.[78] They have powers (exercisable by the diocesan bishop during a vacancy), subject to the consent of the Church Commissioners (who have

---

[70] Endowments and Glebe Measure 1976, ss.15, 19.
[71] *ibid.*, s.18.
[72] *ibid.*, s.32.
[73] *ibid.*, s.24.
[74] *ibid.*, s.20. Where the authorisation of the Commissioners is sought, before making an application the DBF must notify the incumbent, priest-in-charge or churchwardens, and, in certain circumstances, the bishop, all of whom may make representations, which must be considered by the Commissioners before giving their approval, which may be subject to conditions: *ibid.*
[75] *ibid.*, s.25.
[76] *ibid.*, ss.26, 27.
[77] In addition to those provisions described below the Parsonages Measure 1938 contains various powers in relation to the division or improvement of the parsonage during a vacancy in the benefice. It should also be noted that the incumbent has limited powers to lease parsonage property, but the lease must contain a clause to the effect that it will

power to lend money for this purpose), the diocean parsonage board and the bishop, to purchase or erect a house as a parsonage where this is desirable, whether or not the original parsonage has been disposed of.[79] Similarly where the house is inconvenient, too large or for other good reason found to be unsuitable the parsonage may be sold or disposed of subject to the same consents.[80] The patron of the benefice and the PCC have the right to object (but not veto) the proposed action, and any representation they make must be considered by the Church Commissioners.[81] Any moneys received from a sale or exchange of the parsonage must be paid over to the Church Commissioners. They may, at their discretion, apply these to the costs of disposal and associated costs, or for the provision of a new parsonage; otherwise these are held for the benefit of the benefice.[82]

Diocesan parsonages board

8.35 The Repair of Benefice Buildings Measure 1972 requires the diocesan synod either to provide by scheme for the appointment of a diocesan parsonages board or to designate the DBF as the parsonages board.[83] Provision is also made for the appointment of diocesan surveyors, their terms of service and remuneration.

Where a parsonages board is appointed all archdeacons of the diocese are *ex officio* members. At least one-third of the board must be clergy elected by clergy of the diocese, and at least one-third of the board must be laity. The board, which is a body corporate, has the power to enter contracts, hold property, borrow money and execute works, together with such ancillary powers as are provided for in the diocesan scheme. It must present an annual report and accounts to the diocesan synod and the Church Commissioners and comply with any directions given by a resolution of the synod.[84]

Where the DBF is designated as the parsonages board the diocesan scheme must provide for the delegation of its functions to a committee or committees, which may include persons other than members of the DBF and must include adequate representation of clergy and laity.

The board manages a parsonage fund out of which it must defray all its expenditure.[85] The diocesan synod must provide for the submission to it of an estimate of the board's annual expenditure, and may provide by a scheme for the payment of annual contributions by PCC's, or of direct payments by PCCs in respect of repairs to the parsonage house of their own parish,[86] although in some dioceses this contribution is simply included in the parish "quota" (see below).

be avoided if the bishop requires the incumbent to reside in the property: Pluralities Act 1838, s.59. However, generally parsonage property which is not required is transferred to the DBF (see above).

[78] Parsonages Measure 1938, s.9.

[79] *ibid.*, s.2.

[80] *ibid.*, s.2.

[81] *ibid.*, s.3.

[82] *ibid.*, ss.1(5), 5.

[83] Repair of Benefice Buildings Measure 1972, s.1.

[84] *ibid.*

[85] *ibid.*, s.17. Other than that which is defrayed from specific trusts or by direct payments of PCCs.

[86] *ibid.*, s.19.

Repair and maintenance of parsonage houses

The 1972 Measure provides for the maintenance and repair of parsonage **8.36** houses[87] and other buildings belonging to the benefice. The parsonages board must carry out inspections at intervals of not more than five years (and may do so at any time) and the surveyor must on inspecting make a report to the board.[88] The report must specify what repairs are required and the estimated cost for undertaking such repairs, and must indicate whether the works were necessitated by damage caused or aggravated by a deliberate act of, or default by, the present or previous incumbents. In addition it must state whether it would be expedient to undertake improvements to the parsonage, or if necessary to replace it, whether outbuildings appear superfluous and if so state the cost of their demolition, examine the state of the interior decoration, fixtures and fittings of any building, and finally advise on the amount of insurance cover and any special risks which must be insured against.[89] In respect to the need to undertake repairs regard should be had to the building's age, character and prospective life and in the case of a listed building, its special architectural or historic interest must also be noted.[90]

Rights and duties of the incumbent

The incumbent has a duty to take proper care of the parsonage house and must **8.37** notify the board of any repairs which appear to the incumbent to be necessary.[91] They may not make any alterations or additions to the parsonage house or other benefice buildings without consulting the registered patron and without obtaining the consent of the board.[92] A copy of any report made by the parsonages board must be sent to the incumbent together with a notice stating their right to make representations and the date by which these must be made. The board must consider any representations made and give the incumbent an opportunity if they desire to meet them or a committee or representative of the board.[93]

In any case where the report specifies repairs are necessary through damage by, or default of, an incumbent the board may, on completion of the repairs, require the incumbent to pay the whole or part of the cost attributable to that act or default.[94] They may also take proceedings for non-compliance, provided that, in any such proceedings, it shall be open to the defendant to show that the cost is

---

[87] The Repair of Benefices Buildings Measure 1972 applies to a team vicar's house as it applies to a parsonage house (Endowments and Glebe Measure 1976, Sched. 5), which are generally vested in the DBF.

[88] Repair of Benefices Buildings Measure 1972, ss.3, 4, 8.

[89] *ibid.*

[90] *ibid.*, s.2.

[91] *ibid.*, s.13.

[92] *ibid.*, s.21.

[93] *ibid.*, s.4. Where the report refers to repairs arising out of damage by or the default of a previous incumbent they or their personal representatives must also be sent a copy of the report and given like opportunity to make representations, since like provisions as to their liability apply as to current incumbents: *ibid.*, s.13.

[94] Repair of Benefices Buildings Measure 1972, s.13.

not attributable to such act or default or that the amount sought exceeds the cost so attributable.

The board must, after considering any representations made by the incumbent, confirm the surveyor's report with or without variation.[95] It must also, within 12 months of confirming the report commence all repairs to the parsonage house stated to be immediately necessary and execute all others in the time recommended or within the time it considers expedient.[96] Repairs not specified in a report cannot be carried out without the incumbent's consent.[97]

Where it appears to the board and the bishop that a parsonage house or part thereof should be sold, exchanged or demolished the board may decide not to execute any repairs and notify the incumbent of this within six months of the report being confirmed, giving them an opportunity to make representations and notifying them of their right of appeal against the decision to the Church Commissioners.[98]

Payment of outgoings of parsonage house

8.38 The parsonages board may make good to the incumbent or defray general, water or drainage rates and maintenance charges in respect of private roads, party walls or other things maintainable in common.[99] It may also defray the costs of repairs to any residence of the incumbent other than a parsonage house, or to a parsonage house held on lease where the incumbent is liable for repairs.[1] The parsonages board insures the parsonage house,[2] but this cover is unlikely to extend to the incumbent's contents. The incumbent should enquire whether or not this cover extends to them as occupier in respect of third party liability.

Other buildings

8.39 The diocesan scheme may also regulate the carrying out of repairs to benefice buildings, and may authorise the parsonages board to inspect and make reports in respect of residences other than parsonage houses used by clergy and lay workers, and to execute repairs and any other works to these.[3] By express agreement of persons having management and control of such buildings the powers of the parsonage board may also extend to any building held for charitable purposes connected with the Church of England.[4]

Trust property

8.40 As we have already seen much Church property is held on trust by representative owners. Trust schemes, and in particular charitable trusts, are an important

[95] *ibid.*, s.19.
[96] *ibid.*, s.5.
[97] *ibid.*, s.8.
[98] Repair of Benefices Buildings Measure 1972, s.5.
[99] *ibid.*, s.16. It may also, with the incumbent's consent, carry out interior decorations: *ibid.*, s.15. The practice in relation to this varies between dioceses.
[1] *ibid.*
[2] *ibid.*, s.12.
[3] *ibid.*, s.10. As to the housing of unbeneficed clergy see Faull and Rees, "The Church and Housing" (1994) 3 Ecc. L.J. 313.
[4] *ibid.*, s.15.

source of the Church's wealth and these are governed primarily by temporal rather than ecclesiastical law. In particular the law relating to charities, and the question as to what constitutes a valid religious or ecclesiastical trust, is determined by secular law. Although a detailed examination of this area is beyond the scope of a work such as this some general principles may be briefly stated.[5]

Trusts for the advancement of religion and ecclesiastical charities

The purpose to which the trust property is to be put will determine its status. A **8.41** gift will be accepted as charitable if it is for the "advancement of religion" and there is an element of public benefit.[6] As we saw at the beginning of this chapter an ecclesiastical charity is not restricted to purposes connected with the Church of England, indeed gifts for the advancement of religion need not be confined to gifts for the advancement of the Christian faith. The scope of what may constitute an ecclesiastical charity is broad. It includes an endowment held for any lawful spiritual purpose, or for the benefit of any spiritual person or office, the use of a building by any church or denomination whether for worship or otherwise, and funds held for the maintenance of property or for the support or benefit of any of the members of the church or denomination.[7] Public benefit is a question of fact not opinion.[8] It does not mean that any member of the public must be able to benefit from the trust, but that the beneficiaries must include a sufficiently wide group so that the trust cannot be said to be for private purposes.

A trust for the purposes of the Church of England is charitable (it is for precisely these purposes that the Church Commissioners, who have charitable status were founded),[9] and so are gifts to the Church of England. Gifts for particular purposes, such as to a parish church or for the maintenance of its churchyard are all charitable, but care must be taken in framing the terms of the gift or bequest. A gift for the "work of the parish" is not accepted as being for the advancement of religion, and is therefore not charitable.[10] Certain gifts to further religious education or the relief of poverty amongst clergy if not accepted as being for the advancement of religion (and many such endowments are), may nonetheless be charitable since gifts for the relief of poverty and for the purpose of education are also accepted as charitable. Where the gift is expressly stated to be for the benefit of the holder of a specific office it must be clearly stated that it is to be held by that person and their successors as trustees and is not a gift to that individual.[11] Thus gifts to the "incumbent for the time being", "the churchwardens and their successors", or a bishop "for such purposes as he sees fit" are charitable.

[5] See further Martin, *Hanbury and Martin's Modern Equity* (14th ed. 1993); Picarda, *The Law and Practice Relating to Charities* (1995).
[6] *Commissioners of Income Tax v. Pemsel* [1891] A.C. 531.
[7] Local Government Act 1948, s.75(2); Charities Act 1993, s.96.
[8] *Gilmour v. Coates* [1949] A.C. 426.
[9] However, the provisions of the Charities Act 1993 do no apply to any charity of the Church of England administered by the Church Commissioners or any institution administered by them: *ibid.,* Sched. 2.
[10] *Re Stratton, Knapman v. Att.-Gen.* [1931] 1 Ch. 197.
[11] See, *e.g. Re Flinn, Public Trustee v. Flinn* [1948] Ch. 241.

The primary administrative function of a trustee is to give effect to the terms of the settlement as set out in the trust deed. Provided these terms are not contrary to the law, a trustee must despatch their duties to the trust in an honest and efficient manner as required under secular law. In addition the Charity Commission exercise a supervisory function with regard to charitable trusts.[12] For a person to seek to enforce the terms of a trust they must have *locus standi* as a beneficiary of that trust. Failure to fulfil the duties of a trustee will result in a breach of trust and can lead to various sanctions under the civil law.[13]

In cases where the original purpose of the trust can no longer be carried out an application may be made to the Charity Commissioners or the High Court for a *cy pres* scheme (provided it can be established that the settler has a paramount charitable intent) with the intention of substituting a new purpose, as close to the original as is possible, for the trust to fulfil. In cases where a pastoral scheme alters the area of a parish or unites it with another, any charitable trust to benefit the original parish is to be applied to the new parish.[14] Similar provisions exist if the purposes of a trust relates to a specified church which ceases to be used for divine worship, the trust being then applied to the parish church of the parish in which that church was situated.

Parochial trust property

8.42 Provisions exist, under the Incumbents and Churchwardens (Trust) Measure 1964, for the vesting of real and personal property held on permanent trusts established for ecclesiastical purposes of the Church of England, in the DBF. The DBF acts as "custodian" trustee with a representative from the parish (generally the incumbent, a member of the PCC or a churchwarden) acting as "managing" trustee.[15] The managing trustee cannot sell, lease, exchange, charge or take any legal proceedings in respect of the trust property without the consent of the DBF and any other consents required as a matter of law.[16] The 1964 Measure also prohibits incumbents and churchwardens acquiring interests in property to which the provisions would apply without the DBF's consent, with the exception of personal property acquired by gift or under will.[17]

Although the PCC has a general power to acquire property for any ecclesiastical purpose affecting the parish, it cannot acquire any interest in land (other than a short lease) or in any personal property held on permanent trusts, without the consent of the DBF in whom the property will vest as custodian trustee.[18] Church halls, housing for assistant curates, lay ministers, vergers and others, as well as unofficial "parsonage" houses are generally held on such trusts. Where property

---

[12] *ibid.*

[13] Charities Act 1993, s.75.

[14] Pastoral Measure 1983, Sched. 3, para. 11.

[15] Incumbents and Churchwardens (Trust) Measure 1964, s.2.

[16] *ibid.*, s.5. However, with regard to the investment of funds where the DBF is the custodian trustee the Public Trustee Act 1906 applies with the consequence that the DBF must concur with the managing trustees' choice of investment unless this would involve a breach of trust.

[17] Incumbents and Churchwardens (Trust) Measure 1964, s.4.

[18] PCCPM, ss.5, 6.

of any nature vests in the DBF as a result of these provisions, the managing trustee must idemnify the custodian trustee against all liabilities in respect of the property, including all rates, taxes, insurance premiums and outgoings whatsoever and costs incurred in respect of these matters.[19]

Church sharing agreements[20]

The Sharing of Church Buildings Act 1969[21] sets out the framework for the **8.43** sharing of buildings between the Church of England and a number of other churches.[22] The legislation was designed to facilitate two main aims. First the fostering of ecumenical relations and secondly to derive economical benefits from the sharing of financial responsibilities.

The 1969 Act applies to church buildings used, or proposed to be used, as a place of worship, church hall or centre, youth club, or hostel or residence for ordained ministers or lay workers,[23] but cathedral churches and peculiars of the Church of England and any other building of that Church which is situated in an extra-diocesan or extra-parochial place are excluded.[24] Any two or more churches to which the Act applies may make agreements for the sharing of such buildings and for the carrying into effect of such agreements. The agreement may apply to a single building or to two or more such buildings in the same locality, locality not being a term defined.[25] It is expressly stated that nothing in the Act is designed to affect the practice of lending out church buildings temporarily or for a particular occasion to other religious bodies.[26]

Generally the parties to a sharing agreement may provide that the ownership of the shared buildings be vested solely or jointly in all or any of them.[27] However, in the case of consecrated churches of the Church of England it must retain sole ownership, unless authority to make the sharing agreement is given by a pastoral scheme, in which case the church may be in the joint ownership of the

---

[19] PCCPM, ss.5, 6.

[20] See also the Council of Churches for Britain and Ireland, *Under the Same Roof: Guidelines to the Sharing of Church Buildings Act 1969* (1994).

[21] And the Sharing of Church Buildings Measure 1970 which makes consequential extensions to the Pastoral Measure 1983 and to certain other Measures.

[22] The Sharing of Church Buildings Act 1969 applies to the Roman Catholic, Methodist and United Reformed Churches, the Church in Wales, the Presbyterian Church of England, any church of the Baptist or Congregations denomination and any congregation of the Association of Churches of Christ in Great Britain and Ireland: *ibid.*, s.11(1), Sched. 2. In addition any church represented on the General Council of the British Council of Churches or the governing body of the Evangelical Alliance or the British Evangelical Council may give notice that the Act should apply to that church: *ibid.*, s.11(3).

[23] *ibid.*, s.12(1).

[24] *ibid.*, s.10(1).

[25] *ibid.*, s.1(1), (2). Buildings subject to the agreement are held on trust and provision is made to ensure that the purposes of a sharing agreement are exclusively charitable: *ibid.*, s.2. Nor does a sharing agreement affect the application of the Charities Act 1960 to any building owned by the Church of England: *ibid.*, s.8.

[26] *ibid.*, s.13.

[27] *ibid.*, s.1(2).

Church of England and another church or churches.[28] A church which is shared by the Church of England may only become or remain a parish church if it is in the sole ownership of the Church of England, but such a building is not prevented from being designated[29] a parish centre of worship.[30] In cases where the Church of England enters into a sharing agreement in respect of a church building which is used, or to be used, as a place of worship but is not consecrated, that building is only to be consecrated if, under the agreement, it is in the sole ownership of the Church of England.[31] Where a sharing agreement applies to a consecrated church the faculty jurisdiction does not apply to moveables required for the worship of any sharing church other than the Church of England.[32]

8.44   Unless the authority to do so is given by a pastoral scheme no sharing agreement is to be made with respect to an existing residence house of a benefice of the Church of England.[33] In cases where, under a sharing agreement, a separate residence is let to an incumbent in their corporate capacity, that residence is the residence of the benefice during the term of the lease.[34]

With regard to the Church of England the parties to any agreement are the DBF, the incumbent and the PCC, who are required to have the consent of the relevant diocesan bishop and pastoral committee.[35] In respect of other churches the parties will be the persons determined by the appropriate authority of that church who must obtain such consents as that authority determines.[36] The person in whom the building is vested and any managing trustees must also be parties. The agreement must provide for its own termination and may provide for the withdrawal of a church, if that church is not the sole or previous owner of the building.[37] Amendment of the agreement can only occur with the agreement of the parties to it and with the same consents as were required for its original formation.[38]

The agreement must make provision for the finances and other obligations of the parties in respect of the provision, improvement and management of the building. In general the primary responsibility rests with the church which owns the property, or in the case of jointly owned buildings the managing trustees. However, nothing prevents the continuance of any legal powers which persons or bodies have in respect of the application of money for the provision, improvement or management of church buildings, and the duties of the church owning the building or managing trustee may be discharged through the terms of the agreement.[39]

[28] *ibid.*, s.5.
[29] Under the Pastoral Measure 1983, s.29.
[30] The Sharing of Church Buildings Act 1969, s.5.
[31] *ibid.*, s.5.
[32] *ibid.*, s.5.
[33] Sharing of Church Buildings Act 1969, s.7.
[34] *ibid.*, s.7.
[35] Or, in the case of a building held on trust for educational purposes, the consent of the diocesan education board instead of the pastoral committee, together with the approval of the Secretary of State: *ibid.*, s.1(5).
[36] *ibid.*, s.1(3), (4). The agreement is binding on the parties' successors: *ibid.*, s.1(9).
[37] *ibid.*, s.9. Where the agreement concerns two or more buildings it must provide for terminating the sharing of each, so that sharing of one could continue notwithstanding termination of the agreement relating to another: *ibid.*
[38] *ibid.*, s.9.
[39] *ibid.*, s.3.

As a matter of ecclesiastical practice, sharing agreements incorporate constitutional structures in addition to the compulsory and optional statutory terms. Frequently a joint council is established to administer the agreement, consisting of equal numbers of representatives of the churches involved. For the Church of England these representatives would include the incumbent or priest-in-charge, the churchwardens and members selected from the PCC. The functions of such a council will vary but generally it will have power to facilitate joint action, such as repairs and alterations to furnishings and fittings, and to settle questions and disputes which may arise from implementation of the agreement.

In respect of shared buildings used as a place of worship provision must also be made for determining the extent to which such places are available for worship, in accordance with the forms of service and practice of the sharing churches. For a further discussion of such forms and practices and for a wider survey of ecumenical relations in general, see Chapter 12.

Removal of the legal effects of consecration on real property

As we saw earlier the legal effects of consecration in respect of moveables are **8.45** removed when that property is disposed of pursuant to a faculty. However, with regard to real property the legal effects may only be removed by an Act of Parliament, Measure of the Church Assembly or General Synod, or by episcopal action pursuant to these.[40] Although there is nothing at common law to prevent the alienation of consecrated land *per se*,[41] it is unlawful to sell, lease or otherwise dispose of any church, church site, or consecrated land annexed to or belonging to a church or any part of it, other than in pursuance of powers under the Pastoral Measure 1983,[42] the CCEJM, or powers exercisable under any Act of Parliament.[43] However, this does not prevent the grant of a faculty authorising suitable use of a church or in respect of such land which does not involve disposal.

For these purposes "church" is defined[44] as a church or chapel consecrated for the purposes of public worship. Accordingly, in regard to a private chapel not consecrated for public worship, a faculty may be granted for use for secular purposes and the property is not inalienable.[45]

Pursuant to the CCEJM and on the application of the archdeacon a diocesan bishop has the power to make an order in respect of any building or land that, in

---

[40] *Wood v. Headingley-cum-Burley Burial Board* [1892] 1 Q.B. 713 at 725.
[41] Pastoral Measure 1983, s.61.
[42] These powers are exercisable either by a pastoral scheme which may provide for the appropriation of the whole or part of a churchyard or other land annexed to or belonging to a church or a burial ground, and make provision for such property either with or without limitations on its use (as to which see Chap. 5), or in the case of a church or chapel by a redundancy scheme (see below).
[43] Pastoral Measure 1983 s.56; *Vicar and Churchwardens of St Mary Abotts, Kensington v. St Mary Abotts, Kensington Inhabitants* (1873) Tr. Consist. J. 17; *Rector and Churchwardens of St Gabriel, Fenchurch Street v. City of London Real Property Co Ltd* [1896] P. 95 at 101: *Re St Peter's Bushey Heath* [1971] 1 W.L.R. 357 at 360.
[44] Pastoral Measure 1983, s.87(1).
[45] *Re Tonbridge School Chapel (No. 2)* [1993] Fam. 281.

whole or part, it will not be subject to the legal effects of consecration, provided he is satisfied that no purpose will be served by its remaining thus.[46] In particular the faculty jurisdiction will no longer apply. The bishop may impose such conditions and requirements as he thinks fit as to the preservation or disposal of any human remains, the reordering or removal of any tombstones, monuments or memorials commemorating the deceased, and the maintenance of orderly behaviour in or on the property.[47]

The most important example of alienation under Act of Parliament is the power of compulsory acquisition conferred on planning authorities and others. Subject to compliance with certain conditions, such land can be used for the purpose for which it was acquired, notwithstanding any obligation imposed by ecclesiastical law or otherwise, once the prescribed requirements have been observed.[48]

Redundant churches

8.46 If a consecrated church or chapel is judged to be no longer required the only procedure by which it can be closed for that reason is pursuant to a redundancy scheme under the provisions of the Pastoral Measure 1983. Various statutory bodies have been created to advise upon redundant churches and to administer redundancy schemes.

Advisory Board for redundant churches

8.47 The Advisory Board consists of a chairman and six to ten other persons; they are appointed by the two archbishops jointly after consultation with the Prime Minister.[49] The Board advises the Church Commissioners (who make grants out of their funds for its expenses) with regard to the historic and archaeological interest and architectural quality of any church (including the curtilage, and any churchyard or burial ground annexed to it). It also advises on the historic, archaeological and aesthetic qualities of the church's contents, the church's value as part of the landscape and its overall importance. It undertakes such an assessment with a view to determining whether the church should be preserved

---

[46] CCEJM, s.22. He must be satisfied that the property is not held or controlled by any ecclesiastical corporation or by any DBF: *ibid*.

[47] *ibid*. See also *Re St Martin-le-Grand* [1990] Fam. 63. Any such conditions and requirements are local land charges, the bishop being treated as the originating authority, and are enforceable as if the archdeacon was the owner of the adjacent land and the conditions or requirements were negative covenants expressed to be entered into for the benefit of that adjacent land with enforcement being deemed for the benefit of the archdeacon: CCEJM, s.22.

[48] Town and Country Planning Act 1990, ss.238, 239, 240; Town and Country Planning (Churches, Places of Religious Worship and Burial Grounds) Regulations, S.I. 1950 No. 792.

[49] Pastoral Measure 1983, s.41. The Board reports annually to the archbishops and the report is laid before General Synod: *ibid*. The composition of the Board is set out in *ibid*., Sched. 5, paras 1–4.

or demolished. Before advising that a church should be preserved the Board must consult the Churches Conservation Trust as to the funds which the Trust has available for preservation should the property be vested in it.[50]

Churches Conservation Trust

The Trust (previously the Redundant Churches Fund)[51] consists of a chairman and four to six other members, appointed by the Sovereign in consultation with the archbishops through the Prime Minister.[52] Its objectives are the preservation of churches of historic and archaeological interest or architectural quality, together with their contents (vested in the Trust under the Pastoral Measure 1983) in the interests of the nation and the Church of England. The Trust has power to hold, manage, maintain and repair all property vested in it and to acquire property if this would assist in the exercise of these powers to permit occasional or temporary use of the property for purposes considered suitable (including, with the authorisation of the bishop, worship by persons belonging to other christian churches), to let the property on such terms as the Church Commissioners and the Advisory Board may approve,[53] and to carry out such works as are desirable in regard to property to be let.[54] The Trust may also charge entrance fees for admission to such property, raise money by public subscription and appeals, accept gifts and bequests, and may administer and invest sums in its hands and delegate functions to local trustees or bodies.[55]

8.48

Other committees

The Board of Governors of the Church Commissioners must appoint a committee of the Board to exercise such functions as the Board assigns to it in relation to redundant buildings and the preparation of redundancy schemes.[56]

8.49

Each diocese must set up a diocesan redundant churches uses committee, whose duty is to endeavour to find suitable alternative uses for redundant churches in the diocese.[57] It must report to the Church Commissioners when a

---

[50] *ibid.*, s.41.

[51] The Fund was renamed pursuant to the Churches Conservation Trust Pastoral (Amendment) Measure 1994 s.13.

[52] Pastoral Measure 1983, s.44. Its composition is set out in *ibid.*, Sched. 5, paras 13–15. The Church Commissioners may make grants out of their general fund, and the Secretary of State may make grants up to specified amounts with Treasury approval: *ibid.*, s.44; Redundant Churches and Other Religious Buildings Act 1969, s.1. Copies of the Trust's annual report and accounts are laid before Parliament and the General Synod: Pastoral Measure 1983, s.44.

[53] The terms of the leasing may provide that the property shall not be subject to the legal effects of consecration during the currency of the lease. Pastoral Measure 1983, ss.44(7A), 61.

[54] Pastoral Measure 1983, s.44.

[55] *ibid.*

[56] Pastoral Measure 1983, s.43(1). The committee may include persons who are not Commissioners provided the Commissioners constitute a majority.

[57] *ibid.*, s.42. The composition and procedure of the committees is set out in *ibid.*, Sched. 5, paras 5–12.

suitable use or uses has or have been found, or when it has reached the conclusion that no such use will be found, and must also make an annual report.

Declaration of redundancy

8.50 A declaration of redundancy is made by a pastoral scheme,[58] in respect of a church which is not required as a parish church or chapel of ease.[59] Provision is made for the use, care and maintenence of the redundant building and for the ownership of it and land annexed to it to vest in the DBF, or for its demolition.[60] A pastoral scheme itself may make no further provision in regard to the redundant building, save in three exceptional cases. First, in a case where the redundant building is to be replaced by a new church or place of worship the scheme itself may make provision for the building subject to certain conditions.[61] Secondly, where the Church Commissioners are satisfied that a suitable use will be available for the building the pastoral scheme may provide for its appropriation to such use or uses.[62] Finally, where the Commissioners are satisfied no suitable or appropriate use will be available for the building and it appears to them (after consultation with the Advisory Board) to be of such historic and archaeological interest or architectural quality that it ought to be preserved and the Churches Conservation Trust have the resources to repair and maintain it, the pastoral scheme may provide for its transfer (together with any land annexed or belonging to it) to the Trust.[63]

Redundancy scheme

8.51 A redundancy scheme is prepared by the Church Commissioners and must make provision for one of four eventualites. If the Church Commissioners consider that a suitable use or uses appear to have been found the scheme must make provision for appropriating the building or part of it to that use or uses.[64] If such use or uses cannot be found, and subject to the same conditions for transfer of such a building pursuant to a pastoral scheme, it may be vested in the Churches Conservation Trust.[65] Failing this the scheme may provide for the transfer of all

---

[58] As to pastoral schemes generally, see Chap. 5.
[59] Pastoral Measure 1983, s.28. A declaration may be made in respect of a parish church notwithstanding that the parish will have no church at the time the declaration takes effect, but where a parish has no church the bishop must licence a building or part of a building for public worship: *ibid*.
[60] *ibid*., s.28.
[61] *ibid*., s.46.
[62] *ibid*., s.47.
[63] *ibid*., s.47.
[64] *ibid*., s.51. Various supplementary provisions may be made, and in exercising their powers to dispose of any building or land, the Commissioners or DBF may include in the instrument of disposition such covenants as to use as they consider necessary or expedient to give effect to the provisions of the scheme or otherwise to secure the suitable use of the building or land: *ibid*, ss.51, 62.
[65] *ibid*., s.51.

or part of the building to the DBF (with its consent) to be held on such terms as are specified in the scheme. Failing this the scheme must provide for the demolition of all or part of the building not appropriated or provided for by the foregoing provisions.[66]

Save in exceptional circumstances the Church Commissioners must not prepare a redundancy scheme for at least six months after the date the declaration of redundancy takes effect,[67] but must generally prepare such a scheme within three years of the date redundancy was declared. The draft scheme must be served upon various bodies, including the local planning authority, and notice of the draft scheme published. Representations may then be made to the Commissioners.[68] If, following representations, the Commissioners decide not to proceed they must prepare a new draft scheme as soon as possible.[69] A redundancy scheme is confirmed by an Order in Council,[70] but a scheme may be amended either before or after it comes into operation, or its provisions revoked, substituted or complemented by a subsequent scheme.[71]

Upon the declaration of redundancy the redundant building and its contents (with certain exceptions) vests in the DBF.[72] The DBF is responsible for its care and maintenance and the safe keeping of its contents, which it may transfer to some other place for security. The incumbent or priest-in-charge and church-wardens, whilst bearing no financial obligations, must assist the DBF in providing reasonable supervision against damage to the building. With the consent of the bishop and the incumbent or priest-in-charge the DBF may permit the building to be used for worship occasionally, including worship by persons belonging to other Christian churches. Subsequently the property vests in the appropriate body in accordance with the provisions of the pastoral or redundancy scheme.[73]

In cases where a redundant church is vested in either the DBF or the Church Conservation Trust, these bodies may, with the approval of the diocesan bishop and the Church Commissioners, enter into an agreement with the Secretary of State or the Historic Buildings and Monuments Commission for England for the acquisition and preservation of the building.[74]

The proceeds of any sale, exchange or other disposal and the premiums and net rent payable on any lease or licence must be applied in accordance with legislative provisions, the majority of such funds generally going to the diocesan pastoral account.[75]

Before a church is demolished or appropriated to another use the body in whom it is vested must transfer the font, communion table and plate used for Holy Communion to some other church.[76] This other church should be in the

8.52

---

[66] ibid.

[67] ibid., s.49.

[68] ibid., s.50. For the duty to consult interested parties see *Elphick v. Church Commissioners* [1994] A.C. 562.

[69] ibid., s.50.

[70] ibid.

[71] Pastoral Measure 1983, s.57.

[72] ibid., s.49.

[73] ibid., s.59. It vests free of any trust or burial rights: *ibid.*

[74] ibid., s.66.

[75] ibid., s.51.

[76] ibid., s.64. See however *Re West Camel Church; Re Yetton Church* [1979] 2 W.L.R. 501 on disposal of contents in advance of a scheme.

benefice, or if they are not needed in any other church or chapel in the diocese as directed by the bishop. The pastoral or redundancy scheme may also provide for the disposal of other contents (not being tombstones, monuments or memorials), including the vesting of these in either the DBF or the Church Conservation Trust in cases where the church itself is also vested in either of these, and for either of these bodies to assume responsibility for their care and maintenance.[77]

In cases where human remains are believed to be buried in or beneath a redundant building, or any land to which a pastoral or redundancy scheme applies special provisions operate. Until the remains have been removed, and reinterred or cremated, and any tombstones, monuments or memorials have been disposed of, the body or person in whom the property is vested, leased or to whom it is licensed may not, save in limited circumstances, demolish, sell, lease, otherwise dispose of, use, or develop it, or any part of it.[78] If they are satisfied that demolition or the intended use or development will not disturb the remains, these requirements may be dispensed with by order of the Secretary of State, after consultation with the bishop and the Commonwealth War Graves Commission.[79]

A redundant church is not subject to the legal effects of consecration,[80] with the consequence that faculties are not required to authorise disposal of a building, its contents, and land annexed to it. Where a redundant church is vested in either the DBF, Church Commissioners or the Church Conservation Trust, a pastoral scheme may make provision for it to be restored to use as a church.[81] Upon restoration the legal effects of consecration revive.[82]

Cathedral property

8.53 As part of the process of rationalisation brought about pursuant to the Cathedrals Measure 1963, all property of a cathedral is vested in the cathedral's capitular body, or is held by the Church Commissioners on its behalf.[83]

A capitular body, dean, provost or canon has the power to acquire land by *inter vivos* gift or by will. They also have the power to acquire land for gaining access to, or improving, land already held, for certain other specified purposes including improving the amenities of the cathedral, or for any ecclesiastical, educational or other charitable purpose connected with it, or for housing for persons engaged in duties connected with the cathedral. Finally they have the power to sell, grant a

---

[77] Pastoral Measure 1983, s.64.

[78] *ibid.*, s.65.

[79] Pastoral Measure 1983, s.65.

[80] *ibid.*, s.61(1). However, a faculty is required for the removal of the contents of a church between the declaration of redundancy and the making of the final order: *Re West Camel Church* [1987] Fam. 79.

[81] *ibid.*, s.58. The provisions may also apply to buildings acquired by the Secretary of State or by the Historic Buildings and Monuments Commission for England: *ibid.*, s.66(3).

[82] *ibid.*, s.61(3).

[83] Cathedrals Measure 1963, ss.15, 16. Provision also exists whereby the property of a capitular body may be transferred to the Church Commissioners on such terms and for such consideration as the Commissioners consider fair, and for the transfer to a capitular body of property owned by the Commissioners: *ibid.*, s.19.

lease of, mortgage or charge land, and to dedicate land for the purpose of a highway.[84] In all save limited circumstances the consent of the Church Commissioners is required before these powers are exercised.[85] In addition where the transaction concerns a residence the consent of the bishop, dean, provost or residentiary canon normally occupying it is also required, and if the property is allocated for use by a dignitary in respect of whom the Sovereign has the right of presentation, the monarch's consent will also be needed.[86]

The capitular body also has certain powers of investment,[87] and may borrow money for specified purposes.[88] It may, with the consent of the Church Commissioners, use endowment capital for the improvement or development of any property in which it holds an interest other than the cathedral church and buildings ancillary to it.[89] Audited accounts of the cathedral's property and its income must be produced annually. These are transmitted to the Church Commissioners and are also published annually by the administrative body of the cathedral.[90]

Care and maintenance

Although the Cathedrals Measure 1963 made some provision in respect of the care and maintenance of cathedrals and other property for which the capitular bodies had responsibility, there was a total absence of any regulatory framework. In particular, cathedrals were outside the operation of the faculty jurisdiction. Following the report of the Faculty Jurisdiction Commission, *The Continuing Care of Churches and Cathedrals*,[91] the Care of Cathedrals Measure 1990 was introduced. This provided a statutory framework for the care and conservation of cathedrals, akin to the faculty jurisdiction. In addition the Measure provided that a parish cathedral church could in certain circumstances opt to become subject to the faculty jurisdiction of the consistory court, with the effect that the Care of Cathedrals Measure would cease to apply to it.[92] Despite the introduction of a framework for conservation the 1990 Measure contained no provisions relating to enforcement of its provisions. These are contained in the Care of Cathedrals (Supplementary Provisions) Measure 1994, which created a number of procedures for dealing with the carrying out, or threat to carry out, works without the requisite approvals.

8.54

---

[84] *ibid.*, s.20, (1).
[85] *ibid.*, s.20, (2).
[86] *ibid.*, s.20, (3).
[87] *ibid.*, s.21.
[88] *ibid.*, ss.34, 35.
[89] *ibid.*, s.23. Exceptions apply in the case of emergency repairs to the cathedral when the capitular body may borrow from its endowment capital on a short-term basis: *ibid.*, s.25.
[90] *ibid.*, s.38.
[91] (1984). The absence of a regulatory framework for cathedrals threatened the continued existence of the ecclesiastical exemption from planning controls ordinarily applicable to listed buildings: *Report of the Ecclesiastical Committee upon the Care of Cathedrals Measure* (198th Report, 1990). The current system met with a favourable response in the report of the Archbishops' Commission on Cathedrals, *Heritage and Renewal*, (1994) (G.S. No. 1192).
[92] Care of Cathedrals Measure 1990, s.18.

The 1990 Measure created the Cathedrals Fabric Commission. This consists of a lay chairman appointed by the Archbishops of Canterbury and York after consultation with the Secretary of State for the Environment, and a vice-chairman appointed after consultation with the Standing Committee of the General Synod and such organisation as is representative of the deans and provosts. In addition the two archbishops appoint a further 17 members, on the nomination of, or in consultation with, various bodies. These appointments are intended to ensure that the committee contains a broad range of experts from the fields of architecture, archaeology, art, archives, conservation, liturgy and other specialist areas. In addition the General Synod directly elects five members, these being persons who have knowledge of the ways in which cathedral churches are currently used and of their contribution to the work of the Church.[93]

In co-operation with the Cathedrals Fabric Commission each cathedral is required to establish a fabric advisory committee. This committee is to comprise between three and five members appointed by the administrative body of the cathedral who are in holy orders or employed by that body, and a further three to five members appointed by the Commission, after consultation with the cathedral's administrative body. The latter group are to be persons who have demonstrated a special knowledge with respect to the care and maintenance of buildings of outstanding historical interest, and who have a particular interest in the cathedral concerned.[94] The committee must meet at least twice a year and the dean or provost and residentiary canons may attend and speak, but may not vote. In general it is the duty of the cathedral architect and archaeological consultants to attend its meetings.[95]

8.55 Both the Cathedrals Fabric Commission and the fabric advisory committee of each cathedral are required to advise the administrative body of the cathedral on the care, conservation, repair or development of the cathedral, and to consider and determine any application made to it by the cathedral's administrative body, in accordance with the provisions of the 1990 Measure.[96] In addition the Commission has certain other functions including co-operating between itself and relevant organisations, participating in educational and research projects to promote the care and conservation of cathedrals, and maintaining jointly with the Council for the Care of Churches a library of material relating to cathedrals.[97] In exercising their functions the Commission and the fabric advisory committees are to have regard to the fact that the cathedral is the seat of the bishop as a centre of worship and mission.[98]

The functions of the capitular body of a cathedral must be delegated to its administrative body,[99] which is required to make provision for the inspection of all buildings, other than the cathedral church or its ancillary buildings, which the capitular body is liable to repair (either buildings within the cathedral close or allocated as residences of those holding office within the cathedral).[1] The administrative body is now required to compile and maintain an inventory of all

---

[93] *ibid.*, s.3, Sched. 1.
[94] *ibid.*, s.4, Sched. 2.
[95] *ibid.*, s.4, Sched. 2.
[96] *ibid.*, ss.3, 4.
[97] Care of Cathedrals Measure 1990, s.3, Sched. 1.
[98] *ibid.*, s.1.
[99] Cathedrals Measure 1963, s.10(1).
[1] *ibid.*, s.27.

objects in the possession of the chapter which the fabric advisory committee considers to be of architectural, archaeological, artistic or historic interest.[2]

The constitution and statutes of the cathedral must also provide for the appointment of a cathedral architect,[3] the administrative body now being required to consult with the Cathedrals Fabric Commission before making such an appointment.[4] In addition, unless the Commission notifies the administrative body that in its view the archaeological significance of the cathedral does not justify such an archaeological consultant must also be appointed.[5]

The cathedral architect, in consultation with the archaeological consultant, must every five years prepare a written report, detailing any works which they consider need to be undertaken expeditiously.[6] The cathedral's administrative body is also required to keep a record of all works carried out to the cathedral church or in any of its precincts.[7]

8.56 Without authorisation the administrative body must not carry out works on, above or below land vested in the capitular body which would materially affect the architectural, archaeological, artistic or historic character of the cathedral or any building within its precincts being used for ecclesiastical purposes. Neither can it carry out without due authorisation works affecting the immediate setting of the cathedral or any archaeological remains within its precincts. It must not sell, loan or otherwise dispose of any object vested in the capitular body which is of architectural, archaeological, artistic or historic interest, nor may it add permanently to the cathedral any object which would materially affect the architectural, archaeological, artistic or historic character of the cathedral.[8] These prohibitions do not apply to anything done by the administrative body in the furtherance of its duties under the cathedral's constitution and statutes with regard to the ordering of services or the furtherance of the mission of the cathedral, nor to works of a temporary nature, or those which do not affect the fabric of the cathedral.[9]

Applications for authorisation of works and appeals

8.57 Applications for approval are made to the Cathedrals Fabric Commission where proposals for undertaking works may involve the permanent alteration of the fabric, or indeed the demolition of any part of the cathedral or any building within its precincts. Application for approval should also be made if there is a possibility that works may involve the destruction of archaeological remains, or sale, loan or other disposal of works designated as being of architectural, archaeological, artistic or historic interest.[10] An application must also be submitted to the Commission in cases where it declares in writing that the proposals

---

[2] Care of Cathedrals Measure 1990, s.13.
[3] Cathedrals Measure 1963, s.10(1).
[4] Care of Cathedrals Measure 1990, s.12(1).
[5] *ibid.*, s.12(1).
[6] *ibid.*, s.14, (1).
[7] *ibid.*, s.14, (2).
[8] *ibid.*, s.2(1).
[9] *ibid.*, s.2(2).
[10] *ibid.*, s.6.

give rise to considerations of such special architectural, archaeological, artistic or historic interest that it should consider them. In all other cases the application is made to the fabric advisory committee of the cathedral itself,[11] which also has the power to determine whether or not a proposal should be submitted to it or to the Commission.[12]

When an application is made to either the fabric advisory committee or to the Cathedrals Fabric Commission provision is made for display of a notice to the effect that the proposals are available for inspection and that written representations may be made to the body to which the application has been made. This body is under a duty to consider those representations in deciding whether to approve (conditionally or unconditionally) or reject the application. Depending upon the nature of the proposals it is possible that certain other bodies in addition to the body to which application is made may also need to be notified.[13]

Should the fabric advisory committee reject an application it is possible to appeal against such a refusal or approval which is only given by that committee conditionally to the Cathedrals Fabric Commission which can confirm, reverse or vary the committee's decision.[14] A right of appeal against the decision of the Cathedrals Fabric Commission exists to a Commission of Review which has the power to confirm, reverse or vary the Fabric Commission's decision.[15] An appeal may also be made to a Commission of Review where the original application was to the Cathedral's Fabric Commission. In all cases the decision of a Commission of Review is final.[16]

In cases of actual or threatened contravention of the provisions of the 1990 Measure, action may now be taken by the diocesan bishop (acting on his own motion, on the advice of the Cathedrals Fabric Commission, or the allegation of anyone else) pursuant to the Care of Cathedrals (Supplementary Provisions) Measure 1994. This Measure provides that an administrative body may be dealt with in the first instance at a private interview of that body by the bishop. If he considers that such an act has occurred or is threatened he must then, subject to certain conditions, order a special visitation to inquire into the alleged breach. The administrative body is under a duty to obey any direction which the bishop makes at any time during this process, including prior to the interview. Should the bishop consider it necessary or expedient to take further steps he may authorise proceedings to be instituted to seek an injunction or restoration order from the court of the Vicar-General of the province. The court may also order that the special visitation continues on such terms as it considers just or that it is to cease. An appeal lies from the Vicar-General's court to the Court of the Arches or Chancery.[17]

---

[11] ibid., s.6.

[12] ibid., s.5. It also has the power, after consultation with the administrative body and with the agreement of the Cathedrals Fabric Commission, to determine that the requirement for obtaining approval shall not apply to proposals of a specified class: ibid.

[13] ibid., ss.7, 8.

[14] ibid., s.9. The Commission may also be requested to deal with the original application in cases when the committee does not make a determination within three months: ibid.

[15] ibid., s.10. The composition of a Commission of Review is set out in this section. Provision is also made for a Commission of Review to determine an application in cases where the Cathedrals Fabric Commission fails to do so within three months' ibid.

[16] ibid.

[17] Care of Cathedrals (Supplementary Provisions) Measure 1994, ss.1–8.

Finance

Although the Church of England is the established church there is no general **8.58**
provision for financial support to be forthcoming from the State. In earlier times
the Church was supported by gifts, endowments and enforceable tithes. But tithes
having been abolished, the current generation is not endowing the Church to the
same extent that their predecessors did, and the Church is facing serious financial
difficulties as its current assets no longer generate sufficient income to meets its
needs. The Turnbull Commission has recommended radical changes to the
Church's structure for financial management, principally at national, but also at
diocesan level.[18] In particular it proposes that the new Archbishops' Council
should have responsibility for assessing the overall financial resources of the
Church and for undertaking planning in relation to these resources. It would
have the power to redistribute resources within the Church and to allocate the
income from the funds held by the Church Commissioners. The national finance
policies of the Church would be directed by the finance department of the
Council, under the general oversight of the Archbishops' Council itself.[19]

Central Board of Finance

The Central Board of Finance, a company and a registered charity, is the **8.59**
financial executive of the General Synod.[20] The Board's articles of association
provide for the election of a member of each diocese to it. Standing Orders of
the General Synod[21] provide that the Board may submit such reports to the
General Synod as it sees fit on the financial business of the Synod, its subordinate
bodies and of any body in receipt of moneys voted by Synod. In addition to such
reports the Board advises upon the financial implications of any items of business
included on the Synod's agenda.

All bodies which are voted money by the General Synod must lay annual
estimates of expenditure required in the forthcoming year before the Board, the
Board then incorporating (after consultation with the Synod's Standing Committee) the amount which it considers expedient to allocate to that body in the
annual budget which it prepares for the General Synod. In addition to preparing
the annual budget the Board prepares the preceding year's accounts and motions
for the authorisation of expenditure required under the various heads set out in
the budget. This budget funds the various boards and committees of the General
Synod, including the costs of training for full-time ministry, and provides
contributions to various ecumenical bodies including the Lambeth Conference,
the Anglican Consultative Council and the World Council of Churches.

Provision is made for the Board to require any body in receipt of monies voted
by Synod to account for such monies and for the Board to audit the accounts of

[18] *Working as One Body*, The Report of the Archbishops' Commission on the Reorganisation of the Church of England (1995).
[19] *ibid.*, Chap. 5.
[20] It was established under powers conferred on the General Synod by SGM, Sched. 2. In
addition to its company memorandum and articles it is governed by Standing Orders of
the General Synod.
[21] Standing Orders of the General Synod (1995 ed.). (GS 1180, 1180A).

any such body. The Board must report to Synod on any excess expenditure by such bodies, and make recommendations as to any conditions upon which the excess should be condoned and sanctioned. Bodies may also submit supplementary estimates of expenditure, which the Board may in turn submit to Synod for it to make a supplementary vote.

The Board administers the General Synod Fund which covers the costs of the Synod's subordinate bodies and the Central Church Fund which is utilised for the general purposes of the Board. It also holds a legal aid fund on behalf of the General Synod, and as we shall see manages many of the Church's investment funds. The Turnbull Commission has recommended that the functions of the Board should be transferred to the proposed Archbishops' Council, as part of its proposals for centralising control of finance.[22]

Investment functions

8.60   The Central Board of Finance has an important role in the investment of Church funds which is largely regulated by the Church Funds Investment Measure 1958. However, the Measure does not apply to the Church Commissioners whose investment policies have, as we have seen, been the subject of criticism. A statutory scheme pursuant to the 1958 Measure enables the investment of the corporate funds of the Central Board of Finance, the corporate funds of any diocesan authority, the funds of any church educational endowment and any funds held by the Central Board or a diocesan authority or any other person or body upon any trust for exclusively charitable objects connected with the work of the Church of England.[23] The Church of England Pensions Board[24] has the power to invest in this manner as does the capitular body of any cathedral church,[25] and the Churches Conservation Trust.[26]

Investment is either in an investment fund, suitable only for long-term investment, a fixed interest securities fund which is intended to supplement the main investment fund by offering high yield but little inflationary protection for capital, and a deposit fund suitable for smaller or short-term investments. By grouping the funds of contributors together the Board can obtain better returns on its investments.

Contributions are made by paying cash or transferring assets subject to the consent of the Board, the Board having power to invest the money comprised in the funds.[27] In order to record each contributor's interest in the funds each investment fund is divided into income and accumulation shares. The scheme provides for the valuation of such shares, the distribution of income produced,

---

[22] *Working as One Body*, The Report of the Archbishops' Commission on the Reorganisation of the Church of England (1995). Chap. 5.
[23] Church Funds Investment Measure 1958, s.2. Other than a trust which came into operation after February 20, 1958 and which expressly excludes such investment: *ibid*. Otherwise trustees may invest in the funds notwithstanding anything contained in the trust instrument: *ibid*., s.3(1).
[24] Clergy Pensions Measure 1961, s.32(1)(u).
[25] Cathedrals Measure 1963, s.21(1)(b).
[26] Pastoral Measure 1983, s.44(6).
[27] Church Funds Investment Measure 1958.

withdrawals of contributions (on demand from the deposit fund but otherwise monthly) and the winding up of that fund.[28]

The Church Commissioners

The Church Commissioners (themselves a body corporate) are the successors of **8.61** the corporations of Queen Anne's Bounty and the Ecclesiastical Commissioners. The functions of these dissolved corporations, their rights privileges and property which is now held on trust for the purposes of the Church of England, were all transferred to the Church Commissioners in 1947.[29]

The funds of Queen Anne's Bounty, established in 1704 for "the Augumentation of the Maintenance of Poor Clergy" essentially comprised all the revenue from "first fruits and tenths" payable to the Crown following the Reformation. The Ecclesiastical Commissioners were established in 1836 to carry out the recommendations of two Royal Commissions in regard to the raising and distribution of revenues from episcopal duties in the dioceses of England and Wales, and the states of cathedral and collegiate churches. As a consequence of the establishment of such a remit the assets of dean and chapter cathedrals were transferred to the Ecclesiastical Commissioners who held the bulk of Church revenues as one common fund to apply by scheme for such purposes as they saw fit.

Assets originally belonging to the bishops are also vested in the Commissioners, having been transferred pursuant to the Episcopal Endowments and Stipends Measure 1943. For this reason the cost of improvements, repairs and the maintenance of archbishops' palaces and diocesan bishops' see houses are met out of Commissioners' funds.

Church Estates Commissioners

Originally there were 13 Ecclesiastical Commissioners, both spiritual and lay, **8.62** including the two archbishops and the Lord Chancellor. In 1850 three further Commissioners, known as the Church Estates Commissioners, were added to their numbers, and these are now members of the Church Commissioners.[30] Church Estate Commissioners are appointed in the same manner as previously, that is lay members of the Church are appointed by the Sovereign as the First and Second Church Estates Commissioners, and the Third Church Estates Commissioner is appointed by the Archbishop of Canterbury. The First and Third Commissioners hold office during the pleasure of the Crown and Archbishop respectively, whilst, by convention, the Second Church Estates Commissioner (who in contrast to the other two receives no emoluments) is a member of the House of Commons, nominated by the Government of the day, whose appointment lapses on a change of government.

[28] *ibid*.
[29] Church Commissioners Measure 1947, ss.1, 2.
[30] Ecclesiastical Commissioners Act 1850, s.1; Church Property (Miscellaneous Provisions) Measure 1960, s.19(1).

Appointment of Church Commissioners

8.63 The 95 Church Commissioners are either *ex officio*, nominated or appointed. The *ex officio* members are the Archbishop of Canterbury (who acts as chairman), the Archbishop of York, the diocesan bishops of the two provinces of England, the three Church Estates Commissioners, The Lord Chancellor, the Lord President of the Council, the First Lord of the Treasury, the Chancellor of the Exchequer, the Home Secretary, the Speaker of the House of Commons, the Lord Chief Justice, the Master of the Rolls, the Attorney General, the Solicitor General, the Lord Mayors of London and York, and the Vice-Chancellors of the Universities of Oxford and Cambridge. Ten clerks in holy orders and ten lay persons, who are not required to be members of the General Synod, are appointed by the General Synod, for a period of five years. Five deans chosen from amongst their own ranks by the deans and provosts of all cathedral churches as well as the Deans of Westminster and Windsor are elected or appointed for five years. Eight lay persons are nominated, four by the Sovereign and four by the Archbishop of Canterbury, for such period as is determined by the Letters Patent or by the Archbishop respectively. Two from amongst these eight must be, or have been, Queen's Counsel. Finally two aldermen of the City of London are appointed by the Court of Aldermen of the City of London for such period up to five years as the Court determines.[31] Every lay Commissioner, except *ex officio* Commissioners, must before acting make a declaration in writing that they are a member of the Church of England.[32]

Board of Governors

8.64 The Board of Governors is the executive body of the Church Commissioners, most of their business being conducted through it and committees. It consists of the Archbishop of Canterbury as chairman, the Archbishop of York, the three Church Estates Commissioners and 22 other Commissioners appointed by the whole body of Commissioners once in every three years at their annual general meeting, together with up to three further Commissioners co-opted by the Board.[33]

Business of the Commissioners

8.65 The Commissioners hold and administer a General Fund which consists of all the income received in respect of property and funds held by them. This General Fund is used to make grants for stipends, pensions, church buildings and various

---

[31] Church Commissioners Measure 1947, s.1(2), Sched. 1.

[32] *ibid.*

[33] *ibid.*, s.5(1), Sched. 2. Of these 22, six must be diocesan bishops, two deans, six others clerks in holy orders and eight lay persons of whom six must be chosen from amongst the lay Commissioners appointed by the General Synod: *ibid.*

other purposes,[34] and to discharge all obligations to which the income is subject as well as to meet all expenditure which the Commmissioners incur in carrying out their functions. The balance is available for the purpose for which any surplus of the common and corporate funds of its predecessors would have been available.

In addition to the Board of Governors the work of the Commissioners is in the hands of committees[35]—the most important of which are the General Purposes Committee and the Assets Committee,[36] both chaired by the First Estates Commissioner. The General Purposes Committee considers and recommends to the Board how to apply or distribute such sums as the Board may have determined to make available for application and distribution, and on any urgent matters referred to it by the Board.[37] The Assets Committee has exclusive power to act on behalf of the Commissioners in all matters relating to the management of those assets whose income is carried into the Commissioners' General Fund.[38] It has a duty to recommend to the Commissioners what sums are available for distribution by them upon application, and what sums should be appropriated to reserve or reinvestment.

In every financial year the Commissioners hold an annual general meeting as soon as is convenient after the audit of the preceding year's accounts. At this meeting consideration is given to the audited accounts which the Commissioners are required to keep, and to the annual report of the work and proceedings of the Commissioners prepared by the Board of Governors. Within 30 days of the annual general meeting this report, together with the accounts and any resolution referring to them passed by the Commissioners, must be transmitted to the Home Secretary who lays them before Parliament and to the Secretary General of the General Synod who lays them before Synod.[39]

---

[34] The role of the Church Commissioners in respect of church buildings, redundant churches, glebe land, parsonages and cathedrals was considered earlier in this chapter, and their role in regard to pastoral schemes in Chap. 5. See also the Church Schools (Assistance by Church Commissioners) Measure 1958; Church Commissioners (Assistance for Priority Areas) Measure 1988, and Church Commissioners (Loans for Theological Colleges and Training Houses) Measure 1964 (although as a matter of policy loans are no longer made pursuant to the 1964 Measure funding now being derived from the Advisory Board of Ministry).

[35] In addition to the two described below these are the Redundant Churches, Pastoral, Audit and Bishopric Committees.

[36] The General Purposes Committee comprises the three Church Estates Commissioners and between eight to ten other Church Commissioners appointed by the Board of Governors. At least two of these Commissioners must be diocesan bishops, three others clerks in holy orders and at least three lay persons. The Assets Committee comprises the First Church Estates Commissioner, one Commissioner who is a clerk in holy orders appointed for three years by the Board of Governors, between three and five lay Commissioners appointed for three years by the Archbishop of Canterbury and between one and three Commissioners appointed for three years by the Archbishop of Canterbury after consultation with the Board from among the twenty clerks in holy orders and laity appointed as Commissioners by the General Synod. Church Commissioners Measure 1947, s.6(1).

[37] ibid., s.6(2).

[38] ibid., s.6(3). Its powers extending to the sale, purchase, exchange or letting of land, and making, realising and changing investments: ibid.

[39] ibid., ss.4, 11(1), 12.

The Commissioners are not a subordinate body of the General Synod and are under no obligation to consult it or its financial executive (the Central Board of Finance) before exercising any of their functions. The investment policy of the Commissioners has been the subject of some criticism in recent years.[40] In 1991 the issue of the extent to which the Church Commissioners should apply ethical and christian principles to their investment policies came before the High Court.[41] The Vice-Chancellor considered that the primary object of the Commissioners as trustees was the generation of money. Accordingly they could only take account of ethical considerations when making investments to the extent that this would not jeopardise the profitablility of their investments.

The future of the Church Commissioners

8.66 The Turnbull Commission proposes radical changes in regard to the Church Commissioners.[42] In particular it proposes slimming down their numbers from 95 to 15 and transferring all their current functions with the exception of asset management to the new Archbishops' Council.

The smaller number of Commissioners would broadly reflect the current balance between Church and State. They would comprise the First and Second Church Estates Commissioners, three persons appointed by the Crown, the two archbishops, two bishops elected by the House of Bishops, a dean or provost and two clergy, and three lay members elected by the Houses of Clergy and Laity respectively of the General Synod. It is envisaged that there would be no need for a Board of Governors nor a Third Estates Commissioner.

The Commissioners role as independent trustees of centrally held historic assets would remain. Since the State has an interest in the origins of a significant proportion of these assets it is considered appropriate that these should continue to be managed by the Church and State in partnership. Particular concern was expressed that the assets should not be eroded or dispersed, the intention being that they will be ringfenced and only expended by specific legislative authorisation.

Essentially it is proposed that the Commissioners retain the functions of the current Assets Committee together with some of the trustee functions of the Board of Governors. A new Assets Committee would be appointed to oversee day to day management of the Commissioners' portfolio and report directly to them, but it would no longer have exclusive powers. In addition to including some Commissioners the new Committee would comprise people appointed for their professional expertise. An Audit Committee would scrutinise the finances

---

[40] *The Lambeth Report*, a report to the Archbishop of Canterbury by the Lambeth Group and Coopers and Lybrand July 19, 1993, concluded that many of the problems which the Commissioners encountered stemmed from their organisation which is not well suited to present day requirements. The Turnbull Commission was set up in response to the report. See also the report of the House of Commons' Social Security Select Committee (April 1995).

[41] *Harries v. Church Commissioners for England* [1992] 1 W.L.R. 1241.

[42] *Working as One Body*, The Report of the Archbishops' Commission on the Reorganisation of the Church of England, (1995); see especially *ibid.*, Chap. 8. See also *Working as One Body: A Framework for Legislation*, (1996) (G.S. No. 1188).

of the Commissioners, who would report as now to both the General Synod and Parliament.

The need to protect those managing the assets from undue pressure to over-distribute is recognised. The current distance between the Commissioners and their Assets Committee would be echoed in the inter-relation of the Archbishops' Council and the Commissioners, decisions on the application of the income available from these assets being placed in the hands of the Archbishops' Council, acting on advice of its finance committee. The Council would provide the Commissioners with a certificate that the income made available had been spent on the discharge of all trusts and commitments to which the Commissioners' income would have been subject, and the balance spent on the cure of souls in parishes where most required. The Commissioners would continue in their duty to preserve the balance between the need to generate income and maintain the real value of its capital and, in order to prevent it seeking to build its capital at the expense of reducing income, may be placed under a statutory duty to take account of the Council's assessments of the Church's needs.

The Commissioners' role under the Pastoral Measure 1983 would pass to the **8.67** Archbishops' Council, as would their role as the Central Stipends Authority. It is proposed that costs in respect of the archepiscopal and episcopal residences, episcopal expenses and the salaries and pensions of support staff, together with the Commissioners' obligations under the Cathedrals Measure 1963 to pay the stipends of certain cathedral clergy continue to be met out of their funds. This would be met out of the budget set by the Archbishops' Council which would itself be set in regard to these matters in consultation with a bishoprics committee, consisting of 10 members; five nominated by the Church Commissioners and five by the Council.

As we shall see below the Church Commissioners currently hold a pastoral account and a stipends fund for each diocese as well as the diocesan parsonage buildings fund. Under the principle of subsidiarity the Commission proposes that each diocese should take over the responsibility for these funds.

Diocesan boards of finance

The DBF is the financial executive of the diocesan synod, whose funds it holds **8.68** and manages and under whose control it acts. It is a company, regulated by the Companies Acts, its memorandum and articles empowering it to hold property for purposes connected with the Church of England and to transact business in that connection as well as to act as a committee of the diocesan synod.[43]

The diocesan bishop must be an *ex officio* member of the board, and not less than three-quarters of its members must be elected by the diocesan synod or wholly or partly by deanery synods in the diocese. The remainder may be elected, nominated or co-opted as the memorandum provides, but not less than two-thirds of the members elected in total must be members of the diocesan synod and a majority of the members of the company must be laity. The DBF must take

---

[43] Diocesan Boards of Finance Measure 1925, s.1. Its constitution is also deemed to include the furtherance of the work of the Church of England by the exercise of functions under the Endowments and Glebe Measure 1976: *ibid.*, s.40.

steps to ensure that the diocesan member of the Central Board of Finance is, unless already secretary of the DBF, a voting member.[44]

In most dioceses the DBF is required under the Standing Orders of the diocesan synod to submit a report and the preceding year's accounts, together with a draft budget for the next year, to the synod's standing committee, which may make recommendations. The DBF then presents its accounts and budget to the synod. The budget makes provision for every committee and other body responsible to the synod, subject to the prioritisation of resources. The DBF also reports to the synod on any excess expenditure by such bodies, and may make recommendations as to how the excess should be dealt with. Provision generally exists for supplementary budgets to be put forward. In all cases the DBF may not expend any of the synod's funds for which it is responsible without a money resolution.

Diocesan pastoral accounts

8.69   With the commencement of the Pastoral Measure 1968 the Church Commissioners came under a duty to open and hold a pastoral account for each diocese.[45] The Commissioners may pay out of monies held in such accounts expenses incurred for the purposes of the Pastoral Measure 1983 or for any scheme or order under it, and may recompense the Commissioners or the DBF for any monies expended by them on any property vested under the Pastoral Measure, or to further the disposal or use of that property.[46]

Every DBF must prepare an account of the monies paid into or out of the diocesan pastoral account during the year and a statement of the account at the year end, and must send a copy of the audited account to the Commissioners and lay a copy of it before the diocesan synod.[47] If there are insufficient funds to meet such expenditure the Commissioners may make an advance out of their General Fund and may subsequently transfer from that pastoral account into their general account the amount of the advance.[48]

Where it appears to the Commissioners, after consultation with the DBF, that certain monies in the account are not likely to be required for expenditure they must, at the request of the DBF, apply them by grant or loan to certain other purposes. These include the restoration, improvement or repair of churches and parsonage houses in the diocese (including redundant buildings vested in the DBF pending the coming into operation of a redundancy scheme),[49] or for the purposes of any benefice or parish in the diocese, or to another diocese generally or for such purposes as the DBF may specify. Alternatively the money may be transferred to the capital or income account of the diocesan stipends fund.[50]

[44] Church of England (Miscellanous Provisions) Measure 1978, s.5.
[45] Pastoral Measure 1983 s.77(1).
[46] *ibid.*, s.78(1), (2).
[47] *ibid.*, s.77(3), (4).
[48] *ibid.*, s.78(5).
[49] The Commissioners must hold a redundant churches temporary maintenance account and transfer monies payable into it. The funds may be applied to the repair and maintenance of any redundant building vested in the DBF pending the coming into operation of arrangements under a redundancy scheme: *ibid.*, s.78A(1).
[50] *ibid.*, s.78(3), (4). The DBF may only request transfer to an account not held and administered by the Commissioners with their consent: *ibid.*

Diocesan stipends funds

Pursuant to the Diocesan Stipends Fund Measure 1953 the Church Commis- **8.70** sioners maintain a capital and an income account for each diocese, the DBF being entitled to be furnished with the annual accounts.[51] All monies and property which the Commissioners hold and receive for each diocesan stipends fund must be allocated between the capital and income accounts,[52] although these are not credited directly to the account but held by the Commissioners as part of their General Fund and the accounts credited in lieu with a sum charged on that Fund.[53]

Subject to any charge on the income of the fund, money standing to the income account is to be applied in providing and augmenting the stipends or other emoluments of incumbents or assistant curates licensed under seal or other persons who are declared by the bishop to be engaged in the cure of souls within the diocese.[54] Any such application is to be in accordance with directions given by the bishop from time to time and with the concurrence of the DBF.[55] Subject to any charges imposed on it, money standing to the credit of the capital account may, on the request of the bishop with the concurrence of the DBF, be appropriated as an endowment fund held by the Commissioners for any benefice in the diocese or to augment such an endowment.[56] Provisions also exist for the transfer of endowments of benefices to the diocesan stipends funds and the charging of those funds with the payment of stipends and remuneration pursuant to pastoral schemes.[57]

Fees

The Church of England does acquire a small amount of income by means of fees. **8.71** In addition to the fees which the ecclesiastical courts and their officers are entitled to charge (which are considered in Chapter 2) the Ecclesiastical Fees Measure 1986 authorises the making of a Parochial Fees Order in respect of fees for certain offices.[58] A new procedure has been introduced whereby the Order is prepared by the Church Commissioners and laid before the General Synod for approval. It need not be debated if the Standing Committee so determines and no member insists upon a debate, and if it is approved without amendments the Commissioners must make the Order,[59] although it does not come into force until approved by Parliament and sealed by the Commissioners.

---

[51] Diocesan Stipends Fund Measure 1953, s.7.
[52] *ibid.*, s.2.
[53] *ibid.*, s.3.
[54] *ibid.*, s.5. It may also be applied to defraying sequestrator's expenses and in meeting the expenses incurred in repairing and maintaining parsonage houses: *ibid.*
[55] *ibid.*
[56] *ibid.*, s.4.
[57] Pastoral Measure 1983, s.37(k), (1).
[58] Ecclesiastical Fees Measure 1986, ss.1, 2.
[59] If amended the Commissioners may make the Order as amended or withdraw it for further consideration.

The Order[60] sets out the table of fees which are sometimes, in respect of weddings and funerals, referred to as surplice fees. These fees are payable in part to the incumbent[61] and in part to the PCC, although an incumbent may assign fees due to them by deed to the DBF, or give a direction, either generally or in a specific case, that the fee which is due to them should be paid to the minister who performs the service or duty.[62]

As we will see in Chapter 10 fees may not be charged for baptising, but a fee is payable for the issue of the baptismal certificate or a short certificate of baptism. A cutomary offering may also be due at the Churching of Women. Fees are payable in respect of the publication of banns and the certificate issued on publication, and for the solemnisation of matrimony. They are also payable for the conduct of a funeral service in church, for burial in the churchyard or cemetery, for cremation following such a service and for burial of a body or cremated remains on a separate occasion to the church service, in other words when the burial does not immediately follow after the service. Fees are payable where a service is held at the crematorium or cemetery instead of the church, or where a full service is held at the graveside. In the case of fees payable for a minister officiating at a burial which is not in the churchyard or church burial ground or at a crematorium the fees are fixed by the local authority or burial board rather than by the Fees Order. No fees are due for the burial of a still-born child or the funeral or burial of a child dying within a year after birth. A fee is payable for the erection of a monument and fees are payable, as we have seen, for searches to be made of parochial registers.

There appears to be no obligation to demand either the full fee or any fee referred to in the table. Practice varies between dioceses. Many clergy acting on guidance issued by the Church Commissioners[63] recognise a right to waive a fee where there is an acceptable pastoral reason, but others discourage the practice. Fees which are demanded may be recovered as a debt,[64] but no sacrament is to be denied on account of non-payment of money and matrimony must not be hindered or burial denied on account of non-payment of the fee.[65]

The quota system

8.72   The quota system may be regarded as a system of voluntary taxation.[66] Each diocese contributes funds to the Central Board of Finance, the Church Commissioners and the Pensions Board, their proportion being determined in accordance with a table of apportionment based on actual and potential income. approved bv the General Synod. The contribution of each diocese being based upon its income and the income of its parishes.[67]

[60] Parochial Fees Order, S.I. 1995 No. 1160.
[61] During a vacancy in the benefice the fees are payable to the DBF or such other person as the Board, in consultation with the bishop, directs.
[62] Parochial Fees Order, S.I. 1995 No. 1160, Pt II.
[63] Church Commissioners, *A Guide to Church of England Fees* (1986), which states that any departure from collecting fees as a general norm would be undesirable.
[64] Ecclesiastical Fees Measure 1986, s.7.
[65] *Halsbury's Laws of England* (4th ed.), Vol. 14, para. 1194. See also *Burn's Ecclesiastical Law* (4th ed. 1781), Vol. 1, p. 287; Vol. 2, p. 480.
[66] Briden and Hanson, *Moore's Introduction to English Canon Law* (2nd ed., 1992), p. 92.
[67] The annual report of the Central Board of Finance gives details of the current means of apportionment by the General Synod.

Although the income of each of its parishes has been taken into account in assessing its contribution to central funds each diocese has its own arrangements for determining the actual parish quotas or shares from which it derives its own income. Generally, after framing its annual budget the diocesan synod either apportions its expenditure amongst the parishes or delegates this to the deanery synods. The means of assessing parishes varies considerably. In some dioceses the apportionment is based on actual income or ability to pay, whilst in others it is based upon potential income as determined by such criteria as the average number of adults attending services regularly, or the numbers on the electoral roll. As we have seen, in some dioceses the quota takes into account the contribution of the parish to repairs to the parsonage house of the parish, a contribution which may be legally demanded. The quota apportionment itself is not legally enforceable,[68] but were a parish to withhold its share and were it proven that the PCC was not without funds to meet this it is likely that this fact would be taken into account were the PCC in need of diocesan loans or other funding.

Stipends and remuneration

As we have already seen in Chapter 7, the diocesan bishop is not to admit a **8.73** person to holy orders unless he is satisfied that they are provided with an ecclesiastical office. The purpose of this is to ensure that they are provided with a means of support since, except in the case of non-stipendary ministers, a stipend or remuneration is normally attached to an office. In addition as we also saw in that Chapter, a bishop must not licence a deaconess, reader or lay worker unless satisfied that arrangements have been made for the provision of a salary, insurance and retirement pension.

Stipends of parochial clergy

As we have already seen at present the Church Commissioners act as the **8.74** General Synod's Central Stipends Authority, although that function may pass to the proposed Archbishops' Council. The Commissioners also hold the diocesan stipends fund for each diocese, from which is met the cost of stipends and housing of stipendiary ministers in parochial appointments, in other words incumbents, priests-in-charge, team vicars and assistant curates.

Although the Commissioners recommend national maxima and minima for stipends it is the diocese which calculates and determines the actual stipend payable. The Commissioners must apply income standing to the credit of the diocesan stipends fund current account in providing or augmenting the stipends or other emoluments of incumbents, assistant curates licensed under seal and other persons declared by the bishop to be engaged in the cure of souls in the diocese.[69] The funds are to be applied in accordance with directions given from time to time by the bishop, with the concurrence of the DBF, although those

---

[68] See Doe, *The Legal Framework of the Church of England* (1996), pp. 479–482.
[69] Diocesan Stipends Fund Measure 1953, s.5.

directions must be consistent with any directions given by the Commissioners in exercise of their functions as the Central Stipends Authority with respect to the forms and level of pay.[70]

Despite the pooling of endowments to be held for the benefit of the diocesan stipends fund pursuant to the Endowments and Glebe Measure 1976, incumbents have the right to the endowment income generated by their benefice. The Commissioners must pay them a guaranteed annuity of the lesser of either the net annual endowment income of the benefice or one thousand pounds, from the diocesan stipends fund.[71] If the actual net income exceeds one thousand pounds an incumbent who was in office on April 1, 1978 is entitled to receive the excess as an annual personal grant.[72]

The Commissioners have the power to make a payment out of their General Fund towards the stipends of archdeacons who are entitled to an annual grant of not less than the amount payable as the endowment income of the arch-deaconry.[73] The Commissioners must also allocate to the income account of the diocesan stipends fund from their General Fund such sums as were applicable to the emoluments of assistant curates, clerical or lay assistants engaged in the cure of souls chargeable on that Fund.[74]

As we have seen incumbents are entitled to fees in respect of services or offices performed. They are also entitled to customary Easter offerings[75] and may be entitled to other customary offerings. Incumbents and other parochial clergy may also derive income from chaplaincies and other public and educational appointments, from local trusts and from direct parochial giving towards stipends (which ought to be channelled through the diocese and Church Commissioners). When calculating the augmentation grant payable to an incumbent or to any other minister from the diocesan stipends fund, all these sources of income, together with any guaranteed annuity or personal grant, are generally taken into account.

It should be noted that for the purposes of taxation and national insurance all clergy are classified as employed persons in receipt of emoluments.[76] Therefore they pay National Insurance Contributions and are consequently eligible for sickness, maternity and industrial injury benefits.

The episcopacy and cathedral clergy

8.75 An annual stipend is payable to the two archbishops and to diocesan bishops by the Church Commissioners pursuant to the Episcopal Endowment and Stipends Measure 1943, which also gives the Commissioners power to meet the expenses of bishops, and to pay part or whole of the stipend of any suffragan bishop or

---

[70] *ibid.*
[71] Endowments and Glebe Measure 1976, s.1.
[72] *ibid.*, s.2(1).
[73] *ibid.*, s.6.
[74] *ibid.*, s.8.
[75] *Book of Common Prayer*, rubric at end of the Administration of the Lord's Supper or Holy Communion; *Cooper v. Blakiston* [1907] 2 K.B. 688 at 700; [1909] A.C. 104, H.L. See also *Halsbury's Laws of England* (4th ed.), Vol. 14, para. 1207.
[76] *Re National Insurance Act 1911; Re Employment of Church of England Curates* [1911] 2 Ch. 563. The employment status of clergy generally is considered in Chap. 7.

chaplain to the bishop. Over the last decade the Commissioners have provided funds on a discretionary basis for suffragans' expenses, but the Turnbull report has recommended that this practice cease and dioceses (which already provide for the housing of such bishops), once again resume responsibility for their stipends (which would continue to be set nationally) and expenses, although, this proposal is now unlikely to be adopted.[77]

Pursuant to the Cathedrals Measure 1963 the Church Commissioners pay the stipends of the dean or provost and two residentiary canons of each cathedral. Provision is also made under that Measure for the payment of stipends, augmenations, grants, housing costs and expenses of cathedral staff.[78] As we have already seen it is proposed that in future the budgets in respect of these payments and those of the archbishops and bishops should be set by the new Archbishops' Council in consultation with a bishoprics committee.

Pensions

The Pensions Board

The Church of England Pensions Board which was established under the Clergy   **8.76** Pensions Measure 1926 is directly accountable to the General Synod to whom it submits annual reports.[79] The function of the Board is to control and manage the system of pensions established by the Pension Measures (as amended).[80] The Board, which is now in the main governed by the Clergy Pensions Measure 1961, is a body corporate with a chairman and 16 members elected by the General Synod and a further five members appointed by the Church Commissioners.[81]

The Church Commissioners make payments out of their General Fund to the Board for clergy pensions and for pensions for their widows, widowers and dependants. The Board is subordinate to the Commissioners who may give it directions of a general character regarding the performance of its functions, in order to secure a balance between the liability imposed on the Commissioners' General Fund and the resources of that Fund for meeting the liability.[82] Management of the Board's affairs is divided between its General Purposes, Housing and Residential Care and Investments and Finance Committees.

The Board administers the main pensions fund for clergy, together with a further four pension schemes, including a scheme for widows, widowers and dependants of clergy and schemes through which Church organisations make pension provisions for their lay employees. It is also empowered to provide housing for retired clergy, their spouses, widows and widowers. Housing assistance provided under the Church's Housing Assistance for the Retired Ministry

---

[77] *Working as One Body*, The Report of the Archbishops Commission on the Reorganisation of the Church of England (1995), Chap. 8. *Working as One Body: A Framework for Legislation*, (1996) (G.S. No. 1188).

[78] Cathedrals Measure 1963, ss.28–32.

[79] Clergy Pensions Measure 1961, s.34. From time to time the Treasury must appoint an auditor to audit the accounts of any fund or trust administered by the Board: *ibid*.

[80] *ibid*., s.24.

[81] *ibid*., s.21.

[82] *ibid*., s.25.

Scheme funded almost entirely by the Church Commissioners and the costs of running residential and nursing homes are a major expense for the Board.

It has now been acknowledged that the current system whereby pensions are funded by the Church Commissioners cannot continue.[83] Contributions towards pensions in respect of future service will come from the dioceses and be paid into a newly established pension fund. The Turnbull Report proposed that the Pensions Board itself be reconstituted in line with the Pensions Act 1995 which was enacted following the recommendations of the Goode Report.

The new arrangements[84] will mean that the Church Commissioners' existing liability for past service, including service increments will continue but will be limited to that liability alone, although they will make contributions to the new funds. The Commissioners will be empowered to use their capital for pension purposes. It is possibile that their liability in respect of past service will ultimately be met by a transfer of assets to the reconstituted pensions board. The new Pensions Board will comply with the terms of the Pensions Act 1995 and in particular sponsors and members of the pensions scheme will be represented on its governing body. The Board should consist of 15 trustees of whom one-third will be representative of scheme members.[85]

In regard to pensions there will be two separate schemes, one for past and one for future service, the latter being a funded scheme. The funds for the future service scheme will come from the dioceses, through funds raised in the parishes. Because of the significant impact of these contributions on parishes and dioceses, a phased transition for the new system will be initiated, with the expectation that it will be fully operational by 1998.

Entitlement to pensions

8.77 Under the amended Clergy Pensions Measure 1961[86] any clerk in holy orders, a deaconess or a licensed lay worker, referred to as a scheme member, has a right upon their retirement to receive from the Church Commissioners a pension for the remainder of their lives.[87] The Measure also makes provision for the payment of pensions to the widows, widowers and children of scheme members.[88] Contributions are not payable in respect of these pensions by the scheme members. Subject to pensions for service from 1998 being payable out of a fund sponsored by the diocese, it is not envisaged that the new proposals for pensions will affect entitlement.

The right to a pension only arises if a scheme member has completed a period of qualifying pensionable service of not less than two years, or a succession of

---

[83] *Financing Clergy Pensions* (G.S. 1172). See also *Working as One Body*, The Report of the Archbishops Commission on the Reorganisation of the Church of England (1955), Chap. 9.

[84] A draft Measure has been produced.

[85] They would consist of a bishop elected by the House of Bishops, a representative lay employee and three clergy elected by the House of Clergy of the General Synod.

[86] Principally by the Church of England (Pensions) Measure 1988.

[87] Clergy Pensions Measure 1961, s.1(1). Provision is made for the suspension or reduction of pensions in cases where the scheme member who is otherwise entitled to a pension accepts certain ecclesiastical offices or where they perform pensionable service: *ibid.*, s.4.

[88] *ibid.*, s.10, 10A

periods with or without intervals amounting to not less than two years.[89] Qualifying pensionable service means stipendary ecclesiastical service, which is defined as service rendered under the direction of a diocesan bishop or carried out in the furtherance of the sprirtual or administrative work of the church recognised as such by a diocesan bishop.[90]

The right to the pension accrues and its rate is fixed, by reference to office and term of years served and may be augmented at the discretion of the Commissioners.[91] Where a person retires prior to their reaching the retiring age, and such a retirement is made upon the grounds that they have become incapable because of infirmity from carrying out the duties of their office, the right to the pension will accrue if the Board is satisfied, after considering medical evidence, that the infirmity is permanent.[92] Any person who is dissatisfied with the decision of the Board regarding the permanent nature of their infirmity has a right of appeal to a Board of two or more referees appointed by the Pensions Board whose decision is final.[93]

Other questions relating to pensions, such as whether pensionable service has been performed, its length, the date of retirement, and the rights of widows, widowers and dependants, are to be determined by the Pensions Board, but with a right of appeal to the High Court whose decision is final.[94]

---

[89] *ibid.*, s.1(2). In exceptional cases the Church Commissioners may substitute a shorter period: *ibid.*

[90] *ibid.*, (s.112).

[91] Clergy Pensions Measure 1961, s.2.

[92] Clergy Pensions Measure 1961, s.3. In the cases of retirement on grounds of incapacity the pension may be reduced if the scheme member takes up, or is capable of taking up, secular employment: Church of England Pensions Regulations 1988, S.I. 1988 No. 2256.

[93] *ibid.*, s.3.

[94] Clergy Pensions Measure 1961, s.38.

Chapter Nine:
Doctrine and Worship

Worship is central to the life of the Church of England, which expresses and **9.1** organises its public worship principally through formal liturgies. The doctrine of the Church of England upon which all such worship is based is embedded in the Church's liturgies, and many doctrinal disputes within the Church of England have been conducted in regard to worship. Such disputes have tended to be concerned with matters of ritual and ceremonial, most notably in the nineteenth century when the emergence of the high church Oxford Movement and the contemporaneous revival of Evangelicalism led to considerable dispute over such matters as church order and liturgy. However, this century has seen a change in approach to such questions, greater tolerance now being afforded to the various opinions held within the Church. As the Church of England approaches the twenty-first century not only has there been a move towards greater diversity in matters of worship amongst its own membership but also towards ecumenical worship, a subject considered in Chapter 12.

In this chapter we consider the doctrine of the Church of England, its sources, the Church's power to alter that doctrine and the degree of tolerance which the Church extends to its members in doctrinal matters. We examine the principle of conformity of worship which has taken the place of the uniformity imposed following the Reformation, and the authorised liturgies which may be utilised today. We also look at the extent to which permissible departures may be made from these liturgies and the ability of the Church and its ministers to create liturgies where no provision is otherwise made. Matters of ritual and ceremonial are examined as are issues relating to the ornaments and decoration of churches, subjects which are closely allied. Finally we consider the vestments of ministers. The sacraments and offices of the Church themselves form the subject-matter of Chapter 10.

Doctrine

As with its canon law the doctrine of the Church of England is that of the **9.2** Western Catholic Church immediately before the Reformation, subject to modifications both explicit and implicit introduced by the Reformation. The Church of England is a reformed Catholic, and in that sense a "protestant" church, the term "Catholic" being applied to all those churches which maintain the faith and traditions of the Creeds, the Ecumenical Councils and the Church Fathers, together with the practice of the Sacraments and the Episcopate in historical succession from the Apostles.

The Church of England's doctrine is stated in Canon A5 to be "grounded in the Holy Scriptures and in such teachings of the ancient fathers and Councils of the Church as are agreeable to the said Scriptures. In particular such doctrine is to be found in the Thirty-nine Articles of Religion,[1] the Book of Common Prayer[2] and the Ordinal."[3] Any references to doctrine in the Church of England (Worship and Doctrine) Measure 1974 are to be construed in accordance with this statement.[4] To these pre-Reformation formularies and three post-Reformation sources may be added the Canons of 1603, Acts of Parliament and Measures of the Church Assembly and the General Synod, and judgments of the Courts, all of which provide authoritative statements of doctrine, not necessarily right, but binding until altered.[5]

However, although in ascertaining the doctrine of the Church recourse may be made to judgments of the courts as authoritative, these judgments "do not declare doctrine" but extend only to a "consideration of that which is by law established to be the doctrine of the Church of England upon the true and legal construction of the articles and formularies."[6] The extent to which this classic view of the role of the courts is true in practice is a matter of debate. On occasion the Courts have clarified doctrine or settled a doctrinal dispute, a recent example being the judgment of the Court of Ecclesiastical Causes Reserved which determined that a structure which may be referred to as an altar as opposed to a table was permissible in the light of doctrinal developments.[7]

In addition to authoritative sources of doctrine there are others of persuasive authority. These include Acts of Convocations and of the General Synod together with resolutions of these bodies, resolutions of the Lambeth Conference, reports of various commissions and subordinate bodies of the General Synod[8] and in particular the Doctrine Commission. This last Commission is empowered to advise the House of Bishops on doctrinal matters referred to it by that House and to suggest to the General Synod what in its judgment constitutes

[1] The full title of which is "Articles agreed upon by the Archbishops and Bishops of both Provinces and the Whole Clergy in the Convocation holden at London in the year 1562 for the avoidance of Diversities of Opinions and for the Establishing of Consent touching True Religion".
[2] The full title of which is "The Book of Common Prayer and Administration of the Sacraments and other Rites and Ceremonies of the Church according to the Use of the Church of England together with the Psalter or Psalms of David pointed as they are to be sung or said in Churches." This is the definition used in the Church of England (Worship and Doctrine) Measure 1974, with the addition of the words "as altered or amended by an Act or Measure or in accordance with s.1(7) of this Measure:" *ibid.*, s.5(2).
[3] Canon A5.
[4] Church of England (Worship and Doctrine) Measure 1974, s.5(1).
[5] *Moore's Introduction to English Canon Law* (3rd ed., 1992), pp. 49–50.
[6] *Goreham v. Bishop of Exeter* [1850] *Moore's Special Report* 462. See however, *Re St Thomas, Pennywell* [1995] 2 W.L.R. 154 at 160–161 regarding the current status of the Thirty-nine Articles.
[7] *Re St Stephen's, Walbrook* [1987] Fam. 146, as to which see Chap. 10.
[8] See in particular *Doctrine in the Church of England*, the report of the Archbishops' Commission on Christian Doctrine appointed 1922 (1938); *Subscription and Assent to the Thirty-nine Articles*, the Report of the Archbishops' Commission On Christian Doctrine (1968); *The Nature of Christian Belief,* Statement and Exposition by the House of Bishops of the General Synod of the Church of England (1986).

doctrinal issues of concern to the Church of England and to exchange information and advice in doctrinal matters with other Christian churches.[9] Statements
issued by the House of Bishops are also of considerable importance. The
Turnbull Commission has endorsed the practice of the House of Bishops in
issuing papers on doctrine and recommends that it also issues pastoral letters
from time to time.[10]

Although the General Synod is not the only body competent to declare, nor **9.3**
arguably to develop, persuasive doctrine, the declaration of doctrine is restricted
to centralised bodies of the Church or to the courts. As we have seen although
diocesan and deanery synods and PCCs may discuss matters of religious interest
they may not issue any statement purporting to declare the doctrine of the
Church of England.

As the Established Church, the Church of England requires the legislative
sanction of State to effect an alteration in its doctrine. Although it is freedom
from the control of the State which differentiates a voluntary association from an
established church, in regard to the alteration of its doctrine the church of
England has greater freedom than many of the non-established churches which
have fettered themselves to such an extent by the manner in which they came
into being, that they cannot seek to alter their doctrines.[11]

State approval has been given to the alteration of the doctrine of the Church
of England through the enactment of the SGM and Church of England (Worship
and Doctrine) Measure 1974.[12] The doctrines of the Church as set forth in Canon
A5 may themselves only be altered by an amendment to that 1974 Measure but
nonetheless it has been accepted by the courts that the General Synod has an
unlimited power to alter the fundamental doctrines of the Church provided the
correct procedures are followed.[13] As we have seen special procedures exist in
relation to provisions touching upon doctrinal formulae before they may receive
the final approval of the General Synod.[14] Further, all Canons, regulations, form
of service or amendments thereto are to be such as are in the opinion of the
General Synod neither contrary to, nor indicative of, any departure from the
doctrine of the Church of England in any essential matter (the final approval of
the Synod being conclusive evidence that Synod is of that opinion).[15]

There is no general obligation upon the laity to assent to the doctrine of the
Church of England, although an assent is required liturgically from those seeking
baptism, confirmation and Holy Communion. However, as we have seen clergy
and lay ministers are required to make the declaration of assent to the doctrine
and faith of the Church of England on ordination and admission to office.

---

[9] *General Synod, Board and Council Constitutions 1996–2001* (G.S. Misc. 460).
[10] *Working as One Body*, the Report of the Archbishops' Commission on the Organisation
of the Church of England (1995).
[11] This was the situation in *General Assembly of the Free Church of Scotland v. Lord
Overtoun* [1904] A.C. 515, H.L. where a small minority of members of the Free Church
successfully established a breach of trust in relation to church assets when the proposal
of the majority of its members to unite with another church involved a change of
doctrine.
[12] *Halsbury's Laws of England* (4th ed.), Vol. 14, paras. 335, 935.
[13] *R. Ecclesiastical Committee of Both Houses of Parliament, ex p. the Church Society, The
Times*, November 4, 1993.
[14] See Chap. 2.
[15] Church of England (Worship and Doctrine) Measure 1974, s.4(1), (2).

Furthermore the bishops are under a canonical duty to uphold the faith, but are also said to be guardians "of the process of exploration as well as of received truths".[16]

As we shall see in Chapter 11 proceedings may be commenced against the slergy for offences in regard to matters of doctrine. Nonetheless in doctrinal matters the law permits a considerable degree of liberty,[17] and where two interpretations are possible either is permissible. Further there are many matters upon which the formularies are silent and much is therefore left to the conscience of the individual. In England it is generally in the outward expression of doctrine, that is public worship, rather than in exposition of doctrine itself, that the greatest controversies have arisen and where heterodoxy has been challenged, and it is with worship and related matters that the remainder of this chapter is concerned.

Worship[18]

9.4   The architects of the Reformation settlement sought to attain theological unity by the imposition of uniformity. In 1549, in the reign of Edward VI following greater liturgical reform than that undertaken in the reign of Henry VIII, the first English Book of Common Prayer was published and its use made compulsory. Three years later a second Prayer Book was introduced and it is this second book which was reintroduced with important alterations by Elizabeth I following the repeal of the Edwardian enactments and the reintroduction of the Latin rite by Queen Mary. This Prayer Book was subject to further revision in the reign of James I following the Hampton Court Conference in 1604. Further amendments were made to incorporate the reforms of Archbishop Laud and it was reintroduced on the restoration of the monarchy as the Book of Common Prayer after its use was forbidden during the Commonwealth.[19] Subject to minor amendments this Book of Common Prayer has remained in use to the present day.

The principle of uniformity in worship meant that all ministers were required to adhere to the forms of service contained in the Book of Common Prayer and no form or order of common prayers, administration of sacraments, rites or ceremonies was to be openly used other than that which was prescribed in that book.[20]

The principle of conformity

9.5   No variation was permitted from those forms of service contained in the Book of Common Prayer until 1872 when the Act of Uniformity Amendment Act came onto the statute book. Although by the twentieth century attempts were made to

---

[16] *The Nature of Christian Belief*, Statement and Exposition by the House of Bishops of the General Synod of the Church of England (1986) para. 67.

[17] *Goreham v. Bishop of Exeter, (supra)*; *Sheppard v. Bennett* [1871] L.R. 4 P.C. 371 at 408; *Williams v. Bishop of Salisbury* [1863] 2 Moo. P.C. 375.

[18] See Bursell, *Liturgy, Order and the Law* (1996) for a detailed exposition of matters relating to worship.

[19] Act of Uniformity 1662, s.1 (repealed).

[20] Act of Uniformity 1662, s.13 (repealed).

supplement the Book of Common Prayer with alternative forms of liturgy (the rejected Prayer Books of 1927 and 1928 gaining widespread use despite their unlawfulness) it was not until 1965 that alternative forms of service could be authorised. Following the enactment of the Prayer Book (Alternative and Other Services) Measure 1965[21] the principle of uniformity has been replaced by the principle of conformity. Variations are now permitted to the extent that other forms of service are authorised or the minister has a discretion to vary their forms.

Authorisation and alteration of forms of service

The Church of England (Worship and Doctrine) Measure 1974, enabled the General Synod to make provision with respect to worship by Canon, including the power to approve or amend (either for a limited period which may be extended or without limit), continue or discontinue forms of service.[22] Form of service for these purposes includes any order, service, prayer, rite or ceremony whatsoever, including the services for ordination of priests and deacons and consecration of bishops and the catechism or form of instruction before confirmation.[23] The Alternative Service Book 1980 was authorised pursuant to Canon under this procedure.[24] Synod was also empowered under the 1974 Measure to make provision by Canon or regulation for any matter, except the publication of banns of matrimony, to which any of the rubrics contained in the Book of Common Prayer relate;[25] Such Canons or regulations are effective notwithstanding anything inconsistent contained within any of those rubrics.[26]

9.6

The term rubrics derives from the red ink in which the rubrics were and often are still printed, and includes all directions, instructions, tables, prefaces, rules, calendars and other contents of the Book of Common Prayer.[27] However, no amendment or revocation of any of the rubrics effected by any Act or Measure

---

[21] Now repealed: Church of England (Worship and Doctrine) Measure 1974, s.6(3), Sched. 2.

[22] Church of England (Worship and Doctrine) Measure 1974, s.1(1)(a); Canon B2(1). Such approval, amendment, continuance or discontinuance requires a special majority in each House of the General Synod, as to which see Chap. 2.

[23] Church of England (Worship and Doctrine) Measure 1974, s.5(2)

[24] In 1947 the Archbishops issued an abridged version of the Book of Common Paryer incorporating elements of the 1928 Prayer Book. Following the enactment of the Prayer Book (Alternative and Other Services) Measure 1965 the 1947 forms of service appeared as Series 1 in 1966. These together with Series 2 from 1973–8 together form the ASB. Those parts of the ASB authorised under Canon B2 from the date of its publication to 2000 are the services together with the calendars, rules to order the service and the lectionary: ASB. The versions of the psalter authorised for use in conjunction with the ASB are the Prayer Book Psalter, the Revised Pslater, the Liturgical Psalter and the Grail Psalter: ASB, p. 8.

[25] Church of England (Worship and Doctrine) Measure 1974, s.1(1)(b). The powers are wide ranging and the question as to whether any alteration to the Book of Common Prayer or the Ordinal could be made other than in accordance with the 1974 Measure has never been answered: *ex p. Williamson, The Times* March 9, 1994.

[26] Church of England (Worship and Doctrine) Measure 1974, s.1(2).

[27] Church of England (Worship and Doctrine) Measure 1974, s.5(2).

which was itself repealed by the 1974 Measure is affected by that repeal.[28] The provisions in the 1974 Measure have the effect that the rubrics in all authorised forms of service are to be regarded as having equal force.[29]

The Prayer Book is protected since the General Synod's powers[30] must be exercised so as to ensure that the forms of service contained within it continue to be available for use.[31] However, any Canon or regulation made by the General Synod has effect notwithstanding that anything inconsistent with it is contained in any of the rubrics of the Book of Common Prayer.[32]

The Prayer Book (Alternative and Other Services) Measure 1965 gave the Church Assembly power to approve forms of experimental service but did not permit alteration of services set out in the Book of Common Prayer. However, in 1973 the General Synod purported to authorise a code of rules "to order the service" for inclusion in the Book of Common Prayer, and these still remain technically without authority, notwithstanding various subsequent legislative developments.[33]

Provision has been made by the General Synod for the authorisation of proposed new forms of service for experimental periods.[34] Where a form of service is in the course of preparation with a view to its submission to Synod for approval under Canon the archbishops may, after consultation with the House of Bishops, authorise that draft form for experimental use for a period specified by them on such terms and in such places or parishes (so that the congregation consists only of such persons as the archbishops permit) as only they may designate.[35]

Authorised forms of service

9.7 The forms of service now authorised for use in the Church of England are those contained in the Book of Common Prayer, the shortened forms of Morning and Evening Prayer which were set out in the Schedule to the Act of Uniformity Amendment Act 1872,[36] the form authorised by Royal warrant for use on the anniversary of the accession of the reigning sovereign and any forms approved under Canon subject to any amendments so approved,[37] which as we have seen includes the ASB. They also include the *Ministry of the Sick* (1982), *A Service of the Word and Affirmations of Faith* (1993) and the *Series 1 Solemnisation of*

---

[28] *ibid.*, s.6(4), Sched. 3, para. 4.
[29] This view was expressed in *Re St Peter & St Paul, Leckhampton* [1968] P. 495 in respect of The Alternative Services (2nd series).
[30] *i.e.* pursuant to Church of England (Worship and Doctrine) Measure 1974, s.1(1).
[31] *ibid.* Church of England (Worship and Doctrine) Measure 1974, s.1(2).
[32] *ibid.*
[33] See Bursell *Liturgy, Order and the Law* (1996), pp. 6–8.
[34] Church of England (Worship and Doctrine) Measure 1974, s.1(6); Canon B5A.
[35] Church of England (Worship and Doctrine) Measure 1974, s.1(6); Canon B5A.
[36] These shortened forms may be used notwithstanding repeal of the Act itself by the Church of England (Worship and Doctrine) Measure 1974, s.6(3), Sched. 2: *ibid.*, s.6(4), Sched. 3, para. 3. Originally for use on Sundays and certain other days these forms are now authorised for use on any day.
[37] Canon B1(1).

Matrimony and *Burial Services* and *Series 2*[37a] *Baptism and Confirmation Services*, all of which are authorised until the year 2000.[38] Canon B1 requires ministers to have a good understanding of the forms of service used.

In principle each of the forms of service should be regarded as separate and distinct. A form of service which is an amalgam of the Book of Common Prayer and the ASB should not be used save where express provision is made in one form of service for the borrowing of material from another or when the amalgam is not a matter of "substantial importance".[39]

There are also a number of services and other liturgical material which is additional, rather than alternative, to the Book of Common Prayer, the use of which has been commended by the House of Bishops of the General Synod.[39a]

Observance of the rubrics[40]

Until the latter half of the twentieth century the courts had held that all the **9.8** directions in the rubrics of the Book of Common Prayer have the full force of statutory provisions and were to be observed strictly without addition, omission or alteration and without any distinction being made between those things which appear to be important and those which seem trivial.[41] Such pronouncements are of doubtful relevance today due to the repeal, by the Church of England (Worship and Doctrine) Measure 1974, of those provisions of the Act of Uniformity 1662 from which the rubrics derive their force.[42] Even the Book of Common Prayer itself recognised that doubt may arise as to its use and practice, and made provision for referral to the diocesan bishop in cases of doubt.[43]

The view has been expressed that whilst the Book of Common Prayer has statutory authority it should not be construed as a statute and that its rubrics whilst binding must be interpreted in the light of the fact that they are clerical

---

[37a] The Series 1, 2 and 3 services appeared between 1965 and 1980. Although authority was gradually withdrawn from many of them, where they have continued with uninterrupted use in a church or congregation the House of Bishops will regard this use (as opposed to introduction) as a minor variation permissible under canon law: *Public Worship in the Church of England: A Guide to the Law Governing Worship and Doctrine in the Church of England* (6th ed. 1994).

[38] A new Alternative Service Book will be produced to succeed the current ASB as part of a programme generally known as "ASB 2000", under the direction of the Liturgical Commission. A list of the forms of service authorised or commended for use is found in guidance issued by the Standing Committee of the General Synod, *Public Worship in the Church of England: A Guide to the Law Governing Worship and Doctrine in the Church of England* (6th ed. 1994).

[39] *Legal Opinions*, p. 234.

[39a] Such commendation means that the House of Bishops regard this material as being capable of being authorised by a diocesan bishop for use pursuant to Canon B4(3), and if a diocesan bishop makes no direction then ministers may make use of them pursuant to Canon B5(2), matters which are discussed below.

[40] See further Bursell *Liturgy, Order and the Law* (1996), pp. 11–17.

[41] *Martin v. Mackonochie* (1868) L.R. 2 P.C. 365 at 382, 383.

[42] And with the repeal of Canon 14 of the canons of 1603 which enjoined strict observance at the rubrics.

[43] *Book of Common Prayer*, Concerning the Service of the Church.

directives written in the seventeenth century and the elasticity which directives generally require applies to them.[44] In line with this approach the courts have held that a rigorous interpretation should no longer be applied in relation to either the Book of Common Prayer or the ASB.[45]

However, not all rubrics are to be regarded as mere directives, and others which appear only once are to be regarded as applying throughout the whole of the Prayer Book or at least to be indicative of the position in regard to other rites, such as matters of church order.[46] In cases of doubt the matter should be referred to the diocesan bishop.

Occasions for which no provision for forms of service is made

9.9   Pursuant to its powers the General Synod has also made provision by Canon for empowering the Convocations, archbishops and diocesan bishops to approve forms of service for use in any cathedral or church on occasions for which no provision is made by forms of service in the Book of Common Prayer or approved by the General Synod. In addition in the case of the archbishops or any bishop no such form of service must have been approved by Convocation, and in the case of a bishop by the archbishops.[47]

Such a service might for example be for a coronation or national day of thanksgiving. All such forms of services are subject to the requirement that they are neither contrary to, nor indicative of, any departure from the doctrine of the Church of England in any essential matter and must be reverent and seemly.[48]

Provision has also been made to enable the minister having the cure of souls, but not other ministers, to make and to use forms of service considered by them to be suitable on occasions for which no provision is made by the General Synod, Convocations, the archbishops or the bishop and to permit another minister to use such forms.[49] Such forms of service are subject to the same requirements as those made by convocations and the Archbishops and bishops,[50] and any question raised concerning the observance of these must be referred to the bishop in order that he may give such pastoral guidance, advice or directions as he thinks fit.[51]

Permitted variations

9.10   The General Synod has also made provision enabling any minister conducting a service in their discretion to make and use variations which are not of substantial importance in the forms of service contained in the Book of Common Prayer and

---

[44] *St Michael & All Angels, Bishopswearmouth* [1958] 1 W.L.R. 1183 at 1187.
[45] *Re St Thomas, Pennywell* [1995] 2 W.L.R. 154 at 166–168; *Re St John the Evangelist, Chopwell* [1995] Fam. 254.
[46] *Re St Thomas, Pennywell ante* 168–169.
[47] Church of England (Worship and Doctrine) Measure 1974, s.1(5)(a); Canon B4.
[48] Church of England (Worship and Doctrine) Measure 1974, s.4(3); Canon B4.
[49] Church of England (Worship and Doctrine) Measure 1974, s.1(5)(b); Canon B5(1), (2).
[50] Church of England (Worship and Doctrine) Measure 1974, s.4(3); Canon B5(3).
[51] Canon B5(4). Such referral is without prejudice to any proceedings which may be taken under the EJM: *ibid*. The Canon does not identify who may make such a referral nor is referral obligatory.

those forms approved by Synod, Convocations, the archbishops or bishops.[52] It is far from clear what would constitute a variation which is not of "substantial importance", but in cases of doubt the matter may be referred to the bishop in advance of the variation being effected and in practice little difficulty appears to have arisen.[53]

It has been suggested that in seeking to determine whether or not a variation is of substantial importance some guidance may be derived from comparing the rubrics in the Book of Common Prayer with other forms of authorised services; matters in respect of which mandatory directions are given in the former but not in the latter are generally regarded as not of substantial importance.[54] However, this approach must be applied with care and there may be instances, for example manual acts at Holy Communion which, so far as the Book of Common Prayer is concerned, are difficult to justify because of the history of that rite.[55] In determining what are matters of substantial importance the Legal Advisory Board is of the opinion that regard must be had to current practice. Thus, for example, a complete rendering of the Order for the Administration of Holy Communion contained in the Book of Common Prayer is rare and the well established variations such as the omission of the exhortation may be regarded as not of substantial importance.[56]

The provision enabling ministers to make limited variations to forms of service is an extension of the general proposition regarding matters which are *de mininis*.[57] Thus the law recognises[58] that a matter may be so insignificant or trifling that it ought not to become the subject of litigation,[59] and minor alterations including omissions from the forms of services which are not strictly permissible are not to be regarded as falling within the ambit of an ecclesiastical offence, at least if not habitual.[60]

A minister must use only the forms of service so authorised save to the extent that they are permitted to use their discretion.[61] When making the declaration of assent each minister promises that they will in public prayer and in the administration of the sacraments use only the forms of service which are authorised or allowed by Canon. However, the declaration allows for the possibility that in truly private services the authorised forms need not be followed.[62]

---

[52] Church of England (Worship and Doctrine) Measure 1974, s.1(5)(b), Canon B5(1), (2).

[53] The matter is often dealt with in diocesan norms which state that there is no authority to adapt beyond the limit of the alternatives provided within the authroised text: Doe, *The Legal Framework of the Church of England*, (1996) p. 300.

[54] *Re St Thomas, Pennywell* [1995] 2 W.L.R. 154 at 170; *Halsbury's Laws of England* (4th ed.), Vol. 14, para. 941, n. 1.

[55] For a consideration of some of the difficulties see *Re St John the Evagelist, Chopwell* [1995] Fam. 254.

[56] *Legal Opinions*, p. 235.

[57] See further Bursell, *Liturgy, Order and the Law* (1996), pp. 35–42.

[58] *Re St Mary, Tyne Dock* [1954] P. 369 at 382; *Re St John the Evangelist* [1995] Fam. 254.

[59] *Julius v. Bishop of Oxford* (1880) 5 App. Cas. 14 at 226.

[60] *Bennett v. Bonaker* (1828) 2 Hag. Ecc. 25 at 28.

[61] Canon B1(2). The problems this causes in regard to ecumenical services are considered in Chap. 12.

[62] Save in saying Morning and Evening Prayer as required by Canon C26(1) when the authorised services must be used.

This raises the question of what constitutes private prayer. In part the answer will depend upon the circumstances. If a minister reads prayers to their family and household this would contitute private prayer but the reading of services of the Church and possibly the reading of prayers where a person who is not strictly a member of the household is present is likely to go beyond the ambit of private prayer.[63]

Under the previous form of the declaration of assent a minister promised that they would use the forms prescribed by the Prayer Book and none other "except so far as shall be ordered by lawful authority". With the enactment of the Church of England (Worship and Doctrine) Measure 1974, and Canons pursuant to it which no longer make reference to lawful authority, the debate as to its meaning and the extent to which it may justify departures from the authorised forms of service may be regarded as at an end, save in one respect namely the question of the *jus liturgicum* of the archbishops and bishops.

The jus liturgicum[64]

9.11 The controversy over lawful authority overlaps with the question of the *jus liturgicum* of the archbishops and bishops, that is their right to authorise what would otherwise be unlawful. The extent to which this doctrine, which formed part of pre-Reformation canon law, survived the Reformation and the extent to which it now survives is a matter of uncertainty. The issue was of particular concern prior to the revision of the Canons of 1603 and was widely debated following Parliament's rejection of the proposed Prayer Book in 1928.

Since there is no power to override forms of service authorised by statute, Measure or Canon, it is clear that the *jus liturgicum* has been limited by the Reformation settlement. Thus there can be no legal validity in the exercise of the alleged episcopal discretion to allow the use of the deposited Prayer Book of 1928.[65] The decision taken by the bishops to do precisely this in 1929 could not be effective in any case where provision was made by the only lawful Prayer Book, that is the Book of Common Prayer. It would appear however that the *jus liturgicum* survives in regard to liturgical matters over which no provision is made.[66] Thus authorisation of forms from the 1928 Prayer Book or elsewhere would be a lawful exercise of the power, which has now to a large extent been expressly provided for in Canon B4. This also suggests that it survives in regard to the bishops' discretion to settle matters of doubt arising in regard to the Book of Common Prayer.[67]

Necessity

9.12 Departures from the authorised forms of service have also been justified on the basis of the doctrine of necessity. This doctrine was of wider scope in pre-Reformation canon law than in the common law of England and the extent to

[63] *Freeland v. Neale* (1848) 1 R.b. Eccl. 643 at 649, 651.
[64] See further Bursell *Liturgy, Order and the Law* (1996), App. 3; The memorandum on "Lawful Authority" by Vaisey J. in the *Report of the Archbishops' Commission on the Canon Law of the Church of England* (1947); Doe, *The Legal Framework of the Church of England*, (1996) pp. 301–2.
[65] Briden and Hanson *Moore's Introduction to English Canon Law* (3rd ed. 1992) p. 58.
[66] *Martin v. Mackonochie* [1868] L.R. 2 A. & E. 116 at 194.
[67] Bursell *Liturgy, Order and the Law* (1996), pp. 5, 31.

which it has survived the Reformation is a matter of some doubt. However, the doctrine is one known to all branches of English law,[68] and has been recognised in a number of ecclesiastical authorities.[69] Until the introduction of the provisions discussed above enabling departures from the forms of service which are not of substantial importance, this doctrine would have been the only lawful authority under which a priest could administer Holy Communion according to the rite set out in the Book of Common Prayer to a person who was unable by reason of infirmity to kneel, as required by the rubrics.[70]

Such a doctrine would enable a minister to stop taking a service due to their own illness or that of a member of the congregation, or to administer baptism to a dying infant or communion to a baptised and dying person, the latter two cases being mandatory obligations enjoined by Canon in any event.[71] The doctrine might in certain situations such as the exigencies of war, enable a priest to substitute army biscuits for bread or wafers.[72] However, the doctrine of necessity would not enable a lay person to attempt to concentrate the elements in order to administer Holy Communion to a dying person notwithstanding the urgent necessity of administering that sacrament.[73] The sacrament of baptism by contrast may as we shall see be administered by a lay person in an emergency.[74]

Decision as to which forms of service are to be used

The decision as to which of the forms of authorised service, other than the **9.13** occasional offices,[75] are to be used in any church in a parish are to be taken jointly by the minister[76] and the PCC.[77] If there is any disagreement as to which of the authorised services are to be used, so long as the disagreement continues the forms contained in the Book of Common prayer must be used, unless other authorised forms of service were in regular use in the church during at least two of the last four years immediately preceding the date when the disagreement arose and the PCC resolves that those forms are to be used either to the exclusion of or in addition to the forms in the Prayer Book.[78] However, it should

---

[68] See further Doe *The Legal Framework of the Church of England* (1996), p. 49.
[69] See *Beddoe v. Hawkes* (1888) 4 T.L.R. 315; *Hutchins v. Denziloe and Loveland* (1792) 1 Hag. Con. 170; *Rector and Churchwardens of Bishopswearmouth v. Adey* [1958] 1 W.L.R. 1183. For a detailed discussion of the authorities see Bursell, *Liturgy, Order and the Law* (1996), pp. 42–7.
[70] Briden and Hanson *Moore's Introduction to English Canon Law* (3rd ed. 1992) p. 58.
[71] Canon B22(6) requires a minister not to refuse or delay when asked to go and baptise an infant which is weak or in danger of death whilst Canon B15A(1)(d) requires admission to Holy Communion of all who are baptised and in danger of death.
[72] A number of similar examples which occurred during the Second World War are cited by Bursell, *Liturgy, Order and the Law* (1996), p. 44, n. 98.
[73] *Escott v. Martin* (1842) 4 Moo. P.C.C. 104 at 128.
[74] See Chap. 10.
[75] As to the meaning of which see Chap. 10.
[76] Although the Church of England (Worship and Doctrine) Measure 1974 s.1(3)(a) refers to "incumbent" this is defined so as to extend to ministers who are licensed to the charge of a parish or acting as priest-in-charge and a vicar in a team ministry to the extent that the rights of an incumbent are assigned to them: *ibid.*, 5(2).
[77] *ibid.*, s.1(3)(a); Canon B3(1). And in a guild church by the vicar and council: *ibid.*
[78] Church of England (Worship and Doctrine) Measure 1974, s.1(3)(b); Canon B3(2).

be noted that these provisions do not apply to a cathedral or to any part of a cathedral which is a parish church.[79]

Occasional offices

9.14   In the case of the occasional offices, other than the order of confirmation, the decision as to which form is to be used where more than one is authorised is to be made by the minister who is to conduct the service.[80] However, if one of the persons concerned objects beforehand to the form selected and they and the minister cannot agree as to the form to be used, the matter must be referred to the diocesan bishop for his decision.[81] There is no definition of "persons concerned", and whilst this would clearly extend to the couple being married or to the parents or godparents of an infant being baptised it is unclear where the limits are to be drawn and will depend upon the circumstances. A minister who is to take such service (particularly that of the solemnisation of matrimony) would be advised to consult those who appear to them to be the persons concerned well in advance so that agreement may be reached or the bishop's decision obtained.

The decision as to which form of service is to be used for a service of confirmation is to be made by the bishop or archbishop who is to conduct the service, after consultation with the minister of the church where the service is to be held.[82] The bishop or archbishop who is to conduct the ordination of deacons or priests or the consecration of a bishop must likewise decide which form of service to use but without the necessity for any consultation.[83]

Lectionary

9.15   Various changes have been made in regard to the portions of scripture prescribed for use at Morning and Evening Prayer. The Prayer Book (Tables of Lessons) Act 1871 introduced new tables of lessons and directions concerning both lessons and psalms. These lessons and psalms may be substituted on occasions approved or appointed by the bishop with his consent.[84] The Revised Tables of Lessons Measure 1922 introduced alternative tables for use at the minister's discretion, with the proviso that once adopted in any church or chapel they must be continuously followed to at least the end of the ecclesiastical year.[85] A 1955 lectionary[86] has also been used and the range of alternative lessons and

---

[79] Church of England (Worship and Doctrine) Measure 1974, s.1(3) proviso; Canon B3(3).
[80] Church of England (Worship and Doctrine) Measure 1974, s.1(4); Canon B3(4), (5).
[81] Church of England (Worship and Doctrine) Measure 1974, s.1(4); Canon B3(4), (5).
[82] *ibid.*
[83] See n. 81 *ante*.
[84] Prayer Book (Table of Lessons) Act 1871.
[85] Revised Table of Lessons Measure 1922, s.1. The ecclesiastical year ends immediately before the first Sunday in Advent.
[86] Approved by the convocations in 1961.

psalms has been further extended by the alternative services authorised pursuant to Canon.[86a] Certain university colleges may also use special forms of service.[87]

Versions of the Bible

The minister has discretion to use, in place of a portion of scripture which is set **9.16** out and appointed to be read, said or sung, from the Book of Common Prayer, the corresponding passage from any version of the Bible authorised for the purpose by the General Synod.[88] This discretion is subject to the agreement of the PCC or, in the case of the occasional offices, any of the persons concerned objecting beforehand. The Revised Version, the Revised Standard Version, the New English Bible and the Jerusalem Bible have all been authorised and the Revised Psalter of 1963 is deemed to be authorised.[89] Strictly this provision only applies where the passages are "set out" as opposed to specified as in the tables of lessons, leaving open the question of the versions which may be used at Morning and Evening Prayer since these are simply specified in the Table of Lessons within the Book of Common Prayer. A claim for exclusive use of the Authorised Version of 1611 could only be made based upon custom and long usage and the presence of the words "Appointed to be read in churches" on its title page. It would appear that versions of the Bible other than those authorised by the General Synod could be used (subject to the bishop's directions[90]) and not be restrained by legal proceedings, although the point is not free from doubt.[91]

Language

All prayers and services prescribed in and by the Book of Common Prayer are to **9.17** be said or sung in the vulgar tongue, that is in English.[92] Article XXIV of the Thirty-nine Articles of Religion declares that is it plainly repugnant to both the

---

[86a] In 1973 the General Synod purported to authorise a lectionary *Further Alternative Rules to Order the Service together with an Additional Alternative Lectionary*, but this was without legal authority. Arguably its use in Morning and Evening Prayer according to the Book of Common Prayer is permitted by the implied consent of the Ordinary (unless withdrawn) by reason of *The Order How the Rest of Holy Scripture is Appointed to be Read* and if so, it may be similarly used with the ASB by reason of Canon B5(1): Bursell, *Liturgy, Order and the Law* (1996), p. 128. The suggested calendar and lectionaries in *"The Promise of His Glory"* had no authorisation, but may now be authorised pursuant to Canon B4 or B5: Bursell, *ante.*, p. 128. As part of the "ASB 2000" programme a new authorised lectionary, the *Revised Common Lectionary* will be published shortly.
[87] Universities Tests Act 1871, s.6.
[88] Prayer Book (Versions of the Bible) Measure 1965, s.1. See the General Synod *Public Worship in the Church of England: A Guide to the Law Governing Worship and Doctrine in the Church of England* (6th ed. 1994).
[89] *ibid.*
[90] Pursuant to Canon C18(4).
[91] See Bursell *Liturgy, Order and the Law* (1996) p. 63; *Halsbury's Laws of England* (4th ed.), Vol. 14, para. 945, n. 4.
[92] Canon B42 and see *The Book of Common Prayer*, concerning the Services of the Church. The ASB requires the services to be comprehensible to those present.

Word of God and the custom of the primitive Church to have public prayer or to minister the sacraments in a tongue not understood by the people.[93] Latin may only be used in Convocation, the chapels or other public places of the colleges and halls in the universities and the university churches, and in the colleges of Westminster, Winchester and Eton and in such other places of religious and sound learning as custom allows or the Ordinary permits.[94]

The use in addition to the spoken word of sign language during a service[95] when deaf persons are in the congregation is certainly lawful, and where only deaf people make up the congregation the use of sign language alone may be regarded as *de minimis*.[96]

Days to be specially observed

9.18   Canon B6 sets out those days which are to be specially observed. Sundays are to be celebrated as a weekly memorial of the resurrection and kept according to God's will and pleasure, particularly by attendance at divine service, by deeds of charity and by abstention from all unnecessary labour and business. In addition certain other days of the year are designated as days to be specially observed in the Church of England. These include the days set out in the Tables and Rules for the Moveable and Immoveable Feasts prefixed to the Book of Common Prayer, the principal days being Christmas Day, Epiphany, the Annunciation, Easter day, Ascension Day, Whitsunday or Pentecost, Trinity Sunday and All Saints' Day. Days of special observance are also set out in the Table of the Vigils, Fasts and Days of Abstinence which is also prefixed to the Book of Common Prayer. Of these the forty days of Lent, particularly Ash Wednesday and the Monday to Saturday before Easter ought to be specially observed. Good Friday is to be observed by prayer with meditation on the Lord's death and passion by self-discipline and attendance at divine service. In addition the General Synod may approve holy days to be observed generally or provincially, and subject to any directions by the convocation of the province, the Ordinary may approve holy days to be observed locally. The anniversary of the day of accession of the reigning Sovereign is described as a solemn day and a particular service is appointed, which appears in the Book of Common Prayer.[97]

Provision of regular statutory services

9.19   Provision is made for the regular performance of Morning and Evening Prayer, the Litany and Holy Communion. In cathedral churches Morning and Evening prayer, with the inclusion on the appointed days of the Litany,[98] is to be said or

---

[93] As to the marriage of foreigners see Chap. 10.
[94] See n. 92 *ante*.
[95] Chubb, *Lifting up of Hands, A Dictionary of Signs used in Church Services* (1994).
[96] Bursell, *Liturgy, Order and the Law* (1996) p. 67.
[97] The service was authorised by Royal Warrant dated July 26, 1958.
[98] This is to be said or sung after the third Collect at Morning Prayer on Sundays, Wednesdays and Fridays and at other times commanded by the Ordinary: *Book of Common Prayer* rubric preceding the Litany and rubric following the third Collect.

sung daily.[99] In the case of parish churches[1] a similar requirement applies so that the daily offices are to be said or sung at least on Sundays, other principal feast days, Ash Wednesday and Good Friday.[2] Although the Book of Common Prayer indicates that these offices should be said daily,[3] this requirement has been modified in both law and practice. In regard to Holy Communion the normal minimum requirement for both cathedral and parish churches is celebration on all Sundays, feast days and Ash Wednesday, and for parish churches, also Maunday Thursday, subject to the dispensation discussed below.[4] In addition an obligation is laid upon all ministers who have the cure of souls to administer, or cause to be administered, the occasional offices when required.[5]

In parish churches the reading of Morning and Evening Prayer or the celebration of Holy Communion may be dispensed with on an occasional basis as authorised by the minister or PCC acting jointly, or on a regular basis authorised by the bishop on the request of the minister and the PCC acting jointly.[6] In so acting the minister, PCC and bishop must be satisfied that there is good reason for so doing and must have regard to the frequency of such services in other parish churches or places of worship in the benefice as well as ensuring that no church ceases altogether to be used for public worship.[7]

In the case of churches and chapels dependent upon a parish church Holy Communion is to be celebrated as regularly and frequently as may be convenient, subject to the direction of the Ordinary.[8] Where there is more than one parish church or place of worship in a benefice, or where benefices are held in plurality, the minister and PCC acting jointly must make proposals to the bishop as to what services are to be held in each church or place of worship. If the bishop is satisfied with these he may authorise them, or he may give his own directions where no satisfactory proposals are made. In either case he must ensure that no church ceases to be used for public worship altogether.[9]

Family services

In some churches the main act of worship on Sundays takes the form of a **9.20** "Family Service", devised by the incumbent, consisting of scriptural readings, prayers, hymns and possibly a short sermon, unrelated to the authorised forms of service. The Standing Committee of the General Synod has stated that such services are acceptable provided that their use is not so habitual that congregations cease to be familiar with the authorised services. Should this happen family services should be discouraged or their use severely curtailed.[10]

---

[99] Canon B10.
[1] Any church in any parish other than a parish church or any building or part of a building licenced for public worship in any parish designated as a parish centre of worship is deemed to be a parish church for these purposes: Pastoral Measure 1983, s.29(2).
[2] Canon B11, para. 1.
[3] *Book of Common Prayer*, rubric preceding the Order for Morning Prayer.
[4] Canons B13(1), B14(1), (2).
[5] Canon C24(2).
[6] Canon B14A(1).
[7] Canon B14A(1).
[8] Canon B14(3).
[9] Canon B14A(2).
[10] See also the General Synod *Public Worship in the Church of England: A Guide to the Law Governing Worship and Doctrine in the Church of England* (6th ed. 1994).

Sermons

9.21   A sermon must be preached in every parish church a least once each Sunday, except for reasonable cause approved by the bishop of the diocese.[11] Generally provision is made in cathedral statutes for the preaching of sermons. The Book of Common Prayer and ASB provide for the delivery of a sermon or homily after the Creed in the order for Holy Communion, but doubts have arisen as to its necessity and it would appear that it may be omitted.[12] The Book of Common Prayer makes no provision in the order for Morning and Evening Prayer for a sermon whilst the ASB treats it as optional, although a sermon is generally preached on Sundays at these services.[13] A sermon alone, whether or not preceded by a bidding prayer[14] is not a service and therefore is not illegal.[15]

The sermon may be preached by the incumbent or any other minister, reader, deaconess or lay worker, authorised by the bishop.[16] Lay persons who read Morning and Evening Prayer are not authorised to preach. The preacher must endeavour, with care and sincerity, to minister the word of truth to the glory of God and to the edification of the people.[17] Canon B19 permits a specific bidding prayer before any sermon, lecture or homily which must be used in the form or to the effect set out, as briefly as is convenient, but always concluding with the Lord's Prayer. It should be noted that sermons are matters of public interest and are thus open to fair public criticism under the civil law of libel.[18] The law of defamation also applies to sermons and anyone preaching should therefore take care if referring to any identifiable person.

Hymns and other music and liturgical dance

9.22   The principle of conformity of worship does not preclude the minister adding or interpolating hymns, or exercising their discretion as to what portions of the service should be sung.[19] Apart from cathedral or collegiate churches or chapels

---

[11] Canon B18(1).

[12] The Act of Uniformity Amendment Act 1872 (repealed) provided that a sermon, lecture or homily was unnecessary and despite the repeal of this provision it is arguable that the fact that this was unnecessary for many years means that it is a matter not of substantial importance and that it may therefore be ommitted pursuant to Canon B5(1): Bursell, *Liturgy, Order and the Law* (1996), pp. 69–70.

[13] Again this practice was rendered lawful by the Act of Uniformity Amendment Act 1872 (repealed) and would appear to be lawful today as a matter not of substantial importance: Bursell, *Liturgy, Order and the Law* (1996), p. 70.

[14] Canon B19.

[15] Briden and Hanson, *Moore's Introduction to English Canon Law*, p. 80; Bursell, *Liturgy, Order and the Law* (1996), p. 70, who points out that if this argument is wrong and the sermon does constitute a service then, not being authorised, it is illegal.

[16] Canon B18(2).

[17] Canon B18(3).

[18] *Gathercole v. Miall* (1846) 15 M. & W. 319; *Kelly v. Sherlock* (1866) L.R. 1 Q.B. 686; *Botterill v. Whytehead* (1874) 41 L.T. 588.

[19] *Reed v. Bishop of Lincoln* [1892] A.C. 664 at 659–661 P.C.; *Hutchins v. Denziloe & Loveland* (1792) 1 Hag. Con. 170 at 175–180.

where such matters are governed by or are dependent upon special statutes or custom, the final responsibility for the choosing of chants, hymns, anthems, and other settings and for the ordering of music rests with the minister, although they must pay due heed to the advice and assistance of the organist, choir master or director of music if any is appointed.[20] The minister is under a duty to ensure that both the words and music are appropriate to the solemn act of worship and prayer in the House of God as well as to the congregation asembled for that purpose, and to banish all irreverence in the practice and performance of such words and music.[21] It would now appear that liturgical dance may be introduced into a service as a variation which is not of substantial importance, so long as it is reverent, glorifies God and is edifying.[22]

Notices

The minister having the cure of souls is to give adequate public notice in any way which is locally convenient of the feast days and fast days to be observed and of the time and place of services on those days.[23] Although this would appear to be of wide application and relevant to all services being used, this obligation imposed by Canon is in addition to any duties imposed by the rubrics contained in the Book of Common Prayer or the ASB in relation to a particular service.[24]   **9.23**

Some difficulty has been caused by the question of which notices may legally be given in a service, and particularly at a service of Holy Communion. It has been held that notice can only lawfully be given in a Communion service according to the Book of Common Prayer of those holy days included in its Tables,[25] but it is doubtful if such a rigorist approach would be applicable now.[26] This is perhaps emphasised by the fact that in relation to such a service according to the rites set out in the ASB notice may be given not just of holy days listed within it but also of diocesan, local and other commemorations.

Although the matter is not free from doubt it would now appear that any notices may be given so long as they are reverent and seemly,[27] and in practice it is unlikely that objection would be made. Thus notices could for example be given of a forthcoming church fete. So far as notices at other services other than Holy Communion are concerned these would again appear to be lawful so long as they are reverent and seemly.[28]

Register of services

A register book of services must be provided in all churches and chapels in which every service of public worship together with the name of the officiating minister, the preacher (if not the officiating minister), the number of communicants and   **9.24**

---

[20] Canon B20(1), (2).

[21] Canon B20(3).

[22] Bursell, *Liturgy Order and the Law* (1996), p. 79. *A Service of the Word and Affirmations of Faith*, makes express provision for the dramatisation of readings.

[23] Canon B7.

[24] Bursell, *Liturgy, Order and the Law* (1996), p. 82.

[25] *Elphinstone v. Purchas* (1870) L.R. 3 A. & E. 66 at 111.

[26] Bursell, *Liturgy, Order and the Law* (1996), p. 83–84.

[27] Bursell, *Liturgy, Order and the Law* (1996), pp. 85–87. See however Briden and Hanson, *Moore's Introduction to English Canon Law* (3rd ed. 1992), p. 97 where some doubt concerning this is expressed.

[28] Bursell, *Liturgy, Order and the Law* (1996), p. 87.

the amount of alms or other collections must be recorded.[29] If desired notes of other significant events may also be recorded in this book.

Copyright

9.25   It should be noted that in reproducing works (which includes duplicating, photocopying and printing) for worship or other purposes, care needs to be taken to comply with the law relating to copyright. Copyright in the ASB and all authorised alternative services is held by the Central Board of Finance, which permits copying for local use provided certain conditions are met.[30] The Book of Common Prayer and Authorised Versions of the Bible may only be reproduced with permission.[31] In regard to music a code of fair practice is in operation with the result that some copying is permissible.[32]

Video recording of occasional services

9.26   To facilitate the video recording of marriages and baptism services "blanket" arrangments have been made so that the text of these services can be recorded. The arrangments do not cover hymns, anthems, or additional prayers and are also subject to certain conditions, the most important of which is that the recording is not to be sold commercially (although the original recording and a permissible number of copies may be sold to the couple being married or the parents of a baptised infant who commissioned the video).[33] The regulation of video recording of occasional services is now generally subject to diocesan norms which recommend making agreements which impose conditions to prevent disruption of the service.[34] It is for the incumbent to decide whether to permit the recording and for the PCC to decide if it will charge a fee for the use of the equipment in the church.[35]

Obligations upon the congregation

9.27   Obligations in regard to divine service are also enjoined by Canon upon the congregation. These require all persons present at the time of divine service audibly to make the answers appointed in the authorised form of service, and in the due places to join in such parts of the service as are appointed to be said or sung by all present; that is the general confession, the Lord's Prayer, and the

---

[29] Canon F12.
[30] *Legal Opinions* pp, 76–78, which sets out details of how to obtain permission where necessary. See also *Liturgical Texts for Local Use* (1994) which sets out conditions and guidelines in respect of copying for local use.
[31] *ibid*. See n. 30 (*supra*).
[32] Up to date information may be obtained from the Music Publishers Association.
[33] Further guidance and a model notice to permit the use of videoing equipment is set out in *Legal Opinions*, pp. 80–82 and 92–94.
[34] Doe, *The Legal Framework of the Church of England* (1996), p. 371.
[35] See n. 33 *ante*.

Creed.[36] They are also to give reverent attention at the time of divine service, due reverence to the name of the Lord Jesus, and to stand at the Creed, the reading of the Holy Gospel[37] and at the Holy Communion.[38] When the prayers are read and the psalms and canticles said or sung they are to have regard to the rubrics of the service and to locally established custom as to whether they should stand, kneel or sit.[39]

Provision of things appertaining to worship

The PCC is under a duty to see that various things are provided in every church **9.28** and chapel.[40] Thus it must provide for the use of the minister a Bible which includes the Apocrypha and a Book of Common Prayer, both of large sizes, and where there is a pulpit a convenient Bible is to be kept in it for the use of the preacher. Provision should also be made for a service book together with a cushion or desk for use at the communion table.[41] Clean surplices must also be kept and maintained for the use of the minister.[42] Convenient desks for the reading of prayers and God's Word, and, unless it is not required, a decent pulpit for the sermon must also be provided.[43] So also must a font,[44] communion table with communion plate and linen,[45] seats for the people,[46] and a box for the alms of the people.[47] At least one bell is also required, to ring in order to summon the people to divine service.[48]

Bells

In addition to summoning the faithful to worship bells are rung to celebrate **9.29** weddings and festivals and to mark national days of thanksgiving. Muffled bells are sometimes rung at funerals or at times of local or national disaster. It has also been understood that the church bells would be rung as a warning of an invasion during times of war. Although bells have been rung since the seventh century change ringing, which is an art unknown outside the Anglican communion, was not introduced until the middle of the seventeenth century.

Concern has been expressed concerning a potential action for common law nuisance and potential liability under the Environmental Prtotection Act 1990.

---

[36] Canon B9(1).
[37] The reference to the Gospel is to the Gospel at Holy Communion not to the second lesson at Morning and Evening Prayer.
[38] Canon B9(2).
[39] Canon B9(2),
[40] Canon F14.
[41] Canon F9.
[42] Canon F5.
[43] Canon F6.
[44] Canon F1.
[45] Canons F2, F3, F4.
[46] Canon F7(1).
[47] Canon F10. Alms are to be applied to such uses as the minister and the PCC see fit or, if they disagree, as the Ordinary determines: *ibid*.
[48] Canon F8(1). No bell is to be rung contrary to the direction of the minister: *ibid*., F8(2). See Chap 4.

The control of church bells belongs jointly to the incumbent and churchwardens not to the PCC, and they should take care to ensure that the ringing of the bells does not constitute unlawful interference with a person's use and enjoyment of their property, or emit noise which is "prejudicial to health or a nuisance".[49] What would constitute a nuisance is a matter of fact and degree in each case but older authorites have accepted that the ringing of noisy church bells can constitute a nuisance. Particular attention should be paid to the necessity to ring bells early in the morning or late in the evening and to the avoidance of lengthy practice sessions.[50] It should be noted that the consistory court has sanctioned arrangements as to the time of ringing.[51]

Ritual and ceremonial

9.30 We have already considered the principle of conformity of worship. That principle also requires the observance of correct procedure in matters of ritual and ceremonial, and flowing from this requires appropriate controls in respect of matters ancillary to ritual and ceremonial, namely ornaments and decorations. All these matters have given rise to much controversy, and particularly in the nineteenth century, with the emergence of the Oxford Movement and the revival of Evangelicalism, to much litigation between the high and low church factions resulting in a substantial body of reported cases. The subject is a difficult one not least because many of the decisions of the courts are inconsistent, and others are such that a wide divergence between the law and practice of the Church of England has arisen. Today when questions on these matters arise they tend to do so in the context of proceedings for a faculty to authorise a particular ornament or decoration, rather than in the context of the prosecution of a minister for an offence against the laws ecclesiastical.[52]

Guiding principles as to legality

9.31 In ascertaining the legality or illegality of ecclesiastical practices three guiding principles have emerged. First there are things which are ordered and these may not be evaded by an illusory or partial compliance. Secondly there are things which are prohibited and these may not be evaded by any contrivance which, under a different name or appearance, attains the same end. Thirdly there are things which are neither expressly nor by implication ordered or prohibited.[53]

---

[49] Environmental Protection Act 1990, s.76(1)(g).

[50] See *Legal Opinions*, pp. 17–20; Bloor *Clocks, Bells and Cockrels* (1995) 3 Ecc. L.J. 393; Watkin, *A Happy Noise to Hear? Church Bells and the Law of Nuisance* 4 Ecc. L.J. 545; Thomas & Watkin, *Oh, Noisy Bells, be Dumb: Church Bells, Statutory Nuisance and Ecclesiastical Duties*, Journal of Planning and Environmental Law p. 1097.

[51] *Re St Jude, Hampstead, The Times*, August 6, 1909. Older cases suggest that the churchwardens may enter into an agreement to silence the bells or to agree that they may only be rung at specific times: See, *e.g. Martin v. Nutkin* (1724) 2 P. Wms. 266.

[52] Offences in respect of matters of doctrine, ritual and ceremonial are considered in Chap. 11.

[53] *Martin v. Mackonochie* (1868) L.R. 2 A & E 116 at 119, affd. L.R. 2 P.C. 365 at 385.

In general whatever is subsidiary to what is ordered and is in itself both decent and proper and in accordance with primitive catholic use is lawful. Nonetheless the doing of such things must be governed by the living discretion of some person in authority, that person being, as was discussed in Chapter 3, the bishop of the diocese. The function of the bishop is not to resort to a legal judgment but, if he can, to resolve the doubt or[54] if he cannot, to refer the matter to the archbishop. This was the course adopted in the cases of incense, processional lights and the reservation of the sacrament upon which the archbishops pronounced their Opinions (expressly stated not to be judgments in any sense of that term) at Lambeth at the end of the nineteenth century.[55]

The divergence of law and practice

A wide divergence has developed in regard to the law and practice of the Church **9.32** of England with reference to matters of ritual and ceremonial. This divergence was described in the report of the Archbishops' Commission on the Ecclesiastical Courts, which in 1954 expressed the hope that early action would be taken to repeal those parts of the law which were no longer observed and over which recourse to a court of law would no longer be thought proper so that the law reflected modern practice. The report also stated that the law of public worship must be framed in such a way as to allow the full width of tradition within the Church to find a place within the framework, and full allowance be made for variation in ceremonial necessitated by local circumstance.

No comprehensive reform of the law has taken place since that report was made, although some changes have occurred. The enactment of the Church of England (Worship and Doctrine) Measure 1974, enabling alternative forms of service and the recognition for purposes of ecclesiastical jurisdiction of a distinct category of cases in matters of doctrine, ritual or ceremonial, being the most important. It is also evident that there is less inclination to take action in the courts in regard to such matters and this, combined with the willingness of the consistory courts to grant faculties in unopposed cases where the petition might previously have been rejected on grounds of illegality, has led to a more relaxed climate in which considerable variation in matters of ritual and ceremonial now exists.

In looking at questions concerning ritual and ceremonial it should be noted that the law draws a distinction between a rite which consists of services expressed in words, and a ceremony which consists of gestures or acts preceding, accompanying or following the utterance of the ritual words.[56] Much argument has turned upon identifying what constitutes a ceremony although it should be borne in mind when considering the law that there is considerable doubt as to whether or not it would now be applied strictly. That caveat also applies to all the older cases referred to throughout this chapter.

---

[54] *ibid.* However, both the bishop and archbishop can only resolve doubts regarding lawful actions; they cannot authorise that which is unlawful, and the final arbiter of what is legal is always the courts: Bursell, *Liturgy, Order and the Law*, (1996) p. 32.

[55] Macmillan & Co's Official Reports; the Opinions were given on July 31, 1899 and May 1, 1990.

[56] *Martin v. Mackonochie* (1868) L.R. 2 A & E 116 at 135–136.

Processions

9.33 The legality of processions has been called into question,[57] but a ceremonial procession in exercise of the minister's discretion is now lawful.[58] Both *Lent, Holy Week, Easter* and *The Promise of His Glory*,[59] provide for processions.

Candles

9.34 The ceremonial use of candles has been held to be illegal, particularly in processions[60] although candles were never considered unlawful *per se* since their main purpose is to give light. Whilst causing lighted candles to be held either side of a minister when reading the Gospel and the candles are not required to give light, has been held to be illegal as an addition to the ceremonies prescribed by law,[61] the decorative use of candles on or behind the holy table during the celebration of Holy Communion (rather than their use for providing light) has been held to be legal provided that the lighting of the candles does not take place during the celebration and provided that the candles are not used for ceremonial purposes.[62]

However, all these decisions are now of doubtful validity in the context of changing liturgical practices. The ASB provides for the giving of a lighted candle during the service of baptism, and for a candle, which may be the paschal candle[63] to be made ready from which other candles may be lighted.[64] Moreover, both *Lent, Holy Week, Easter* and *The Promise of His Glory*,[65] provide for services of light which include the lighting of candles (which may on appropriate occasions be held by the congregation) and processions with candles, whilst the latter also contains a Candlemas service also involving a procession with candles. Given these developments it is now unlikely that the ceremonial use of candles is illegal[66]; thus they could be used pursuant to the minister's discretion in any other appropriate service.

[57] *Elphinstone v. Purchas* (1870) L.R. 3 A & E 66 at 96–97.
[58] *Re St John the Evangelist, Chopwell* [1995] Fam. 254.
[59] Forms of service commended by the House of Bishops of the General Synod.
[60] *Elphinstone v. Purchas* (*ante*); *Sumner v. Wix* (1870) L.R. 3 A & E 58; *Martin v. Mackonochie* (1868) L.R. 2 P.C. 365 at 387, P.C. 388; *Read v. Bishop of Lincoln* [1892] A.C. 644 at 666, P.C.; *Rector and Churchwardens of Capel St Mary, Suffolk v. Packard* [1927] P. 289 at 304; *Re St Mary Tyne Dock* [1954] P. 369 at 379. The Archbishops last century were of the opinion that there is no authority to warrant carrying lights in processions: Opinions of Lambeth, July 31, 1899, n. 55 *ante*.
[61] *Sumner v. Wix* (*ante*).
[62] *Read v. Bishop of Lincoln* [1891] P. 9; on appeal [1892] A.C. 644, P.C. Previously such use had been considered illegal. In the court of the Archbishop of Canterbury, Archbishop Benson reviewed the subject in detail, leading the Privy Council to conclude that the Archbishop's review afforded new matters for consideration. In all subsequent cases the Archbishop's decision has been accepted as being correct. See *e.g. Re St Saviour's, Walthamstow* [1951] P. 147.
[63] Previously the legality of a paschal candle depended upon whether it was to be used in ceremonial: *Re St Mary Tyne Dock* (*ante*).
[64] P. 248 and n. 4 before the Baptism of Children at p. 241.
[65] Forms of service commended by the House of Bishops of the General Synod.
[66] *Re St John the Evangelist, Chopwell* [1995] Fam. 254; *Re St Thomas, Pennywell* [1995] 2 W.L.R. 154 at 169.

Incense

The ceremonial use of incense has been held to be illegal.[67] However, it should   **9.35**
not be inferred that the liturgical use of incense is permanently excluded from
the church's ritual. It has been held that, notwithstanding that there is no
authority for the use of incense in the public worship of the Church of England,
and its use during statutory services may well be illegal, its use during other new
services is probably lawful if sanctioned by the bishop exercising the *jus
liturgium*.[68] This was the opinion of the archbishops in the last century, who were
also of the view that the time for greater tolerance regarding its use would come,
and it is evident from their statements that there is no doctrinal objection to
incense.[69] Given liturgical developments that time may be regarded as having
come, and it would seem probable that the use of incense is now legal in all
services at the discretion of the minister, extending to censoring of both the
clergy and congregation.[70] In any event it should be noted that there is certainly
nothing to prevent the use of incense for fumigatory purposes so long as it is not
done ceremoniously.[71],

Ornaments and decorations

"Ornament" in ecclesiastical law is used in the larger sense of the word   **9.36**
"*ornamentum*" meaning all the articles used in the performance of the service
and rites of the church, including for example holy tables,[72] rather than in its
modern sense of embellishment. Ornaments proper are therefore distinguished
from those things which are decorations, furnishings or fittings of the church.

   The category of things lawful and ordered is determined primarily by the
"Ornaments Rubric" in the Book of Common Prayer and by a group of Canons[73]
headed "Of things appertaining to Churches", which may be regarded as being
supplemental to the Rubric, and designed to silence old controversies.[74] The
Rubric which concerns both ornaments of the church and of the minister,
declares that such ornaments as were in use by the authority of Parliament in the
second year of the reign of Edward VI shall be retained. Its precise meaning and

---

[67] *Martin v. Mackonochie* (1868) L.R. 2 A & E 116 at 215; *Sumner v. Wix* (1870) L.R. 3 A
 & E 58; *Rector and Churchwardens of Capel St Mary, Suffolk v. Packard* [1927] P. 289 at
 305 *c.f.* n. 47 before.
[68] *Re St Mary, Tyne Dock* [1954] P. 369 at 380.
[69] Opinions of Lambeth, July 31, 1899, n. 55 *ante*.
[70] *Re St John the Evangelist, Chopwell* [1995] Fam. 254 where the liturgical use of incense
 was held to be a variation which was not of substantial importance and which was
 therefore permissible purusant to Canon B5(1); Bursell, *Liturgy, Order and the Law*,
 (1996), p. 77.
[71] *Re St Mary, Tyne Dock* [1954] P. 369 at 380. Opinions of Lambeth, July 31, 1899, n. 55
 ante.
[72] *Westerton v. Liddel, Horne,* etc. (1855) Moore's Special Report at 156, 157 cited with
 approval by the Court of Ecclesiastical Causes Reserved in *Re St Michael and All Angels,
 Great Torrington* [1985] Fam. 81 at 89.
[73] Canons F1–F12.
[74] *Halsbury's Laws of England* (4th ed.), Vol. 14, para. 960.

effect has been disputed, it not being clear whether the Rubric refers to the ornaments authorised by the first Prayer Book (introduced in the third year of Edward VI's reign) or to the ornaments in use before that Book's introduction. In regard to ornaments of the church the courts have been more concerned with the use to which they have been put than whether they were in use by the authority of Parliament. The difference between the two interpretations therefore really only concerned the ornaments of ministers and ceased to be of any practical effect with the introduction of the Vestures of Ministers Measure 1964.[75]

Ornaments of the church

9.37   "Ornaments of the church" in the rubric refers to those articles the use of which in the service and ministrations are prescribed by the First Prayer Book of Edward VI.[76] Thus the Rubric provides for the use of an English Bible, the new prayer book, a poor man's box, a chalice, a corpas, a paten and a bell.[77] The Canons[78] as we have seen require a font (with cover), a holy table, articles of communion plate and linen, a reading desk and pulpit, seats for the use of parishioners and others, at least one church bell, a Bible, a Book of Common Prayer, a service book for use at the communion table, an alms box and the necessary register books.

Although the Canons exclude issues of the legality of ornaments as far as possible, they leave in place aesthetic control over the appearance of such objects to the Ordinary by exercise of the faculty jurisdiction. Whilst the Court of Ecclesiastical Causes Reserved has discussed the distinction between the introduction of an object ordered by Canon, which it was said did not generally require the authorisation of a faculty, and an item not ordered but legal which did,[79] this cannot have been intended to remove the court's control over the aesthetics of such objects. Rather it is suggested that it is simply an affirmation of the principle that *de minimis* matters, if uncontroversial aesthetically or otherwise, do not usually require a faculty.[80] The scope of that *de minimis* principle in such cases has however been somewhat reduced by the provisions which enable an archdeacon to grant a faculty in unopposed cases[81] in which the DAC do not object to the introduction of articles other than an aumbry which may be used for the lawful performance of divine service or the rites of the church.

Articles not expressly provided for by either the Rubric or Canons may be permitted. In the case of ornaments their use must be consistent with and subsidiary to the services of the church,[82] in other words their use must be consistent with lawful ceremonial. For decorations the test for legality is whether

---

[75] *ibid.*, paras., 961, 970; *Moore's Introduction to English Canon Law* (3rd ed. 1992), pp. 98, 101.
[76] *Re St Michael and All Angels, Great Torrington* [1985] Fam. 81 at 89–90.
[77] *ibid*.
[78] Canons F1–F12.
[79] *Re St Michael and All Angels, Great Torrington* [1985] Fam. 81 at 89–90.
[80] *Newsom*, p. 124.
[81] As to which see Chap. 11.
[82] *Martin v. Mackonochie* (1868) L.R. 2 P.C. 365 at 391.

or not they are in danger of being used for purposes of veneration or adoration.[83] In this context the courts have sought to distinguish between objects which are legitimate aids to devotion and those which are likely to attract or encourage superstitious reverence or to inculcate erroneous doctrine. "Superstitious reverence" has itself been open to diverse interpretation. The nineteenth century view, that it should not be limited to cases of the actual worshipping or adoration of images contrary to Article XXII of the Thirty-nine Articles of Religion,[84] has given way in recent times to a more relaxed approach where the courts are slow to find the possibility of such reverence arising.[85] Since 1950 only a tabernacle, a sanctuary gong and bell, and stations of the cross, all of which are discussed below, and portable candle holders, have been held to be illegal.

Crosses, as emblems of the Christian faith may be used as decorations in the absence of superstitious reverance provided they are not fixed to the communion table.[86] Crucifixes and sculptured images are subject to the same test of legality.[87] Painted windows, pictures, representations in glass, wood and stone are thus generally free from objection unless there is a danger of superstitious reverence,[88] or of inculcating erroneous doctrine. Thus a petition to erect a plaque over a font was refused on the ground that it depicted a scene inconsistent with doctrine relating to baptism.[89]

Holy tables and appurtenances

A convenient and decent table of wood, stone or other suitable material must be **9.38** provided in every church and chapel for the celebration of Holy Communion and must stand in the main body of the church or in the chancel where Morning and Evening Prayer are appointed to be said.[90] Any dispute as to where it shall stand is to be determined by the Ordinary.[91] What constitutes such a table is considered in Chapter 11. It should be noted that it is not unlawful to raise the table above the floor of the church[92] nor to curtain the back and north and south ends of the table so long as this does not prevent the minister, if they so wish, from officiating at the north end.[93]

---

[83] *Vincent v. Rector and Churchwardens of St Magnus the Martyr,* etc., [1925] P. 1 at 11, 12.

[84] *Clifton v. Ridsdale* (1876) 1 P.D. 316.

[85] See, *e.g. Re St Mary, Tyne Dock* [1954] P. 369; *Re St Peter, St Helier, Morden, & St Olave, Mitcham* [1951] P. 303.

[86] *Westerton v. Liddel, Horne,* etc., (1855) Moore's Special Report; *Vicar and Churchwardens of Wimbledon v. Eden, Re St Mark's, Wimbledon* [1908] P. 167.

[87] *Halsbury's Laws of England* (4th ed.) Vol. 14, para. 964, n. 2 set outs a comprehensive selection of the many cases upon this subject.

[88] *Clifton v. Ridsdale* (1876) 1 P.D. 316 at 358, affd. *sub nom. Ridsdale v. Clifton* (1877) 2 P.D. 276 P.C.; *Vicar and Churchwardens of St John, Pendlebury v. Parishioners of St John, Pendlebury* [1895] P. 178; *Vincent v. Rector and Churchwardens of St Magnus the Martyr,* etc., [1925] P. 1 at 16.

[89] *Re St Edward the Confessor,* Mottingham [1983] 1 W.L.R. 364.

[90] Canon F2(1); *Book of Common Prayer,* rubric preceding the Order for the Administration of the Lord's Supper or Holy Communion.

[91] *ibid.*

[92] *St Andrew's, Haverstock-Hill* (1909) 25 T.L.R. 408.

[93] *Vicar and Churchwardens of Wimbledon v. Eden, Re St Mark's, Wimbledon* [1908] P. 167.

An additional[94] and even a third[95] holy table may be sanctioned on the grounds of convenience. Whether that part of the church in which the additional table is situated should be partitioned from the rest of the church is a matter for the court granting the faculty; it is not essential to its existence.[96] Where necessary a credence table (a small table or ledge on which the bread and wine are placed before being consecrated) may be lawfully placed in the church as subsidiary to the administration of Holy Communion.[97]

The table must be kept in a sufficient and seemly manner, and from time to time repaired.[98] During divine service it must be covered with a covering of silk or other decent stuff, and at the celebration of Holy Communion with a fair white linen cloth.[99] A sufficient number of fair white linen cloths for covering the table and other fair linen cloths for the priest's use during Holy Communion must be provided and maintained.[1]

Every church or chapel must be provided with a chalice for the wine and a paten or other vessel for the bread, which must be fashioned from gold, silver or other suitable metal. A cruet or flagon is also required for bringing wine to the communion table and a bason for the reception of alms and other devotions is also included amongst the items of communion plate.[2] It is the minister's duty to see that the communion plate is kept washed and clean, ready for Holy Communion.[3] A ciborium (a goblet shaped lidded vessel to hold consecrated wafers) is not illegal and may be used during the administration of Communion, or in a church where reservation has been approved as a receptacle for the reserved sacrament.[4]

The placing of candles upon the holy table has already been discussed. Although the use of two single candlesticks is the traditional and recognised use in the Church of England it is within the discretion of the diocesan chancellor to authorise the use of more than this should they consider it to be proper so to do.[5] Vases of flowers may be placed on the table and kept there during divine service provided these are used purely as decorations.[6]

---

[94] *Re St James the Great, Buxton, Vicar of St John the Baptist, Buxton v. Parishioners of St John the Baptist, Buxton* [1907] P. 368.
[95] *St Margaret's, Toxteth Park* (1924) 40 T.L.R. 687 where it was said that a stronger case could be made out for three rather two; *Re St Mary, Tyne Dock* [1954] P. 369 at 381.
[96] See n. 94 *ante*.
[97] *Westerton v. Liddel, Horne*, etc., (1855) Moore's Special Report at 187.
[98] Canon F2(2); *Book of Common Prayer*, rubric preceding the Order for the Administration of the Lord's Supper or Holy Communion.
[99] *ibid*.
[1] Canon F4.
[2] Canon F3(1).
[3] Canon F3(2).
[4] *Re St Mary, Tyne Dock (no. 2)* [1958] P. 156.
[5] *Re St Saviour's, Walthamstow* [1951] P. 147 where six were allowed. Six were also permitted in a three further cases including *Re St Mary, Tyne Dock* [1954] P. 369 at 379 (although portable candle holders were not allowed). Earlier cases where the number of candlesticks were reduced to two must now be doubted, unless the larger numbers of sticks are being put to ceremonial use.
[6] *Elphinstone v. Purchas* (1870) L.R. 3 A & E 66.

Sanctuary lamps and votive candles

A sanctuary lamp on the altar of a memorial chapel has been authorised by **9.39** faculty.[7] In the Church of England red sanctuary lights are a call to prayer, white lamps indicate the Blessed Sacrament is reserved. Blue lights are customarily held in a Lady Chapel.[8] A stand for votive candles is not illegal, where it is introduced as an aid to private devotion. However, it should be noted that the use of electric lights in the form of imitation candles has been disapproved of.[10]

Sanctuary gongs and bells

A sanctuary gong and sanctuary bells have been held to be illegal ornaments.[11] **9.40** The court has also refused to permit the bells of the church to be used from the interior as a sanctuary bell.[12] Despite this the ringing of a sanctus bell to focus the attention of worshippers, or a bell to draw the attention of those unable to attend church themselves is now legal.[13]

Receptacles for the reserved sacrament

In Chapter 10 the practice of reservation of the sacrament is considered. In **9.41** determining the lawfulness of receptacles to house the reserved sacrament the court will have regard to the existence of episcopal sanction for the practice ot reservation and the conditions under which it is granted. There is now a body of authority for the issue of a faculty for an aumbry (a closed recess in the wall) in a church where the bishop has approved the practice of reservation.[14] Where such a

---

[7] Re All Saints, Leamington Priors [1963] 1 W.L.R. 806.

[8] Legal Opinions, p. 219.

[9] Re St John the Evangelist, Chopwell [1995] Fam. 254. However, such stands are not to be used in the performance of the rites and services of the Church: Westerton v. Liddel, Horne etc. (1855) Moore's Special Report at 156; Re St Thomas, Pennywell [1995] 2 W.L.R. 154 at 171.

[10] Re St Andrew's Dearnley [1981] Fam. 50.

[11] Re St Mary, Tyne Dock [1954] P. 369 at 379 following Elphinstone v. Purchas (1870) L.R. 3 A & E 66 on appeal sub nom. Hebbert v. Purchas (1871) L.R. 3 P.C. 605. However, in Re St Mary, West Fordingham (1956 unreported) (1991) 2 Ecc. L.J. 250 a faculty was granted for a bell intended as a sanctus bell when there was no other bell in the church, it being held that the good resulting from its being used as a proper church bell outweighed its ringing on occasions as Holy Communion which might strictly be a breach of good order.

[12] Vicar and Churchwardens of St John the Evangelist, Clevedon v. All having Interest [1909] P. 6; Re St Mary, Tyne Dock (no. 2) [1958] P. 156.

[13] Re St John the Evangelist, Chopwell [1995] Fam. 254. See also Bursell, Liturgy, Order and the Law (1996) pp. 78–9.

[14] Re Lapford (Devon) Parish Church [1954] P. 416; affd. on appeal [1955] P. 205; Re St Mary, Tyne Dock [1954] P. 369; Re St Michael and All Angels, Bishopwearmouth [1958] 1 W.L.R. 1183; Re St Peter and St Paul, Leckhampton [1968] P. 495.

faculty is granted it is normally stipulated that the aumbry is set in a wall of the church in a position not immediately behind or above a holy table.[15] This accords with the rubrics set out in the rejected Prayer Book of 1928 which provided for an aumbry to be set in the north or south wall of the sanctuary of the church or any chapel thereof, or a wall in some other part of the church approved by the bishop, so long as it was not immediately behind or above a holy table. Far from treating an aumbry as an illegal ornament modern authorities have taken the view that they are not an ornament at all but simply a cupboard which is part of the furnishings of the church.[16] The aumbry is often covered by a curtain and is generally accompanied by a light to indicate the presence of the sacrament.[17] It should be noted that any such faculty is expressed to operate only until further notice so as to enable the court to keep control in case of any abuse.[18]

A tabernacle (a small ornamented cupboard or box in the middle of the altar) has been held to be illegal and to be so notwithstanding the terms in which the bishop may have authorised reservation of the sacrament.[19] In contrast a hanging pyx (from the latin "pyxis" a small box) does not appear to be illegal, although there is conflicting authority on the question.[20] The difference between a tabernacle and a pyx is not an obvious one although historically a pyx was common in England before the Reformation whereas tabernacles were not.[21] Most recently there have been cases where a "sacrament-house", a decorated box or cupboard standing on its own legs, was permitted as a receptacle.[22] A *ciborium* (a chalice shaped vessel with a lid used to contain sacramental bread) may be used to contain the reserved sacrament within the aumbry.[22a]

[15] *Re Lapford (Devon) Parish Church (ante)*. In *Re St Peter and St Paul, Leckhampton* (*ante*) the faculty authorised the reconstituiton of an ancient aumbry behind the central subsidiary altar at the east end of the church.

[16] *Re Lapford (Devon) Parish Church (supra)*; *Rector and Churchwardens of Bishopwearmouth v. Adey (supra)* at 1185.

[17] *Re St Mary Magdalene. Altofts* [1958] P. 172; *Re St Michael and All Angels, Bishopwearmouth* (*ante*) at 1191.

[18] *Re St Mary, Tyne Dock (no. 2)* [1958] P. 156 at 166.

[19] *Capel St Mary v. Packard* [1927] P. 289; Re Lapford (Devon) Parish Church (*ante*); *Re St Mary, Tyne Dock (supra)*. Although the illegality of a tabernacle was doubted in *Re St Thomas, Pennywell* [1995] 2 W.L.R. 154 at 172.

[20] The observations of the Dean of the Arches in *Re Lapford (Devon) Parish Church* [1955] P. 205 suggest a hanging pyx is illegal but in *Re St Nicholas, Plumstead (Rector and Churchwardens)* [1961] 1 W.L.R. 916 it was held that a hanging pyx was an ornament but a faculty was granted to hang it from a *baldachino* (canopy) which was around and above an altar in a chapel.

[21] *Re St Nicholas, Plumstead (Rector and Churchwardens) (supra)* at 918, 919, 920.

[22] *Re St Matthew, Wimbledon* [1985] 3 All E.R. 670; *Re St John the Evangelist, Brierley* [1989] Fam. 60; *Re St Thomas, Pennywell* [1995] 2 W.L.R. 154.

[22a] *ibid.* at 171. A ciborium is also of course used to contain the sacramental bread at Holy Communion.

Holy water, stoups and aspergill

Although a holy water stoup has been held to be illegal,[23] there is also authority **9.42**
that a faculty may be granted for such a stoup,[24] thus indicating that there can be
no doctrinal objection to this. The making of the sign of the cross using water, at
least outside a service, would seem to be a matter of private devotion.[25] *A Service
for the Feast of the Baptism of the Lord*,[26] goes further stating that water may be
sprinkled over the people, left in vessels at the door for them to make the sign of
the cross, or poured over the threshold. Thus the use of holy water is now
accepted as being lawful, at the discretion of the minister, this extending to the
sprinkling of the clergy and congregation from an aspergill.[27]

Stations of the cross

Stations of the cross are not intrinsically unlawful[28] and it would appear that the **9.43**
same tests should apply to them as should be used in relation to other images.
However, a faculty may only be granted to authorise their introduction until
further order to give the court control over any abuse. It should be noted that in
cases where the stations of the cross have been authorised this authorisation has
extended to all 14 stations notwithstanding that four (St Veronica and the three
falls of Our Lord) have no scriptural authority.

Thuribles

The use of incense has never been prohibited in all cases and as we have seen the **9.44**
liturgical use of incense in authorised services now appears to be permissible.
Accordingly a thurible or censor and an incense boat are lawful.[29]

Holy oil

Although there is no provision in the Book of Common Prayer for the use of **9.45**
holy oil such annointing is now provided for in the Laying on of Hands and
Annointing,[30] whilst the ASB provides for collects and readings for the Blessing

---

[23] *Hebbert v. Purchas* (1871) 3 P.C. 605 at 651; *Davey v. Hinde* [1903] P. 221 at 237; *Rector and Churchwardens of Capel St Mary, Suffolk v. Packard* [1927] P. 289 at 306.
[24] *Re St Mary, Tyne Dock* [1954] P. 369 at 382 where a faculty was granted for a stoup in the vestry on the principle that admission was *de minimis* and that it was an aid to private devotion; *Re St John the Evangelist, Chopwell* [1995] Fam. 264.
[25] Bursell, *Liturgy, Order and the Law* (1996), pp. 76, 40.
[26] *The Promise of His Glory*.
[27] *Re St John the Evangelist, Chopwell ante*. In reliance upon Canon B5(1) as not being a matter of substantial importance.
[28] *Re St Peter, St Helier, Morden, & Re St Olave, Mitcham* [1951] P. 303; *Re St Mary, Tyne Dock* [1954] P. 369; *Re St Agustine's Brinksway* [1963] P. 364. In *Re St Mary the Virgin, West Moors* [1963] P. 390 the stations were held to be illegal.
[29] *Re St Mary, Tyne Dock* [1954] P. 369, where these were permitted to be introduced for limited purposes and *Re St John the Evangelist, Chopwell* (*ante*) where the use of incense for liturgical purposes was approved and a faculty granted for the introduction of a thurible and stand.
[30] In *Ministry to the Sick*.

of the Oils and for the annointing of candidates for confirmation[31]. A cruet for holy oil which is no more than a receptacle to contain such oil is thus lawful.[32]

Confession table and boxes

9.46 A confession table and chair may be authorised where they are intended for use in the hearing of voluntary confessions[33]; so may a confession box, although this is not regarded as part of the regular church furniture and fittings.[34]

Vestments of ministers

9.47 As discussed earlier in this chapter the ornaments or vestments of ministers like those of the church, were governed by the Ornaments Rubric, the effect of which was subject to much dispute until the enactment of the Vestures of Ministers Measure 1964 (now repealed). Whilst the 1964 Measure and now the modern Canons[35] retained the provisions of the Rubric and of the Act of Uniformity 1558, they have permitted considerable latitude in the vestments allowed to be worn today. In particular it should be noted that the Church of England does not attach any particular doctrinal significance to the diversities of vesture permitted and that the vesture of ministers is not to be understood as implying any doctrines other than those contained in the formularies of the Church.[36]

At Morning and Evening Prayer and for the occasional offices a minister is required to wear a cassock and a surplice with a scarf or stole or an alb (a long white linen vestment with sleeves) with a stole.[37] At Holy Communion the celebrant wears a cassock and surplice with a scarf or stole or a cassock and alb with a stole, to which if a stole is worn other customary vestments[38] may be

---

[31] p. 252.

[32] *Re St Mary Tyne Dock* [1954] P. 369 at 382.

[33] *ibid*. at 94, 95 (where the Deputy Dean of the Arches set aside an order for the removal of a confession box); at 380.

[34] *Roffe-Silvester v. King* [1939] P. 64; *Rector and Churchwardens of Capel St Mary, Suffolk v. Packard (ante)*. Bursell, *Liturgy, Order and the Law*, (1996) p. 227 says that confession boxes are illegal, citing *Davey v. Hinde* [1901] P. 95; *Rector and Churchwardens of Capel St Mary, Suffolk v. Packard (ante)*. However, although in the latter case (which concerned an ordinary kneeling stool to be used for confession) the Dean of the Arches stated that it was probably advisable that confessions be heard in open church rather than a vestry or a confession box, and referred to *Davey v. Hinde (supra)* and *Brdford v. Fry* [1903] P. 221 as examples of cases where confession boxes had been removed by faculty since they were not part of the regular furniture and fittings recognised by the Church of England, he did not go so far as to state that they were illegal.

[35] Canon B8, which largely follows the wording of the Vestures of Ministers Measure 1964.

[36] Canon B8(1).

[37] Canon B8(4), (5).

[38] The customary vestments being the chasuble (a long sleeveless outer vestment), for a priest; the dalmatic for a deacon; amice (a linen scarf worn under the alb); the maniple (an ornamental band worn on the left arm by the celebrant at Holy Communion); and stole.

added.[39] The gospellor and epistoler if any, wears a cassock with surplice or alb to which other customary vestments[40] may be added.[41] At their discretion the minister may wear a cope (a large ceremonial cloak) on any appropriate occasion, and when they wear a scarf may if entitled to do so wear the hood of their degree. It should be noted that the use of a black gown for preaching whilst now uncommon is permissible.[42]

Notwithstanding the provisions of Canon B8 no minister is to change the form of vesture in use in the church or chapel in which they officiate without ascertaining by consultation with the PCC that such change is acceptable.[43] In the case of any disagreement with the PCC the minister must refer the matter to the bishop, whose direction is to be obeyed.

It should also be noted that the fact that a form of vesture is not specifically authorised does not make it unlawful. The clerical collar, often known as a dog or Roman collar, which was widely adopted in England in the nineteenth century has no specific authorisation. Nor is specific mention made of a cassock, it perhaps being assumed that this was the basic garment upon which the other vestments would rest. Nor is any mention made of headgear but the use of a biretta (or a skull-cap) for protection may be lawful.[44]

The vestments of bishops has not been the subject of either legislation or litigation. The "magpie" robes of rochet (a white surplice with tight sleeves) with a black chimere (a sleeveless gown) with black wristbands is regarded as the choir habit although bishops frequently wear their Convocation robes with scarlet chimere and wristbands. Copes, mitres, rings and pectoral crosses would all appear to be lawful. A bishop's cassock is purple although there is no rule regarding the colour of any cassocks save those of Chaplains to the Sovereign (including Honorary Chaplains in the Armed Services) and other appointments in the Royal Household, whose cassocks are scarlet.[45]

A reader should wear a cassock, surplice, the hood of their degree if appropriate and a blue scarf.[46] Servers, choristers and others have also not been the subject of regulation nor litigation.

---

[39] Canon B8(3).
[40] See n. 38 *ante*.
[41] Canon B8(3).
[42] *Re Robinson, Wright v. Tugwell* [1897] 1 Ch. 85, C.A.
[43] Canon B8(2).
[44] *Elphinstone v. Purchas* (1870) L.R. 3 A & E 66 at 94 *sub nom. Hebbert v. Purchas* (1871) L.R. 3 P.C. 605 at 651.
[45] Directive from the Lord Chamberlain 1982.
[46] Regulations respecting Readers, accepted by the House of Bishops on January 15, 1991. The previous regulations included the wearing of their badge of office which would still be legal: Bursell, *Liturgy, Order and the Law* (1996) p. 96, n. 354.

Chapter Ten: Sacraments and Offices

A sacrament is defined in the Catechism in the Book of Common Prayer as "an **10.1** outward and visible sign of an inward and spiritual grace given unto us, ordained by Christ himself, as a means by which we receive the same and a pledge to assure us thereof." The Catechism also states that there are two sacraments generally necessary to salvation, namely Baptism and the Lord's Supper, whilst Article XXV of the Thirty-nine Articles of Religion states that only these two sacraments "were ordained of Christ" in the Gospel. That Article goes on to declare that the other five commonly called sacraments, that is confirmation, penance, orders, matrimony and extreme unction are not sacraments of the Gospel, leaving their precise theological nomenclature unclear.

The word "office"comes from the Latin *officium* meaning a duty, divine office being the worship which was enjoined as a duty. Office is frequently used in contradistinction to sacrament since the daily offices are treated as preparation for Holy Communion. However, reference is also made to the constant offices of Morning and Evening Prayer and Holy Communion to distinguish these from the occasional offices of Baptism, Confirmation, Holy Matrimony, the Burial of the Dead, the Visitation of the Sick, and the Churching of Women. A complete list of all the offices would also include the Litany, the Commination Service from the Book of Common Prayer and the Thanksgiving for the Birth or Adoption of a Child, The Renewal of Baptismal Vows and the Service to be used Before a Funeral from the ASB.

In this chapter we consider the sacraments of baptism (together with the renewal of baptism vows) and Holy Communion and issues associated with Holy Communion such as the practice of the reservation of the sacrament. We examine the daily offices of Morning and Evening Prayer and the occasional offices: confirmation, the churching of women and thanksgiving for the birth or adoption of a child, the ministry to the sick, exorcism, confession and absolution, commination, and the conduct of funeral services. In particular we look in detail at the solemnisation of matrimony, which ministers undertake as officers of the State with the consequence that the requirements of secular law must be strictly complied with to effect a valid marriage.

Holy Communion

The central act of worship in both the Western and Eastern Catholic Church **10.2** focuses upon the sacrament of Holy Communion or the Lord's Supper, some-times also known as the Eucharist, Mass or Liturgy. The celebration of this sacrament of the body and blood of Christ involves the consecration of the elements of bread and wine by the priest and their reception by the communicants, and associates the participants in the sacrifice of Christ's death upon the cross and the eternal offering of his life for mankind.

Celebrant or eucharistic president

10.3   Only a person who has been ordained priest by episcopal ordination may consecrate and administer the sacrament of Holy Communion.[1] As we saw in Chapter 7 a PCC or administrative body of a cathedral may pass resolutions preventing a woman priest celebrating Holy Communion in that parish or cathedral, it being an offence to act in contravention of such a resolution.

When celebrating Holy Communion according to the rites of the ASB the bishop should preside if he is present,[2] although the rite in the Book of Common Prayer assumes that he will not.[3] No provision is made for concelebration and is therefore a matter to be resolved by the diocesan bishop.[4]

Although they may not preside as a deacon's functions include assisting the priest in ministering the Holy Communion and in its distribution and reading the Holy Scriptures especially the Gospel.[5] It is customary for the deacon to administer the chalice whilst the priest administers the paten but there is no reason why a deacon should not administer the paten.

A lay person may distribute the Holy Communion, if specifically authorised by the bishop under regulations made by the General Synod.[6] Such a person must be baptised and confirmed, and the incumbent or priest-in-charge must apply in writing to the bishop and the application must be supported by the churchwardens.[7] Subject to the bishop's general directions a lay person may also, at the invitation of the minister, read the Epistle and Gospel and the prayer of intercession.[8] A lay person may also preside over the Ministry of the Word where

[1] Canon B12(1). It cannot be celebrated by a lay person even in an emergency: *Escott v. Martin* (1842) 4 Moo. P.C. 104 at 128.

[2] ASB, p. 115, n.2.

[3] *Book of Common Prayer*, the rubric before the administration of Communion in the Order for the Administration of the Lord's Supper or Holy Communion states that the minister shall receive Communion themselves and proceed to deliver the same to the bishops if any be present. However, although under this rite a bishop would generally not preside the rubric is not to be regarded as a matter of order preventing him from doing so: Bursell, *Luturgy, Order and the Law* (1996), p. 99, n. 9.

[4] Bursell, *Liturgy, Order and the Law* (1996), p. 99.

[5] *The Ordinal*, Form and Manner of Making of Deacons.

[6] Canon B12(3). Regulations on the Administration of Holy Communion passed by the Church Assembly in November 1969, which remain in operation. The regulations are reproduced as an annexure to the *Canons of the Church of England* (5th ed. 1993).

[7] Permission is a matter for the bishop's discretion, but lay distribution of the elements has been the subject of diocesan norms, many of which require the consent of the PCC as well as the churchwardens and that the person concerned be over 17 years old. Permission is often given for a fixed term and may lapse on a vacancy in the benefice: Doe, *The Legal Framework of the Church of England* (1996), pp. 338–339. A deaconess is authorised to distribute the sacrament under Canon D1(3)(b), and readers and lay workers may be authorised purusant to Canons E4(2)(c) and E7(4)(b).

[8] Canon B12(4).

necessity dictates.[9] It is not clear what necessity this is directed at, nor what their ministry would encompass.[10] A lay person cannot make the greeting, say the Collect, give the Absolution, the peace and the blessing, nor consecrate the elements, and presumably cannot preach a sermon.

Location

The general rule is that unless they have prior permission from the bishop no **10.4** priest shall celebrate Holy Communion other than in a consecrated building or other building licensed for the purpose within their cure.[11] However, it would appear, as we saw in Chapter 5 that the permission of the bishop is needed in regard to a proposal to conduct a celebration in the open air.

The main exception to the general rule regarding celebration in consecrated buildings is celebration in a private house where there is a person who is sick, dying, or so impotent that they cannot attend church, and who is desirous of receiving the sacrament.[12] As we saw in Chapter 6 the bishop may licence a minister to celebrate Holy Communion in colleges, schools, hospitals and public or charitable institutions, and a chaplain ministering in a house in which there is a chapel may also celebrate Holy Communion there subject to certain restrictions.

Number of communicants

The minimum obligations as to the frequency of celebration of Holy Communion **10.5** were considered in Chapter 9. Whether that requirement is to be subject to the additional requirement of the presence of a sufficient number of communicants is not clear.[13] The Book of Common Prayer states that Holy Communion should not be celebrated unless there are a convenient number to communicate with the priest at their discretion.[14] The purpose of this rubric being to prevent solitary masses.[15] However, the priest's discretion is limited by a further provision that even if there are not more than 20 qualified communicants in the parish there is to be no Communion unless four, or at least three, communicate with the priest.[16] Even in regard to the Communion of the Sick the Book of Common Prayer requires that at least two persons other than the priest communicate save in cases of infectious diseases. The requirements as to the number of communicants does not appear in the ASB and in practice the limitation set out in the

[9] ASB, p. 115.
[10] This may be aimed at matters such as the president losing their voice. See further Bursell, *Liturgy, Order and the Law* (1996), p. 99.
[11] Canon B40.
[12] Canon B37(2).
[13] Bursell, *Liturgy, Order and the Law* (1996), p. 105 suggests that the requirement as to numbers cannot be used to circumvent the requirement as to frequency of celebration.
[14] Rubrics at the end of the Order for the Administration of the Lord's Supper or Holy Communion. The ASB states that the president and the people receive Communion: ASB, p. 143, n. 46; p. 196, n. 37.
[15] Bursell, *Liturgy, Order and the Law* (1996), p. 103.
[16] See n. 14 *ante*.

Book of Common Prayer is of no effect today when it is common for the priest to communicate alone with the sick person. Furthermore although it has been held in the nineteenth century to be an ecclesiastical offence to communicate with less than three other communicants, unless administering to the sick,[17] in recent times there has been much latitude in the observance of these requirements in regard to services held in the church and it is not uncommon for there only to be a priest and a server. As a matter of law the requirement as to numbers may now be regarded as a matter of discretion for the minister provided at least one other person is present.[18]

Persons to be admitted to Holy Communion

10.6   All members of the Church of England who have been confirmed in accordance with the rites of that Church, or who are ready and desirous of being confirmed, or have been otherwise episcopally confirmed with unction of the laying on of hands, are entitled to be admitted to Holy Communion.[19] So too are those who are baptised persons and who are communicant members of other churches which subscribe to the doctrine of the Holy Trinity and who are in good standing in their own church.[20] The words used are mandatory not permissive so that the incumbent has no discretion.[21] If such a person regularly receives Communion over a long period which appears likely to continue indefinitely, the minister must however set before that person the normal requirement for communicant status.[22] However, having set these before them the decision whether to comply rests with the individual.[23] Any baptised person in immediate danger of death may also be admitted[24] as may any baptised person who is authorised to be admitted under regulations of the General Synod.[25] Where a minister is in doubt as to the communicant status of any person they should refer the matter to the diocesan bishop or other Ordinary.[26]

Any member of the Church of England ready and desirous of being confirmed may receive Holy Communion and this may extend to children under 18 years of age, provided that they fulfil the conditions, although it would be unusual to admit a child before puberty.[27] In regard to young children it is common practice

---

[17] *Parnell v. Roughton* (1874) L.R. 4 P.C. 46; *Clifton v. Ridsdale* (1876) 1 P.D. 316.

[18] Bursell, *Liturgy, Order and the Law* (1996), p. 105.

[19] Canon B15A(1)(a).

[20] Canon B15A(1)(b).

[21] *Legal Opinions*, p. 5.

[22] Canon B15A(2).

[23] *Legal Opinions*, p. 5.

[24] Canon B15A(1)(c).

[25] Canon B15A(1)(d). Although to date no relgulations have been made.

[26] Canon B15A(3).

[27] The issues surrounding the admission of children to Communion before confirmation are considered in Reardon, *Christian Initiation; Communion before Confirmation*, the Report of the Working Party of the General Synod's Board of Education on Christian Initiation and Participation in the Eucharist (1985). As to diocesan norms see Doe, *The Legal Framework of the Church of England* (1996), p. 346. The admission of unconfirmed children to Holy Communion was raised in the November 1996 group of sessions of the General Synod and is under active consideration. Some local experiments have been authorised by diocesan bishops.

for them to go to the altar rail and receive a blessing at the time of distribution of communion. If confirmed or ready and desirous of this, the mentally handi-capped are entitled to receive the sacrament, and the policy of the Church of England is that such persons should be encouraged to become communicant members of the Church.[28]

Duty to communicate

A positive duty is imposed by canon upon all confirmed members of the Church **10.7** of England to receive Holy Communion regularly, and especially at the festivals of Christmas, Easter and Whitsun (Pentecost).[29] The Book of Common Prayer also contains a provision to the effect that all parishioners shall communicate at least three times a year of which Easter is to be one.[30] Persons intending to communicate are strictly required to signify their names to the minister at least some time the day before,[31] but this is a requirement which has now fallen almost entirely into dissuse. In any event lack of notice would not appear to be sufficient grounds for a minister to refuse admission to Holy Communion, and the entire practice may have been no more than a courtesy or convenience.[32]

Lesser excommunication

A minister may not without lawful cause deny the sacrament to any person who **10.8** devoutly and humbly desires it.[33] If the minister is persuaded that a person ought not to be admitted by reason of malicious and open contention with their neighbours or other grave and open sin without repentance, the minister must give an account of this to the Ordinary and obey their order and direction in the matter.[34] Until this procedure has been followed, and in accordance with any order or direction the minister warns the person not to come to the Lord's table, the minister may not refuse them the sacrament.[35] The only exception is where the matter is one which is a case of grave and immediate scandal to the congregation. In such a case the minister is not to admit them, but to give an account to the Ordinary within seven days and obey the Ordinary's order and directions[36] It should be noted that before making an order or direction in either case the Ordinary must afford the person concerned the opportunity for an

---

[28] Bayley, *The Local Church and Mentally Handicapped People* (1984); Doe, *The Legal Framework of the Church of England* (1996), p. 347.
[29] Canon B15(1).
[30] *Book of Common Prayer,* rubric at the beginning of the Order for the Administration of the Lord's Supper or Holy Communion.
[31] *ibid.*
[32] Bursell, *Liturgy, Order and the Law* (1996), p. 103.
[33] Sacrament Act 1547, s.8. The right to receive communion is enforceable in the civil courts at common law: *R. v. Dibdin* [1910] P. 57 at 107.
[34] Canon B16(1); *Book of Common Prayer,* rubric at the beginning of the Order for the Administration of the Lord's Supper or Holy Communion.
[35] *ibid.*
[36] See n. 34 *ante.*

interview. Exclusion from the Lord's table in this manner is sometimes referred to as a "lesser excommunication".

A minister contemplating exclusion needs to exercise great care not least because (aside from the lack of charity involved) this could involve an action against them for defamation in the secular courts. "Grave and open" sin means more than being a sinner as all persons are sinners, and "grave and immediate" scandal must be still more serious. It has been said that this involves a course of life which is in conflict with Christian morality and causes offence to the public conscience.[37]

Whether a lawful cause for exclusion is limited to the matters specified in the opening rubric of the Order for the Administration of the Lord's Supper or Holy Communion in the Book of Common Prayer, or whether it could include other breaches of church discipline is not clear. As a matter of law it would appear unlikely that the sacrament could be refused to a person who had contracted a marriage valid in temporal law, but invalid in ecclesiastical law,[38] although in practice bishops have on occasion assumed the right to exercise discretion in regard to persons divorced who have remarried during the lifetime of a former spouse.[39]

The elements

10.9 The churchwardens of every parish with the advice and direction of the minister must provide a sufficient quantity of bread and wine for communicants.[40] It suffices that the bread is such as is usually eaten[41] but it would appear that bread may be leavened or unleavened,[42] thus permitting the use of wafer bread. The bread must be of the best and purest wheat flour that can conveniently be got and the wine must be good and wholesome and the fermented juice of the grape.[43] It may be that those who are unable due to a medical condition to eat

---

[37] *Thompson v. Dibdin* [1910] A.C. 533, H.L. A sin cannot be open if known only to the minister: *R. v. Dibdin (ante)* at 137. It has been suggested that where such a person makes a general confession repenting of their sins and receives absolution as part of the congregation they must be admitted: Doe, *The Legal Framework of the Church of England* (1996), p. 344.

[38] *Banister v. Thompson* [1908] P. 362; *R. v. Dibdin* [1910] P. 57, C.A.; affd *sub nom. Thompson v. Dibdin* [1912] A.C. 533, H.L.

[39] An Act of the Convocation of York in 1938 provides that a minister may exclude from Communion a divorced person who has remarried within the lifetime of a former spouse. However, the matter must be referred to the bishop who, if satisfied that the admission ought not to give grave offence to the Church nor "would be to the hurt of their own souls", may direct that they are not to be excluded, where they have resided in the diocese, for the preceding six months. The decision of the bishop in such a case is to be accepted as final in the province including all other dioceses within it. A similar Act for the Province of Canterbury was revoked by the General Synod in 1982.

[40] Canon B17(1).

[41] *Book of Common Prayer*, rubric at the end of the Order for the Administration of the Lord's Supper or Holy Communion.

[42] A provision referring to unleavened bread was contained within the Prayer Book (Miscellaneous Provisions) Measure 1965, s.3(3) (repealed) which may indicate the legality of unleavened bread notwithstanding earlier decisions to the contrary.

[43] Canon B17(1).

gluten or to take alcohol can of necessity be provided with a separate wafer or non-alcoholic wine, although in order to prevent diversity their receiving only wine or bread respectively may be more appropriate.[44] The bread is to be brought to the communion table in a paten or convenient box and the wine in a convenient cruet or flagon,[45] and the Holy table is to be covered with a fair white linen cloth.[46] It is the duty of the minister to keep the communion plate washed and ready.[47]

Ante-Communion

The Order for Holy Communion as set out in the Book of Common Prayer comprises two elements, the Ante-Communion which ends with a prayer for the church militant, and the Communion itself. Although the rubrics direct (and the ASB makes similar provision) that the Ante-Communion be said on Sundays and other holy days even though no Communion is to follow this is a requirement which is generally no longer observed.   **10.10**

Collections

During the reading of the offertory, which forms part of the Ante-Communion, the deacons, churchwardens or other fit persons appointed[48] receive the alms for the poor and other devotions of the people in a decent "bason" provided for the purpose by the parish.[49] This bason is then reverently brought to the priest who humbly presents it and places it upon the holy table. The disposal of such alms is to be for such uses as the minister and PCC jointly determine, or if they disagree as the bishop directs, the alms forming part of the general funds of the PCC.[50] It should be noted that it is evident from the rubrics that it is not unlawful, although neither is it obligatory, to announce the objects of the collection beforehand. Nor, where Holy Communion is combined with another service, is it illegal to take two collections.[51]   **10.11**

Position of celebrant and manual acts

Holy Communion must be celebrated distinctly, reverently and in an audible voice.[52] The rubric in the Book of Common Prayer directs that the priest shall, at the opening prayers of the Communion itself, stand at the north side of the table.   **10.12**

---

[44] Bursell, *Liturgy, Order and the Law* (1996), p. 109.
[45] Canon B17(1).
[46] Canon F2(2).
[47] Canon F3(2).
[48] The appointment is made by the priest: *Cope v. Barber* (1872) L.R. 7 C.P. 393 at 403. If a priest performs this function then they perform a lay function: *ibid.*
[49] Canon F3(2).
[50] PCCPM, ss.7(iv), 9(3); Canon B17A.
[51] *Marson v. Unmark* [1921] P. 163.
[52] Canons B13(1), B14(1).

In the period when the rubric was first framed the table was lengthwise in most parish churches with the shorter sides facing east and west, or moved into this position in the body of the church for a celebration (giving rise to the idea that the altar should be moveable). Only later did the table come to be placed altarwise, giving rise to a longrunning dispute as to whether the priest was still required to stand at the north end or should stand at the west side, or whether the priest was at liberty to move to the west side after the opening prayers. Decisions of the courts have made clear that considerable latitude is to be permitted on the interpretation of these issues, and in particular it has been held that it is not an ecclesiastical offence for a priest to stand on the west side of the table at any time during the Holy Communion.[53]

However, the courts have held that all manual acts, such as the traction or breaking of the bread, should be visible to all communicants, this being the effect of the rubric directing that these should be "before the people".[54] Whilst it should be noted that there is no authority for the increasingly common practice of the priest standing on the east side (that is behind the table) facing westwards towards the congregation, this, as opposed to standing on the west side, does have the advantage of rendering such acts more visible. However, where such a practice has not been prevalent the minister ought not to introduce this unilaterally.[55]

Administration

10.13 Whenever they celebrate Holy Communion every minister must receive the sacrament themselves.[56] The rubric of the Prayer Book then requires them to administer it to the other communicants, delivering it into their hand when they kneel. The so-called "black rubric" at the end of the Order for the Administration of the Lord's Supper or Holy Communion emphasises that the act of kneeling does not imply any adoration of either the sacramental bread or wine, or any corporeal presence of Christ's natural flesh and blood. The bread and wine remain in their natural substances and Christ's natural body and blood are in Heaven. Unless necessity requires otherwise the sacrament must be administered to the people in both kinds, that is both bread and wine.[57] In addition to the examples considered above this would also include a person too sick to take anything but liquids.

The question has arisen as to the lawfulness of the priest consecrating the wine in a lipped chalice or flagen and administering the wine by pouring it into individual cups held by each communicant. The rubrics of the Book of Common Prayer and the words of the ASB contemplate that the wine will be administered to each communicant in a common cup, delivered (as required by canon law and statute) into their hands. Accordingly the use of individual cups, which raises various issues as to their provision, cleansing and so forth, as well as drawing an unacceptable division between the minister and communicants if the minister

---

[53] *Reed v. Bishop of Lincoln* [1892] A.C. 644, P.C. at 665.
[54] *Ridsdale v. Clifton* (1877) 2 P.D. 276, P.C. at 343–344.
[55] *Howell v. Holyroyd* [1897] P. 198.
[56] Canon B12(2).
[57] Sacrament Act 1547, s.8.

drinks from the chalice or flagon, is considered unlawful.[58] The exception would be in cases of necessity, recognised by the Sacrament Act 1547, where for example there was fear of contracting a contagious disease. However, it is suggested that the elements may be lawfully administered by adopting the practice of intinction (from the latin *intingere* to dip in) that is by the priest delivering the bread to the communicant who then dips it into the cup which is held by the priest but which the communicant lays his other hand upon as he dips the bread.[59] It should also be noted that the unlawfulness of individual cups does not prevent the consecration of wine in a flagon which is then poured into several chalices for administration by several ministers or others at services with a large congregation where a number of communicants receive from each chalice[60]. The same principle would apply so that more than one paten could be used for the bread.

In a number of cases particularly during the nineteenth century the legality of certain ceremonies connected with the consecration of the elements has been brought into question. Before considering these it is helpful to consider briefly eucharistic doctrine, since theological considerations underpin all such disputes. The doctrine of transubstantiation (whereby it is held that the physical accidents or characteristics of the bread and wine remain unchanged but the substance becomes the body and blood of Christ) is incompatible with Anglican doctrine being expressly repudiated by Article XXVIII of the Thirty-nine Articles of Religion. It is however clear that great emphasis is placed upon the sacramental character of what occurs during the consecration of the elements, and it should be noted that a repudiation of the doctrine of transubstantiation does not involve a rejection of the doctrine of the Real (as opposed to corporeal) Presence.[61] Article XXVIII declares that the body of Christ is given, taken and eaten, only after an heavenly and spiritual manner, by faith, which has been expressed by some as the doctrine of consubstantiation.

Certain practices have been held to be unlawful. The mixing of the wine with water in, and as part of, the Communion service has been held to be illegal.[62] So too has a change of the priest's posture by kneeling or prostration during the prayer of consecration, this being directly contrary to the rubrics which state that the priest should remain standing.[63] Article XXV declares that the sacraments were not ordained by Christ to be carried about, but that we should duly use them, whilst Article XXVIII states that the sacrament was not by Christ's ordinance to be reserved, carried about, lifted up and worshipped. In line with this the elevation of the elements after consecration has been held to be unlawful.[64] So too has the performance of a ceremony of ablution or cleansing of

10.14

---

[58] *Legal Opinions* pp. 138–142.
[59] *Legal Opinions*, pp. 138–142.
[60] *Legal Opinions*, pp. 138–142.
[61] *Sheppard v. Bennett* (1871) L.R. 4 P.C. 371.
[62] *Read v. Bishop of Lincoln* [1892] A.C. 644 at 658, P.C. In the *Opinions of Lambeth* issued July 31, 1899 (Macmillan & Co. Official Reports) the archbishops were of the view that although the wine of passover was a mixed cup so that there was no objectio.i to mixing beforehand, there is no record of Our Lord having mixed the cup afresh for the purposes of the sacrament itself.
[63] *Martin v. Mackonochie* (1868) L.R. 2 P.C. 365; (1869) L.R. 3 P.C. 52; (1870) L.R. 3 P.C. 409.
[64] *ibid.*

the vessels as a distinct and integral part of the service, as opposed to the cleaning by the minister of all remains by reverent consumption without ceremony or prayers as required by the rubrics.[65]

Reservation of the sacrament

10.15   Perhaps the greatest controversy of all has been that concerning the practice of reservation of the sacrament, whereby a portion of the consecrated elements is set aside for subsequent administration to persons other than those present at the service where consecration took place. It is important to distinguish between the three distinct forms this practice may take. The first, which it is claimed does not constitute reservation at all, involves treating sick persons not actually in the church but who are living close by as part of the congregation. The consecrated elements are then taken out of the church and administered to these people at the same time as they are administered to the rest of the congregation, so that it cannot be said that what is sent out is part of what remains after the service is over. The second form is to set aside a portion of the sacraments for administration, after the service, to those known to be sick at the time of the service or retained for use in case of sudden emergency. The final form is to reserve the sacrament for administration after the service to those who cannot attend for reasons other than incapacity, such as conditions of work.

In addition to references to Articles XXV and XXVIII, set out above, those opposed to reservation rely upon the rubric at the end of the Order for the Administration of Holy Communion which directs that if any of the bread and wine remain it shall not be carried out of the church but reverently consumed. A counter argument is that this rubric was directed at the practices of puritan extremists who would otherwise take home what remained of the elements for ordinary consumption. It is also noteworthy that until its repeal in 1967 a section of the Brawling Act 1553 provided for the protection of the sacrament and the receptacle for holding it. Perhaps the strongest argument for the practice has been that based upon the doctrine of necessity, which has been discussed in Chapter 9. Particularly in modern times when priests have increasing demands upon their time, individual celebrations at the homes of the sick are not practicable.

The deposited Prayer Books of 1927 and 1928 would have permitted the practice in regard to reservation in an aumbry set into the church wall as part of an alternative Order for the Communion of the Sick. In 1929, in exercise of their *jus liturgicum*, the bishops issued a statement[66] to regulate the practice of reservation on the lines laid down by the deposited Prayer Books, notwithstanding the technical illegality of the practice. Under the practice laid down by the bishops the diocesan bishop is entitled to authorise reservation in a prescribed place of safety for purposes which he defines. Usually these are for the communion of the sick (which had been contemplated by the two Prayer Books) but may extend to some groups of parishioners whose work prevents them from being at church services. Although the practice of reservation was held in older

[65] *Read v. Bishop of Lincoln (ante).*
[66] The Canterbury resolution is set out in full by the Dean of the Arches in *Re Lapford (Devon) Parish Church* [1955] P. 205 at 213. The York resolution was in similar terms.

cases to be illegal, in the light of the bishops' statement and modern liturgical developments, it has been accepted by the courts as being allowable so long as episcopal sanction is obtained, and the conditions under which this is granted are observed.[67] Indeed it has been held that the rubrics of the ASB, which are not in the same terms as those of the Book of Common Prayer but simply say that the bread and wine which is not required for the purposes of communion is to be consumed at the end of the distribution or after the service, in fact permit reservation.[68]

Baptism

Baptism is the sacrament by which a person is admitted into the Church, and it is also the sign of regeneration or new birth to a life in the Spirit.[69] Its essential elements are the immersion of the candidate in water, or the affusion or pouring of water over them in the name of the Trinity. Immediately after baptism the cross is signed upon the forehead of the baptised[70] but this forms no part of the substance of the sacrament being simply in remembrance of the cross and following the practice of the primitive and apostolic church.[71]   **10.16**

Baptism provides a legal and valid initiation into the Church,[72] and is a precondition for admission to Holy Communion, confirmation, ordination and admission to various legal offices and institutions. Baptism has been regarded by many as a prerequisite to salvation.[73] However, whatever views may have been held in the past the ASB requires that parents be assured that the question of ultimate salvation or of the provision of a Christian funeral for an infant who dies do not depend upon whether or not the child has been baptised.[74]

Being a sacrament it is appropriate that baptism should if possible be administered by a priest.[75] However, a deacon is required to baptise in the

---

[67] The legal position was fully discussed in *Bishopswearmouth v. Adey* [1958] 1 W.L.R. 1183. See also *Re Lapford (Devon) Parish Church* [1955] P. 205; [1954] P. 416, C.A.; *Re St Mary's Tyne Dock* [1954] P. 369; *Re St Nicholas, Plumstead* [1961] 1 W.L.R. 916; *Re St Peter & St Paul, Leckhampton* [1968] P. 495; *Re St Matthew's Wimbledon* [1985] 3 All E.R. 670. See also *Newsom*, pp. 138–141.

[68] See *Re St Peter & St Paul, Leckhampton (ante)*.

[69] Article XXVII of the Thirty-nine Articles of Religion and see the Book of Common Prayer and ASB.

[70] *Book of Common Prayer*, rubrics in the Ministration of Publick Baptism of Infants, of Private Baptism of Children and of Baptism to Such as are of Riper Years; Canon B21.

[71] Canon B25.

[72] *Kemp v. Wickes* (1809) 3 Phill. 264 at 275.

[73] Although there has been considerable speculation and controversy over the centuries as to the precise theological significance of baptism the Church of England is not swift to condemn any view as long as it is not inconsistent with the little stated in the Articles of Religion and the Book of Common Prayer: Briden and Hanson, *Moor's Introduction to English Canon Law* (3rd ed., 1992), p. 62. *Gorham v. Bishop of Exeter* [1850] Moore's Special Report 462.

[74] ASB, *Emergency Baptism*.

[75] The ASB provides that the parish priest should normally adminsiter baptism but may delegate this to any lawful minister: ASB, p. 241, n. 1. Presumably this is when the priest themselves cannot be present.

absence of a priest,[76] and a deaconess may also be authorised by the bishop to do so, again in the absence of the priest.[77] Furthermore baptism by ministers of other churches[78] or by a lay person in the name of the Trinity is good and effectual,[79] and even it would appear baptism administered by a non-believer.

A decent font with a cover to keep it clean must be provided in every church or chapel in which baptism is to be administered[80]. The font bowl must only be used for water at the administration of baptism and for no other purpose.[81] These requirements relate to the traditional font. Modern liturgical thinking concerning fonts capable of permitting baptism by affusion, immersion or submersion and their location are considered in Chapter 11.

Age of candidates

10.17 Baptism may take place at any age but the Church of England favours infant baptism whenever possible. Article XXVII of the Thirty-nine Articles of Religion states that baptism of young children is to be retained in the Church and the Book of Common Prayer says that parents should be admonished not to delay baptism longer than the first or second Sunday after birth, unless there is a great or reasonable cause.[82]

The Book of Common Prayer draws a distinction between infants and children and those of riper years, whereas the ASB distinguishes between children not old enough to answer for themselves and adults.[83] In practice the distinctions are not likely to cause difficulties if it is borne in mind that in the case of a person of riper years or of an adult they will be confirmed as soon thereafter as may be convenient. Those of riper years could therefore include for example those who are not yet 18 years of age. The ASB provides that in the case of children able to respond they should, at the discretion of the priest, answer the questions with their parents and godparents.[84]

In regard to those who are mentally handicapped but no longer children and whose ability to answer for themselves may be in doubt, there is no reason why baptism should be denied. Recourse may be had to the Book of Common Prayer which provides that one of the forms of infant baptism is to be used in the case of those who were not baptised in infancy but have not yet come to years of discretion to answer for themselves.[85]

[76] *The Ordinal*, Form and Making of Deacons.
[77] Canon D1,(4)(b).
[78] In *Kemp v. Wickes* (*ante*) the Dean of the Arches specifically referred to baptisms in the Roman Catholic, Greek and Presbyterian Churches and by the Calvanistic Independents: *ibid.*, at 270–271.
[79] *Kemp v. Wickes* (*supra*); *Escott v. Mastin* (1843) 4 Moo. P.C.C. 104; *Nurse v. Henslowe* (1844) 3 Note of Cases 272; *Titchmarsh v. Chapman* (1844) 3 Notes of Cases 370; *Cope v. Barber* (1872) L.R. 7 C.P. 373 at 402.
[80] Canon F1(1).
[81] Canon F1(3).
[82] *Book of Common Prayer*, introductory rubric to the Private Baptism of Children.
[83] See also Canon B24(1) which refers to those of riper years who are also able to answer for themselves.
[84] p. 241, n. 2.
[85] *Book of Common Prayer*, rubric at the end of the Ministration of Baptism of such as are of Riper Years. See also Bursell, *Liturgy, Order and the Law* (1996), pp. 137–8.

Duty to baptise children

Whether or not the Church of England should adopt a liberal and inclusive **10.18** approach to baptism or whether it should seek to restrict the rite to those children for whom there is some prospect of their being brought up in the Christian faith has been a matter of some debate.[86] However, under the present law a minister with the cure of souls is generally under a duty to baptise children, subject in certain cases to the right to delay. In particular a minister must not refuse or delay to go and baptise any infant within their cure if informed of the weakness of, or danger of death, of that infant and that they are desired to go and baptise the child.[87]

Provided that due notice has been given and the provisions relating to godparents observed (which the minister may insist on) a minister may only refuse to baptise an infant within their cure or delay for the purpose of preparing or instructing the parents or guardians or godparents.[88] The canon does not specify the grounds upon which such preparation or instruction may be warranted and is not clear whether for example lack of intent to bring up the child as a Christian would be sufficient reason to delay, nor is it clear if the minister must refuse or merely has a discretion to delay in appropriate cases. If the minister does refuse or delay unduly the parents, guardians or godparents may apply to the diocesan bishop who must make such directions as he thinks fit after consultation with the minister.[89] A refusal or unlawful or unreasonable delay may consitute an offence of ministerial neglect of duty, and a conscientious objection would not of itself be sufficent to justify refusal.[90]

Notice to be given in respect of the baptism of children

Due notice should be given before a child is brought to the church to be **10.19** baptised. Although the Book of Common Prayer says that this should be given overnight or in the morning before Morning Prayer,[91] Canon B22(1) states that normally at least a weeks notice should be given.[92] Where a minister intends to baptise an infant whose parents reside outside the boundaries of their cure, unless the names of one of them are on the electoral roll of that church, the minister should not proceed to baptise without having sought the goodwill of the minister of the parish in which the parents reside.[93]

---

[86] See Reardon, *Christian Initiation: A Policy for the Church of England* (1991). (G.S. Misc. 365).

[87] Canon B22, (6).

[88] Canon B22(4).

[89] Canon B22(2). There is no specific right of appeal from the bishop's decision although the matter could become the subject of a judicial review or of an application to the European Court of Human Rights. See Doe, *The Legal Framework of the Church of England* (1996), p. 317.

[90] *Bland v. Archdeacon of Cheltenham* [1972] Fam. 157.

[91] *Book of Common Prayer*, introductory rubric to the Publick Baptism of Children.

[92] It is not clear to whom this notice should be given, but it is to be inferred that it is the minister with the cure of souls.

[93] Canon B22(5). The duty is only to seek the goodwill not to obtain it.

Parents and guardians

10.20   Ecclesiastical law does not define parents or guardians with the consequence that the secular law will apply to determine who these are and who therefore has parental responsibility.[94] It is doubtful that the minister has a duty to enquire into the bona fides of a person who holds themselves out as a parent or guardian unless there is reason to doubt this, but once such doubt arises appropriate enquiries should be made and the matter resolved before baptism takes place.[95] Where only one parent or guardian approaches the minister enquiries should be made as to the existence and attitude to baptism of the other parent or guardian, so that they may be instructed in their responsibilites. Although it is usual for the consent of a parent to be sought this does not appear to be a prerequisite for baptism and, for example, in the case of an emergency baptism it may not be possible to obtain such consent.[96]

Godparents

10.21   Unless the person is of sufficient age to answer for themselves there must be no fewer than three godparents, save that where three cannot be conveniently obtained, one godfather and one godmother will suffice.[97] For a male child there should be two godfathers and a godmother and for a female child two godmothers and one godfather. Parents may be godparents for their own children provided there is at least one other godparent.[98] At the ministration of baptism the godparents are required to make the appropriate answers on behalf of the child and it is they who name the child and give it what becomes its christian name.[99]

Godparents are to be persons who will faithfully fulfil their responsibilities both by their care for the children committed to their charge and by the example of their own godly living.[1] The minister must instruct parents or guardians of an

---

[94] Under the Children Act 1989 if a child's father and mother are married to each other at the time of its birth each has parental responsibility, but if they are not married a father can only gain such under the provisions of that Act by order of the Court: *ibid.*, ss.4, 12. An adoption order gives parental responsibility to those adopting the child and the rights of natural parents and of guardians are thereby extinguished: Adoption Act 1976, s.12.

[95] Bursell, *Liturgy, Order and the Law* (1996), p. 136.

[96] However, care should be taken if it is known that one parent is opposed that the question of baptism is not made the subject of an application to the secular court. Doe, *The Legal Framework of the Church of England* (1996), p. 317, n. 47 refers to one such application being made pursuant to the Children Act 1989 by a muslim father opposed to such baptism which the mother of the child wished to be carried out, but the outcome of that case cannot be traced.

[97] Canon B22(1); *Book of Common Prayer*, introductory rubric to the Publick Baptism of Children.

[98] *ibid.* If a parent is baptised on the same occasion as their child provided they are baptised first they may become a godparent: ASB, p. 225, n. 2.

[99] *Book of Common Prayer*, rubrics in the Ministration of Publick Baptism of Children.

[1] Canon B23(2).

infant that the same responsibilities rest upon them as are required of the godparents.[2] An Act of Convocation in the province of Canterbury recommends that ministers visit godparents and parents in their homes to enquire as to their fitness and explain the meaning of the sacrament and their responsibilities.[3]

No person may be a godparent (or what is now termed a sponsor of a candidate of riper years) unless they have been baptised and confirmed, although the minister has the power to dispense with the requirement of confirmation in any case where in their judgment "need so requires".[4] It is not clear what situations this is intended to encompass but appears to give the minister wide discretion. There is no procedure to enable parents of a child to remove a godparent or substitute another person. However, there is no legal significance in a particular person being a godparent and therefore no objection to parents making an informal arrangement with other persons to act as additional godparents.[5]

Usual time and place of baptism

Baptism is normally to be administered on Sundays or other holy days at public worship.[6] This is so that the most people may be present and the congregation may witness the reception of the newly baptised person into the church and be reminded of their own profession at baptism.[7] **10.22**

Private or emergency baptism

The minister is enjoined to warn the people that they should not have their children baptised in their houses without grave cause and necessity.[8] However, both the Book of Common Prayer and the ASB provide brief forms of private baptism for use when a child has to be baptised at home or in hospital in an emergency. In the case of a private baptism the child is not signed with the cross.[9] Where a minister baptises a child in a hospital or nursing home and the parents of the child reside outside that minister's cure and their names are not on the electoral roll, the minister must send their names and addresses to the minister of the parish in which they reside.[10] **10.23**

---

[2] Canon B22(3).

[3] Smethurst, Wilson, Riley (eds) *Acts of Convocations* (revised ed. 1961) pp. 67–68.

[4] Canon B23(4). Proposals were discussed in the November 1996 group of sessions of the General Synod, under which godparents would no longer be required to be Christians nor to assert their belief in God but only to be sympathetic to the Christian faith, the aim being to make the baptism service more inclusive.

[5] *Legal Opinions*, p. 137.

[6] Canon B21; *Book of Common Prayer*, introductory rubric to the Publick Baptism of Children.

[7] Canon B21; *Book of Common Prayer*, introductory rubric to the Publick Baptism of Children.

[8] Canon B22(9).

[9] *Book of Common Prayer*, Private Baptism of Children; ASB, Emergency Baptism.

[10] Canon B22(7).

Emergency baptism may of course be administered if necessary by a lay person. The giving of a name is not essential in the case of an emergency or private baptism but should be given if possible.[11] There is no express provision for the emergency baptism of adults in danger of death although this may be implied in the ASB.[12]

If any infant which is baptised privately lives it is to be brought to the church and received by the minister into the congregation of Christ's flock, being signed with the cross.[13] If the validity of the former baptism cannot be verified then the child is conditionally rebaptised.[14]

Baptism of those of riper years

10.24 A separate office is provided for the baptism of those of riper years or adults. It is the minister's duty to see that such a candidate is properly instructed in the principles of the Christian religion and to exhort them to prepare themselves with prayers and fasting to receive the sacrament with repentance and faith.[15] Notice of any such baptism must be given by the minister to the diocesan bishop or whosoever he appoints one week before.[16] Such a person chooses three or at least two godparents to be sponsors who are ready to present the candidate at the font and to remind them of their Christian profession and duties.[17]

Administration of baptism

10.25 In the case of an infant the Book of Common Prayer contemplates that the child will normally be baptised by total immersion, although it states that if the child is weak it will suffice to pour water over it.[18] In spite of this in modern times most children are baptised by affusion (possibly in recognition of the tendency of very young children to catch a chill) rather than immersion. Sprinkling is also lawful. The ASB states that a threefold administration of water (whether by dipping or pouring) is an ancient practice of the Church and is commended as testifying to the faith of the Trinity, although a single administration is lawful and valid.[19] This ASB rite also contemplates that the sign of the cross may be made in oil blessed for the purpose.[20] The ASB makes provision for family baptism when parents and

---

[11] *Book of Common Prayer*, Private Baptism of Children; ASB Emergency Baptism.

[12] This contemplates verification of their baptism by the person baptised in an emergency in contrast to verification on its behalf in the case of a child: ASB, p. 280, n. 109.

[13] Canon B22(8); *The Book of Common Prayer*, rubrics in the Ministration of the Private Baptism of Children. If the minister of the parish performed the baptism they must certify that the baptism was according to the law: *ibid*.

[14] *ibid*.

[15] Canon B24(1); *Book of Common Prayer*, introductory rubrics to the Baptism of Such as are of Riper Years.

[16] Canon B24(2). Such a person is to be confirmed by the bishop as soon as is convenient: Canon B24(3).

[17] Canon B23(3).

[18] *Book of Common Prayer*, rubrics in the Ministration of the Publick Baptism of Children.

[19] ASB, p. 226, n. 11.

[20] *ibid*., p. 225, n. 3.

children may be baptised together, stating that it is fitting that the children are baptised immediately after their parents.[21] The rites of public baptism in both the Book of Common Prayer and the ASB require that a name must be given, and this may consist of more than one part.[22] Any name given should not be wanton.[23]

Conditional baptism and renewal of baptismal vows

Admission into Christ's church is something which can occur only once and thus **10.26** baptism cannot be repeated. However, where there is doubt as to whether or not a person has been baptised the Book of Common Prayer and the ASB both make provision for conditional baptism. Despite calls to regulate the position of those who request rebaptism[24] (usually because they question the validity of their first baptism as an infant on the grounds that it lacked a genuine response to faith) any such request should therefore always be refused. A rite for the renewal of baptismal vows is provided in the ASB which may be used on appropriate occasions including Easter, New Year and in conjunction with baptism, confirmation and Holy Communion.

Registration of baptisms

A register of public and private baptisms must be kept by the minister of every **10.27** parish and by the minister of every chapelry where baptism may be administered,[25] and every minister must observe the law relating to the registration of baptisms.[26] The prescribed particulars[27] must be entered by the person who performed the ceremony as soon as possible after solemnisation in the register, who must also sign it.[28]

Where baptism is performed in any place in a parish other than the parish church by a person who is not a minister of the parish, the person performing the baptism must, as soon as possible thereafter, send the incumbent or priest-in-charge of the parish a certificate signed by them containing specified particulars.[29] In the case of a ceremony being performed in an extra-parochial place which does not have its own register the person who performs the baptism must send a

---

[21] *ibid.*, p. 225, n. 2.
[22] *Legal Opinions*, p. 182.
[23] Bursell, *Liturgy, Order and the Law* (1996), p. 150, relying on the application of pre-Reformation canon law.
[24] Reardon *Christian Initiation: A Policy for the Church of England* (1991, G.S. Misc. 365).
[25] Parochial Registers and Records Measure 1978, ss.1, 2; Births and Deaths Registration Act 1836, s.1. The 1978 Measure is also applied to cathedrals, collegiate churches and chapels of colleges and hospitals: *ibid.*, s.5. The minister of a conventional district must also comply with the requirements by sending a certificate to the incumbent or priest-in-charge of the parish certifying when and where the ceremony was performed: *Legal Opinions*, p. 16.
[26] Canon B39(1).
[27] The form is set out in the Parochial Registers and Records Measure 1978, Sched. 1.
[28] *ibid.*, s.2(1).
[29] Parochial Registers and Records Measure 1978, s.2(2). The form of the certificate is set out in *ibid.*, Sched. 1.

certificate to the incumbent or priest-in-charge of such adjoining parish as the bishop may direct.[30] On receiving any such certificates the incumbent or priest-in-charge must enter the particulars to which the certificate relates in the register of baptisms.[31]

Where a person's name appears on the birth certificate as that of the father of the child the baptismal register should follow the birth certificate. If no birth certificate is produced or if the certificate does not show who the father is no person's name can be entered as the father of an illegitimate child without his consent.[32] The same principles should be applied in the case of a married woman who leaves her husband and goes to live with another man whose name she assumes and by whom she has a child. The register has no place for the surname of the child. The register cannot be altered where a second husband accepts the child of his wife's first marriage and wishes the baptismal register to be amended to save the child from the knowledge that he is not the father.[33] Nor is there power to enter the name of a child born to parents in the Foreign or Armed Services in the register of a parish in England in which they normally reside.[34] The register may be annotated in the case of a person legitimised after baptism,[35] and provision is made for the correction of any error within one month of its discovery by an entry in the margin.[36]

Fees

10.28   Since baptism is a sacrament it was, under general ecclesiastical law to be administered free of charge (unless there was a local custom to the contrary). The Baptismal Fees Abolition Act 1872[37] expressly provides that no fee or reward may be demanded by any minister, clerk in holy orders, parish or vestry clerk, warden or any other person in respect of the administration or registration of baptism. Fees may however be charged for a short form of the certificate or a search of the register.[38]

Confirmation

10.29   Confirmation is the laying on of hands by the bishop upon persons who are baptised and instructed in the Christian faith and are come to years of discretion.[39] Confirmation is regarded as an important rite by the Church of

[30] *ibid.*, s.2(3).
[31] *ibid.*, s.2(4).
[32] *Legal Opinions*, p. 15.
[33] *Legal Opinions*, p. 15.
[34] *Legal Opinions*, p. 15.
[35] Baptismal Registers Measure 1978, s.1.
[36] Parochial Registers and Records Measure 1978, s.4, this must take place in the presence of the parents of the child to whom the entry relates or, in the case of their death or absence, the presence of the churchwardens: *ibid*. The error must be corrected by an entry in the margin of the register book without altering the original and must be signed by the person making it and attested by the persons in whose presence it is made and the date added: *ibid*.
[37] Baptismal Registers Measure 1961, s.1.
[38] *ibid.*, s.2.
[39] *Book of Common Prayer*, Order of Confirmation.

England yet almost nothing is said as to its meaning. Its theological significance is also a matter of dispute although it is generally agreed that it is the bestowal of the Holy Spirit to strengthen the candidate in their baptismal vows which have either been reaffirmed, or, in an older candidate, just taken.[40] In the Western Church it is commonly asserted that confirmation became separated from the rite of baptism as the result of infant baptism becoming the norm. But in the Eastern Church where infant baptism is also the norm, the infant is baptised, confirmed and receives the first Holy Communion in a single service shortly after birth. Although the rite of confirmation came to stand alone in the Western Church, theologically there appears to be no justification for its separation from the rite of baptism and it is therefore best regarded as a completion of the baptismal rite.

Godparents of baptised infants are to take care that they are brought to the bishop to be confirmed as soon as they are able to say the Apostles' Creed, the Lord's Prayer and the Ten Commandments and are further instructed in, and can render an account of, their faith according to the Church Catechism.[41] The minister having the cure of souls must satisfy themselves that these requirements are satisfied in regard to all candidates before presenting them to the bishop.[42] At confirmation the child affirms for themselves what was affirmed for them by their godparents at their baptism and each child should have a godparent as witness to their confirmation.[43] Although the Book of Common Prayer refers to everyone having a godparent as witness to their confirmation this does not appear in the ASB and is not a requirement for a valid confirmation. Indeed it could not be since it may well be the case that all the candidate's godparents have died.

The age at which confirmation takes places varies but 12 and 16 are common ages. Those who are baptised when they are of riper years should be confirmed by the bishop as soon as convenient after their baptism,[44] indeed are often baptised and confirmed on the same occasion. The desire of the Church of England to encourage the mentally handicapped to be confirmed and thus to become communicant members of the Church was discussed earlier, and it is therefore to be presumed that some degree of latitude may be extended with regard to their ability to fulfil all the criteria required, such as giving an account of their faith.[45]

10.30 A minister who has the cure of souls must diligently seek out children and others who they think are suitable to be confirmed, and instruct them in the Christian faith and life as set out in the Bible, the Book of Common Prayer and the Catechism.[46] Diocesan norms generally provide that candidates undergo a course of instruction prior to confirmation. The minister must satisfy themselves that those whom they present to the bishop for confirmation have been validly

---

[40] Briden and Hanson, *Moore's Introduction to English Canon Law* (3rd ed., 1992), p. 64. See also Dix, *The Theology of Confirmation in Relation to Baptism* (1946); Behrens, *Sacrament of Grace: The Theology, Practice and Law of the Roman Catholic Church and the Church of England* (1995).

[41] *Book of Common Prayer*, exhortation at the end of the Administration of Publick Baptism of Infants and rubric following the Catechism.

[42] Canon B27(3).

[43] *Book of Common Prayer*, rubric following the Catechism.

[44] Canon B24(3); *Book of Common Prayer*, rubric following the Ministration of Baptism to Such as are of Riper Years.

[45] See Doe, *The Legal Framework of the Church of England* (1996), p. 331.

[46] Canon B27(2).

baptised, ascertaining the date and place of such baptism.[47] In cases where the minister is doubtful about the candidate's baptism they are to be conditionally baptised by the minister before being presented to the bishop.[48] Before or at the time assigned for confirmation the minister gives the bishop the names of the candidates together with their ages and dates of their baptism.[49]

Confirmation is performed by the diocesan bishop or another bishop acting on his behalf,[50] although the bishop may delegate parts of the service other than the confirmation itself to other ministers.[51] Generally the minister presents the candidates to the bishop.

The bishop may for good reason add to or alter the Christian name of any a person who is confirmed,[52] by confirming them under the new name (which should be stated in full to indicate which, if any, parts of the original name have been retained) which is then deemed under the law of the Realm to be their lawful Christian name.[53] In such cases the bishop signs a certificate of his having confirmed the person by that name, which is noted in the register of confirmation[54] and, as a matter of good practice, should be noted in the margin of the register of baptisms although the register itself cannot be altered. It is also advisable although strictly unnecessary that a statutory declaration of the change of name be made.[55] All confirmations must be recorded in the register of confirmations kept for that purpose in every church or chapel.[56]

Reception into the Church of England

10.31 Canon B28 deals with reception into the Church of England. Any person who desires to be received into the Church of England who has not been baptised or the validity of whose baptism has been called into question, must be instructed and either baptised or conditionally baptised, such baptism constituting their reception into the Church of England. A person who has been baptised but not episcopally confirmed must, if they desire to be formally received into the Church of England, be recieved by the rite of confirmation after appropriate instruction. It should be noted that in some churches in christendom confirmation may be performed by a priest using oil blessed by the bishop. This would not constitute episcopal confirmation and thus the candidate for reception into the Church of England would require confirmation. In cases where the candidate is not ready to be received by confirmation they must be received by the parish priest with appropriate prayers.[56a]

---

[47] Canon B27(4).
[48] Canon B27(5).
[49] Canon B27(2).
[50] Canon B27(1).
[51] *The Book of Common Prayer* only provides for delegation of the reading of the Preface but the ASB provides for full delegation other than confirmation itself.
[52] *Re Parrott, Cox v. Parrott* [1946] Ch. 183.
[53] Canon B27(6).
[54] Canon B39(2).
[55] *Legal Opinions*, p. 182.
[56] Canon B39(2).
[56a] A rite of reception into the Church of England will be included in the new Alternative Service Book being prepared under the "ASB 2000" programme.

Those who have been episcopally confirmed by unction (that is the administration of oil) or by the laying on of hands must first receive instruction. They may then, with the permission of the bishop, be received into the Church of England according to the form of reception approved by General Synod or with other appropriate prayers. If a priest such a candidate may only be received into the Church of England by the diocesan bishop of his commissary.

Holy matrimony[57]

The nature of holy matrimony

The solemnisation of matrimony in church is an attestation in the presence of **10.32** God and the Church by a man and a woman of their consent and marital contract to cohabit with each other and only each other, and on the Church's part its blessing of their union.[58] The doctrine of the Church of England holds that marriage is a permanent, life-long union, of one man and one woman to the exclusion of all others until they are parted by death.[59] Marriage is for the procreation and nuturing of children, the hallowing and right direction of the natural instincts and affections and for the mutual society, help and comfort which the one ought to have of the other in both prosperity and adversity.[60] When application is made to them for a marriage in their church it is the duty of any minister to explain this doctrine to the parties.[61]

Divorce and remarriage

Until the State's introduction of divorce, in the modern sense of that term, both **10.33** Church and State followed Western Catholic canon law as to the nature of marriage. Now a divergence has arisen which is difficult to reconcile with the statement that the secular and ecclesiastical law are one. Although both agree that marriage springs from a contract the traditional stance of the Western Church has been that marriage is an indissolvable union creating a relationship akin to that of parent and child, the nature of marriage being determined by divine law. Although the Church has always accepted the right of the State to terminate the legal consequences of marriage it has adhered to the view that the parties remain husband and wife despite the legal nexus being broken.

Some argue that the Established Church cannot be at variance with the State. Accordingly secular legislation in the nineteenth century which brought into

---

[57] The following works offer guidance — *Suggestions for Guidance of the Clergy with Reference to the Marriage and Registration Act* (1982, HMSO); *Anglican Marriage in England and Wales: A Guide to the Law for the Clergy* available from the Faculty Office, The Sanctuary, Westminster, London, SW1 3JT.

[58] *Book of Common Prayer*, Form of Solemnisation of Matrimony; *Harrod v. Harrod* (1854) 1 K. & J. 4.

[59] Canon B30(1). This doctrine is expressed and maintained in the *Book of Common Prayer*, Form of Solemnization of Matrimony: Canon B30(2).

[60] *ibid.*

[61] Canon B30(3).

being divorce as it is now understood is simply to be taken as part of the overall process of legislation arising from the Reformation. The counter argument is that such erastianism is in conflict with the Western Catholic position which regards the Church's authority as limited to that delegated by Christ. Consequently the Church is not permitted to make alterations to the framework of divine law itself, but only has the power to legislate with regard to incidentals. On such a view a second union, whilst one of the parties to the first remains alive, is not theologically a marriage.[62]

A measure of compromise has been reached in respect of the differing views of Church and State. Accordingly the secular law recognises the right of a minister of the Church of England to decline to marry those entitled by law to be married if one or both of the intended parties to the marriage has been divorced and that former spouse is still living.[63] A minister may also decline to allow such a marriage to be solemnised in a church or chapel of which they are the minister.[64]

The Church has been under some pressure to reappraise its theology on marriage and to bring ecclesiastical law into line with the secular law. The present position which allows considerable discretion to individual ministers and relies upon such guidelines as may be issued by the bishop, creates a wide divergence in practice between both dioceses and individual parishes.

10.34 Resolutions concerning marriage and divorce which were declared an Act of Convocation[65] state that remarriage after divorce during the lifetime of a former partner always involves a departure from the true principle of marriage. Accordingly the Church should not allow the use of the marriage service in the case of anyone who has a former partner still living. That Act also declared that whilst affirming its adherence to Christ's principle and standard of marriage the Church of England recognised that the actual discipline of particular christian communions in the matter has varied widely. It also held that the Church of England was competent to enact such a discipline of its own in regard to marriage as might from time to time appear most salutary and efficacious.

In 1981 the General Synod carried a motion to the effect that whilst it considered that marriage should always be undertaken as a lifelong commitment, it nonetheless recognised that there were circumstances in which a divorced

---

[62] Briden and Hanson, *Moore's Introduction to English Canon Law* (3rd ed., 1992), pp. 72–74.

[63] Matrimonial Causes Act 1965, s.8(2).

[64] *ibid.*

[65] On October 1, 1957 published as an annexure to *The Canons of the Church of England* (5th ed. 1993). These resolutions were first passed by the Convocation of Canterbury in 1937 and then reaffirmed by it with modifications in 1957. The Convocation of York passed similar resolutions in 1938. Although essentially the same the York resolutions differ from those of Canterbury by declaring that both divorce and remarriage involve a departure from Christ's teaching and that the lifelong obligation is inherent in every marriage between Christians however solemnised, thus where two persons have contracted a legal marriage during the lifetime of a former partner of either of them, and either or both wish to be baptised or partake of Holy Communion the minister must refer the matter to the bishop who must have regard to the church's standard of marriage and to the pastoral care of the parties. Similar pastoral regulations relating to the sacraments existed for the province of Canterbury, but these were revoked by the General Synod in 1982. The York pastoral regulations have not been revoked and are therefore strictly operative.

person might be married in church during the lifetime of a former spouse. It considered that no action should be taken to repeal or modify the resolutions of the Convocations until a report had been prepared. Subsequently in 1984 such a report, prepared by the House of Bishops, was rejected with the consequence that the resolutions remain in force. However, notwithstanding this the House of Bishops issued guidelines in 1985[66] since they considered that provision ought to be made for clergy who held the view that a second marriage was theologically permissible.

The guidelines state that in regard to the past marriage applicants will be free to marry in church if the dissolved relationship was one which, either in its original intention or in the way it developed, failed to acquire the nature and purpose of marriage as taught by Christ.[67-68] A person is also free to remarry if the primary reason for the breakdown of the marriage was the arbitary action of the other party or if they were divorced against their will. Finally, a person will be free to remarry if they have turned to Christ and this has caused an incompatibility of spirit which love could not overcome. In regard to the present attitude and approach of the applicants they will be required to demonstrate that the new relationship was not the direct cause of the breakdown of the past marriage and to demonstrate a mature view of the circumstances of the divorce; a failure to accept any responsibility for the breakdown generally being taken as a sign of immaturity. The applicants should also show that they are growing in an understanding of Christian marriage and that they intend to seek God's help in sustaining their proposed marriage.

The majority of diocesan norms follow the guidelines issued by the House of Bishops, although some still adhere to the resolutions of the Convocations and emphasise that remarriage is not the normal practice. Those diocesan regulations which follow or incorporate the guidelines generally impose a duty to consult the bishop, but leave the final decision to the minister concerned. The justification for such consultation is to achieve a uniformity of practice throughout the diocese. However, since the norms themselves only become operative when the minister concerned feels able to conduct a second marriage. The practice will obviously vary from parish to parish, depending upon the views of the incumbent or priest-in-charge.[69]

A decree of divorce is the dissolution[70] of an undoubted marriage and it is the remarriage of such divorcees which is the cause of tension both within the Church and between Church and State. However, in regard to a decree of nullity, that is the declaration that what appears to be a marriage but is not in fact so (in other words an annulment), Church and State are essentially[71] in

---

[66] *Marriage Discipline* being a Report issued by the House of Bishops of the General Synod February 13, 1985 (G.S. 669).

[67-68] For example, if there was no free consent, persistent infidelity or a unilateral decision not to have children.

[69] Doe, *the Legal Framework of the Church of England* (1996), pp. 378–79.

[70] A marriage is only dissolved by a decree absolute not a decree nisi and any cleric proposing to publish banns or to solemnise the marriage of a divorcee would be advised to obtain sight of a copy of the decree absolute.

[71] There is one divergence even here. Canon law has always considered that for a marriage to be void the ground upon which the declaration of nullity is granted must have existed at the time the marriage took place. Therefore although the State accepts it as such, the

agreement.[72] Space does not permit of a review of the law relating to nullity. Briefly it may be said that a marriage void *ab initio*[73] never existed whereas a voidable marriage[74] may only be impugned by one of the parties to it, and is taken to exist unless and until it is declared void by a court of competent jurisdiction. Thus if a marriage is void or is declared to be void[75] the parties to it may be regarded as never having been married and issues of remarriage do not arise.

Recognition of marriages by the Church which fulfil secular requirements

10.35 In consequence of its position as the Established Church the Church of England only recognises as a valid marriage that which complies with secular legal requirements. The Church being of the view that marriage arises by the mutual agreement of parties, who being free to do so take each other to the exclusion of all others, it also accepts any legal formula which fulfils these requirements. Accordingly the Church of England recognises the validity of civil marriages or those of other religious bodies, save where one of the parties is divorced and has

Church cannot regard a wilful refusal to consummate as a ground for a declaration of nullity, since it did not exist at the time of the ceremony. Were the view ultimately to prevail that theologically a marriage is not completed by the parties accepting each other as man and wife, but requires consummation, then the views of Church and State would be fully reconciled: Briden and Hanson, *Moore's Introduction to English Canon Law* (3rd ed., 1992) pp. 74–76. See also *Marriage in Church and State* Lacey (revised ed., 1947), pp. 198 *et seq.; The Church and the Law of Nullity of Marriage*, (1955) being the Report of a Commission appointed by the Archbishops of Canterbury and York in 1949.

[72] Acts of the Convocations in 1938 recognised as valid reasons for declaring a marriage null and void the same grounds as were then recognised by the State in the Matrimonial Causes Act 1937. Smethurst, Wilson & Riley (eds) *Acts of the Convocations* (revised ed. 1961) p. 92.

[73] A marriage may be declared void on one of six grounds namely where; the parties are within the prohibited degrees of relationship; one of the parties was under the age of 16 the parties have intermarried in disregard of certain requirements; at the time of the ceremony one of the parties was already married; where the parties were not respectively male and female; in the case of a polygamous marriage entered into outside England and Wales either party was at the time of the marriage domiciled in England or Wales: Matrimonial Causes Act 1973, s.11.

[74] A marriage is voidable on six grounds namely that; the marriage has not been consummated owing to the incapacity of one of the parties to consummate it; that the marriage has not been consummated owing to the wilful refusal of the respondent to consummate it; at the time of the marriage either party, though capable of giving a valid consent, was suffering whether continuously or intermittently from a mental disorder of such a kind or to such an extent as to render them unfit for marriage; at the time of the marriage the respondent was suffering from a venereal disease in a communicable form; that at the time of the marriage the respondent was pregnant by some man other than the petitioner: Matrimonial Causes Act 1973, s.12.

[75] A decree of nullity avoids a voidable marriage, but any marriage which is void *ab initio* does not require such a decree. However, before agreeing to conduct a ceremony of marriage in relation to a person whose previous "marriage" was void, the minister should either obtain sight of any decree which was made or seek advice.

a spouse still living. In this the Established Church of England differs from the Roman Catholic Church, which in some countries refuses to recognise the secular ceremony upon which the State insists, regarding the ceremony in church as the effective marriage.

Service after civil ceremony

Where the marriage has already been solemnised in the presence of a superinten-   **10.36** dent registrar the parties may wish to add a Church of England service of solemnisation. In such cases they must give notice to the minister,[76] who may, if they see fit,[77] use such form of service as may be approved by the General Synod so long as the canons and any regulations of the General Synod are observed.[78] An adaptation of the marriage service is required to make clear that a valid marriage has already occurred, but the service may still only be read or celebrated by a person entitled to solemnise marriages according to the rites of the Church of England.[79] Since the marriage has already taken place, and thus cannot be invalidated or superseded by the church service, there must be no banns, licence or certificate authorising such a marriage and no record of it must be entered in the marriage registers provided by the Registrar General.[80] The provisions themselves only apply to a civil marriage, but presumably they must also apply where there has been any other prior legally valid marriage such as in a Roman Catholic church or abroad.[81]

The House of Bishops have commended the use of *Services of Prayer and Dedication after Civil Marriage*.[81a]

Conditional marriage

In cases where it is thought that there has been a breach of the formalities in an   **10.37** earlier marriage ceremony great care must be taken before another ceremony is performed, and the minister should consult the diocesan registrar for advice. No provision is made in the Book of Common Prayer or the ASB for conditional marriages and it is suggested that the rites for the solemnisation of marriage

---

[76] The parties are required to produce their marriage certificate and pay any customary fee: Marriage Act 1949, s.46(1).

[77] The use of the term "sees fit" clearly indicates that the minister has a discretion as to whether or not to conduct such a service.

[78] Marriage Act 1949, s.46(1); Marriage (Registrar General's Licence) Act 1970, s.11(2); Canon B36(1). In fact no such service has been approved by the General Synod (under Canon B2) and thus any form of service approved by the diocesan bishop may be used instead, or one which the minister having the cure of souls considers suitable and which they may permit other ministers to use. The House of Bishops have commended the use of *Services of Prayer and Dedication after Civil Marriage* (1985).

[79] Marriage Act 1949, s.46(3).

[80] *ibid.*, s.46(2); Canon B36(2).

[81] Bursell, *Liturgy, Order and the Law* (1996), p. 192.

[81a] 1985. Although these services need not be taken by a priest only a priest should give the blessing (as the text makes clear) and the Absolution should be varied from "you" to "us".

contained within these are not really appropriate, although a variation of them similar to that used in respect of conditional baptism would be permitted.[82] The second ceremony should be recorded in the marriage register but the marital status recorded as "previously went through a form of marriage" giving the date and place of that first ceremony.[83]

In the case of persons who have been legally divorced but who wish to remarry each other it would appear that they are entitled to be remarried according to one of the authorised rites without variation.[84] The normal theological objections to remarriage of divorced persons cannot apply. However, a minister who does not accept that a second marriage whilst a former spouse is living is theologically permissible does so on the basis that the first union was indissolvable by human action (whilst recognising that its legal consequences may be terminated by secular law). Such a minister is likely to have a conscientious objection to "remarrying" a couple in such circumstances, since they would regard them as already married. As we have seen a minister may decline to marry a couple where one of the parties has been divorced and has a former spouse still living, and it is submitted that the provision would apply equally to protect a minister from remarrying a couple.[85]

Requirements for marriage

10.38 English law lays down strict requirements for the solemnisation of a valid marriage. As marriage officers of the State ministers of the Church of England have a weighty responsibility towards those whom they seek to marry, since if careful regard is not paid to the legal requirements the marriage may be invalidated in the eyes of the State. Since the Church requires compliance with the temporal laws before it recognises a marriage as valid, the marriage will also be invalid in the eyes of the Church. It was the desire to have marriages declared invalid, prior to the ready availability of divorce or judicial separation in secular law, which has lead to a large body of case law on the subject, much of which is now only of historical interest.

The majority of enactments relating to marriage were consolidated in the Marriage Act 1949.[86] Marriage in the Church of England can be solemnised after publication of banns, on the authority of a special or common licence, or on the authority of a certificate issued by the superintendent registrar, all of which are considered below.[86a]

[82] Bursell, *Liturgy, Order and the Law* (1996) p. 194. However, it would appear that the unaltered marriage service may be used: *Piers v. Piers* (1849) 2 H.L. Cas. 331.

[83] *Suggestions for Guidance of the Clergy with Reference to the Marriage and Registration Act* (1982, HMSO), p. 3

[84] Bursell, *Liturgy, Order and the Law* (1996), p. 194, n. 382.

[85] Since the minister would nonetheless wish to encourage a reconciliation they would no doubt give consideration to offering the couple a service similar to that for the renewal of baptism vows (devised pursuant to Canon B5) at which they could renew their commitment to each other following a civil ceremony of marriage having taken place.

[86] The Marriage Act 1949 does not unless otherwise expressly provided extend to Scotland or Northern Ireland: *ibid.*, s.80(2). Certain provisions do not apply to Wales: *ibid.*, s.80(3), Sched. 6. The Act does not affect any law or custom relating to marriages of members of the Royal Family: *ibid.*, s.79(5).

[86a] Marriage according to the rites of the Church of England cannot be solemnised on the authority of the Registrar General's licence: Marriage (Registrar Generals Licence) Act 1970, s.1(1).

With the exception of divorced persons who have a former spouse still living and in certain cases of affinity between the parties which are discussed below, two persons legally qualified to intermarry are entitled to be married according to the rites of the Church of England in an authorised place after banns, if one of them possesses the legal qualification of residence for that parish church or centre of worship. This right extends to persons who are not members of the Church of England[87] and although the point has never been conclusively determined it would appear that even where both parties are unbaptised a person could not lawfully be refused.[88] When an application is made to a minister for matrimony to be solemnised it is their duty to inquire whether there is any impediment.[89] A minister[90] is thus under a duty to solemnise the marriage of those parishioners who fulfil the legal requirements, and commits an ecclesiastical offence if they refuse to do so.[91]

Mixed marriages

Since the common understanding with regard to the marriage of persons by banns is that it extends to those who are unbaptised it follows that there is no legal bar to mixed marriages, that is marriages between a member of the Church of England and another faith or none. However, Guidelines issued by the House of Bishops[92] in relation to marriage by common licence, which as we shall see is a matter for the discretion of the diocesan bishop, are generally not issued unless one party is baptised. It is also the policy to require a statement from a non-baptised party that they do not reject the Christian faith and desire marriage in Church, the crucial test being whether the parties are prepared to move towards a vision compatible with Christian understanding. Similar criteria are operated in   **10.39**

---

[87] *Agar v. Holsworth* (1758) 2 Lee 515; *R. v. James* (1850) 3 Car. & Kir. 167 at 175, C.C.R.; *Jones v. Robinson* (1815) 2 Phil. Ecc. R. 285.

[88] See Doe, *The Legal Framework of the Church of England* (1996), pp. 363–364 for a discussion of this principle.

[89] Canon B33.

[90] It is not entirely clear to whom this obligation relates. Clearly it relates to the minister with the cure of souls and may extend to the minister to whom application for marriage is made so long as they are licensed to the parish; Bursell, *Liturgy, Order and the Law* (1996), p. 157, n. 5.

[91] *Agar v. Holdsworth* (1758) 2 Lee 515. Doe, *The Legal Framework of the Church of England* (1996), pp. 358–362 questions both this authority and the general proposition and concludes that the duty to solemnise survives as "a powerful legal fiction." He says at p. 368 that is has "acquired the force of law" so that it is doubtful if the existence of the right could now be successfully challenged. See also Bursell, *Liturgy, Order and the Law* (1996), p. 182 as to the generally held view that an ecclesiastical offence would be committed by refusal. Both Doe at pp. 365–368 and Bursell at p. 182 consider the consequences which might flow from a refusal including the possible actions which might be taken in the secular courts. Doe is of the opinion (p. 368) that a writ of *mandamus* to compel the minister would not lie since an alternative remedy is available in the form of civil marriage. An action for damages may lie although it may be difficult to quantify the loss.

[92] *Guidelines for the Celebration of Mixed Faith Marriages in Church* (1992). See also *The Marriage of Adherents of Other Faiths in Anglican Churches*, the Report of the Inter-Faith Consultative Group of the Board of Mission to the House of Bishops (1992).

regard to marriage by special licence. The Guidelines also deal with liturgical considerations and state that whilst nothing should be omitted from the marriage service additions such as a reference to the faith of the non-Christian party may be appropriate.

Same sex

10.40   In English law a marriage may only be contracted between a man and a woman not between two persons of the same sex. Nor can a person change their sex by means of a medical operation which effects a "sex change" for the purposes of marriage.[93] It is suggested that the question of whether a minister may use a service of blessing for such persons (pursuant to Canon B5 since no other provision is made in the Book of Common Prayer or the ASB) will depend in part at least upon the extent to which the service resembles one of marriage.[94]

Age requirements and consents for persons under 18

10.41   Each party to the marriage must be at least 16 years of age and any purported marriage with a child under this age is void.[95] Where a party to the marriage is under 18 years of age and is not a widow or widower special requirements apply and the consent of parents or guardians is required. Ecclesiastical law does not define who the parents or guardians are and therefore the general law as to their identity applies.

Where the marriage is to be solemnised by a common licence (that is where the marriage is to be celebrated without the publication of banns) in addition to the requirement of a sworn declaration which is discussed below, the consent of specified person or persons is required.[96] No minister is to solemnise a marriage without such consent.[97] However, consent may be dispensed with if the ecclesiastical authority granting the licence is satisfied that it cannot be obtained by reason of absence or inaccessibility or by reason of the person required to give it being under any disability, and there is some other person whose consent is also required.[98] If there is no other person required to give consent then the Master of Faculties may dispense with the consent, or the court may consent on an application made to it.[99] The court may also give its consent where the person

---

[93] *Corbett v. Corbett (otherwise Ashley)* [1971] P. 83.
[94] Bursell, *Liturgy, Order and the Law* (1996), p. 160.
[95] Marriage Act 1949, s.2: Cnon B31(1).
[96] Marriage Act 1949. s.3(2), Sched. 2. The specified persons being: any parent with parental responsibility; each guardian (if any); the person with whom the child minor lives or is to live or (if now over the age of sixteen years) did live, as the result of a residence order; the local authority where a care order is in force. Consent need not be express but may be implied, although consent must be expressly retracted: *Hodgkinson v. Wilkie* (1795) 1 Hag. Con. 262.
[97] Canon B32.
[98] Marriage Act 1949, s.3(1).
[99] *ibid.*

whose consent is required refuses it. It should be noted, however, that a marriage solemnised without the requisite consent is nonetheless valid.[1]

Where a marriage is intended to be solemnised after banns any person whose consent would otherwise have been required to the marriage may openly or publicly declare or cause to be declared their dissent in the church or chapel where the banns are published, at the time of publication, whereupon publication of the banns is void.[2] A minister who solemnises the marriage of a child after publication of banns without the consent of the parents or guardians is not liable to ecclesiastical censure unless they had notice of the dissent of any persons entitled to give it,[3] but will have committed an offence under the Marriage Act 1949, which is considered below. Nothing in the Marriage Act 1949 regarding consent dispenses with the necessity to obtain the consent of the High Court to the marriage of a ward of court.[4]

Prohibited degrees of kindred and affinity

The parties must not be within the prohibited degrees of kindred and affinity, **10.42** and any such purported marriage is void.[5] The Marriage Act 1949 provides that certain marriages will not be void by reason only of affinity if both the parties to the marriage were over 21 years of age at the time of the marriage and the younger party had not, before attaining 18 years, been a child of the family of the older party.[6] That Act also provides that certain marriages will not be void by reason of affinity where both parties were over 21 when the marriage was solemnised and certain persons related to one of the parties have died. Any minister solemnising such a marriage would be advised to do so on a common or special licence or registrar's certificate in order to ensure that the legal formalities are complied with and the proper evidence obtained.

Exceptions to minister's duty to solemnise marriage

The exception to the minister's duty to solemnise, where one or both of the **10.43** intended parties to the marriage has been divorced and that former spouse is still living, was discussed above. However, it would appear that whilst a minister is not obliged to marry such a person they may be obliged to publish banns.[7]

[1] *R. v. Birmingham Inhabitants* (1828) 8 B. & C. 29.
[2] Marriage Act 1949, s.3(3).
[3] *ibid.*, s.3(4).
[4] *ibid.*, s.3(6).
[5] *ibid.*, s.1(1), Sched. 1; Canon B31(2). Kindred or consanguinity refers to persons related by blood (whether whole, half or by legal adoption) whilst affinity refers to persons who are spouse or former spouses or relatives by blood of a spouse or former spouse.
[6] See n. 5 *ante*.
[7] An aggrieved party might be able to apply to the High Court for an order that the incumbent publish the banns, although since the matter would be in the judge's discretion and since the Marriage Act 1949 provides an alternative remedy of a superintendent registrar's certificate, such an order might not be granted: *Legal Opinions*, p. 163. The practical value of obtaining the publication of banns is not clear since the minister of the church or chapel could still decline to celebrate the marriage or allow it to be conducted in the church or chapel in which the publication occured.

A minister is also not obliged to solemnise a marriage or permit such a marriage in the church or chapel of which they are the minister which would, but for the provisions of the Marriage (Prohibited Degrees of Relationship) Act 1986, have been void by reason of the degree of affinity between the parties.[8] Under earlier statutes a minister was not liable to penalty or censure for refusing to publish banns or solemnise marriages between a man and his deceased wife's sister, or deceased brother's widow, or between persons and their nephews or nieces by marriage. It would appear that this right is still preserved.[9]

Place for solemnisation of marriage

10.44 The registrar of each diocese must send to the Registrar General of England and Wales, within 15 days of January 1 of each year, a list of all chapels in the diocese in which marriages may lawfully be solemnised according to the rites of the Church of England.[10] The registrar must distinguish between those chapels which have a parish, chapelry or other ecclesiastical division annexed to them, those which are licensed by the bishop for limited districts, and those licensed under enactments relating to naval, military and air force chapels. The Registrar General is then under a duty to make out and cause to be printed a list of all such chapels and all registered buildings yearly, a copy of which is sent to every registrar of marriages and superintendent registrar.[11]

The sharing of a church under the Sharing of Church Buildings Act 1969 does not alter the requirements for registration of the building as a place where marriages may be solemnised according to the rites of the Church of England, but simply enables it also to be registered as a place where non-conformist marriages may be solemnised. Save where an Anglican church is subject to such a sharing agreement, it cannot be used for the solemnisation of marriages according to the rites of the Roman Catholic or other non-Anglican church, but only according to the rites of the Church of England.[12]

It should be noted that the provisions of the Marriage Act 1949 relating to marriages according to the rites of the Church of England apply, with certain exceptions and subject to certain modifications, to naval, military and air force chapels as if those chapels were a parish church.

Marriage after banns must normally be solemnised in a church or chapel in which banns may be published.[13] Exceptions are where two or more benefices are held in plurality or where by virtue of a pastoral scheme there are two or more

---

[8] Marriage Act 1949, s.5A.
[9] The Marriage Act 1949, s.79(10) provides that nothing in that Act is to enable proceedings to be taken in an ecclesiastical court which could not have been taken if the Act has not been passed. Nothing in s.79 of that Act is to be taken as prejudicing the operation of s.16(1) of the Interpretation Act 1978 which provides that the repeal of any enactment does not, unless a contrary intention appears, revive anything not in force or existing at the time when the repeal takes effect, and there is nothing in the Marriage Act 1949 which directly imposes an obligation to solemnise such marriages.
[10] Marriage Act 1949, s.73.
[11] Marriage Act 1949, s.73.
[12] *Legal Opinions*, p. 172.
[13] Marriage Act 1949, s.12(1).

parishes or parish churches in the area of a single benefice.[14] In the latter case if the bishop does not give directions as to which of the parish churches banns may be published in or the marriage solemnised in then it is for the parishioners to specify their preference, or if they do not do so, for the incumbent to decide.[15] In cases where persons reside in a parish which has a parish centre of worship that place is deemed to be a parish church for all the purposes of the Marriage Act 1949 with one exception.[16] Where such a place has been designated[17] as a parish centre but there is in fact no parish church in the parish as we saw in Chapter 4 they may elect to be married either in the parish centre of worship or in the parish church of the adjoining parish.

Marriage by common licence must be solemnised in the parish church of the **10.45** parish or the authorised chapel of the ecclesiastical district in which one of the parties had their usual place of residence for 15 days immediately before the grant of the licence, or in the usual place of worship of one of the parties.[18]

Marriage in a private house or anywhere except a church or chapel, other than under a special licence, is an ecclesiastical offence.[19] Any person who knowingly and wilfully solemnises a marriage according to the rites of the Church of England (other than a marriage under a special licence or of a person who is house-bound or detained) in any place other than a church or other building in which banns may be published commits an offence which carries a maximum sentence of 14 years' imprisonment,[20] and such a marriage is, if the parties marry knowingly and wilfully, void.[21]

It should be noted that although a marriage may now be solemnised at "approved premises" on the authority of a superintendent registrar's licence, such a marriage may not be solemnised according to the rites of the Church of England.[21a]

Marriage of house-bound and detained persons

Persons who are house-bound, that is persons who ought not by reason of illness **10.46** or disability to be moved from their home or other place where they are at the time (and such is likely to remain the position for at least three months), persons detained in a hospital other than under certain provisions of the Mental Health Act 1983 relating to short term detentions, or persons detained in a prison or place to which the Prisons Act 1952 applies, may now by virtue of the Marriage Act 1983 be married at the place where they are house-bound or detained, under the authority of a superintendent registrar's licence.[22]

[14] *ibid.*, s.23; Pastoral Measure 1983, Sched. 3, para. 14(4).
[15] *Legal Opinions*, p. 161.
[16] Marriage Act 1949, s.29.
[17] Pursuant to the Pastoral Measure 1983, s.29(1).
[18] Marriage Act 1949, s.15.
[19] *Middleton v. Crofts* (1736) 2 Atk. 650. Although this would no longer be the case in regard to house-bound persons.
[20] Marriage Act 1949, s.75(1)(c). No prosecution may be commenced after the expiration of three years from the commission of the offence: *ibid.*, s.75(4).
[21] Marriage Act 1949, s.25.
[21a] Marriage Act 1949, ss.26(1)(bb), 46B(4).
[22] Pursuant to *ibid.*, s.26(1)(dd).

Marriage in Cathedrals

10.47   A parish cathedral church is in the same position in both secular and ecclesiastical law as any parish church. Cathedrals with a dean and chapter are extra-parochial places which may be authorised by the bishop as a place where marriages may be celebrated. Such licence is likely to extend only to marriages where one or both parties reside in the close or precincts.[23] If the cathedral is authorised by the bishop marriage can also be celebrated there under the authority of a superintendent registrar's licence provided the dean and chapter consent. If the cathedral is not an authorised place marriage can only be celebrated within it on the authority of a special licence.[24]

Place for publication of banns

10.48   Banns are normally published in the parish church of the parish in which the two parties to the marriage reside, or if they reside in different parishes, in the parish church of each parish in which they reside. The exception is where one of them resides in a chapelry or district for which the bishop has licensed a chapel for the publication of banns and solemnisation of marriage, when the banns may be read in that authorised chapel.[25] Where persons reside in an extra-parochial place the provisions must be read as referring to the authorised chapel of that place.[26] For the purpose of publishing banns a parish in which there is no parish church or chapel or none in which divine service is usually solemnised every Sunday, is taken as belonging to any adjoining parish or chapelry.[27]

Banns may also be published in any parish church or authorised chapel which is the usual place of worship of the parties to be married or one of them, notwithstanding that neither resides in the parish or chapelry to which the church or chapel belong.[28] However, such banns are to be additional to, not in substitution for, the banns required in the place of residence.[29] No person can claim a church or chapel to be their usual place of worship unless enrolled on the electoral roll of the area in which the church or chapel is situated, but enrollment is sufficient evidence that such is their usual place of worship.[30]

A retired clerk in holy orders cannot have their name entered on the electoral roll of a parish. Accordingly where a clerk wishes to be married at their usual

---

[23] Persons who are declared habitual worshippers for the purposes of a scheme under CRR, r. 27, do not appear to constitute persons on a church electoral roll for the purposes of the law of marriage, and thus if they do not reside within the cathedral boundaries, are not entitled to be married in the cathedral after the publication of banns: *Legal Opinions*, p. 170.

[24] *Legal Opinions*, p. 170.

[25] Marriage Act 1949, s.6(1). Special provision is made where a church is being rebuilt or repaired: *ibid.*, s.18(1).

[26] *ibid.*, s.6(2).

[27] *ibid.*, s.6(3). Similar provision is made in regard to extra-parochial places having no authorised chapel: *ibid*.

[28] *ibid.*, s.6(4).

[29] *ibid.*, s.6(4).

[30] *ibid.*, s.72(1).

place of worship which is not the parish church of either party and the other party to the marriage is not entered on the electoral roll, they can do so only under the authority of a special licence.[31]

Residence

The law relating to residence requirements for the publication of banns and the **10.49** granting of common and superintendent registrar's licences is far from clear and is susceptible of more than one interpretation. Ministers will therefore have to exercise their own judgment in the case of banns together with, in the case of common licences, directions and guidance given by the bishop or vicar-general of the diocese.

The requirement that one of the parties resides in the parish[32] does not have to be satisfied over a period of time, and refers to the date when the application for the calling of the banns is given to the minister. The better view is that the person who arrives in the parish with the sole intention of being married there rather than making it their permanent home and is physically present at the relevant date is resident for this purpose.[33] However, if residence does connote permanence it would appear that, looking at the matter on the relevant date, permanence means more than residence for a limited period (as is the case with common or superintendent registrar's licences) and thus a person coming to the parish with the sole intention of being married there would not qualify.[34]

For common licences the requirement is that one of the persons to be married has their usual place of residence in the parish for 15 days before the grant of the licence.[35] This would appear not to require physical presence in the parish for those 15 days and would therefore include persons who claim the parish as their home although they are actually living elsewhere during that time, for example a student at college or a person employed on a short-term secondment abroad.[36] However, it would not extend to those who have set up a permanent residence elsewhere and are simply "visiting" the parish when they do return. The distinctions may not always be easy to draw. A student in a college hall of residence or person working abroad may have nowhere else to go except the parental home when returning from abroad. In contrast a person who has cohabited elsewhere for a period of time and returns to the parish in order to be married would not on this view qualify as resident.[37]

The alternative view is that the focus is on the 15 days period so that the test is what is usual for that period. Thus the person who arrived in the parish in order to marry there is usually resident if for example they took (and actually stayed in rather than left a suitcase there) bed and breakfast accommodation, whilst the person away from home during that period would not be resident.[38]

---

[31] *Legal Opinions*, p. 169.
[32] Marriage Act 1949, s.6(1).
[33] *Legal Opinions*, pp. 166–169; see also *Anglican Marriage in England and Wales: A Guide to the Law for the Clergy* (1982 HMSO).
[34] See n. 33 *ante*.
[35] Marriage Act 1949, s.15(1)(a).
[36] *Legal Opinions*, pp. 166–169; See also *Anglican Marriage in England and Wales: A Guide to the Law for the Clergy* (1982) HMSO).
[37] *ibid*.
[38] See n. 36 *ante*.

For a superintendent registrar's certificate the requirement is that the person reside for the period of seven days immediately before the giving of the notice.[39] Again the person who arrives in the parish in order to marry would appear to satisfy this test. Guidelines issued to Registrar's instruct them to treat as "resident" persons who are temporarily absent from a home within the district, but who retain a room for their use and keep possessions there and who return when they have an opportunity. This would include those whose usual place of residence was the district (even though the statute does not use that word), but not those who have become visitors, having a permanent residence of their own.

Banns of matrimony[39a]

10.50 A minister is not obliged to publish banns unless the parties intending to be married give at least seven days notice of the date on which they first wish the banns to be published.[40] The parties are required to deliver or cause to be delivered a notice in writing, dated on the day on which it was delivered, stating the christian and surname and place of residence of each and the period during which each has resided at their place of residence.[41] A minister need not insist on this notice, but if they fail to exercise due diligence and marry persons one of whom is not resident in the parish they would be liable to ecclesiastical censure[42] (though the marriage itself would be valid). Solemnisation of a marriage without due publication of banns, unless the marriage was solemnised on the authority of a special or common licence or certificate of a superintendent registrar, is a felony with a maximum sentence of 14 years' imprisonment.[43]

Banns must be published in an audible manner in the form of words prescribed in the rubric prefixed to the Office of the Solemnisation of Matrimony in the Book of Common Prayer.[44] All other rules prescribed by that rubric concerning the publication of banns and solemnisation of matrimony are to be observed, so far as these are consistent with Part II of the Marriage Act 1949.[45] Banns must generally be published on the three Sundays preceding the solemnisation of marriage during morning service, or if there is no morning service on a Sunday when they are to be published, during evening service.[46] Although publication need not occur in three successive weeks, where there is an excessive interval

---

[39] *ibid.*, s.34.

[39a] Proposals to obviate the need for banns or to modify the requirements relating to them were considered by the General Synod at the November 1996 group of sessions. See also "The report of a working party on the Legal Preliminaries to Marriage" (1994) 3 Ecc. L.J. 323.

[40] *ibid.*, s.8.

[41] *ibid.*, s.8.

[42] *Nicholson v. Squire* (1809) 16 Ves. 259 at 261; *Wynn v. Davies and Weever* (1835) 1 Curt. 69 at 83, 84.

[43] Marriage Act 1949, s.75(1)(b). No prosecution may be commenced after the expiration of three years from the commission of the offence: *ibid.*, s.75(4).

[44] *ibid.*, s.7(2); Canon B35(2). It is sufficient if the substance of this form is used: *Standen v. Standen* (1791) Peake 45 at 48. A form is also now set out in the ASB p. 285, n. 1.

[45] *ibid.*

[46] Marriage Act 1949, s.7(1). This modifies the rubric in the Book of Common Prayer, Form of Solemnisation of Matrimony.

between publications the incumbent or priest-in-charge should consider starting the process again.[47]

Save for limited exceptions publication must be by a minister.[48] However, where a minister does not officiate on any Sunday in a church or other building where banns are to be published at the service at which it is usual to publish banns in that church or building, the banns may be published by a minister at some other service at which banns may be published.[49] In such circumstances the banns may also be published by a lay person during the course of a public reading (authorised by the bishop) of a portion or portions of the service of Morning or Evening Prayer.[50] That public reading is required either to be at the hour at which the service at which it is usual to publish banns normally occurs, or at such hour as the bishop may authorise. A lay person may not publish banns pursuant to the above provisions unless the incumbent, minister in charge or other minister nominated by the bishop has made or authorised the requisite entry to be made in the register book of banns.[51] The only other exception to the general rule is in the case of a marriage where one of the intended parties is a naval officer, seaman or marine on board a ship, where banns may be published on board the ship and a certificate of publication issued.[52]

Particular problems arise in the case of churches which are subject to a sharing agreement under the Sharing of Church Buildings Act 1969, or churches in local ecumenical projects where the main morning service may not be a Church of England service. Publication should not occur at a service which is not performed according to the rites of the Church of England or authorised by Canon, since this would appear to be unlawful.[53] Furthermore the right of a lay person to publish banns would appear to be limited to the case of Morning or Evening Prayer according to the rites of the Church of England.[54]   **10.51**

Both the Marriage Act 1949 and the Book of Common Prayer contemplate that the true names of the persons will be stated together with the parish or parishes in which they reside. There is no need to state the parties marital status. A person's true name is not necessarily that given in baptism together with the original surname.[55] A person may have adopted a name by which they are generally known so that this assumed name overrides the true name. In such circumstances the name by which the person is generally acredited is their true name for the purpose of banns.[56] Using the original name of a person where they have acquired another name may be an act of concealment and not due publication, but use of the original name is only wrong where the other name has been so far obtained by repute as to obliterate the original.[57] A woman generally changes her surname on marriage and the name conferred on her by marriage will become her actual surname unless obliterated by repute.[58] Generally, where

---

[47] *Legal Opinions*, p. 162.
[48] Marriage Act 1949, s.9(1).
[49] *ibid.*, s.9(2).
[50] *ibid.*, s.9(2).
[51] *ibid.*, s.9(2).
[52] *ibid.*, s.14.
[53] *Legal Opinions*, p. 163.
[54] *ibid.*
[55] *Diddear v. Faucit* (1821) 3 Phil. Ecc. R. 580.
[56] *Dancer v. Dancer* [1949] P. 147.
[57] *Fendall v. Goldsmid* (1877) 2 P.D. 263.
[58] *ibid.*

the wrong name has been used in the publication of banns the effect on the validity of the marriage will depend upon whether it was used with the intention of concealing one or more of the parties' identity.[59]

If an objection is made when calling the banns (other than in the case of persons under 18 years of age) the certificate of publication must be endorsed or amended stating that such an objection has been made.[60] The circumstances of the allegation must then be investigated before the marriage takes place.

10.52 The PCC of a parish must provide a register book of banns, for every church and chapel in the parish in which marriages may be solemnised.[61] All banns must be published from this book and not from loose papers. After each publication the entry in the book must be signed by the person publishing the banns or some person under their direction.[62] Where a lay person publishes the banns they must sign the book and they are deemed to be the officiating minister for this purpose.[63]

Where the parties to the intended marriage do not reside in the same parish or ecclesiastical district a minister must not solemnise a marriage in the parish or district within which one resides without production of a certificate that the banns have been published in the parish or district in which the other resides, or in such other parish or chapelry as is permitted, in accordance with the statutory provisions.[64] Where the parties wish to be married in the usual place of worship of one of them although neither resides in the parish or chapelry to which that place of worship belongs, the minister of the place may only solemnise the marriage on production of a certificate or certificates of publication of banns in the parish or district in which the parties do reside, or other lawful place.[65] Any certificate of publication of banns must be signed by the incumbent or minister in charge of the church or building in which the banns were published or by a minister nominated by the bishop.[66]

Where a marriage is to be celebrated in England or Wales between parties one of whom resides in England and Wales and the other in Scotland, Northern Ireland or the Republic of Ireland, a certificate given in accordance with that law and custom that banns have been published or proclaimed is a sufficient certificate in respect of the party resident outside England or Wales.[67]

If a marriage is not solemnised within three months after the completion of the publication of banns the publication is void.[68] Accordingly no minister may solemnise a marriage on the authority of those banns.

Where one party to the intended marriage is a foreigner the Legal Advisory Commission recommends that the marriage should be by licence rather than by

---

[59] *Chipchase v. Chipchase* [1942] P. 37.
[60] *Legal Opinions*, p. 164.
[61] Marriage Act 1949 s.7(3); Canons F11(1), F14. In the case of an authorised chapel or extra-parochial place the reference to PCC is construed as a reference to the chapel warden or other officer exercising analogous duties; Marriage Act 1949, s.7(4).
[62] Marriage Act 1949, s.7(3).
[63] *ibid.*, s.9(3).
[64] *ibid.*, s.11(1), (3).
[65] *ibid.*, s.11(2), (3).
[66] *ibid.*, s.11(4) For this purpose the certificate of the person who actually published the banns may not be sufficient.
[67] *ibid.*, s.13.
[68] *ibid.*, s.12(2).

banns. On receiving a request for such a licence the diocesan registrar can then be consulted to afford an opportunity of ensuring that the legal requirements of the foreigner's country have been complied with.[69]

Common and special licences

Ecclesiastical authorities have the power to grant licences dispensing with certain **10.53** requirements in respect of the solemnisation of marriage, although in granting these they are under a duty to observe the law relating to the subject.[70] Common licences may be granted by the archbishops, diocesan bishops and all others[71] who by ancient right have been accustomed to issue them.[72]

A common licence may authorise the solemnisation of marriage without the publication of banns at a lawful place and time, within the areas of the jurisdiction of the person issuing the licence,[73] in other words it cannot authorise a marriage to take place outside lawful hours or in a special place.

The Archbishop of Canterbury may grant a common licence throughout England.[74] He may also grant a special licence (a remnant of the old legatine jurisdiction) for the solemnisation of marriage without the publication of banns at any convenient time or place, including places not otherwise licensed for marriages, throughout all England.[75] In practice such licences are usually not granted for marriages outside the usual lawful hour or in a building other than that used for Anglican worship, and a real connection with the parish church or chapel must be shown. Further it is normally issued subject to the condition that the marriage must take place within three months of the grant.[76] The conditions applied to the grant of such a licence (and of a common licence) in the case where one party to the proposed marriage is not baptised and of another faith or none have already been considered. It should be noted that as a matter of practice neither a special nor common licence is granted where both parties are unbaptised, or generally where one is divorced and has a former spouse still living.[77]

---

[69] *Legal Opinions*, p. 165.
[70] Canon B35(1).
[71] Seemingly a reference to ecclesiastical judges and their surrogates: Marriage Act 1949, s.16(4). Since this is a dispensing power this would include vicar-generals who normally delegate such matters to a surrogate: Ecclesiastical Licences Act 1533, s.9; Marriage Act 1949, s.16(4); *Halsbury's Laws of England* (4th ed.), Vol. 14, para. 1023; *Anglican Marriage in England and Wales: A Guide to the Law for the Clergy*, (1982) para. 9.
[72] Marriage Act 1949, s.5(c); Canon B34(1).
[73] Canon B34(3).
[74] *ibid*.
[75] Marriage Act 1949, s.5(b); Canon B34(2). Application is made for such a licence to the Faculty Office of the Archbishop of Canterbury, 1, The Sanctuary, Westminster, London, SW1 3JJ.
[76] *Anglican Marriage in England and Wales: A Guide to the Law for the Clergy*, (1982) paras 9, 10; *Legal Opinions* p. 165.
[77] *Anglican Marriage in England and Wales: A Guide to the Law for the Clergy*, paras 9, 10; *Legal Opinions* p. 165.

10.54   The obtaining of common licences is a matter of favour not right and no appeal lies against a refusal.[78] However, an appeal does lie against the refusal of the Archbishop of Canterbury to grant a special licence.[79]

Before a common licence is granted a sworn declaration must be made by one of the parties to the intended marriage before a surrogate or other person having the authority to grant it.[80] That party must declare that they believe there to be no impediment of kindred or alliance or any other lawful cause nor suit commenced in any court to bar or hinder the solemnisation of the marriage in accordance with the licence; that for 15 days immediately before the grant of the licence one of the parties to the marriage had their usual place of residence in the parish or other ecclesiastical district in which the marriage is to be solemnised, or that the parish church or authorised chapel in which the marriage is to be solemnised is the usual place of worship of one of them; where one of the parties not being a widow or widower is a minor the consent of the person or persons whose consent is required by statute has been obtained, or that the necessary consent has been dispensed with, or that the court has consented, or that there is no person whose consent is required.[81] A person who makes a false declaration in order to obtain a marriage licence is guilty of an offence.[82]

In cases where the marriage would otherwise be void by reason of affinity[83] the person granting the licence must not do so unless satisfied that the conditions under which that marriage are permitted are satisfied.[84] Accordingly evidence must be produced and declarations made by the parties that those conditions are satisfied.

The grant of a common licence may be opposed by entering a caveat, signed by or on behalf of the person opposing it, stating their place of residence and ground of objection.[85] No licence may then be issued until the caveat is transmitted to the judge out of whose office the licence is to issue, and that judge has certified to the diocesan registrar that they have examined the matter of the caveat and are satisfied that it ought not to obstruct the grant of the licence. Where the person who entered the caveat withdraws it the judge need not examine or certify he has examined the matter unless the ground of objection was that one of the additional conditions required in respect of marriages which would otherwise be void, referred to above, was not satisfied. In such cases the judge must examine and certify he has examined the matter, notwithstanding withdrawal of the caveat.[86]

Both a common and special licence can only be used for the marriage of the parties for whose marriage it was intended to be obtained, but provided it

---

[78] *Halsbury's Laws of England* (4th ed.), Vol. 14, para. 1023, n. 7.

[79] Ecclesiastical Licences Act 1533, s.11. A writ would issue from Chancery enjoining the archbishop to show clause whereupon the Lord Chancellor may allow the cause, or if they see fit enjoin the archbishop, or if he refuses commission two other bishops, to grant the licence. *ibid.*, ss.11, 12.

[80] Marriage Act 1949, s.16(1).

[81] *ibid.*

[82] Perjury Act 1911, s.3(1).

[83] *i.e.* where the marriage must fulfil the requirements of the Marriage Act 1949, s.1(3), (5).

[84] *ibid.*, s.16(1A), (1B).

[85] *ibid.*, s.16(2), (2A), (2B).

[86] Marriage Act 1949, s.16(2), (2A), (2B).

identifies them sufficiently the licence need not state their true names and addresses.[87] A common licence is void if the marriage does not take place within three calendar months of its grant and no minister may then solemnise the marriage on its authority.[88] Where a marriage is solemnised by licence the responsibility as to whether the requirements as to marriage law upon which it was granted have been observed rests with the bishop by whose authority the licence is granted.[89] If such a licence is produced to a minister authorising the marriage of persons in their church or chapel they are required by canonical obedience and the rights of the parties to solemnise the marriage according to the licence.[90] If from their knowledge of certain facts a minister refuses to solemnise the marriage in spite of the licence they do so at their own peril,[91] but a delicate line must be drawn since a minister who solemnises a marriage when it appears evident that a condition for the marriage is not satisfied has been severely criticised.[92] It is suggested that unless confident that the requirements for a lawful marriage do not exist a minister should solemnise the marriage.

Superintendent registrar's certificate

A marriage according to the rites of the Church of England may be solemnised **10.55** on the authority of a certificate of a superintendent registrar in any church or chapel in which banns of matrimony may be published.[93] It may also be issued in respect of a place specified in the notice in regard to the marriages of house-bound or detained persons, that place being the place where the person usually resides which includes the place where that person is for the time being.[94]

In general a marriage on the authority of a registrar's certificate may be either by licence issued by the registrar or without. However, in the case of a church or chapel in which marriages may be solemnised according to the rites of the Church of England, or any church or chapel belonging to it or licensed for the celebration of divine worship according to the rites of it, the registrar may not issue a licence.[95] Nor may a licence be issued in respect of a church of chapel to which a sharing agreement relates except for a marriage to be solemnised otherwise than according to the rites of the Church of England.[96]

A registrar's certificate may be issued for the solemnisation of matrimony in any church or authorised chapel, even if it is not within the registration district in which either of the parties resides, provided it is the usual place of worship of one of the parties.[97] However, a certificate is merely permissive. The consent of

---

[87] *Cope v. Burt* (1809) 1 Hag. Con. 434; affd (1811) 1 Phil. Ecc. I.R. 224.
[88] Marriage Act 1949, s.16(3).
[89] *Tuckniss v. Alexander* (1863) 32 L.J. Ch. 794.
[90] *Tuckniss v. Alexander* (1863) 32 L.J. Ch. 794.
[91] *ibid.*
[92] *Millet v. Rouse* (1802) 7 Ves. 419.
[93] Marriage Act 1949, s.17.
[94] *ibid.*, ss.17, 26(1)(dd); Marriage Act 1983, s.1.
[95] Marriage Act 1949, s.26(2) (as amended). Nor may such a licence be issued in respect of the marriage of a detained or house-bound person at that person's residence according to the rites of the Church of England: *ibid.*
[96] Sharing of Church Buildings Act 1969, s.6(3).
[97] Marriage Act 1949, s.35(3).

the minister of the church or chapel is still required and the marriage must not be celebrated by a person other than a minister of the Church of England.[98]

A marriage on the authority of a superintendent registrar's certificate must not be solemnised until 21 days after the day on which notice was entered in the marriage notice book.[99] It may then be solemnised on any date thereafter within three months from the date notice was entered. If not solemnised within that period the notice of marriage and the certificate are void and no person may then solemnise the marriage on its authority.[1]

Solemnisation of matrimony

10.56 No person may solemnise a marriage according to the rites of the Church of England unless they are a clerk in holy orders.[2] Further such a marriage should usually be solemnised by a priest, although it may be solemnised by a deacon.[3] A person in holy orders may not solemnise their own marriage.[4]

A minister or lay person who is a member in good standing with a church to which the Church of England (Ecumenical Relations) Measure 1988 applies[5] and is a baptised person may be invited to assist at the Solemnisation of Matrimony if authorised to perform a similar duty in their own church.[6] The marriage itself and the final blessing would be conducted by the Anglican minister, but the rest of the service, including preaching, could be taken by the other minister or person except at a marriage service which includes Holy Communion. Only an episcopally ordained priest of a church whose Orders are recognised and accepted by the Church of England could preside.[7] The person invited to assist could sign the register as a witness.

Since a minister of the Scottish Epicsopal church may officiate in any church or chapel belonging to the Church of England under the same conditions as if admitted into holy orders by a bishop of a diocese in the Church of England,[8] this places them in the same position, within the provinces of Canterbury and York, as clergy of the Church of England and accordingly they may celebrate a marriage in England according to the rites of the Church of England.

A marriage solemnised according to the rites of the Church of England must, unless it is by special licence, conform to the general requirements as to the time of day when it may be solemnised. Accordingly a marriage must be solemnised between 8.00 a.m. and 6.00 p.m.,[9] which means completing the entire authorised

---

[98] Marriage Act 1949, s.17.

[99] *ibid.*, s.31(4).

[1] *ibid.*, s.33(1), (2) A person who knowingly solemnises a marriage in contravention of any of these provisions is guilty of an offence and liable to imprisonment for a term not exceeding five years: *ibid.*, s.75(2)(d), (e). No prosecution may be commenced after the expiration of three years from the commission of the offence: *ibid.*, s.75(4).

[2] Church of England (Ecumenical Relations) Measure 1988, s.3(b).

[3] See Chap. 7.

[4] *Beamish v. Beamish* (1861) 9 H.L. Cas. 274.

[5] See Chap. 12.

[6] Canon B43(1)(1)(e).

[7] Church of England (Ecumenical Relations) Measure 1988, s.3(a).

[8] Episcopal Church (Scotland) Act 1964, s.1(1).

[9] Marriage Act 1949, s.4; Canon B35(3).

service by 6.00 p.m.. A person who knowingly and wilfully solemnises a marriage outside those hours is guilty of an offence,[10] although a marriage solemnised outside the required hours is not void.[11] Whilst a marriage according to the rites of the Church of England must be solemnised in the presence of two witnesses in addition to the officiating minister,[12] where it takes place in the presence of only one witness it is not invalid.[13]

The marriage should take place in the body of the church[14] in the presence of the congregation. The essential elements of the ceremony have been held to be the reciprocal agreement of the parties to take each other for wedded wife and wedded husband until parted by death, the joining together of their hands and the pronouncement by the minister that they are man and wife.[15] However, for civil purposes the marriage is complete after the plighting of troth and all that follows, including the giving of the ring, the joining of hands and publication by the minister of the marriage, is symbolic and declaratory of the marriage having taken place.[16] Since the certificate which the minister gives afterwards states that the marriage was solemnised according to the rites of the Church of England the ceremony should be in accordance with the form of Solemnisation of Matrimony in the Book of Common Prayer, ASB or other authorised service. Nonetheless as a matter of secular legal requirement it is not essential that the language of the marriage service be used nor the rubrics observed.[17] Nor is it essential that the parties repeat the words of the service and hence deaf and dumb persons may be legally married.[18] The giving away of the woman is not essential.[19] Neither is the adjuration by the parties that there is no lawful impediment to their marriage.[20]

If at the ceremony anyone alleges that there is any impediment to the marriage **10.57** and is willing to be bound to prove their allegation, with sufficient surities, then the service must be deferred.[21] However, this does not mean that if the person is not willing to be bound the ceremony should go ahead. Although their reluctance to be bound may indicate a lack of seriousness the minister must decide, and if there was real doubt the minister would be entitled to delay the ceremony.[22] In

---

[10] And liable to a term of imprisonment not exceeding 14 years: Marriage Act 1949, s.75(1)(a). No prosecution may be commenced after the expiration of three years from the commission of the offence: *ibid.*, s.75(4).

[11] *Catterall v. Sweetman* (1845) 1 Rob. Eccl. 304 at 317.

[12] Marriage Act 1949, s.22; Canon B35(4).

[13] *Wing v. Taylor* (1861) 2 Sw. & Tr. 278 at 286.

[14] Although a marriage held in the vestry has been held to be valid: *Wing v. Taylor (ante)*.

[15] *Harrod v. Harrod* (1845) 1 K. & J. 4 at 15, 16; *Beamish v. Beamish* (1861) 9 H.L. Cas. 274 at 339.

[16] *Beamish v. Beamish (ante)* at 329, 330.

[17] *Beamish v. Beamish (ante)* at 329, 330, 331.

[18] *Harrod v. Harrod (ante)* at 16.

[19] *More v. More* (1741) 2 Atk. 157.

[20] *Beamish v. Beamish (ante)* at 329, 330, 331.

[21] *Book of Common Prayer*, Form of Solemnisation of Matrimony. Now the only means of binding sureties would be by deed: Bursell, *Liturgy, Order and the Law* (1996), p. 188.

[22] The ASB gives no guidance as to how a minister should proceed if an impediment is alleged, but Series 1 Solemnisation of Matrimony suggests that once objection is made the ceremony must be adjourned, in contrast to the Book of Common Prayer where the minister would need to be sure of their ground before declining to proceed: Bursell, *Liturgy, Order and the Law* (1996), p. 189.

all cases where serious doubt arises a minister should be aware of their duty to prevent an improper marriage.[23]

As was discussed in Chapter 9, save in certain colleges, all services must be conducted in English. Where an English person is marrying a foreigner who is not resident in England and does not speak English or where English is not the first language of the parties to the marriage or the congregation, the service must still be conducted in English to be in accordance with the rites of the Church of England.[24] However, the minister is also obliged to ensure that the parties to be married understand the service, and needs to ensure that the essential parts of the service, that is the charge, promises and vows are translated by an interpreter. The Legal Advisory Commission strongly urges the minister to choose the interpreter independently and to ensure that they are not a relative or friend of the couple.[25] The interpreter should sign the marriage register as one of the witnesses.

We also saw in Chapter 9 that the choice as to the form of service lies with the minister, although the couple concerned have a right of appeal to the bishop. Where the ASB rite is to be used the minister must inquire the day before the marriage which form of vows the couple have agreed to use.[26]

Although the Book of Common Prayer envisages a sermon declaring the duties of man and wife, since the preaching of the sermon is in any event discretionary[27] this subject need not be regarded as obligatory.[28] The Book of Common Prayer states that the newly-married persons should receive Holy Communion at the time of their marriage or as soon as is convenient thereafter, whilst the alternative forms of service make provision for occasions when the marriage service is combined with Holy Communion.

The marriage of more than one couple may take place at the same time so long as the formalities are separately complied with in regard to each couple,[29] and appropriate minor variations may be made to the service accordingly.

Although tickets may be issued for a wedding no parishioner can be refused admission on the grounds that they are not in possession of such a ticket.[30] It is for the minister of the parish to decide what music is to be played, what hymns or anthems are to be sung, and what furnishings or flowers should be placed in or about the church for the occasion.[31] The videoing of marriage was discussed in Chapter 9.

The throwing of paper confetti within the churchyard is now prohibited in many parishes. The incumbent, who as we saw in Chapter 8 has the freehold of the churchyard, is entitled to impose such a restriction.

---

[23] *Beamish v. Beamish (ante).*

[24] There is one statutory exception to this. Is any place in which the Welsh language is commonly used the authorised translation into Welsh of the declaratory and contracting words may be used if the parties wish: Registration of Marriages (Welsh Language) Regulations 1986, S.I. 1986 No. 1445.

[25] *Legal Opinions*, p. 171.

[26] p. 285, n. 6.

[27] As it is in the ASB although the Series 1 rite states that a sermon should be preached if there is no Holy Communion.

[28] Bursell, *Liturgy, Order and the Law* (1996), p. 190.

[29] *Suggestions for Guidance of the Clergy with Reference to the Marriage and Registration Act* (1982), p. 3.

[30] *Legal Opinions*, p. 225.

[31] Canon B35(5).

Registration of marriage

A minister who solemnises a marriage according to the rites of the Church of **10.58**
England must register that marriage.[32] Failure to do so can lead, on summary
conviction, to the imposition of a fine.[33] Registration must be in duplicate,[34] in
the prescribed form,[35] in two of the marriage books furnished by the Registrar
General for England and Wales.[36] Marriage register books must be kept in every
parish church and chapel where marriage is to solemnised and must be
maintained and kept in accordance with statutes and Measures relating to them
and any rules and regulations made thereunder.[37] Each entry must be made in
consecutive order from the beginning to the end of the book and the number of
each entry in the two duplicate books must be the same.[38] The entry must be
signed by the minister, the parties to the marriage and two witnesses.[39]

Where a marriage is solemnised according to the rites of the Church of
England at the residence of a person who is either house-bound or detained, the
marriage must be registered in the marriage register books of any church or
chapel which is in the same parish or extra-parochial place as the place where the
marriage is solemnised, or if there is no such church or chapel, in the adjoining
parish.[40]

Any person who wilfully or knowingly makes or causes to be made a statement
for the purpose of being inserted in the register any false statement as to any of
the particulars required is guilty of an offence.[41] A minister who discovers an
error in the entry, either in form or substance, and within one calendar month
after discovery corrects it, incurs no penalty.[42] Correction must occur in the
presence of the parties to the marriage, or if they are dead or absent, in the presence of the superintendent registrar and two other credible witnesses.[43] The entry
is corrected in the margin without any alteration to the original entry, the
correction being signed and dated. Where an error in the original entry is not
discovered until after the certified copy has been sent to the superintendent
registrar a certified copy of the erroneous entry and the marginal entry must be
delivered to the registrar.[44]

The incumbent or curate in charge of every church or chapel in which **10.59**
marriages may be solemnised according to the rites of the Church of England
must make and deliver a true copy, certified under their hand, of all entries in the
marriage book kept by them at quarterly intervals. These copies must be
delivered in the months of January, April, July and October and relate to the

---

[32] Marriage Act 1949, s.53(a), (d).
[33] *ibid.*, s.76. Prosecution must be within three years of the commission of the offence: *ibid.*
[34] *ibid.*, s.55.
[35] Registration of Marriage Regulations 1986 S.I. 1986 No. 1442, r. 10, Sched. 1.
[36] Marriage Act 1949, s.54.
[37] Canon F11(1), (2).
[38] Marriage Act 1949, s.55.
[39] Marriage Act 1949, s.55.
[40] *ibid.*
[41] Perjury Act 1911, s.3(1)(b).
[42] Marriage Act 1949, s.61.
[43] Marriage Act 1949, s.61.
[44] *ibid.*

period of three months ending with the last day of the month immediately before the month in which the copy is required to be made. If no marriage has been entered during this period this fact must be certified. Failure to submit certified copies can lead, on summary conviction, to the imposition of a fine.[45]

The marriage books must be kept safely by the incumbent or minister in charge until filled.[46] Careless loss or injury to such books can result, on summary conviction, to the imposition of a fine.[47] Once filled one copy must be delivered to the superintendent registrar and the other remains in the custody of the incumbent or curate in charge.[48] The incumbent or curate in charge must allow searches to be made in the marriage books at all reasonable hours and, on payment of a prescribed fee, must give a certified copy of any entry.[49]

Where any church or chapel ceases to be used for the solemnisation of marriages any marriage register books must be delivered to the incumbent of the church which is or becomes the parish church of the parish in which the church or chapel where marriages are to cease is situate.[50] Unless they are the only marriage register books for that parish they are sent to the Registrar General to be formally closed.[51]

Funeral services[52]

10.60　The right of a parishioner and certain other persons to be buried in the parish churchyard or burial ground, the reservation of gravespace and the erection of monuments to the deceased as well as the subject of exhumation are all matters considered in Chapter 11, whilst fees in regard to funerals were considered in Chapter 8. Here we consider the conduct of the funeral service itself and the requirements surrounding this.

Cremation

10.61　The use of the term funeral as opposed to that of burial service in the ASB reflects the fact that many dead bodies are now cremated. Cremation is lawful in connection with Christian burial.[53] The prohibition against the cremation of a

---

[45] Marriage Act 1949, s.76. Prosecution must be within three years of the commission of the offence: *ibid.*

[46] *ibid.*, s.59. They may be given to a minister who is to solemnise a marriage of a housebound or detained person in advance of that solemnisation who then comes under a obligation to keep them safely and return them as soon as is reasonably practicable: *ibid.*, 55(5).

[47] Marriage Act 1949, s.76. Prosecution must be within three years of the commission of the offence: *ibid.*

[48] *ibid.*, s.60.

[49] *ibid.*, s.63.

[50] *ibid.*, s.62(1).

[51] *ibid.*, s.62(1).

[52] For more detailed consideration see Smale, *Davies' Law of Burial, Cremation and Exhumation* 1994 (6th ed. revised).

[53] Canon B38(3). Indeed the incumbent's rights pursuant to the Cremation Act 1902 not to perform the burial service in certain circumstances has now been repealed: Church of England (Miscellaneous Provisions) Measure 1992, ss.2(5), 17(2), Sched. 4, Pt. II.

person who has left a written direction to the contrary has been revoked, the decision how best to honour the wishes of the deceased now being left entirely to relatives and others responsible for the funeral.[54]

Where the body is to be cremated the burial service may precede, accompany or follow the cremation, and may be held in the church or in the crematorium.[55] The ashes should be reverently disposed of by a minister in a churchyard or other burial ground or on an area of land designated by the bishop for the purpose or at sea.[56] The bishop may designate an area for the sole purpose of the burial of cremated remains[57] but the use of the term "on" an area in the Canon supports the scattering of ashes on both land and sea.[57a]

Minister's obligation to perform funeral service

Subject to the exceptions described below, a minister is obliged to say (or arrange **10.62** for the performance of) the office for the burial of the dead in respect of the corpse of ashes of any person entitled to such burial in a churchyard or burial ground under their control, according to the rites of the Church of England.[58] Many parishes are situated either wholly or partially in an area which is chargeable with the expenses of a cemetery or where a cemetery or crematorium has been designated by the bishop as for the use of that parish. In such cases the minister is under the same obligation to perform funeral services at that cemetery or crematorium as they are to perform services in the churchyard of the parish.[59] The duty to perform or to arrange the performance of such services applies regardless of whether the deceased was a member of the Church of England or even a Christian.

The only requirement is that due notice be given to the minister.[60] No guidance is given as to what constitutes sufficient notice, but it would seem that the convenience of the minister is an important consideration,[61] as would

---

[54] *Legal Opinions*, p. 27.

[55] Canon B38(4)(a). A funeral service at a crematorium may only be performed in accordance with directions given by the diocesan bishop Canon B38(7). The same applies to service in cemeteries: Canon B38(7).

[56] Canon B38(4)(b).

[57] See Chap. 11.

[57a] By an Act of Convocation (operative only in the province of York) ashes may be disposed of in consecrated or dedicated ground by burial or by strewing them reverently on the surface of the ground and lightly covering them with earth. To scatter them broadcast without any covering is unseemly or irreverent and cannot be recommended: Smethurst, Wilson and Riley (eds), *Acts of the Convocations* (revised ed. 1961) p. 158.

[58] Canon B38(2). These are either persons deceased within the minister's cure or on the electoral roll of their parish. Thus it may be presumed that minister refers to the incumbent or priest-in-charge and not to an assistant curate. A breach of the duty of burial by a minister is an ecclesiastical offence: *Halsbury's Laws of England* (4th ed.), Vol. 14, para. 1357. Such a breach may also be an offence at common law and give rise to an action in damages: *Halsbury's Laws of England* (4th ed.), Vol. 10, para. 1135.

[59] Church of England (Miscellaneous Provisions) Measure 1992, s.2(4); Local Authorities' Cemeteries Order 1977 S.I. No. 204 of 1977, art. 17.

[60] *Titchmarsh v. Chapman* (1844) 3 Curt. 703, 840.

[61] *ibid*.

presumably be time to ascertain whether any of the exceptions applied and to prepare a reverent interment.[62] The urgency of the situation would also be relevant, the burial of a corpse being more so than the interment of ashes.

Exceptions

10.63   The first exceptions are those set out in the rubric of the Book of Common Prayer, and Canon B38, namely where a person dies unbaptised, or is excommunicate "for some grievous and notorious crime and no man can testify to his repentence", or being of unsound mind has laid violent hands upon themselves.[63] In regard to the unbaptised it should be remembered that as was discussed earlier in this Chapter baptism by a dissenting minister or a lay person is valid, and thus such persons are not within the exception. Further where there is uncertainty the deceased's proper baptism should be presumed.[63a] Excommunication has not been a pressing issue in the twentieth century. It is no longer included in the list of possible punishments pursuant to the EJM and despite the fact that it is still recited as an exception in the revised canons it is doubtful if it has any force today.[64]

So far as suicides are concerned the exception only applies to those who take their own life whilst of sound mind.[65] In practice the usual verdict of the coroner is to record a verdict that the deceased took their life while the balance of their mind was temporarily disturbed, and this has been treated as bringing such cases outside the exception.[66] However, if the coroner does not record such a verdict the minister's own opinion as to the state of mind of the deceased cannot prevail over that of the coroner.[67]

In all these cases where the burial office may not lawfully be used and the minister is to use[68] such form of service as may be prescribed or approved by

---

[62] Bursell, *Liturgy, Order and the Law* (1996), p. 205.

[63] *Book of Common Prayer*, rubric before the Order for the Burial of the Dead. Canon B38(2). The exception also extends to those executed for high treason: Phillimore, *Ecclesiastical Law of the Church of England*, Vol. 1, pp. 667–668. See also *Re St Edmund's Churchyard, Gateshead* [1995] 3 W.L.R. 253 at 259.

[63a] This accords with the legal *maxim omnia praesumuntur rite esse acta*. See also Cripps, Church and Clergy (8th ed.) p. 566.

[64] It is possible that a person excommunicated by a church of competent jurisdiction outside England but dying in England could be caught by this exception.

[65] Older authorities refer to the taking of one's own life at the time of years of discretion as well as when the deceased was in their senses: *Clift v. Schwabe* (1846) 3 C.B. 437 at 472–476; *Dufaur v. Professional Life Assurance Co.* (1858) 25 Beav. 599 at 602.

[66] Briden and Hanson, *Moore's Introduction to English Canon Law* (3rd ed. 1992), p. 82.

[67] See Bursell, *Liturgy, Order and the Law* (1996), p. 213, Phillimore, *Ecclesiastical Law of the Church of England*, (2nd ed. 1895), Vol. 1, pp. 669–670; *Cooper v. Dodds* (1850) 2 Rob. Ecc. 270.

[68] The wording of Canon B38(2) means that it is not clear whether the authorised form of service must be used in such cases or must be used upon the request of the person having charge of the funeral. It is suggested that the former interpretation is correct but Doe, *The Legal Framework of the Church of England* (1996) takes the opposite view.

the Ordinary.[69] Such persons are not to be denied burial in consecrated ground nor are they to be denied a funeral service; it is only the burial office which may not lawfully be used. In cases of doubt as to whether the exceptions apply the minister must refer the matter to the bishop and obey his order and direction.[70]

The second exception to the use of the burial office are cases where any relative, friend or legal representative having charge of or being responsible for the burial, gives the prescribed written notice that it is intended that the burial shall take place without the office.[71] That person may request the minister to use the form of service prescribed or approved by the Ordinary for cases where the burial office may not lawfully be used.[72] Alternatively the burial may take place without any religious service or with such Christian and orderly religious service at the grave as the person having charge or being responsible thinks fit.[73] A Christian service includes every religious service used by any church, denomination or person professing to be a Christian.[73a] A non-Christian service is not possible.

Anyone whom that person invites or authorises to do so may conduct such a service or take part in any religious act at it,[74] thus permitting unordained persons to conduct funeral services in these circumstances. However, if the Church of England burial service is to be read it is not clear this must be authorised by the incumbent of the parish in which the burial ground is situated, but it would appear that such authorisation is not required.[75]

---

[69] Burial Laws Amendment Act 1880, s.13; Prayer Book (Further Provisions) Measure 1968, s.5; Canon B38(2). If an alternative service for suicides has been approved by General Synod that must be used for such persons instead unless the person having charge or being responsible for the burial requests otherwise: *ibid*. To date no such service has been approved. It should be noted that the minister cannot use any other form of service notwithstanding Canon B5(2): Bursell, *Liturgy, Order and the Law*, (1996) p. 220 *et seq.*

[70] Canon B38(6). Although not felicitously worded this provision must be aimed at the question of whether any of the exceptions apply not whether an authorised service may be used: Bursell, *Liturgy, Order and the Law*, (1996), p.200, n. 8.

[71] Burial Laws Amendment Act 1880, s.1, Sched. A. See also Local Authorities' Cemetries Order 1977 S.I. No. 204 of 1977, art. 5(5). In the ordinary course of events the person responsible is not the funeral director unless they are acting on the instructions of the relation, friend or legal representative in charge of the funeral: Bursell, *Liturgy Order and the Law*, (1996), p. 199, n. 6.

[72] See n. 69 *ante*.

[73] Burial Laws Amendment Act 1880, s.6. Notice must be given in accordance with the Burial Act 1900, s.8. As to order see *ibid*., s.6; Local Authorities' Cemeteries Order 1977 S.I. No. 204 of 1977, art. 18. Everyone must be given free access to the churchyard or graveyard where the funeral is taking place: Burial Laws Amendment Act 1880, s.6.

[73a] Burial Laws Amendment Act 1880, s.6.

[74] See n. 73 *ante*.

[75] *Legal Opinions* p. 28 suggests that the authorisation is required, but in spite of the generality of the dictum of Lord Coleridge C.J. in *Wood v. Headingley-cum-Burley Burial Board* [1892] 1 Q.B. 713 at 729 this view appears contrary to the express wording of the Burial Laws Amendment Act 1880: Bursell, *Liturgy, Order and the Law*, (1996), p. 201, n. 22.

Performance of service by deaconesses, readers and lay workers

10.64   It should be noted that deaconesses, readers and lay workers may be authorised to bury the dead and to read the burial service before, at or after a cremation.[76] Thus again unordained persons may conduct funeral services, but they may only do so with the goodwill of the persons responsible and at the invitation of the minister of a parish or extra-parochial place.[77] Goodwill apears to imply that consent is not required but that the service may be conducted by such persons in the absence of opposition.[78] Those who have charge of or are responsible for a funeral may therefore insist upon it being conducted by an ordained minister. Otherwise, subject only to the exceptions discussed above, only an ordained minister may officiate at a funeral on consecrated ground, even where that consecrated ground is a cemetery not a churchyard.[79]

Location

10.65   The minister[80] of one parish may perform a funeral service in any crematorium or cemetery which is situated in another parish without the consent of the incumbent of that parish if certain conditions are met. Either the deceased died in that minister's parish, or was resident[81] there, or their name was on the church electoral roll immediately before death.[82] A person licensed[83] to perform funeral services on premises forming part of or belonging to a university, college, school, hospital or public or charitable institution may perform a funeral service for the deceased who was resident in, employed by or enrolled as a student in the institution, in any cemetery or crematorium, without the consent of the incumbent in whose parish it is performed.[84] However, a funeral service performed at a cemetery or crematorium must only be performed in accordance with directions given by the bishop.[85] Apart from these exceptions the consent of the incumbent of the benefice is required before a minister may conduct a funeral service, and if

---

[76] Canon D1(4)(c), E4,(2A), E7(5)(c). Where the cure is vacant the invitation is made by the rural dean: *ibid*.

[77] See n. 76 *ante*.

[78] Bursell, *Liturgy, Order and the Law*, (1996), p. 200, n. 17.

[79] *Johnstone v. Friend* (1860) 6 Jur, N.S. 28; *Wood v. Headingley-cum-Burley Burial Board* (*ante*) at 729.

[80] Minister for these purposes means the incumbent, or where the benefice is vacant the priest-in-charge and where no such curate is appointed the rural dean, and where a special cure of souls of the parish has been assigned to a team vicar: Church of England (Miscellaneous Provisions) Measure 1992, s.2(6). However, an assistant curate, deaconess, reader or lay worker would require the consent of the incumbent of the parish in which the funeral is performed: *Wood v. Headingley-cum-Burley Burial Board* (*ante*) at 729.

[81] The term has its ordinary or natural meaning and is normally a matter of fact and degree: Bursell, *Liturgy, Order and the Law*, (1996), p. 203, n. 35.

[82] Church of England (Miscellaneous Provisions) Measure 1992, s.2(1), (2); Canon C8(2).

[83] Under the Extra-Parochial Ministry Measure 1967, s.2.

[84] Church of England (Miscellaneous Provisions) Measure 1992, s.2(3); Canon C8(2).

[85] Canon B38(7).

the minister who is to conduct the service is from a different diocese the consent of the bishop is also required. It should be noted that the conducting of funeral service's in undertakers' chapels, which are essentially resting places for corpses, whether within the incumbent's benefice or not, is almost certainly unlawful.[86]

Burial in unconsecrated ground

In limited cases the deceased person may have had a right of interment in **10.66** unconsecrated ground provided under an Act relating to burial. The person having charge or responsibility for the funeral may if they think fit have the burial performed in that ground according to the rites of the Church of England by a minister willing to perform it.[87] A minister cannot be obliged to perform such a service,[88] but where they do they are not liable to censure or penalty for doing so if they would otherwise be entitled to use the service had the burial ground, cemetery or building on it been consecrated.[89] Where a body is buried according to the rites of the Church of England in unconsecrated ground the minister, on coming to the grave, must first bless it.[90]

The Burial

The responsibility for digging the grave is upon the executors or those responsible for the funeral arrangements. The incumbent's duty is only to indicate the place at which the grave is to be dug and the depth; there is no obligation to provide a grave digger.[91]

The right to burial is only to burial in the usual manner.[92] Although the mode of burial may be out of the ordinary, for example in an iron coffin, vault or with unusual accompaniments[93] it must be reverent.[94]

Subject to the provisions already discussed enabling those in charge of the funeral to give notice that the burial shall be without the burial office, one of the authorised burial services must be read at the time of burial if it is in consecrated ground.[95] The service may be taken entirely at the graveside or partially at the graveside and partially in church.[96]

---

[86] *Legal Opinions*, pp. 134–136.
[87] Burial Laws Amendment Act 1880, s.12.
[88] *Rugg v. Kingsmill* (1868) 5 Moo. P.C.C.N.S. 79 at 89, 90.
[89] See n. 87 *ante*.
[90] Canon B38(5).
[91] *Legal Opinions,* p. 25.
[92] *Winstanley v. North Manchester Overseers* [1910] A.C. 7 at 16.
[93] *ibid*.
[94] See for example, *Gilbert v. Buzzard* (1821) 2 Hag. Con. 333 at 344 regarding the necessity for the corpse to have some involucra or covering if not a coffin.
[95] *Kemp v. Wickes* (1809) 3 Phil, Ecc. R. 264 at 295.
[96] *Book of Common Prayer*, rubrics at the beginning of the Order for the Burial of the Dead, ASB, Series 1 Burial Services. This latter service provides that burial may precede the service in church and the prayers. See also Bursell, *Liturgy, Order and the Law* (1996), pp. 209–210.

Sermons and eulogies

The ASB makes provision for a sermon at a funeral service and whilst the Book of Common prayer does not do so, the inclusion of a sermon would seem to be a *de minimis* addition. If it has a Christian content a sermon would also embrace an "eulogy" to the deceased, but would be required to be preached by those who may deliver such sermons.[97] However, if such an eulogy is not a sermon it would appear to be a *de minimis* addition which could be delivered by anyone provided it was reverent and seemly.[98]

Burial of children

10.67 The ASB provides a special service for the funeral of a child.[99] The "Funeral Service for a Child Dying near the Time of Birth" specifically envisages that it may be used if the burial has already taken place, and may be used at church, crematorium, hospital or home. The Prayers after the "Birth of a Still-born Child" or the "Death of a Newly-born Child" in the ASB may both be used at the burial or cremation of such a child, and it would seem permissible to include prayers from these services where the burial rite from the Book of Common Prayer is used.[1] The ASB also makes provision for the combination of the "Funeral of Child" with a service of Holy Communion whilst the "Order for the Burial of the Dead" provides for occasions when an adult and child are buried together.

Burial at sea

10.68 The Book of Common Prayer provides for a special form of words of committal for a service of burial at sea whilst the ASB provides variations for such circumstances.

Other services

The ASB also provides for a service which may be used before a funeral, where the body is brought to church the day before or which may be said in the home before the body is taken to the church. An "Order for the Burial of the Dead" in the Series 1 Burial Services also provides for the service in church to be used as a memorial service apart from the funeral.

Certificate of disposal

10.69 It should be noted that a body may not be disposed of until a certificate for disposal has been issued by the registrar of births and deaths or a corresponding order made by the coroner.[1a] This certificate or order should be produced to the

[97] Bursell, *Liturgy, Order and the Law* (1996), p. 210.
[98] *ibid*.
[99] As does the Series 1 Burial Service.
[1] Bursell, *Liturgy, Order and the Law* (1996), p. 212.
[1a] Births and Deaths Registration Act 1926, s.2.

incumbent, but they may proceed without if satisfied by a written declaration that this has been left behind or mislaid and will be produced to him later or a duplicate certificate obtained.[2] A minister is under a duty to register a burial as soon as possible in the prescribed manner,[3] save where a non-Anglican burial takes place in the churchyard under the Burial Laws Amendment Act 1880 when the person having charge of the funeral is responsible.[4] The burial of still-born children must be authorised by certificate or coroner's order and the burial must not proceed without production of the actual certificate.[5] In cases where no other arrangements can be made burial is regulated by the Public Health (Control of Diseases) Act 1984.[6]

Register

In every parish church and chapel where its churchyard or burial ground is used **10.70** for burials a register book of burials must be provided which must be kept in accordance with the statutes and Measure relating to it and rules and regulations made thereunder.[7] Any minister[8] who officiates at a burial according to the rites of the Church of England[9] must, as soon as possible after the burial has taken place, enter in the appropriate register book of burials the particulars required relating to the burial and sign the register.[10]

Where a burial occurs in an extra-parochial place (unless it takes place in the burial ground of a church or chapel for which a register book is provided) the minister who officiates must as soon as possible after the burial send to the incumbent (or priest-in-charge) of such adjoining parishes as the diocesan bishop may direct a certificate signed by them certifying when and where the burial took place and containing the particulars required for the registration.[11] On receiving the certificate the incumbent must enter particulars of the burial to which the certificate relates in the appropriate register book.[12]

---

[2] *Legal Opinions*, p. 26.

[3] Parochial Registers and Records Measure 1978, s.3. The Births and Deaths Registration Act 1926, s.3 requires the incumbent of the parish to notify the registrar of the date and place and means of disposal of the body within 96 hours of burial. Compliance with the secular law is enjoined by Canon B39(1).

[4] By virtue of the definition of "person effecting the disposal" in s.12 of the Birth and Deaths Registration Act 1926.

[5] *ibid.*, s.5.

[6] s.46.

[7] Canon F11(1), (2).

[8] Minister for these purposes includes any person who is authorised to bury the dead according to the rites of the Church of England: Parochial Registers and Records Measure 1978, s.3(5).

[9] The requirement regarding entry in the register does not apply to a cemetery in which an Act incorporating the Cemeteries Clauses Act 1847 applies or in a cemetery provided amd maintained by a burial authority within the meaning of section 214 of the Local Government Act 1972: Parochial Registers and Records Measure 1978, s.3(1), (4).

[10] Parochial Registers and Records Measure 1978, s.3(1); Canon B39(1).

[11] Parochial Registers and Records Measure 1978, s.3(2).

[12] *ibid.*, s.3(3). The words "According to the certificate of _____ received by me on the _____ day of _____."

If an error is discovered by a person required to register a burial in the form of substance of an entry it may be corrected within one month of the discovery by an entry in the margin of the register book without altering the original.[13]

Prayers for the dead

10.71   Prayers for the dead and notices inviting such prayers are not illegal.[14] Prayers for the dead do not fall under the same condemnation as the doctrine of purgatory[15] with which they are sometimes erroneously linked, being of a much earlier date than that doctrine.[16] Accordingly unless they actually involve the doctrine of purgatory.[17] or any notice inviting such prayers contains erroneous doctrine[18] they are permissible. Since the publication of the revised Prayer Book of 1928 (rejected by Parliament) which contained prayers for the dead, the practice has become more widespread.

Morning and Evening Prayer

10.72   At the Reformation the old offices of Matins, Lauds, Prime, Terce, Sext, None, Vespers and Compline were replaced by two daily offices known as Morning and Evening Prayer, which are often called Matins and Evensong.[19] The old offices have revived in Anglican religious orders whilst Compline has also been revived (in English) in some parishes. Such services, which are voluntary extras are not unlawful, but are not part of the official worship of the Church of England, with one exception, namely Night Prayer, which is itself based upon the old office of Compline.

The service of Night Prayer, set out in *Lent, Holy Week, Easter,* was commended by the House of Bishops of the General Synod, and is now published as a separate edition, with the intention that it be used as a late evening service adaptable to other parts of the Church year.[20] It is far from clear who is to act as the minister, and since it is also envisaged that the service may be used at home, it may be that anyone may so act.[21]

---

[13] The correction must be made in the presence of two persons who were present at the burial to which the entry relates or the churchwardens of the parish to which the register book belongs. The marginal entry must be signed by the person making the entry and must be attested by the persons in whose presence it is made, and the date of the entry must be added: Parochial Registers and Records Measure 1978, s.4.

[14] *Rector and Churchwardens of St Mary, Suffolk v. Packard* [1927] P. 289; *Re Parish of South Creake Parish* [1959] 1 W.L.R. 427.

[15] Thirty-nine Articles of Religion, Article XXII.

[16] *Breeks v. Woolfrey* (1838) 1 Curt. 880.

[17] *ibid*; *Re Parish of South Creake* (ante); *Re St Mary the Virgin Ilmington* [1962] P. 147.

[18] *Rector and Churchwardens of St Mary, Suffolk v. Packard* [1927] P. 289; *Re Parish of South Creake* (ante).

[19] Briden and Hanson, *Moore's Introduction to English Canon Law* (3rd ed. 1992), p. 78.

[20] The service is intended to be used in accordance with the provisions of Canon B5(2), but it is not clear whether the adaptions have in fact been commended by the House of Bishops.

[21] Bursell, *Liturgy, Order and the Law* (1996), p. 234.

The requirements as to when Morning and Evening Prayer must take place have been considered in Chapter 9. Both must be said or sung distinctly, reverently and in an audible voice.[22] Save in the case of the exceptions set out below the minister of the parish together with all other ministers licensed to serve there shall make provision for the daily offices to be said or sung in the parish church.[23] The Book of Common Prayer directs that a bell be tolled at a convenient time beforehand so that the people may join them.[24] Alternatively provision may be made for these services to take place elsewhere as may best serve to sustain the corporate spiritual life of the parish and the pattern of life enjoined upon ministers, after consultation with the PCC.[25]

Save in cathedral churches readers and such other lay persons as the bishop of the diocese may authorise can say or sing the daily offices, save for the Absolution.[26] In place of the Absolution they read the collect for the twenty-first Sunday after Trinity.[27] So too may some other suitable lay person at the invitation of the minister or, where the minister is incapacitated or the cure is vacant, at the invitation of the churchwardens.[28] The practice of any lay person whom the minister considers suitable reading the lessons is longstanding and whilst no specific provision is made for this it would not appear to be unlawful.[29]

In addition to the forms of Morning and Evening Prayer in the Book of Common Prayer, the shorter forms set out in the Schedule to the Act of Uniformity Amendment Act 1872 may still be used, whilst the ASB also provides for shorter forms of these services with or without a sermon, lecture or reading of a homily. Although doubts arose in the nineteenth century as to whether Morning Prayer, the Litany and Holy Communion according to the Book of Common Prayer might be used separately it is now clear that they can be.[30]

---

[22] Canons B10(1), B11(1).

[23] Canon B11(2).

[24] *Book of Common Prayer*, concerning the Service of the Church.

[25] Canon B11(2).

[26] Canon B11 (1); *Book of Common Prayer*, Order for Morning Prayer and Order for Evening Prayer, rubric following the general confession.

[27] See the rubric inserted in The Book of Common Prayer, Morning and Evening Prayer after the Absolution by the Prayer Book (Further Provisions) Measure 1968, s.1(2). Although this Measure is repealed the provision remains in force: Church of England (Worship and Doctrine) Measure 1974, s.6(4), Sched. 3, para. 4. No alternative provision was made in relation to the ASB but see "A Service of the Word and Affirmations of Faith", (1993) Appendix, which now regulates the matter. The rubrics of both the Book of Common Prayer and "A Service of the Word and Affirmations of Faith" refer to situations when no priest is present and thus a deacon should likewise not pronounce the Asbolution.

[28] See n. 26 *ante*.

[29] The Prayer Book (Further Provisions) Measure 1968 s.1(5) provided that nothing in the Book of Common Prayer was to be taken as preventing the reading of any lessons by a lay person, but it was repealed and not replaced in 1975. The rubrics in the Book of Common Prayer do not say who is to read the lessons, simply that the minister is to announce them.

[30] Doubts were resolved by the Act of Uniformity Amendment Act 1872 and despite the repeal of this Act it is clear that they may still be used separately: Bursell, *Liturgy, Order and the Law* (1996), p. 121.

Indeed the Litany is probably best regarded as a separate service.[31] However, the ASB does provide for the incorporation of the Litany in the longer forms of Morning and Evening Prayer.[32] Morning and Evening Prayer both end with the Grace in the Book of Common Prayer, but the ASB provides that it may end with a blessing.[33]

A "Service of the Word" has been authorised as an alternative to Morning and Evening Prayer. However, this is not intended for daily use but to provide a structure for Sunday and weekday services of an occasional nature.[34]

Churching of women

10.73   The full title in the Book of Common Prayer is the "Thanksgiving of Women after Childbirth, commonly called the Churching of Women." Although the language of the rubric at the beginning and in the opening words to be spoken by the priest indicate that the office is mandatory its actual use varies considerably[35] and in some parishes has fallen into disuse. The ASB provides the alternative "Thanksgiving for the Birth of a Child", and a form of service for "Thanksgiving after Adoption".

The potential implication that the churching of women should be the first public service attended by the mother[36] is not supported by the fact that the ASB provides that the alternative "Thanksgiving for the Birth of a Child", may be in the home or in the hospital at the priest's discretion.[37]

The rubrics in the Book of Common Prayer direct that the woman is to come into the church decently apparelled and to kneel down in some convenient place determined by custom or at the direction of the Ordinary. If there is a celebration of Holy Communion she should receive this. She is also enjoined to offer the accustomed offerings.[38]

The rubrics also indicate that the service is to be conducted by a priest, but the bishop may authorise a deaconess or a lay worker to church women at the

---

[31] This would accord with the Act of Uniformity Amendment Act 1872, s.5 and the definition of "form of service" in the Church of England (Worship and Doctrine) Measure 1974, s.5(2). See also Bursell, *Liturgy, Order and the Law* (1996), p. 127.

[32] Note 10, at p. 46. Any doubt is also resolved by Canon B5(1).

[33] The practice of following this by hymns during one of which a collection may be taken, possibly a sermon and a blessing, whilst not unlawful, forms part of a separate service: Briden and Hanson, *Moore's Introduction to English Canon Law* (3rd ed. 1992), p. 79. It would appear that a deacon may either pronounce the blessing or may alter it by virtue of Canon B5(1) to an inclusive form of joint petition by themselves and the congregation: Bursell, *Liturgy, Order and the Law* (1996), p. 126.

[34] *A Service of the Word and Affirmations of Faith* (1993), p. 7.

[35] Briden and Hanson, *Moore's Introduction to English Canon Law* (3rd ed. 1992), p. 81–82.

[36] *ibid*.

[37] Bursell, *Liturgy, Order and the Law*, (1996), p. 223 suggests that the use of the service from the Book of Common Prayer at home or in hospital would be permissible.

[38] The ASB makes no reference to such offerings and it would appear that this duty is now abrogated or at least is abrogated in all parishes other than those not bound by a standard table of fees under the Ecclesiastical Fees Measure 1962, s.2(4): Bursell *Liturgy, Order and the Law*, (1996), p. 223.

invitation of the minister.[39] The same principles apply to the alternative services of thanksgiving for birth and adoption. Somewhat curiously therefore a deacon cannot perform any of these services.[40]

Ministry to the sick

Upon being informed that any person in their parish is sick or in danger of death the minister must resort to them as soon as possible, to exhort, instruct and comfort them in such manner as they consider most needful and convenient.[41] A form of service for this purpose, entitled "Order for the Visitation of the Sick" is set out in the Book of Common Prayer, whilst the General Synod has authorised the forms of service in "The Ministry to the Sick". In addition the House of Bishops of the General Synod has commended a form of service, "Ministry at the Time of Death". **10.74**

Where a parishioner is sick, in danger of death or so impotent that they cannot go to church and is desirous of receiving Holy Communion the minister must visit them as soon as may be, and unless there is grave reason to the contrary, must minister the sacrament to them at such place and time as may be convenient.[42] This expression would include any institution, the person's home or anywhere where an emergency arises.

The Communion of the Sick and the practice of reservation of the sacrament for administration to the sick has already been considered earlier in this Chapter. The ASB provides an alternative form of eucharistic service which may be shortened if the needs of the patient require it. The reserved sacrament may be administered to the sick by deacons, deaconesses and readers and any lay worker can be authorised to administer Holy Communion (including to the sick) by the bishop.[43]

As is evident from the rubrics before the Absolution, "The order for the Visitation of the Sick" must be taken by a priest. However, the "Service of Commendation at the Time of Death" in the Ministry to the Sick may be led by a priest or by any other Christian person, although the blessing should only be given by a priest, and "Ministry at the Time of Death" has alternative forms of service when the minister is a deacon or lay person.

If a person wishes the priest may lay hands upon them and may annoint them with oil on the forehead with the sign of the Cross.[44] Alternative Forms of Service for the Laying on of Hands and Annointing, contained in the "Ministry to the Sick", have been approved. Pure olive oil must be used which has been consecrated by the diocesan bishop or otherwise by the minister themselves in accordance with that service.[45]

---

[39] Deaconesses and Lay Ministry Measure 1972, s.1; Canons D1(4)(b), E7(5)(b).
[40] See Bursell, *Liturgy, Order and the Law*, (1996), p. 223.
[41] Canon B37(1).
[42] Canon B37(2).
[43] Canons B12(3), D1(3)(b), E4(2)(c), E7(4)(b); *Legal Opinions*, p. 4.
[44] Canon B37(3).
[45] Canon B37(3).

Exorcism

10.75   No provision is made in the Book of Common Prayer for exorcism nor in the Revised Canons, although the Canons of 1603 provided that ministers were not to attempt exorcism without first obtaining the licence of the bishop. In a statement to the General Synod[46] the Archbishop of Canterbury indicated that it should only be performed by an experienced person authorised by the diocesan bishop, and in collaboration with medical treatment and in the context of prayer and sacrament and be followed by continuing pastoral care.

Commination

10.76   The service of commination or the denouncing of God's anger and judgment against sinners, set forth in the Book of Common Prayer, appears to have fallen into disuse. Although the matter is not beyond doubt if taken, it would appear that the service should be conducted by a clerk in holy orders.[47]

Confession and Absolution

10.77   The sacrament of penance as it is often called, consists of confession with repentance and Absolution. The Book of Common Prayer makes provision for both public and, inappropriate circumstances, private penance. In the office of Holy Communion there is a general confession followed by Absolution, as there is in the Orders for Morning and Evening Prayer. Private confession is not obligatory,[48] but as discussed in Chapter 9 confession tables and chairs or boxes are permitted in churches. It should be noted that no minister may exercise the ministry of Absolution in any place without the permission of the minister having the cure of souls therein other than in respect of persons in danger of death or if there is some other urgent or weighty cause.[49]

Private confession and Absolution are enjoined in the Exhortation which is read after the prayer for the Church in the service of Holy Communion and in the Order for the Visitation of the Sick. This states that the sick person is to be moved to make a special confession of their sins if they feel their conscience troubled with any weighty matter. After such confession the priest then pronounces Absolution.[50]

Only a priest may pronounce Absolution. Where the sacrament is distributed other than by a priest it is suggested that the bishop's authorisation should provide that where the Book of Common Prayer form is used the communicant makes an act of penitence and the person administering the sacrament should say a prayer such as the Collect for the 21st Sunday after Trinity and where the ASB form is used "you" in the Absolution should be replaced by "us".[51]

---

[46] 30 June, 1975,
[47] Bursell, *Liturgy, Order and the Law* (1996), p. 226.
[48] *Rector and Churchwardens of Capel St Mary, Suffolk v. Packard* [1927] P. 289.
[49] Canon B29(4).
[50] Repeated in Canon B29(3).
[51] *Legal Opinions*, p. 4.

Canon B29[52] states that it is the duty of baptised persons to examine their lives and to confess to God. It states that if there is anyone who cannot quieten their conscience by these means and who requires further comfort or counsel they should come to some discreet and learned minister to receive the benefit of Absolution together with "ghostly counsel and advice".[53]

The seal of the confession

The only part of the Code of Canons of 1603 which has not been repealed is the proviso to Canon 113.[54] This imposes an obligation upon the priest not to break the "seal of the confession" under pain of irregularity. Thus a priest would commit an ecclesiastical offence were they to disclose matters revealed to them in the course of a private confession.[55] There is one exception in respect of "such crimes as by the law of this Realm (the priest's) own life may be called into question for concealing the same". To what exception this in fact refers is obscure. Treason would seem to be the only candidate.[56] **10.78**

To what extent the secular courts would consider such a communication privileged, so that the priest could refuse to answer questions relating to it, is unclear. Pre-Reformation canon law, which remains unaltered in this respect, imposes an obligation of secrecy and the Book of Common Prayer which has statutory authority may be taken to have embodied what was already the law.[57]

Nonetheless the question remains one of considerable doubt, and the weight of opinion tends towards a view that the seal is not absolutely privileged.[58] The **10.79**

---

[52] Canon B29(1), (2).

[53] Doe, *The Legal Framework of the Church of England* (1996), p. 350 suggests because of the use of may in the Canon the penitent's only right is to make the request and the priest has a lawful discretion both to refuse to hear the confession or, having heard it, to refuse Absolution on the ground that the penitent has no intention of amending their life.

[54] An amendment was proposed to Canon 113 in the Report of the Archbishops' Commission on Canon Law, *The Canon Law of the Church of England*, (1947). The recommendation was not followed on the grounds that developments in the modern law of evidence created difficulties regarding the enactment of a revised canon: *The Canons of the Church of England* (1969) p. xii.

[55] Halsbury's Laws of England, (4th ed.), Vol. 14, para. 1047; Bursell, *Liturgy, Order and the Law*, (1996), p. 227 and Briden and Hanson, *Moore's Introduction to English Canon Law*, (3rd ed. 1992), pp. 83–84 and see the works referred to in n. 67 *post*. Doe, *The Legal Framework of the Church of England*, (1996), pp. 353–354 disagrees, and suggests that the rule against disclosure binds only in conscience, this being the view of the Doctrine Commission, (see Doctrine in the Church of England, the Report of the Commission on Christian Doctrine appointed by the Archbishops, (1938), pp. 197–198), and the assumption in 1959 when Convocations passed a resolution reaffirming as "an essential principle of Church doctrine" the seal of confession (see Smethurst, Wilson & Riley eds, *Acts of the Convocations* (revised ed. 1961) p. 165.

[56] Re St Edmund's Chapel, Gateshead [1995] 3 W.L.R. 253 at 258–259.

[57] Briden and Hanson, *Moore's Introduction to English Canon Law*, (3rd ed. 1992), p. 84.

[58] Bursell, "The Seal of the Confessional" (1990) 2 Ecc. L.J. 84; Winkworth *The Seal of the Confessional and the Law of Evidence* (1952); Nokes "Professional Privilege" (1950) 66 L.Q.R. 88; Badeley *The Privilege of Religious Confessions in English Courts of Justice* (1865). See also Elliott, "An Evidential Privilege for Priest-Penitent Communications", (1994) 3 E.L.J. 274.

Criminal Law Revision Commission declined to recommend that communications between priest and penitent be privileged.[59] A trial judge nonetheless has discretion to exclude such evidence.[60] It may also be possible for the penitent, or possibly the Church in a representative capacity, to seek an injunction[61] preventing the information being disclosed in civil proceedings. Were a court to attempt to force a priest to disclose such a communication they should seek legal representation so that the matter could be argued before the Court.

[59] The Criminal Law Revision Committee, 11th Report (1972) paras 273–274.
[60] Police and Criminal Evidence Act 1984, ss. 76, 78, 82. See also Doe, *The Legal Framework of the Church of England*, (1996), pp. 354–355.
[61] As to injunctions *quita timet*, see *Argyll v. Argyll* [1967] Ch. 302; *Stephens v. Avery* [1988] Ch. 449 as to matters of confidentiality.

Chapter Eleven: Ecclesiastical Jurisdiction

Despite its unitary nature, as we saw in Chapter 1 English law has two distinct **11.1** branches, one known as ecclesiastical law administered by the ecclesiastical courts and another consisting of general law administered by the temporal courts. This separation of ecclesiastical and secular jurisdiction dates from the reign of William I. Prior to the Norman Conquest both ecclesiastical and secular causes were tried in the courts of the hundred or of the shire in which the bishop sat with secular officials. In 1072 an ordinance was issued forbidding the bishop to hear ecclesiastical pleas in the secular courts and prescribing that all cases relating to the cure of souls be tried in the church courts. It is from this date that we can trace the development of the court of the archdeacons and those of the bishops and archbishops.

In this chapter we consider the development and the present day scope of ecclesiastical jurisdiction, together with the role of the secular courts in reviewing the decisions of ecclesiastical courts, as well as the role of the secular courts in reviewing those administration actions of officers of the Church which fall outside the scope of ecclesiastical jurisdiction. We look at the system of the ecclesiastical courts, their officers, proceedings, costs and fees, and the legal aid system in respect of criminal cases. The faculty jurisdiction which occupies the majority of the time before the consistory courts is examined, and finally we consider the now limited criminal jurisdiction of the ecclesiastical courts.

Development and present day scope of ecclesiastical jurisdiction

Following the separation of the ecclesiastical and secular courts after the Norman **11.2** Conquest the ecclesiastical courts developed a wide field of jurisdiction in both civil and criminal matters. Within the civil jurisdiction these included matrimonial and testamentary causes and matters incidental to these such as probate and grants of administration. Within the criminal jurisdiction their ambit extended beyond offences of the clergy in connection with their office, to crimes of the laity of ecclesiastical cognisance, such as heresy and defamation.

From the reign of Stephen, if not before, appeals from the ecclesiastical courts were made to Rome.[1] Where the ecclesiastical courts exceeded their jurisdition

---

[1] For the origins and development of the ecclesiastical jurisdiction see further Makower, *Constitutional History of the Church of England* (English translation), pp. 384 *et seq.* and Appendix 1; *Report of the Archbishops' Commission on Ecclesiastical Courts* (1954); Phillimore, *Ecclesiastical Law* (2nd ed.), pp. 1108–1109; *Holdsworth's History of English Law* (7th ed.), pp. 614 *et seq.*

they were restrained by prohibition issuing from the King's Courts,[2] such writ being a means by which potential papal usurpation was kept in check in the Realm.

The Reformation brought relatively few changes to the ecclesiastical courts. Thomas Cromwell's supression of the study of canon law in the universities meant that ecclesiastical lawyers qualified in civil or Roman law at the universities before practising out of Doctors' Commons. Founded in 1511 as a college of ecclesiastical advocates, Doctors' Commons were essentially an ecclesiastical version of the Inn of Courts of the common lawyers, and thus became the recognised centre for the study of canon law and the place where professional training in ecclesiastical law took place.[3] Previously ecclesiastical judicial appointments had been resticted to those who were in holy orders (which might be minor orders) with academic training in canon law, but following the supression of the study of canon law in the universities laymen who were doctors of civil law became eligible to hold such appointments.[4]

From 1532 appeals from the ecclesiastical courts which had previously been made to Rome were prohibited, and the following year these appeals together with those from the archbishop's court were directed to be made to the King in Chancery.[5] The High Court of Delegates, which was constituted to hear appeals, remained the supreme court of appeal in ecclesiastical causes until it was superseded by the jurisdiction of the Judicial Committee of the Privy Council[6]. With these exceptions the system of ecclesiastical courts system continued just as it had done before the Reformation.

In the middle of the nineteenth century the jurisdiction of the ecclesiastical courts was curtailed and their cognisance in a number of matters removed. These included jurisdiction in testamentary matters and in cases of intestacy which were transferred to the Court of Probate, and in matrimonial causes which were transferred to the Divorce Court.[7] This curtailment led to the closure of Doctors' Commons and with it the disappearance of the distinct profession of ecclesiastical lawyers who had held a virtual monopoly of the ecclesiastical courts.

As doctrinal controversies grew pressure for further reform developed. Prosecutions of clergy for offences of ritual and ceremonial together with the enactment of the Public Worship Regulation Act 1874 (now repealed) fuelled resentment. Between 1833 and 1952 six commissions made proposals for the reform of the system before a report by the Archbishops' Commission on Ecclesiastical Courts in 1954 led to the enactment of the Ecclesiastical Jurisdiction Measure 1963 (EJM).

---

[2] 18 Edw. 1 (Writ of Consultations) (1289) (repealed).

[3] *The Canon Law of the Church of England*, Reports of the Archbishops' Commission on Canon Law (1947), pp. 52, 53.

[4] Ecclesiastical Jurisdiction Act 1545 (repealed).

[5] Ecclesiastical Appeals Act 1532, s.3 (repealed); Submission of the Clergy Act 1533, s.4 (repealed).

[6] Submission of the Clergy Act 1533, s.4 (repealed); Privy Council Appeals Act 1832, s.3 (repealed); see also the *Report of the Archbishops' Commission on Ecclesiastical Courts* (1954), pp. 23, 24.

[7] Court of Probate Act 1857 (repealed); Matrimonial Causes Act 1957 (repealed); Ecclesiastical Courts Act 1855 (repealed).

Ecclesiastical Jurisdiction Measure 1963

The EJM reformed the ecclesiastical court system and abolished obsolete **11.3** jurisdictions. In addition to various repeals the Measure declared that any canon, constitution, decretal or other like instrument forming part of the law ecclesiastical which was inconsistent with the provisions of the Measure should, to the extent of the inconsistency, cease to have effect.[8] The perogative of the Crown, and the existing procedure relating to the confirmation of the election of bishops, the mode of appointment, the office and duties of vicars-general of provinces or dioceses, the visiatorial powers of archdeacons, and the jurisdiction of the Master of the Faculties, were expressly preserved, the Measure having no effect upon any of these.[9] Nor did it have any effect upon any power of the High Court to control the proper exercise by the ecclesiastical courts of their functions.[10] Although the EJM brought about widespread reform, sweeping away the complex system created by a mutliplicity of courts and other tribunals, the new system and procedures which it introduced are, as we shall see, themselves cumbersome and impractical in regard to the operation of part of its appellate jurisdiction.

As with the secular courts the work of the ecclesiastical courts is divided into civil and criminal cases. A further division is then made between those ecclesiastical cases which are concerned with doctrine, ritual or ceremonial known as reserved cases and all others which are called conduct or ordinary cases.

Scope of ecclesiastical jurisdiction

The scope of the present day jurisdiction of the ecclesiastical courts is limited to **11.4** the protection of consecrated land by means of the faculty jurisdiction, enforcing discipline upon the clergy and adjudicating upon and enforcing certain civil rights in connection with ecclesiastical matters and property. However, some matters of ecclesiastical law fall within the jurisdiction of the secular courts.[11] Amongst these, as we have seen, are appeals relating to determinations of questions relating to clergy pensions by the Pensions Board, an action of *quare impedit* for disturbance of rights of patronage, and proceedings to enforce an order relating to the deposit of parochial registers and records. But subject matter is not a definitive test in ascertaining the appropriate procedure. For example, the ownership of chattels in a church is justicable by either the secular or ecclesiastical courts, and the forum in which the matter is litigated will depend upon the context in which the matter arises. Where a matter of general law arises incidentally for consideration in a case before the ecclesiastical courts that court

---

[8] EJM, s.87.

[9] *ibid.*, s.83(2).

[10] EJM, s.83(2).

[11] For a discussion of the distinction between that part of the ecclesiastical law enforced by the ecclesiastical courts and that enforced by the secular courts see *Att.-Gen. v. Dean and Chapter of Ripon Cathedral* [1945] Ch. 239. See also *Caudrey's Case* (1591) 5 Co. Rep. 1a; Denning, "The Meaning of Ecclesiastical Law" (1944) 60 L.Q.R. 235.

will ascertain the general law and apply it accordingly.[12] Thus, for example, an ecclesiastical court has a right to determine a boundary dispute, ordinarily a matter in the secular sphere, prior to granting a faculty to erect a fence.[13] Similarly where a matter of ecclesiastical law arises incidentally in a matter before the secular courts it will ascertain and apply that ecclesiastical law.[14]

Judicial review by the secular courts

11.5   The ecclesiastical courts are within their own sphere of jurisdiction as unfettered as the High Court is in secular causes.[15] Nonetheless the High Court does exercise control over the proper exercise of that jurisdiction.

As we have seen the power of the now Queen's Bench to issue a writ of prohibition to restrain the ecclesiastical courts acting in excess of their jurisdiction pre-dates the Reformation. It would appear that all ecclesiastical courts and appellate bodies, including the Judicial Committee of the Privy Council when exercising jurisdiction in an ecclesiastical suit, are liable to an order of prohibition.[16]

The ecclesiastical courts may render themselves liable to the issue of an order of prohibition by hearing a matter not within their jurisdiction,[17] which includes a violation of the common law principles of natural justice.[18] However, prohibition does not issue where the ecclesiastical court has merely exercised its jurisdiction erroneously.[19] Generally it will also not issue where one object of the suit is within the jurisdiction of the ecclesiastical court, since a presumption operates that the court will not exceed its jurisdiction.[20]

An application for an order of prohibition is made to the High Court pursuant to Order 53 of the Rules of the Supreme Court, the modern procedure for which belongs to that branch of administrative law known as judicial review. In addition to orders of prohibition, Order 53 is concerned with applications for orders for *mandamus* and *certiorari* (to correct or quash proceedings in the inferior court).

It is accepted that where an ecclesiastical court declines to exercise jurisdiction in a case within its sphere it may be compelled by *mandamus* to take cognisance of the matter.[21] However, it has been assumed, on the basis of the decision of the

---

[12] *Att.-Gen. v. Dean and Chapter of Ripon Cathedral (ante)* at 245.

[13] *Re St Peter & St Paul, Scrayingham* [1992] W.L.R. 187.

[14] *Att.-Gen. v. Dean and Chapter of Ripon Cathedral (ante)* at 245.

[15] *R. v. Chancellor of St Edmundsbury and Ipswich Diocese, ex p. White* [1947] 1 K.B. 263 at 274.

[16] *Mackonochie v. Lord Penzance* (1881) 6 App. Cas. 424, H.L.

[17] *Corven's Case* (1612) 12 Co. Rep. 105 at 106; 3 *Coke's Institute* (1680) Vol. 3, p. 202; *Veley v. Burder* (1841) 12 A & E. 265; *R. v. Twiss* (1869) L.R. 4 Q.B. 407; *Re Bateman* (1870) L.R. 9 Eq. 660; *R. v. Tristam* [1902] 1 K.B. 816, C.A. A common law right of action may also lie against the bishop or chancellor and damages may be recovered: *Beauain v. Scott* (1812) 3 Camp. 388; *Ackerley v. Parkinson* (1815) 3 M. & S. 411.

[18] *ex p. Story* (1852) 12 C.B. 767 at 777; R. v. North, ex p. Oakley [1927] 1 K.B. 491, C.A.

[19] *R. v. Judicial Committee of the Privy Council, ex p. Smyth* (1835) 2 C.M. & R. 748; *Proud v. Price* (1893) 69 L.T. 664 at 665; *Macknochie v. Lord Penzance (ante)*.

[20] *Hallack v. Cambridge University* (1841) 1 Q.B. 593; *R. v. Twiss* (1869) L.R. 4 Q.B. 407; *Macknochie v. Lord Penzance (ante)*.

[21] *R. v. Archbishop of Canterbury* (1856) 6 E. & B. 546; *R. v. Arches Court Judge* (1857) 7 E. & B. 315; *R. v. Bishop of London* (1889) 24 Q.B.D. 213, C.A.; *sub nom Allcroft & Lighton v. Lord Bishop of London* [1891] A.C. 666, H.L.

Court of Appeal in *R. v. Chancellor of St Edmundsbury and Ipswich Diocese, ex parte White*[22] that an order of *certiorari* does not lie from the High Court to an ecclesiastical court. Lord Wrottesley, in delivering the leading judgment in *ex parte White*, explained that the principle reason why no historical precedent for such existed was the reluctance of the King's Bench to interpret ecclesiastical law and the desire not to remove into that Court proceedings not capable of being determined there. Prohibition would issue to prevent the ecclesiastical court transgressing the limits of its jurisdiction, but no process was available from the common law courts to control or correct them in the exercise of their jurisdiction.[23]

Judicial review pursuant to Order 53 lies in respect of "inferior courts". **11.6** Whether the ecclesiastical courts are an "inferior court" for these purposes is a matter of doubt.[24] However, if prohibition lies to an ecclesiastical court pursuant to Order 53 it is to be assumed that for these purposes it is an inferior court, and it is therefore difficult to draw a distinction between an order of prohibition and *certiorari*. In 1992 the Divisional Court[25] felt bound to follow the decision of the Court of Appeal in *ex parte White*, but nonetheless questioned the logic of its reasoning, asserting that the distinction was "devoid of logic" and expressed an expectation that the Court of Appeal would "reconsider the distinction at the first opportunity".[26] However, until such opportunity presents itself, *ex parte White* remains as authority for the proposition that an order of *certiorari* would not run to the ecclesiastical courts.

The powers of the High Court to review proceedings of the ecclesiastical courts may at present be limited to orders of prohibition and *mandamus*. However, recently a further power of review has emerged with the European Court of Human Rights entertaining an application against the ecclesiastical courts in respect of a criminal charge, and indicating that it would in an appropriate case be prepared to hear a matter involving bias and thus a breach of civil rights by a tribunal which was supposed to be independent and impartial.[27]

Judicial review of administative actions and quasi-judicial decisions

It is far from clear to what extent judicial review is available in respect of the **11.7** decisions, acts and omissions of ecclesiastical bodies and officers, in order to determine whether they have exceeded, abused or failed in the exercise of their powers and functions. Judicial review depends upon two factors, first that the function of the officer or body complained of is a public one, and secondly that no other remedy is available.[28] Bodies established and regulated by statute are thus subject to review, and this will include many of the Church's bodies,

---

[22] [1948] 1 K.B. 195.

[23] *ibid*. at 214, 216.

[24] *ibid*. at 205–206, 219–220.

[25] *R. v. Chancellor of Chichester Consistory Court, ex p. News Group Newspapers Ltd & Others* [1992] C.O.D. 48.

[26] *ibid*. at 49.

[27] *Re Tyler* (1994) 3 E.L.J. 348, European Commission of Human Rights, Application No. 21283/93.

[28] *R. v. Chief East Berkshire Health Authority, ex p. Walsh* [1984] 3 All E.R. 425.

including the majority of its tribunals, since they are established pursuant to Measures.[29] Judicial review will also extend to non-statutory bodies where there is a sufficient public element and thus it may be that judicial review is also available in respect of a range of non-statutory committees and other bodies. The law relating to judicial review is developing on a case by case basis and it is thus difficult to generalise as to which bodies may in future be held subject to judicial review.[30]

Jurisdiction over the laity

11.8   Amongst the many obsolete jurisdictions abolished by the EJM was that of the criminal jurisdiction of the ecclesiastical courts over the laity.[31] However the Measure did not destroy all other jurisdiction over them. The extent to which this jurisdiction would now be invoked, if at all, is extremely limited.[32] It has been suggested that since the ecclesiastical courts retain jurisdiction over the moral life and orthodoxy of the laity this jurisdiction might still be invoked in respect of persons such as chancellors and churchwardens,[33] deaconesses, readers and licensed lay workers. In practice it is doubtful if such action would be taken; there is no reported case of the courts attempting to do so since 1965 when the EJM came into force.

Ecclesiastical courts, their judges and officers

The consistory court

11.9   In each diocese[34] there is a court of the bishop called the consistory court, except in the diocese of Canterbury where it is known as the commissary court.[35] The consistory court has original jurisdiction to hear and determine a cause of faculty for authorising in respect of land in the diocese or anything on such land,[36] the

---

[29] See, *e.g. Harris v. Church Commissioner* [1992] 1 W.L.R. 1241.

[30] See further Doe, *The Legal Framework of the Church of England* (1996), pp. 128–129, 139–141 Gordon, *Judicial Review Law and Procedure* (2nd ed. 1995).

[31] EJM, ss.17, 69, 82(1)(c).

[32] See Doe, *The Legal Framework of the Church of England*, pp. 231–233.

[33] Briden and Hanson, *Moore's Introduction to English Canon Law* (2nd. ed., 1992), p. 112; Dale, *Law of the Parish Church* (4th ed.), p. 113 expresses the alternative view.

[34] For the purposes of the EJM an extra-parochial place including any exempt place or peculiar other than a royal peculiar is deemed to be within the diocese surrounding it: *ibid.*, s.66(3).

[35] *ibid.*, s.1(1); Canon G1(1). Unless the context otherwise requires references to the consistory court and chancellor include references to the commissary court of Canterbury and the commissary general of that court respectively: EJM, s.66(2); Interpretation Measure 1925, s.3.

[36] The faculty jurisdiction of the court is limited to land or anything on it over which it had jurisdiction immediately before the passing of the Ecclesiastical Jurisdiction Measure: EJM, s.6(2).

doing of anything for which a faculty is required. It may also grant a faculty for the sale of books from a library within the diocese. The court now also has jurisdiction to hear and determine proceedings for an injunction or restoration order under section 13 of the CCEJM.[37]

Except in cases where the offence is a reserved matter the consistory court has original jurisdiction in proceedings in which a priest or deacon is charged with an offence under the EJM, where the accused either held preferment or resided in the diocese at the time when the offence was alleged to have been committed.[38] Original jurisdiction also exists in proceedings upon any *jus patronus* awarded by the bishop, certain proceedings under the Pluralities Act 1838 in regard to the recovery of penalties and forfeitures, proceedings in respect of illegal trading and any other proceedings which it had jurisdiction to hear and determine immediately before the passing of the EJM and which were not expressly abolished by that Measure.[39]

The Chancellor

The judge of the consistory court is the chancellor of the diocese.[40] The **11.10** chancellor is the Official Principle of the bishop, is appointed by the diocesan bishop by letters patent, and is second only to the bishop in the diocese.[41] Before appointing a person to be chancellor the bishop must consult the Lord Chancellor and the Dean of the Arches and Auditor.[42] A person appointed to be chancellor must be at least 30 years of age and may be either a barrister or a solicitor with a seven year general qualification within the meaning of section 71 of the Courts and Legal Services Act 1990 or a person who has held high judicial office.[43] If a lay person is to be appointed the bishop must also satisfy themselves that the person is a communicant.[43a] A person now appointed may only hold two chancellorships.[44] Somewhat surprisingly there is no longer a requirement that the chancellor must be versed in ecclesiastical law, in contrast to the requirement for a registrar.

Before entering into the execution of their office the chancellor must take the oath of allegiance and the appropriate judicial oath before the diocesan bishop or in open court, in either case in the presence of the diocesan registrar, who must record this.[45] If a lay person they must also make and subscribe the appropriate declaration of assent under the same conditions.[46]

A chancellor may resign by an instrument addressed to and served on the bishop. They may also be removed by the bishop if the Upper House of

---

[37] EJM, s.6; Canon G1(1).
[38] EJM, s.6; Canon G1(1).
[39] EJM, s.6; Canon G1(1).
[40] See n. 35 *ante*.
[41] EJM, ss.2(1), 13(2). They also have the functions of official principal to archdeacons: *ibid*., s.7(2).
[42] *ibid*., s.2(1A).
[43] *ibid*., s.2(2); Canon G2(2).
[43a] As to the meaning of communicant see Chap. 2.
[44] *ibid*., s.2A; Diocesan Chancellorship Regulations, S.I. No. 1841 of 1993, which apply to appointments made on or after October 1, 1993.
[45] EJM, s.2(5)(a); Canon G2(3).
[46] Church of England (Worship and Doctrine) Measure 1974, s.2; Canon G2(3).

Convocation of the relevant province passes a resolution that they are "unfit to act or incapable or acting". Otherwise a chancellor holds office until they reach the age at which a circuit judge is obliged to retire (provision being made for the completion of cases pending)[47] although their tenure may be extended by the bishop.[48]

A deputy chancellor may be appointed by the bishop for the period where, for any reason, the chancellor is unable to act as such or where the office is vacant. Such a deputy has all the powers and duties of the office for the period of such incapacity or vacancy. The chancellor may also, with the consent of the bishop, appoint a person to act as deputy for a period not exceeding 12 months or for a period specified in the instrument of appointment, during which, or for which, that person has all the powers and duties of the office.[49] Such deputy must be a fit and proper person and is subject to the same qualifications as the chancellor and is required to take the same oaths and declarations in like manner.[50]

11.11 The chancellor often advises the bishop on legal or other questions arising in the administration of the diocese (notwithstanding the position of the registrar) and may also often advise clergy of the diocese. The chancellor is one of the Queen's judges in the Queen's court and acts in that court as an Ordinary, independent of the bishop. Being independent of the bishop they may hear causes in which the bishop has an interest, and there is no right of appeal from the chancellor to the bishop.[51]

It has been the custom in a few dioceses for the bishop to reserve to himself the right to exercise his Ordinary jurisdiction, either by himself or in conjunction with his chancellor.[52] The position is now governed by the EJM which appears (since any reservation cannot be in conflict with statute law) to render such reservation legally effective only in faculty proceedings, which may be heard by the bishop alone or with the chancellor if provision for such is made by the letters patent appointing the Chancellor.[53] However, the practice of the bishop of hearing faculty cases has been criticised on the grounds that it is "antiquated and regrettable" involving a breach of the constitutional principle of the separation of powers.[54]

Substitute judge for criminal trial

11.12 If the chancellor is of the opinion that it is not expedient for them to preside at proceedings against a priest or deacon for an ecclesiastical offence they may certify this fact to the bishop.[55] They may then, with the bishop's consent, appoint

---

[47] EJM, s.2. This does not apply to a chancellor in office on April 24, 1976: *ibid*.
[48] Extension cannot go beyond the age at which a pusine judge of the High Court must vacate office: *ibid*.
[49] EJM, s.4.
[50] Hill, *Ecclesiastical Law* (1995), p. 346 disagrees, stating that a deputy need only be a fit and proper person.
[51] *ex p. Medwin* (1853) 1 E. & B. 609 at 616.
[52] *R. v. Tristam* [1902] 1 K.B. 816, C.A.
[53] EJM, s.46(1). See also *Halsbury's Laws of England,* (14th ed.), Vol. 14, para. 1278.
[54] *Re St Mary's Barnes* [1982] 1 W.L.R. 531 at 532 *per* Garth Moore Ch. See also *Newsom*, p. 17.
[55] EJM, s.27.

another person who in the chancellor's opinion possesses sufficient experience in criminal law and procedure. Such a person must consent, and must possess all the qualifications for appointment as a chancellor, and is subject to the same requirements as to oaths and the declaration of assent as the chancellor.[56]

Vicar-General

Nothing in the EJM affects the mode of appointment, the office and duties of **11.13** vicars general of dioceses,[57] and in practice the letters patent issued by the bishop also constitute the chancellor vicar-general of the diocese. The office is an ancient one at common law and comprises duties of an administrative and supervisory nature which are largely undefined.[58] It is in their capacity as vicar-general that the chancellor issues marriage licences (generally through a deputy known as a surrogate).

Registrar

For each diocese there is a registrar who performs the functions conferred on the **11.14** registrar of the diocese and the registrar of the consistory court, as well as acting as the bishop's legal adviser,[59] the office of legal secretary to the bishop having been abolished.[60] The appointment is made by the bishop, after consultation with the bishop's council and the standing committee of the diocese, and may be held by two persons acting jointly.[61] With the consent of the bishop the registrar may appoint a fit and proper person as deputy registrar for such period or purpose specified in the instrument of appointment, such a deputy having all the powers and duties of the registrar, the appointment ceasing when a new registrar is appointed.[62]

In cases where, in the opinion of the bishop, the registrar is unable or unlikely to be able to perform the duties of the office and there is no deputy he may request the registrar of the province to appoint such a person.[63] There is no statutory provision as to the qualifications of a registrar. By Canon they are required to be a person who has a general qualification within the meaning of section 71 of the Courts and Legal Services Act 1990, who is learned in the ecclesiastical laws and the laws of the Realm, and a communicant.[64] They are also required by Canon to take and subscribe the same oaths in like manner as required of a chancellor and to make the declaration of assent.[65] The registrar

---

[56] EJM, s.27.
[57] *ibid.*, s.83(2)(d).
[58] Canon C18(3) See also Pearce, "Roles of the Vicar-General, etc," (1990) 6 E.L.J. 28; Coningsby, "Chancellor, Vicar-General, Official Principle" (1990) 2 E.L.J. 273.
[59] Ecclesiastical Judges and Legal Officers Measure 1976, s.4.
[60] As to potential problems arising from the merger of roles and the possibility of short term appointments being made to meet these, see *Newsom*, p. 20.
[61] Ecclesiastical Judges amd Legal Officers Measure 1976, s.4.
[62] *ibid.*
[63] See n. 61 *ante.*
[64] Canon G4(2).
[65] Canon G4(3).

may resign, or their appointment be terminated by the bishop with the consent of the archbishop on 12 months notice; otherwise they retire, currently at 70 years of age.[66]

The registrar sits as clerk of the consistory court. Provision is made for the appointment of another practising solicitor in cases where the chancellor considers that the registrar ought not to sit because they have been personally connected with the proceedings.[67] The registrar also carries out the functions previously undertaken by the archdeacon's registrar, but its not required to attend archdeacon's visitations.[68]

Examiners and assessors

11.15 Provision is made for the establishment of panels of examiners and assessors whose respective purposes are to hold preliminiary inquiries into complaints respecting offences under the EJM triable in the consistory court and to sit with the chancellor in the trial of a priest or deacon.[69] Through a committee the dicosean synod is responsibile for establishing these panels. The panel of examiners must comprise not less than three barristers or solicitors who are communicants and who possses such experience as the chancellor considers appropriate. There are two panels of assessors; one consisting of six priests, the other of six lay persons who are communicants, from which two from each panel are selected for a trial.

Court of the Arches and the Chancery Court of York

11.16 The Court of the Arches of Canterbury (so named because it sat, and sometimes still does sit, in the arched crypt of St Mary le Bow in the City of London) and the Chancery Court of York are the courts of the archbishops of the two provinces, each having only appellate jurisdiction.[70] They have jurisdiction to hear and determine appeals from all judgments, orders or decrees of the consistory courts of the province, other than reserved causes of faculty.[71] If the court considers that the case does involve a matter of doctrine, ritual or ceremonial it may, notwithstanding the chancellor's certificate to the contrary, refer the appeal to the Court of Ecclesiastical Causes Reserved.[72] However, the courts may hear appeals from interlocutory orders of the consistory court in reserved cases.[73]

The courts have jurisdiction to hear and determine appeals in proceedings for an injunction or restoration order under section 13 of the CCEJM.[74] They may

---

[66] Ecclesiastical Judges and Legal Officers Measure 1976, s.5.
[67] FJR, r. 27.
[68] Ecclesiastical Judges and Legal Officers Measure 1976, s.7(2); Church of England (Miscellaneous Provisions) Measure 1992, s.13.
[69] EJM, s.30, Sched. 2.
[70] *ibid.*, s.1(2)(a); Canon G1(2).
[71] EJM, s.7(1). Proceedings concerning *jus patronus* are also excluded: *ibid.*
[72] *ibid.*, s.10(5).
[73] *ibid.*, s.7(1).
[74] *ibid.*, s.7(1).

also hear appeals from orders, judgments or decrees of the Vicar-General's court.[75] An appeal to the court lies at the instance of either party in a civil suit with the leave of the consistory court or the Vicar-General's court, or if leave is refused by those courts with the leave of the Dean of the Arches and Auditor.[76] In a criminal suit an appeal lies at the instance of either party on a question of law and the defendant on a question of fact.[77]

The Dean of the Arches and Auditor is a judge in both courts. Styled Dean of the Arches in the Court of the Arches and Auditor in the Chancery Court, the Dean is appointed by the two archbishops acting jointly, with the Sovereign's approval signified by warrant. The Dean must be a person who has a 10 year general qualification within the meaning of section 71 of the Courts and Legal Services Act 1990, or a person who has held high judicial office and, if a lay person, must be a communicant.[78] The Dean is the official principal of both archbishops in their capacity as metropolitans, Vicar-General of the province of Canterbury but not of York, and Master of Faculties.

Before entering into the execution of the office the Dean must take the oath of allegiance and the appropriate judicial oath before each of the archbishops or in open court, and in the presence of the provincial registrar. If a lay person they must also make the appropriate declaration of assent under the same conditions.[79] The Dean may resign or be removed by both the archbishops acting jointly if the Upper House of each Convocation resolves that the Dean is incapable of acting or is unfit to act; otherwise the Dean retires at 75 years of age.[80] Provision is made for the appointment of a deputy by the archbishops where the Dean is unable to act or in the case of a vacancy, and the Dean may also, with the consent of the archbishops, appoint a deputy.[81]

Two judges of both the Court of the Arches and Chancery Court are clerks in holy orders appointed by the prolocutor of the Lower House of convocation of the relevant province. The other two are lay persons who possess such experience as the Lord Chancellor considers appropriate, appointed by the House of Laity of General Synod after consultation with the Lord Chancellor.[82] All four are required to take the same oaths, and in the case of the lay persons, make the declaration of assent, in the same form and manner as the Dean, and the same provisions relate to resignation, removal and tenure as in the case of the Dean.[83] The others judges for each court are all the diocesan chancellors[84] of the relevant province.[85]

11.17 In the case of an appeal from a judgment of the consistory court given in proceedings in which a priest or deacon is charged with an offence under the EJM the appeal must be heard by all the judges of the court except the diocesan chancellors. In all other cases the appeal must be heard by the Dean and two diocesan chancellors designated by him.[86]

---

[75] *ibid.*, s.(1A). As to which see Chap. 8.
[76] EJM, s.7(1).
[77] EJM, s.7(2).
[78] *ibid.*, s.3; Canon G3.
[79] EJM, s.13(1).
[80] EJM, s.3; Canon G3.
[81] EJM, s.4.
[82] EJM, s.3; Canon G3.
[83] EJM, s.3; Canon G3.
[84] Except the Chancellor of the Diocese in Europe.
[85] EJM, s.3; Canon G3.
[86] EJM, s.47(1).

There is a registrar of the province for each of the two provinces who performs the functions conferred on the registrar of the province and of the registrar of the Court of the Arches or Chancery Court, and acts as the archbishop's legal adviser.[87] The appointment is made by the archbishop, in certain circumstances after consulting the standing committee of General Synod. In regard to the holding of the office, the appointment of a deputy and tenure, the provisions are broadly the same as for a diocesan registrar, save that the archbishop acts instead of the bishop.[88]

The Privy Council

11.18   The Judicial Committee of the Privy Council has jurisdiction to hear and determine appeals from judgments of the Court of the Arches and Chancery Courts in faculty causes other than reserved cases,[89] although it has not yet heard such an appeal since the EJM came into force. As we have already seen the Privy Council also has jurisdiction to hear appeals against pastoral and redundancy schemes and appeals against schemes prepared by the Cathedrals Statutes Commission.

Courts of Ecclesiastical Causes Reserved

11.19   The EJM brought into being the Court of Ecclesiastical Causes Reserved which has jurisdiction over both provinces.[90] It has original jurisdiction to hear and determine proceedings in which a priest or deacon, bishop or archbishop is charged with a reserved offence,[91] and all suits of *duplex querela*.[92] The Court also has appellate jurisdiction in respect of appeals from judgments, orders or decrees of consistory courts in reserved faculty causes, for which no leave of appeal is required.[93]

The Court is constituted by five judges, all appointed by the Sovereign, two of whom must be persons who hold or have held high judical office and who make declarations that they are communicants, and three who are or must have been diocesan bishops.[94] When trying a cleric charged with an offence the court must also sit with not less than three and not more than five advisors selected by the Dean of the Arches and Auditor from a panel of eminent theologians and liturgiologists drawn up by the Upper Houses of the Convocations of Canterbury and York acting jointly with the approval of the two Lower Houses.[95]

Commissions of Convocation and Review

11.20   Provision was made in the EJM for the appointment of commissions presided over by the Dean of Arches and Auditor, with original jurisdiction to hear and determine cases where a bishop or archbishop is charged with a conduct offence.

---

[87] Ecclesiastical Judges and Legal Officers Measure 1976, s.3.
[88] *ibid.*
[89] EJM, ss.1(3)(d), 8(1); Canon G1(5).
[90] EJM, s.1(3)(b); Canon G1(3).
[91] EJM, s.10(1).
[92] As to which see Chap. 5.
[93] EJM, s.10(1).
[94] EJM, s.5.
[95] *ibid.*, s.45(2).

The commission's decision and it should be noted that one has never yet sat is subject to review by a Commission of Review.[96]

Commissions of Review, for which the EJM also makes provision for appointment, may also review the findings of the Court of Ecclesiastical Causes Reserved.[97] Again, since the Measure came into force such a commission has not sat. Except in proceedings charging an offence, where only the defendant may seek review on a question of fact, any party to the proceedings may apply for a review on a question of either law or fact.[98] Application is made by petition to the Sovereign, and upon this being lodged a commission would be directed under the Great Seal to five persons nominated by the Sovereign. Three of these persons must be Lords of Appeal who make a declaration that they are communicants and two must be Lords Spiritual sitting as Lords of Parliament.[99] In cases involving questions of doctrine a commission must sit with five advisors which it selects from a panel constituted for this purpose.[1] Each member of the commission is required to state their own opinion, the judgment being according to the opinion of the majority.

Other courts and tribunals

The Court of Faculties, faculty here being used in the sense of a privilege or **11.21** special dispensation granted as an indulgence by the Archbishop of Cantebury, is of ancient origin. It arises from the transfer of legatine powers to the Archbishop of Canterbury by the Ecclesiastical Licences Act 1533, which vested in him the power to grant dispensations.[2] The court, which is not in fact judicial in nature, is presided over by the Master of Faculties, who is the same individual as the Dean of the Arches. The Court has jurisdiction over the appointment and removal of notaries public.[3] It may also issue such faculties and licences, for example special marriage licences, as the Archbishop of Canterbury can grant in the province of York and in his own province.[4]

Archdeacons' courts were abolished by the EJM,[5] although as we shall see the archdeacon has the power to grant faculties in certain limited circumstances where the chancellor has delegated this authority. For the sake of completeness mention here should also be made of the newly constituted Vicar-Generals' courts, which as we saw in Chapter 8 has jurisdiction to grant injunctions and restoration orders in respect of acts done or threatened in contravention of the Care of Cathedrals Measure 1990.

As we have seen throughout this work various tribunals and appeal procedures have also been established pursuant to both Measures and Canons.[6]

---

[96] EJM, ss.1(2)(b), 3(a), 9, 35, 36; Canon G1(2)(b), (3)(b).
[97] EJM, s.1(3)(c); Canon G1(4).
[98] EJM, s.11.
[99] EJM, s.11.
[1] *ibid.*, s.48(2), (3).
[2] *Coke's Institute's*, (1680) Vol. 4, p. 337.
[3] Public Notaries Act 1801; Public Notaries Act 1843; *Re Champion* [1906] 86.
[4] Canon C17(7).
[5] EJM, s.82(2)(a).
[6] See further Doe, *The Legal Framework of the Church of England* (1996), pp. 130–139.

These include tribunals to hear appeals under the Incumbents (Vacation of Benefices) Measure 1977; tribunals to hear appeals relating to the conduct of elections pursuant to the CRR and enrolment in the register of clerical and lay electors or a church electoral roll; and an appeals procedure against the summary revocation of the bishop's licence in respect of unbeneficed clergy or lay ministers to the archbishop. It should be noted that all these tribunals and procedures operate, as we have seen, under their own rules and are not therefore subject to the practice and procedure of the ecclesiastical courts.

Practice and procedure of the ecclesiastical courts

Rules of procedure

11.22   The procedure and practice of the modern ecclesiastical court system is largely governed by rules made pursuant to the relevant enactments. The CCEJM established a rule committee for the purpose of making rules to carry into effect the provisions of that Measure, the EJM, the Faculty Jurisdiction Measure 1964, the Care of Cathedrals Measures 1990 and 1994, and certain other matters.[7] The Dean of Arches and Auditor, who normally acts as chairman, and nine other specified persons sit on all such committees, but the composition of the remaining places and the number of its members varies according to the particular rules to be made.

Unless repealed or amended rules made under former provisions continue in force.[8] Any rules made under these new provisions must be laid before General Synod and cannot come into force unless approved by it, with or without amendments.[9] The common law rules or any analogies with those rules are not applicable to the ecclesiastical courts unless expressly provided for. Where no relevant rules are applicable, the customary rules of the ecclesiastical courts with any necessary modifications will apply.

A party to proceedings in the ecclesiastical courts may be legally represented. Barristers, as successors to the advocates in Doctors Common's, and solicitors[10] both have rights of audience. In disciplinary proceedings either party may be represented by a friend or advisor at the hearing of an interlocutory application and in subsequent proceedings by counsel or a solicitor.[11]

A hearing may be held in any place convenient to the court, commission, committee or enquiry established or held by or under the provisions of the EJM and the Vicar-General's courts.[12] However, due regard must be paid to the convenience of the parties and witnesses. In practice most hearings in chambers

---

[7] CCEJM, ss.25, 26.

[8] *ibid.*, s.27.

[9] CCEJM, s.27.

[10] Solicitors Act 1974, s.19(1)(c). Before they held such rights solicitors with management of cases in the ecclesiastical courts were known as proctors, acting by proxy for the litigant with control of the action.

[11] EJM, ss.24(2), 33(5), 42(4); Ecclesiastical Jurisdiction (Discipline) Rules 1964, S.I. 1964 No. 1755 r. 61.

[12] EJM, s.80.

are held in the diocesan registry. Hearings in open court in faculty causes are often held in the church in respect of which the proceedings arise, and for these purposes a church is a court.[13] A hearing held in a church affords the opportunity of viewing the subject matter of the dispute which may otherwise be a matter of some delicacy.[14]

Any court or commission established under the EJM and the Vicar-Generals' courts have the same powers as the High Court in relation to the attendance and examination of witnesses and the production and inspection of documents.[15] Any act or omission in connection with proceedings before such court or commission, or in connection with an order (which includes an injunction or special citation) made by such commission or court, which is or would have been a contempt had the court or commission the power to commit for contempt, may be certified by the judge, presiding judge or presiding member of the commission to the High Court for it to deal with the matter.[16] A failure to comply with a condition subject to which a faculty was granted would for example be a contempt, as would taking photographs of those involved in proceedings in the court and its precincts.[17] The High Court may after inquiring into the alleged act or omission, and after hearing witnesses and any statement offered in defence, exercise the same jurisdiction and power as if the contempt had been a contempt of the High Court.[18]

The binding force of precedent

The EJM gave statutory recognition to the principle of the binding force of precedent, a doctrine not fully accepted in ecclesiastical law until the nineteenth century.[19] Under the principle of *stare decisis* judges are bound to follow earlier decisions of the court in which they are sitting or those of courts which are superior to it since these decisions have the authority of law. However, only the *ratio decidendi* of a decision, that is the actual rule or reason which was applied or given as the determinent in reaching the decision, represent the law. All other judicial statements which are set forth in the decision, known as *obiter dicta*, are merely persuasive. However, one of the difficulties in English law is to identify which elements of a decision represent the *ratio*, and in older writings on ecclesiastical law there may have been a tendency to give undue weight to cases when citing them as authorities because of a failure to observe the proper distinction between the *ratio decidendi* and *obiter dictum*.[20]

11.23

Not all questions concerning the application of the doctrine to the new system created by the EJM were settled by that Measure, since it did not deal fully with

---

[13] *Re St Andrew's, Heddington* [1978] Fam. 121.

[14] *Salsbury v. Woodland* [1970] 1 Q.B. 324.

[15] EJM, s.81(1).

[16] *ibid.*, s.81(2), (3), (4); See *R. v. Editor of Daily Herald, ex p. Bishop of Norwich* [1932] 2 K.B. 402 as to the High Court's inherent jurisdiction over the "inferior" consistory court.

[17] Criminal Justice Act 1925, s.41; *Re St Andrew's Heddington (ante).*

[18] See n. 16 *ante.*

[19] EJM, ss.45(3), 48(5), (6).

[20] *Halsbury's Laws of England* (4th ed.) Vol. 14, para. 1271.

the status of decisions of a number of courts in the ecclesiastical hierarchy. Generally courts are bound to follow decisions on questions of law given by higher courts exercising a superior jurisdiction. Accordingly the consistory courts in the provinces of Canterbury and York are bound by decisions of the Arches Court of Canterbury and the Chancery Court of York respectively, and these two courts are bound by any applicable decisions of the Judicial Committee of the Privy Council.

Decisions of the Privy Council given before the commencement of the EJM relating to matters of doctrine, ritual and ceremonial are not binding upon the Court of Ecclesiastical Causes Reserved or a Commission of Review.[21] This exemption may have arisen in the nineteenth century due to resentment of the fact that the final court of appeal in ecclesiastical causes was a secular body, but it leaves open the question of whether these courts are so bound in non-doctrinal matters. It would appear that consistory courts when considering doctrinal matters arising in faculty cases, are bound by decisions of the Privy Council. So too, it would seem, are the Arches and Chancery Courts, when acting as the court of final appeal, although the matter is not beyond doubt.[22]

11.24   A decision by a court of co-ordinate jurisdiction, although it may be of persuasive value, is not binding (although in many instances the ecclesiastical courts have applied such persuasive decisions in effect adopting them).[23] In addition the decisions of the provincial courts are only binding in that province. Thus a decision of the Arches Court does not bind the Chancery Court or vice versa,[24] and decisions of the Arches Court bind consistory courts in the province of Canterbury but not of York, whose consistory courts are bound only by decisions of the Chancery Court.[25] Both the Court of Arches and the Chancery Court are each bound by their own previous decisions.[26] A consistory court is bound by its own previous decisions, but is not bound by those of a consistory court of another diocese whether or not they are both within the same province.[27]

The binding effect of an earlier decision of the same court creates some difficulties. A Commission of Review is bound by decisions of a previous Commission unless new information or evidence is adduced which was not before the Commissioners on a previous occasion.[28] However, the rule of *stare decisis* may be relaxed under ecclesiastical law in a final court of appeal. Acordingly the Privy Council has been prepared to examine the reasons for an earlier decision and to take a different view of the law.[29] It has been suggested by the Dean of the Arches that some latitude would be permissable in the Arches and Chancery

---

[21] EJM, ss.45(3), 48(5), (6).

[22] *Halsbury's Laws of England* (4th ed.) Vol. 14, para. 1271.

[23] Doe, *The Legal Framework of the Church of England* (1996), pp. 156–157.

[24] *Halsbury's Laws of England* (4th ed.) Vol. 14 para. 1271. *Rector and churchwardens of Bishopswearmouth v. Adey* [1958] 1 W.L.R. 1183 at 1189; *Re St Stephen's, Walbrook* [1987] Fam. 146; *Re St John the Evangelist, Chopwell* [1995] Fam. 254.

[25] See *Re St Mary, Tyne Dock (No. 2)* [1958] P. 156 at 169.

[26] *Re Lapford (Devon) Parish Church* [1955] P. 205 at 208, C.A. *Reed v. Bishop of Lincoln* [1892] A.C. 644 at 654, 655.

[27] *Rector and Churchwardens of Bishopwearmouth v. Adey* [1958] (*ante*) at 1189; *Re Rector and Churchwardens of St Nicholas, Plumstead* [1961] 1 W.L.R. 916 at 918; *Re St John the Evangelist, Chopwell* (*ante*).

[28] EJM, ss.48(6).

[29] *Read v. Bishop of Lincoln* [1892] A.C. 644 at 654, 655, P.C.

Courts where there was strong reason to depart from an earlier decision.[30] However, it was also said that such latitude would not extend to the consistory court.[31] The reason for drawing this distinction is not entirely clear, but this opinion does accord with the consensus of judicial opinion that no such right exists with regard to the consistory courts.[32]

Finally it should be noted that when considering a matter of ecclesiastical law the secular courts must ascertain that law, but they are not bound by a decision of the highest ecclesiastical court. Neither are the ecclesiastical courts bound by decisions of the secular courts, although again when issues of general law arise they are under an obligation to determine what that law is.[33]

Interpretation of ecclesiastical legislation

The principles by which the ecclesiastical courts construe legislation are essen- **11.25** tially the same as those employed in the secular courts, although subject to some modification in examining the circumstances giving rise to the Act or Measure.[34] The Interpretation Act 1978 applies to Measures of the Church Assembly and of the General Synod as it does to Acts of Parliament, thus imposing the same principles of construction upon these.[35] In addition the Interpretation Measure 1925 gives definitions of a limited number of terms, whilst most Measures themselves contain an interpretation section defining some of the terms used within them, which will be applied unless the context otherwise requires.

Although they have often adopted a literal approach, frequently in order to ascertain the intention of the legislation the ecclesiastical courts will adopt a purposive approach,[36] enquiring into the historical circumstances which gave rise to the provision[37] and where appropriate the construction put upon it by contemporaneous and long-usage.[38] Recourse is also made to commentators and to other materials where legislation proves difficult to interpret.[39]

---

[30] *Re Lapford (Devon) Parish Church (ante).*
[31] *Re Lapford (Devon) Parish Church (ante).*
[32] See, *e.g. Re Rector and Churchwardens of St Nicholas, ꞏ ꞏꞏmstead (ante).*
[33] *Mackonochie v. Lord Penzance* (1881) 6 App. Cas. 424 at 431, 447, 460, H.L.; *Att.-Gen. v. Dean and Chapter of Ripon Cathedral* [1945] 1 Ch. 239 at 246.
[34] *Halsbury's Laws of England* (4th ed.), Vol. 14, para. 401.
[35] Interpretation Measure 1978, s.22.
[36] As to principles of statutory construction generally see *Cross on Statutory Interpretation* (2nd, ed., 1987). See also Doe, *The Legal Framework of the Church of England* (1996), pp. 151–153.
[37] *Herbert v. Purchas* [1872] L.R. 4 C.P.; *Ridsdale v. Clifton* (1877) 2 P.D. 276 at 331. In *R. v. Ecclesiastical Committee of both Houses of Parliament, ex p. Williamson, The Times* November 25, 1994, the court was prepared to apply the rule in *Pepper v. Hart*, [1993] A.C. 593 enabling recourse to debates of Parliament when there is ambiguity in a statute. Whether this principle will ever be extended to debates of the Church Assembly or General Synod in regard to Measures is not certain, but there seems to be no objection in principle to doing so, since it would merely constitute part of the historical enquiry.
[38] *Goreham v. Bishop of Exeter* (1849) E.R. 1221 at 1223; *Ridsdale v. Clifton (ante) Re St Luke's Chelsea* [1976] Fam. 295; *Re St Nicholas, Baddesley Ensor* [1983] Fam. 1.
[39] See, *e.g. Re St Martin-le-Grand, York* [1990] Fam. 63.

Fees, costs and legal aid

Fees and costs

11.26 Fees for the performance of certain duties by any legal officer, or in connection with ecclesiastical proceedings, are fixed by Fees Orders made pursuant to the Ecclesiastical Fees Measure 1986, by the Fees Advisory Commission. Certain other fees are fixed by the chancellor.

Any court or commission having jurisdiction under the EJM and the Vicar-Generals' courts have the power, at any stage of the proceedings, to order any party to give security for costs.[40] Costs in this context, and in that of an order for costs, includes "fees, disimbursements, expenses and remuneration".[41] This provision enables the court to obtain not only security for costs of another party, but also, unlike the secular courts, the court fees themselves including the cost of the hearing and expenses in relation to it. It is commmon for the petitioner to be required to give security in costs to cover the fees of the registrar or chancellor.

Any court, commission, committee or examiner has discretion to make an order against any party for the payment of taxed costs, or a specified proportion of such taxed costs, up to a specified stage in the proceedings or of a specified gross sum in lieu of taxed costs, although account must be taken of the fact that a party has received or is receiving legal aid.[42] Taxation is the procedure by which allowable costs are determined, a procedure carried out by the registrar.[43] Where any party is dissatisfied they may appeal to the chancellor of the diocese in which the proceedings took place, who may confirm or vary that decision.[44] In the exercise of the delegated authority to grant faculties an archdeacon does not have the power to make any order as to costs. Where they consider that a question arises as to payment of costs the matter must be referred to the chancellor.[45]

Costs ordered to be paid may be recovered, by the person in whose favour the order was made, as a contract debt in either the county or High Court, depending upon the amount due, the registrar's certificate stating the sum due to be paid under an order being conclusive evidence of the facts certified.[46] Any sum ordered to be paid by the consistory court in or consequent upon proceedings for a faculty shall, if the county court so orders, be recoverable by execution from that court or otherwise as if payable under an order of that court,[47] which appears to allow execution to be obtained directly in such cases.

The costs and expenses of all court, commissions committees and examiners constituted or appointed under the EJM for the purpose of disciplinary proceedings must be met, so far as not payable by anyone else, by the Central Board of Finance.[48] The Board must also pay the costs and expenses of the Vicar-Generals' courts.[49]

---

[40] EJM, s.60(1).
[41] *ibid*., s.60(4).
[42] *ibid*., s.60(2), (3).
[43] EJM, s.60(4).
[44] *ibid*., s.60(5).
[45] CCEJM, s.14(5).
[46] EJM, s.61(1).
[47] FJM, s.11.
[48] EJM, s.62.
[49] EJM, s.62.

Costs in faculty cases

In unopposed faculty cases the petitioner bears the cost of obtaining the faculty   **11.27**
unless the court orders otherwise. In a contested case the consistory court (and to
a lesser extent the appellate courts) exercise discretion, so that the general rule,
applicable in the secular courts, that costs follow the event, (in other words costs
are recoverable by successful parties and paid by the losing party or parties) need
not necessarily apply.[50-51] Indeed the initial onus is on the petitioner because of
the initial obligation upon them to prove their case.[52] In particular the court may,
if it considers opposition to a petition to have been reasonable, direct that the
parties should bear their own costs.[53-54] The court may also, where an opponent
has been partially successful, order that the applicant pay a proportion of that
opponent's costs.[55] It is also not uncommon, where a faculty is obtained for the
sale of a church treasure, for the petitioners to recoup the cost of obtaining the
faculty from the proceeds of the sale.[56]

In two instances the court has specific power to order that costs be paid by a
"defaulting" party. The first is where in faculty proceedings by any person it
appears to the court that any other person who is a party to the proceedings was
wholly or partially responsible for any act or default in consequence of which the
proceedings were instituted. In such cases it may order the whole or any part of
the costs and expenses of, and consequent upon the proceedings, including
expenses incurred in carrying out any work authorised by the faculty (so far as
those costs and expenses have been occasioned by that act or default), to be paid
by the person responsible.[57] The court also has the power to add a person
responsible or alleged to be responsible as a further party to the proceedings by
special citation. An example of such a person would be an architect or
monumental mason acting without a faculty. The citation requires that person to
attend court at the time and place specified, and failure to comply without
reasonable excuse is a contempt of court. Such a citation must not be issued
unless the court is satisfied that the proceedings were instituted less than six years
after the act or default, although provisions exist for extending that time in cases
of concealment from the archdeacon of the act or default.

The second instance where costs may be awarded against a defaulting party are
cases where the court issues a faculty to an archdeacon to carry out work in
default of the work being carried out by another person.[58] In such a situation
where the work is carried out by the archdeacon the costs of this work must be
paid for by the defaulter. Cost orders may also be made in proceedings for
injunctions or restoration orders pursuant to section 13 of the CCEJM.[59]

[50-51] For a general discussion see *Newsom*, pp. 205–207, and for a discussion of competing
merits see *Re St Peter & St Paul, Scrayingham* [1992] 1 W.L.R. 92, C.A.. See *Re St Mary
the Virgin, Sherbourne* [1996] 3 All E.R. 769 at 774–776 for guidelines on costs in respect
of appeals from the consistory court, and for a summary of the position on costs in
faculty cases generally.

[52] *Re St Catherine's, Leconfield* [1992] 3 All E.R.

[53] See n. 51 *ante*.

[54] *Re St Catherine's, Leaconfield* [1992] 3 All E.R.

[55] See, *e.g. Re West Camel Church etc.* [1979] Fam. 79.

[56] See, *e.g. Re St Mary-le-Bow* [1984] 1 W.L.R. 1363 at 1368–1369.

[57] CCEJM, s.13.

[58] *ibid.*, s.12(2).

[59] Faculty Jurisdiction (Injunction and Restoration Orders) Rules 1992, S.I. 1992 No. 284,
r. 11.

Where the archdeacon (or such other person as the bishop may appoint) institutes or intervenes in proceedings, following the written approval of the bishop, who himself acts only after consultating with the DBF, the archdeacon will not be liable for costs. Any expenses or costs which they are ordered by the court to pay will be paid by the DBF.[60] Conversely, where costs are awarded against another party in favour of the archdeacon the DBF may enforce this.

Legal aid

11.28 The General Synod maintains a legal aid fund to which it and the Church Commissioners contribute.[61] The fund is administered by a Legal Aid Commission which authorises payments out of the fund by means of a certificate. The Standing Committee of the General Synod is empowered to make rules to give effect to and prevent abuse of the legal aid system and in respect of certain other matters.[62]

Applications may be made by an accused person in respect of proceedings in any ecclesiastical court or before any commission, committee, bishop or examiner in respect of an offence under the EJM; by the incumbent concerned in proceedings on an enquiry by a provincial tribunal pursuant to the Incumbents (Vacation of Benefices) Measure 1977, Part I; by a person entitled to compensation pursuant to Schedule 4 in proceedings under the Pastoral Measure 1983, Schedule 4 (including any interview by a pastoral committee); by the appellant in proceedings under any canon made in pursuance of the Church of England (Legal Aid and Miscellaneous Provisions) Measure 1988, s.7 against the revocation of a licence granted to a minister, deaconess, lay reader or stipendary reader by the appellant; and in proceedings on an appeal under section 50 of the EJM against an intended deposition of a priest or deacon from holy orders.[63]

In deciding whether to grant legal aid the Commission must have regard to all the circumstances of the case. In particular it must consider the financial resources of the applicant and their spouse and not grant aid if it appears that the applicant could proceed without it.[64]

The applicant must also show that they have reasonable grounds for taking, defending or being a party to proceedings.[65] Payments may be made to cover the whole or part of the costs incurred by the applicant after the date the certificate is issued.[66]

No person other than those set out above is entitled to legal aid. However, the Church Commissioners may at their absolute discretion, if satisfied that the costs and expenses are reasonable in amount, pay all or part of the costs incurred by an archbishop or bishop (who is not the accused) in respect of certain proceedings authorised, taken or simply contemplated. The proceedings are

---

[60] CCEJM, s.16(4).
[61] Church of England (Legal Aid) Measure 1994, s.1.
[62] *ibid.*, s.4; Church of England (Legal Aid) Rules 1988, S.I. 1988 No. 1175, S.I. 1990, No. 1438, S.I. 1993 No. 1840.
[63] Church of England (Legal Aid) Measure 1994, s.2(1), Sched. 1.
[64] *ibid.*, s.2(5).
[65] *ibid.*, s.2(6).
[66] *ibid.*, s.2(2), (3), (4).

limited to those in respect of an offence under the EJM or in relation to any declaration pursuant to a judgment, order or decree of a secular court, or proceedings in the Vicar-Generals' court.[67] They may also likewise meet the costs of a person nominated to promote such proceedings.

The faculty jurisdiction[68]

As we saw in Chapter 8 the act of consecration brings the land so consecrated **11.29** and everything on or under it within the jurisdiction of the Ordinary, and usually also within the faculty jurisdiction. Cathedrals are normally excluded, being subject as we saw to an alternative process under the Care of Cathedrals Measures, although a parish church cathedral may be brought within the faculty jurisdiction. Also excluded are peculiars and the chapels of colleges in the Universities of Oxford and Cambridge.[69] In addition to consecrated property some buildings licensed for public worship which are merely dedicated are brought within the jurisdiction, as is the curtilage or land surrounding a church which will include churchyards which are not themselves consecrated. The faculty jurisdiction has a long history, probably dating back to shortly after the conquest,[70] although the present extent of the jurisdiction dates back to the nineteenth century when controversies over ornaments and other matters led to the establishment of the principle that the contents of a church as well as the church itself were within the jurisdiction.

A faculty is a licence or dispensation authorising works of alteration, including repairs, renovations, removals and additions to the fabric or contents of a church and to churchyards. A faculty is also required for various purposes such as the sale of church treasures and the erection of monuments within churchyards and other burial grounds. Ministers and churchwardens are under a duty to comply with the requirements of the faculty jurisdiction.[71]

Generally a faculty enables a person to do something, but does not order that it be done,[72] although a restoration order will have this effect. The previous position that a faculty was not revocable save in cases of fraud unless the court specifically reserved its power to do so no longer applies[73]; the chancellor now has the right to amend or set aside a faculty where it is just and expedient to do so. Where the court does still reserve power of revocation to itself it uses the words "until further order". A faculty may also be granted subject to conditions.[74] In particular the conditions may require that the work be supervised by the archdeacon or any person nominated by the court. Where a faculty is granted to someone other than the archdeacon and the court considers that the work should be carried out it may provide that in default of that person carrying out the work a faculty will issue to the archdeacon.[75] A confirmatory faculty (which must come

---

[67] EJM, s.58.
[68] For further detailed consideration of the faculty jurisdiction see *Newsom*.
[69] As to which see Chap. 6.
[70] *Lee v. Hawtrey* [1898] P. 161 at 167.
[71] Canon, F13(3).
[72] *Re St Mary, Tyne Dock (No. 2)* [1958] P. 63 at 74.
[73] FJR, r. 30.
[74] CCEJM, s.12(1).
[75] *ibid.*, s.12(2).

before the chancellor) may be issued to legitimate a situation,[76] although such a faculty cannot be retrospective.[77] A remedial faculty may also be obtained to regularise a situation since acts done unlawfully cannot be undone without such a faculty.[78-79]

Ecclesiastical law has a tradition of flexibility which has persisted notwithstanding acceptance of the doctrine of binding force of precedent. The discretionary character of the courts' jurisdiction is still referred to in modern judgments, particularly those given in faculty proceedings. However, such discretion as the court possess is restricted by the existing law whose boundaries it cannot go beyond.

Cases not dealt with by the consistory court

11.30   Although the faculty jurisdiction is wide ranging the consistory court does not in practice exercise its right to intervene in three situations. The first are matters which are *de minimis*. The chancellor of the diocese is required (after consultation with the DAC) to issue written guidelines as to those matters which are considered to be of such minor nature that they may be undertaken without a faculty.[80] For obvious reasons no exhaustive definition can be given, but a prudent churchwarden, PCC or minister will consult the archdeacon in respect of anything not within the chancellor's guidelines as to which there is any doubt regarding its nature before undertaking the work.

The second situation is the introduction of monuments into the churchyard with the permission of the incumbent, priest-in-charge, rural dean or archdeacon acting for the chancellor, which is considered in more detail below. The third situation is where cases are dealt with on a non-contentious basis by the archdeacon pursuant to the powers of the consistory court which are delegated for this purpose, and this again is considered below. The former procedure whereby the archdeacon could, on the application of the incumbent and churchwardens, issue a certificate authorising works in a limited class of cases no longer exists, although any such certificate previously granted continues in force as if it were a faculty granted under the new procedure.[81]

Diocesan Advisory Committee

11.31   Each diocese has a Diocesan Advisory Committee whose primary function is to act as an advisory body on matters affecting places of worship in the diocese. Schedule 2 of the CCEJM sets out the functions of the DAC. It is required to advise the bishop, chancellor, archdeacons, PCCs, intending applicants for faculties, the pastoral committee and persons engaged in the planning, design or building of new places of worship in the diocese not being places within the

[76] FJR, r. 9(1).
[77] See, *e.g. Re St Mary's Baron-upon-Humber* [1987] Fam. 41.
[78-79] See, *e.g. Kensit v. Rector of St Ethelburga, Bishopsgate Within* [1900] P. 80; *Re Escot Church* [1979] Fam. 125; *Re St John's with Holy Trinity, Deptford* [1995] 1 W.L.R. 721.
[80] CCEJM, s.11(8).
[81] *ibid.*, s.14.

jurisdiction of the consistory court. The DAC may also advise such other persons as it considers appropriate. In particular it should give advice to the persons specified on matters relating to the granting of faculties, the DAC having become an important part of the operation of the faculty jurisdiction. The DAC has a large number of specified functions but the most important are to offer advice upon the architecture, archaeology, art and history of places of worship and their use, care, planning, design and redundancy, the use and care of the contents of such places and the use and care of churchyards and burial grounds.

In carrying out its functions the DAC must have regard to the rites and ceremonies of the Church of England.[82] Section 1 of the CCEJM further provides that any person or body carrying out functions of care and conservation pursuant to its provisions or any other enactment or rule of law must have due regard to the role of a church as a local centre of worship and mission.

Schedule 1 of the CCEJM provides for the membership and constitution of the DAC. The chairman is appointed by the bishop after consultation with the bishop's council, the chancellor and the Council for the Care of Churches. The bishop must also appoint a secretary, after consultation with the chairman and with the chief administrative officer of the diocese. The DAC comprises all the archdeacons of the diocese, together with two persons appointed by the bishop's council from the elected members of the diocesan synod. Not less than ten other persons are to be appointed by the bishop's council, three of them after consultation with the Historic Buildings and Monuments Commission for England (generally known as English Heritage), the relevant association of local authorities and the national amenity societies (as defined). In making these appointments the bishop's council must ensure that the persons appointed have between them knowledge of the history, development and use of church buildings, Church of England liturgy and worship, architecture, archaeology, art and history, and experience of the care of historic buildings and their contents. In addition a number of members (not exceeding a third of the total number) may be co-opted by the DAC with the consent of the bishop. At the request of the DAC the bishop may also appoint suitably qualified persons to act as consultants. Any member who ceases to hold the qualifications of their appointment ceases to be a member forthwith, and provision is made for the filling of casual vacancies. Tenure is until the formation of the second new diocesan synod following the last appointments, although all members who fulfil the citeria for appointment are eligible for re-appointment.

The constitution of each DAC must provide for such matters as quorums and the establishment and powers of sub-committees.[83] The expenses of the DAC are met by the DBF to the extent that it has approved those expenses in advance.[84] The DAC is required at the end of each year to make a report of its work and proceedings, which is laid before the diocesan synod (whose secretary sends a copy to the Council for the Care of Churches).[85] It is also required to make a scheme for the inspection of each church in the diocese and to appoint a qualified person to care for the churches in the diocese, matters which were considered in Chapter 8.

11.32

---

[82] *ibid.*, s.2(5).
[83] *ibid.*, s.2(3).
[84] *ibid.*, s.2(6).
[85] *ibid.*, s.2(7).

Section 15 of the CCEJM provides that the chancellor must seek the advice of the DAC before making a final determination in any cause of faculty or issuing a permanent injunction or making a restoration order. The only exceptions are where the action relates to exhumation or reservation of a grave space, or where the matter is sufficiently urgent to justify not seeking advice. Likewise an archdeacon must also consult the DAC before making a final determination in a cause of faculty, with the same exceptions regarding exhumation and reservation of grave space, but not urgency. The DAC must keep a register of all petitions referred to it available for inspection by the public.[86] The FJR also provide that an applicant should seek the advice of the DAC prior to lodging a petition.[87] The applicant should submit all necessary plans and documents detailing the proposed work.

The function of the DAC is to give advice, not to approve proposals.[87a] Once it has reached a decision upon any proposals it sets out in a certificate whether it recommends, does not recommend or objects to the proposals.[88] The question has been raised as to liability of members of the DAC for negligent advice. There is no statutory provision for members, and this is a difficult issue.[89] In many dioceses the DBF has taken steps to insure members and all members of DACs would be advised to ensure adequate cover is in place.

Procedure in faculty cases

11.33 Procedure in respect of faculty cases in the consistory court is governed by the Faculty Jurisdiction Rules 1992.[90] However, these are not fully comprehensive and where no provision is applicable the judge should be guided so far as is practicable by the Rules of the Supreme Court.[91] The FJR set out, in Appendix B, specimen forms to be followed in the preparation of the documentation.

The petitioner

11.34 Proceedings are initiated by the lodging of a petition in the registry of the consistory court. Generally the petitioner will have sought the advice of the DAC in advance, and it is certainly desirable that they should. Proceedings may be initiated by the archdeacon of the archdeaconry in which the parish concerned is situated, the minister and churchwardens of the parish concerned, or any other person appearing to the court to have a sufficient interest in the matter.[92] Under

---

[86] FJR, r. 15(3).

[87] *ibid.*, r. 3(1).

[87a] *Re St Andrew, Cheadle Hulme* [1994] 1 W.L.R. 880. The consistory court has sole responsibility for the grant of faculties: *ibid.*

[88] For further details as to the advice of the DAC see *Newsom*, pp. 42–46.

[89] As to which see *Legal Opinions*, pp. 98–104 and see *Newsom*, pp. 46–47.

[90] S.I. 1992 No. 2882.

[91] FJR, r. 31.

[92] CCEJM, s. 16. In *Re St John's with Holy Trinity, Deptford* [1995] 1 W.L.R. 721 this included auctioneers who sought a confirmatory faculty in respect of the sale of items already removed from the church.

the CCEJM the archdeacon is deemed to have an interest as is any person on the electoral roll of the parish who does not reside within the parish, whose interest is deemed to be that of a parishioner. Although not explicitly specified a PCC would certainly be said to have an interest. The legislation deliberately does not set out an exhaustive test. Previously the test was whether the prospective petitioner had a personal interest and it would appear that this test still applies when the court has to determine whether there is sufficient interest.[93]

General citation

The petition is lodged with any necessary designs, plans or other documents **11.35** together with the recommendation of the DAC if this has been obtained.[94] Save in cases of exhumation or reservation of a grave space, a general citation must also be prepared detailing the work to be carried out, and this must be displayed in accordance with the FJR.[95] If the petitioner is a minister or churchwarden it is prepared by them and is displayed immediately, otherwise the registrar gives directions as to its display. The registrar may also if necessary direct that amendments be made to it. This is important because any faculty granted in respect of an incorrect or insufficiently published citation is a nullity, as is one where there is no citation at all.[96]

The general practice is that the citation must be displayed for a period of not less than 14 days, including at least one Sunday when the church is used for worship, but the registrar has the power to extend this period. Where the citation relates to a parish church or churchyard it must be displayed both inside and outside the church on notice boards or by the principal door or other prominent position and in all other cases in similar positions in addition to these. The registrar may also direct that the citation be placed elsewhere in the parish concerned in a place visible to the public. Additional directions for display (such as publishing in newspapers) must or may be given by the chancellor in certain cases.[97]

Once displayed in accordance with the FJR and any directions given, the citation must be returned to the registrar with a certificate of execution. To determine whether or not failure to comply in some minor regard would render publication void is a difficult question in the light of the FJR. Previously it has been held that where the object of publication, that is giving the public notice, had been achieved publication was merely irregular not void,[98] and a minor breach would probably still be so regarded under the new rules. The FJR expressly provides that non-compliance with any of the rules is not to render the proceedings void unless the chairman so directs, and thus allows for the exercise of some discretion.[99]

The general citation instructs any parishioner, person on the electoral roll or person having a lawful interest who wishes to object, to deliver a written notice of

---

[93] As to those having *locus standi* see also *Newsom*, pp. 51–56.
[94] FJR, r. 3.
[95] *ibid.*, r. 5(1), (2), (5).
[96] *Re St Cuthbert's Doveridge* [1983] 1 W.L.R. 845.
[97] FJR, r. 5(1).
[98] *Re St Michael The Archangel, Brantham* [1962] 1 W.L.R. 1067.
[99] FJR, r. 30.

objection in the form set out at the bottom of the citation. Objection must be made at the latest seven days after the expiry of the notice period, anyone who objects being treated as as an opponent for the purposes of costs.[1]

Exhumation and reservation of grave space

11.36 No general citation is required in cases of exhumation and reservation of grave space. In the case of exhumation the chancellor may dispense with a citation and issue a faculty forthwith if satisfied that any near relatives of the deceased and persons whom, in the opinion of the chancellor, it is reasonable to regard as being concerned with the matter, are petitioners or consent to the grant of the faculty.[2] In cases of reservation of grave space the chancellor may dispense with general citation and direct that any persons who are not petitioners be specially cited. If the chancellor does not dispense with general citation in cases of either exhumation or reservation of grave space then the registrar must complete a general citation.[3]

Special citation

11.37 Special citation normally occurs where the general citation is also served upon a particular person or body. The chancellor has a general power to direct special citation and must in certain cases direct this.[4] In cases which affect a grave or memorial maintained by the Commonwealth War Graves Commission the Commission must be cited. In addition in certain cases involving alterations or extensions to listed buildings, works affecting the archeological importance of a church, or the demolition of the exterior of an unlisted church in a conservation area, it is necessary to cite English Heritage and certain other bodies including the local planning authority and national amenity bodies.[5] Those bodies who are required to be cited have 28 days to send notice of objection or comments. If only comments are sent the body does not become a party. Notice of the petition analogous to special citation must or may also be given in certain circumstances, including to some of the same bodies (limiting the application of special citation), and to the Council for the Care of Churches if an article or a matter or artistic interest is involved; if the petition relates to the demolition or partial demolition of a church notice must be published in the London Gazette.[6]

A special citation may also issue against a person who is alleged to have been wholly or partly responsible for an act or default in consequence of which the proceedings were instituted.[7] In order to be made responsible for any costs such a person should be added as a party.

Special citation is always a matter for the chancellor and where a special citation might be required in proceedings before the archdeacon the matter should be referred by the registrar to the chancellor[8]

[1] *ibid.*, r. 15(1).
[2] *ibid.*, r. 12(8), (9).
[3] *ibid.*, r. 12(8), (9).
[4] FJR, r. 12.
[5] *ibid.*, r. 12.
[6] *ibid.*, rr. 12, 14; CCEJM, s.17(4), (5). See also *Newsom*, pp. 66–68.
[7] CCEJM, s.13(2).
[8] Under FJR, r. 9(1)(c).

Opponents

The categories of those who may be opponents are wider than those who may **11.38** petition. The FJR provide that in addition to parishioners and those on the electoral roll any interested person may object to a proposed faculty.[9] Interested persons are defined as including the relevant archdeacon, the PCC, the local planning authority for the area, and any national amenity society defined in the CCEJM (to which the Dean of the Arches has now added the Twentieth Century Society).[10] Previously these bodies could only assist through nominated witnesses and could not be a party to the proceedings. Any other body designated by the chancellor for the purpose of the petition may also become an opponent. This provision would enable the DAC or the Council for the Care of Churches to take part in their own right in cases where it is not appropriate to have their objections subsumed in the intervention of the archdeacon, for example where the archdeacon does not agree with the views of those bodies. Finally any person appearing to the chancellor to have a lawful interest in the subject matter of the petition may become a party.

Archdeacon's faculty

Rule 6(1) of the FJM specifies those matters over which the archdeacon may **11.39** have jurisdiction. The petition must be unopposed and the DAC must either recommend or not object to the proposals. Further, the archdeacon has no jurisdiction if the works or purposes are not within Appendix A to the FJM, which is divided into over 30 categories. Nor has the archdeacon jurisdiction in cases involving conservation issues which require special citation of English Heritage and certain other bodies including the local planning authority and national amenity bodies.[11]

If the registrar decides the case falls within the archdeacon's jurisdiction the petition is indorsed accordingly.[12] In cases of doubt, or where it appears to the registrar that the proposal raises a question of law, or contains issues pertaining to the doctrine, ritual or ceremonial of the Church of England, or which affect the legal rights of any person or body, the matter must be referred to the chancellor.[13] It appears that the registrar need not wait until the period of objection is over before indorsing the petition, and the archdeacon may grant a faculty *nisi* on condition that no objection is received.[14] If such an objection is then received the case must be remitted to the chancellor and the archdeacon's faculty is a nullity; otherwise it may be issued by the registrar at the end of the period for lodging notices of objection. However, the archdeacon cannot make a final determination until the advice of the DAC, has been sought and presumably obtained.[15]

[9] FJR, r. 15.
[10] *ibid.*, r. 15.
[11] *i.e,* under FJR, r. 12(3).
[12] *ibid.*, r. 6(2).
[13] *ibid.*, r. 9(1).
[14] *ibid.*, r. 6(4), (5).
[15] *ibid.*, r. 6(3).

The archdeacon must decline to act if they are the minister of the parish to which the petition relates or have been personally involved to the extent that it is inappropriate for them to act. The archdeacon can also decline to act for any reason.[16] In either case the matter is then referred to the chancellor. If the archdeacon is of the opinion that the matter needs to be dealt with as one of urgency without the advice of the DAC, or requires the grant of an interim faculty, injunction or restoration order, or gives rise to any question as to the payment of costs, whether or not a petition has been lodged, the registrar is notified and the matter referred immediately to the chancellor to give such licence or other direction as they consider fit.[17] All matters not allocated to and retained by the archdeacons are dealt with by the chancellor.

Licence for temporary re-ordering

11.40   Rule 8 FJR provides for the minister and a majority of the PCC to apply to the archdeacon for a licence for a scheme of re-ordering for a period not exceeding 12 months. A licence may only be granted where the archdeacon is satisfied that the scheme does not involve interference with the fabric of the church, nor fixing any item to the fabric, nor disposal of any fixture. They must also be satisfied that where the scheme involves moving any item this is done by competent persons with proper safeguards for storage of the item so that it can be readily reinstated. Where the archdeacon declines to grant the licence, application may be made to the chancellor to authorise the scheme by means of an interim faculty (an interim faculty being a licence or order in respect of works or purposes pending final determination of a petition of faculty for such). The archdeacon's licence cannot be extended (although a further licence may be granted). However, if a petition is lodged not later than two months before the expiry of the licence for a chancellor's faculty the scheme is deemed to be authorised until determination of the petition by the chancellor.

Pleadings

11.41   Once notice of objection has been given the registrar directs the objector to lodge written particulars, setting out the detailed grounds of objection, which must be served on the petitioner within 21 days.[18] The petitioner may, or may be directed by the registrar to, serve an answer within 21 days.[19] If a party objects to any part of the pleadings on grounds that they are irrelevant or bad in law they may within 14 days serve a notice to this effect together with their reasons and serve it on the other parties, who have 14 days to serve and lodge amended pleadings.[20] If no amended pleadings are received the matter is placed before the chancellor who decides if it is to be resolved at a preliminary hearing or at the general hearing of the case,[21] which closes the pleadings.

[16] *ibid.*, r. 7(1), (2).
[17] *ibid.*, r. 7(3).
[18] *ibid.*, r. 15(3).
[19] *ibid.*, r.17(1).
[20] *ibid.*, r. 17(2).
[21] *ibid.*, r. 17(3).

All time limits referred to may be extended on an application to the registrar or chancellor, notwithstanding that time has already expired.[22] All pleadings must be in writing and signed by the party concerned or their solicitor or counsel, be lodged at the registry, and a copy must be served on the other parties.[23] Service may be effected under the FJR by leaving the documents at the proper address or sending them by post to that address, the proper address being the usual or last known address of the person or body or the address of their solicitor, if any, acting in the proceedings.[24]

Appearance by archdeacon

In some cases which are unopposed the chancellor may consider that the interests of justice would best be served by the matter being argued by the archdeacon.[25] The purpose of the archdeacon appearing was explained by the Deputy Dean of the Arches in *Re St Gregory, Tredington*,[26] when criticising the failure of the archdeacon to appear in that case, and the failure of the courts to utilise the provision often enough. It enables the petitioner's witnesses to be cross-examined, witnesses for various bodies to be examined in chief, and for the law to be thoroughly argued. It is desirable that the archdeacon should be represented by solicitors or counsel and arrangements are made for the costs of this. Where the archdeacon is asked by the chancellor to appear it is inconsistent with their duty to the court to support the petitioners, and in cases where the archdeacon does support the petitioners arrangements should be made for an acting archdeacon or a person to act in the archdeacon's stead.[27]

11.42

If, after ascertaining the strength of opposition, a petitioner wishes to withdraw the petition they may only do so with the leave of the court, since expenses will have been incurred and accordingly an order for such costs must be considered.

The chancellor must give directions where any issues remain outstanding at the close of pleadings.[28] Since the petition usually only summarises the proposals the case may not be set out fully until the petitioner's answer to the particulars of objection. For this reason such directions are of particular importance, since further pleadings may be necessary.

This provision also enables documents to be agreed and any facts not in dispute to be conceded. These matters are dealt with on a summons for directions, held by the judge or registrar. Orders as to the number of expert witnesses who may be called and exchange of their proofs may be made,[28a] as

---

[22] *ibid.*, r. 29.

[23] *ibid.*, rr. 15, 17.

[24] *ibid.*, r. 28.

[25] CCEJM, s.16(2).

[26] [1972] Fam. 236 at 239–40. These remarks of the Deputy Dean were reiterated by the Court of Ecclesiastical Causes Reserved in *Re St Michael & All Angels, Great Torrington* [1985] Fam. 81 at 91.

[27] CCEJM, s.16(3). An acting archdeacon in *Re St Mary, Barton-on-Humber* [1987] Fam. 41, and the failure to appoint such an archdeacon was implicitly criticised by the Dean of Arches in *Re All Saints, Melbourn* [1990] 1 W.L.R. 833 at 834. See also *Re St Thomas, Pennywell* [1995] 2 W.L.R. 154 where a solicitor was appointed to act instead of the archdeacon, effectively as *amicus curiae*.

[28] FJR, r. 18.

[28a] Proofs of expert witnesses are to be disclosed in advance of the hearing in accordance with R.S.C. 0.38: *Re St Martin's, Ashton-upon-Mersey* [1981] 1 W.L.R. 1288.

may any other matter, since the rule is of wide application. An order for security for costs may be made, and any objection to pleadings to be dealt with as a preliminary issue determined. It should be ascertained whether the parties are prepared to have the case dealt with by written representations.

Written representations

11.43 Unopposed cases and cases where there are no facts in dispute or no great differences between the parties may be suitable for disposal by written representations, pursuant to Rule 25 of the FJA, where the parties agree to this. In such cases it would appear that the general principle is that there should be no order as to costs.[29] The procedure cannot be used in a case for demolition or part demolition of a church where evidence must be heard in open court from the Council for the Care of Churches.[30] The petitioner has 21 days in which to lodge a written statement in support of their case together with supporting evidence and each opponent has 21 days to lodge a statement in reply with any supporting evidence. The petitioner then has a further 14 days to lodge a response. At any stage the chancellor may revoke the direction that the matter be determined by written representations and direct an oral hearing. If this does not occur the chancellor determines the matter on the pleadings and written statements.

The hearing

11.44 Where the petitioner is unopposed, or the opponent party is in default of pleadings having failed to plead, the chancellor may grant the faculty without a hearing; otherwise a hearing must take place. In unopposed cases the chancellor may sit in chambers; otherwise the hearing is in open court. The hearing itself generally follows the practice of the Chancery Division in the High Court: thus the petitioner presents their case, followed by the opponents, with the petitioner being allowed a right of reply[31]; the procedure is, however, complicated by the possible introduction of non-party witnesses.

Generally evidence must be given orally, but the chancellor may direct on their own motion or by application that some evidence may be given by affidavit or before an examiner.[32] Having received such a statement the chancellor is entitled to direct that the maker of it attend for cross-examination, and failure to do so will render the statement inadmissable in all but exceptional circumstances with the leave of the judge.

Public petitions are wholly inadmissable, unless the party presenting it gives sworn evidence as to the representations made to the signatories.[33] The proper means of obtaining the views of the parish is for the churchwardens or bishop's officers to make proper enquiries and report these on oath to the court,[34] but even this evidence must be viewed with caution since it is technically hearsay.

---

[29] *Re St James, New Malden* [1993] 3 W.L.R. 861 at 865.
[30] CCEJM, s.17(4).
[31] The practice is described in *Kino v. Rudkin* (1877) 6 Ch. D. 160 at 163–164.
[32] The procedure and requirements as to time are set out in FJR, r. 20.
[33] *Rector & Churchwardens of Capel St Mary, Suffolk v. Packard* [1927] P. 289 at 300.
[34] This occurred in *Re St Luke's, Chelsea* [1976] Fam. 295 at 317–318.

Provision is made for non-party witnesses to give evidence. This procedure contrasts with the position in the secular courts where such witnesses may only be called with the consent of the parties and where the powers of the judge to question such witnesses are considerably curtailed. Seven days notice must be given to the parties regarding these witnesses and where they are summoned by the chancellor the nature of the evidence required must be given.[35] These witnesses may be cross-examined by any party, and with leave from the chancellor are themselves able to ask questions of parties.[36] In cases involving demolition or part demolition of a church the Council for the Care of Churches may apply to give evidence, and any other person may apply and give evidence unless the chancellor considers their evidence vexatious or frivolous.[37] In cases concerning articles or matters of historic or artistic interest the Council for the Care of Churches may send a report to the chancellor (the substance of which must be disclosed to the parties) or apply to give evidence, and it may apply to give evidence in all other cases.[38] English Heritage may also apply in any case, whether or not it has been specially cited.[39] The chancellor may also summon a member of the DAC, the Council for the Care of Churches or any other person to give evidence where it is considered relevant and the person willing to give it.[40] This enables the chancellor to deal with cases where there is no opponent party, but there is an issue between the petitioner and the DAC, a not uncommon occurance.

Onus of proof

The burden of proof is on those who propose changes[41]: they must bring evidence **11.45** in favour of the grant, the civil standard of proof, that is the balance of probabilities, being applied. Recent decisions have suggested that the court should be slow to grant a faculty to the detriment of private property where those objections were objectively real and sensible,[42] but that unless there is good reason for refusing the faculty it should be granted.[43] A petitioner is not entitled as of right to a faculty which lies in the judicial discretion of the chancellor upon the evidence before them.

The wishes of the parishioners are an important factor to be taken into account. However, even if the parishioners were to hold a unanimous opinion, it is a matter of some uncertainty as to whether their views would prevail, although in practice the courts have only ever considered cases where a majority of parishioners are agreed.

In the nineteenth century the Dean of the Arches, Lord Penzance, was critical of any matter being decided upon the wishes of the majority of parishioners,

---

[35] FJR, r. 24(2).
[36] *ibid.*, r. 24(3).
[37] CCEJM, s.17(4); FJR, r. 21.
[38] FJR, r. 22.
[39] *ibid.*, r. 23.
[40] *ibid.*, r. 24(1).
[41] *Peek v. Trower* (1881) 7 P.D. 21 at 27.
[42] *Re St Peter & St Paul, Upper Teddington & Others* [1993] 1 W.L.R. 852.
[43] *Re St James, New Malden* [1993] 3 W.L.R. 861 at 865.

since it would remove judicial discretion.[44] However, in recent years both appellate courts have criticised and overturned decisions on the basis that insufficient weight was given to the parishioners' views.[45] In *Re St Stephen's Walbrook*[46] the Court of Ecclesiastical Causes Reserved appears to have held that where the technical evidence was evenly balanced the views of the parishioners should prevail, in contradistinction to the views of both Lord Penzance (which were cited in that judgment) and the Dean of the Arches in *Re St Mary's Banbury*,[47] who adopted the opinions of Lord Penzance.

Listed buildings

11.46   The two cases referred to above have also produced a divergence of opinion between the two appellate courts as to the approach to be adopted in regard to listed buildings, where the evidence in favour of a grant may be subject to stringent tests. The Dean of the Arches in *Re St Mary's, Banbury* stated that a faculty affecting the character of a listed building should only be granted in wholly exceptional circumstances, "showing a necessity for such change".[48] This approach was criticised in *Re St Stephen's, Walbrook*, on the basis that the concept of "proved necessity", was not found in the Town and Country Planning Act 1971 which sets out the considerations to be borne in mind by the secular authorities, and that the discretion of the court must be exercised in the context of the building's use as a church.[49] In *Re All Saints Melbourn*[50] the Dean of the Arches considered the guidelines which he had given in *Re St Mary's, Banbury* in the light of the observations of the Court of Ecclesiastical Causes Reserved, pointing out that they were just guidelines and not rules of law and were not in his view in conflict with circulars issued by the Department of the Environment. He added however that if it were accepted that the presumption should be against change then "adversely affect" might be better than "affect".

---

[44] *Nickalls v. Briscoe* [1982] P. 269 at 283.

[45] In addition to the cases cited in the text see *Re St Michael & All Angels, Great Torrington* [1985] Fam. 81; *Re All Saints, Melbourn* [1990] 1 W.L.R. 833. See also *Newsom*, pp. 84–85.

[46] [1987] Fam. 146, *per* Sir Ralph Gibson.

[47] [1987] Fam. 136.

[48] *ibid*. at 145 and see *Re All Saints, Melbourn* [1990] 1 W.L.R. 833, applied *Re St Barnabas, Dulwich* [1994] 2 W.L.R. 545 where it was stated that there was no conflict between the decisions in *Re St Mary's* and *St Stephen's, Walbrook* and see *Re St James Shirley* [1994] Fam. 134. It should be noted that listed buildings are new governed by the Planning (Listed Buildings and Conservation Areas) Act 1990.

[49] For a full discussion see *Newsom*, pp. 85–87. See also *Re St Mary the Virgin, Sherbourne* [1996] 3 All E.R. 769 at 781–782, C.A. approving the principles set out in *Re St Helen's Bishopsgate* (1993) (unreported) which were commended in *Re St Luke the Evangelist, Maidstone* [1995] Fam. 1, namely that three questions need to be considered: have the parishioners proved a necessity for the work for the pastoral well-being of the parish or some other compelling reason; will any of the works adversely affect the character of the church as a building of special architectural and historic interest; and if the answer to the second question is yes, is the necessity such that nonetheless the court should exercise its discretion to grant the faculty.

[50] [1990] 1 W.L.R. 833 at 843, 844.

Injunctions, restoration and place of safety orders

Injunctions and restoration orders

The CCEJM gave the consistory court powers to issue injunctions to prevent **11.47** threatened illegal acts and restoration orders to restore the status quo following such an illegal act.[51] However, a restoration order cannot usually be made in respect of acts done more than six years before the proceedings, although special provisions apply in cases where the act has been concealed.[52] Restoration orders are in effect mandatory injunctions.[53]

The powers to grant such injunctions and orders are governed by the Faculty Jurisdiction (Injunctions and Restoration Orders) Rules 1992.[54] The archdeacon or any person having sufficient interest may make an application in writing supported by affidavit.[55] Service takes place only if the application contains a hearing date provided by the registrar, and must be served at least two days before that date.[56] If faculty proceedings have already commenced service must be on all parties to those proceedings, in addition to the person against whom the order is sought and the relevant minister and archdeacon (if these are not the applicant).[57] Provision is made for the lodging of affidavit evidence by way of reply[58] and for leave for oral evidence to be given at the hearing, which is otherwise conducted on affidavit evidence.[59] The injunction or restoration order may be on such terms as the chancellor considers just (although the time for doing any act must be stated) and directions may be given for the institution of faculty proceedings.[60]

In situations of great urgency an applicant may apply to the chancellor without effecting service and the chancellor may grant an injunction on terms that it remains in force for not more than 14 days.[61] The application is then served and directions are giving for the hearing of that application.

The chancellor also has power to order injunctions or make restoration orders on their own motion, although this may not be exercised in the case of a restoration order without considering if a special citation should be issued and whether the person to whom it is issued should be given an opportunity to be heard.[62] The chancellor may also vary, extend or discharge any order as they think fit.[63] Failure to comply with an injunction or order is a contempt of court.[64]

---

[51] CCEJM, s.13(4), (5), (6).
[52] ibid., s.13, (8), (9), (10).
[53] For a discussion of this see *Newsom*, pp. 199–200.
[54] S.I. 1992 no. 2884.
[55] ibid., rr. 3, 4.
[56] ibid., r. 5.
[57] ibid., r. 5.
[58] ibid., r. 6.
[59] ibid., r. 7.
[60] ibid., r. 7.
[61] ibid., r. 8(1).
[62] ibid., rr. 8(2), 9.
[63] ibid., r. 10(2).
[64] CCEJM, s.13(11).

Place of safety orders

11.48   Section 21 of the CCEJM conferred a new power on archdeacons to order that an article of architectural, artistic, historical or archaeological value appertaining to a church in the archdeaconry, which is exposed to danger of loss or damage, should be removed from it and deposited in a place of safety. However, a record or register within the meaning of section 10 of the Parochial Registers and Records Measure 1978 is excluded, there being as we have seen separate powers to protect these.[65] Save in urgent cases the archdeacon must notify the church-wardens, the PCC, DAC and any person having custody of the article, all of whom have 28 days to make representations. If the order is not complied with the archdeacon can apply to the consistory court for a mandatory order. Once the article is removed the archdeacon must apply to the court for a faculty authorising retention in the safe place.

Appeals from the consistory court

11.49   Matters relating to all appeals to the Courts of the Arches and Chancery Court and the Court of Ecclesiastical Causes Reserved are provided for in the Ecclesiastical Jurisdiction (Faculty Appeals) Rules 1965.[66] An appeal from the consistory court to the appellate courts must be instituted within 28 days after judgment or 14 days after the chancellor's certificate, whichever is the later, although an application for an extension may be made. The chancellor's certificate as to whether or not the cause involves a point of doctrine, ritual or ceremonial (not whether the appeal itself may involve such a question), determines which court the appeal is made to.[67] As we have seen, any party may appeal with the leave of the consistory court or, if this is refused, with leave from the Dean of the Arches and Auditor.[67a]

Notice of appeal and the chancellor's certificate are lodged and copies served on every party. In addition two copies are served upon the diocesan registrar, one of which the registrar must have affixed to the principal door of the church concerned.[68] The appellant must apply in writing to the chancellor for a signed copy of any notes made by them and of the judgment.[69] All relevant documents and exhibits must also be available,[70] and the court has discretionary power, exercised only in exceptional circumstances, to hear oral evidence, including new evidence.[71] The court may draw any inferences of fact which might have been

---

[65] As to which see Chap. 8.

[66] S.I. 1965 No. 251.

[67] EJM, s.10(3).

[67a] The principles upon which leave should be granted are set out in *Re St Mary the Virgin, Sherbourne* [1996] 3 All E.R. 769 at 772.

[68] Ecclesiastical Jurisdiction (Faculty Appeals) Rules 1965, S.I. 1965 No. 251, r. 4.

[69] *ibid.*

[70] *ibid.*, r. 8.

[71] See *Re St Gregory, Tredington* [1972] Fam. 236. The principles to be applied are set out in *Re St Mary the Virgin, Sherbourne* (*ante*) at 772–773 these being similar to those followed in the secular courts, requiring a proof together with an explanation as to why the evidence was not adduced earlier and its importance to the appeal.

drawn by the consistory court.[72] The appellate court may give any judgment or direction which ought to have been given in the consistory court or may remit the matter with directions for rehearing and determination by that court.[73]

Faculties in particular cases

Faculties relating to the fabric of the church

Except for *de minimis* matters, a faculty is required in order for works of repairs, **11.50** renovation, alteration, addition or demolition to be undertaken to the fabric of the church. In certain cases where the work is to affect the church's external appearance planning permisison under the secular law may also be required, as distinct from listed building consent in respect of which, as we saw in Chapter 8, there is an exemption.

In the case of demolition or partial demolition, except in an emergency,[74] a faculty now can only be granted on limited grounds. Even relatively minor matters such as a chimney stack will generally fall within the definition of partial demolitions, although some matters may still be regarded as *de minimis*. Minor part demolition may be authorised on the ground that it is necessary for the repair or alteration of the church, or in order to reconstruct the part which is to be demolished.[75] In such cases the court must be satisfied, after consultation with the DAC, that the proposed work when completed will not materially affect either the internal or external appearance of the church or its architectural, archaeological, artistic or historic character. If the court is not satisfied then provisions relating to the obtaining of the consent of the bishop, notification of certain bodies, and certain other procedural requirements must be complied with.[76]

Those provisions and the grounds upon which demolition may otherwise be ordered are set out in the CCEJM.[77] A faculty may not be granted for demolition or part demolition unless the court is satisfied that another church or part of a church will be erected on the site or curtilage to take the place of that church or the part to be demolished or, in the case of partial demolition, that the part left standing will be used for a substantial period for public worship. As was discussed earlier such a faculty cannot be granted without a full hearing in open court. In a case where a faculty is granted a consequential direction as to the removal of any human remains or contents of the building should be made.[78]

---

[72] *Re St Edburga's, Abberton* [1962] P. 10; *Re St Gregory, Treddington* [1972] Fam. 236; *Re St Michael & All Angels, Great Torrington* [1985] Fam. 81; *Re St Stephen's Walbrook* [1987] Fam. 146; *Re St Mary's Banbury* [1987] Fam. 136; *Re All Saints, Melbourn* [1990] 1 W.L.R. 833 at 839.

[73] Ecclesiastical Jurisdiction (Faculty Appeals) Rules 1965, S.I. 1965 no. 251, r. 8.

[74] As to which CCEJM, s.18 applies.

[75] *ibid.*, s.17(3)(b).

[76] *ibid.*, s.17(6).

[77] *ibid.*, s.17. There are yet further requirements in the case of listed buildings or buildings in a conservation area: *ibid.*

[78] See *Re St Luke, Cheetham* [1978] Fam. 144 at 147–148.

In cases of proposed extensions to churches[79] for purposes ancillary to worship the status of the ground upon which it is proposed to build needs to be considered. This may be consecrated or unconsecrated burial ground or curtilage of the church or burial ground. As we saw in Chapter 8 where a burial ground is disused any proposed building is, unless the land is released from the constraints of that Act, subject to the restrictions imposed by the Disused Burials Grounds Act 1884. In the case of consecrated land which is not a disused burial ground the restrictions on the secular use which were considered in Chapter 8 apply, and thus limit the purposes for which an extension may be erected. An extension of the church and a building for ancillary purposes of worship or an ecclesiastical building such as a school would all appear to be permissible. Where a faculty for an extension is granted it is desirable that conditions should be imposed to ensure that the extension is not used for purposes unsuitable to part of a church.[80] Directions as to the removal of any human remains will need to be considered as will faculties for the removal of tombstones and monuments.

The secular use of consecrated land has already been considered in Chapter 8. It should be noted that where a licence is granted to permit secular use this should always be made under the authority of a faculty, the incumbent (if there is one), the PCC and prospective licensee all being petitioners.[81]

Faculties relating to contents of churches

11.51   Petitions are often lodged in respect of a scheme to authorise the rearrangement of moveables and fixtures such as pews, with or without additions to or subtractions from the existing contents. Such schemes for re-ordering may be justified by developments in the approach to the physical framework of worship which have occurred throughout the Church's history, and require a balance to be struck between the wishes and needs of the congregation and the claims of the conservationist.[82] The most important principle to have emerged in such cases is that schemes for re-ordering should be reversible, since the needs and tastes of future generations must be borne in mind.[83–84] Particular problems may emerge where there is a divergence of opinion amongst the congregation as to the adoption of a scheme, a situation more likely to occur when, as is becoming common, large numbers on the electoral roll do not live in the parish but choose to come to a particular church because of the style of worship conducted there.

The right to occupy a pew obtained by faculty, prescriptive right or by Act of Parliament was considered in Chapter 8. The effect that such rights may have upon a scheme for re-ordering became apparent in *Re St Mary's, Banbury*.[85] Since

---

[79] See also The Council for the Care of Churches, *Church Extensions and Adaptions* (1996).

[80] As to which see *Newsom*, pp. 108–109.

[81] Various procedural matters were discussed in *Re St Mary, Aldermary* [1985] Fam. 101. Care should be taken that appropriate insurance cover is obtained.

[82] *Re Holy Innocents, Fallowfield* [1982] 3 W.L.R. 666 at 667 sets out guidelines.

[83–84] *Re St Stephen's, Walbrook* [1987] Fam. 146. See also *Re St Mary's, Banbury* [1987] Fam. 136; *Re All Saints, Melbourne* [1990] 1 W.L.R. 833; *Re St Luke the Evangelist, Maidstone* [1994] 3 W.L.R. 1165.

[85] [1986] Fam. 24; [1987] Fam. 136.

such rights were perpetual and were to an identifiable pew or seat and could not be removed by faculty the pews themselves could not be removed permanently without the owner's consent.

Under the chancellor's powers of delegation the archdeacon may authorise the installation of new heating and lighting systems where the DAC consider that the work will not result in a material alteration to, the appearance of the church. The archdeacon may also authorise the installation or alteration of sound reinforcement systems where the DAC certifies that it approves or does not object. Although heating, lighting and sound reinforcement are important matters and form the subject of faulty petitions, there is no recent reported case upon such work which offers assistance in this area.

Carpets have also not been the subject of reported decisions although unreported cases suggested that a faculty to permit extensive carpeting will only be permitted in older churches where these lack architectural merit.[85a]

Organs, which are generally the most expensive item in the church, require specialist advice regarding their repair and replacement. Expert opinion differs over the merits of pipe organs and electrostatic or computerised organs,[86] and advice should be sought at an early stage.[87]

Bells to bring the people to divine service are also expensive items. An **11.52** archdeacon may authorise *in situ* repairs, but nothing should be done to the bells without expert advice. Although bells are frequently the subject matter of faculty petitions the lack of reported cases suggests that in practice proper advice is sought on their installation and repair so that the matter is uncontroversial.

Canon F1 provides that a font should stand as near to the principal entrance of the church as is convenient unless there is a custom to the contrary or the Ordinary otherwise directs, and in as spacious and well ordered surroundings as possible. However, in the light of a statement by the House of Bishops[88] setting out current liturgical thinking on baptism, the chancellor now has a discretion and thus the strict requirements of the Canon may be mitigated.

Prior to the Bishops' statement it was accepted that there is no rule of law or Canon which prevents a second font, and sometimes application has been made for a second font, two reported cases[89] being concerned with pools for baptism by immersion, assurances being obtained in one[90] that the practice of infant baptism by affusion would not be discouraged nor rebaptism permitted. However the statement by the House of Bishops anticipates one font in which baptism by

---

[85a] *Re St Michael the Archangel, South Malling & Others* (1991) (unreported) 1991 2 Ecc. L.J. 251. The relevant factors to be taken into account were considered in *Re Wadsworth Parish Church* (unreported) 3 Ecc. L.J. 260.

[86] See *Re St Mary's Lancaster* [1980] 1 W.L.R. 657; *Re St Martin's Ashton-upon-Mersey* [1981] 1 W.L.R. 1288.

[87] For a further discussion see *Newsom*, pp. 113–116.

[88] Response of the House of Bishops to questions raised by diocesan chancellors of June 1992, the text of which is set out in *Re St James' Church, Shirley* [1994] Fam. 134, where a faculty was granted for a single font enabling baptism by immersion. The conflict between Canon and such statements by the House of Bishops was considered in Chap. 2.

[89] *Re St Barnabas, Kensington* [1991] Fam. 1; *Re St George's, Deal* [1991] Fam. 6.

[90] *Re St Barnabas, Kensington* (*ante*).

affusion, immersion (that is pouring water over the whole body only parts of which are submerged), or submersion becomes the norm, and states that anything other than one font would be an anomaly.[90a] The statement also makes clear that the one font need not be by the door (to signify the entry into Christ's Church), but can be at the centre of the church and congregation.

Prior to the introduction of the Holy Table Measure 1964 it had been accepted that the holy table must be moveable. Section 1 of that Act provides that it may be moveable or immoveable and of wood, stone or any other suitable material. The question of what may constitute such a table and the history of the subject was considered exhaustively by the court of Eccleisastical Causes Reserved in *Re St Stephen's, Walbrook*.[91] The court concluded that such a table could include a structure that might properly be referred to as an altar. Basing its decision upon recent ecumenical developments the court stated that since the doctrine of eucharistic sacrifice (which is not that of a repetition of the sacrifice at Calvary) can lawfully be held there can be no objection to an altar. Thus a faculty was granted to enable the introduction of a cylindrical piece of marble weighing over 10 tons. The position of the table and other related matters have already been considered in Chapter 9.

The issues relating to moveables, that is to ornaments and decorations have also been considered in Chapter 9. As to the question of title to such chattels, although this is justifiable in the consistory court[92] as well as in the secular courts, the former may be the more appropriate forum since, whomsoever title vests the chattels in, cannot be removed from the church without a faculty.[93]

11.53 As we saw in Chapter 8 a faculty is also required for the disposal, whether by sale or otherwise, of any chattel. The principles governing such cases were considered by the Court of the Arches in *Re St Gregory's, Tredington*.[94] Church-wardens who have the legal title in such goods may sell them with the consent of the PCC under authority of a faculty. However, to obtain a faculty they will need to demonstrate a "special reason", and in considering such the court must take account of the "special character" of the ministry of the particular church. Redundancy of the article in question or financial emergency or both are the commonest grounds. A faculty granting permission may impose a condition requiring a specified period to elapse before sale,[95] enabling for example museums to have an opportunity to bid. Provision is usually made for the application of the proceeds of sale. Provision should also be made for proper commemoration of the person in whose memory or by whom the article was given. Should the church wish to loan one of its treasures to a museum or to the cathedral treasury a faculty is required and adequate arrangements must be made for security and insurance.

[90a] See Stancliffe, "Baptism and Fonts" (1994) 3 Ecc. L.J. 140; *Re Emmanuel, Loughborough* (1995) (unreported) 3 Ecc. L.J. 430 where a faculty for a single new font for infant and adult baptism was granted. See Ch. preferring the reasoning of Bishop Stancliffe in "Baptism and Fonts" (*ante*) and the reasoning in *Re St Nicholas, Gosforth* (unreported) to that of Newsom Ch. in *Re St Barnabas, Kensington* (*ante*), and *Re St George's Deal* (*ante*).

[91] [1987] Fam. 146.

[92] *Re St Mary of Charity, Faversham* [1986] Fam. 143.

[93] *Re Escot Church* [1979] Fam. 125 at 127.

[94] [1972] Fam. 236.

[95] CCEJM, s.12(1)(b).

Cremated remains may be buried in a church under authority of a faculty, but it is a privilege to be exercised sparingly,[96] and is generally to be confined to the benefactor of a church or a person closely connected with it such as the incumbent.[96a] Faculties have been granted for columbaria, a device to hold caskets containing ashes.[97] Burial of a dead body within a church would now be wholly exceptional and there is no reported case in recent years of faculty for this being granted. A memorial tablet within the church is also a matter of privilege, and a faculty will again only be granted in exceptional cases.[98] Such cases might be the exceptional character or outstanding service of the person, or the desire to commemorate an important aspect of local or national history.[99] Aesthetic considerations must also be taken into account. The ownership of such memorials and of all monuments and tombstones has already been discussed in Chapter 8.

Faculties relating to churchyards and burial grounds

11.54 All persons (or strictly speaking their personal representatives who will have to enforce the right[99a] who are parishioners[99b] or who die in the

---

[96] *Re Kerr* [1894] P. 284; *Re St Peter's, Folkstone* [1982] 1 W.L.R. 1283.

[96a] Similarly faculties have been granted in the past to permit burials in church for persons of "pre-eminent sanctity of life": *Gilbert v. Buzzard* (1820) 3 Phil. Ecc. R. 348. However, see *Re St Peter's Folkestone (supra)* at 1286 wherein it is said that since the Second World War faculties, in the province of Canterbury, for the burial of cremated remains have only been granted for the burial of cremated remains in church on four occasions and none have been granted for the burial of bodies in church.

[97] In effect pigeon holes, the term comes from the latin for pigeon. For discussion of this practice see *Newsom*, p. 142.

[98] *Dupuis v. Parishioners of Ogbourne St George* [1941] P. 11 19 at 121.

[99] The Dean of the Arches outlined the criteria to be considered in *Re St Margaret's, Eartham* [1981] 1 W.L.R. 923.

[99a] Although enactments commonly treat the right as being in the deceased person. The right is said to crystalise when the person dies: *Re West Pennard Churchyard* [1991] 4 All E.R. 124 at 126. Strictly the right must vest in whoever has responsibility for disposing of the body and arranging the funeral. Where no other arrangements can be made burial is regulated by the Public Health (Control of Diseases) Act 1984, s.46. An executor, administrator or other person on whom the law imposes a duty to bury the deceased cannot deprive them of their common law right to burial: *Re Kerr* [1894] 284 at 293. However, pursuant to the Anatomy Act 1984, s.4, the Secretary of State may grant a licence to carry out anatomical examinations if a person expressed a request, either orally or in writing, in the presence of two witnesses during their final illness, that their body should be so used.

[99b] Personal representatives are entitled to remove a body to the parish of residence and demand its burial there: *Legal Opinions*, p. 24. On a union of parishes pursuant to a pastoral scheme persons resident in the united parish have the rights of parishioners in respect of burials in that parish, save that any parishioner who before union had rights of burial in a churchyard in the parish will, for so long as that churchyard remains open, continue to have those rights and will not become entitled by virtue of the union to rights of burial in any other churchyard: Pastoral Measure 1983, Sched. 3, para. 15. On the creation of a new parish, other than by union, parishioners retain their original

parish[1] have a right to be buried in the parish churchyard or burial ground if there is one.[2] That common law right is extended by statute to those whose name is on the electoral roll of the parish[3] and to the burial of cremated remains.[4] The right exists regardless of whether the person is a member of the Church of England or even a Christian. In all other cases the consent of the minister of the parish (either the incumbent, priest-in-charge, licensed curate or rural dean) is required.[5] In deciding whether to consent the minister must have regard to any general guidance given by the PCC in respect to the matter.[6] The incumbent's refusal to bury a person who has no right of burial cannot be challenged in the consistory court.[7]

Graveyards are frequently buried over more than once but care must be taken not to disturb remains without a faculty.[8] The fact that the remains of the deceased are in a particular place does not give their descendents the right of burial nearby.[8a] Although there is no right to burial in a particular place a gravespace may be reserved by faculty for either a parishioner or other person.

rights of burial until they obtain rights of burial in the new parish at which point the original right ceases: *ibid*. Where any person by virtue of a pastoral scheme or order altering parish boundaries comes to reside within a different parish they will have the rights and privileges in respect of burial enjoyed by parishioners of that different parish and no other: *ibid*. This may have unfortunate consequences for those whose relatives are buried in their previous parish before the alteration of the boundary since they will no longer have the right to be buried in the same churchyard.

[1] *ex parte Blackmore* (1830) 1 Bd. & Ad. 122 at 123; R. *v. Stewart* (1849) 12 Ad. & E. 773 at 778. Even if the person has only just come into the parish or is passing through and dies in a road accident for example, *Legal Opinions*, p. 24.

[2] *Maidman v. Malpas* (1794) 1 Hag. Con. 205; R. *v. Coleridge* (1819) 2 Bd. & Ad. 806; *Kemp v. Wickes* (1809) 3 Phil. Ecc. R. 264; *Re Kerr* [1894] P. 284 at 293. The right is enforceable in both secular and ecclesiastical jurisdictions: *Halsbury's Laws of England* (4th ed.) Vol. 10, para. 1118. In the secular courts it is enforceable by mandamus: R. *v. Coleridge* (*supra*). For more detailed consideration of this and other issues discussed in this section see Smale, *Davies Law of Burial, Cremation and Exhumation* (6th ed., 1993).

[3] Church of England (Miscellaneous Provisions) Measure 1976, s.6(1).

[4] Church of England (Miscellaneous Provisions) Measure 1992, s.3(1). The right does not extend to closed churchyards or burial grounds when a faculty would be required. However, a faculty is often granted to permit part of a churchyard (including a closed churchyard) to be set aside for interment of ashes. A bishop may consecrate land in the diocese for the sole purpose of burying cremated remains. *ibid*., ss.(3). Doe, *The Legal Framework of the Church of England* (1996) at p. 396 n. 102 suggests that the right to burial of cremated remains may also be a common law right and thus express provision was unnecessary.

[5] Church of England (Miscellaneous Provisions) Measure 1976, s.6(2), (3). The incumbent does not have the right to derogate from the parishioners' rights in the soil by parishioners signified by the PCC: *Re St Mary Magdalene, Lyminister* (1991) (unreported) 2 E.L.J. 127.

[6] *ibid*.

[7] *Re St Nicholas, Badesley Ensor* [1983] Fam. 1. The court will not entertain an application for a faculty where the minister does not consent unless the minister gave and then withdrew consent and the non-parishioners have acted upon this and would be prejudiced: *ibid*.

[8] *Re Dixon* [1892] P. 386; *Newsom*, p. 153.

[8a] *Fryer v. Johnson* (1755) 2 Wils. 28.

With a right of burial, it is for the minister, or a non-parishioner[9] to precribe the position where a burial is to take place.[10]

Reservation of gravespace was a lucrative source of income for some incumbents at the turn of the century but the discretion for granting such rests entirely with the consistory court.[11] The consistory court may also grant a faculty conferring an exclusive right of burial in a particular vault or part of the churchyard.[11a] Any right for the exclusive use of any particular part of the churchyard, burial ground or other consecrated land for the purposes of sepulture, however granted or acquired, will cease on April 15, 2064 unless granted or enlarged or continued by a faculty issued after April 15, 1964.[12] Records of burials and reserved grave space should be kept.[13] Failure to do so has led to at least one unfortunate case where the person entitled to the space has been granted a faculty to exhume remains buried there in error.[14]

On closure of a churchyard or burial ground (as to which see Chapter 8) all rights of burial in it are destroyed.[14a] In the case of a disused burial ground (which may not be closed if that ground is consecrated) it appears that a faculty may be granted to authorise burials.[14b] Where a churchyard or burial ground is

[9] For a fuller discussion see P. Sparkes, "Exclusive Burial Rights" (1991) 2 E.L.J. 133; *Re Marks (deceased) ante*; *Halsbury's Laws of England* (4th ed.) Vol. 14, para. 1315; *Newsom*, p. 170; *Legal Opinions*, p. 26. Church of England Miscellaneous Provisions) Measure 1976, s.6(2).

[10] *Re West Pennard Churchyard* [1992] 1 W.L.R. 32; *ex parte Blackmore* (1830) 1 B. & Ad 122; *Re Marks (deceased) The Times*, Oct. 28, 1994.

[11] *Re West Pennard Churchyard* [1991] 1 W.L.R. 32. It is freely granted to a petitioner with legal rights of burial where there is plenty of space in the churchyard: *ibid.* Doubt was however cast on this view in *Re St Mary, Dodleston* [1996] 1 W.L.R. 456; the persons in respect of whom the reservation was sought being young and thus might only have a tenuous connection with the parish in future. The PCC may adopt general guidance to an incumbent concerning reservations and may adopt a practice of always opposing petitions for reservations, but although the views of the PCC will be taken into account they will not be binding on the consistory court: *Re West Pennard Churchyard (ante)*.

[11a] *Rugg v. Kingsmill* (1868) L.R. 2 P.C. 59. Such grants may be limited to a particular family so long as they remain parishioners or to a person and their heirs and family: *Magnay v. Rector, Churchwardens and Parishioners of the United Parishes of St Michaels, Paternoster Royal and St Martin, Vintry* (1827) 1 Hag. Ecc. 48. The precise nature of the right is unclear; it is similar to but not the same as an easement: *Re Hendon Churchyard* (1910) 27 T.L.R. 1.

[12] FJM, s.8. The provisions do not apply to burial grounds provided under the Burial Acts 1852–1906, or the Public Health (Interments) Act 1879.

[13] Under rules pursuant to the CCEJM, s.26(3)(b).

[14] *Re St Luke's, Holbeach Hurn* [1991] 1 W.L.R. 16.

[14a] *Re West Pennard Churchyard (ante)* at 126. However, it should be noted that closure may only relate to one part of the churchyard or burial ground not to the entirety. Thus as a general rule once closed a burial ground can no longer be used for the burial of corpses but whether in fact any burials may take place will depend upon the precise terms of the Order or Orders in Council applicable to it: *Legal Opinions*, p. 61. The most usual exceptions are for burial in vaults or family graves or to permit the burial of a named person with a close relative: *Halsbury's Laws of England* (4th ed.) Vol. 10, para. 1207, n. 2. For the procedures involved in tracing an Order in Council see *Legal Opinions*, pp. 61–62. It is an offence to bury remains in a closed churchyard or burial ground contrary to the terms of an Order in Council: Burial Act 1855, s.2.

[14b] Open Spaces Act 1887, s.4; Disused Burial Grounds Act 1884; Disused Burial Grounds (Amendment) Act 1981, s.5.

closed a person similarly does not have the right to burial of their cremated remains. However, burial of cremated remains may be authorised by faculty and consequently the prohibition does not apply when the burial is in accordance with a faculty or in an area which has been set aside for the burial of cremated remains generally.[14]

Once buried in consecrated ground a body cannot be re-interred without a faculty permitting exhumation. Ordinarily in cases of exhumation a licence is required from the Secretary of State but where exhumation is from and re-interment is to take place in consecrated ground such a licence is not required.[15]

11.55   A faculty for exhumation will only be granted upon the application of the executors or members of the family for reasons approved by the court, or on the application of any other party on grounds of necessity or public convenience, and will in the latter cases only be granted if re-interment in other consecrated ground is to take place.[16] Such orders are often sought where a church is to be extended or altered. Exhumation will only be granted in strong and compelling circumstances.[17] The underlying assumption is that the court must protect the remains of the deceased, when it was the express or presumed intention of all taking part that the remains were to be finally laid to rest once and for all.[18] However, where the application is one made on private grounds the court will be guided by the wishes of the deceased or members of their family, friends or personal representatives.[18a] In the case of an application for public purposes the

---

[14c] Church of England (Miscellaneous Provisions) Measure 1992, s.3(1); *Legal Opinions*, p. 25; *Newsom*, p. 154. Doe, *The Legal Framework of the Church of England* (1996), p. 399 suggests that the burial of cremated remains in churchyards and burial grounds closed by Orders in Council prior to 1902, when cremation was put on a statutory footing, may be lawful without a faculty, provided the Order does not prohibit the burial of cremated remains. Doe also disagrees with commentaries which suggest that a faculty is required to authorise all burials of cremated remains in closed churchyards and burials grounds and disagrees that *Re Kerr* [1894] p. 284 is authority for that proposition. Since the Church of England (Miscellaneous Provisions) Measure 1992, s.3(1) refers only to burial, it may be that the scattering of ashes does not require a faculty: Doe, *The Legal Framework of the Church of England* (1996), p. 399. However, it may be advisable to seek legal advice before so doing.

[15] Burial Act 1857, s.25. This interpretation has been agreed with the Home Office: *Legal Opinions*, pp. 28–29. If the body is exhumed from unconsecrated ground and re-interred in consecrated ground then a licence for exhumation and a faculty for re-interment are required, but it is not clear whether in cases of exhumation from consecrated ground and re-interment in unconsecrated a licence is required for re-interment although a faculty would be required for exhumation: *Re Holy Trinity, Freckleton* (1995) (unreported) 3 Ecc. L.J. 429. The position of unconsecrated churchyards which fall within the jurisdiction of the consistory court (as to which see Chapter 8) is not entirely clear but it would apear that both a faculty and a licence are required for exhumation. Exhumation may also occur pursuant to a coroner's orders: Coroners' Act 1980, ss.1, 4.

[16] *Re Dixon* [1892] P. 386 at 393–394; *Re Matherson* [1958] 1 W.L.R. 246 at 248 it was said that the court should be slow to impose fetters upon the exercise of its discretion since unforeseen circumstances making exhumation desirable could arise.

[17] The authorities on exhumation were reviewed in detail in *Re Church Norton Churchyard* [1989] Fam. 37.

[18] *Re St Peter's Churchyard, Oughtrington (ante)*. *Re Smith (deceased)* [1994] 1 All E.R. 90 following *Re Atkins* [1989] 1 All E.R. 14 and *Re St Luke's, Holbeach Hurn (ante)*.

[18a] *Re Dixon (supra)*; *Holy Trinity, Freckleton (supra)*.

court will consult the wishes of the deceased's relatives so far as this is possible, as to where the remains should be removed to.[18b]

The Church of England makes no distinction in canon law between a corpse and the ashes of a cremated body: both should be treated with the same dignity and reverence.[19] Although the physical differences between a corpse and ashes cannot be ignored the court should make no distinction and should not give undue weight to the fact that disinterment and removal of ashes buried in a casket is simpler and less expensive than disinterment of a corpse and unlikely to pose a risk to health. In particular it should resist any tred towards regarding the remains of relations as portable, to be taken from place to place so that the grave or place of interment may be visited more easily.[20]

No new monument may be introduced into a churchyard without a faculty, although in practice the chancellor is content to delegate the authority to grant permission for ordinary tombstones to the incumbent or priest-in-charge, or during a vacancy the rural dean. Such power of delegation is either implied or granted by express delegation. Where delegation is express it is subject to the cases falling within churchyard rules[21] and is generally subject to requirements that the proposed monument has the unanimous support of the PCC and that there is no opposition by any significant body of opinion in the parish. Powers may also be delegated to archdeacons in regard to monuments not strictly complying with the churchyard rules where these have the unanimous support of the PCC and are approved by the DAC. Such permission is not irrevocable; it merely dispenses with the immediate need to apply for a faculty. If the matter comes before the chancellor they are not bound by the granting of such permission.

As has been recognised it is often difficult for an incumbent to resist acceding to a request. Matters of taste are of great relevance. A memorial incorporating colour photographs of the deceased, "alien" to an English country churchyard, will not be permitted.[22] Certain types of material, such as marble and polished granite, are now generally prohibited, local stone being favoured.[23] Inscriptions have caused much difficultly. The grounds upon which these are rejected being generally ones of taste, although it has also been held recently that an inscription upon a public monument should be of a formal nature, diminutive pet names or nicknames being avoided. Thus whilst "father" is acceptable, "dad" is not.[24]

[18b] *Rector of St Helen's, Bishopsgate v. Parishioners of Same* [1892] P. 259; *Newsom*, p. 172.

[19] *Re Atkins* above.

[20] *ibid.*

[21] Advice upon these regulations and upon the subject of churchyards generally will be found in Burman and Stapleton, *The Churchyards Handbook*, (3rd ed. 1988). These regulations are merely parameters within which monuments may be introduced and they do not confer any rights, and a PCC may operate its own more stringent rules within these guidelines: *Re St Martin's, Hereford* (unreported) 4 Ecc. L.J. 606. The fact that another monument was incorrectly authorised by the incumbent is irrelevant: *Re St Mary, Grendon* (unreported) (1991) 2 Ecc. L.J. 64. So too is the fact that other monuments of a type now outwith the rules are already in the churchyard: *Re All Saints, Orpington* (unreported) (1990) 2 Ecc. L.J. 65. Further where the previous incumbent has unlawfully permitted a memorial their successor may obtain a faculty to remove it: *Re St Peter's Weston Favell* (unreported) (1991) 2 Ecc. L.J. 228.

[22] *Re, St Mary's, Fawkham* [1981] 1 W.L.R. 1171 at 1175.

[23] See, *e.g. Re St Paul, Hanging Heaton* [1968] 1 W.L.R. 1210.

[24] *Re Holy Trinity Churchyard*, Freckleton [1994] 1 W.L.R. 1588.

Difficult situations can also arise where competing parties, such as spouses and former spouses, wish to erect a monument,[25] and great tact is frequently called for. In practice the power to control monuments is rarely exercised in burial grounds not belonging to the church, and indeed the faculty jurisdiction is generally exercised sparingly in relation to municipal cemeteries.[26]

It should be noted that the tide is turning against the use of individual plaques (especially at ground level) for cremated remains. The use of a single wall plaque, or a limited number of monuments or a Book of Commemoration in the church are now being favoured.[26a] A Book of Commemoration could include parishioners who had donated their body to medical research or whose body had not been recovered, for example, because they had been lost at sea.

11.56   Faculties are often required for the re-ordering of churchyards requiring the movement of monuments and tombstones. *Re St James' Heywood*[27] sets out many of the considerations to be borne in mind. As we saw in Chapter 8 memorials and tombstones are privately owned and cannot, prima facie, be interfered with without the consent of their owners. However, in certain circumstances an order for removal, demolition, alteration or other work may be made without such consent or where reasonable efforts to trace the owner have failed, notwithstanding that a faculty was originally granted giving the right to erect the monument.[28] A faculty for such removal will not be granted where the owner satisfies the court that within a reasonable time they are able to remove it themselves and effect any consequential repairs to other property which the court may require to be carried out as a result of such removal.[29]

The criminal jurisdiction

11.57   "Criminal suit" in the ecclesiastical courts refers to proceedings in which a person is charged with an offence against the laws ecclesiastical. Although those proceedings are similar to the trial of a criminal charge in the secular courts, the many offences against the ecclesiastical laws are not "criminal" in the usual sense, and for this reason the term disciplinary proceedings is perhaps to be preferred. The exercise of this jurisdiction by the ecclesiastical courts has traditionally been justified on the basis that it is good for the soul.[30]

---

[25] See, *e.g. St Mark's Haydock (No. 2)* [1981] 1 W.L.R. 1167.

[26] *Re West Norwood Cemetery* [1994] 3 W.L.R. 820. *Re Cosgrove* (1996) (unreported) 4 Ecc. L.J. 607 suggests that the powers of the consistory court under CCEJM, section 13 to issue injunctions may not be exerciseable where the default occurs in a burial ground managed by a local authority. However, the case was complicated by the fact that the breach was of a pre-existing contractual reservation not a reservation by faculty.

[26a] *Re St Edmund, West Kingsdown* (unreported) (1989) 5 Ecc. L.J. 5. See also Burman and Stapleton, *The Churchyards' Handbook* (3rd ed. 1988) p. 65. A faculty would be required for a Book of Commemoration together with a glass case or lecturn to house or display it.

[27] [1982] 1 W.L.R. 1289.

[28] FJM, s.3.

[29] *ibid.*

[30] Phillimore, *Ecclesiastical Law* (2nd ed.), Vol. 2 pp. 837, 838; *Caudrey's Case* (1591) 5 Co. Rep. 1a at 66.

Proceedings may be instituted under the EJM against an archbishop, a diocesan, suffragan or any other bishop, or a priest or deacon who when the offence was alleged to have been committed held preferment in a diocese or resided there, a diocese for this purpose extending to extra-parochial places including peculiars.[31] Proceedings in respect of a reserved offence may only be instituted if the offence was committed within the provinces of Canterbury and York, but this limitation does not apply to any other offence.[32] The fact that the offence charged in a criminal suit before the ecclesiastical court could also have been the subject of a prosecution in the secular courts does not prevent the ecclesiastical proceedings.[33]

"Offences against the laws ecclesiastical" include statutory offences (under relevant Acts of Parliament or Measures), offences in respect of ecclesiastical matters under the common law, and breaches of post-Reformation canons.[34] All violations of the law and breaches of Canons and other ecclesiastical laws and all diobedience on the part of the clergy to the lawful commands of the bishop constitute an ecclesiastical offence.[35] Many statutory offences have been repealed, but save where a contrary intention appears the repeal does not affect the existence of any corresponding common law offence. The EJM expressly provides that the repeal by it of any Measure under which proceedings could have been taken for an ecclesiastical offence does not prevent proceedings for that offence being taken under the EJM.[36] As we shall see a number of offences remain cognisable under both statutory provisions and the common law.

Offences of doctrine, ritual or ceremonial

The doctrine of the church has been considered in Chapter 9. Heresy,[37] avowing **11.58** blasphemous[38] and impious opinions contrary to the Christian religion,[39] depraving the Book of Common Prayer and maintaining doctrines repugnant to the Thirty-Nine Articles of Religion,[40] are all offences of doctrine, and all appear to

---

[31] EJM, ss.17, 66(3). This extension does not enlarge the jurisdiction of the consistory court: *ibid.*, s.66(4). Further nothing in the EJM authorises proceeding against a holder of an office in a royal peculiar: *ibid.*, s.83(3) which is expressed to be subject to the Ecclesiastical Commissioners Act 1840, s.29, which makes provision in respect of rectories annexed to canonries of Westminster.

[32] EJM, s.15.

[33] *Bishop of Ely v. Close* [1913] P. 184 at 194, 195.

[34] *Halsbury's Laws of England* (4th ed.), Vol. 14, para. 1352; *Matthew v. Burdett* (1703) 2 Salk. 412; *Bishop of Exeter v. Marshall* (1868) L.R. 3 H.L. 17 at 47, 54; *Bannister v. Thompson* [1908] P. 362 at 385.

[35] *Halsbury's Laws of England* (4th ed.) Vol. 14, para. 1353; Ayliffe, *Parergon Juris Canonici Anglicani* (2nd ed. 1734), p. 208; Goldolphin *Repertorium Canonicum* (3rd ed. 1687) at pp. 306, 307; *Rugg v. Bishop of Winchester* (1868) L.R. 2 P.C. 223 at 235; *Coombe v. De la Bere* (1881) 6 P.D. 157.

[36] EJM, s.14(2).

[37] *Williams v. Bishop of Salisbury* (1864) 2 Moore PCCNS 375.

[38] As to this being an offence in secular courts see Chap. 12.

[39] *Bland v. Archdeacon of Cheltenham* [1972] Fam. 157 at 165.

[40] The term being used in the archaic sense of vilifying, defaming or treating with contempt.

be still cognisable at common law, notwithstanding the repeal of various relevant enactments.[41]

Heresy is the holding of a false opinion repugnant to some point of doctrine clearly revealed in scripture, either essential to or of high importance to the Christian faith.[42] As a matter of law heresy is that which prior to 1559 was adjudged heretical by authority of the canonical scriptures, or by any of the first four General Councils, or was declared such by any other General Council by express word of the canonical scriptures, or which since 1559 may have been, or may be determined by Parliament with the assent of the clergy in Convocation to have been, considered as heresy.[43] The articles charging heresy must state clearly the obnoxious opinions and the exact terms in which it is said they were uttered or published.[44] Many matters of doctrine are open to every member of the Church to decide for themselves according to conscientious opinion, these not having been decided by the Church of England.[45]

In considering cases of depravity in regard to the Book of Common Prayer and maintaining doctrines repugnant to the Thirty-Nine Articles the courts generally exercise a degree of latitude. That latitude may also be seen in recent legislation, which provides for the protection of "essential" Church doctrine.[46] It may well be that cases upon such matters, which generally relate to earlier enactments, are now inapplicable in the context of the modern legislative framework and in a theological environment which recognises that the questioning and creative process is a necessary part of Christian discipleship.[47] The prosecution of a minister for such offences would now appear to be only a remote possibilty.[48]

Ritual and ceremonial was also considered in Chapter 9. As with matters of doctrine although the statutory offences have been largely repealed, offences of ritual and ceremonial remain cognisable under the common law. Illegal ceremonial practices and the use of illegal ornaments could constitute an ecclesiastical offence, as could contravention of the law relating to conformity of worship, but again in practice the prospect of such a prosecution is remote.

[41] *Halsbury's Laws of England* (4th ed.), Vol. 14, para. 1354.
[42] *Burn's Ecclesiastical Law* (14th ed.), Vol. 2, pp. 304, 305; Ayliffe, *Parergon Juris Canonici Anglicani* (2nd ed. 1734) p. 288.
[43] Act of Supremacy 1558, s.20 (repealed) with a saving for any principle or rule of law or equity affirmed, recognised or delivered by, in or from any enactment thereby repealed: Statute Law Revision Act 1863, s.1.
[44] *Williams v. Bishop of Salisbury (ante)*.
[45] *Goreham v. Bishop of Exeter* (1850) Moore's Special Report 462, P.C.
[46] Church of England (Worship and Doctrine) measure 1974, s.4.
[47] *The Nature of Christian Belief* a Statement and Exposition by the House of Bishops (1986); Doe, "Obedience to Doctrine in Canon Law" (1992) Denning L.J. 23.
[48] Despite reports to the contrary in the press this position is actually confirmed by the recent case of the Reverend Anthony Freeman, the former part-time priest-in-charge of Stapleford in the diocese of Chichester, who published a book in which he was alleged to have cast doubt upon the objective reality of God. The Reverend Freeman also held the post of Continuing Ministerial Education Officer for the diocese, a post which it was widely felt that he could not continue in whilst maintaining such views. Since his parochial ministry was only part-time and no other post could be found for him in the diocese to provide him with a full-time stipend, the bishop of Chichester revoked the Reverend Freeman's licence. However, there was no question of a prosecution in regard to a doctrinal offence nor was it suggested that the Reverend Freeman could not have remained simply as priest-in-charge had he been in a parish where it carried with it a full stipend.

Conduct offences

The two main conduct offences are conduct unbecoming the life and work of a **11.59** clerk in holy orders and neglect of duty. Unlawful trading,[49] failure to reside on the benefice and simony[50] have been considered in earlier chapters. It is also an offence for which proceedings may be taken under the EJM for a bishop to act in contravention of a declaration, and for a bishop, priest or deacon to act in contravention of a resolution, made pursuant to the Priests (Ordination of Women) Measure 1993.[51]

A clerk in holy orders may commit an ecclesiastical offence by making any alteration to the fabric, fittings or ornaments of a church or churchyard without a faculty,[52] an offence for which they could be censured by monition. An incumbent, and no doubt a priest-in-charge, who prevents the churchwardens entering the church to care for it, also commits an offence.[53]

Officiating without permission is an ecclesiastical offence. The offence is committed if a clerk officiates in a diocese without the licence of the bishop[54] or in a parish without the incumbent's consent, save in those limited exceptions which the law permits.[55] An offence is also committed if a clerk in holy orders performs any function which, by virtue of a censure pronounced upon them pursuant to the EJM, they are disqualified from performing.[56] A priest or deacon who sought to assume to exercise the episcopal function of ordination would commit an offence.[57]

An overseas minister commits an offence, for which proceedings may be taken under the EJM, if they officiate as a priest or deacon within the provinces of Canterbury or York without the permission of the archbishop.[58] Any minister who knowingly allows such a overseas minister to officiate in any church in their charge also commits an offence. Similarly it is an offence for an overseas bishop to perform any episcopal function in a diocese within the two provinces unless he has either the commission of the diocesan bishop or the consent and licence of the relevant archbishop.[59]

---

[49] See Chap. 7.

[50] See Chap. 5.

[51] Priests (Ordination of Women) Measure 1993, s.5. See also Chap. 7.

[52] *St Pancras Vestry v. Vicar & Churchwardens of St Martin's-in-the-Fields* (1860) 6 Jur. N.S. 540; *Lee v. Vicar & Churchwardens of Herne* (1892) Trist. 217. The more usual course would to seek costs and expenses from such a person who would have committed a trespass; as to which see earlier in this chapter.

[53] *Bellars v. Geast* (1741) *Rotheray's Precedents* No. 157, p. 77.

[54] *Colfatt v. Newcombe* (1705) 2 Ld. Raym. 1250; *Smith v. Lovegrove* (1755) 2 Lee 162; *Barnes v. Shore* (1846) 8 Q.B. 640; *Nesbitt v. Wallace* [1901] P. 354. See also Chap. 7.

[55] *Richards v. Fincher* (1873) L.R. 4, A. & E. 107; *Wood v. Headingly-cum-Burley Burial Board* [1892] 1 Q.B. 713 at 729; *Nesbitt v. Wallace* [1901] P. 354; See also Chap. 5.

[56] EJM, s.5; *Nesbitt v. Wallace (supra)*.

[57] *Bishop of St Albans v. Fillingham* [1906] P. 163.

[58] Overseas and Other Clergy (Ministry and Ordination) Measure 1967, s.1(6). See also Chap. 12.

[59] *ibid.*, s.4(3).

Conduct unbecoming and neglect of duty

11.60   Conduct unbecoming the office and work of a clerk in holy orders and serious, persistent, or continuous neglect of duty are both offences expressly recognised by section 14(1)(b) of the EJM. It is expressly provided that as regards either offence no proceedings are to be taken against a person in respect of their political opinions. Conduct unbecoming is not defined. It is presumed to cover contraventions of the Canons as to the life of the clergy,[60] but all conduct prescribed by general ecclesiastical law would seem to be encompassed.[61] However, if such conduct is itself an ecclesiastical offence it appears that it should be specifically charged as such rather than as conduct unbecoming.[62] Modern Canons are less specific than those of 1603, but the general intention to prohibit all immoral, dishonest or improper conduct is still apparent. Acts which have been held to constitute the offence include drunkeness,[63] habitual swearing and ribaldry,[64] writing a rude letter to a parishioner,[65] collection of alms on false pretences,[66] taking and demanding exorbitant fees[67] and lewd and indecent conduct, adultery, fornication and incontinence.[68]

Neglect of duty is taken to mean the failure without due cause to perform an ecclesiastical duty,[69] and thus would appear to relate almost entirely to those with preferments to which such duties are attached.[70] The duties, and thus potential failures, are wide ranging, although many of the reported cases relate to failures to perform the offices or administer the sacraments.[71] Again if the failure is itself an ecclesiastical offence it should be charged as such.[72] Such a failure must be serious, persistent or continuous.[73] Neglect does not mean negligence and neglect of duty does not mean breach of a duty of care, although absence of negligence or showing good cause for the action taken, such as making diligent enquires of parties to a marriage, may be a defence.[74] However, in the absence of just cause being shown the court will infer that there was no such excuse.[75] It should be noted that a conscientious objection to perform the duty is not a defence unless there is express legal provision for this,[76] such as that in regard to the marriage of divorced persons.

[60] As to which see Chap. 7.
[61] *Bishop of Ely v. Close* [1913] P. 184 at 193.
[62] *Bland v. Archbishop of Cheltenham* [1972] Fam. 157.
[63] *Burder v. Speer* (1841) 1 Notes of Cases 39; *Bishop of Rochester v. Harris* [1893] P. 137.
[64] *Moore v. Bishop of Oxford* [1904] A.C. 283, P.C.
[65] *Bland v. Archbishop of Cheltenham* [1972] Fam. 167.
[66] *Fitzmaurice v. Hesketh* [1904] A.C. 266, P.C.
[67] *Burgoyne v. Free* (1829) 2 Hag. Ecc. 456 affd. *sub nom. Free v. Burgoyne* (1830) 2 Hag. Ecc. 662.
[68] *Kitson v. Loftus* (1845) 4 Notes of Cases 323.
[69] *Bland v. Archbishop of Cheltenham* [1972] Fam. 167.
[70] As to which see Chaps. 5 and 7.
[71] In the case of marriage there may also be an offence against the secular laws.
[72] *Bland v. Archbishop of Cheltham* [1972] Fam. 167.
[73] *ibid.*
[74] *Nicholson v. Squire* (1809) 16 Ves. 259.
[75] *Bennett v. Bonaker* (1830) 3 Hag. Ecc. 17 at 39.
[76] *Bland v. Archbishop of Cheltenham* (*ante*) citing the unreported case of *Watkins-Grubb v. Hilder* (1965).

Procedure in respect of deacons and priests

The Ecclesiastical Jurisdiction (Discipline) Rules 1964[77] regulate disciplinary **11.61** proceedings. The Rules provide for the forms to be used and set out prescribed forms in the Appendix. They also contain detailed provisions for service of documents (including personal service, and where this is impracticable substituted service) and the calculation of time. Proceedings are not rendered void by non-compliance with the Rules, unless the court or commission before whom the proceedings are pending so directs.[78] However, the tribunal may set the proceedings aside as being irregular, either wholly or in part, or may direct that they be amended or otherwise dealt with in such manner and on such terms as the court thinks fit.[79]

Proceedings against a priest or deacon charging an offence under the EJM are instituted by way of complaint laid before the registrar of the relevant diocese.[80] The complaint may only be made by certain persons. These must be an authorised complainant (that is a person authorised by the bishop to lay a complaint under the relevant provisions of the EJM), or in the case of an incumbent of a parochial benefice, or a stipendary curate licensed to such a benefice (which would include a priest-in-charge) or a curate-in-charge of a conventional district, by six or more persons of full age whose names are on the electoral roll of the parish.[81]

Proceedings may not be instituted unless the act or omission alleged to constitute the offence (or the last such if a series) occurred within three years ending on the day on which the complaint is laid.[82] However, in the case of an offence for which the accused has been convicted in the secular courts, whether on indictment or summarily, the complaint may be laid within six months of the conviction becoming conclusive, notwithstanding that the three years have elapsed.[83]

Within 28 days of a complaint being made the complainant must serve personally upon the accused a copy of the complaint together with a supporting affidavit.[84] The accused must then complete forms as to their address for service.[85] A priest or deacon against whom proceedings are pending may be inhibited (known as inhibition *pendente lite*) by the diocesan bishop from performing any services of the church.[86] Although it has many common features, the procedure which then follows differs depending upon whether the complaint concerns a reserved or conduct matter.

---

[77] S.I. 1964 No. 1755.
[78] Ecclesiastical Jurisdiction (Discipline) Rules 1964, r. 65. For the purposes of this rule all proceedings before trial are deemed to be pending in the trial court or commission.
[79] *ibid.*
[80] EJM, s.18(1).
[81] *ibid.*, s.19.
[82] *ibid.*, s.16.
[83] *ibid.*
[84] *ibid.*, s.18(3); Ecclesiastical Jurisdiction (Discipline) Rules 1964, r. 4(1), (2).
[85] EJM, *ibid.*, r. 4(3).
[86] EJM, s.77. As to inhibition generally see below.

Interview

11.62 As soon as possible after the laying of the complaint the bishop must afford the accused and complainant the opportunity of a private interview, and may thereafter decide that no further step should be taken with regard to the matter of the complaint, in which case he notifies the parties and the registrar accordingly.[87] Although efforts are therefore made to deal with pastoral problems without recourse to litigation, the bishop may nonetheless decide that the appropriate course is to refer the complaint for inquiry by an examiner, and notify the registrar accordingly.[88]

In a conduct case it is also open to the bishop on the application of the accused, and after consultation with the complainant, to pronounce a censure[89] upon the accused, which precludes any further steps being taken.[90] If the bishop decides not to pronounce censure his decision must be notified in writing to the parties and recorded in the district registry, and if he decides to do so the censure must be reduced to writing and the parties given notice of the date and time of pronouncement, although only the registrar is obliged to attend.[91]

Inquiry

11.63 Where the complaint is referred an inquiry must be held to determine if the accused has a case to answer.[92] In a conduct case the inquiry is conducted by an examiner selected by ballot from a panel appointed by the diocesan synod,[93] and in a reserved case it is conducted by a committee of the relevant convocation.[94] The parties (that is complainant and accused) may be represented by friends or advisers before any inquiry or meeting of the committee which they are asked to attend.[95]

Evidence before an inquiry or committee is given by affidavit.[96] However, a deponent may be requested by the examiner or committee to give oral evidence on oath and must also do so if an application is made by either party to this effect.[97] The complainant must lodge originals and copies of their affidavits with the registrar and must give notice of those witnessses whom they intend to call to give oral evidence.[98] Copies of these are served personally on the accused who then lodges their own affidavits and a list of those to be called to give oral evidence on their behalf.[99] Without the leave of the registrar no further evidence

---

[87] *ibid.*, ss.23, 39.
[88] EJM, ss.23, 39.
[89] As to censure see below.
[90] EJM. s.31. The application must state the extent to which the accused admits the offence and the allegations contained in the complaint.
[91] Ecclesiastical Jurisdiction (Discipline) Rules 1964, r. 11.
[92] EJM, ss.24(1), 42(2).
[93] *ibid.*, ss.23(1)(b); 30, Sched. 2, Pt. 1.
[94] *ibid.*, s.42(2), (3).
[95] *ibid.*, ss.24(2), 42(4).
[96] *ibid.*, ss.24(3), 42(5).
[97] *ibid.*, ss.23(3), 42(5).
[98] Ecclesiastical Jurisdiction (Discipline) Rules 1964, rr. 7(1). 30(2).
[99] *ibid.* rr. 7(3), 30(3).

can be laid before the inquiry or committee.[1] The registrar must give 14 days' notice of the date of the inquiry, and since this must (unless postponed) take place within 28 days of the examiner or committee being selected,[2] this allows only 14 days for the exchange of evidence.

The inquiry or committee may decide there is no case to answer, in which case it announces its decision and no further steps may be taken.[3] If it decides there is a case to answer the offence must be specified,[4] and a person nominated to promote the complaint.[5] However, the committee which considers reserved cases has an additional power to dismiss the complaint (after considering the evidence and any statement of the accused and any representations by their bishop).[6] It may do this where it is of the opinion that the offence charged is too trivial to warrant further proceedings, or was committed under extenuating circumstances, or that further proceedings would not be in the interests of the Church of England.[7] Given the committee's wide discretion to dismiss a complaint, particularly on the last of these grounds, and given also the general theological tolerance which is now exhibited by the Church in matters of doctrine, a prosecution in a reserved case is likely to be pursued only as a measure of last resort. In cases where the committee dismisses the complaint it must notify Convocation, and no further steps may be taken in connection with the offence.[8]

Interlocutory applications

Applications made to a registrar before trial (including those made before the completion of an inquiry) are known as interlocutory applications. They must be made in writing, lodged with the registrar and a copy served on the other party.[9] Unless the written consent of that other party is lodged as well, or the registrar is satisfied that party does not object, or unless the Disciplinary Rules provide otherwise in respect of the particular application, a hearing must be fixed at which both parties are entitled to attend.[10] At such a hearing either party may appear or be represented by a friend or adviser, or if the inquiry is concluded by counsel or a solicitor.[11] A person required to perform an act in the proceedings within a specified time may apply to the registrar for an abridgment or for an extension of time, notwithstanding that in the latter case the time may already have expired.[12] All applications, including those referred to below, to the trial court, may be granted on such terms as the person or body granting them considers just.[13] Either party has a right of appeal against the decision of the

11.64

---

[1] *ibid* rr. 7(4), 30(4).
[2] *ibid.*, rr. 8, 31. Either party may apply to the registrar for postponement of the hearing.
[3] EJM, ss.24(5), 42(8), (10).
[4] *ibid.*, ss.24(4), 42(6).
[5] *ibid.*, ss.25, 43. The promotor has the right to promote to the exclusion of all others: *ibid.*, s.70.
[6] *ibid.*, s.42(7), (10).
[7] EJM, s.42(7), (10).
[8] *ibid.*, s.42(7), (10).
[9] Ecclesiastical Jurisdiction (Discipline) Rules 1964, r. 60(1), (2).
[10] Ecclesiastical Jurisdiction (Discipline) Rules 1964, r. 60(3), (4).
[11] *ibid.*, r. 61.
[12] *ibid.*, r. 63.
[13] Ecclesiastical Jurisdiction (Discipline) Rules 1964, r. 60(5).

registrar, either to the trial judge, or if the application was made before the conclusion of the inquiry, to the examiner or committee.[14]

By means of this application procedure either party may apply to the registrar or to the court of trial for orders in respect of documents or witnesses. Thus an order may be made for production of documents for inspection pre-trial, or at the trial, or for the attendance of witnesses.[15] The trial court may also make such orders of its own motion.

Pre-trial matters

11.65 Within 28 days of their nomination the promoter must lodge articles charging the offence or offences with the registrar and serve these personally on the accused.[16] The promoter can apply to the examiner, committee or to the court where the trial is to be held, for leave to include particulars of any offence disclosed by the evidence before the inquiry or committee, either in substitution for or in addition to the particulars of the offences specified,[17] in which case time for service may be extended. The articles must allege all facts required to constitute the offence.[18]

The accused has 14 days after service upon them in which they may lodge an "answer" with the registrar and serve a copy of this on the complainant.[19] An answer must admit or deny each offence, and may also admit or deny or give the accused's account or explanation of the facts alleged to constitute each offence.

Trial

11.66 The trial takes place within 28 days of the lodging of articles, although it may be postponed by either party or by the trial judge.[20-21] The procedure is as close as possible to that of a trial conducted by the Crown Court exercising criminal jurisdiction.[22] If the accused is to be convicted each offence must be proved beyond reasonable doubt.

In a conduct case the chancellor or substitute judge sits in the consistory court with four assessors[23] chosen by ballot from a panel. The chancellor or judge has the functions of a judge of the Crown Court exercising criminal jurisdiction, whilst the assessors have the same function as a jury in the Crown Court.[24] The

---

[14] *ibid* r. 60(6).
[15] *ibid.*, r. 62.
[16] *ibid.*, rr. 12(1), 34(1).
[17] *ibid.*, rr. 12(2), (3), 34(2), (3). As to the hearing of such an application and if leave is refused see *ibid.* rr. 12, 34.
[18] *Bland v. Archdeacon of Cheltenham* [1972] Fam. 157 at 168.
[19] Ecclesiastical Jurisdiction (Discipline) Rules 1964, rr. 13, 35.
[20-21] *ibid.*, rr. 14, 36.
[22] EJM, ss.28(a), 45(1)(a).
[23] The practice of disclosing the name of the accused and witnesses to the assessors and asking for the details of the nature and extent of their acquaintance with the acused so that the chancellor may decide if this is such as would disqualify the assessors has been commended in *Burridge v. Taylor* [1992] 1 All E.R. 437.
[24] EJM, s.28(e). The Crown Court replaces the former Court of Assize. As to the role of assessors see also *Bland v. Archdeacon of Cheltenham* [1972] Fam. 157 at 163, 169.

assessors must be unanimous,[25] and if they cannot agree the chancellor may discharge them.[26] The chancellor must then consider within 14 days, after such consultation with the parties and their representatives as may be appropriate, whether to order a re-trial or to pronounce the accused acquitted.[27]

In a reserved case the Court of Ecclesiastical Causes Reserved sits with advisers, the decision being according to the opinion of the majority of the court.[28]

The trial court may allow the promoter to withdraw charges or amend articles (but not so as to charge a new offence), and the accused to put in or amend answers on such terms as it considers just.[29] If the accused admits an offence or any act or omission alleged the court may treat it as proved and dispense with evidence of it.[30] The rules regarding the admissibility of evidence and as to whether a witness is competent or compellable are the same as in a Crown Court exercising criminal jurisdiction.[31] Evidence is given orally in open court, unless a witness is permitted to make a deposition because of ill health.[32] The court has the power to direct that any person or class of persons be excluded during any part of the proceedings in the interests of justice.[33] This includes the assessors in a case before the consistory court,[34] their position being akin to a jury excluded from certain parts of a trial in the Crown Court. It would also extend to the press.

If the accused is found guilty the court must decide the censure, which must be reduced to writing and pronounced in open court, although this need not occur in the presence of the accused.[35]

Appeals

If an appeal is lodged against a judgment, order or decree of the court in proceedings charging an offence or claiming a penalty or forfeiture against a priest or deacon, the censure or award of the court is suspended until the appeal is determined.[36] However, this does not apply to an inhibition *pendente lite*. **11.67**

An appeal lies from the consistory court to the Court of the Arches or Chancery Court, at the instance of either party on a question of law and the accused on a question of fact.[37]

The appellant must lodge six copies of the notice of appeal with the registrar of the appellate court (and lodge a copy with the diocesan registrar and serve a copy on the other party) within 28 days of the decision of the consistory court.[38]

---

[25] EJM, s.28(e).
[26] EJM, s.29.
[27] *ibid.*
[28] *ibid.*, s.45(1)(f).
[29] Ecclesiastical Jurisdiction (Discipline) Rules 1964, rr. 16, 37(1).
[30] Ecclesiastical Jurisdiction (Discipline) Rules 1964, rr. 16(4), 37(4).
[31] EJM, ss.28(c), 45(1)(c).
[32] Ecclesiastical Jurisdiction (Discipline) Rules 1964, rr. 17, 38.
[33] EJM, ss.28(f), 45(1)(e).
[34] *ibid.*
[35] *ibid.*, ss.28(g), (h), 45(1)(g), (h).
[36] *ibid.*, s.73.
[37] *ibid.*, s.7.
[38] Ecclesiastical Jurisdiction (Discipline) Rules 1964, r. 39.

The notice must state the grounds of appeal, and if only part of the judgment is appealed state which part, and unless leave is granted by the appellate court the appellant is not entitled to rely upon any other grounds.[39]

If the accused appeals on a question of fact the judge's notes and all documents and exhibits used in the consistory court must be available.[40] The court may require or allow all documents or exhibits produced at trial to be produced before it, and it may also require or allow a shorthand note of the proceedings of the consistory court to be used.[41] It may also require or allow all witnesses who gave evidence before the consistory court to give evidence before it or an examiner.[42] In exceptional circumstances new witnesses may be required or allowed to give evidence. On an appeal on a question of law the same provisions apply to the extent that the court considers necessary for the purpose of examining any matter of fact relevant to the determination of that question.[43]

The court determines the question raised by the appeal by a majority opinion of all the judges.[44] It may thereupon confirm, reverse or vary any finding of the consistory court appealed from, or remit the case to the consistory court with its determination for the consistory court to take such proceedings as it directs.[45] Any remitted proceedings continue as the original trial. The appellate court may vary a censure, or impose a censure for any offence in respect of which it confirms, varies or makes a finding of guilt, or remit the decision as to censure to the consistory court.[46]

The accused in a reserved case before the Court of Ecclesiastical Causes Reserved may petition the Queen for a review of the finding on a question of fact, and either party may petition on a question of law.[47] The petition must state the grounds of appeal and must, where the judgment comprised findings in respect of two or more offences, specify the findings appealed.[48] The Clerk of the Crown in Chancery must then appoint a registrar of the commission which will hear the appeal.[49]

The same rules as to judge's notes, shorthand notes, exhibits, documents and witnesses, considered above in relation to an appeal from the consistory court, would apply.[50] The commission must determine the questions before it, judgment being that of the majority, although each member must state their opinions.[51] Thereupon it could confirm, reverse, or vary the finding or remit the case, and on making a finding of guilt vary or impose a censure or remit the decision to the trial court.[52]

---

[39] *ibid.*, r. 39(4). Appeals may be withdrawn or amended *ibid.*, r. 40.
[40] *ibid.*, r. 42.
[41] *ibid.*, r. 42.
[42] *ibid.*, r. 42.
[43] *ibid.*, r. 42.
[44] EJM, s.47(1).
[45] Ecclesiastical Jurisdiction (Discipline) Rules 1964, r. 43.
[46] Ecclesiastical Jurisdiction (Discipline) Rules 1964, r. 43.
[47] EJM, s.11(2)(a).
[48] Ecclesiastical Jurisdiction (Discipline) Rules 1964, r. 44.
[49] Ecclesiastical Jurisdiction (Discipline) Rules 1964, r. 44.
[50] *ibid.*, r. 47.
[51] EJM, s.48(4).
[52] Ecclesiastical Jurisdiction (Discipline) Rules 1964, r.48.

Procedure in respect of bishops and archbishops

A somewhat different procedure operates in regard to a criminal charge against a   **11.68**
bishop or archbishop. Whereas the Lords Temporal have lost the right to be tried
by their fellow peers, trial of the Lords Spiritual in the ecclesiastical courts occurs
pursuant to special provisions, differentiating them from priests and deacons.

Briefly the differences between these proceedings and those against priests and
deacons are as follows. The complaint is laid before the registrar of the relevant
province instead of the diocesan registrar.[53] Thereafter an interview is held by the
archbishop in the case of a bishop accused of a reserved offence.[54] A complaint
against a bishop in a conduct case and any complaint against an archbishop are
automatically referred for inquiry.[55] In a conduct case the inquiry is conducted by
an episcopal committee assisted by a legal assessor, and in a reserved case by a
committee of Convocation, with a different constitution to that required for a
priest or deacon.[56] If there is a case to answer a conduct trial is conducted by a
commission of Convocation and a reserved case by the Court of Ecclesiastical
Causes Reserved.[57] Determination by either body or court is according to the
opinion of the majority of its members.[58] In a conduct case the court must reduce
its findings to writing, publish it to the accused and such other persons as it
considers should have notice and send a copy to the relevant (or in the case of an
archbishop the other) archbishop.[59] Where the accused is an archbishop the
finding is to be laid before a joint meeting of the Upper Houses of both
Convocations, which must determine the censure to be pronounced by the other
archbishop where the finding is one of guilt.[60] In the case of a bishop the finding
is laid before the Upper House of the relevant Convocation which determines
the censure to be pronounced by the archbishop where the finding is one of
guilt.[61]

Censures

Five censures may be pronounced against a person found guilty of an offence   **11.69**
under the EJM: deprivation, inhibition, suspension, monition and rebuke.[62] In
general only one censure may be pronounced, although inhibition may be
pronounced for the same period as suspension.[63] The court has the power to
accept the accused's assurance of future submission and not to pronounce a
censure where it is satisfied that the offence will not be repeated.[64] However,

[53] EJM, s.18(1).
[54] *ibid*., s.40.
[55] *ibid*., ss.33(2), 41,
[56] *ibid*., ss.33(2), (3), (4), 42(2), (3)(b).
[57] *ibid*., ss.9, 10(1)(a)(ii), 32, 38.
[58] *ibid*., ss.36(g), 45(1)(f).
[59] *ibid*., s.36(h).
[60] *ibid*., s.37(1).
[61] *ibid*., s.37(2).
[62] *ibid*., s.49(1).
[63] *ibid*., s.49(6).
[64] *Read v. Bishop of Lincoln* [1892] A.C. 644 at 669, P.C.

normally a censure will be pronounced following a finding of guilt, although the court has discretion as to its leniency in the absence of express enactment.[65] The court acts in a judicial not a pastoral capacity, with the effect that the paramount consideration is the gravity of the offence rather than the good of the parish.[66] However, the court may take into account all relevant considerations, and in cases where the gravity of the offence warrants deprivation this would include considering the interests of the parish.[67] Certain convictions, orders and findings of the secular courts which are considered below may also render a clerk in holy orders subject to ecclesiastical censure without further trial.

Deprivation

11.70   Deprivation is the removal from any preferment or preferments and the disqualification from holding any other preferment in the future, save on certain conditions.[68] In the case of bishop, priest or deacon the disqualification does not extend to a preferment to which a diocesan bishop subsequently appoints them with the consent of the relevant archbishop and, in the case of a priest or deacon, with the additional consent of the bishop of the diocese in which the proceedings were instituted.[69] The disqualification itself may cease if the archbishop so directs when consenting to such an appointment.[70]

Deprivation cannot be imposed for a reserved offence unless the court is satisfied that the accused has been admonished on a previous occasion in respect of another offence of the same, or substanially the same, nature.[71] The sentence should only be pronounced if warranted by the gravity of the offence, not passed simply in order to remove an incumbent from a parish however desirable such a course might be pastorally.[72] It should be noted that deprivation does not render void any spiritual act which is carried out by a deprived cleric.[73]

Deprivation following secular proceedings

11.71   A priest or deacon,[74] bishop or archbishop,[75] is liable to deprivation without further trial if convicted of an offence in the secular courts and a sentence of imprisonment (whether or not suspended) is passed.[76] They are also to liable on

[65] *ibid*; Martin v. Mackonochie (1882) 7 P.D. 94 at 99, P.C.
[66] *Coombe v. De la Bere* (1881) 6 P.D. 157 at 169; *Bland v. Archdeacon of Cheltenham* [1972] Fam. 157 at 171.
[67] *ibid*.
[68] In the case of an archbishop, bishop or any preferment other than a parochial benefice where the right to appoint vests in the Sovereign, the sentence only has effect if confirmed by Order in Council.
[69] EJM, s.49(5).
[70] EJM, s.49(5).
[71] *ibid*., s.49(3).
[72] *Bland v. Archdeacon of Cheltenham* (*ante*).
[73] *Costard v. Winder* (1600) Cro. Eliz. 775.
[74] EJM, s.55.
[75] *ibid*., s.56.
[76] Suspended sentence is defined in *ibid*., s.55(7). The Criminal Justice Act 1967, s.39(1) was repealed and replaced by the Power of the Criminal Courts Act 1967, s.22(1), which now applies to the EJM by virtue of the Interpretation Act 1978.

the making of certain orders in matrimonial and other family proceedings in the secular courts. In the case of divorce where the decree has been made absolute, or a judicial separation, relevant findings are that the spouse was entitled to rely upon adultery, unreasonable behaviour or desertion.[77] Relevant orders are a matrimonial order made against them by a magistrates court,[78] or an order made against them on the grounds of wilful neglect to maintain their spouse, or a child of the family or an affiliation order.[79]

The court in which the conviction, or order was obtained or made must cause a certificate, which is signed by the registrar, clerk or other proper officer of the court, to be sent to the bishop of the diocese in which it sits.[80] In an ecclesiatical court the certificate is conclusive proof that the act specified has been committed by the person to whom it relates.[81]

The clerk in holy orders is liable to deprivation from any preferment held or from holding preferment from the date the conviction, decree, order or finding becomes conclusive, although this is again subject to the bishop's right which was discussed above to make such a future appointment. A conviction, order or decree from which there is no appeal becomes conclusive on the date it is made. Where a conviction, order or decree is subject to appeal and an appeal is made, it becomes conclusive on the date when the appeal is dismissed, or abandoned or proceedings finally concluded; where no appeal is made it becomes conclusive on the date when the time limit for appealing expires, or where no time limit is specified, two months from the date of the conviction, order or decree.[82]

Once the conviction, decree, order or finding becomes conclusive the diocesan bishop must refer the matter to the relevant archbishop with his own recommendations as to the action to be taken and a copy of any written representations which the priest or deacon has made to him.[83] Unless on considering all the circumstances, including the bishop's recommendations and the minister's own written representations, the archbishop determines that no such declaration should be made he must make a declaration of deprivation and disqualification.[84] However, no declaration may be made after the expiry of three years from the date the conviction, decree, order or finding becomes conclusive.[85]

A declaration can be made by the archbishop, bishop or his commissary, but in any case the provincial or diocesan registrar should if practicable give the

---

[77] They would also be liable to deprivation where, in the case of a divorce where the decree has been made absolute, or a judicial separation, the spouse is found to be entitled to rely upon adultery, unreasonable behaviour or desertion, or where there is a finding in a matrimonial cause that they have committed adultery. However, under the Family Law Act 1996 it is no longer necessary to allege "fault" in order to establish the irretrievable breakdown of a marriage, so that a finding of adultery, unreasonable behaviour or desertion will not be established by the secular courts in any matrimonial proceedings.
[78] *i.e.* under the Domestic Proceedings and Magistrates' Courts Act 1978, s.2.
[79] *i.e.* under the Matrimonial Causes Act 1973, s.27.
[80] EJM, s.79. the certificate must be preserved in that or another diocesan registry, at the bishop's direction: *ibid.*
[81] *ibid.*
[82] EJM, s.79(1).
[83] *ibid.*, s.55(2).
[84] *ibid.*, s.55(3).
[85] *ibid.*, s.55(3A).

minister not less than 14 days notice of the time and place where it will be made, so that they have an opportunity to be present.[86] If no sentence is to be pronounced the archbishop informs the minister and the bishop of his decision.[87] A bishop or archbishop against whom a conviction, decree, order or finding as set out above is made is also liable to deprivation and disqualification, the procedures being put into effect by the relevant archbishop.[88]

Where a sentence of deprivation or disqualification is made under these provisions it takes effect subject to the provisions of the EJM relating to censures.[89] Accordingly the same consequences ensue as if the deacon, priest, bishop or archbishop had been found guilty of an offence under that Measure and censure pronounced against them.

Deposition from holy orders

11.72   Where a sentence of deprivation has been pronounced upon a priest or deacon their diocesan bishop may depose them from holy orders by sentence,[90] a process commonly known as unfrocking. No further legal proceedings are required, but the bishop must serve the minister and the diocesan registrar with notice of his intention and the minister has a right of appeal to the archbishop within one month.[91] The bishop must wait until the time for appealing has passed or any appeal dismissed before pronouncing sentence. A bishop or archbishop may only be deposed following deprivation by a resolution of the Upper House of the relevant Convocation.[92] Before so doing the House must notify him and consider any written representations made as well as give him an opportunity to be heard before it personally.

The effect of deposition is the same as if a deed of relinquishment had been executed under the Clerical Disabilities Act 1870,[93] which the bishop had on the day of deposition caused to be registered.[94] However, as we have seen, deposition does not serve to remove the indelible character of the order from which the clerk is deposed.[95]

A free pardon from the Crown operates in both secular and ecclesiastical matters. Accordingly the incapacities of any minister who was deprived or deposed and who receives a free pardon cease, and they will be restored to any preferment previously held if it has not been filled in the meantime.[96]

Inhibition and suspension

11.73   Inhibition is the disqualification of a minister from exercising the functions of their order for a specified period of time.[97] Where a priest or deacon is accused of any offence under the EJM, or in a secular court of any criminal offence or

[86] *ibid.*, s.55(4).
[87] *ibid.*, s.55(3).
[88] *ibid.*, s.56.
[89] *ibid.*, s.57.
[90] *ibid.*, s.50.
[91] Pursuant to the Ecclesiastical Jurisdiction (Discipline) Rules 1964, rr. 49, 50.
[92] EJM, s.51.
[93] See Chap. 7.
[94] EJM, s.52.
[95] See Chap. 7.
[96] *ibid.*, s.53.
[97] *ibid.*, s.49(1)(b).

any act constituting an ecclesiastical offence, the bishop in whose diocese they hold preferment may, at any time during which the proceedings are pending, inhibit them *pendente lite*.[98] The bishop may only do so where he considers that this is desirable in the interests of the Church due to the nature of the offence charged. Where he does consider this to be the case a notice is served upon the minister inhibiting them from performing any services of the Church within the diocese from a specified date until the proceedings are concluded,[99] although this inhibition may be revoked at any time.[1]

As we have seen a censure of inhibition may be pronounced in respect of the same offence and for the same period of time as that for which a censure of suspension is pronounced. However, neither inhibition nor suspension may be pronounced in respect of a reserved offence unless the court is satisfied that the accused has been admonished on a previous occasion in respect of another offence of the same or substantially the same nature.[2]

Suspension is the disqualification for a specified time of a clerk from exercising or performing any right or duty that forms part of, or is incidental, to their preferment, or residing in the house of residence or within such distance thereof as may specified, without leave of the bishop.[3] A bishop or archbishop may also be suspended. In all cases of suspension and inhibition arrangements must be made for the performance of the relevant duties by another clerk. An incumbent inhibited *pendente lite* may nominate such a person, whom the bishop must licence provided he approves them.[4] In all other cases the bishop appoints a person or persons.[5]

A minister inhibited or suspended must not interfere with the person appointed to discharge their duties.[6] Save in a case of inhibition *pendente lite* they must not reside in the house of residence belonging to the office, unless, in the case of an incumbent the bishop permits this for special reasons.[7] However, an incumbent will not be liable for non-residence during this period. No minister may be re-admitted to their benefice or permitted to exercise the functions of their order unless they satisfy the bishop of their good conduct during the period of inhibition or suspension.[8]

Monition

Monition is an order to do or to refrain from doing a specified act.[9] Historically **11.74** monition was considered to be a warning or command which should be followed by a coercive sanction in the case of disobedience, and it appears to have been a

---

[98] *ibid*., s.77(1).
[99] *ibid*., s.77(1).
[1] *ibid*., s.77(4).
[2] *ibid*., s.49(3).
[3] *ibid*., s.49(1)(c).
[4] *ibid*., s.77(2).
[5] *ibid*., ss.71(4)(1), (3), 77(3).
[6] *ibid*., ss.74(1), 77(5).
[7] *ibid*., s.74.
[8] *ibid*., s.49(2).
[9] *ibid*., s.49(1)(d).

general (but not invariable) rule of law that it should precede, suspension or excommunication.[10] Although monition may be the sentence or part sentence pronounced upon the merits at the end of an ecclesiastical cause, it can be issued at the beginning or during proceedings.[11] Its purpose is to prevent the commission or omission of acts which would constitute an ecclesiastical offence or to rectify an act which constituted the commission of such an offence, and it is usually accompanied by an order for costs against the accused.[12]

Rebuke

11.75   Rebuke is not defined,[13] but means precisely what it suggests. The offence is condemned, but there is no disqualification or penalty, although costs may be awarded against the accused.

Excommunication

11.76   Excommunication in the meaning of the law of the English church is not merely expulsion from the Church of England, but from the Christian Church as a whole.[14] Although the ecclesiastical court formerly had the power to pronounce a sentence of excommunication[15] it is no longer amongst the censures which may be pronounced in respect of an offence under the EJM. Nonetheless that Measure itself appears to contemplate the possibility of an extra-judicial excommunication, providing that no person suffering excommunication is to be imprisoned.[16] So also does Article XXXIII of the Thirty-nine Articles of Religion, which provides that a person who is excommunicated is to be taken as a heathen and publican until openly reconciled and received into the Church by a judge who has the authority to do so. Burial according to the rites of the Church of England may be denied to a person declared excommunicate for "some grevious or notorious crime", where there is no evidence of repentence.[17] Such extra-judicial excommunication would extend to the laity and would presumably, in the absence of reconciliation, disqualify them from holding any office for which communicant status of the Church of England is a requirement.

A new procedure for clergy discipline?

11.77   The criminal jurisdiction of the ecclesiastical courts has recently been the subject of review by a working party of the General Synod, which has made various recommendations regarding a completely new system for clergy discipline.[18]

---

[10] Gibson's *Codex Juris Ecclesiastical Anglicani*, (2nd ed. 1761), pp. 1046, 1048; *Mackonochie v. Lord Penzance* (1881) 6 App. Cas. 424 at 433, H.L.; *Enraght v. Lord Penzance* (1882) 7 App. Cas. 240 at 247, H.L.

[11] *ibid.*

[12] *Burn's Ecclesiastical Law* (14th ed. 1842), Vol. 3, p. 191.

[13] EJM, s.49(1)(e).

[14] *Kemp v. Wickes* (1809) 3 Phill. Ecc. R. 264.

[15] As to the history of which see *Report of the Archbishops' Commission of Ecclesiastical Courts* (1954).

[16] EJM, s.82(4).

[17] Canon B38(2).

[18] *Under Authority*, the report of the General Synod Working 14 Party Reviewing Clergy Discipline and the Working of the Ecclesiastical Courts (1996) (GS 1217).

Since the coming into force of the EJM and the writing of the report no disciplinary cases have come before the Court of Ecclesiastical Causes Reserved and only three have reached a trial before the consistory court. In part this is thought to be due to the Church's experience of the current legislation, not least in regard to the high financial costs involved, which had the effect of inhibiting the bringing of proceedings. Although it is envisaged that the new procedure would be more flexible and should be less expensive in individual cases, it is acknowledged that any reduction in the costs of individual cases is likely to be offset by an increased number of cases being brought.

Under the new system, which would apply to all clerks in holy orders,[19] the following would constitute ecclesiastical offences: wilful disobedience to, or breach of, the laws ecclesiastical; neglect, culpable carelessness or gross inefficiency in the performance of the duties of the office; conduct inappropriate to, or unbecoming, the office and work of a clerk in holy orders; teaching, preaching, publishing or professing doctrine or belief incompatible with that of the Church of England as expressed within its formularies; conviction in a secular court of an offence for which a sentence of imprisonment can be imposed. In addition where a cleric is involved in a divorce or judicial separation a review of the circumstances should be made to establish whether there are grounds for invoking the disciplinary process.[20] As no disciplinary proceedings would be taken in respect of the political opinions of a cleric, the committee has recommended the removal of the protection in respect of political activity, so that were a cleric to commit a secular offence or neglect their clerical duties as a consequence of political activity action could be taken.

All disciplinary complaints, whether involving matters of doctrine, ritual or ceremonial or conduct offences, would be dealt with under one procedure, and there would no longer be a separate procedure for bishops and archbishops, (although they would be entitled to a fellow bishop as the clerical member of the new proposed tribunal).

The working party recommends a new independent national forum—the Clergy Discipline Tribunal—for adjudicating all disciplinary complaints, instead of the diocesan consistory courts and the Court of Ecclesiastical Causes Reserved. The tribunal would be under the overall direction of a legally qualified President and administered on a day to day basis by a registrar. In any particular

---

[19] The report expressed concern regarding the circumstances in which the licence of unbeneficed clergy may be withdrawn, and the lack of protection which such clergy enjoy in contrast to those with freehold offices. The working party recommends that the law relating to unbeneficed clergy should be amended so that fixed term licences are no longer revocable on notice. In cases where a cleric continues in office after the expiry of a fixed term three months notice should be given of termination of the appointment and if they continue in office for more than 12 months the licence should become an indefinite one. Licences should generally be for a fixed term but where they are or become indefinite these should not be revocable for disciplinary reasons. The effect of this would be that the church's disciplinary procedures should be followed for unbeneficed clergy as they would be for those with a freehold office.

[20] This is to take account of the fact that under the newly enacted Family Law Act 1996 it is no longer necessary to allege "fault" in order to establish the irretrievable breakdown of a marriage, so that a finding of adultery, unreasonable behaviour or desertion for which a cleric could face automatic depreciation will not be established by the secular courts in any matrimonial proceedings.

case the tribunal would have a legally qualified chairman drawn from an established panel, together with a lay and clerical member also drawn from specially established panels, making three members in total. The chairman would rule on points of law but otherwise decisions would be taken by a majority of the members. In cases of doctrine, ritual or ceremonial, special assessors would be appointed by the House of Bishops to assist the tribunal. The procedures of the tribunal would be governed by Rules and the standard required to convict would be, as now, proof beyond reasonable doubt. In general disciplinary proceedings would be held in private, although the decision would be made public.

Appeals against a decision of the tribunal would be made to the Court of the Arches or Chancery Court, the Dean of the Arches and Auditor hearing the appeal with two tribunal chairmen. Appeals could be made as of right against any penalty imposed, or with leave on a point of law, or where it is alleged that the decision is unreasonable.

The report also recommends the establishment of a new body, the Clergy Discipline Commission, comprised of members of the General Synod, whose function would be to maintain the lay and clergy panels from which members of the tribunal would be drawn and a panel of investigators to advise the bishops and act as a policy and resource body. Prosecutions would be the responsibility of the Legal Services Department (if the proposals of the Turnbull Commission are adopted) or under the auspices of the General Synod. The Legal Services Department would consider cases referred to it, decide whether the allegations disclosed constituted an ecclesiastical offence, appoint an investigator to gather evidence, oversee the investigation, consider the evidence obtained and, if it considers a prosecution justified, issue proceedings and conduct the prosecution.

11.78   The report recommends that bishops be given assistance under the new system in order to reconcile their disciplinary and pastoral roles. At the same time their role in clergy discipline should be reaffirmed, and under the new system the bishop would be involved at an earlier stage and have greater flexibility.

The procedure for making complaints would be simpler; a letter to the diocesan bishop being sufficient. Upon receiving a written complaint (which at that stage would not be a "formal" complaint) the bishop would have four weeks during which he, or a person to whom he delegates the task, would make soundings about the complaint.

The bishop would then take one of four options[21]: dismiss the complaint as vexatious; decide that the complaint although with substance was a minor one and deal with the matter under a minor complaints procedure[22]; because the gravity of the complaint is difficult to assess deal with the matter under the minor complaints procedure unless the seriousness of the complaint becomes more

---

[21] The bishop will also be able to direct that the matter be dealt with under the Incumbents (Vacation of Benefices) Measure 1977 procedures where this is more appropriate. Presumably this would only apply to cases where disciplinary procedures are not appropriate since, as we saw in Chapter 5, these procedures are not to be used as an alternative to disciplinary procedures.

[22] A minor complaints procedure whilst outside the remit of the working party has been suggested at its request by the Clergy Conditions of Service Steering Group, and is set out as Appendix C to *Under Authority*.

obvious; where the complaint is serious[23] invoke the disciplinary processes and invite the complainant to complete an official complaint form.

Once formal proceedings are commenced the bishop would, after investigation, adopt one of four courses of action: to take no further action; refer the matter for conciliation; impose a penalty where the cleric consents to this and decide that the complaint should be prosecuted.

However, the report recommends that the bishop should not have the final veto, as now, as to whether a complaint is prosecuted. Instead, if he decides not to take any formal action in respect of a complaint from an individual or a parish the complainant would have the right to a review of the bishop's decision by the Clergy Discipline Commission which could, if it so decided, refer the matter to the legal department. If the Commission declined to do so then the complainant would have the residual right of bringing a prosecution at their own expense.

The report proposes new censures to be known by the more generally understood term of "penalties", these being removal from office, disqualification, prohibition, injunction, conditional discharge, deferred sentence, rebuke and absolute discharge.

Removal from office would replace deprivation and revocation of a licence and would mean no more than the loss of the current preferment. Removal of itself would allow the cleric to seek an alternative position and would be appropriate in cases where they had simply inadequately met the challenges of the current post, but in more serious cases would be combined with disqualification or prohibition.

Disqualification would prevent the cleric obtaining a new appointment. Prohibition would be either for a specified period of time or an indefinite period, but where an indefinite prohibition of the exercise of orders is imposed the bishop may proceed to deposition from holy orders. In cases of disqualification, or indefinite prohibition where the bishop does not proceed to deposition the cleric may in due course apply to the tribunal for the lifting of the penalty. A cleric would also be able to request the tribunal to remove a record in most cases beyond a certain period.

An injunction would be a monition but "with teeth", the cleric being either restrained from doing, or required to do, a specified act, and would be in contempt of court if the injunction was not obeyed. A conditional discharge would replace monition in less serious cases. If the condition were broken within a specified period the cleric would be liable to receive a penalty for the original offence.

Deferred sentence would give the tribunal the opportunity to determine a **11.79** penalty in the light of the cleric's conduct during that period. Rebuke is the only one of the old censures which would remain. Absolute discharge would acknowledge the technical existence of an offence in cases where even a rebuke is considered unnecessary.

Where the bishop gives censure by consent the same penalties should be available to him except that, in the case of prohibition or an injunction, the matter should be referred to the tribunal, since disregard of the latter would be a contempt of court.

---

[23] The report recommends that the bishop retain the power to inhibit a cleric *pendente lite* in cases of serious allegations but under a new procedure for suspension. If suspended a cleric would have the right to apply to the tribunal for a review and any suspension would be for a definite period of time, or until proceedings were issued by the tribunal unless it renewed the suspension.

The report recommends that resignation by the accused prior to disciplinary proceedings should not be acted upon without adequate time for reflection, and that any such resignation should not, as now, enable the cleric to circumvent the resignation being recorded as a disciplinary matter.

At present the Archbishops maintain a "Caution List"[24] (available only to diocesan and area bishops) which is in two parts. The first part records those upon whom censure has been passed pursuant to the EJM (whether as the result of disciplinary proceedings or by consent, or following secular proceedings) and and is uncontroversial. The second part records those who are under pastoral discipline, but inclusion in this part is only advisory not mandatory, and its existence has led to a sense of injustice.

The report recommends that the first part of the list become the record for the new disciplinary procedures. The second part would then include a much smaller group of those who resign before proceedings are taken but who are likely to have faced censure and those against who some warning should be given, for example in cases of pastoral inadequacy which do not amount to an offence. Further clergy should be informed if their name is on the list and what is recorded against it, and be given an opportunity to challenge both inclusion and that information.[25]

In addition to the above proposals the working party recommended the promotion of greater awareness of new disciplinary procedures by issuing all ordinands with an explanation. It also recommended the formulation of a Code of Practice containing guidance covering all aspects of clergy discipline.

Finally, although outside its own remit the working party considered what other changes would be needed to compliment the new disciplinary system[26] These changes cover three areas, the need for a procedure for minor complaints which fall short of the need for discipline; clarifying the boundaries of ministerial review[27] so that this is clearly demarcated from disciplinary procedures; and suggesting a grievance procedure to enable clerics to express concern when they feel poorly handled by senior clergy.

---

[24] Likely to soon be renamed the "Lambeth and Bishopthorpe Register".

[25] If their name is included following disciplinary proceedings the appeal would be to the tribunal, otherwise to the relevant archbishop. In the latter case this builds upon the recent innovation that a bishop now informs a cleric that their name is to be included upon the list, and the archbishop contacts them indicating the details which have been given by the bishop and inviting them to comment.

[26] See Appendix C to *Under Authority*.

[27] Arrangements for ministerial review were considered by the General Synod in the November 1995 group of sessions.

Chapter Twelve: The Anglican Communion and Ecumenical Relations

"Forasmuch as the Church of Christ has for a long time past been distressed **12.1** by separations and schisms among Christian men, so that the unity for which Our Lord prayed is impaired and the witness to his gospel is grievously hindered, it is the duty of clergy and people to do their utmost not only to avoid occasions of strife but also to seek in penitence and brotherly charity to heal such divisions."

Thus Canon A8 sets out the duty to seek reconciliation with other Christian Churches, a duty which the Church of England seeks to fulfill in its continuing efforts at improving relations with other churches. As head of the Anglican Communion the Archbishop of Canterbury is the focus of unity for the Anglican churches worldwide, and the Church of England is in communion with a number of other Churches both in the United Kingdom and abroad. Further efforts at reconciliation are constantly being made, evidenced most recently in the Porvoo and Meissen Declarations.

Both the Sharing of Church Buildings Act 1969 and the Church of England (Ecumenical Relations) Measure 1988 have enabled the Church of England to take great strides in improving its relations with other churches. The sharing of buildings, and greater participation in ecumenical worship and in local ecumenical projects have all led to an increased awareness and desire for still closer relations. In 1972 the Church of England considered uniting with the Methodist Church. That proposal was rejected, but has once again been raised as a possibility and such a union may yet take place early in the twenty-first century.

Since the Reformation religious toleration in England has been a slow but gradual process and as this century draws to a close there is almost total religious freedom for those of all faiths or of none. One of the questions which the Church of England has faced in recent years is whether or not it should remain as the Established Church, but the debate over disestablishment is outside the scope of this book.

In this chapter we look at the Anglican Communion and the Lambeth Conference, those churches which are in communion with the Church of England and the ministry of overseas clergy. We consider the provisions concerning worship in shared buildings, ecumenical relations with other churches and the involvement of the Church of England in local ecumenical projects. Finally we look briefly at the question of religious tolerance and the offence of blasphemy.

The Anglican Communion

12.2   The Church of England is that branch of the catholic and apostolic church established in England. It is also part of the world-wide Anglican communion, a fellowship of those churches which have an historical association with the British Isles, share a common doctrine, are in communion with the See of Canterbury and recognise the Archbishop of Canterbury as their focus of unity. Amongst its members are the Scottish Epicopal Church, the Church in Wales, the Church of Ireland, the Anglican Church in Australia, and the Episcopal Church in the United States of America.[1]

The Church in Wales

12.3   The part of the Church of England which extended to, and existed in, Wales and Monmouthshire was disestablished on March 31, 1920 by the Welsh Church Act 1914 and became known as the Church in Wales. On disestablishment all cathedral and ecclesiastical corporations in the Church in Wales were dissolved, the ecclesiastical courts and persons in Wales ceased to exercise jurisdiction and the ecclesiastical law of the Church in Wales ceased. Welsh bishops and clergy were no longer represented in Convocation and neither they nor the laity are represented in the General Synod. No bishop of the Church in Wales sits in the House of Lords and its clergy are not disqualified from being elected to the House of Commons.

The Welsh Church Act 1914 empowered the members of the Church in Wales to frame a constitution and regulations for the general management and government of the Church. From the date of disestablishment the existing ecclesiastical law and rules of the Church of England, together with any alterations made to these according to the Welsh Church's constitution are binding upon its members on a consensual basis.[2] The property of the Welsh Church is held on behalf of that Church or its members as if the property had been expressly placed upon trust for persons bound by these terms, the majority of its property having been transferred to the Representative Body of the Church

---

[1] It also includes the Anglican Churches of Canada, Korea, Mexico, Papua New Guinea and the Southern Cone of America, the Anglican Churches in Aotearoa, New Zealand and Polynesia, the Episcopal Churches in Jersualem and the Middle East and in the Philipines, the Episcopal Anglican Churches of Brazil, the Church of the Provinces of Burundi, Central Africa, the Indian Ocean, Kenya, Melanesia, Myanamar, Nigeria, Rwanda, South East Asia, Southern Africa, Sudan, Tanzania, Uganda, West Africa, the West Indies and Zaire, the Holy Catholic Church in Japan, the Spanish Reformed Episcopal Church and the Lusitanian Church (of Portugal). For further details see *The Church of England Yearbook*, published annually by Church House Publishing. See also Rowell, "Anglican Identity, Historical, Ecumenical and Contemporary Reflections", 4 Ecc. L.J. 454.

[2] See *Welsh Church Commissioners v. Representative Body of the Church in Wales* [1940] Ch. 607; *Representative Body of the Church in Wales v. Tithe Redemption Commission* [1944] A.C. 228, H.L. See Also *General Assembly of the Free Church of Scotland v. Ouverton* [1904] A.C. 515, H.L.

in Wales following disestablishment.[3] The province of Wales is almost conterminous with the principality with the exception of some border parishes, and is divided into six dioceses; Bangor, Brecon and Swansea, Llandaff, Monmouth, St Asaph and St Davids.

Church of Ireland and Scottish Episcopal Church

As we saw in Chapter Two, the Church of England was united with the Church of Ireland between 1800 and 1871, at which date the Church of Ireland was disestablished. We also saw in that Chapter that Scotland has its own established Kirk. Its Anglican church, the Scottish Episcopal Church, is not an established church. A person ordained by a bishop of the episcopal church in Scotland who has not held a benefice or other ecclesiastical preferment in England or Ireland is not entitled to be admitted or instituted to such preferment in England without the consent of the diocesan bishop in which the preferment is situated.[4] Before such a minister is admitted or instituted or licensed to any curacy they must make and subscribe before the bishop the same declarations and subscriptions required by law upon ordination by a bishop of the Church of England.[5] The same restrictions are not applied to clergy of the Church of Ireland or Church in Wales.

12.4

A minister of the Scottish Episcopal Church may officiate in any church or chapel in England belonging to the Church of England if invited to do so by the minister having the cure of souls, without the permission of the diocesan bishop, subject to the same conditions as would have been applicable to a minister ordained by a diocesan bishop in the Church of England.[6] Identical provisions now apply to ministers of the Church of Ireland whose position was previously unclear.[7]

Overseas churches

Although the Crown claims supremacy in all matters ecclesiastical as well as temporal throughout its dominions,[8] in practice this is limited by modern constitutional developments. Furthermore, since the introduction of English law into a colony did not carry with it English ecclesiastical law,[9] the Anglican

12.5

---

[3] See further *Halsbury's Laws of England* (4th ed.), Vol. 14, paras 322–331; Watkin, "Disestablishment, Self-Determination and the Constitutional Development of the Church in Wales", and Doe and Lambeth, "The Status and Enforceability of the Rules of the Church in Wales" in Doe (ed.), *Essays in Canon Law* (1992); Watkin, "Vestiges of Establishment: the Ecclesiastical and Canon Law of the Church in Wales" (1991) 2 Ecc. L.J. 110; Brown, "What of the Church in Wales?" (1993) 3 Ecc. L.J. 20.
[4] Episcopal Church (Scotland) Act 1864, s.5.
[5] *ibid*. As to those requirements see Chap. 7.
[6] Episcopal Church (Scotland) Act 1964, s.1. Such permission extending to the solenmisation of matrimony: Bursell, *Liturgy, Order and the Law* (1996), p. 177, n. 216.
[7] Church of England (Miscellaneous Provisions) Measure 1995, s.1.
[8] Thirty-nine Articles, Art. xxxvii.
[9] *Re Lord Bishop of Natal* (1865) 3 Moo. PCCNS 115 at 152.

churches in the Commonwealth are not established churches, but are voluntary associations whose constitutions are contractually enforceable under secular law. Many of them, whilst not established in the full sense of that term, have been given statutory recognition and powers by their countries' legislature.

The overseas churches within the Anglican Communion whilst wholly autonomous are organised on a synodical basis, it being the accepted policy of the Anglican Communion that the dioceses should be grouped into provinces and provincial synods instituted.[10] Within the limitations imposed by the constitutions of its various members a provincial synod may make rules for the regulation and discipline of the Church.

The Lambeth Conferences

12.6 The Anglican Communion holds periodic conferences of bishops, under the presidency of the Archbishop of Canterbury. These conferences of bishops have no legal basis, although statements issued by it carry great weight. This body relies for its authority upon voluntary acceptance of the resolutions which it passes by the various churches who are represented.[10a] The first conference met in 1867 and at present Lambeth Conferences take place every ten years, the next being in 1998. To co-ordinate the Anglican Communion between these conferences a Central Consultative Body of the Lambeth Conference was formed, consisting of not less than 18 members appointed by the Archbishop of Canterbury after consultation with metropolitans and presiding bishops of the Communion.[11]

An Anglican Consultative Council was also established in 1969 which meets every two years. The Council, which is under the presidency of the Archbishop of Canterbury, has members from each church or province in the Anglican Communion. The Council has no legislative powers but acts as a forum for consultation and liaison. It co-operates with the World Council of Churches and seeks to encourage Anglican participation in the ecumenical movement.[12] Pan-Anglican congresses have also been held from time to time, attended by clerical and lay representatives from all the dioceses in the Anglican Communion. The Anglican Communion also maintains an Anglican centre in Rome.[13]

The Lambeth Quadrilateral

12.7 Of great importance to ecumenical relations is the Lambeth Quadrilateral, a statement made by the Lambeth Conference of 1888[14] which established four fundamental conditions for Church unity. These conditions are the acceptance of: the Holy Scripture, as containing all things necessary to salvation; the Apostles'

[10] Report of the Lambeth Conference 1930, pp. 157–160.
[10a] Stephenson Anglicanism and the Lambeth Conferences (1978); Kemp, "Legal Implications of Lambeth", (1989) 5 Ecc.
[11] Report of the Lambeth Conference 1930, Resolution 50.
[12] For further details see *The Church of England Yearbook*.
[13] For further details see *The Church of England Yearbook*.
[14] Report of the Lambeth Conference 1888, pp. 24, 81–91.

Creed as the symbol of baptism and the Nicene Creed as a sufficient statement of the Christian faith; the two domincial sacraments of baptism and the Lord's Supper; and the historic epicopate locally adapted in methods of administration. In considering their relations with other churches and in particular when looking to reunion, the churches of the Anglican Communion have applied the criteria set forth in the Quadilateral.

Churches in communion with the Church of England

The Church of England is also in full communion with a number of other **12.8** churches which do not form part of the Anglican Communion. Amongst these are many churches which have evolved from a union of Anglican churches with churches of other Christian traditions such as the Church of South India together with the Old Catholic Churches in the Netherlands, Austria, Czechoslovakia, Germany, Poland, Switzerland, Croatia and the United States of America.[15]

The Church of England also has special relations with a number of foreign churches which are commonly referred to as the Nordic and Baltic Lutheran Churches, these being parts of the Western Catholic Church which identified with the teaching of Martin Luther in the sixteenth century and ceased to be in communion with the Bishop of Rome. Formal conversations between these churches and the British and Irish Anglican Churches resulted in the Porvoo Common Statements in 1993 recommending that the participating churches establish a relationship of communion, with structures for collegial consulation and an interchangeable ministry by approving the Porvoo Declaration, which the General Synod did in July 1995.

Similarly the Mesissen Declaration approved by the General Synod in July 1990[16] provides for the Church of England and the Evangelical Church in Germany (a communion of 25 member churches) to live in closer fellowship but without as yet interchangeable ministries, and commits these churches to work towards full visible unity.

A further category of churches are those with whom the Church of England is in intercommunion,[17] these being churches which have maintained the historic three-fold ministry and which subscribe to the doctrine of the Holy Trinity. Thus, as we have seen, baptised persons who are communicant members of churches which subscribe to the doctrine of the Holy Trinity may be admitted to Holy Communion in the Church of England, and in many such churches reciprocal arrangements exist in respect of members of the Church of England.

The CCR in their original form referred to another church of the Anglican Communion or an overseas church in communion with the Church of England, but as amended simply refers to a church in communion with the Church of

---

[15] Amongst the Churches with which the Church of England is in communion are the Churches of North India and Pakistan, the Churches in South Asia, the Church of Bangladesh, the Holy Catholic Church in China, Mar Thoma Syrian Church and the Malabar Independent Syrian Church. For further details see *The Church of England Yearbook*, published annually by Church House Publishing.

[16] Proclaimed an Act of Synod on January 29, 1991.

[17] *Intercommunion Today*, the report of the Archbishop's Commission on Intercommunion (1968); *Report of the Commission on Reciprocal Intercommunion* (1973).

England, drawing no distinction between the two. Likewise the Overseas and Other Clergy (Ministry and Ordination) Measure 1967 refers only to those churches in communion with the Church of England, suggesting that in fact the distinction between members of the Anglican Communion and these other churches in communion is no longer significant. Whether or not a Church is in communion with the Church of England for the purposes of the CRR or the 1967 Measure is a matter to be determined by the the Archbishops of Canterbury and York whose decision is conclusive.[18] The Archbishops have the same power to determine under the 1967 Measure whether the Orders of any church are recognised and accepted by the Church of England, although such churches are not in communion with the Church of England.

Ministry of overseas clergy

12.9 For the purposes of the Overseas and Other Clergy (Ministry and Ordination Measure 1967 an overseas bishop of an overseas diocese is defined as meaning a bishop of the Church of England, or a church in communion with it, of a diocese outside the provinces of Canterbury, York, Ireland, Wales or Scotland.[19] An overseas minister is one who has been ordained priest or deacon by an overseas bishop, or by a bishop of the provinces of Canterbury and York at the request of an overseas bishop[20] with a view to exercising their ministy in an overseas diocese.[21] For these purposes the Diocese in Europe is treated as being in the province of Canterbury so neither its bishops nor any clergy are treated as overseas bishops or clergy.[22]

An overseas bishop, or a bishop consecrated in a church not in communion with the Church of England whose Orders are accepted and recognised, cannot perform any episcopal functions, including ordination, in any diocese in the provinces of Canterbury and York other than at the request of (and by the commission in writing of) the diocesan bishop, with the consent and licence in writing of the provincial archbishop.[23] Women bishops of the Anglian Communion consecrated overseas or of other churches, would not be permitted to

---

[18] CRR, r. 54(5); Overseas and Other Clergy (Ministry and Ordination) Measure 1967, s.6(2).

[19] Overseas and Other Clergy (Ministry and Ordination) Measure 1967, s.6.

[20] *ibid.*, s.5(1); Canon C5(3). The bishop must endorse on the Letters of Orders that the ordination was under the section in pursuance of the request of the overseas bishop. Where the person to be ordained is not a citizen of the United Kingdom and Colonies the bishop who ordains them may dispense with the oath of allegience: Overseas and Other Clergy (Ministry and Ordination) Measure 1967, s.5(2); Canon C13(2). The Archbishops of Canterbury of York may grant the person ordained temporary permission to officiate in the relevant province before going overseas: Overseas and Other Clergy (Ministry and Ordination) Measure 1967, ss.1, 5(3).

[21] Overseas and Other Clergy (Ministry and Ordination) Measure 1967, s.6.

[22] Diocese in Europe Measure 1980, s.6.

[23] Overseas and Other Clergy (Ministry and Ordination) Measure 1967, s.4(1). To perform such functions without permission is an offence for which proceedings may be taken pursuant to the EJM: *ibid.*, 4(3). A person ordained priest or deacon by a bishop acting on such a request is deemed to have been ordained by the bishop making the request for the purposes of the 1967 Measure: *ibid.*, s.4(3).

perform episcopal functions in England, since their ministry is not accepted canonically,[24] but such female bishops are nonetheless owed respect and courtesy.[25]

Similarly an overseas minister or person episcopally ordained priest or deacon in a church not in communion with the Church of England whose Orders are accepted and recognised, may not officiate as priest or deacon in the provinces of Canterbury or York other than in accordance with permission granted by the relevant archbishop.[26] The effect of this permission which must be in writing and may be for a specified period of time, is that the overseas minister has all the rights and is subject to the same duties and liabilites as they would have possessed and been subject to had they been ordained by a diocesan bishop in England.[27]

A minister granted permission to officiate by the archbishop may only do so in any place after recieving the permission of the bishop or other Ordinary (except in a case where any minister of the Church of England would not need such permission.[28] Similarly they must only exercise their ministry in any place where they do not have the cure of souls with the permission of the minister having that cure (except in a case where any minister of the Church of England would not need such permission).[29]

Worship in shared buildings and ecumenical relations

Worship in shared buildings

In Chapter 8 we considered the requirements for the sharing of church buildings. **12.10**
In the case of such buildings which are used as a place of worship the sharing

---

[24] See the Statement of the Archbishop of Canterbury (also speaking on behalf of the Archbishop of York) to the General Synod in 1989. Regardless of whether there is a strict legal prohibition against their ministry it is evident that the Archbishops would not give their consent or licence.

[25] See the *Report of the Archbishop of Canterbury's Commission on Communion and Women in the Episcopate* (1989); and for a general discussion of the issues see *Episcopal Ministry*, The Report of the Archbishops' Commission on the Episcopate (1990).

[26] *ibid.*, ss.1, 3; Canon C8(5). To perform such functions without permission is an offence for which proceedings may be taken pursuant to the EJM: Overseas and Other Clergy (Ministry and Ordination) Measure 1967, s.1(6). The provision does not apply to an overseas deacon who is ordained priest by the bishop of a diocese in the province of Canterbury and York otherwise than at the request of an overseas bishop: *ibid.*, s.1(7). Nor does it apply to any person ordained deacon or priest on the request and by the commission of a bishop of a diocese in the provinces of Canterbury and York: Canon C8(5). Where a minister who has been granted such permission is to be admitted to a benefice or other office to which section 5 of the Clerical Subscription Act 1865 applies and they are a citizen of the United Kingdom and Colonies the person who admits them may dispense with the oath of allegiance: Overseas and Other Clergy (Ministry and Ordination) Measure 1967, s.2; Canon C13(2).

[27] This includes, in the case of a priest or deacon of a United Church (*i.e.* the Churches of North and South Indian, Bangladesh and Pakistan) who is granted permission to officiate for a limited period of time, the right to exercise their ministry in another church to which the Church of England (Ecumenical Relations) Measure 1988 applies: Church of England (Ecumenical Relations) Measure 1988, s.4.

[28] Canon C8(2), and see Chap. 7.

[29] Canon C8(4), and see Chap. 5.

agreement must make provision for determining the extent to which it is available for worship.[30] The agreement may provide for the holding of joint services on such occasions as are approved by the sharing churches, and in the case of the Church of England may dispense with the holdings of statutory services on Sundays and other days[31] as may be necessary.[32]

A minister, reader or lay preacher of one sharing church may, if invited by a minister, reader or lay preacher of another church with which they share, take part in conducting worship in that building in accordance with the forms of service of that other church, notwithstanding any statutory or other legal provision. However, this right must be exercised in accordance with any rules or directions given by either church and to any limitation imposed by or under the sharing agreement.[33]

Apart from these specific provisions the participation of the communities of each sharing church in each other's worship is subject to the practice and disciplines of those churches, as if they worshipped in separate buildings. Accordingly the terms of any sharing agreement to which the Church of England is a party and the extent to which its ministers may become involved in joint worship, are themselves governed by the position in regard to ecumenical arrangements regarding shared liturgy.

Ecumenical relations

12.11   The Church of England (Ecumenical Relations) Measure 1988 and Canons B43 and 44 promulged pursuant to it, make provision for relations with other churches and for local ecumenical projects respectively.[34] The Measure follows an interim Code of Practice issued by the House of Bishops in 1980 and flows from the growth of the relationship between the Church of England, Roman Catholic and Free Churches over recent years. The Measure[35] and hence the Canons relate to any church which is designated by the Archbishops of Canterbury and York as a church to which they apply, all such churches being required to subscribe to the doctrine of the Holy Trinity[36] and to administer the sacraments of baptism and Holy Communion[37] and to be churches to which the Sharing of

---

[30] Sharing of Church Buildings Act s.4.

[31] See Chap. 9.

[32] Canon C8(2), and see Chap. 7.

[33] *ibid.*

[34] A Code of Practice regarding ecumenical relations was also drawn up in 1989 under the authority of General Synod. In some dioceses the terms of the Code of Practice have been incorporateld into diocesan regulations. See also *Multi-Faith Worship ? Guidance on the situations which may arise*, published on behalf of the House of Bishops by the Inter-Faith Consultative Group of the General Synod's Board of Mission (1993) (G.S. Misc. 411).

[35] Church of England (Ecumenical Relations) Measure 1988, s.5.

[36] This excludes the Unitarian Church, but essentially includes all other Christian denominations.

[37] This excludes the Salvation Army and the Society of Friends (Quakers).

Church Buildings Act 1969[38] applies.[39] The 1988 Measure required that any Canon made pursuant to it should not enable any person who has not been episcopally ordained priest in a church whose Orders are recognised and accepted by the Church of England to preside at the Holy Communion according to the use of the Church of England, or to permit any person other than clerk in holy orders of the Church of England to solemnise a marriage according to its rites.[40]

Canon B43 enables clerks in holy orders, deaconesses, readers and lay workers of the Church of England to take part in worship in accordance with the forms and practice of other churches, and for places of worship of the Church of England to be made available for such worship, and to enable members of other churches to participate in public worship in accordance with forms of service and practice of the Church of England.[41]

An incumbent[42] is able to invite (in writing) a baptised minister or lay person who is good standing with their own church to say or sing Morning or Evening Prayer or the Litany, read the Holy Scriptures and preach at any service, lead the intercession at the Holy Communion and to lead prayers at all other services, to assist at baptism or the solemnisation of matrimony, or conduct a funeral service and to assist in the distribution of the holy sacrament to the people at Holy Communion, provided the person invited is authorised to perform a similar duty in their own church.[43]

The invitation to perform such duties (other than in connection with a service **12.12** of ordination or confirmation in any parish church or other place of worship may only be given if the approval of the bishop has been obtained where it relates to the saying of Morning and Evening Prayer or the Litany, preaching or assisting at baptisms and marriages and conducting funerals on a regular basis. The bishop's consent is also required when the invitation extends to assisting in the distribution of the holy sacrament. In the case of any invitation to assist at a baptism or marriage or to conduct a funeral the consent of those persons concerned is required. Finally in the case of invitations to say Morning or Evening Prayer or the Litany, to preach at any service, or to assist in the distribution of the holy

---

[38] See Chap. 8.
[39] Those churches designated are the Baptist Union, Methodist, Moravian and United Reformed Churches and the Roman Catholic Church in England and Wales, the Congregational Federation, the International Ministerial Council of Great Britain, the Greek Orthodox Archdiocese of Thyateria and Great Britain, the Council of African and Afro-Caribbean Churches, the Free Church of England, Southam Road Evangelical Church Banbury, the Assemblies of God in Great Britain and Ireland and the New Testament Church of God. It is anticipated that further churches will be designated in due course. See Also *The Church of England Yearbook.*
[40] The Church of England (Ecumenical Relations) Measure 1988, s.3.
[41] The Church of England (Ecumenical Relations) Meassure 1988, s.1.
[42] For the purposes of Canon B43 the incumbent in relation to a parish includes the rural dean when the benefice is vacant, the priest-in-charge in cases where a suspension period within the meaning of the Pastoral Measure 1983 applies, or vicar in a team ministry to whom a special care of the souls within the parish has been assigned: Canon B43(12).
[43] Canon B43(1) (1).

sacrament the approval of the PCC[44] is required.[45] In the case of a service of ordination or confirmation the invitation may only be given by the bishop, subject to the approval of the incumbent and PCC.[46] Essentially the same conditions apply in regard to invitations to perform any duties in a cathedral church.[47]

A bishop who receives an invitation from a person authorised by another church to take part in a service may in the course of that service perform any duty assigned to him provided that the duty is, or is similar to, a duty which he is authorised to perform in the Church of England. Before accepting the invitation the bishop must obtain the approval of the incumbent of the parish in which the service is to take place, and if this is in another diocese, the approval of the bishop of that diocese. He must also obtain the consent of the archbishop of the province if the invitation is to take part in the ordination or consecration of a minister of another church, or to participate in a service of confirmation, or to preside at the Holy Communion.[48]

A priest or deacon who receives an invitation from a person authorised by another church to take part in a service may likewise in the course of that service perform any duty assigned to them provided that the duty is, or is similar to, a duty which they are authorised to perform in the Church of England. Before accepting the invitation they must obtain the approval of the incumbent of the parish in which the service is to take place. If the invitation is to take part in the ordination or consecration of a minister of another church, or to preside at the Holy Communion they must also obtain the approval of bishop of the diocese in which the service is to take place. Where the invitation is to take part in any service on a regular basis the approval of the bishop of the diocese and of the PCC of the parish in which the service is to take place are both required.[49]

12.13   Neither an archbishop nor a bishop are to give their approval for a bishop, priest or deacon to preside at Holy Communion unless satisfied that there are special circumstances which justify acceptance of the invitation, and that the rites and elements to be used are neither contrary to, nor indicative of any departure from the doctrine of the Church of England in any essential matter.[50] Where a bishop or priest accepts an invitation to take part in a service of ordination or consecration they may not do any act (by the laying on of hands or otherwise) which is a sign of conferring Holy Orders, unless the relevant church is an episcopal church with which the Church of England has established intercommunion.[51]

A deaconess, reader or lay worker of the Church of England who receives an invitation from a person authorised by another church to take part in a service

---

[44] In cases under the Canon where the approval of the PCC is required this may be given in respect of the performance of such duties as may be specified, by such persons or class of persons as is specified, and may be given generally, for an unlimited period or subject to a specified limitation regarding duration or occasion: *ibid.*, B43(8).

[45] Canon B43(1), (2).

[46] *ibid.*, B43(1), (3).

[47] *ibid.*, B43(1), (4). The consent of the dean and chapter or, in the case of a parish church cathedral the cathedral chapter, is required instead of the incumbent, and no consent is required from the PCC.

[48] *ibid.*, B43(2).

[49] *ibid.*, B43(3).

[50] *ibid.*, B43(4).

[51] *ibid.*, B43(5).

may likewise in the course of that service perform any duty assigned to them provided that the duty is, or is similar to, a duty which they are authorised to perform in the Church of England. Before accepting the invitation they must obtain the approval of the incumbent of the parish in which the service is to take place and, where the invitation is to take place in any service on a regular basis, the approval of the bishop of the diocese and of the PCC of the parish in which the service is to take place.[52]

Where the approval of the incumbent is required in order for a priest, deacon, deaconess, reader or lay worker to accept any of the foregoing invitations and the relevant incumbent refuses, an appeal may be made to the bishop of the diocese in which the service is to be held. If, after considering the views of the applicant and incumbent, the bishop considers that the consent was unreasonably withheld he may authorise the applicant to take part in the service in question, and must inform the incumbent of his reasons for so doing in writing.[53] There appears to be no procedure for an appeal if an incumbent refuses approval to a bishop, nor if a bishop refuses approval.

With the approval of the PCC and the diocesan bishop the incumbent may invite members of another church to take part in joint worship with the Church of England, or to use a church in the parish for worship in accordance with the forms and practices of that other church on such occasions as the bishop may specify in his approval,[54] and similar provisions apply to a cathedral church.[55]

Joint worship is not defined, but every minister of the Church of England is under a duty to use only authorised forms of service, or in the case of a minister with the cure of souls, to exercise their discretion in cases where no provision is made.[56] Since no form of joint worship has been approved it would appear that a minister would have to exercise discretion but a difficulty arises since the definition of incumbent for the purposes of the Canon is wider than those having the cure of souls to whom the exercise of such discretion is permitted.[57] Thus only incumbents could exercise discretion to make provision for such joint worship.

Local ecumenical projects

Canon B44 enables a diocean bishop to enter into an agreement with the **12.14** appropriate authority of each participating church for participation by the Church of England in a local ecumenical project established, or to be established, in respect of an area within his diocese. He may also make special provision as to the ministry of ordained ministers, deaconesses, readers and lay workers beneficed or licensed to a parish wholly or partly within the area of the project, or ministering in, or licensed to, any cathedral church in that area.[58] In cases where a clerk in holy orders is licensed to an institution in the diocese under section 2

---

[52] *ibid.*, B43(6).
[53] *ibid.*, B43(7).
[54] *ibid.*, B43(9).
[55] *ibid.*, B43(10).
[56] Canons B1(2), B5(2).
[57] See Bursell, *Liturgy, Order and the Law* (1996), pp. 228–229.
[58] Church of England (Ecumenical Relations) Measure 1988, s.2.

of the Extra-Parochial Ministry Measure 1967, the diocesan bishop may also enter an agreement for the participation of the Church of England in a local ecumenical project established, or to be established, for that institution and to make special provision in regard to the ministry in that institution of clerks in holy orders.[59]

The bishop may only enter into any agreement in regard to a project established in an area comprising the whole or part of any parish, or which is extended to any parish, with the consent of the incumbent[60]; 75 per cent of those present at voting at a meeting of the PCC; either the annual parochial church meeting or a special parochial church meeting; and the diocesan pastoral committee after consultation with the relevant deanery synod or its standing committee.[61] Any such agreement is to have effect for the period specified, which is to be no longer than seven years, although the bishop may agree to an extension for further periods of up to seven years.[62]

Where the project is amended to include a church which was previously not within the project, or an additional congregation of a participating church, the Church of England is not to continue to participate unless the diocesan bishop agrees.[63] However, the bishop must not agree to extend the period of an agreement or to continue in an amended project unless he has consent of the relevant incumbent, PCC and the diocesan pastoral committee. He may also revoke any agreement after consultation with the appropriate authority of each participating church, each PCC concerned and the diocean pastoral committee.[64]

Where the bishop has agreed to participation in a project he may, after consulting with the PCC of each parish, make special provision by written instrument (which may be amended or revoked) for ministry in the area of the project. He may also exercise his canonical powers with regard to worship and pursuant to these may dispense with the requirement for the holding of statutory services, authorise a minister to celebrate Holy Communion in buildings not licensed or consecrated for the purpose and exercise all the powers already discussed in relation to Canon B43. In addition he may authorise ministers of any other participating church to baptise in a place of worship of the Church of England according to the rite of that other church, with the goodwill of the persons concerned.[65]

12.15 The bishop may authorise a priest of the Church of England to preside at a service of Holy Communion in accordance with a rite authorised by any participating church, and authorise the holding in a place of worship of the Church of England of services of Holy Communion presided over by a minister of any other participating church. The bishop may also make provision for the holding of joint services with any other participating church, including services of baptism and confirmation.[66] However, all such authorisation is subject to the condition that the bishop is satisfied that the rite and the elements to be used are

---

[59] Church of England (Ecumenical Relations) Measure 1988, s.2.
[60] The defintion in Canon B44 is the same as in Canon B43, see n. 42, *ante*: Canon B44(9).
[61] Canon B44(1).
[62] Canon B44(2).
[63] *ibid.*, B44(2).
[64] *ibid.*, B44(3).
[65] *ibid.*, B44(4).
[66] *ibid.*, B44(4).

not contrary to, nor indicative of any departure from, the doctrine of the Church of England in any essential matter.[67]

In cases where the bishop authorises a service of Holy Communion at a place of worship belonging to the Church of England which is to be presided over by a minister of another church, notice of the holding of such service is, as far as is practicable, to be given on the Sunday before, with an indication of the rite to be used and the church to which the minister who is to preside belongs. No such service, regardless of the form used, is to be taken or held to be a celebration of Holy Communion according to the use of the Church of England. Save at the express wish of an individual sick communicant no portion of the bread and wine consecrated at such a service is to be carried out of the church.[68]

Before exercising any of his powers in regard to ministry and services the bishop must consult the authorities of the other churches participating in the project and must also ensure that public worship according to the rites of the Church of England is maintained with reasonable frequency in any parish, with particular regard to the celebration of Holy Communion on Christmas Day, Ash Wednesday, Easter and Ascension Days and Pentecost.[69]

Similar provisions apply in regard to a project established, or to be established in the area of any cathedral church,[70] or in respect of an institution.[71]

Religious tolerance and the offence of blasphemy

Religious tolerance

Although the Church of England is the Established Church there is within England and the rest of the United Kingdom almost total religious freedom to practice any religion, whether Christian or non-Christian, or not to practice any religion at all.[72] The United Kingdom is a signatory to the European Convention of Human Rights which prescribes a right of freedom of religion subject only to those limitations which may be necessary in a democratic society.   **12.16**

Since the intention at the Reformation was to oust the jurisdiction of the Pope in England such disabilities as existed were directed in the main at Roman Catholics, and some vestiges of these restrictions do still remain.[73]

As we saw in Chapter Two the Sovereign may not be a Roman Catholic, and neither may their consort.[74] Although the Prime Minister may be a Roman Catholic should they be so they would not be able to advise on the exercise of the

---

[67] Since all services are required to be authorised and the minister having the cure of souls may only exercise their discretion where no other provision is made, any service of baptism and confirmation must be according to the Book of Common Prayer or ASB. Bursell, *Liturgy, Order and the Law* (1996) pp. 228–229.

[68] Canon B44 (4), (3), (c).

[69] Canon B44(5).

[70] Canon B44(6).

[71] Canon B44(7).

[72] See *Halsbury's Laws of England* (4th ed.), Vol. 14, paras 1386–1435.

[73] See *Halsbury's Laws of England* (4th ed.), Vol. 14, paras 1386–1435.

[74] Act of Settlement 1700, s.2.

Crown's ecclesiastical patronage, including appointments to bishoprics,[75] and these functions would need to be undertaken by another minister who was not a Roman Catholic. The Lord Chancellor may also be a Roman Catholic and were this to occur special provision would have to be made by the Sovereign in Council for the exercise of the Lord Chancellor's functions in respect of the Church of England, including those in relation to visitations and patronage.[76]

In general religous bodies are in the same position as any secular body or association. On occasion the State has intervened and legislated in regard to such bodies, for example by the Methodist Church Union Act 1929 and the United Reformed Church Act 1972, but in general their regulation is based simply on contractual principles, with their property normally being being held on trust for the purposes of the association. Their ministers may enjoy certain privileges such as exemption from jury service, their registered places of worship and certain other buildings may enjoy exemption from council tax, and their property may be the subject of charitable trusts, but the overriding principle is one of toleration rather than of active assistance to these bodies.

Blasphemy

12.17   The Christian religion is still afforded some limited protection by the common law offences of blasphemy,[77] such statutory offences having been repealed. A blasphemous libel is committed where a person publishes any matter attacking the Christian religion, God, Christ, the Bible or the formularies of the Church of England, which is such as to utrage and insult a Christian's feelings.[78] It should be noted that it is the nature of the attack rather than the attack itself which constitutes the offence. It is not blasphemous to speak or publish opinions hostile to the Christian religion or to deny the existence of God if the publication is couched in decent and temperate language. Although publication must be intentional the crime is one of strict liablity and thus the issue of whether the defendant intended to blaspheme is irrelevant,[79] and it may be that the other common law offence of blasphemy which is committed simply by speaking may also be an offence of strict liability.

The European Court of Human rights rejected a claim that the confinement of the offence of blasphemous libel to Christianity offended the Convention on Human Rights.[80] However, the continued existence of the offence has met with

---

[75] Roman Catholic Relief Act 1828.

[76] Lord Chancellor (Tenure of Office and Discharge of Ecclesiastical Functions) Act 1974, s.1.

[77] See Kenny "The Evolution of the Law of Blasphemy" (1992) 1 C.L.J. 127; Walter, "Blasphemy, Ancient and Modern (1990).

[78] *Bowman v. Secular Society Ltd* [1917] A.C. 406, H.L.

[79] *Whitehouse v. Lemon and Gay News Ltd* [1979] A.C. 617, H.L. The case resurrected the law of blasphemy after a period of desuetude.

[80] *Gay News Ltd and Lemon v. United Kingdom* (Application 8710/79) (1982) 5 E.H.R.R. 123. See also *Wingrove v. United Kingdom* (Application 19/1995), *The Times*, December 5, 1996.

increased criticism which has led to calls either for its abolition or alterntively for its extension to other faiths.[81]

---

[81] *Whitehouse v. Lemon and Gay News Ltd (ante), per* Lord Scarman at 658; and see *R. v. Chief Metropolitan Stipendiary Magistrate, ex p. Choudhury* [1991] 1 Q.B. 429 at 452 (a case concerning *The Satanic Verses* by Salman Rushdie. See also *Offences against Religion and Public Worship*, Law Com. Working Paper No. 79 (1981); Spencer, "Blasphemy, The Law Commission's Working Paper" (1981) Crim. L.R. 810; Law Com. Report No. 145 (1985); *Report of the Archbishop of Canterbury's Working Party on Offences against Religions and Public Worship* (1988) (G.S. Misc. 286); Routledge, "Blasphemy, the Report of the Archbishop of Canterbury's Working Party on Offences against Religions and Public Worship" (1989) 4 Ecc. L.J. 27; Elliott, "Blasphemy and Other Expressions of Offensive Opinion" (1993) 3 Ecc. L.J. 70. The Law Commission's Report No. 145 was laid before Parliament together with a draft bill proposing the abolition of the offence of blasphemy without any replacement; this being the recommendation of the majority. The minority proposed a new offence to cover the major religions within society, a view also favoured by the Archbishop of Canterbury's working party which in effect proposed an offence constituted by an intention to publish material with the purpose of wounding or outraging religious feelings.

Index

Worship—*cont.*
confession table and boxes, 9.46
conformity, principle of, 9.1, 9.5
congregation, obligations on, 9.27
copyright, 9.25
days to be specially observed, 9.18
decorations, 9.36
divergence of law and practice, 9.32
family services, 9.20
feast days, 9.18
forms of service,
alteration of, 9.6
authorisation of, 9.6
authorised, 9.7
decision as to use of, 9.13
occasions for which no provision is
made, 9.9
generally, 9.1
greater diversity in matters of, 9.1
guiding principles as to legality, 9.31
history of, 9.4
holy oil, use of, 9.45
holy tables and appurtenances, 9.38
holy water stoups and aspergill, 9.42
hymns, 9.22
incense, use of, 9.35, 9.44
jus liturgicum, 9.11
language, 9.17
lectionary, 9.15
legality, guiding principles as to, 9.31
liturgical dance, 9.22
maintained schools, in, 3.35
ministers, vestments of, 9.47
music, 9.22
necessity, doctrine of, 9.12
notices, 9.23
occasional offices, 9.14
occasional services, video recording of,
9.26, 10.57
ornaments,
church, of, 9.37
meaning, 9.36
parish place of, 4.5
permitted variations, 9.10

Worship—*cont.*
Prayer Book. *See* **Book of Common
Prayer**
private prayer, 9.10
processions, 9.33
provision of things appertaining to, 9.28
pyx, 9.41
register of services, 9.24
regular statutory services, provision of,
9.19
reserved sacrament, receptacles for, 9.41
ritual and ceremonial, 9.30
rubrics,
meaning, 9.6
observance of, 9.8
sacrament-house, 9.41
sanctuary,
gongs and bells, 9.40
lamps, 9.39
sermons, 9.21
shared buildings, in, ecumenical
relations and, 12.1, 12.10
St Paul, conduct set out by, 1.2
stations of cross, 9.43
tabernacle, 9.41
thurible, use of, 9.44
uniformity, principle of, 9.4, 9.5
versions of Bible, 9.16
vestments of ministers, 9.47
video recording of occasional services,
9.26, 10.57
votive candles, 9.39
See also **Divine service; Doctrine**
Written representations
faculty case, procedure in, 11.43

York, Archbishop of
powers and duties of, 2.37
style of, 2.36
See also **Chancery Court of York**
York, province of
convocations, 2.39–2.41
Youth club
sharing agreements, 8.43–8.44